DUMBARTON OAKS TEXTS

VII

LETTERS OF GREGORY AKINDYNOS

CORPUS FONTIUM HISTORIAE BYZANTINAE

CONSILIO SOCIETATIS INTERNATIONALIS
STUDIIS BYZANTINIS PROVEHENDIS DESTINATAE
EDITUM

VOLUMEN XXI

GREGORII ACINDYNI EPISTULAE

EDIDIT, ANGLICE VERTIT,
ET ADNOTAVIT
ANGELA CONSTANTINIDES HERO

SERIES WASHINGTONENSIS
EDIDIT IHOR ŠEVČENKO

In aedibus Dumbarton Oaks

Washingtoniae, D.C.

MCMLXXXIII

LETTERS OF GREGORY AKINDYNOS

GREEK TEXT AND ENGLISH TRANSLATION

by

ANGELA CONSTANTINIDES HERO

Dumbarton Oaks

Research Library and Collection

Washington, D.C.

1983

Manufactured in the United States of America by
Sheridan Books, Inc., 450 Fame Avenue, Hanover, PA 17331 | (717) 632-3535

LIBRARY OF CONGRESS CATALOGING IN PUBLICATION DATA
Akindynos, Gregorios, ca. 1300–ca. 1349.
Letters of Gregory Akindynos.
(Dumbarton Oaks texts ; 7) (Corpus Fontium Historiae Byzantinae ; 21)
text and translation by Angela Constantinides Hero.
Includes index.

ISBN 978-0-88402-107-0 (hardcover: alk. paper)
ISBN 978-0-88402-448-4 (paperbound: alk. paper)
LCCN permalink: https://lccn.loc.gov/82024263

1. Hesychasm—History—Sources.
I. Hero, Angela Constantinides, 1926–2014.
II. Title. III. Series.
IV. Series: Corpus fontium historiae Byzantinae ; v. 21.
V. Series: Series Washingtonensis.
BX384.5.A3813 1983
281'.5 82-24263

In accordance with the rules adopted by the
International Commission
for the Edition of Sources of Byzantine History,
the text and translation of this volume have been verified
by Ihor Ševčenko.

EU GPSR Authorised Representative
LOGOS EUROPE, 9 rue Nicolas Poussin, 17000, La Rochelle, France
E-mail: Contact@logoseurope.eu

TABLE OF CONTENTS

PREFACE

The hesychast controversy is the last of the major dogmatic disputes in the history of Byzantium. Aside from its importance for the subsequent development of Eastern Orthodox theology, its cultural and socio-political aspects are of unquestionable interest to the historian. The involvement of the Palamites and their opponents in the civil war of 1341–47, the disputed attitude of both parties toward the West, and the alignment with the anti-Palamites of such groups as the intellectuals and the Zealots make the study of this many-faceted conflict a prerequisite to a fuller understanding of the complex events of the mid-fourteenth century.

In the hesychast controversy Akindynos played the part of a protagonist, and the historical and prosopographical value of his correspondence has been noted by the various scholars who have already published thirty-one of his seventy-six surviving letters. The present edition was undertaken at the suggestion of Father John Meyendorff, under whose mentorship I edited the fifty-nine letters which were unpublished at the time and which I submitted to Fordham University in 1975 as a doctoral dissertation. I am deeply grateful to Professor Meyendorff not only for suggesting this topic to me, but also for providing me with the results of his personal research and for generously sharing with me his unique knowledge of Palamism. I am also greatly indebted to Professor Ihor Ševčenko who as my teacher at Columbia University introduced me to the study of manuscripts. My work has benefited immensely from his constant interest and invaluable advice. Grateful acknowledgment is also due to Dr. Alice-Mary Talbot for generously going over the text and translation and for helping to improve their accuracy with her suggestions and advice.

In his analysis of eighteen letters of Akindynos, the late Fr. Raymond J. Loenertz expressed the hope that his study would facilitate the work of the future editor of Akindynos' correspondence. Even a brief glance at my commentary will prove how far he has succeeded and how much I remain in the debt of this eminent Byzantinist.

The preparation of this edition would not have been possible without

the generosity and moral support of my husband. Loving thanks go to him and our two sons for their encouragement and understanding.

Finally, I would like to express my appreciation to Dumbarton Oaks and to the Corpus Fontium Historiae Byzantinae for including in their series of texts this edition of the letters of Gregory Akindynos. I am particularly indebted to Professor Peter Topping, Advisor for Byzantine Publications at Dumbarton Oaks, for his help and unfailing kindness, to Dr. Frances Kianka for her careful editing, and to Miss Julia Warner, Associate Editor, and Mr. Glenn Ruby, Publishing Manager, for seeing this manuscript through the press.

Angela Constantinides Hero
Queens College of the
City University of New York

INTRODUCTION

I. THE LIFE OF AKINDYNOS

According to the testimony of his adversaries,[1] Akindynos was of Bulgarian extraction and came from the vicinity of Prillapos, the present day Prilep in southern Yugoslavia.[2] Akindynos does not contest this testimony nor, in fact, does he ever refer to his ancestry. Only once, in answer to his opponents' disparaging remarks about his obscure origin,[3] he concedes that he may come from a "rustic race of shepherds," but points out that so did the revered patriarchs of the Old Testament and even Moses and David.[4]

His real name is unknown. Palamas informs us that Gregory was his monastic name and Akindynos the name he adopted for reasons of prestige.[5] Equally un-

[1]Information about the early life of Akindynos must be carefully culled from the sparse references in the correspondence and polemical writings of Palamas, the *Encomium* of Patriarch Philotheos, and the unpublished homily on the Sunday of Orthodoxy by Patriarch Kallistos which contains an eyewitness account of Akindynos' visit to Mt. Athos (see excerpt published by Meyendorff from *Patmiacus 366*, fols. 414^{v}–415^{r}: *Introduction*, 61 note 88). Of Akindynos' own writings only the *Iambics* (PG, 150, cols. 843A–862A) contain a brief allusion to his ancestry, and the two first letters to Gregoras (Letters 1 and 2) provide an insight into their author's literary interests and early associations.

[2]Cf. Kallistos, *Homily on the Sunday of Orthodoxy*, cited in Meyendorff, *Introduction*, 62 note 90; Philotheos of Selymbria (copying Kallistos), *Vita Macarii*, ed. Papadopoulos-Kerameus, *Μαυρογορδάτειος Βιβλιοθήκη, Ἀνέκδοτα Ἑλληνικὰ* (Constantinople, 1892–93), 57; Palamas, *Ὅτι Βαρλαὰμ καὶ Ἀκίνδυνος ..., Συγγράμματα*, II, 265, lines 7–8; *idem*, *Ἀναίρεσις γράμματος Ἰγνατίου, Συγγράμματα*, II, 633, lines 12–14.

[3]Palamas, Πρὸς Γαβρᾶν, *Συγγρ.*, II, 348, lines 27–32: *Πόθεν γὰρ ἂν ταῦτα καὶ μεμύηται; παρὰ τῶν γεννησάντων; ἀλλ' οὐδ' ὄνομα τούτων ἔχει τις εἰπεῖν, πλὴν ὅτι τῶν ἔσθ' ὅπου τῶν δυτικῶν ἐσχατιῶν ὁδοστατούντων καὶ λωποδυτούντων ἢ τῶν τοῦτο πασχόντων, μᾶλλον δὲ ἀντιπασχόντων παρὰ τῶν ὁμόρων ἦσαν*. See also Kalothetos, *Κατὰ τοῦ κινδυνεύσαντος Ἀκινδύνου, Συγγράμματα*, 142, lines 37–38: ... ὃς (*sc.*, Akindynos) *οὐκ ἐγκαλυπτόμενος καὶ τὴν πατρικὴν ἐνδὺς σισύραν*...

[4]Ἴαμβοι, PG, 150, col. 859A: *εἰ γὰρ ἡμεῖς ἐκ γένους κτηνοτρόφου καὶ χωρικῶς ἔχοντος ὡς κτηνοτρόφου*... In his first letter to the Cypriot Lapithes, Akindynos described himself as a poor and insignificant man pitted against the aristocratic and renowned Palamas (Letter 42, lines 41–50).

[5]Ἀντιρρητικὸς 3, 3, 106, *Συγγρ.*, III, 238, lines 22–31. Akindynos allegedly claimed that his name was indicative of the safety and orthodoxy of his beliefs; cf. Palamas, *ibid.*, and Dishypatos, *Poem*, 737, lines 563–64. Such puns on his name are discreet and rare in his letters; see Letter 68, line 4 and, perhaps, Letter 26, line 15 and Letter 69, line 5. More frequent are his references to the Pala-

known is the date of his birth. But, whatever his background, he succeeded in acquiring a good education. His correspondence attests not only to his rhetorical training and familiarity with classical literature, but also to his association with a select coterie of Byzantine intellectuals. According to Kallistos, Akindynos grew up in Pelagonia (present day Bitolj), but was educated in the cosmopolitan city of Thessalonica.[6] There, as we learn from his letters, he was the student of the notable philologist Thomas Magistros and of a lesser known personality, the archdeacon Bryennios, with both of whom he remained in contact until the last years of his life.[7] We do not know, however, the identity of his other teacher who allegedly committed suicide before 1342.[8]

Following his studies in Thessalonica, Akindynos spent some time in the neighboring city of Berroia where he taught grammar to the sons of some prominent local families.[9] It was probably during his stay in Berroia that he came in contact with Gregory Palamas who as a newly ordained hieromonk spent the years 1326 to 1331 at a hermitage near that Macedonian town.[10] From Akindynos' correspondence we know that the two were already acquainted by the end of 1330. For upon his return from a trip to Constantinople that year, Palamas presented Akindynos with a copy of an astronomical treatise by Nikephoros Gregoras. The author had intended it for Joseph the Philosopher, but, since that learned monk happened to die at that time, Palamas, who knew Akindynos' scholarly interests, handed it to him.[11]

His acquaintance with the prominent hesychast probably influenced Akindynos' decision to become an Athonite monk. When Palamas was forced by the Serbian incursions to leave Berroia in 1331 and return to Mt. Athos, Akindynos visited him at his hermitage of St. Sabbas near the Great Lavra and sought with his encouragement to be admitted to that monastery. But, despite the support of his powerful sponsor, he was rejected by the monks not only at Lavra but also at the monasteries of Iberon, Philotheou and Petra. Both Palamas and his follower, Pa-

mites as "Παλαμναῖοι" (murderous, abominable); see commentary on Letter 25, line 15. Palamas, in turn, called him "*πολυκίνδυνος*" ('Αντιρρητικὸς 3, 21, 96, *Συγγράμματα*, III, 230, line 28), and Philotheos styled him "*ψευδώνυμος*" (*Encomium*, PG, 151, col. 603A), while Kalothetos entitled one of his discourses against him Λόγος *κατὰ τοῦ κινδυνεύσαντος* 'Ακινδύνου (*Συγγράμματα*, 141).

[6]Kallistos who holds Akindynos' Hellenic learning responsible for his heresy writes in his homily: *'Ετράφη δὲ κακῶς εἰς* Πελαγονίαν, *ἑλληνικὴν δὲ παιδείαν ἐν τῇ μεγαλουπόλει* Θεσσαλονίκῃ *ἐξήσκησεν, ἐκεῖσε γὰρ καὶ τὸν σπινθῆρα τῆς ἀσεβείας ὤδινεν* (cited in Meyendorff, *Introduction*, 62 note 91).

[7]See Letter 56, lines 75–76 and Letter 58, line 26.

[8]In his letter to John Gabras dating from the end of 1342, Palamas remarked contemptuously that Akindynos could not have been initiated in the study of theology either by his obscure and knavish ancestors or by his teachers, one of whom hanged himself while the other (*sc.*, Barlaam) rebelled against the orthodox faith and ran away to live among the impious; see Πρὸς *Γαβρᾶν*, *Συγγράμματα*, II, 348–49.

[9]Philotheos, *Encomium*, PG, 151, cols. 650D–651A.

[10]Meyendorff, *Introduction*, 58.

[11]See Letter 1, lines 30–38 and commentary.

triarch Kallistos have left eyewitness accounts of this event. Recalling, after an interval of twenty years, the visit of Akindynos to the Holy Mountain, Kallistos ascribed to Divine Providence the future heretic's failure to remain among the hesychasts; but some of his remarks intimate that what in fact disposed the monks against Akindynos was his attempt to win them over with his Hellenic learning.[12] Palamas refers to the same incident in an *Antirrhetic* written at the height of the controversy where he too portrays Akindynos as a victim of his profane studies and explains that he had endeavored to save him at the time by taking him under his tutelage.[13]

Akindynos' letters, on the other hand, contain no allusion to the Athonite episode, only references to his close association with Palamas and the hesychasts whose sincere and artless piety he extolls in writing to their detractor, the Calabrian monk Barlaam.[14]

After his abortive efforts to settle on Mt. Athos, Akindynos returned to Thessalonica from where in 1332 he addressed two letters to Gregoras. What prompted him to write to the distinguished polymath was his admiration for his writings on astronomy. Gregoras had recently emerged victorious from his debate with Barlaam, and Akindynos alluded to the latter's resentment when he assured Gregoras that, unlike some other men of letters, he personally rejoiced at his accomplishments and rising fame. His flattery elicited a friendly response from Gregoras and the exhilarating news that he had shown Akindynos' letter to the Emperor and commended it for its style.[15] But theirs was not destined to be a close association. Though Akindynos dedicated some iambics to his prominent acquaintance and repeatedly wrote either to praise one of his works or to urge him to assume the leadership of the opposition to Palamism,[16] Gregoras treated him with indifference.[17]

It was in Thessalonica that Akindynos met Gregoras' rival, the Calabrian humanist Barlaam, who was destined to play such a fatal role in his life. His letters indicate that he and Barlaam had known each other before the latter's confrontation

[12] Kallistos, *Homily on the Sunday of Orthodoxy*, cited in Meyendorff, *Introduction*, 61 note 88.

[13] Ἀντιρρητικὸς 7, 16, 59, Συγγράμματα, III, 505, lines 11–32.

[14] See commentary on Letter 16, lines 27–28; and also the letters to Barlaam: 7, lines 78–84; 10, lines 79–82 and 93–107.

[15] Letter 1, lines 1–6, 39–45; Letter 2, lines 87–101.

[16] A short poem which Akindynos wrote in honor of Gregoras' own poem praising the almond tree (Εἰς τὴν ἀμυγδαλῆν ἐγκώμιον) has been published by S. G. Mercati in "Sulle poesie di Niceforo Gregora," *Bessarione*, 34 (1918), 98 (= *Collectanea byzantina I* [Rome, 1970], 151). During the crisis, Akindynos sent two more poems to Gregoras, first to complain about his neutrality and later to congratulate him on his first *Antirrhetics* against Palamas; see commentary on Letter 43, lines 2–3 *infra*. See also Letters 18, 19, and 44.

[17] In his *History*, Gregoras mentions Akindynos only briefly and incidentally, once when he quotes Kantakouzenos' address to the council of 1351 (XVIII, 8: II, 906, line 9) and another time when he declares his own agreement with the Church's verdict against Barlaam and Akindynos (XXVII, 17: III, 139, lines 3–6). Gregoras' only surviving letter to Akindynos is the one he addressed to him at the initiation of their correspondence; see commentary on Letter 2.

with Gregoras in the winter of 1331–32.[18] However, Palamas' claim that Akindynos was the student of Barlaam[19] is not substantiated by their correspondence. His letters to Barlaam, which were written before the Calabrian's condemnation and therefore have no reason to conceal such an association, leave no doubt that Akindynos belonged to the intimate circle of Barlaam's friends, but give no indication either in context or in general tone that he was his student. In these letters Akindynos counsels Barlaam as an equal and is outspokenly critical of his vanity and intransigence without ever showing for him the deference he accords to his acknowledged teachers, Magistros and Bryennios.[20] However, even if theirs was not a student-teacher relationship in the strict sense, they enjoyed a close association and had even shared lodgings for a long time.[21]

Aware of this relationship, Palamas, who was not personally acquainted with Barlaam, addressed to Akindynos shortly after the Feast of Pentecost, on 19 May 1336, a letter criticizing Barlaam's anti-Latin treatises which had appeared in the aftermath of the negotiations for reunion of the Churches in 1335.[22] Attacking the fundamental method of his Latin opponents' argumentation, Barlaam maintained that the Aristotelian method of demonstration did not apply to divine realities because the latter are beyond empirical knowledge and therefore beyond demonstration.[23] Akindynos shared Barlaam's views and had already objected mildly when Palamas used the term "demonstrative" to define his own discourses against the Latins. Palamas claimed, therefore, that it was for Akindynos' benefit as well that he undertook in his letter to defend at length the use of demonstrative syllogisms in theology which more than any other discipline has to do with necessary, unchanging, eternal principles.[24]

[18] See Letter 10, lines 17–30. According to Philotheos of Selymbria (*Vita Macarii* [cited in note 2 *supra*], 57), Barlaam and Akindynos met in Thessalonica after the latter's return from Mt. Athos. However, this information, which is not confirmed by any other source, must be inaccurate, because Barlaam left Thessalonica in 1330 (cf. commentary on Letter 10, lines 17–29) and Akindynos visited Palamas on Mt. Athos when the latter returned there *ca.* 1331. As Meyendorff correctly observes, Akindynos' long friendship with Palamas, which preceded his brief visit to the Holy Mountain (cf. Kallistos, *Homily*, in Meyendorff, *Introduction*, 61 note 88), must have been formed during the years that Palamas spent in Berroia, *ca.* 1326–31; see *Introduction*, 62.

[19] Palamas, Πρὸς Γαβρᾶν, *Συγγράμματα*, II, 325, lines 21–23; Πρὸς Φιλόθεον, *Συγγράμματα*, II, 527, line 25; Ἀντιρρητικὸς 3, 1, 1, *Συγγράμματα* III, 161, line 13. It must be noted that after the publication of the tome of 1341 which did not condemn Akindynos by name but any follower of Barlaam, it was very important for the Palamites to present Akindynos as Barlaam's disciple.

[20] Compare Letter 7, lines 7–10, 114–117; Letter 9, lines 11–37, 79–82, 109–115; Letter 10, lines 318–323, with Letters 56 and 58.

[21] Cf. Palamas, Α´ πρὸς Ἀκίνδυνον, *Συγγράμματα*, I, 203, lines 15–16.

[22] On the chronology of the preliminaries of this dispute between Palamas and Barlaam, see the recent study of R. Sinkewicz, "A New Interpretation," 489–96, where the reasons for proposing these dates are discussed in detail. For the date of Palamas' first letter to Akindynos, see *ibid.*, 495–96.

[23] For an excellent analysis of Palamas' first letter to Akindynos in light of the latest research, cf. Sinkewicz, "A New Interpretation," 494–500.

[24] Palamas, Α´ Πρὸς Ἀκίνδυνον, *Συγγράμματα*, I, 217, lines 8–11. Palamas' two discourses against the Latins bear the title *Λόγοι ἀποδεικτικοὶ* in some of the manuscripts which have preserved

Forced into the role of mediator which he was to retain until the council of June 1341, Akindynos conveyed Barlaam's answer to Palamas and quoted him as saying that whereas demonstration had various meanings, he had chosen to deal in his treatise with logical demonstration, in the Aristotelian sense, because this was the method used by western theologians to arrive at knowledge of God. By placing, therefore, that knowledge beyond the reach of human intelligence he believed that he had done a service to the pious theologians of the East who were reared in the apophatic tradition. Akindynos suggested tactfully that this explanation ought to be satisfactory and counseled against an unbecoming dispute between two "philosophers."[25] At the same time he recommended restraint to Barlaam, cautioning him not to "aim his arrows at a man who was not ignorant of the art of archery."[26] But his conciliatory efforts did not succeed. Dispensing with his services, Barlaam and Palamas began to correspond directly as their debate over the Aristotelian theory of knowledge and its application to the *gnosis* of God developed eventually into a dispute over the conception of *theosis* and the hesychast method of prayer. Thus began the second phase of Barlaam's quarrel with Palamas in which Akindynos played a decisive role not only because of his friendship with the contending parties, but also because of his access to the Patriarch.

Akindynos was in Constantinople when Barlaam lodged his first complaint with the Synod before the summer of 1337, accusing the hesychasts of heresy.[27] Neither his letters nor the writings of his opponents contain any hint of the reasons for which he left Thessalonica, nor of his occupation in the capital.[28] His frequent representations to Patriarch Kalekas in behalf of the hesychasts indicate that he was well acquainted with him and able to wield a certain influence, but we do not know in what capacity.[29] His status undoubtedly profited from the patronage of Princess Eulogia Choumnaina-Palaiologina, daughter of Nikephoros Choumnos, who became a nun after the death of her husband the Despot John Palaiologos. It seems that Akindynos met this scholarly and wealthy woman soon after his arrival at the capital and, according to the Palamite sources, her loyalty and liberality proved invaluable to him during the controversy.[30]

---

them; cf. PG, 150. col. 833; Meyendorff, *Introduction*, Append. I, 340; Sinkewicz, "A New Interpretation," 495 note 4. The discourses have been edited by B. Bobrinsky in Συγγράμματα, I, 23–153.

[25] See Letter 5, lines 42–72.

[26] Letter 10, lines 32–33.

[27] See Akindynos, *Report*, 86; Darrouzès, no. 2178. On Barlaam's first charges against the hesychasts, see Meyendorff, *Introduction*, 70–71. For a detailed history of the hesychast controversy, see *ibid.*, 65–128. For the revised chronology and excellent analysis of the most significant stages of the controversy (1337–51), see Darrouzès, pp. 136–268.

[28] It is possible that Akindynos continued to earn his living as a teacher in Constantinople. Dishypatos' remark that the majority of Akindynos' following consisted of young people lends a certain plausibility to this assumption; see *Poem*, 723, lines 6–9.

[29] Weiss agrees that Akindynos' role on the eve of the council of June 1341 was that of a very influential man; see *Kantakuzenos*, 105.

[30] See commentary on Letter 6, line 7.

In the dispute between Barlaam and the monks, Akindynos showed no qualms about opposing his friend. Despite the unpleasant memories of his brief stay at Mt. Athos, he strongly defended the monks against what he considered Barlaam's unnecessary intrigue. In the *Report* he presented to the Patriarch during the controversy, Akindynos wrote that when Barlaam pressed his first charges against the hesychasts, he personally protested to the Patriarch against this dangerous interference, and consequently Barlaam had to leave the capital after having been threatened with punishment by Kalekas. When Barlaam returned in the last months of 1340, bringing with him his treatise *Against the Messalians*, in which he accused Palamas and his fellow-monks of Messalianism, Akindynos again rejected his demand to join him in the attack against the hesychasts. Instead, accompanied by a group of monks he visited the Patriarch and in his presence read aloud from Barlaam's writings and criticized his views on the hesychast method of prayer and the divine light of the Transfiguration.[31]

Akindynos claimed to have opposed Barlaam at the time by all that he "said and wrote,"[32] and his correspondence confirms this claim. His four surviving letters to Barlaam[33] date from 1340, after Barlaam's return from Avignon, to the eve of the council in the spring of 1341. They contain repeated indictments of Barlaam's conceit and contentiousness which Akindynos held responsible for his friend's involvement in unnecessary and at times humiliating disputes, first with Gregoras, then with the Cypriot Lapithes, and finally with Palamas and the Athonites for whose piety Akindynos had nothing but unqualified praise.[34]

Though firmly opposed to Barlaam's interference, Akindynos was nevertheless beginning to share his doubts as to the orthodoxy of Palamas' theology. He admitted to Barlaam that he was disturbed by what he had to say about Palamas' doctrine of the divine grace,[35] but expressed skepticism as to the accuracy of Barlaam's interpretation,[36] refusing to pass judgment before he acquired a firsthand knowledge of Palamas' views. At the same time he warned Barlaam that it was an offense to call anyone a heretic before he was so declared by a synod and stressed the danger of attacking a man of Palamas' stature and prestige, predicting that not only the monks but all other segments of society would rally to his support.[37] To

[31] *Report*, 86–87; Darrouzès, no. 2201.

[32] *Ibid.*, 87.

[33] In an excerpt published by Allatius, Akindynos speaks of letters and discourses that he addressed to Barlaam concerning his errors (PG, 150, col. 875C). To my knowledge, no such discourses have survived, unless Akindynos used the term *λόγοι* for the long Letters 9 and 10.

[34] Letter 10, lines 17–58, and note 14 *supra*.

[35] Letter 8, line 4; Letter 9, lines 67–72. Akindynos probably revealed his misgivings to some of the hesychasts at the preliminary meetings with the Patriarch; see Kalothetos, *Κατὰ τοῦ Ἀκινδύνου πρὸς τὸν πατριάρχην κῦρ Ἰωάννην*, *Συγγράμματα*, 238, lines 78–81: *παρῆν τοῖς τότε λεγομένοις καὶ ὁ ψευδάδελφος ἡμῶν ... ὃς καὶ παρὼν οὐκ ἠνέσχετο μὴ λυπεῖν ἡμᾶς λόγοις ἀντιθέτοις, μᾶλλον δὲ Βαρλααμικοῖς.*

[36] Letter 9, lines 46–47; Letter 10, lines 197–99.

[37] Letter 8, lines 7–18; Letter 9, lines 62–67, 74–75.

Barlaam's imputation that his attitude reflected his partiality to Palamas, he answered by reminding him how he had earlier displeased his spiritual father by not hesitating to defend Barlaam's anti-Latin treatises.[38] Finally Akindynos declared his determination to remain faithful to the teaching of the Fathers, disregarding the newfangled theology of either of his two friends.[39]

Once more his advice for moderation fell on deaf ears. By the spring of 1341, Palamas and the monks had already signed two tomes condemning Barlaam without the Patriarch's approval. Their rash move enabled their opponent to charge them with organizing clandestine assemblies, a serious canonical offense for which, according to Akindynos, many in the capital urged Kalekas to condemn Palamas immediately.[40] Rejecting such drastic measures, the Patriarch wrote to the metropolis of Thessalonica summoning Palamas to appear before the Synod at Constantinople and account for his acts. The tone of the patriarchal summons and the fact that it was not addressed directly to Palamas but to his superiors, thereby creating the impression that he had already been judged guilty, disturbed Akindynos. He, therefore, first wrote and then visited the Patriarch to plead that such a letter was not in keeping with Kalekas' "gentleness and humanity."[41]

Probably unwilling to alienate as powerful a group as the monks, the Patriarch relented and, since the summons could not be recalled because Barlaam had already dispatched it, he addressed a letter to Palamas which Akindynos describes as "the kind that Palamas would have wished for."[42] This time he entrusted it to Akindynos who sent it together with a covering letter in which he alluded to his role in obtaining this patriarchal favor and also hinted briefly at his reservations concerning the doctrine of the divine grace which Palamas had explained to him in a recent letter from Thessalonica.[43] Up to that time he had doubted the accuracy of Barlaam's interpretation of this doctrine, but after reading his spiritual father's letter, he was inclined to agree with Barlaam and feared that Palamas had left himself open to Barlaam's charge of ditheism by the use of certain terms.[44] For this reason he wrote to

[38] Letter 10, lines 191–94.

[39] Letter 10, lines 195–208.

[40] *Report*, 87; Darrouzès, no. 2204.

[41] *Report*, 87.

[42] *Ibid.*

[43] See Letter 11. See also commentary on lines 8–9 of this Letter.

[44] The term that Akindynos found objectionable and later repeatedly attacked in his writings is the expression *θεότης ὑφειμένη*, which Palamas uses in this letter in reference to the divine grace: *Ἔστιν ἄρα θεότης ὑφειμένη κατὰ τους θεοσόφους θεολόγους, δῶρον οὖσα τῆς ὑπερκειμένης*. See Nadal, ed. "La rédaction première," 252, lines 10–12. Nadal argues convincingly that the original text of Palamas' third letter to Akindynos has been preserved in Akindynos' refutation of that letter, and that the text published by Meyendorff (*Θεολογία*, 24 [1953], 557–82 = Palamas, *Συγγράμματα*, I, 296–312 = Meyendorff, *Byzantine Hesychasm, Study III*) represents an expanded and edited version composed by Palamas, probably, for the benefit of Athanasios of Kyzikos who had refused to sign the *Tome* of 1341, because he had been shown what must have been the original copy of Palamas' third letter to Akindynos, not "falsified writings," as Palamas claimed. See Nadal, *op. cit.*, 233–85. In Meyendorff's edition of this letter the controversial passage reads: *Ἔστιν ἄρα θεότης ὑφειμένη κατὰ τοὺς*

the monk David Dishypatos who was then on retreat in the remote hermitage of Paroria in Thrace. Akindynos expressed the hope that this trusted friend of Palamas would convince him to eliminate from his writings all possible cause for criticism. His own advice, he explained, might not be as effective since he had earlier aroused Palamas' suspicions by defending Barlaam on the issue of the indemonstrability of divine realities. Akindynos also informed Dishypatos of his latest efforts on behalf of Palamas and revealed to him his serious fears for the peace of the Church, noting with apprehension that Palamas appeared extremely stubborn while, on the other hand, Barlaam's accusations against him did not seem altogether unjustified.[45]

Illuminating as Akindynos' correspondence is for the history of the origins of the controversy and the preliminaries of the council of June 1341, it sheds no light on the proceedings of that council. His account of the events that led to his condemnation is found in his *Report*, not a totally unimpeachable witness, since Akindynos wrote it in the spring of 1343 in order to justify the Patriarch's and his own opposition to Palamism.[46] According to the *Report*, Palamas arrived at Constantinople and while awaiting the convocation of the council stayed with Akindynos. When the latter questioned him about Barlaam's charges and revealed his own misgivings concerning the doctrine of the divine grace, Palamas sought to reassure him by explaining that it was "nothing new" and that Akindynos was disturbed because he did not comprehend "the mysteries of contemplative men."[47] Failing to persuade Akindynos, he urged him to assist him in the fight against Barlaam and professed himself willing to eliminate the objectionable terms from his writings, once Barlaam had been defeated.[48]

The council that the Patriarch convoked to hear Barlaam's charges against Palamas and the monks was held on 10 June 1341 at the Church of St. Sophia in the presence of Patriarch Kalekas and his Synod, the Emperor Andronikos III and the lay dignitaries. It lasted one day and, according to the Tome of 1341, it disposed of the charges of Bogomilism against the monks by contrasting passages from Barlaam's works with relevant quotations from the writings of the Fathers. The session ended with the Emperor's speech summing up the conclusions of the debate and condemning Barlaam's theories on prayer and the created character of the light of the Transfiguration.[49]

θεοσόφους θεολόγους, ὡς κἀνταῦθ' εἶπεν ὁ μέγας Διονύσιος, ἡ θέωσις, δῶρον οὖσα τῆς ὑπερκειμένης οὐσίας τοῦ Θεοῦ (*Θεολογία*, 577, lines 27–29; *Συγγράμματα*, 306, lines 18–20).

[45] Letter 12, lines 36–52.

[46] The *Report* can be accurately dated on internal evidence. Akindynos presented it to the Patriarch and the Synod while Palamas was a refugee at the church of St. Sophia; see *Report*, 92. On the date of Palamas' exercise of the right of asylum in that church, see commentary on Letter 27, line 171.

[47] *Report*, 87–88.

[48] *Ibid.*, 88. This agreement is not mentioned by any other source, but the fact that Palamas never repudiated such a claim may be a tacit admission of its incontestability. Indeed, the manner in which he allegedly answered Akindynos' objections seems to be in keeping with his low opinion of Akindynos' theological training; see, for example, his letter to Gabras, *Συγγράμματα*, II, 348, lines 25–27.

[49] *Συνοδικὸς τόμος*, PG, 151, cols. 681B–691D; Miklosich-Müller, I, 203–15.

Palamas charged later that Akindynos was not present at the council. Protesting his claims that he had stood up to Barlaam and refuted his errors concerning the divine light, Palamas wrote that Akindynos was not even present at the synod at the time but had run away on purpose.[50] The accuracy of this information cannot be verified, because the testimony of Akindynos is incomplete on this point. He writes that he appeared with Palamas before the Patriarch and the other bishops and fully supported Palamas on all matters, except the matter of the new doctrine, which neither of them mentioned—he out of trust in Palamas' promise to eliminate it eventually from his writings, and Palamas from fear of being detected. Accordingly, he concludes, Palamas read only from his works that dealt with the hesychast prayer, bringing forth only a few unimpeachable excerpts about the divine light, and thus "with our common consent Barlaam was beaten."[51]

There is little doubt that this statement refers to a preliminary meeting with the Patriarch and the Synod,[52] but not to the actual session of the council, about which Akindynos has nothing to say. Was he, then, absent from the council, or did he walk out before the matter of the divine grace was taken up, perhaps in tacit support of his spiritual father who was to adduce this later as evidence that Akindynos was in agreement with Barlaam? Unfortunately, the available evidence does not permit a definite answer.

Both Akindynos and the Tome of 1341 agree, however, that the Patriarch insisted on avoiding a doctrinal inquiry, and Akindynos claims that out of respect for Kalekas' wishes he did not protest when the council condemned Barlaam without examining his charges against the Palamite doctrine of the divine grace.[53] He sought nevertheless to convince Palamas to suppress it and honor their agreement prior to the council, but he complains that the hesychast leader, emboldened by his success, paid no heed to his protests and entreaties.[54]

Akindynos' persistent representations to Palamas in the aftermath of the synod of June concerning their doctrinal differences are also attested by the Palamite monk Kalothetos who provides the additional information that, in an attempt

[50] Πρὸς 'Αθανάσιον Κυζίκου, *Συγγράμματα*, II, 413, lines 9–13: *Καὶ τοῦτο οὐχ ἅπαξ ἢ δὶς εἰπὼν ἀπήλλαξεν, ἀλλὰ καταπεποίκηλταί οἱ πᾶς ὁ λόγος τοῖς δυσὶ τούτοις, ὅτι τε διανέστη καὶ ἀντέστη καὶ νενίκηκε τὸν* Βαρλαὰμ *εἰς τὸ φῶς ἐκεῖνο βλασφημοῦντα, καὶ ταῦτα μηδὲ τῇ συνόδῳ τηνικαῦτα παρών, ἀλλ'ἀποδρὰς ἐπίτηδες.*

[51] *Report*, 88.

[52] That such a meeting took place is evident from the complaint of Athanasios, the bishop of Kyzikos, that he was not invited to the hearing of the case prior to the council (Τόμος *συνοδικός*, PG, 151, col. 692B). See also Darrouzès, no. 2206.

[53] *Report*, 88; Τόμος *συνοδικός*, PG, 151, col. 681B–D; Miklosich-Müller, I, 203–4. Gregoras agrees that Barlaam was not allowed to argue his case against Palamas' theology from fear of stirring a major dogmatic dispute (*Hist.*, XI, 11: I, 558). Athanasios of Kyzikos was also left unsatisfied by the hurried proceedings of the council. One of the reasons he cites for his delay in signing the Tome of 1341 is that he had been denied permission at the council to read certain documents he had brought with him. (PG, 151, col. 692C).

[54] *Report*, 88.

to settle the matter, Palamas and eighteen of his followers met with Akindynos at the monastery of Patriarch Athanasios I on Xerolophos.[55] It was an animated meeting and after "arguments, disputations, questions, answers, objections, and counter-objections," Akindynos wrote out and signed an agreement with Palamas,[56] only to repudiate it the following day.[57] His retraction angered the Palamites, and at their insistence a second synod was convoked in July.[58]

Any attempt to reconstruct the proceedings of this synod stumbles upon the conflicting testimony of the contending parties; upon the strange silence of the Tome of 1341 which, though published after that council, totally ignores it; and finally upon the Patriarch's ambiguities in his interpretation of the Tome.

According to the Palamite sources, this second synod, which was presided over by the Grand Domestic John Kantakouzenos in place of the recently deceased Emperor Andronikos III, was as large as the first and, after failing to move Akindynos from his intransigent opposition to Palamas' theology, condemned him for holding unorthodox beliefs and falsely accusing the hesychast leader.[59]

[55]Kalothetos, *Κατὰ τοῦ 'Ακινδύνου πρὸς τὸν πατριάρχην κῦρ 'Ιωάννην*, *Συγγράμματα*, 240–41. On this meeting, which was probably the result of the Patriarch's conciliatory efforts (*Report*, 88), see also Philotheos, *Encomium*, PG, 151, col. 600D.

[56]Kalothetos, *ibid.*, 241, lines 154–56; Philotheos, *ibid.*; Dishypatos, *Poem*, 727, lines 150–51. Such a document has been preserved; see ed. Meyendorff, *Introduction*, 86 note 86; and "Le tome synodal de 1347," 226 notes, 93–97: Τὸ *τοῦ 'Ακινδύνου οἰκειόχειρον γράμμα. 'Επεὶ συνεληλύθαμεν καὶ συνεζητήσαμεν περὶ τῆς διαφορᾶς ἧς εἴχομεν πρὸς ἀλλήλους, ἐφάνη δὲ χάριτι Θεοῦ ὅτι οἱ πατέρες πρὸς οὓς εἶχον τὴν διαφωνίαν ἐν οἷς λέγουσι καὶ γράφουσι σύμφωνοί εἰσιν ἀλλήλοις καὶ τοῖς ἁγίοις, κἀγὼ συμφωνήσας αὐτοῖς κατὰ πάντα, τὴν παροῦσαν συμφωνίαν εἰς ἀσφάλειαν οἰκειοχείρως ἔγραψα. Γρηγόριος ὁ 'Ακίνδυνος*. During the persecution that followed his ordination Akindynos signed another such statement (see p. xxviii, *infra*), and Palamas ironically styled him a "chameleon" (*'Αναίρεσις γράμματος 'Ιγνατίου*, *Συγγράμματα*, II, 633, lines 21–24).

[57]Kalothetos, *Κατὰ τοῦ 'Ακινδύνου πρὸς τὸν πατριάρχην κῦρ 'Ιωάννην*, *Συγγράμματα*, 241, lines 170–73. In an extract from his writings published by Allatius, Akindynos renounces such an agreement with Palamas and affirms his determination to remain faithful to the doctrines of the Church (PG, 150, col. 877A–B): *Μηδεὶς ἀκούων συγκαταβῆναί με εἰς συμφωνίαν τῷ Παλαμᾷ, ἄλλο τι νομιζέτω φρονῆσαι παρὰ τὰ παραδοθέντα ἡμῖν παρὰ τῆς ὑγιεστάτης καὶ πᾶσι φανερᾶς καὶ ὡμολογημένης θεολογίας· ἐπὶ γὰρ τῷ στέργειν αὐτὰ τὰ τῶν θεολόγων ῥήματα, ὡς ἔχουσι κείμενα, συνεφώνησα, οὐκ ἐπὶ τῷ ἑτέραν τινὰ φωνὴν καὶ προσθήκην ἢ τοῦ καλοῦ Παλαμᾶ ἢ τοῦ Βαρλαὰμ παραδέξασθαι* ...

[58]Kalothetos, *Κατὰ τοῦ 'Ακινδύνου* ..., *Συγγράμματα*, 242, lines 180–82. That the synod against Akindynos was convoked in July and not in August, as commonly thought, is confirmed by the date of the copy of the Tome of 1341 in the patriarchal registry, which reads: July of the Ninth Indiction (Miklosich-Müller, I, 216). Loenertz was the first to observe that this date agreed with the Short Chronicle of 1352, according to which, Kantakouzenos—whose presence at the synod is attested by several sources—had left the capital in July and did not return until 28 August; see "La chronique brève de 1352," *OCP*, 30 (1964), 61. As Darrouzès notes, the date of August, shown on the signed text of the Tome (ed. Dositheos, PG, 151, col. 692B), does not refer to the session of the council but to the signing of the Tome which was not concluded until some time after that session. See Darrouzès, nos. 2212–14, and pp. 168 (*Date*) and 170 (*Date*).

[59]Palamas, *'Αναίρεσις γράμματος 'Ιγνατίου*, *Συγγράμματα*, II, 633, lines 16–30; Phi-

Akindynos' own account, as preserved in his *Report*, is neither detailed nor explicit, though it sheds some light on the proceedings. He was obviously summoned to the council as a defendant, for he says that he answered the Patriarch's call and appeared at the synod, though he was aware of his opponents' designs on his life.[60] The Patriarch was present and, at his command, Theodore Dexios, the future staunch Akindynist, read a chapter from St. Basil on the incomprehensibility of God.[61] In his continued effort to avoid a doctrinal dispute, Kalekas was probably anxious to put an end to the debate by emphasizing the futility of such inquiries, but Akindynos implies that he acted in his favor and that the patristic lesson so disarmed his enemies that when deprived of further arguments they resorted to violence. Two monks who accompanied him were severely beaten and he barely escaped death.[62]

---

lotheos, *Encomium*, PG, 151, 596B–C; Kantakoukouzenos, *Hist.*, II, 40: I, 556–57; Kalothetos, *Λόγος κατὰ τοῦ Ἀκινδύνου…, Συγγράμματα*, 242, lines 183–94. Kantakouzenos speaks of several arguments between the two opponents and Kalothetos mentions several attempts by the Patriarch and the civil authorities to counsel Akindynos, but a more precise account is given by the monk Mark in his address to the Patriarch (*Coisl. Gr. 388*, fol. 305ᵛ). Complaining that Akindynos, in a letter to one of his friends in Thessalonica, had described the synod of July as a synod inspired by the devil, Mark reminds Kalekas that he had presided over that synod and, together with his fellow-bishops, the civil dignitaries, the men of letters, the monks and all the other faithful, had condemned Akindynos who could only say in his defense that he believed in one God in three hypostases and did not accept two gods, one higher and the other lower. Therefore, "he was convicted and mocked by the judges for holding, indeed, the evil beliefs of which he falsely accuses others. Wherefore he was publicly condemned and reproached, for he was not only found guilty of holding the wrong doctrines but also of falsely accusing others." See this passage in Weiss, *Kantakouzenos* (110 note 718) where, however, the last sentence is omitted: *διὸ καὶ κατεδικάσθη καὶ κατηγορήθη παρρησίᾳ ὡς φωραθεὶς κακόδοξος, οὐ μόνον δὲ ἀλλὰ καὶ τοὺς ἄλλους διαβάλλων*. An excerpt from Mark's account has also been published by Meyendorff in *Introduction*, 87 note 91. Unlike the other sources quoted above, Mark does not mention the presence of Kantakouzenos at the synod, but his silence as well as the tactful allusion of Kalothetos to "those who were then in charge of the government" are probably due to the fact that both authors were addressing the Patriarch and were careful to avoid any reference to his archenemy.

[60] *Report*, 88–89.

[61] *Ibid.*, 89. In his edition of the *Report*, Uspenskij has left out this long passage (*Monac. Gr. 223*, fols. 53ʳ–53ᵛ), which is St. Basil's *Epistle to Eunomios* (*Epist.* XVI, PG, 32, cols. 280B–281A). The same passage is also found in the *Tenth Antirrhetic* against Eunomios by Gregory of Nyssa (PG, 45, col. 828A–C). Though Kalekas did not explicitly deny his presence at the council of July, his rather ambiguous account of that council written at the height of the controversy (cf. *Περὶ τόμου*, PG, 150, col. 901A–B) led to the belief that, contrary to Palamite claims, he abstained from the synod (cf. M. Jugie, "La controverse palamite," *DTC*, XI^2, col. 1782). Loenertz considers the Patriarch's presence established by the testimony of Akindynos, but believes that Kalekas walked out before the end of the council because he was dissatisfied with the unruly proceedings (cf. "Dix-huit lettres," 84). Had that been the case, however, would Akindynos have failed to cite such concrete evidence in his favor?

[62] *Report*, 89. See also Letter 26, lines 51–52; Letter 42, lines 60–61; Letter 63, lines 19–20; *Address to Hierotheos*, 199; *Antirrhetic V* (*Monac. Gr. 223*, fol. 322ʳ): *δεινοὶ γάρ εἰσι καὶ ἀπειλαῖς φοβῆσαι καὶ παραστήσασθαι τοὺς μὴ σφίσιν ἑπομένους αὐτόθεν, οὐ γλῶτταν μόνον ἀκόλαστον καὶ ὑβρίστριαν ἀσελγῶς ἐπαφίεντες αὐτοῖς, ἀλλὰ καὶ χειρῶν νόμῳ χρώμενοι καὶ μετὰ τοσαύτης ἡδονῆς τὸ τῶν μὴ πειθομένων αὐτοῖς αἷμα κατασκευάζοντες ἐκχεῖσθαι μεθ' ὅσης οἷον αὐτοὶ πίνουσι καὶ διαχέονται· διαβολὰς δὲ καὶ συκοφαντίας καὶ ὕβρεις ἀτοπω-*

He writes that as a result of these disorders the Patriarch and the Church turned against the hesychasts and, consequently, the latter persistently pressed the Patriarch to issue a tome exonerating them.[63]

Nevertheless, in his *Fifth Antirrhetic*, the most vehement of his polemical writings, Akindynos claims that after the reading of the passage of St. Basil, which was as damaging to Palamas as to Eunomios against whom it was written, the synod condemned Palamas and ordered the burning of his impious doctrines.[64] This claim, however, is not substantiated by any other source whatsoever, nor does it agree with his account in the *Report* where by carefully avoiding discussion of the decision of the council and by dwelling upon the unruly conduct of his enemies and the abuse they inflicted upon him, he indirectly confirms their boast that they had won the day.

The text of the *Tome* of 1341 is as silent as Akindynos about his condemnation,[65] and, while the reasons for the failure to record the synod of July remain conjectural,[66] we can say with certainty only that there is no evidence that Akin-

---

τάτας αἷς χρῶνται κατὰ τῶν εἰρημένων ἑῶ, οὐ γὰρ ἄδηλα τοῖς πλείστοις λέγω, οὐδ'ἔλαθεν ἐκείνοις τὰ ξίφη καὶ ἡ τῶν φόνων παρασκευὴ καθ'ἡμῶν ἣν ἐφάνησαν οὗτοι συνεσκευακότες. In the same discourse (fol. 323r), Akindynos accuses the Palamites of having unsuccessfully employed a certain Monemvasiote to assassinate him after the synod of July: *πάντα τρόπον ἐσπούδαζον ἐκκήρυκτον ἐμὲ γενέσθαι τῆς ἐκκλησίας, παραδοῦναι τῷ πλήθει, καὶ οὐχὶ τοῦτο μόνον, ἀλλά με καὶ ὅπως ἀναιρεθῆναι γένοιτο ... καί τις ἤδη καθεῖτο Δωριεὺς ἀνὴρ ἐπὶ τὴν πρᾶξιν αὐτοῖς, ὃς μεταγνοὺς τὴν ἐγχείρησιν ἀπέστη τε ταύτης καὶ τὸ δρᾶμα ἐξεῖπε.* (For the meaning of Δωριεὺς as used by Akindynos, cf. commentary on Letter 52, line 20). The violence of the crowd at the synod is also attested by the Palamite sources which, in turn, interpret it as a sign of the public's animosity against Akindynos; see Palamas, Περὶ θείων ἐνεργειῶν, Συγγράμματα, II, 135, lines 26–28; Kalothetos, Πρὸς τὸν ἐν μοναχοῖς αἰδέσιμον Σάβαν, Συγγράμματα, 365, lines 55–60.

[63] *Report*, 89.

[64] *Antirrhetic V* (*Monac. Gr. 223*, fols. 322v–323r): *Τοῖς δὲ ἦν διὰ σπουδῆς οὐ ταῦτα μόνον, ἀλλὰ καὶ περὶ ἐμοῦ πεῖσαι τοὺς πειθομένους αὐτοῖς συναποκεκηρῦχθαι δή με καὶ αὐτὸν τῷ Βαρλαὰμ ὡς δὴ ταὐτὰ φρονοῦντα διὰ τοῦ γράμματος, τὸ γράμμα μὲν μὴ δεικνύουσι, λέγουσι δὲ ἀπὸ στόματος καὶ δὴ καὶ ὑπό τινων, ὡς εἶπον, πιστευομένοις· οἷς οὐ συνέβη παρεῖναι τότε τοῖς γινομένοις, ὅθ'ὑμῖν ἐμοῦ μικρὸν παραδείξαντος τὰς δυσσεβείας αὐτοῦ, ἡ σὴ κορυφαία θειότης προβαλλομένη τὰ πρὸς τοῦτον οὐχ ἧττον ἢ τὸν Εὐνόμιον ἀντιρρητικὰ τοῦ μεγάλου καὶ σοφοῦ Βασιλείου, κατέγνω μετὰ τῶν ἄλλων πάντων θείων ἀρχιερέων αὐτοῦ, καὶ πυρὸς τροφὴν ἀπεφήνασθε γενέσθαι χρῆναι τὰς βεβήλους καινοφωνίας αὐτοῦ.*

[65] Only its title, in the edition of Dositheos (PG, 151, col. 679), links Akindynos' name with that of Barlaam, stating that the *Tome* was issued on the "great synods which confuted and rejected the impiety of Barlaam and Akindynos."

[66] For the political considerations that might have influenced the publication of the *Tome* and for the role of Kantakouzenos in the events of July, see Meyendorff, *Introduction*, 88–89; Weiss, *Kantakouzenos*, 110–113. The sources agree unanimously on one point: the difficulties that the Palamites encountered in securing the *Tome*. The Patriarch maintains that Kantakouzenos forced him to issue this document; see Περὶ τοῦ τόμου, PG, 150, col. 901B. Akindynos confirms the Patriarch's claim that he was reluctant to satisfy the Palamites' demand and says that when the hesychasts secured the *Tome* they became arrogant and abusive because they enjoyed the support of the all-powerful Kantakouzenos; see *Antirrhetic V* (*Monac. Gr. 223*, fol. 321v): *γράμμα μὲν ἐπέθετο τῇ ἐκκλησίᾳ δοῦναι αὐτῷ, λόγῳ μὲν ἐφ' οἷς Βαρλαὰμ ἑάλω, ἔργῳ δὲ διανοούμενος τούτῳ τὴν ἑαυτοῦ βεβαιῶσαι δυσσέβειαν·*

dynos signed at the time a statement of submission. Therefore the view that the *Tome* contains no reference to his condemnation because he signed such a document must be rejected.[67]

The *Tome*, however, contains two clauses which had a direct impact on Akindynos. The first clause decrees that if anyone prefers the same charges against the

---

τῆς δὲ μὴ πειθομένης ἐπὶ πολύ, μόλις ὅμως, διὰ τὴν πρόδηλον μὲν τοῦ Βαρλαὰμ ἀναχώρησιν παρὰ Λατίνους, ἄμετρα δὲ μηχανήματα τούτων συνεχῶς ἐσκεμμένων καί τινα χώραν ἐχόντων τότε, μήπω δεικνύντων ὁποῖοι φανήσονται τοῦ γράμματος τετυχηκότες ... (fols. 322ʳ–ᵛ): *Τὸ γράμμα δὴ περιφέροντες ταῦτα πάντα εἰργάζοντο, δυνάμει γὰρ ἐχρῶντο τῇ τότε μὲν τὰ μέγιστα δυναμένῃ, μετὰ ταῦτα δὲ διὰ τὴν τότε περιουσίαν τυραννεῖν ἐπικεχειρηκυίᾳ.*

On the other hand, Palamas and Kalothetos attribute their troubles to the interference of the Akindynists, who both threatened and cajoled the members of the Synod in order to prevent the *Tome* first from being properly written and then from being signed; see Palamas, *'Αντιρρητικὸς* I, 8, 49, *Συγγράμματα*, III, 72, line 25–73, line 40: *Πᾶσαν μὲν πρότερον ἔθεντο σπουδὴν μηδαμῶς ἀναγράπτους τὰς συνοδικὰς διαγνώσεις γεγενῆσθαι· τοῦτο δὲ μὴ δυνηθέντες, ὡς εἶδον ἤδη τὸν ὑπὲρ τῆς ἀληθείας συνοδικὸν τόμον γεγραμμένον, καὶ ὅσον οὔπω μέλλοντα τοῖς πανιέροις τῶν ἀρχιερέων ἐνσημανθήσεσθαι γραφαῖς, διανιστῶσιν ἑαυτούς, τί μὲν οὐ λέγοντες, τί δὲ οὐ πράττοντες, ὥστε κωλῦσθαι τελεσθῆναι ταῖς ὑπογραφαῖς. περιῄεσαν γὰρ τῶν ἀρχιερέων ἕκαστον, ἀπειλοῦντες ἅμα καὶ θωπεύοντες, νῦν μὲν μῶμον λέγοντες ἐποίσειν τῇ κατ'αὐτοὺς ἱερωσύνῃ τὴν ὑποσημείωσιν, νῦν δ'ἐξαίροντες ἐν μέρει τούτων ἕκαστον καὶ μὴ δεῖν ἀκόλουθα τοῖς ἄλλοις πράττειν συμβουλεύοντες.* Kalothetos, *Κατὰ 'Ακινδύνου καὶ Βαρλαὰμ τῶν κακοδόξων*, *Συγγράμματα*, 112, lines 49–54: *'Οπόσα δ'ἡμῖν προσέστη, τὸ μὴ τὸν ἱερὸν τόμον ὑπογραφικαῖς σημειώσεσι κατασφαλισθῆναι ἢ καὶ αὐτὸν μὴ προβῆναι τὸν θεῖον τόμον ὡς ἐχρῆν, οἶδεν ἡ δίκη καὶ ἡμεῖς οἱ τότε τοῖς πατριαρχείοις συχνὰ παραβάλλοντες, δι'ἃ καὶ τραχεῖς τισιν ἐδόξαμεν καὶ πάνυ τοι ἀπαίδευτοι καὶ σχῆμα πρὸ τοῦ σεμνότητος περικεῖσθαι. ἴσασι τὰ ἐμὰ τῶν ποδῶν πέλματα καὶ τῶν ἐμοὶ συννόμων καὶ πάνυ τοι τοῦτο ἴσασιν.* The Palamite testimony is particularly interesting because it intimates that Akindynos was not totally annihilated at the synod of July and that his accusations against his opponent's doctrines must have aroused some doubts among the ecclesiastical hierarchy which the turbulent proceedings of that council did not entirely dispel. The case of the bishop of Kyzikos who refused to sign the *Tome* until he had examined Palamas' own writings supports this assumption; see PG, 151, col. 692B–D. It must also be noted that whereas, according to Kantakouzenos, thirty-six bishops attended the synod of June, only seven signed the *Tome*; see Kantakouzenos, *Letter to the Bishop of Carpasia*, ed. J. Darrouzès, "Lettre inédite de Jean Cantacuzène relative à la controverse palamite," *REB*, 17 (1959), 15; Palamas, *op. cit.*, 73, line 6; Meyendorff, *Introduction*, 91. It seems, therefore, that the synod of July was not an undisputed Palamite triumph, and for this reason the powerful Grand Domestic might have compromised with the Patriarch and agreed to its omission from the *Tome* of 1341 and to the anonymous condemnation of Akindynos.

[67] Such a statement is quoted by Palamas, but it can be accurately dated on internal evidence to the persecution that followed Akindynos' ordination; see p. xxviii note 106 *infra*. Meyendorff (*Introd.*, 87) and Weiss (*Kantak.*, 111 note 724) date it to August 1341, but do not attribute to it the anonymous condemnation of Akindynos, as do P. Chrestou (*Συγγράμματα*, II, 17); B. Phanourgakes (*"Αγνωστα ἀντιπαλαμικὰ συγγράμματα τοῦ Γρηγορίου 'Ακινδύνου*, *Κληρονομία*, 4² [1972], 294–95); and K. Pitsakes (*Γρηγορίου 'Ακινδύνου ἀνέκδοτη πραγματεία περὶ* [*Κωνσταντίνου*;] *'Αρμενοπούλου*, *'Επετ. Κέντρ. 'Ερευν. 'Ιστορ. 'Ελλην. Δικαίου*, 19 [1972], 128). For his opponents' claim that Akindynos owed his anonymous condemnation to the generosity of his fellow monks, who were thus providing him with the opportunity to repent, see the passage from the letter of an anonymous Palamite cited by Meyendorff (*Introduction*, 88 note 98), and Kalothetos, ⟨*Κατὰ 'Ιωάννου Καλέκα*⟩, *Συγγράμματα*, 296, lines 366–68.

monks as Barlaam he will be subject to the same condemnation.[68] Palamas referred to this clause when he declared his opponent condemned and for this reason portrayed him as a Barlaamite,[69] while Akindynos vehemently protested this accusation.[70]

The second clause, whose aim was obviously to put an end to the dogmatic dispute, forbids anyone to make any oral or written pronouncements on dogma.[71] This injunction was eventually violated by both adversaries, but in the immediate aftermath of the council of July it was strictly enforced only in the case of Akindynos. He complained later that while Palamas could write at the time "numerous wily tracts" against him, he was not permitted even to make a sound.[72] Palamas confirms this,[73] and, whereas Akindynos attributes the Patriarch's attitude to his desire for the preservation of peace in the Church,[74] he interprets it in terms of Kalekas' secular pursuits and ambitions during the political crisis that developed shortly after the synod of July. He writes that when the Patriarch assumed the regency in October 1341 following the coup d'état of Alexios Apokaukos and the defection of Kantakouzenos, he sought unsuccessfully to win his support by offering him the sees of Monemvasia and Thessalonica and finally exploiting his feud with Akindynos.[75] Accordingly, Kalekas suggested to him in the spring of 1342 that if he should cooperate, Akindynos, who had again started to "agitate and talk non-

[68] PG, 151, cols. 691D–692A.

[69] See, for example, *Δευτέρα πρὸς Μακάριον*, *Συγγρ.*, II, 540, line 3; *Ἀναίρεσις γράμματος Καλέκα*, *ibid.*, 601, lines 7–8; *Ἀναίρεσις γράμματος Ἰγνατίου*, *ibid.*, 649, line 8; *Ἀναίρεσις ἐξηγήσεως Καλέκα*, *ibid.*, 658, line 28 – 659, line 1; *Ἀντιρρητικὸς* 2, 3, 11, *Συγγρ.*, 3, 92, lines 26–27; *Ἀντιρρητικὸς* 6, 24, 91, *Συγγρ.*, 3, 455, lines 18–19. Akindynos is called a Barlaamite in the titles of some of Palamas' polemical writings; see, for example, *Διάλεξις ὀρθοδόξου μετὰ Βαρλααμίτου*, *Συγγράμματα*, II, 164; *Πρὸς τὸν αὐτὸν αἱρεσιώτην τῆς τοῦ Βαρλαὰμ κακοδοξίας Ἀκίνδυνον ... λόγος ἀντιρρητικὸς δεύτερος*, *Συγγράμματα*, III, 85. See also the titles of Kalothetos' *Second* and *Fourth Antirrhetics* against Akindynos, *Συγγράμματα*, 111 and 159.

[70] See, for example, his statement published by Allatius, *De ecclesiae occidentalis et orientalis perpetua consensione*, 802: PG, 150, col. 875C–D; also, *Ἡ τοῦ Παλαμᾶ ὁμολογία ἀνεσκευασμένη*, ed. Candal, *OCP*, 29 (1936), 402, lines 4–9; *Ἡ ἐπιστολὴ τοῦ Παλαμᾶ ἀνεσκευασμένη*, *Monac. Gr. 223*, fol. 36ᵛ: *Καὶ μή με συκοφαντήσῃς ὡς τοῦ Βαρλαὰμ τούτοις τοῖς λόγοις ἀντιποιούμενον· οὐ γὰρ εἰ ταῦτά σου βελτίων ὁ Βαρλαὰμ καὶ ὀρθότερος, ἤδη καὶ πάντα ὀρθός ... μέσοι δὲ ὄντες ἡμεῖς Παλαμᾶ καὶ Βαρλαάμ, τὰ τούτων ὀρθὰ παραδεχόμενοι, τὰ μὴ τοιαῦτα ἀποστρεφόμεθα, εἰ καὶ ὑπ'ἐκείνου μὲν Παλαμῖται παρόντος ἠκούομεν, σὺ δὲ αὖ νῦν Βαρλααμίτας καλεῖς.* *Ibid.*, fol. 50ᵛ: *Καὶ πρό γε τούτων τῷ Βαρλαὰμ ἀντειρήκαμεν ὑπὲρ τῆς ἱερᾶς καὶ ἀσφαλοῦς ἡσυχίας ... καὶ δηλοῦσιν οἱ πρὸς ἐκεῖνον ἡμῖν γεγενημένοι λόγοι παρόντες καὶ φαινόμενοι, ἐν οἷς καὶ τὰ μὴ παντάπασιν εὐλόγως ἐκεῖνα κατὰ σοῦ γεγραμμένα οὐ τῆς τυχούσης ἐπιτιμήσεως ἔτυχε.* *Antirrhetic II*, *Monac. Gr. 223*, fol. 168ᵛ: *Ἴσθι τοίνυν ἡμᾶς οὔτε κατὰ σὲ οὔτε κατὰ τὸν σὸν Βαρλααμίτην ἁπανταχοῦ φρονοῦντας, ἀλλὰ δυοῖν τῶν παρ' ὑμῖν ἐναντίων μέσην οἰκοῦντας τῆς εὐσεβείας χώραν τὴν ἀνεπίληπτον.*

[71] PG, 151, col. 692A–B; Miklosich-Müller, I, 216.

[72] Letter 42, lines 105–9.

[73] Palamas, *Πρὸς Φιλόθεον*, *Συγγρ.*, II, 528, lines 17–19.

[74] Letter 42, lines 110–111.

[75] *Ἀναίρεσις γράμματος Καλέκα*, *Συγγράμματα*, II, 618, line 32 – 619, line 3; *Πρὸς σεβασμιωτάτους γέροντας*, *ibid.*, 510, line 25; Dishypatos, *Poem*, 726, lines 119–21.

sense," would be silenced.[76] Akindynos complained later that during this period he was nearly abandoned by all. He was forced, therefore, to write secretly and hurriedly in defense of his beliefs while he spent most of his time running all over the city in his effort to extinguish the "fires of heresy."[77] From this period probably date his appeal to a justice general who favored Palamas and his letters to Gregoras and to the young scholar Styppes in which he refers to the controversy in discreet and subdued tones while emphasizing occasionally the pain that his disagreement with his old friends was causing him.[78]

He was slowly given more freedom, however, as the Patriarch's negotiations with Palamas broke down in the spring of 1342 and Kalekas decided to begin canonical proceedings against the hesychasts' leader on charges that he had defied the Tome's injunction by engaging in written polemics against his opponent.[79] In May 1342 Akindynos accompanied by several monks appeared at a council organized against Palamas by the Patriarch with the support of Eulogia Choumnaina.[80] The following summer he played an active role in the events that culminated in the condemnation of Palamas. He claimed that he alerted the Patriarch to the danger of the unceasing dissemination of Palamas' innovative doctrines, and Palamas accused him of having indeed organized the two synods that condemned him *in absentia* that summer.[81] A few months later, at the beginning of 1343, he emerged as the Patri-

[76] *Πρὸς Φιλόθεον*, *Συγγράμματα*, 2, 531, lines 26–28.

[77] See Letter 42, lines 132–40; and Palamas, *Θεοφάνης*, *Συγγράμματα*, II, 259, line 28 – 260, line 3, where Akindynos is accused of violating the Tome's injunction through his oral propaganda. According to Palamas, it was the Princess Irene-Eulogia Choumnaina who sheltered Akindynos during those troubled days, and whenever his opponents came searching for him she appeared herself and engaged them in theological discussions; cf. *'Αντιρρητικὸς* 7, 5, 9–10, *Συγγράμματα*, III, 467, line 29 – 468, line 29.

[78] Letters 15–18.

[79] Palamas writes that sometime before their final breakup that spring the Patriarch allowed Akindynos to agitate against him, and when he personally complained to him, Kalekas turned a deaf ear, because he was already angered by his refusal to modify his political position; see *Πρὸς Φιλόθεον*, *Συγγράμματα*, II, 530, line 30 – 531, line 11. See also Philotheos, *Encomium*, PG, 151, col. 603A. The Palamites repeatedly accused Akindynos of profiting from the Patriarch's political ambitions and lack of theological training; see, for example, Palamas, *'Αντιρρητικὸς* 1, 8, 50, *Συγγράμματα*, III, 73, lines 11–12; *'Αντιρρητικὸς* 2, 15, 71, *ibid.*, 135, line 31 – 136, line 1; Kalothetos, *Κατὰ Βαρλαὰμ καὶ 'Ακινδύνου τῶν κακοδόξων*, *Συγγράμματα*, 113, lines 60–63; 120, lines 290–93; *Κατὰ τοῦ 'Ακινδύνου πρὸς τὸν πατριάρχην κῦρ 'Ιωάννην*, *ibid.*, 242, line 204–243, line 208; *Πρὸς Γρηγόριον Στραβολαγκαδίτην*, *ibid.*, 372, lines 103–4; Dishypatos, *Λόγος*, 93, lines 5–7. Kalekas, on the other hand, claimed that, in contrast to Palamas, Akindynos had complied with his request and provided him with a confession of faith; see *Περὶ τόμου*, PG, 150, 902A. See also, Kalothetos, *Πρὸς τὸν ἐν μοναχοῖς αἰδέσιμον Σάββαν ...*, *Συγγράμματα*, 367, lines 141–43. As already commented by Darrouzès (no. 2233, *Critique*: p. 184), this must be the *Confession of Faith* preserved in *Monac. Gr.* 223, fols. 14^r–16^v.

[80] Palamas, *Πρὸς Φιλόθεον*, *Συγγράμματα*, II, 535, lines 14–21.

[81] *Report*, 90; Palamas, *Πρὸς τοὺς σεβασμιωτάτους γέροντας*, *Συγγρ.*, II, 512, lines 13–16. Palamas also writes that Akindynos had sent some polemical tracts to Thessalonica and Berroia that

arch's official theological spokesman when at Kalekas' behest he presented to him and the Synod his treatise entitled *Dialogue of the Impious Palamas with an Orthodox*, a refutation of his opponent's *Dialogue of an Orthodox with a Barlaamite*.[82] This was followed, in the spring of the same year, by the *Report* to the Patriarch and the Synod in which he gave an account of the controversy up to that point and reaffirmed the orthodoxy of his own beliefs.[83] At the same time he wrote to his friends both in and outside the capital, inveighing against Palamas' doctrines and emphasizing his opponent's condemnation and the Court's opposition to Palamism.[84] The latter he ascribed to the influence of Sabbas Logaras,[85] an otherwise unknown personage, whose association with high Palatine dignitaries, and especially with the *megas doux* Apokaukos, proved extremely valuable to Akindynos in 1345.[86]

Another man of letters whose support Akindynos hailed enthusiastically in the summer of 1343 was John Gabras. Described by both Akindynos and Palamas as an

---

summer, though he did not dare show them in the capital; see Ἀντιρρητικὸς 2, 1, 5, Συγγράμματα, III, 88, lines 5–10; 89, line 24–90, line 8.

82 See commentary on Letter 25, lines 11–15. In complying with the Patriarch's order, Akindynos also wrote the antirrhetic treatises preserved in *Monac. Gr. 223*, fols. 16^{v}–26^{r} and 65^{r}–363^{v}. See his statements to that effect in the excerpts published by Uspenskij from the *Second Exposition Against Palamas' Heresies* (*Monac. Gr. 223*, fol. 67^{r}; *Synodikon*, 94) and *Antirrhetic II* (*Monac. Gr. 223*, fol. 164^{r}; *Synodikon*, 95); also in his last *Antirrhetic* (*Monac. Gr. 223*, fol. 336^{r}): Ἐγὼ δὲ ἤδη μοι νομίζω τὸ σὸν ἐπίταγμα, θειότατε δέσποτα ..., διηνύσθαι εἰς δύναμιν ... ἀπέδωκα δὲ καὶ Θεῷ καὶ τῇ σῇ μετὰ Θεὸν εὐμενείᾳ τὴν δυνατὴν ὀφειλήν ... *Ibid.*, fols. 358^{v}–359^{r}: Ἔχει μὲν ἤδη τετελεσμένην εἰς δύναμιν τὴν ἐμὴν ἡ σὴ κορυφαία θειότης εὐπείθειαν, δέονται δὲ οἱ λόγοι καὶ ἀξιοῦσι μὴ μάτην τὴν τοσαύτην ἀναλωκότες φροντίδα περιοφθῆναι ... The precise dating of these works must await their forthcoming edition by Fr. J. S. Nadal. I believe, however, that most of these seven treatises were written between the fall of 1342 and the spring of 1343, because in a letter dating from the spring of 1343 Akindynos wrote to a friend in Thessalonica that he was sending him some of his "many" refutatory discourses written at the Patriarch's behest; see Letter 27, lines 148–56. From the same period must date his *Iambics* which allude to the condemnation of Palamas and his doctrines; see PG, 150, col. 855B. On the other hand, the moderate and conciliatory tone of his refutation of the third letter of Palamas indicates that it was written very early, perhaps even before the synod of July; see *Monac. Gr. 223*, fols. 32^{r}–51^{r}.

83 Missing from Uspenskij's edition is the patristic florilegium which Akindynos attached to his *Report* in support of his refutation of Palamas' doctrines. On the date of the *Report*, see note 46 *supra*.

84 His letters contain at times whole diatribes against the Palamite doctrine of the divine energies; see, for example, Letter 27, lines 81–128 and Letter 40, lines 9–201. For references to Palamas' condemnation, see Letter 26, lines 58–61; Letter 27, lines 161–63; Letter 28, lines 31–34; Letter 30, lines 48–50; Letter 40, lines 126–27. On the attitude of the Empress, see Letter 28, line 30; Letter 32, lines 42–45; Letter 34, lines 40–41; Letter 39, line 64; Letter 40, lines 127–29. His opponents describe Akindynos as a zealous polemicist who sent his writings everywhere and canvassed the city for support; see Palamas, Ἀντιρρητικὸς 2, 8, 28; 16, 74, Συγγράμματα, III, 104, line 30 – 105, line 4, 137, lines 7–16; Kalothetos, Κατὰ Βαρλαὰμ καὶ Ἀκινδύνου τῶν κακοδόξων, Συγγράμματα, 120, lines 284–93; Πρὸς Γρηγόριον Στραβολαγκαδίτην, Συγγράμματα, 367, lines 100–107. Letters 27, 33, and 40 are indeed covering letters which he sent with polemical tracts to Thessalonica.

85 Letter 34, lines 39–44. Logaras wrote two discourses criticizing both the theology and the literary style of Palamas; see Letters 35 and 36.

86 On Logaras' support of Akindynos during the troubled period following his ordination, see Letter 51.

accomplished writer,[87] Gabras composed an anti-Palamite tract.[88] But his opposition to Palamism was short-lived. Wooed by both opponents, he eventually changed his convictions and joined the ranks of the hesychasts.[89] Akindynos sought also to rouse against the Palamites his old teacher, the noted Thessalonian philologist Thomas Magistros, but his appeals failed to elicit a response for, although the old scholar approved of his former student's position, he did not become an active anti-Palamite.[90] Amongst Akindynos' own students, the hetaeriarch Andronikos Tzimiskes of Berroia and the Thessalonian Isaris originally shared their teacher's views and in the spring of 1343 acted as carriers of Akindynos' letters and writings to his friends in Macedonia.[91] Later they both converted to Palamism, but, whereas Tzimiskes remained a staunch Akindynist long after his teacher's death, Isaris, who was a wealthy landowner, joined the Kantakouzenists in Thessalonica and barely escaped death in the Zealot uprising of 1345.[92]

In May 1344, Patriarch Kalekas and the young Emperor John V accompanied the *megas doux* Apokaukos on an expedition against Kantakouzenos in Thrace.[93] They stayed in Heraclea until the month of August when the Empress suddenly recalled them to Constantinople.[94] During Apokaukos' absence from the capital, Anna's advisers urged her to come to terms with Kantakouzenos.[95] The projected negotiations encouraged the Palamites and seriously disturbed Akindynos. He wrote to the Patriarch warning him that the "Palamite hydra" had again raised its head and expressing his confidence that the Patriarch upon his return would put an end to his opponents' subversive activities, while the legitimate Emperor would punish them for their disloyalty.[96] That he found it necessary in the same letter to reaffirm his own personal loyalty to Kalekas, the Emperor, and the true faith[97] indicates that his enemies had sought to discredit him to the Empress with the accusation to which Anna proved very sensitive at the time of his ordination, namely, that Akindynos was a heretic according to the decisions of the council presided over by her late husband.[98]

[87] See commentary on Letter 32, line 11.

[88] See commentary on Letter 32, lines 40–42.

[89] On Gabras, see commentary on Letter 32.

[90] See commentary on Letters 33 and 56.

[91] Letter 27, line 2 and Letter 28, lines 14–15. The *protonotarios* Michael Kaballaropoulos also acted as a carrier of letters and information between Akindynos and his friends in Berroia; see commentary on Letter 28, line 11.

[92] On Tzimiskes, see commentary on Letter 27, line 2. On Isaris, see *ibid.* and Letters 59 and 73.

[93] Kantakouzenos, *Hist.*, II, 68:II, 421; III, 71:II, 432–35; Gregoras, *Hist.*, XIV, 3–6:II, 702–10; *Chronica*, I, Chronicle 8, § 42, p. 83; commentary *ibid.*, II, 258–59.

[94] Kantakouzenos, *Hist.*, III, 71:II, 432; 437–38; Gregoras, *Hist.*, XIV, 5:II, 710–11; *Chronica*, I, Chronicle 8, § 43, p. 83; commentary *ibid.*, II, 259–60.

[95] Kantakouzenos, *Hist.*, III, 72:II, 437.

[96] Letter 38, lines 31–46.

[97] *Ibid.*, lines 17–18.

[98] The Palamite monk Mark Kyrtos did write to the Patriarch against Akindynos that summer and also publicly accused him of impiety and disloyalty to the Emperor; see Letter 37, lines 46–48 and 38–40.

But the return of the Patriarch to Constantinople and the failure of the negotiations with Kantakouzenos checked the Palamite resurgence and stiffened the government's attitude towards the enemies of the regime, just as Akindynos had hoped.

On 4 November 1344 the Patriarch convoked a synod which condemned and excommunicated Palamas, and formally deposed Isidore—the bishop-elect of Monemvasia and leader of the Palamite party during the incarceration of Palamas—for disciplinary reasons as well as disloyalty to the Emperor.[99] Then he proceeded to rid himself of another embarrassing situation. The injunction prohibiting doctrinal teaching to anyone under the rank of bishop and the Patriarch's subsequent policy toward Palamas, whom he had condemned under the terms of that injunction, rendered incongruous the position of Akindynos as the Patriarch's official theological spokesman.[100] He decided, therefore, to raise Akindynos to the episcopate.[101] But his plans hit upon an unexpected obstacle. They were revealed to the Empress just as he was preparing to ordain his protégé to the diaconate. The Patriarch's opponents convinced Anna that the ordination of Akindynos would annul the decision of the council over which the late Emperor had presided, and she acted with alacrity to restrain the Patriarch and prevent an affront to the memory of her husband.[102] But

[99] On the condemnation of Palamas, see Arsenios of Tyre, *Tome* (Mercati, *Notizie*, 205), and Darrouzès, no. 2249. On the deposition of Isidore, see Mercati, *Notizie*, 199 and 202; Kalekas, *Πατριαρχικὸς λόγος, δι' οὗ ἀποκηρύττει τὸν Παλαμᾶν* ..., PG, 150, col. 893B–C (hereafter, Kalekas, *Encyclical*); *idem*, *Περὶ τοῦ τόμου*, PG, 150, col. 903A–B; Darrouzès, no. 2250.

[100] See Kalekas, *Encyclical*, PG, 150, col. 892C–D. Akindynos was aware of the limitations imposed upon him by his status as a plain monk; cf. Letter 25, lines 2–4; Letter 42, lines 125–26. In defense of his polemical activity he repeatedly quoted the Pauline precept to "resist profane innovations" (II Tim. 2:16) and in his first letter to Lapithes pointed out that history offered many an example of plain monks who had spoken up for orthodoxy; see Letter 42, lines 128–31. He also argued that Palamas did not have a right to teach either, since he was only a monk; see *Dialogue of the Impious Palamas with an Orthodox*, *Marc. Gr. 155*, fol. 93r: ... *καὶ ταῦτα οὐδαμόθεν ἔχοντα τὸ τῆς διδασκαλίας ἀξίωμα· οὔτε γὰρ Χριστός, οὔτε ἀπόστολος, οὔτε προφήτης, οὔτε ἐπίσκοπος εἶ ἀλλὰ μοναχὸς καὶ ἀναχώρησιν ἐπαγγελλόμενος*. Unlike Akindynos, however, Palamas was an ordained monk; see Meyendorff, *Introduction*, 58.

[101] Palamas, Β΄ Πρὸς *Μακάριον*, *Συγγράμματα*, II, 540, lines 2–4; Arsenios of Tyre, *Tome*, in Mercati, *Notizie*, 205.

[102] Palamas, Β΄ Πρὸς *Μακάριον*, *Συγγράμματα*, II, 540, lines 4–12; *Ἀναίρεσις γράμματος Καλέκα*, *Συγγράμματα*, II, 592, lines 14–25; Meyendorff, ed., "Le tome synodal de 1347," 216, lines 174–80; Kalothetos, Πρὸς *τὸν ἐν μοναχοῖς αἰδέσιμον Σάβαν* .... *Συγγράμματα*, 364, line 32 – 371, line 48: *Ὁποῖα δ' ἀμφοῖν συνηνέχθη καὶ πρὶν τὸ χρῖσμα δοῦναι τῷ ἀλάστορι, ἀκούοις ἄν· γνωρίζεται τὰ περὶ τούτου τῇ αὐγούστᾳ καὶ τοῖς ἐν τέλει πᾶσι, καὶ πάντων ὁμοῦ ἐν δεινῷ τῷ πράγματι τιθεμένων καὶ μεστῶν θορύβου γενομένων καὶ καινοτομίαν ἀποκαλούντων τῶν πώποτε, τί γίνεται; πρεσβεύεται ἡ θαυμασία αὐγούστα μετὰ τῶν περὶ αὐτὴν πρὸς τὸν πατριάρχην ... ὁ δὲ παρεκρούσατο τὴν πρεσβείαν καὶ προσανεκάλεσεν αὐτοῖς, ἄγνωμον εἶναι εἰπὼν οὕτω προσφέρεσθαι αὐτῷ ὥς τινι τῶν πάντα ῥᾴστων καὶ εὐεπιχειρήτων. ἀλλὰ καὶ αὖθις ἡ βασιλίς, χεῖλος ἓν ὥσπερ μετὰ τῶν περὶ αὐτὴν γενομένη, διαπρεσβεύεται πρὸς τὸν πατριάρχην δριμύτερον, "μηδέν σοι," λέγουσα, "καὶ τῷ Ἀκινδύνῳ. τὰ μὲν γὰρ ἄλλα πάντα ἀνεῖταί σοι, ἱερά, ναοί, ἀσκητήρια, ἡσυχαστήρια, μονάζοντες, ἱερεῖς, ἐπίσκοποι, καὶ χρῶ τούτοις ὡς ἐφεῖταί σοι. τουτὶ δὲ τὸ κατὰ τὸν παρόντα, εἰ μὲν ἔφθη γεγονός, ὡς μὴ γεγονὸς ἔχω·*

the imperial rebuke did not intimidate Kalekas. He proceeded defiantly with the ordination, and when the Palamites raised a great turmoil, he reacted with vengeance.[103] He convoked a synod which confirmed the condemnation and excommunication of the Palamites.[104] The retaliation of the Empress was equally swift. Overstepping her authority, as even the exuberant Palamas admits, she declared the ordination uncanonical by a decision of the Senate and the concurrence of the Pala-

---

εἰ δ' οὐ γέγονε, μηδὲ γένηται. τούτου γὰρ ἐκβάντος, ὥς γε σὺ προείλου, ἀνατέτραπται πάντως ἡ τοῦ ἁγίου μου αὐτοκράτορος καὶ ὁμοζύγου ἀδέκαστος κρίσις ...."

[103] Palamas, Β΄ Πρὸς Μακάριον, *Συγγράμματα*, II, 540, lines 12–20: *Ὡς δ' ἐκεῖνος ἀπειθήσας, τὴν ἄθεσμον ταύτην ἤνυσε πρᾶξιν καὶ ὁ θόρυβος παρὰ τῆς πόλεως ἤρθη πολὺς εὐθὺς καὶ οἱ μὲν κατεβόων, οἱ δὲ καὶ ῥῆξιν ἠπείλουν, οἱ δὲ καὶ ἀπερράγησαν ἤδη τῆς ὑπ' αὐτὸν ἐκκλησίας, ὁ δὲ ἀντέκειτο πρὸς πέρας ἄγειν τὸ βούλημα προθυμούμενος ... καὶ τοῖς βασιλείοις ἐπιδημήσας, καθ' ἡμῶν δεινὸν ἔπνει καὶ δεινῶς ἐμεμήνει καὶ πάντα πράττων ἑωρᾶτο καὶ πάντα λέγων ἠκούετο* ... The ordination of Akindynos must have taken place sometime between November 1344 and January 1345. The validity of this date is supported by the following: 1) According to Palamas (*ibid.*, 539, line 26 – 540, line 4), Kalekas proceeded to ordain Akindynos after sending to the Athonites an imperial writ against Palamas. This missive, which has not survived, he dispatched in place of his own letter which has been preserved and is dated November, Thirteenth Indiction; see Palamas, *ibid.*, 539, lines 10–15; Miklosich-Müller, I, 238–42; PG, 152, cols. 1269D–1273A. 2) The persecution which followed Akindynos' ordination ended before the murder of Apokaukos on 11 June 1345; see Letter 51 and commentary. 3) Akindynos was still in hiding when he sent his second letter to Lapithes. According to Palamas, this letter was written nearly four months after the protests that followed his ordination and forced him to a sign a declaration accepting the decisions of the council of June 1341; see commentary on Letter 46. Even if this letter dates from as late as May 1345, the ordination could not have taken place later than January of that year.

[104] This second synod is attested by both Kalothetos and Akindynos. That it simply confirmed the condemnation of the Palamites, which had already been decided, is evident from Kalothetos' account of the sequence of events. In his letter to the monk Sabbas, Kalothetos writes first that in order to justify the ordination of Akindynos, the Patriarch wrote and sent to the various monasteries his encyclical denouncing Palamas and his followers. Kalothetos then goes on to say that when the opposition of the Court reached its peak Kalekas convoked a synod of his newly appointed bishops which confirmed his encyclical. See *Συγγράμματα*, 365, lines 74–366, line 110: *Βουληθεὶς γὰρ τὴν κατὰ τὸν Ἀκίνδυνον πρᾶξιν ἀκίνδυνον ποιῆσαι ... λύειν ἐπιχειρεῖ ἀτόπῳ τὸ ἄτοπον ... γράφει τοίνυν καὶ ἐγχειρίζει τοῖς αὐτοῦ διακομισταῖς τὰ ἐκεῖνον μᾶλλον ἢ ἡμᾶς ἀποκηρύττοντα αὐτοῦ γράμματα ... οἱ δὲ σπουδὴν θέμενοι διῆλθον ταχέως τὰς πλείους τῶν θείων μονῶν ... Ἀλλ' ἡ συνετωτάτη αὐγούστα τοῦτο γνοῦσα μετὰ τῶν ἐν τέλει, τί μὲν οὐκ εἶπε, τί δ' οὐ καθήψατο τοῦ πατριάρχου, τί δ' οὐκ ἐπέπληξεν αὐτῷ φανερῶς καὶ ἀφανῶς; ... Ἐπεὶ δ' ἑώρα καὶ αὖθις τοῖς ὅλοις ἑαυτὸν ἡττημένον καὶ ᾐσχυμένον ... συγκροτεῖ σύνοδον μετὰ τῶν νεοπλάστων αὐτῷ ἐπισκόπων, μηδὲν εἰδυίας τῆς ἁγίας ἡμῶν δεσποίνης μηδέ τινος τῶν περὶ αὐτήν. Ὡς δ' ἀνηνέχθη τοῦτο τῇ αὐγούστᾳ, ἐνσκήπτει τῷ πατριάρχῃ λῦσαι τὸν σύλλογον. Ὁ δ' ὀξύρροπος ὢν πρὸς τὰ φαῦλα, ἀλλ' οὐ πρὸς τὰ χρηστά, παρεκρούσατο τὰς αὐτῆς ἐντολὰς καὶ εἰς ἔργον ἄγειν προθυμεῖται τὰ αὐτοῦ διαβούλια. Ἀλλ' ἐκεῖ μὲν καθ' ἡμῶν κυροῦται τὰ τῆς αὐτοῦ γνώμης καὶ τρόπου οὐδὲν ἐλλελοιπότα γράμματα· ἐκεῖ τὸ τῆς ἀποκηρύξεως γραμμάτιον, ὧδε τὸ τῆς ἀθωώσεως καὶ ἀναρρήσεως· ἐκεῖ τὸ τῆς ἀδικίας, ὧδε τῆς δικαιοσύνης* ...

Akindynos also affirms that when the Palamites raised a furor over his ordination, the Patriarch called a synod against them and that it was attended by the Patriarch of Antioch and other Asiatic prelates; see Letter 50, lines 108–110.

mite bishops.[105] Akindynos suffered imprisonment and persecution and had to sign a statement accepting the decision of the synod against Barlaam.[106]

The furor surrounding his ordination forced Akindynos to pass over in silence what must have been for him an event of momentous importance. In his correspondence there is only one reference to his ordination. Writing to the hieromonk Matthew, a former follower who had suddenly defected, he boasted that opposition to his ordination resulted in the expulsion from the Church of Palamas and his followers.[107] Allusions to the persecution that followed his ordination, on the other hand, are more frequent though vague and impossible to decipher without the information provided by his opponents. In his letter to the Thessalonian scholar Branas he writes, for example, that the friendship and support of men like him make the

[105] Palamas, Ἀναίρεσις γράμματος Καλέκα, *Συγγρ.*, II, 592, lines 26–32: Ὡς δ' ἐκεῖνος *τὸν ἔξω τῆς εὐσεβείας* Ἀκίνδυνον *εἴσω τοῦ βήματος τῆς ἐκκλησίας φέρων ὤθησε ... καταχρῆται καὶ αὕτη λυσιτελῶς καὶ δικαίως τῇ ἐξουσίᾳ καὶ τὸν ἐν ἱερατείᾳ γενόμενον ἀνίερον* Ἀκίνδυνον *ἐξωθεῖ τῆς ἱερᾶς ἐκκλησίας* ... Β´ Πρὸς Μακάριον, *Συγγρ.*, II, 540, lines 25–28: Καὶ *δὴ βουλὴ καὶ ψῆφος συγκλήτου δικαιοτάτη, συναινούντων καὶ τῶν ἐν ἀρχιερεῦσιν ἐκκρίτων, ἀκυροῖ μὲν ὡς ἄθεσμον τὴν ἐπ'* Ἀκινδύνῳ *χειροτονίαν, ἐκβαλοῦσα δὲ τοῦτον τῆς ἐκκλησίας ὥσπερ τι κοινὸν ἄγος πόρρω ποι ῥιπτεῖσθαι διακελεύεται* ...

[106] Palamas, Ἀναίρεσις γράμματος Καλέκα, *Συγγρ.*, II, 593, lines 1–4: ... *εἶθ' ὡς πάντολμον καὶ ἀλλόκοτον καὶ κατὰ τῆς ἱερωσύνης μᾶλλον ἢ πρὸς ἱερωσύνην χωρήσαντα, πληγῶν καὶ δεσμῶν καὶ καθειργμῶν δικαιοῖ*. This passage is quoted by the synodal tome of 1347 (ed. Meyendorff, "Le tome synodal de 1347," 216, lines 186–88). According to Kalothetos, the Patriarch offered as a justification for the ordination of Akindynos a brief confession of faith which Akindynos had presented to him: Ἀλλὰ *καὶ αὖθις πληττόμενος ὁ τῆς ἐκκλησίας προστάτης ὑπὸ πάντων, ὅτι τὸν οὕτως ἔχοντα κακοδοξίας ἱερωσύνης ἠξίωσε, τοιάδε φάσκει·* "Δέδωκέ *μοι ὁμολογίαν καὶ διὰ τοῦτο τοῦτον ἱερωσύνης ἠξίωσα*" ... *ἀλλὰ πρότερον μὲν μακροῖς τισι καὶ περιοδικοῖς γράμμασι ἐνεχείρισέ σοι ὁμόλογον τὴν κακοδοξίαν αὐτοῦ, ἀποστάσιον τῆς εὐσεβείας σαφῶς· νῦν δὲ πρὸς ἐξαπάτην τῶν ἁπλουστέρων βραχυσύλλαβόν τινα πλασάμενος ὁμολογίαν ἐγχειρίζει σοι ταύτην. ἀλλ' ἐψεύσθη γε τῶν ἐλπίδων μάτην ὀνειροπολήσας ταῦτα· πάντες γὰρ ὡσανεὶ ὑπογραφὴν καὶ σφραγῖδα ἡγήσαντο ταύτην τῶν προτέρων αὐτοῦ κακοδόξων γραμμάτων*. (Πρὸς *Σάββαν μοναχόν, Συγγράμματα*, 367, line 132 – 368, line 147). This confession is obviously the document quoted by Palamas in his sixth *Antirrhetic*: Ἀλλ' *αὐτὸς πάλιν ἡνίκα θωπείαις ἅμα καὶ δώροις κλέψας τοὺς πρὸς αὐτὰ κεχηνότας, τοῖς ἐν τῷ σεπτῷ βήματι συνεξητάσθη καὶ παραυτὰ φωραθεὶς παρὰ τῶν ἐκκρίτων ἀρχιερέων ἐγγράφως ἀπεχειροτονεῖτο καὶ παρὰ τῶν εὐσεβῶν βασιλέων καὶ τῶν ὀρθοδόξων ἁπλῶς ἁπάντων ὥς τι μύσος τῶν τῆς ἱερᾶς ἐκκλησίας περιβόλων ἠλαύνετο, λίβελλον συγγραψάμενος τῆς ἑαυτοῦ τάχα δόξης, θαρρῶν ἀπατῆσαι πάντας εἴπερ ἑαυτοῦ καταψεύσαιτο, κἂν εἰ μηδ' οὕτως ἐκφυγεῖν ἐδυνήθη τὴν καταδίκην, πάντων συνεγνωκότων ἔργῳ τἀληθές, ὡς ἐπὶ πανδήμου συνόδου βεβαίως ἀναφανέν· ἐπὶ τούτου τοίνυν αὐτοῦ τοῦ λιβέλλου πάλιν φησίν, "ἡμεῖς ἀποδεχόμεθα καὶ ἐκ ψυχῆς ἀσπαζόμεθα καὶ τὴν ἐπὶ τῇ παρουσίᾳ τοῦ εὐσεβεστάτου καὶ μακαρίτου καὶ ἀοιδίμου βασιλέως ἡμῶν συναθροισθεῖσαν σύνοδον καὶ ἀπελέγξασαν καὶ ἀποπέμψασαν ὅσα τῷ* Βαρλαὰμ *περὶ τοῦ ἀπροσίτου καὶ θείου φωτὸς τῆς μεταμορφώσεως εἴρηται βλασφήμως καὶ κακοδόξως"· τελευτῶν δ' ἐπὶ τοῦ λιβέλλου τούτου φρονεῖν οὕτω καὶ τούτοις ἀεὶ ἐμμένειν διισχυρίζεται καὶ μηδέποτ' ἄλλως φρονήσειν, κἂν εἰ μυρίους τις ἐπάγοι τούτῳ θανάτους*. (Ἀντιρρητικὸς 6, 1, 4, *Συγγρ.*, III, 381, line 23 – 382, line 6). The reference to Akindynos' ordination in this text proves that, contrary to P. Chrestou's assertion, the *Antirrhetics* of Palamas were not all written before the end of 1344; see *Συγγράμματα*, III, 24.

[107] Letter 50, lines 106–10.

"present persecution" preferable to a life of leisure, but adds nothing as to the nature or the cause of this persecution.[108] Even more cryptic are his remarks to Lapithes, the Cypriot man of letters whose unexpected support brought Akindynos at this time a much needed solace and encouragement. An admirer and correspondent of Gregoras, Lapithes evidently became interested in the controversy through a group of Cypriot anti-Palamites gathered around Hyakinthos, a monk at the monastery of Hodegetria in Constantinople and later metropolitan of Thessalonica.[109] Lapithes' first letters, in which he requested precise information about the history of the dispute and the writings of the leading opponents, found Akindynos in hiding. Unable to satisfy fully his correspondent's request, Akindynos sent Lapithes only his refutations of Palamas' *Third Letter* and *Dialexis*, with the vague excuse that the turbulent times prevented him from sending his more important polemical tracts.[110] At one point, however, he was forced to confess that his situation was so precarious that he thought of fleeing to Cyprus and asked Lapithes to prepare a shelter for him there.[111]

From his hideout[112] Akindynos remained in touch with the Patriarch[113] and pursued his polemical activity spurred on by his new supporter who wrote from distant Cyprus that even Akindynos' resistance to Palamism was weak.[114] His principal targets were the uncommitted or μέσοι, as he called them, whose apathy he vehemently attacked.[115] The most notable among these was the polymath Gregoras to whom Akindynos addressed an impassioned appeal urging him to imitate the example of their Cypriot friend and not allow Constantinople to be surpassed by the provinces in the contest for orthodoxy.[116] His persecution, however, lasted only a few months. Sabbas Logaras used his influence at Court to reconcile him with the *megas doux*,[117] who had been a strong opponent of his ordination, and the Patriarch, in defiance of the Empress and the Senate, promoted him from the diaconate to the

[108] Letter 41, lines 37–38.

[109] Lapithes' first letter concerning the controversy was addressed to Hyakinthos; see Letter 44, lines 37–38.

[110] See Letter 42, lines 166–69; 192–203; Letter 46, lines 41–51; Letter 47, lines 2–21. The difficulty he experienced in sending Lapithes his refutation of Palamas' *Dialexis* and the fact that he sent only his commentaries on Palamas' works, not his *Antirrhetics*, indicate that he had no ready access to his papers and also that he was afraid to send out his more vehement polemical tracts.

[111] Letter 42, lines 184–86.

[112] The Tome of 1347 states that Akindynos was sentenced to "be thrashed and bound and confined, but he escaped through subterranean hollows" (Meyendorff, ed., "Le tome synodal de 1347," 216, lines 198–99).

[113] See Letter 47, lines 49–55, where he writes to Lapithes that he is sending him the patriarchal tomes against Palamas at the behest of the Patriarch.

[114] Letter 42, lines 38–39.

[115] Letter 41, lines 155–83.

[116] Letter 43.

[117] Letter 51, lines 20–44. This reconciliation must have occurred shortly before the murder of Apokaukos on 11 June 1345. On this date, see commentary on Letter 51. On Apokaukos' opposition to the ordination of Akindynos, see commentary on Letter 51, line 25.

priesthood.[118] In a letter to an unknown supporter Akindynos confessed that he had emerged from his ordeal more powerful than before.[119] His enemies claim that he played a leading role in Kalekas' campaign to rid the ecclesiastical hierarchy of dissident elements,[120] and his own letters attest to his elation at the appointment of Iakobos Koukounares to the see of Monemvasia and the Cypriot Hyakinthos to that of Thessalonica.[121] In the autumn of 1345 he wrote several letters to Thessalonica recommending the new metropolitan to his friends there and at the same time congratulating them for their perseverance during the persecution they suffered earlier that summer.[122] Hyakinthos proved, indeed, a dedicated anti-Palamite.[123] During his tenure in Thessalonica, Palamism experienced a temporary setback, but his brief episcopate was the last cause Akindynos had for rejoicing. His own career came to an end even before the death of that prelate in the spring of 1346.[124]

The feud with the Empress over his ordination of Akindynos and the murder of the *megas doux* Apokaukos on 11 June 1345 marked a turning point in the Patriarch's career. While Kantakouzenos was rapidly winning the war, the Empress took a more active part in the doctrinal aspects of the religious controversy. In January 1346, the later patriarch Philotheos Kokkinos addressed to her on behalf of the Athonites two dogmatic treatises defending Palamas against the charge of ditheism.[125] Subsequently, she demanded and received from both Palamas and Akindynos a doctrinal statement.[126] In Akindynos' case this document shows that he was al-

[118] Palamas, *'Αναίρεσις γράμματος* Καλέκα, *Συγγράμματα*, II, 601, lines 11–19: ... *καὶ τὸν 'Ακίνδυνον τοῦτον ἐπὶ διαβολῇ πάντως ἡμῶν τε καὶ τῆς συγκλήτου πάσης, ἔτι δὲ καὶ τῆς φωτὸς δίκην εἴπερ ποτὲ τηνικαῦτα διαυγασάσης βασιλικῆς εὐσεβείας, σεαυτῷ νῦν ἐπ' αὐτοῦ τοῦ θείου συνῆψας βήματος, βεβαιωτὴς αὐτοῦ καὶ προστάτης γενόμενος ... καὶ κατέλεξας ἐν ἱερεῦσι τὸν μὴ τὸν βίον μόνον ἀλλὰ καὶ τὸ σέβας ἀνίερον.* As Meyendorff points out (*Introduction*, 114 note 87), the fact that Akindynos is designated as hieromonk in some of the manuscripts that have preserved his works (*Marc. Gr. 155*, fols. 17^r, 35^v, 80^r, 91^v; *Barber. Gr. 291*, fol. 218^r) is further evidence that he had been ordained priest. Akindynos must have been ordained priest following his persecution, because Palamas says that the Empress ordered his arrest immediately after his ordination to the diaconate; see *'Αναίρεσις γράμματος* Καλέκα, *Συγγράμματα*, II, 592, line 26–593, line 4.

[119] Letter 53.

[120] See the excerpt from the work of an anonymous Palamite published in Mercati, *Notizie*, 221: note 2: *ἀλλὰ καὶ οἱ νεόφυτοι αὐτοῦ ἀρχιερεῖς οὕτως ὑπέγραψαν πάντες, προεβλήθησαν δὲ οἱ πλείονες ὑπὸ τοῦ 'Ακινδύνου, πρότερον στέρξαντες τὰ αὐτοῦ.* See also Darrouzès, no. 2256, where other pertinent sources are cited.

[121] Letter 52, lines 2–54.

[122] Letter 56, lines 70–81; Letters 57 and 58.

[123] On Hyakinthos, see commentary on Letter 44, line 38. On his persecution of the Palamites in Thessalonica, see *ibid.*

[124] The inference from a letter of Akindynos to Lapithes is that the death of Hyakinthos was contemporary with the collapse of the dome of St. Sophia, which is accurately dated to 19 May 1346; see Letter 60, lines 70–72 and commentary.

[125] Meyendorff, *Introduction*, 117 and 314.

[126] Palamas, *Πρὸς "Ανναν Παλαιολογίναν*, *Συγγράμματα*, II, 545–47; Akindynos, *'Ομολογία πρὸς τὴν δέσποιναν*, ed. Candal, "La confesión de fe antipalamítica de Gregorio Acíndino," *OCP*, 25 (1959), 216–26.

ready in disgrace. For after stating his beliefs and affirming that his enemies had falsely accused him of the heresies of which they were themselves guilty, he ended his confession of faith by promising the Empress that he would remain quiet, if she gave orders that he was to be left undisturbed.[127] He was, evidently, in trouble, and the Patriarch was either unable or unwilling, in the face of an imminent Kantakouzenist victory, to lend him further support. In fact the evidence from the correspondence of Akindynos indicates that Kalekas abandoned his protégé before he was himself deposed. In a desperate plea for help in "the storm" that had overtaken him, Akindynos reminded the Patriarch of his services to him and the Emperor and complained that since the Patriarch had turned away from him he was the prisoner of his enemies whose calumnies had won in the end.[128] His letter to Lapithes, dating from the early summer of 1346, confirms that Akindynos by that time was already in distress. To this distant follower he confessed that he was in a "host of troubles" for which he desperately needed his help.[129]

By this time, of course, the Patriarch's authority was rapidly declining. While on 21 May 1346 the victorious John Kantakouzenos was crowned emperor at Adrianople, the dissident bishops gathered in that city deposed John Kalekas primarily on the grounds of his association with Akindynos.[130] The same charge, in addition to sacrilege, heresy and simony, was brought against him the following September by six members of the synod who had been confined by him to their cells. They, too, petitioned the Empress for his deposition.[131] On 2 February 1347, before mounting ecclesiastical and political pressure, just as Kantakouzenos was preparing to enter the capital, Anna convoked a synod presided over by herself and her young son John V. This council, at which neither Kalekas nor Akindynos appeared, deposed the Patriarch, confirmed the *Tome* of 1341, and declared Akindynos and his followers excommunicated and expelled from the Church. Its decisions were confirmed by a second council held a week later in the presence of Kantakouzenos and were incorporated in the synodal tome of 1347.[132]

[127] Ὁμολογία, 226, lines 11–18. Candal dates this confession to the end of 1347, i.e., after Akindynos' final condemnation (*op. cit.*, 253). It is, however, unlikely that Anna would have reopened the case of Akindynos after it had been decided by a synod presided over by herself and her son. We know from the *Tome* of 1347 that shortly before his deposition by the dissident bishops in May 1346 Kalekas had also submitted to the Empress a dossier in which he attacked the theology of Palamas and accused him again of misinterpreting the *Tome* of 1341; cf. Meyendorff, ed., "Le tome synodal de 1347," 217, lines 205–17; see also Palamas, Ἀναίρεσις ἐξηγήσεως Καλέκα, Συγγράμματα, II, 649–70, and Darrouzès no. 2261. We can, therefore, safely assume that these doctrinal statements by the protagonists in the dispute were presented to Anna in the spring of 1346.

[128] See Letter 63.

[129] See Letter 60, lines 2–22.

[130] Kantakouzenos, *Hist.*, III, 92: II, 564–65; Πρόσταγμα, PG, 151, col. 771D; Gregoras, *Hist.*, XV, 5: II, 762; "Le tome synodal de 1347," ed. Meyendorff, 217, lines 209–17; Darrouzès, no. 2262.

[131] Ἀναφορὰ τῶν ἀρχιερέων, PG, 151, cols. 767D–770D; Darrouzès, no. 2263.

[132] Kantakouzenos, *Hist.*, IV, 3: III, 23; Πρόσταγμα, PG, 151, cols. 771C–772B; "Le tome synodal de 1347," 218–24; Darrouzès, nos. 2269 and 2270.

Akindynos survived his sentence by one year. His disappointment as well as his desperate effort to hold on to a diminishing following are registered in his "Et tu, Brute" letters to the friends who were abandoning him and the messages of consolation and encouragement to those who remained loyal and shared his lot.[133] Two men disillusioned him in particular, the jurist Harmenopoulos and the court dignitary Maximos Kalopheros. Harmenopoulos had taken part in the anti-Palamite activities of the metropolitan Hyakinthos of Thessalonica,[134] but in the summer of 1347[135] he declared his disenchantment with both parties in the controversy and accused them equally of contentiousness and heresy.[136] Kalopheros, on the other hand, who had opposed Palamas and inveighed against him in public while at Constantinople,[137] left the capital after the arrival of Kantakouzenos and went to Mt. Athos where he joined forces with the hesychasts.[138] Another severe blow, though one for which Akindynos was prepared since the summer of 1345, was the final defection of his former student, the wealthy Thessalonian landowner Isaris who barely escaped with his life during the Zealot uprising. Akindynos bitterly reproached the selfish political interests that motivated his transfer of allegiance.[139]

The fear of being arrested forced Akindynos to go into hiding and to reject Kantakouzenos' offer to come forward and receive a fair trial.[140] His refusal either to

[133] See Letters 67–76.

[134] *Address to Hierotheos*, ed. Pitsakes, 193: *Οὐ ταῦτα παρ' ἡμῶν ἀεὶ πρότερον ἤκουσας; οὐ ταῦτα καὶ λαβεῖν παρ' ἡμῶν ἠξίωσας πέρυσι, καὶ λαβὼν ἀπῄεις ἐπ' Ἄθῳ κἀκεῖθεν ἐπὶ Θεσσαλονίκης, λαμπρόν τι πνέων κατὰ τῶν Παλαμναίων; μεθ' ὧν καὶ τῷ Θεσσαλονίκης ἀληθινῷ ποιμένι, τοὺς λόγους τούτους ἀμυνομένῳ τὴν ἐκκλησίαν τὴν αὐτοῦ διασπῶντας, Ὑακίνθῳ τῷ ἱερῷ συνηγώνισαι, καὶ τοὺς ἀγῶνας γράψας ἀπέσταλκάς μοι αὐτός τε καὶ ἀδελφός;*

[135] The *Address* can be dated to the spring of 1347 at the earliest, on the basis of Akindynos' statement that he had been proclaiming his beliefs for the last six years (*Marc. Gr. 155*, fol. 81ᵛ): *Τίς γὰρ ἡμᾶς οὐκ οἶδε ταῦτα νῦν ἐξ ὅλων ἐνιαυτῶν βοῶντας καὶ κεκραγότας*; Pitsakes, who reads against the MS *ἐξ ὅλων ἐνιαυτῶν* (p. 192), disregards this evidence and dates the *Address* to autumn 1346–January 1347 (p. 135).

[136] *Address to Hierotheos*, 188.

[137] Letter 70, lines 17–18.

[138] *Ibid.*, lines 14–17 and Letter 76.

[139] Letters 59, 71, and 73. With one of those puns favored by the Byzantines, Philotheos informs us that a certain Kaloeidas was another staunch Akindynist who defected to Palamas (*Encomium*, PG, 151, col. 608B): *Τούτοις καὶ τῶν ὁμιλητῶν Ἀκινδύνου καὶ φίλων εἷς τις συνῆν ... καλὸς μέν πως τὸ εἶδος ἐκ γένους καλούμενος, δυσειδὴς δὲ τὸν τρόπον τέως καὶ τὴν γλῶτταν ἀκόλαστος, εἰ καὶ τοῦτον μετὰ βραχὺ θαυμαστῶς ἡ δεξιὰ τοῦ Ὑψίστου ἠλλοίωσε.* An attendant to the governor-elect of the Peloponnese, Kaloeidas had been entrusted with the delivery of Akindynos' *Iambics* to his fellow-Akindynists there, but before leaving for his post he miraculously converted to Palamism (*ibid.*, cols. 608A–609D). The relationship of this individual to the *sebastos* Michael Kaloeidas, the friend and correspondent of Gregoras, cannot be determined (Guilland, *Correspondance*, 306).

[140] Kantakouzenos, *Hist.*, IV, 24: III, 179: *Καὶ μετ' ἐκεῖνον αὖθις τὸν Ἀκίνδυνον, ἐπεὶ κρυπτόμενος αὐτὸς ἑτέρους προσέπεμπε καὶ παρέπειθε θορυβεῖν, ὡς ἀδίκως ὑπὸ τῆς ἐκκλησίας διαστροφὴν τῶν δογμάτων ἐγκαλοῖντο ... οὐ περιεῖδον ἀλλ' ἐπὶ τὴν ἐξέτασιν ἐκέλευον χωρεῖν καὶ τυγχάνειν τῶν δικαίων, καὶ πίστεις παρεῖχον ἐπὶ τῷ πείσεσθαι προσδοκᾶν μηδὲν δεινόν,*

recant or keep silent finally led to his exile. In the first months of 1348 he addressed a moving farewell to his followers in which he reviewed his whole struggle and urged them to remain steadfast in their principles and carry on the resistance. Turning to the City, he paid tribute to its beauty as he described with emotion his dwelling place on a quiet hill by the sea from where he often gazed tearfully on the beauty of the Asiatic coast across the Bosphoros and painfully reflected how he was to be deprived of it all, not by barbarian enemies but by the war that was being waged against the pious.[141]

He died in exile before May 1348.[142] Three years later, he was again condemned by the Council of 1351 and his name was inserted in the *Synodikon of Orthodoxy* among those of other heretics anathematized every year on the first Sunday of Lent.[143]

δεδοικέναι γὰρ ἔλεγε μὴ εἰρχθῇ. αὐτὸς δὲ οὐδὲν ἧττον καὶ μετὰ τὰς πίστεις ἀπεκρύπτετο καὶ ἠγνοήθη μέχρι τελευτῆς. In his *Farewell Address*, Akindynos admits that he had been hiding and blames it on the harassment by his enemies who pursued him unrelentingly and had set a price on his head: *Ἄνδρες εὐσεβεῖς καὶ φιλόθεοι, ὧν καὶ πρὸ πολλοῦ μὲν ὥσπερ μέλος μελῶν συμφυὲς ἀπερράγην ὑπὸ τῶν τεμνόντων καὶ τὴν θεότητα ... καὶ παρ' ὧν οὐκ ἀπέλαβον τῶν φιλτάτων παρόντων, οὐ γὰρ ἐξῆν ὑπὸ τῶν διωκόντων καὶ λαβεῖν εἰς ὄλεθρον, ὡς ἴστε, ῥινηλατούντων. νῦν δὲ καὶ πόρρω τῆς πόλεως τῆς ὑμετέρας ἐλαυνόμενος ἄπειμι, τοῦ κακοῦ τελέως κατακρατήσαντος τῆς ἐκκλησίας.* (*Marc. Gr. 155*, fol. 17ʳ) ... *διὰ ταῦτα διώκομαι καὶ θηρεύομαι θηριωδέστατα· πωλοῦσί μου τὴν ἅλωσιν οὐκ ὀλίγων οἱ θηρευταὶ τοῖς ὠνουμένοις ἀσμένως ἐπὶ τῷ διασπᾶσθαι* (*ibid.*, fol. 34ʳ). The date of this *Address* can be inferred from the author's statement that his friends had cared for him for much longer than a year during his persecution (*ibid.*, fol. 32ʳ: ... *καὶ τὸν ὅλον ἐνιαυτόν, καὶ πολὺ τούτου πλέον, ὡς ἡμερῶν ἑβδομάδα ἐδείξατε*). Since Akindynos was already in hiding when the council of February 1347 was convoked and died before May 1348, he must have left for exile at the beginning of 1348.

[141] See *Marc. Gr. 155*, fols. 32ᵛ–33ʳ: Χαῖρε *πᾶσα ἡ πόλις· τὸ θαυμάσιον ἔδαφος· οἱ ξένοι παράδεισοι καὶ τὰ ἐν τούτοις ἡσυχαστήρια οἷς ἔχαιρον διαφερόντως· καὶ τέλος τὸ ἐμόν ποτε ἀγαπητὸν οἰκητήριον, ὁ πρὸς θαλάσσῃ λόφος, τὸ τῆς πόλεως κράτιστόν τε καὶ καθαρώτατον, τὸ ἐν τῇ πόλει μάλιστα ἐρημικόν τε καὶ ὄρειον· αἱ πρὸς τῇ πόλει νῆσοι ταῖς* Σποράσι *καὶ* Κυκλάσι *προσόμοιοι· τὰ ἀντιπέραν κάλλη οἷς προσωμίλουν ὡς ἥδιστα ἀπὸ τοῦ λόφου, πρὸς αὐτὰ τετραμμένου καὶ συνεχοῦς αὐτοῖς εἶναι δοκοῦντος τῷ θεατῇ. ἀφ' οὗ περιαλγὴς θεωρῶν πρὸς ἐκεῖνα καὶ δακρυώδης ἐγενόμην πολλάκις, ἐννοῶν οἵων ἡ πρὸς τὸ θεῖον ἡμᾶς ἐστέρησεν ἀγνωμοσύνη ... ἀφῃρέθην δὲ οὐχ ὑπὸ βαρβάρων ἐθνῶν καὶ πάλαι θεομάχων, ἀλλ' ὑπὸ τοῦ κοινοῦ τοῦδε τῶν εὐσεβῶν πολέμου.*

[142] The date of Akindynos' death was established by Meyendorff (*Introd.*, 132 note 2) on Philotheos' information that Akindynos was already dead when he and Gregoras met in Heraclea a year after his ordination as metropolitan of that city (*Contra Gregoram* VII, PG, 151, col. 924C). Since Philotheos was ordained soon after the elevation of Isidore to the patriarchal throne on 17 May 1347 (Philotheos, *Vita Isidori*, ed. Papadopoulos-Kerameus, 118–19), Akindynos' death must have occurred before May 1348.

[143] See *Tome* of 1351, PG, 151, col. 758A; Darrouzès no. 2324; *Synodikon*, ed. Gouillard, 81. The information by Nicholas Komnenos Papadopoulos, a late 17th-cent. Greek Jesuit, that Akindynos had a grandson who composed a *Historia victoriarum Gregorii Acindyni* (Fabricius, *Bibl. gr.*, XI, 607) is not substantiated by any other source.

II. DESCRIPTION OF MANUSCRIPTS

1. *Monacensis Gr. 223* (= Mn)

Late fourteenth to early fifteenth century. Parchment (except for six flyleaves and an extraneous addition of seven paper folios marked consecutively on both sides 1–14. Four of these folios have been inserted between the first and fourth flyleaf at the beginning of the MS and the other three between the last parchment folio and the flyleaf at the end). 21.3×17.4cm. I+4+IV+363+3+I. Single column of 31–37 lines (e.g., fols. 156ʳ, 117ʳ, 8ʳ).

Collation: 8×8(64), 11(75), 36×8(363).

Hands: a) parchment folios 1ʳ–65ʳ, 66ʳ–164ʳ, 196ʳ–363ʳ. Similar to *Vat. Gr. 984* (1354—A. Turyn, *Codices Graeci*, pl. 125).

b) 65ᵛ.

c) 164ʳ–195ᵛ.

d) paper folios 1–14.

Decoration: Ornate initials (1ʳ, 164ʳ, 197ᵛ).

Inks: Dark brown and black for text; vermilion for title on fol. 32ʳ, erasures (73ʳ, 73ᵛ, 74ʳ, 74ᵛ), and marginal numbering of the Letters.

Binding: Brown leather.

Previous owner: Methusala Kabbades, an otherwise unknown monk, whose name appears on paper folio 14: Τὸ *βιβλίον* Ἀκίνδυνος Μαθουσαλᾶ (*μον*)*αχ*(*οῦ*) *τοῦ* Καββαδῆ *ἐστιν οὗ καὶ τὰ γράμματα ἴδια*. Since this subscription is by the same hand as the paper folios, Kabbades was the scribe of these folios alone and not of the whole MS, as M. Candal supposes ("Escrito de Pálamas desconocido [Su 'Confesión de fe' refutada por Acíndino]," *OCP*, 29 [1963], 358).

Contents:

Paper folios:

1–2 Θεωρία *on the Transfiguration*.

2–9 *Four* Θεωρίαι *on Melchizedek* (Heb. 7:1–4).

9 Θεωρία *on the Transfiguration* by Maximos the Confessor.

10–13 Θεωρία *on Natural and Written Law*.

14 Θεωρία *on the Conversation of Christ with Moses and Elias during the Transfiguration*.

Parchment folios:

1ʳ–14ʳ Akindynos, Seventeen letters (Letters 3–4, 21, 23, 32–33, 37, 40–41, 45, 55, 60–61, 65–66, 69–70).

14ʳ–16ᵛ ____________ *Confession of Faith*.

16ᵛ–26ʳ ____________ *Brief Exposition of Palamas' Heresies*.

26ʳ–32ʳ ____________ *Refutation of Palamas' Confession of Faith*, ed. Candal, 357–440.

32ʳ–51ʳ ____________ *Refutation of the Third Letter of Palamas*.

51^r–64^r ______________ *Report to the Patriarch*, ed. Uspenskij, *Synodikon*, 85–94.

64^r–64^v ______________ *Another Confession*.

65^r–124^r ______________ *Another Exposition and Refutation of Palamas' Heresies*.

124^v–163^v ______________ *First Antirrhetic against Palamas*.

164^r–197^v ______________ *Second Antirrhetic*.

197^v–236^r ______________ *Third Antirrhetic*.

236^r–313^v ______________ *Fourth Antirrhetic*.

313^v–363^v ______________ *Fifth Antirrhetic*. A critical edition of the works of Akindynos is being prepared by J. S. Nadal; cf. "La rédaction première," 238 note 1.

The only manuscript wholly dedicated to the writings of Akindynos, Mn contains seventeen of his letters, two of which are also found in *Marcianus Gr. 155*. As will be discussed in greater detail below, a comparison of the variants of these two letters—the only items that the two MSS have in common—leads to the conclusion that these manuscripts are independent of each other, with Mn representing an earlier tradition.

On Mn, see I. Hardt, *Catalogus codicum manuscriptorum bibliothecae regiae bavaricae* (Munich, 1806), 454–60.

2. *Marcianus Gr. 155* (= M):

Late fourteenth century. Paper. 27.7×20.3cm. Four flyleaves, 205 folios. Single column of 26–34 lines (e.g., fols. 16^v, 74^v).

Collation: 1×14(14), 4×4(30), 11(41), 6(47), 6×8(95), 2(97), 12×8(193), 4(197), 8(205) (two folios with the number 201).

Hands: a) 1^r–17^v. Similar to *Marcianus Gr. 431* (1343—A. Turyn, *Dated Greek Manuscripts*, pl. 159).

b) 17^r–17^v. Similar to *Vat. Gr. 127* (1372—Turyn, *Codices Graeci*, pl. 143).

c) 18^r–34^v.

d) 35^v–98^v. Similar to *Vat. Gr. 616* (1354—Turyn, *Codices Graeci*, pl. 126).

e) 99^r–198^v. Similar to *Regin. Gr. 57* (1358—Turyn, *Codices Graeci*, pl. 130).

f) 199^r–205^v.

Watermarks: a) Flute (Italy, 14th cent.); cf. M. Briquet, *Les filigranes. Dictionnaire historique des marques du papier dès leur apparition vers 1282 jusqu'en 1600* (Paris, 1907; reprint, Amsterdam, 1968), no. 3340; V. Mošin-S. Traljić, *Les filigranes des XIIIe et XIVe SS* (Zagreb, 1957), no. 2339 (e.g., fol. 7).

b) Cross-bow (Italy, 14th cent.); cf. Briquet, no. 703; Mošin-Traljić, no. 205 (e.g., fols. 22, 37, 51, 61, 201).

c) Pear (Italy, 14th cent.); cf. Briquet, no. 7373; Mošin-Traljić, no. 4273 (e.g., fols. 101, 104, 107, 111).

Decoration: Simple headpiece (99r); moderately ornate initials (e.g., 17r, 36r, 99r).

Inks: Brown and black for text; vermilion for titles and initials.

Binding: Brown leather.

Previous owner: Cardinal Bessarion, whose name appears on fol. 1r: *κτῆμα Βησσαρίωνος καρδιναλίου τ(ῆς) τῶν Τούσκλ(ων)*.

Contents:

1r–16v Fragment of the *Synodic Tome* of 1351.

17r–34r Akindynos, *Farewell Address to his Followers*.

34v–35r Blank.

35v Akindynos, *Index of Contents of Book I*: Τοῦ *σοφωτάτου καὶ λογιωτάτου καὶ τιμιωτάτου ἐν ἱερομονάχοις κυροῦ* Γρηγορίου *τοῦ* Ἀκινδύνου *βιβλίον πρῶτον. πίναξ ἀκριβὴς τοῦ παρόντος βιβλίου· α΄) ἐπιστολαὶ πρὸς διαφόρους πεμφθεῖσαι κατὰ τῆς τοῦ* Παλαμᾶ *δυσσεβείας να΄. β΄) λόγος πρὸς μοναχὸν* Ἱερόθεον, *πρὸς* Ἀρμενόπουλον *ἀποτεινόμενος, ὅς* Ἀκινδύνῳ *κατὰ τὰ δόγματα συμφωνῶν, ἀντιφέρεσθαι οὐκ' οἶδ' ὅπως ᾑρεῖτο. γ΄) ὁ πολύθεος διάλογος* Παλαμᾶ *ἀνεσκευασμένος. δ΄) ἡ ὁμολογία αὐτοῦ. ε΄) ἡ ἀπολογία περὶ ὧν πρὸς τῶν* Παλαμητῶν *σεσυκοφάντηται· ἔκθεσις ἐπίτομος τῶν πονηρῶν αὐτῶν καὶ δυσσεβῶν δογμάτων. στ΄) ἑτέρα ἔκθεσις τῶν αὐτῶν δυσσεβημάτων. ζ΄) ἕτερος λόγος κατὰ τῶν αὐτῶν πολυθέων δογμάτων. η΄) συλλογιστικὰ κεφάλαια κατὰ τῶν αὐτῶν δογμάτων ριη΄ ἐν οἷς καὶ αὖθις ἑτέρα ἔκθεσις τῶν τοῦ* Παλαμᾶ *αἱρέσεων. θ΄) λόγος πρὸς* Ἴσαριν *κατὰ τῶν αὐτῶν δογμάτων. ι΄) στίχοι ἰαμβικοὶ κατὰ τῶν αὐτῶν αἱρέσεων φζ΄*. Of the works listed in the above *Index*, only the first three are found in M. The iambic poem against Palamas' heresies has been preserved in *Barberinus Gr. 291*, fols. 224v–225v (ed. Allatius, *Graecia Orthodoxa*, I, 756–69=PG, 150, cols. 843A–861A), but we have no way of knowing whether the *Confession*, the *Expositions*, and the *Discourse* against Palamas (items δ΄–ζ΄ of the *Index*) were the same as those preserved in Mn under similar but not identical titles; see page xxxv *supra*.

36r–79r ———— Fifty-one letters (Letters 6, 14–20, 22, 24–32, 34–36, 38–39, 42–44, 46–54, 56–59, 62–64, 67–68, 70–76).

79v–91v ———— *Address to Hierotheos*, (ed. K. Pitsakes).

91v–98v ———— Fragment of the *Dialogue of the Impious Palamas with an Orthodox*.

94r–194v Prochoros Kydones, *Treatise on the Question of Essence and Energy*. A superscription on fol. 1r identifies Prochoros as the author of this treatise: Τοῦ Προχόρου *πραγματεία ἀρίστη εἰς τὸ περὶ οὐσίας καὶ ἐνεργείας ζήτημα*. In the early 17th cent., J. Gretser, the editor of the

first two books of this treatise, attributed it to Akindynos, thereby creating the false impression that Akindynos was a disciple of Western scholasticism; cf. G. Mercati, *Notizie*, 1–2.

195^{r}–198^{v} *Patristic Florilegium.*

199^{r}–205^{v} Philotheos Kokkinos, patriarch of Constantinople, *Vita Sabbae* (fragment). A superscription on fol. 199^{r} by a hand different from that of the text identifies this fragment of the *Vita* as an autograph of Philotheos: *Τὸ παρὸν τετράδιόν ἐστιν ἐκ τοῦ βίου τοῦ ἁγίου Σάββα οὗ τὸ ἐπίκλην* Τζίσκος· *συνεγράφη δὲ παρὰ τοῦ χρηματίσαντος πατριάρχου* Φιλοθέου τοὺ Κοκκίνου· *ὅπερ τετράδιον ἐκομίσθη παρά τινος τῶν ἐκείνου γνωρίμων ἐξ αὐτῆς τῆς βίβλου αὐτοῦ ληφθὲν καὶ ἥτις διὰ τῶν ἐκείνου ἐγράφη χειρῶν.*

M has preserved the bulk of Akindynos' correspondence: 51 letters, of which two are also in Mn, a third in *Vat. Gr. 1086*, and a fourth in *Vat. Gr. 1122*. Like those in the other MSS, the letters in M are not grouped together in accordance with any arrangement, chronological or otherwise.

On this manuscript, see A. M. Zanetti, *Graeca D. Marci Bibliotheca* (Venice, 1740), 88.

3. *Scorialensis Gr. Φ–III–11* (= S):

Fourteenth century. Paper. 22.5×16.3cm. 7 flyleaves, 254 folios (two folios with the number 133; three folios with the number 237; no folio marked 201; no folio marked 207, but two folios with the number 208). Single column of 29–41 lines (e.g., fols. 230^{v}, 19^{r}, 2^{r}, 12^{r}, 11^{v}).

Collation: 1×8(8), 1×7(15), 1×6(21), 1×5(26), 9×8(98), 1×12(110), 5×8(150), 1×7(157), 4×8(183), 1×4(193), 1×8(201), 3×7(222), 1×8(230), 1×5(235), 1×6(241), 2×8(257).

Hands: a) 1^{r}–12^{r}. Similar to *Vat. Gr. 605* (1326/27—Turyn, *Codices Graeci*, pl. 104).

b) 12^{r}–14^{v}. Similar to *Udine, Bibl. Arcivescovile, ms. 264* (1317—Turyn, *Dated Greek Manuscripts*, pl. 100).

c) 16^{r}–20^{v}. Similar to *Vat. Gr. 175* (1321/22—Turyn, *Codices Graeci*, pl. 97).

d) 22^{r}–26^{v}.

e) 27^{r}–50^{v}. Similar to *Naples, Bibl. Nazionale, ms. III. 22* (1331/32—Turyn, *Dated Greek Manuscripts*, pl. 146).

f) 51^{r}–58^{r}. Similar to *Ambros. Gr. C 126* (1294/95—Turyn, *Dated Greek Manuscripts*, pl. 62).

g) 58^{v}. Similar to *Florence, Bibl. Laurenziana, ms. Plut. 28, 16* (1381/82—Turyn, *Dated Greek Manuscripts*, pl. 204).

h) 59^{r}–82^{v}.

i) 83^r–156^v. Similar to the scholia in *Marc. Gr. 183* (1358—Turyn, *Dated Greek Manuscripts*, pl. 181).

j) 157^r–208^v.

k) 208^{r}bis–210^v; 212^r–213^r. Similar to *Vat. Gr. 22* (1342/43—Turyn, *Codices Graeci*, pl. 118). Untidy version of the same hand on fols. 210^v–211^r and 212^r–214^r.

l) 214^r–214^v.

m) 215^r–215^v. Similar to *Regin. Gr. 42* (1339—Turyn, *Codices Graeci*, pl. 112).

n) 216^r–217^r; 218^r–221^v.

o) 217^v.

p) 222^r–229^r. Similar to *Marc. Gr. 183* (1359—Turyn, *Dated Greek Manuscripts*, pl. 182).

q) 230^r–234^v. Similar to *Marc. Gr. XI 6* (1321—Turyn, *Dated Greek Manuscripts*, pl. 109).

r) 235^r–254^v. Similar to *Marc. Gr. 183* (1359—Turyn, *Dated Greek Manuscripts*, pl. 182).

s) 254^v.

Watermarks: a) Letter B (Italy, 14th cent.); cf. Briquet, no. 7964; Mošin-Traljić, no. 5149 (e.g., fol. 24).

b) Greek cross (Italy, 14th cent.); cf. Briquet, no. 5422; Mošin-Traljić, no. 3536 (e.g., fols. 30, 36, 38, 43).

c) Greek cross (Italy, 14th cent.); cf. Briquet, no. 5420; Mošin-Traljić, no. 3521 (e.g., fol. 39).

d) Circle (Italy, 14th cent.); cf. Briquet, no. 3184; Mošin-Traljić, no. 2015 (e.g., fol. 96).

e) Cross (Italy, 14th cent.); cf. Briquet, no. 5765; Mošin-Traljić, no. 3585 (e.g., fols. 161, 178).

f) Unicorn (France, 14th cent.); cf. Briquet, no. 15773; Mošin-Traljić, no. 5916 (e.g., fol. 206).

g) Escutcheon (France, Italy, 14th cent.); cf. Briquet, no. 890; Mošin-Traljić, no. 524 (e.g., fols. 232, 234).

Decoration: Simple geometric headpieces and ornate initials (e.g., fols. 32^r, 43^r, 1^r, 51^r).

Inks: Brown and black for text; vermilion for titles, initials, quotations (e.g., fols. 2^r, 6^r), marginal notes (e.g., fols. 1^v, 6^v, 7^r, 8^v, 9^r), and decorations.

Binding: Light brown leather.

Previous owner: Unknown. Perhaps the sixteenth-century Spanish bibliophile Juan Páez de Castro; see G. De Andrés, *Catálogo de los Codices Griegos de la Real Biblioteca de el Escorial* (Madrid, 1965), II, 64.

Contents:

S is a miscellany containing mainly excerpts from medical, astronomical, philosophical, and theological texts. Its contents have been described in detail by

G. De Andrés (*Catálogo de los Codices*, 60–63). I will, therefore, add here only the following remarks: The anonymous letter on fols. 213ʳ–214ᵛ is addressed to Matthew Kantakouzenos in the Peloponnese and attests to his close association with the anti-Palamite John Kyparissiotes. See my edition and translation, "An Unknown Letter to Matthew Kantakouzenos," in *Okeanos* (Festschrift Ihor Ševčenko), *Harvard Ukrainian Studies*, 7 (1983).

The two homilies in the name of an anonymous metropolitan on fols. 222ʳ–229ʳ (*Λόγος παραινετικὸς εἰς τοὺς ἐξελθόντας μετὰ τῶν ἁγίων εἰκόνων ὡς ἐκ προσώπου τοῦ μητροπολίτου*; the second homily has no superscription) are not addressed to a besieged populace, as suggested by V. Laurent ("La direction spirituelle à Byzance," 51 note 4), but to the inhabitants of a city suffering from the effects of severe drought who had gone out in procession to pray for rain. This unidentified city was near a river and had an imperial residence and a colony of foreign merchants.

Fols. 230ʳ–234ᵛ contain four letters of Akindynos (Letters 7–9, 13). These letters, as well as the correspondence of the Princess Eulogia Choumnaina-Palaiologina with her spiritual director on the succeeding folios (235ʳ–254ᵛ), appear anonymously in the MS. Their authorship was first established on the basis of internal evidence by Laurent (*ibid.*) who also expressed the view that Akindynos' letters were autograph. External considerations support this opinion. There are neither superscriptions nor ornate initials at the beginning of each letter, and fols. 230ʳ, 231ʳ, 231ᵛ, 233ʳ, 233ᵛ, and 234ʳ show traces of editorial interference: erasures, deletions, and additions both between lines and in the margins. These changes, which appear to be by the same hand as the text, modify it in the manner of an author revising his correspondence. For instance, the corrector of the letters deletes sentences by crossing out whole lines (e.g., fol. 231ʳ, line 9: *ὁρᾷς ἣν ἐγὼ περὶ σὲ γνώμην ἔχω*; fol. 231ᵛ, lines 8–11: *εἰ δὲ καὶ αὖθις εἴποις, οὐ φροντὶς Ἱπποκλείδῃ φησὶν ἡ παροιμία· ἕως ἂν οὐχ ὡς ἄν τις εἴποι πάντως οὕτω τὰ πράγματα ἔχῃ, ἀλλ' ὡς ἂν ἡ φύσις αὐτὰ καταδείξειε*; *ibid.*, lines 15–16: *ὡς θιασώτην, οἶμαι, σοφοῖς ἀνδράσιν ἀποδεικνύμενον*); substitutes one sentence for a group of sentences (e.g., fol. 231ʳ, lines 13–16, where he changes *σκοπεῖν πρὸς τὰ κρατοῦντα ἤθη παρὰ τοῖς εὐσεβέσι, τά τε ἔθεσι νόμιμα καὶ τὰ δέλτοις ἱεραῖς παραδοθέντα, οἷς, ὥσπερ ἔφην, ἁπλῶς τε καὶ πεποιθότες νῦν οἱ τῶν ἀρετῶν ἕπονται ζηλωταὶ καὶ μιμηταὶ τῶν πατέρων σὺν τοῖς κατ' ἦθος ἔργοις* to *σκοπεῖν πρὸς τὰ κρατοῦντα ἤθη παρ' οἷς ὢν ταῦτα κινεῖς ἀνέδην*); recasts a whole line (e.g., fol. 231ʳ, bottom line, where he crosses out *τοῦ πονηροῦ, πειρᾶσθε ἀναταράττειν καὶ κύματα ἐγείρειν ἀλλόκοτα* and writes underneath *τοῦ διαβόλου, δεινῷ ταράττετε κλύδωνι καὶ στάσει χαλεπῇ κατασείετε*); adds words or sentences (e.g., fol. 230ʳ, line 4, he adds *ἀναγκαῖον καὶ ἀψευδὲς* to *τηρεῖν αἱρεῖσθαι τὸ καθαρὸν ἐν τῷ λέγειν*; *ibid.*, line 6, he adds *τῶν φιλοσόφων* to *φιλονεικίας*; *ibid.*, line 19, after *ἐπεχείρησας πείθειν* he adds in the left margin *σοὶ γὰρ οὐκ ἐμοὶ δοκοῦντα πρὸς τὸ πεῖσαί με λέγεις*, then crosses out this sentence and writes above it *οὐ γὰρ ὡσαύτως ἐγώ τε καὶ σὺ περὶ τούτων φρονοῦμεν, ἐξ ὧν με πάντως προσεδόκησας πείσειν*); changes

words (e.g., fol. 230^{r}, line 7, *πειθόμενος* into *ἀκροώμενος*; fol. 231^{r}, line 3, *μοναχῶν* into *σπουδαίων*; fol. 233^{v}, bottom line – fol. 234^{r}, line 1, *νεμεσεῖν* into *φθονεῖν*); leaves space for a quotation from Barlaam's letter, which he later inserts (fol. 231^{v}, line 5); and finally crosses out a whole letter by drawing a diagonal line across the page (fol. 234^{r}). A corrector who takes such liberties with the text cannot be a scribe or a later editor. He must be the author himself.

The presence in S of the letters of Akindynos and the correspondence of his staunchest supporter, the royal nun Eulogia Choumnaina-Palaiologina, may not be the result of pure coincidence. The letter to Matthew Kantakouzenos, written by a close friend of Kyparissiotes, an anti-Palamite leader, as well as the other contents of S, especially the medical and philosophical collectanea, suggest that the Spanish manuscript came from an anti-Palamite milieu and was perhaps the property of a man of letters from the entourage of the scholarly princess.

4. *Ambrosianus Gr. 290* (*E 64 sup.*) (= A):

Fifteenth century. Paper. 22×14.8cm. Three flyleaves, 264 folios. On this manuscript, see E. Martini-D. Bassi, *I manoscritti greci de la biblioteca Ambrosiana* (Milan, 1906), 319–25.

According to the catalogue of the *Ambrosiana*, A is a miscellany containing mainly theological texts and some excerpts from rhetorical works. Folios 67^{r}–75^{v} are taken up by four letters of Akindynos (Letters 5 and 10–12). These letters—one of which is addressed to Barlaam, another to Dishypatos, and two to Palamas—antedate the controversy and constitute important documents for the study of its origins.

5. *Vaticanus Gr. 1086* (= V):

Second half of fourteenth century. Paper and parchment. 236 folios. For a detailed description of this manuscript, see P. L. M. Leone, "Per l' edizione critica dell' epistolario di Niceforo Gregora," *Byzantion*, 46 (1976), 27–29.

Among the correspondence of Gregoras, V has preserved on fols. 218^{v} and 224^{v}–226^{v} three letters of Akindynos addressed to that distinguished polymath (Letters 1–2, 18). Two of these are the earliest surviving letters of Akindynos, while the third, which is also found in M, dates from the period of the controversy. Professor I. Ševčenko kindly informed me that two marginal notes which appear on fol. 218^{v} (*Αὕτη ἡ ἐπιστολή ἐστι τοῦ Ἀκινδύνου πρὸς τὸν Γρηγορᾶν* and *Ζήτει τοῦ αὐτοῦ μετὰ φύλλα ιδ´ καὶ στίχους ἰαμβικοὺς πρὸς τὸν αὐτόν*) are by the hand of Gregoras. For Gregoras' other autograph annotations in V, see Ševčenko, "Some autographs of Nicephorus Gregoras," *ZVI*, 8^{2} (1964) 445–46 (reprinted in *Society and Intellectual Life* ..., Study XII).

6. *Vaticanus Gr. 1122* (= W):

Fifteenth century. Paper. 234 folios. On this manuscript, see Mercati, *Notizie*, 2 note 3, and P. Canart-V. Peri, *Sussidi bibliografici per i manoscritti Greci della Biblioteca Vaticana*, ST, 261 (Vatican City, 1970), 540–41.

Folios 199[r]–200[v] contain one letter of Akindynos (Letter 56) inserted between the *Dialogues on the Procession of the Holy Spirit* by Niketas of Maroneia, Archbishop of Thessalonica, and a series of excerpts from the *Treatise on the Question of Essence and Energy* by Prochoros Kydones. This letter is also found in M.

Relationship of Manuscripts

Only four letters of Akindynos have been preserved in more than one manuscript: Letters 32 and 70 are found in Mn and M, Letter 18 in M and V, and Letter 56 in M and W.

A collation of Mn and M shows the following textual differences:

a) choice of words: *αἰδέσιμον* Mn: *αἰδούμενον* M (letter 32, line 13); *ὡς* Mn: *ὥστε* M (32, 39); *πιθανοτάτων* Mn: *πιθανοτήτων* M (32, 60); *κακοδοξούντων* Mn: *οὐκ εὐσεβούντων* M (32, 62); *ἔπραξας* Mn: *ἔδρασας* M (Letter 70, line 1); *διετέθημεν* Mn: *ἠνιάθημεν* M (70, 19); *ἀναπεπηδήκαμεν* Mn: *ἀναπεπνεύκαμεν* M (70, 24); *καρδίᾳ* Mn: *γνώμῃ* M (70, 34); *καινοφωνίαις* Mn: *πλάναις* M (70, 56); *ἠθέλησε* Mn: *ἐπῄνεσε* M (70, 58); *ὑπὲρ* Mn: *πρὸς* M (70, 62).

b) word order: *πάντων ἀνιαθεὶς* Mn: *ἀνιαθεὶς ἁπάντων* M (70, 37); *ἡμᾶς λέγειν* Mn: *λέγειν ἡμᾶς* M (70, 54).

c) style: *τῶν δ' εὐσεβείᾳ κεκοσμημένων τὸ πάσχειν μὲν καὶ ἀκούειν τὰ παρὰ τῶν ἀντιδόξων* Mn: *τῶν δὲ τῆς εὐσεβείας τὸ πάσχειν τε καὶ ἀκούειν παρὰ τῶν ἀντιδόξων ἃ παρὰ τῶν ἀσεβῶν τοὺς εὐσεβοῦντας εἰκὸς* M (32, 63–64); *οἶσθα ὅπερ* Mn: *οἶσθα δ' ὅπερ* M (32, 77); *τὴν εὖ ῥέουσαν γλῶτταν* Mn: *τί ῥέουσαν εὖ;* M (70, 4–5); *τοὺς δυσμενεῖς ἀνῄρεις* Mn: *τοὺς δυσμενεῖς ἅμα φανεὶς ἐτρέπου* M (70, 6); *ἀντικειμένῳ ξίφει* Mn: *τμητικωτάτῳ λόγῳ* M (70, 13); *μεθ'οὗ* Mn: *μεθ' οὗπερ* M (70, 18); *ἀρετῆς ἁπάσης ἀμφισβητῶν τοῖς ἄκροις* Mn: *ἀρετῆς πάσης ἕνεκα τοῖς ἀρίστοις συντρέχων* M (70, 36); *γνώσει γὰρ ἀληθεῖ καὶ σοφίᾳ ἧς ἐραστὴς σὺ καὶ τρόφιμος, οὐδὲν ἀλογίας ἀλλοτριώτερον ἧς Παλαμᾶς ὁ τεράστιος* Mn: *γνώσει γὰρ ἀληθεῖ καὶ σοφίᾳ ἧς ἐραστὴς σὺ καὶ τρόφιμος, οὐ Παλαμᾶς ὁ τεράστιος τὴν ἀλογίαν οὐχ ἧττον ἢ τὴν ἀσέβειαν, οὐδὲν ἀλογίας καὶ ἀφροσύνης ἀλλοτριώτερον* M (70, 51–53); *ἀλλ' ὥσπερ πέπλον εὐσεβείας ἐξύφηνεν τῷ Θεῷ εἰς τέλος δι' ὁμοίας τῆς γλώττης τὸν χαριέστατον* Mn: *ἀλλ' ὥσπερ πέπλον εὐσεβείας εἰς τέλος τὸν χαριέστατον ἐξυφᾶναι τῷ Θεῷ δι' ὁμοίας τῆς γλώττης* M (70, 83–84).

Futhermore, Mn omits 12 words found in M: [Τῷ Γαβρᾷ] (32, title);

[*θειοτάτη*] *βασιλίς* (32, 42); [*καθαρωτάτη*] *μήτηρ* (32, 43); *αἵρεσιν* [*δυσσεβεστάτην*] *οὖσαν*, *ἀλλὰ* [*καὶ*] *ἀλόγιστον καὶ ἀνοητοτάτην* (70, 49); *καίτοι ταῦτα μὲν ἡμᾶς λέγειν*, [*ὡς οἶσθα*,] *αὐτὸς Παλαμᾶς ἐξηνάγκασε* (70, 54); *ὁ γὰρ τοῖς ἄλλοις* [*πρότερον*] *ἀπηχθημένος* (70, 61); *ἀντὶ* [*τοῦ*] *ἀοράτου καὶ ἀνειδέου θεοῦ* [*μεμορφωμένον*] (70, 73–74); while M omits 10 words found in Mn: *πάσχειν συνέβαινε* [*πρότερον*] (32, 23); *Τιμόθεος* [*ὁ αὐλητὴς*] (32, 36); [*ἐμπεσὼν*] *ἐν μέσοις τοῖς βασιλείοις* (70, 18); [*ὁ*] *Ἄθως* (70, 23); *ἀναγκασθεὶς* [*βασιλικῇ δυνάμει*] *πρεσβεῦσαι* (70, 39); *ἀτοπώτατα* [*καὶ ἀμαθέστατα*] *καί*, *ὡς εἰπεῖν*, *γραωδέστατα* (70, 78); *χρυσῆς* [*σου*] *γλώττης* (70, 82).

Since such differences can only be the result of editorial interference, the question arises which of the two manuscripts has preserved the earlier version of the text of the letters. The reading *βασιλικῇ δυνάμει*, which is found only in Mn and describes under what authority a certain emissary was dispatched to Serbia, indicates the author's familiarity with specific circumstances. Its omission in M, therefore, suggests that either an editor other than the author revised this MS, discarding such information as unimportant and sacrificing it to stylistic considerations, or Akindynos deliberately deleted it. As to the second possibility, I believe that if we consider this omission together with two specific additions in M, we will observe a certain pattern which may prove enlightening.

In Letter 32, the editor of M embellishes the references to the Empress-mother Anna of Savoy by adding the epithets *θειοτάτη καὶ καθαρωτάτη* (*ἡ δὲ θειοτάτη βασιλὶς ἡμῶν καὶ βασιλέως καθαρωτάτη μήτηρ*), whereas in Letter 70 he eliminates the phrase *βασιλικῇ δυνάμει* which qualified *ἀναγκασθεὶς* and might have been interpreted as offensive to Kantakouzenos. Are such emendations the work of a later editor or do they reflect a last minute effort by Akindynos to placate a hostile Court? The latter probability added to the substantial number of differences between the two manuscripts indicates, in my opinion, that Mn has preserved an earlier form of the letters, while M represents a version edited by the author himself.

Of the two MSS, however, Mn has preserved a more complete and accurate form of the text, since what must be an oversight of the copyist of M, rather than a deliberate emendation, has resulted in an omission and an incorrect transcription which play havoc with the syntax of two whole periods in the text of Letter 70 as transmitted by M. Compare: *ὡς δὲ καὶ ἄλλος καὶ μάλα ἄλλος ἐπῆλθεν ἀπὸ τοῦ θείου Ὄρους μηνύοντες οὐχ ὅτι μόνον τοῖς ἱεροῖς Λαυριώταις ἐναρίθμιος εἶ, ἀλλ'ὅτι καὶ* . . . Mn: *ὡς δὲ* . . . *μηνύοντες τοῖς ἱεροῖς Λαυριώταις ἐναρίθμιος εἶ, ἀλλ'ὅτι καὶ* . . . M (lines 24–27); *εἰ δὲ τούτων ἀποστὰς* . . . *τὰ πάτρια δόγματα πρεσβεύειν ἠθέλησε, μάλα θαρρῶν ἀποφαίνομαι ὡς οὐδεὶς ἂν ἁπάντων ἔφθη* . . . *ἐμὲ εἰς φιλίαν καὶ θεραπείαν ἐκείνου* Mn: *οὐδὲ τούτων ἀποστὰς τὰ πάτρια δόγματα πρεσβεύειν ἐπῄνεσε, μάλα θαρρῶν ἀποφαίνομαι ὡς* M (lines 56–58).

M and V, which have one letter (18) in common, are also independent of each other. In one instance V omits two sentences which are found in M and constitute an amplification on a preceding statement (*τὸ νόθον ἐλήλαται, τὸ γνήσιον ἀντεισῆκται· τὸ μὲν ὡς κίβδηλον ἐληλεγμένον, τὸ δ' ὡς ἀκήρατον δοκιμασθέν· [ὧν τὸ μὲν οὐκ οἶδ' ὅπως πρότερον ἐσιωπᾶτο, τὸ δ' ἐν ἐπαίνου μοίρᾳ λεγόμενον εἰς Κωνσταντῖνον, οὐδὲν μᾶλλον ἐσέμνυνεν ἢ καθῄρει τὸν μέγαν τῆς ὑπαρχούσης δόξης*] V); and in another it omits two words which are essential to the syntax of a sentence (*οὗ τὸ κεφάλαιον ἥ τε περὶ τὸ θεῖον ἐπιστήμων εὐλάβεια καὶ σωφροσύνη καὶ τὸ τῆς ἀμαθίας καὶ πλάνης περὶ αὐτὸ [τῶν ταύταις] περιπιπτόντων ἐκ δαιμονίας οἰήσεως ἐλεγκτικὸν* V; cf. lines 14–18; 27–30). On the other hand, the copyist of M, because of an oversight, omitted the first of two clauses which begin with the same word, thus rendering incoherent the final paragraph of the letter (*ὥστ' [οἴκοθεν οἴκαδε πέμψας ἡμῖν τοὺς λόγους,] οἴκοθεν αὖθις οἴκαδε δέχου καὶ νῦν ἰόντας, μᾶλλον δὲ τοὺς αὐτοὺς καὶ πεμπομένους καὶ μένοντας, τὸ μὲν τῇ δέλτῳ, τῷ δὲ τῇ ἐπιστήμῃ* M [lines 32–35]). Although the two MSS are not related, M obviously has preserved an expanded version of the letter as edited by Akindynos. Only the author himself could have amplified his statement about the critical evaluation of evidence in Gregoras' encomium of Constantine the Great by alluding to specific instances of such evidence which Gregoras had accepted or rejected.

Finally, a comparison between the variants of M and W, which also share only one letter (56), shows that W diverges from M primarily in spelling, containing errors arising from itacisms. The two MSS are closely related, since W repeats the same error of omission as M (*τῶν ὑπερκειμένας καὶ ὑφειμένας θεότητας κατατεμνόντων τὸ θεῖον ἀνέχεσθαι* [line 22–23]) and displays identical marginal compendia in the same places in the text (*σῆ(μείωσαι) α΄, β΄, γ΄, δ΄, ε΄, στ΄*). Furthermore, as noted above, W contains, in addition to the letter of Akindynos, several excerpts from the treatise of Prochoros Kydones on *The Question of Essence and Energy* which is also found in M. I hesitate, however, to define W as an apograph of M, because in one instance it contains an extra word, and in another the copyist writes and subsequently erases two words which do not exist anywhere in that part of M and cannot, therefore, be explained in terms of a visual error (Letter 56, ad appar. 32, 58).

III. PREVIOUS EDITIONS AND STUDIES OF AKINDYNOS' CORRESPONDENCE

The first of Akindynos' letters to be published were the two that he addressed to Gregoras from Thessalonica (1, 2). Accompanied by a Latin translation, they

were included in the Bonn edition of Gregoras' *History* which appeared in 1829.[144] In 1865, J. P. Migne reprinted them in his *Patrologia Graeca*.[145]

At the end of the nineteenth century, the Russian historian Th. Uspenskij transcribed from Mn four letters (37, 60, 65, 70) and an excerpt from Letter 40. His transcription, which contains several errors and omissions, is appended to his edition of the *Synodikon*.[146]

After another interval of more than fifty years, a series of Akindynos' letters began to appear. In 1954, I. Ševčenko edited the letter to Nicholas Kabasilas (14); in 1957, R. J. Loenertz published a critical edition of a select group of nine letters from M (50, 52, 56–58, 70, 72, 74, 76); and in 1960, V. Laurent published an edition, translation of, and commentary on the letter to Dishypatos (13).[147] Four years later, the Greek scholar E. Tsolakes edited the last of Akindynos' letters to Gregoras (44).[148] Because this letter refers to Akindynos in the third person, its authorship was originally disputed by R. Guilland.[149] But his doubts were not shared by either Loenertz or Meyendorff, both of whom accepted the manuscript's assignation of this letter to Akindynos.[150] Tsolakes, on the other hand, agrees with Guilland and believes that it was written by a member of Akindynos' immediate entourage. He argues that Akindynos would not have made use of the third person in reference to himself throughout the letter and points out that at the very end the author clearly distinguishes himself from Akindynos when he states in the first person plural: *Διόπερ αὐτὸν οὐ μόνος 'Ακίνδυνος, ἀλλὰ καὶ πάντες Χριστιανοὶ οἱ μίαν θεότητα τρισυπόστατον ὁμολογοῦντες . . . ὡς τῆς ἐσχάτης ἀσεβείας μετὰ τοῦ πατρὸς αὐτῷ τοῦ Σατανᾶ πατέρα εἰκότως ἀποστρεφόμεθα*.[151]

I do not find Tsolakes' argument sufficiently persuasive. As Loenertz has pointed out, other ancient and medieval writers employed the third person in referring to themselves.[152] In fact, an example similar to that of our letter occurs in a contemporary document, Palamas' *Refutation of the Patriarch of Antioch*, where the author alternates between the third person singular and the first person plural in writing about himself.[153] Moreover, certain statements in this letter regarding op-

[144] Cf. vol. I, pp. LXIX–LXX; LXXXVI–LXXXVIII.

[145] PG, 148, cols. 68D–70A; 84C–86D.

[146] Pp. 75–84. Uspenskij erroneously transcribed as part of the letter to Maximos (70) an adjacent letter (65) which appears in the MS without superscription.

[147] Ševčenko, "Nicolaus Cabasilas' Correspondence," 53 note 4; Loenertz, *Epistulae*; Laurent, "L'assaut avorté," 144–62.

[148] *Γεώργιος Λαπίθης*, 84–96.

[149] *Correspondance*, 282 note 8.

[150] Loenertz, "Dix-huit lettres," 81 note 1; Meyendorff, *Introduction*, 127 notes 155, 157.

[151] Tsolakes, *Γεώργιος Λαπίθης*, 91.

[152] Loenertz, "Dix-huit lettres," 81.

[153] *'Αναίρεσις γράμματος 'Ιγνατίου*, *Συγγράμματα*, II, 640, lines 6–15: *Τί δ' ὁ πράξεις συνοδικὰς δῆθεν καθ' ἡμῶν καὶ γράμματα προφασιζόμενος; ἆρα τῶν ἀνακηρυξάντων ἡμᾶς ἐπ' εὐσεβείᾳ μεγάλων ἐκείνων συνόδων ἀνήκοος, ὧν ἐν θατέρᾳ μὲν καθ' ἣν τὸ τοῦ Βαρλαὰμ κράτος ὁ Παλαμᾶς ἔσχε ... τῆς ἑτέρας δὲ καθ' ἣν ὁ αὐτὸς Παλαμᾶς ἐπὶ τοῖς αὐτοῖς ἀντι-*

position to Palamas' doctrines outside the Empire and Lapithes' censure of Akindynos for his allegedly mild resistance to Palamism are found in the *Address to Hierotheos* and in some of the other contemporary letters of Akindynos.[154] It must also be noted that Akindynos' favorite quotation from St. Paul (2 Tim. 2:16), which appears in many of his letters, occurs here too (line 64). In view of this evidence, I believe that the question of the authorship of this letter must be settled in favor of Akindynos.

Finally, to the above editors of Akindynos' correspondence must be added A. Vassilikopoulou-Ioannidou who in 1976 published the letter to the metropolitan of Corinth (67); H. V. Beyer who, in the same year, edited one of the letters to Gregoras (17) and a large part of another (43); A. Karpozilos whose edition of the 17 letters contained in the Munich manuscript appeared in 1977; and G. I. Passarelli who published a transcription of the letter to the Metropolitan of Philadelphia (48) in 1980.[155]

Studies

The only study devoted exclusively to the correspondence of Akindynos is the valuable historical and prosopographical commentary on eighteen select letters which R. J. Loenertz published in 1957.[156] On the other hand, summaries of and excerpts from various letters have appeared in several studies as scholars made use of the information from Akindynos' correspondence in their articles or monographs.

In 1927, R. Guilland included summaries of the six letters to Gregoras, along with a brief biographical sketch of Akindynos, in his *Correspondance*, and four years later an excerpt from one of these letters (18) was published by G. Mercati in his *Notizie*.[157] In 1959, J. Meyendorff in his fundamental work on Gregory Palamas derived important historical and prosopographical information from a thorough study of Akindynos' correspondence.[158] In 1961, K. Kyrres studied certain letters in connection with the role played by Cypriot anti-Palamites in the hesychast contro-

---

λέγοντα τὸν 'Ακίνδυνον ᾔσχυνε ... ἆρ'οὐχὶ τὸν ἐπὶ ταύταις εἶδε ταῖς δυσὶ μεγίσταις ἐφ' ἡμῶν συνόδοις προβάντα τόμον, ὃς τὸν μὲν Παλαμᾶν ....

[154] *Address to Hierotheos*, 195–96. Commenting on these statements, Pitsakes also notes the similarity between the two documents and assigns this letter to Akindynos, rejecting Guilland's view that it was written by someone other than Akindynos (cf. *ibid.*, 139 note 27). See also Letter 42, lines 38–39; Letter 49, lines 11–12; Letter 74, lines 7–18.

[155] Vassilikopoulou-Ioannidou, *'Ανέκδοτος ἐπιστολή*, 92; Beyer, *Antirrhetika I*, 108–9; Karpozilos, *Letters*; Passarelli, *Macario*, 32 note 28. A transcription of the first letter of Akindynos to Palamas is included in R. E. Sinkewicz' unpublished doctoral dissertation, *The Doctrine of the Knowledge of God in the Initial Discussions between Barlaam the Calabrian and Gregory Palamas* (Oxford, 1979), Appendix I, 242–48.

[156] "Dix-huit lettres."

[157] *Correspondance*, 274–76, 281–83, 293–97; *Notizie*, 12 note 2.

[158] *Introduction*, 55–128.

versy, and in 1964 D. Polemis included an excerpt from one of the letters to Barlaam (10) in his edition of Gregoras' Ἀντιλογία.[159] More recently, G. Weiss made extensive use of Akindynos' correspondence in his monograph on John Kantakouzenos, and I. Ševčenko commented on some of the letters in his report on society and intellectual life in the fourteenth century. H. V. Beyer included a detailed analysis of Akindynos' correspondence with Gregoras in his edition of the latter's first *Antirrhetics*.[160] Several references to the letters can also be found in K. Pitsakes' edition of Akindynos' address to Hierotheos; in D. Tsames' editions of the Palamite authors Dishypatos and Kalothetos; and in J. Darrouzès' *Regestes*.[161]

IV. PRESENT EDITION

With the exception of Letters 18, 32, 56, and 70, Akindynos' correspondence has been transmitted by single witnesses. In the following edition, Letters 6, 14–20, 24–32, 34–36, 38–39, 42–44, 46–54, 56–59, 62–64, 67–68, 70–76 are based on M; Letters 3–4, 21, 23, 33, 37, 40–41, 45, 55, 60–61, 65–66, 69 on Mn; Letters 7–9, 13 on S; Letters 5, 10–12 on A; and Letters 1–2 on V.

Since S is an autograph, I have edited the corrected version and registered all deletions and erasures in the critical apparatus. In the case of Letters 32 and 70, I have opted for M rather than Mn, since, for reasons discussed above, M appears to have preserved a version edited by the author himself. For the same reasons, I have chosen M and not V as the basis for Letter 18. In both cases, however, variants of Mn and V have been accepted when obviously correct or more complete. Letter 56 is also based on M because W differs from M only in its inferior spelling.

M, Mn, S, A, and V are excellent manuscripts requiring only the conventional changes in punctuation and accentuation, especially that of the proclitics and enclitics, the addition of the iota subscript, and the correction of itacisms.

The translation, though not literal, is hampered by the hard-to-render theological terms and especially by the assonances, puns, and other devices of Akindynos' rhetorical style. For example, the word εὐσέβεια appears often in the text in the sense of orthodoxy (the correct faith). However, since the author uses it either in conjunction with or in antithesis to its cognates (εὐσεβής, ἀσέβεια, ἀσεβής), I have translated it throughout as "piety" in order to retain the nuances of the rhetorical style.

[159] Kyrres, Ὁ Κύπριος ἀρχιεπίσκοπος Θεσσαλονίκης Ὑάκινθος, 95–107; *idem.*, Ἡ Κύπρος καὶ τὸ ἡσυχαστικὸν ζήτημα, 28–31; Polemis, Ἀντιλογία, 51 note 2.

[160] Weiss, *Kantakuzenos*, 102–37; Ševčenko, "Society and Intellectual Life in the Fourteenth Century," 70–72, 74, 87; Beyer, *Antirrhetika I*, 55–57, 108–9.

[161] Akindynos, *Address to Hierotheos*, 124, 133, 139–42, 207; Dishypatos, Λόγος, 17–18, 28; Kalothetos, Συγγράμματα, *passim*. Darrouzès, nos. 2204–5, 2242, 2246–7, 2256, 2262.

In the translation of all Scriptural passages, I follow the L. C. Brenton translation of the *Septuagint* (London, 1844) and the *New English Bible* (Oxford-Cambridge, 1961).

Finally, in order to achieve a better historical perspective, I have arranged the letters according to chronological order on the basis of internal evidence. The reasons for the date assigned to each letter are discussed in the commentary along with all other historical information. This edition would benefit substantially from a doctrinal commentary, but this must be entrusted to the competence of a theologian.

LIST OF ABBREVIATIONS

Actes de Chilandar: L. Petit-B. Korablev, eds., *Actes de Chilandar*, *Vizantijskij Vremennik*, 17 (1911), *Suppl.*

Akindynos, *Address to Hierotheos*: G. Akindynos, *Λόγος πρὸς Ἱερόθεον μοναχόν*, ed. K. Pitsakes, *Γρηγορίου Ἀκινδύνου ἀνέκδοτη πραγματεία περὶ* (Κωνσταντίνου;) *Ἀρμενοπούλου*, Ἐπετηρὶς Κέντρου Ἐρεύνης Ἱστορίας Ἑλληνικοῦ Δικαίου, 19 (1972), 111–216

_______ *Dialogue of the Impious Palamas with an Orthodox*: G. Akindynos, *Διάλογος τοῦ κακοδόξου* Παλαμᾶ *μετὰ ὀρθοδόξου*, *Marcianus Gr. 155*, fols. 91v–98v

_______ *Report*: G. Akindynos, *Λόγος πρὸς τὸν μακαριώτατον πατριάρχην κῦρ* Ἰωάννην *καὶ τὴν περὶ αὐτὸν σύνοδον διεξιὼν ὅπως ἡ τοῦ* Παλαμᾶ *καὶ* Βαρλαὰμ *φιλονεικία τὴν ἀρχὴν συνέστη*, ed. Th. Uspenskij, *Sinodik v nedelju Pravoslavija* (Odessa, 1893), 85–94

Barlaam, *Epistole Greche*: Barlaam, *Barlaam Calabro Epistole Greche: primordi episodici e dottrinari delle lotte esicaste*, ed. G. Schirò, *Istituto Siciliano di Studi Bizantini e Neogreci, Testi*, I (Palermo, 1954)

Beck, *KTL*: H. G. Beck, *Kirche und Theologische Literatur im byzantinischen Reich* (Munich, 1959)

Beyer, ed., *Antirrheticka I*: H.-V. Beyer, *Nikephoros Gregoras. Antirrhetika I. Einleitung, Textausgabe, Übersetzung und Anmerkungen*, Wiener Byzantinische Studien, 12 (Vienna, 1976)

_______ "Eine Chronologie": H.-V. Beyer, "Eine Chronologie der Lebensgeschichte des Nikephoros Gregoras," *JÖB*, 27 (1978), 127–55

BZ: *Byzantinische Zeitschrift*

Chronica: *Chronica Byzantina Breviora*, ed. P. Schreiner, *Die byzantinischen Kleinchroniken*, Corpus Fontium Historiae Byzantinae, 12/1–3 (Vienna, 1975–79)

Darrouzès, *Offikia*: J. Darrouzès, *Recherches sur les* ΟΦΦΙΚΙΑ *de l'église byzantine*, *Archives de l'Orient chrétien*, II (Paris, 1970)

_______ *Regestes*: J. Darrouzès, *Les Regestes des actes du Patriarcat de Constantinople, vol. I: les actes des Patriarches, fasc. V, Les regestes de 1310 à 1376* (Paris, 1977)

Demetrakos, *Lexikon*: D. B. Demetrakos, Μέγα *λεξικὸν τῆς* Ἑλληνικῆς *γλώσσης*, 9 vols. (Athens, 1933–51)

Dennis, *The Letters of Manuel II Palaeologus*: G. T. Dennis, *The Letters of Manuel II Palaeologus. Text, Translation and Notes*, Dumbarton Oaks Texts, IV (Washington, D.C., 1977)

Dishypatos, Λόγος: D. Dishypatos, *Δαβὶδ Δισυπάτου λόγος κατὰ* Βαρλαὰμ *καὶ* Ἀκινδύνου *πρὸς* Νικόλαον Καβάσιλαν, ed. D. Tsames, *Βυζαντινὰ* Κείμενα *καὶ* Μελέται, 10 (Thessalonica, 1973)

________ *Poem*: D. Dishypatos, Τοῦ *θαυμαστοῦ καὶ σοφοῦ μοναχοῦ* Δαβὶδ *τοῦ* Δισυπάτου *πρὸς τοὺς* 'Ακινδύνου *στίχους*, ed. R. Browning, "David Dishypatos' Poem on Akindynos," *Byzantion*, 25–27 (1955–57), 714–45

DOP: *Dumbarton Oaks Papers*

DTC: *Dictionnaire de Théologie Catholique*

EO: *Echos d'Orient*

'Επ.'Ετ.Βυζ.Σπ.: 'Επετηρὶς 'Εταιρείας Βυζαντινῶν Σπουδῶν

Fatouros, ed., *Die Briefe des Michael Gabras*: G. Fatouros, *Die Briefe des Michael Gabras (ca. 1290–nach 1350). I: Einleitung, Addressaten, Regesten, Register. II: Text*, Wiener Byzantinische Studien, 10/1–2 (Vienna, 1973)

Gregoras, *Florentios*: Nikephoros Gregoras, Φλωρέντιος, ed. P. L. M. Leone, *Niceforo Gregora, Fiorenzo o intorno alla Sapienza*, Byzantina et Neohellenica Neapolitana, Collana di Studi e Testi, 4 [Naples, 1975])

Grumel, *Chronologie*: V. Grumel, *La Chronologie*, *Traité d'Études Byzantines*, I (Paris, 1958)

Guilland, *Correspondance*: R. Guilland, *Correspondance de Nicéphore Grégoras; texte edité et traduit par R. Guilland* (Paris, 1927)

Horologion: Τὸ *μέγα* 'Ωρολόγιον, ed. M. I. Saliveros (Athens, n.d.)

Janin, *Géographie ecclésiastique*: R. Janin, *La géographie ecclésiastique de l'empire byzantin. I. Le siège de Constantinople et le patriarcat oecuménique. 3, Les églises et les monastères* (Paris, 1953)

JÖB: *Jahrbuch der Österreichischen Byzantinistik*

JÖBG: *Jahrbuch der Österreichischen Byzantinischen Gesellschaft*

Kalothetos, Συγγράμματα: 'Ιωσὴφ Καλοθέτου Συγγράμματα, ed. D. Tsames, Θεσσαλονικεῖς Βυζαντινοὶ Συγγραφεῖς, I (Thessalonica, 1980)

Karpozilos, *Letters*: A. Karpozilos, "Seventeen Letters of Gregorios Akindynos (Cod. Mon. Gr. 223)," *OCA*, 204 (1977), 65–117

Kourouses, Αἱ *ἀντιλήψεις περὶ τῶν ἐσχάτων τοῦ κόσμου*: S. Kourouses, Αἱ *ἀντιλήψεις περὶ τῶν ἐσχάτων τοῦ κόσμου καὶ ἡ κατὰ τὸ ἔτος* 1346 *πτῶσις τοῦ τρούλλου τῆς ἁγίας* Σοφίας, 'Επ.'Ετ.Βυζ.Σπ., (1969–70), 211–50.

________ Μανουὴλ Γαβαλᾶς: S. Kourouses, Μανουὴλ Γαβαλᾶς, *εἶτα* Ματθαῖος *μητροπολίτης* 'Εφέσου (1271/2–1355/60) (Athens, 1972)

Krumbacher: K. Krumbacher, *Geschichte der byzantinischen Litteratur von Justinian bis zum Ende des oströmischen Reiches*, 2nd ed. (Munich, 1897)

Kyrres, 'Ο Κύπριος *ἀρχιεπίσκοπος* Θεσσαλονίκης 'Υάκινθος: K. Kyrres, 'Ο Κύπριος *ἀρχιεπίσκοπος* Θεσσαλονίκης 'Υάκινθος (1345–46) *καὶ ὁ ρόλος του εἰς τὸν ἀντιπαλαμιτικὸν ἀγῶνα*, Κυπριακαὶ Σπουδαί, 25 (1961), 91–122

________ 'Η Κύπρος *καὶ τὸ ἡσυχαστικὸν ζήτημα*: K. Kyrres, 'Η Κύπρος *καὶ τὸ ἡσυχαστικὸν ζήτημα κατὰ τὸν* XIV *αἰῶνα*, Κυπριακαὶ *Σπουδαί*, 26 (1962), 21–31

Laurent, "L'assaut avorté": V. Laurent, "L'assaut avorté de la horde d'or contre l'empire byzantin (printemps-été 1341)," *REB*, 18 (1960), 144–62

________ "La direction spirituelle à Byzance": V. Laurent, "La direction spirituelle à Byzance: La correspondance d'Irène-Eulogie Choumnaina Paléologine avec son second directeur," *REB*, 14 (1956), 48–86

Leutsch-Schneidewin: eds. E. L. Leutsch and F. G. Schneidewin, *Corpus Paroemiographorum Graecorum*, 2 vols. (Göttingen, 1839; reprint, Hildesheim, 1965)

Loenertz, "Chronologie de Nicolas Cabasilas": R. J. Loenertz, "Chronologie de Nicolas Cabasilas, 1345–1354," *OCP*, 21 (1955), 205–31 (reprinted in *Byzantina et Franco-Graeca* [Rome, 1970], 303–28)

———— ed., *Correspondance*: R. J. Loenertz, *Démétrius Cydonès Correspondance*, 2 vols. (Vatican City, 1956–60)

———— "Dix-huit lettres": R. J. Loenertz, "Dix-huit lettres de Grégoire Acindyne analysées et datées," *OCP*, 23 (1957), 114–44; reprinted in Loernertz, *Byzantina et Franco-Graeca* (Rome, 1970), 81–110. All references are to this edition.

———— *Epistulae*: J. R. Loenertz, "Gregorii Acindyni epistulae selectae IX," Ἐπ.Ἑτ. Βυζ.Σπ., (1957), 89–109

Makrembolites, *Dialogue*: Alexios Makrembolites, *Διάλογος πλουσίων καὶ πενήτων· τίνας ἂν εἶπον λόγους πένητες πρὸς πλουσίους καὶ τίνας αὖ πρὸς τοὺς πένητας οὗτοι*, ed. I. Ševčenko, "Alexios Makrembolites and His Dialogue between the Rich and the Poor," *ZVI*, 65 (1960), 203–28

———— *Εἰς τὴν ἁγίαν Σοφίαν*: Alexios Makrembolites, *Εἰς τὴν ἁγίαν Σοφίαν πεσοῦσαν ὑπὸ πολλῶν κατὰ συνέχειαν γενομένων σεισμῶν*, ed. Kourouses, *Αἱ ἀντιλήψεις περὶ τῶν ἐσχάτων τοῦ κόσμου*, 235–40

Mercati, *Notizie*: G. Mercati, *Notizie di Procoro e Demetrio Cidone, Manuele Caleca e Teodoro Meliteniota ed altri appunti per la storia della teologia e della letteratura bizantina del secolo XIV*, Studi e Testi, 56 (Vatican City, 1931)

Meyendorff, *Introduction*: J. Meyendorff, *Introduction à l'étude de Grégoire Palamas* (Paris, 1959)

———— "Le tome synodal de 1347": "Le tome synodal de 1347," ed. J. Meyendorff, *Recueil des Travaux de l'Institut d'Etudes Byzantines, Mélanges G. Ostrogorsky*, 8 (Belgrade, 1963), 209–27 (reprinted in J. Meyendorff, *Byzantine Hesychasm* [Variorum Reprints (London, 1974)], Study VII)

Miklosich-Müller: F. Miklosich and J. Müller, *Acta et diplomata graeca medii aevi sacra et profana*, 6 vols. (Vienna, 1860–90)

Nadal, ed. "La rédaction première": J. S. Nadal, "La rédaction première de la Troisième lettre de Palamas à Akindynos," *OCP*, 40 (1974), 233–85

OCA: *Orientalia Christiana Analecta*

OCP: *Orientalia Christiana Periodica*

Palamas, *Διάλεξις*: Gregory Palamas, *Διάλεξις ὀρθοδόξου μετὰ* Βαρλααμίτου, ed. G. Mantzarides, *Συγγράμματα*, II, 164–218

———— *Συγγράμματα*: G. Palamas, *Λόγοι Ἀποδεικτικοί, Ἀντεπιγραφαί, Ἐπιστολαὶ πρὸς Βαρλαὰμ καὶ Ἀκίνδυνον, Ὑπὲρ Ἡσυχαζόντων*, eds. B. Bobrinsky, P. Papaevangelou, J. Meyendorff, P. Chrestou, *Γρηγορίου τοῦ Παλαμᾶ Συγγράμματα*, I (Thessalonica, 1962); *Πραγματεῖαι καὶ Ἐπιστολαὶ γραφεῖσαι κατὰ τὰ ἔτη* 1340–1346, eds. G. Mantzarides, N. Matsoukas, B. Pseutongas, *Γρηγορίου τοῦ Παλαμᾶ Συγγράμματα*, II (Thessalonica, 1966); *Ἀντιρρητικοὶ πρὸς Ἀκίνδυνον*, eds. L. Kontoyiannis, B. Phanourgakes, *Γρηγορίου τοῦ Παλαμᾶ Συγγράμματα*, III (Thessalonica, 1970)

Passarelli, *Macario*: G. I. Passarelli, *Macario Crisocefalo (1300–1382), l'omelia sulla festa dell'Ortodossia e la basilica di S. Giovanni di Filadelfia, OCA*, 210 (Rome, 1980)

PG: Patrologiae cursus completus, Series Graeca, ed. J. P. Migne

Philotheos, *Encomium*: Philotheos Kokkinos, patriarch of Constantinople, *Λόγος ἐγκωμι-*

αστικὸς εἰς τὸν ἐν ἁγίοις πατέρα ἡμῶν Γρηγόριον, ἀρχιεπίσκοπον Θεσσαλονίκης, τὸν Παλαμᾶν, PG, 151, cols. 551A–656C

——— *Vita Isidori*: Philotheos Kokkinos, patriarch of Constantinople, *Βίος καὶ πολιτεία καὶ ἐγκώμιον τοῦ ἐν ἁγίοις πατρὸς ἡμῶν Ἰσιδώρου πατριάρχου Κωνσταντινουπόλεως*, ed. A. Papadopoulos-Kerameus, *Zapiski istoriko-filologičeskago fakul'teta Imperatorskago S.-Peterburgskago Universiteta*, 76 (1905), 51–149

——— *Vita Sabbae*: Philotheos Kokkinos, patriarch of Constantinople, *Βίος καὶ πολιτεία τοῦ ὁσίου καὶ θεοφόρου πατρὸς ἡμῶν Σάββα τοῦ Νέου τοῦ ἐν τῷ Ἄθῳ ὄρει ἀσκήσαντος*, ed. A. Papadopoulos-Kerameus, *Ἀνάλεκτα Ἱεροσολυμιτικῆς Σταχυολογίας* (St. Petersburg, 1898), V, 190–359

Polemis, *Ἀντιλογία*: D. Polemis, *Ἡ πρὸς τὸν Βαρλαὰμ διένεξις τοῦ Γρηγορᾶ.* ' Ἡ Ἀντιλογία,' *Ἑλληνικά*, 18 (1964), 44–72

Ps.-Kodinos, *Traité des Offices*: Pseudo-Kodinos, *Traité des Offices*, ed. J. Verpeaux (Paris, 1966)

REB: *Revue des Études Byzantines*

Ševčenko, "Alexios Makrembolites' Dialogue": I. Ševčenko, "Alexios Makrembolites and His 'Dialogue between the Rich and the Poor'," *ZVI*, 65 (1960), 187–228 (reprinted in I. Ševčenko, *Society and Intellectual Life in Late Byzantium* [Variorum Reprints (London 1981)], Study VII)

——— "Anti-Zealot Discourse": I. Ševčenko, "Nicolas Cabasilas' 'Anti-Zealot' Discourse. A Reinterpetation," *DOP*, 11 (1957), 81–171 (reprinted in *Society and Intellectual Life* ..., Study IV)

——— "Nicolaus Cabasilas' Correspondence": I. Ševčenko, "Nicolaus Cabasilas' Correspondence and the Treatment of Late Byzantine Literary Texts," *BZ*, 47 (1954), 49–59 (reprinted in *Society and Intellectual Life* ..., Study X)

——— "Society and Intellectual Life in the Fourteenth Century": I. Ševčenko, "Society and Intellectual Life in the Fourteenth Century," *Actes du XIVe Congrès international des Études byzantines, Bucarest, 1971, vol. I* (Bucharest, 1974), 69–92 (reprinted in *Society and Intellectual Life* ..., Study I)

R. E. Sinkewicz, "A New Interpretation": R. E. Sinkewicz, "A New Interpretation for the First Episode in the Controversy Between Barlaam the Calabrian and Gregory Palamas," *Journal of Theological Studies*, 31^2(1980), 489–500

ST: Studi e Testi

Synodikon, ed. Gouillard: J. Gouillard, ed., *Le Synodikon de l'Orthodoxie*, *Travaux et Mémoires*, 2 (Paris, 1967), 1–316

Triodion: *Τριῴδιον κατανυκτικόν*, Apostolike Diakonia (Athens, 1960)

Tsolakes, *Γέωργιος Λαπίθης*: E. Tsolakes, *Ὁ Γεώργιος Λαπίθης καὶ ἡ ἡσυχαστικὴ ἔριδα*, *Ἑλληνικά*, 18 (1964), 84–96

Turyn, *Dated Greek Manuscripts*: A. Turyn, *Dated Greek Manuscripts of the Thirteenth and Fourteenth Centuries in the Libraries of Italy* (Illinois, 1972), 2 vols.

——— *Codices Graeci*: A. Turyn, *Codices Graeci Vaticani saeculis XIII et XIV scripti* ... (Vatican City, 1964)

Uspenskij, *Synodikon*: Th. Uspenskij, *Sinodik v nedelju Pravoslavija (Le Synodikon de l'orthodoxie)* (Odessa, 1893)

Vassilikopoulou-Ioannidou, *Ἀνέκδοτος ἐπιστολή*: A Vassilikopoulou-Ioannidou, *Ἀνέκδοτος ἐπιστολὴ τοῦ Γρηγορίου Ἀκινδύνου πρὸς τὸν μητροπολίτην Κο-*

ρίνθου Ὑάκινθον, Πρακτικὰ Α΄ Διεθνοῦς Συνεδρίου Πελοποννησιακῶν Σπουδῶν (Athens, 1976), II, 91–97

Weiss, *Kantakuzenos*: G. Weiss, *Joannes Kantakuzenos—Aristokrat, Staatsmann, Kaiser und Mönch—in der Gesellschaftsentwicklung von Byzanz im 14 Jahrhundert* (Wiesbaden, 1969)

ZVI: *Zbornik Radova Vizantoloskog Instituta, Srpska Akademija Nauka*

All citations of Byzantine historians refer to the Bonn edition, unless otherwise stated.

LIST OF SIGNS

TEXT

* * *	lacunae codicis
⟨ ⟩	addenda
[ ]	delenda
...	singula pro litteris ponuntur puncta quae nec legi nec suppleri certe possunt
† †	crucibus amplectuntur corruptelae

APPARATUS

Mn	*Monacensis Gr. 223*
M	*Marcianus Gr. 155*
S	*Scorialensis Gr. Φ–III–11*
S^1	ejus corrector
A	*Ambrosianus Gr. 290 (E 64 sup.)*
V	*Vaticanus Gr. 1086*
V^1	ejus corrector
W	*Vaticanus Gr. 1122*

TEXT and TRANSLATION

ΓΡΗΓΟΡΙΟΥ ΑΚΙΝΔΥΝΟΥ ΕΠΙΣΤΟΛΑΙ

1. Τοῦ Ἀκινδύνου ἐκ Θεσσαλονίκης πρὸς τὸν Γρηγορᾶν

Βαλσαμὼν ὁ γενναῖος, φίλος ὢν ἐμοὶ καὶ φίλους πάντας ὑπερβαλλόμενος τὰ πρὸς ἐμέ, ἀντ' ἄλλης τινὸς λαμπρᾶς καὶ μεγάλης εὐεργεσίας—ᾔδει γάρ μέ σού τε καὶ τῶν σῶν συγγραμμάτων σφόδρα περικαόμενον—φέρων ἐνεχείρισέ μοι τὴν σὴν ἐκείνην ἐπιστολὴν τὴν περὶ τῶν ἐν οὐρανῷ τοὺς ἀγνοοῦντας διδάσκουσαν· ἀρκείτω δὲ τοῦτ' ἀντὶ παντὸς ἐπαίνου τοῖς γράμμασι, μᾶλλον δὲ εἰς ὅσον ἂν ἡμεῖς ἰδεῖν τε καὶ εἰπεῖν ἐξικοίμεθα, μὴ ὅσον ἐκείνῃ προσῆκεν, εὐμενῶς ἐκείνη τε δεχέσθω καὶ ὁ πατήρ.

Ἐγὼ δὲ παραλαβὼν καὶ διεξιὼν τό τε βάθος τῆς διανοίας τό τε τῆς ἑρμηνείας Ἑλληνικὸν καὶ τὸ τῶν λέξεων ἀνθηρὸν ἐξ Ἀττικοῦ τοῦ λειμῶνος καὶ ποικιλίαν ἐνθυμημάτων ἐκ τῶν Πλάτωνος θησαυρῶν (εἰ μὴ παντάπασιν ἄπιστος ἐγὼ τὰ τοιαῦτα) καὶ πᾶσαν, ὡς ἔπος εἰπεῖν, τὴν μεθ' ὥρας κατασκευὴν αὐτῆς, οὐχ ὅσον μὲν εἰκὸς ἦν, οὐδ' ἐγγύς, ὅπερ εἶπον, θαυμάσας δ' οὖν εἰς δύναμιν τὴν ἐμαυτοῦ, τοῖς σφόδρα ζητοῦσι—πολλοὶ δὲ οὗτοι—διέδωκα. καὶ ἦλθε διὰ πάντων τὸ θαῦμα, καὶ πολλαχοῦ σοι θέατρα καθειστήκει διὰ κρότου καὶ πηδημάτων, ἄλλων ἄλλα θαυμαζόντων, μᾶλλον δὲ πάντα πάντων, ὅση γε δύναμις ἑκάστῳ. ἀλλ' οὕτω μὲν ἡδονῇ τοὺς ἀνθρώπους τῶν γραμμάτων ἐξήρτησας, ἃ δὲ ὠφέληκας τῇ διδαχῇ τούς τε τὴν αὐτὴν ἐπιστήμην σοι μετιόντας, τούς τε μή, τοὺς μὲν ἃ μηδαμῶς ᾔδεσαν μεμαθηκότας, τοὺς δ' ἃ σφαλερῶς, ἐπηνωρθωμένους καὶ τἀκριβὲς ἐγνωκότας, τούτων τίς οὐχ ὁμολογεῖ σοι χάριτας μείζους ἤπερ ἔχων τυγχάνει;

Ἐκείνην ἐγὼ [fol. 225r] τὴν ἐπιστολὴν ὑπὸ ποικιλοφόρμιγγος ἀοιδᾶς τοῦ Θηβαίου ποιητοῦ συντεθῆναι, μὴ μάτην,

---

1: 25–26 Pindarus, *Olymp.*, IV, 3

1: V 224v–225r. Gregoras, *Hist.*, I, LXIX–LXX =PG, 148, 68D–70A.
2–3 ὑπερβαλόμενος V

LETTERS OF GREGORY AKINDYNOS

1. To Gregoras from Thessalonica

The noble Balsamon, who is a friend of mine and surpasses all friends in his regard for me, knows that I am fired with admiration for you and your works. Therefore, instead of some other splendid and great kindness, he brought and handed to me that letter of yours which instructs the ignorant in celestial matters. So let me write just this instead of all other praise. Or rather let both the letter and its author receive favorably as much attention and discussion as I could give to it, rather than what the letter deserves.

I took it, then, and studied its depth of meaning as well as its classical style and the flower of its vocabulary, picked from an Attic meadow, and the variety of arguments from the Platonic treasures (unless I am altogether untrustworthy in such matters); in short, I may say, its whole graceful composition. I did not admire it as much as it deserves, not even nearly so, as I said before. Nevertheless, admire it I did to the best of my ability; then I passed it on to those who were eagerly asking for it, and they were many. Admiration came over everyone, and in many places audiences gathered in your honor, with everyone admiring something different in your letter by clapping and leaping. Or rather they all admired everything, each according to his ability. This is how you bound men with delight at your writings. As for the help you provided with your teaching, alike for those who pursue the same studies as you and for those who do not: the latter have learnt what they did not know at all, while the former had their erroneous notions corrected. For this help, who would not concede to you a gratitude even greater than he can really afford?

I think I was not wide of the mark in considering that letter to have been composed by the Theban poet's "melody, accompanied by varied notes of the lyre". I

οἶμαι, νενόμικα· ἐκείνην τῆς παρὰ Πλάτωνι κατ' οὐρανὸν Ἀφροδίτης ὑπείληφα γέμουσαν. οὐ μὴν ἀλλὰ καὶ πολλ' ἕτερα τῆς σῆς γενναίας καὶ γνώμης καὶ γλώττης δημιουργήματα παρ' ἐμοί σοι συνῆκται καὶ διὰ θαύματος ἄγεται, εἴπερ ἃ πέπομφας Ἰωσὴφ ἐκείνῳ τῷ μακαρίτῃ καὶ σοφωτάτῳ διὰ τοῦ θεσπεσίου καὶ σοφοῦ Παλαμᾶ διὰ μνήμης ἔχεις, πρὸ γὰρ δυοῖν ἐτοῖν τοῦτό γε· ὃς ἐπειδὴ τὸν φιλόσοφον εὗρε παρὰ τὸν ἐκ μάλα πολλοῦ πεποθημένον οἰχόμενον—ᾔδει δὲ ἄρα καὶ οὗτος δεινὸν ἐμὲ τῶν σῶν ἐραστὴν καὶ ὡς, εἰ κομιεῖ τὸ βιβλίον, τὰ μέγιστά μοι χαρισάμενος ἔσται—φέρων ἐγκεχείρικε, φιλοτιμότατα προσειπών· "δέξαι λόγους ὧν ἤρας." ἀνθ' ὧν παρ' ἡμῶν οὐ μικράς τινας κεκόμισται χάριτας, ἀλλ' οἵας οὐ μέμψασθαι.

Ἐκ τοσούτου σφοδροὺς ἐραστὰς εἶχες ἡμᾶς, ὦ μέγα κῦδος Ἀχαιοῖσι, λέγω δὴ τοῖς Ἕλλησιν. εἰ μὴ μᾶλλον τοὐναντίον· πολλοὺς τῶν ἐν λόγοις τὸν βίον κατατριψάντων αἰσχύνει τὰ σὰ τῇ ὑπερβολῇ καὶ λυπεῖ, ἀλλ' οὐχ ἡμᾶς γε, εἰ καὶ μηδὲν τὸ ἡμέτερον πρὸς τὸ σὸν πέλαγος τῆς σοφίας, ὦ βέλτιστε. μάλιστα μὲν οὖν καὶ συγχαίρομεν, καὶ ψήφους ἥδιστά σοι τῆς κατὰ πάντων νίκης ἐκφέρομεν. εἴ σοι τοίνυν καὶ αὐτῷ τῶν δικαίων τι δόξειε—δόξει δ', οἶμαι—μὴ τὸν οὕτω τῶν σῶν ἐραστὴν μόνον εἶναι τῶν Ἀργείων ἀγέραστον, μηδὲ μόνοις τοῖς πρὸς τοὺς ἄλλους σοι γράμμασιν, ἀλλ' ἤδη καὶ τοῖς πρὸς αὐτὸν ἐντρυφᾶν, ἐπιστελεῖς καὶ ἡμῖν καὶ δείξεις ὡς οὐ μάτην ἐρῶμεν. εἰ δὲ μήπω τεθεαμένος τὴν σὴν χρυσῆν κεφαλήν, μηδ' ἄλλως ἄγαν ἐγνωσμένος σοι γράφω, μὴ τοῦτο θρασύτητος ἀλλ' ἔρωτος οἴου. εἰ δὲ ψυχὴ σώματος τιμιωτέρα, τῷ βελτίονι δήπου σύνεσμεν, εἰ ψυχῆς αὖ ἔγγονα τὰ συγγράμματα.

2. Τοῦ αὐτοῦ πρὸς τὸν αὐτὸν

Οὐδὲν θαυμαστὸν ἴσην Κλεοδήμῳ σε δόξαν ἀποφέρεσθαι πρὸς ἀνθρώπων· ἀλλ' ἐκεῖνο θαυμαστόν, εἰ μὴ πλέον ἔχεις ἢ κατ' ἐκεῖνον κλέους, εἴπερ ὁ μὲν ὄρνιθάς τινας ἑαυτὸν ᾄδειν ἐδίδασκε, περιεργαζόμενος δήπου καὶ ὅθεν οὐκ ἐνεδέχετο δόξαν θηρώμενος—ταῦτ' ἄρα καὶ περιττὸς ἄν, οἶμαι, μᾶλλον ἢ ἐπαινετὸς ἐδόκει τοῖς ᾐσθη-

---

27–28 cf. Platonem, *Sympos.*, 180d ‖ 39–40 Homerus, *Il.*, 9, 673; 14, 42; *Od.*, 3, 79; 12, 184 ‖ 46–47 cf. Homerum, *Il.*, 1, 119

---

49 σῆν V

2: V 225ʳ–226ᵛ. Gregoras, *Hist.*, I, LXXXVI–LXXXVIII =PG, 148, 84C–86D.

thought it replete with Plato's celestial Aphrodite! Besides this I have collected many other products of your noble thought and speech, and I hold them in admiration; that is, if in fact you remember (for this happened two years ago) what you sent to that most wise Joseph of blessed memory, with the divine and wise Palamas. When Palamas found that the philosopher had gone near to Him for Whom he had yearned for so long—and he apparently knew that I am an ardent lover of your works and that if he should bring me the book, he would do me the greatest favor—he brought and handed it to me saying most generously, "Take the book that you fell in love with!" In return, he won from me no trivial gratitude, but such as he could not complain about.

For so long you enjoyed my ardent love, O "great glory of the Achaeans" (I mean, of course, the Hellenes)! Unless the opposite may rather be true. For your achievements bring shame and sorrow by their superiority to many men who have spent their life in literary pursuits. That is not indeed the case with me, although I am nothing in comparison with your ocean of wisdom, my excellent friend. In fact I rejoice with you especially and am delighted to cast my vote for your victory against all comers. If, therefore, you too should think that it is unfair—and I believe that you will consider it so—for the man who loves your works so much to be "the only man among the Argives to go without a prize," and that he should delight only in the letters that you write to others, rather than in those that you write to him, you will send me a letter also and show that my love is not in vain. And if I write to you without having yet set eyes on your golden face or being otherwise known to you very much, do not consider this a sign of impudence, but of love. And if the soul is held in higher honor than the body, then we are associated through the better element: if, that is, written works are the progeny of the soul.

2. To the same from the same

It is not at all amazing that you receive from men the same honor as Kleodemos. But what is amazing is that you do not enjoy greater fame than he, for all he did was to teach some birds to sing about him, simply wasting his efforts and hunting out glory from impossible places. As a result I think that he would have even seemed eccentric rather than praiseworthy to those who saw through his trick.

2

μένοις τὸ τέχνασμα—[fol. 225v] σὲ δὲ οὐκ ὄρνιθες, οὐδ' ἑτέρα συσκευή τις τοιαύτη πεπλασμένη, τῷ μηδὲν ἔχειν οἴκοθεν ἀναπεφάνθαι σοφόν, εἰς ἀσόφου σοφίας ἐπίδειξιν, ἀλλὰ λόγων κάλλος τε καὶ δύναμις μέγαν πανταχῇ γῆς κηρύττουσι καὶ πείθουσιν ἕκαστον μηδένα πρὸ τοῦ σφετέρου πατρὸς αὐτῶν ἄγειν Ἑλλήνων—οἷοι νῦν εἰσιν Ἕλληνες—ὥσπερ τὰ Ὁμήρου τὸν Ὅμηρον καὶ τὰ Πινδάρου τὸν Πίνδαρον καί, εἰ βούλει γε, τὰ Δημοσθένους τὸν Δημοσθένην καὶ ὁντινοῦν εἴποι τις ἂν ἕτερον ἐκείνου δὴ τοῦ χοροῦ.

Καὶ μὴν οὐχ ὅπως οἱ σοί σε λόγοι κηρύττουσιν, οὐδ' ἀνθρώπων οἱ τῆς σῆς θεσπεσίας φωνῆς γεγευμένοι καὶ ἀπολελαυκότες, ἀλλ' ἤδη καὶ τὰ οὐράνια, ἥλιος αὐτὸς καὶ σελήνη καὶ ἄστρα, κατὰ τὴν σὴν ὑφήγησιν ἡμῖν ἐκλείποντά τε καὶ πάλιν φαινόμενα καὶ ὡς ἔχει κινούμενα. ὥστ' οὔτ' αὐτὸς εἰκότως ἀπορεῖν μοι δοκεῖς ὅτῳ τρόπῳ καὶ παρ' ἡμῖν εὐδοκίμηκας, οὔτ' ἐγώ μοι δοκῶ πως ἀπεικότως ἁλῶναί σου. ἀλλ' οὐδὲ μόνος τῶν ἄλλων ἁπάντων ἁλοίην ἐγώ, οὐχ οὕτως ἀπειροκάλως ἔχω, ἀλλ' ὅτι φύσιν ἔχει τὰ σὰ χειροῦσθαι καὶ τῶν ἄλλων ἁπάντων τοὺς αὐτοῖς ἐντυγχάνοντας, καθάπερ τὰ Σειρήνων μέλη τοὺς διαπλέοντας, διὰ τοῦτο καὶ αὐτῷ μοι συμβέβηκεν αὐτῶν ἐξηρτῆσθαι.

Οὐ μὴν οὐδ' ἐκεῖνό μοι πάνυ δοκεῖς ἀκριβῶς ἐσκεμμένος εἰπεῖν, ὡς ἄρα μηδὲν τῶν ἀνθρωπείων τοῖς ἀνθρώποις ὁμολογεῖται, ἀλλ' ὃ μὲν οὗτος τεθαύμακεν, ἐκείνῳ φαῦλον, καὶ τοὔμπαλιν. ἐγὼ γὰρ ὅτι μὲν δυσχερὴς ἡ τῶν καλῶν ἐστι γνῶσις οἶδα κοὐκ ἀπαρνοῦμαι τὸ μή. πῶς γάρ; μέγα βοώσης τῆς παροιμίας ὅτι χαλεπά ἐστι τὰ καλὰ ὅπως ἔχοι μαθεῖν. ὅτι μέντοι τὰ καλὰ μαθεῖν οὐκ ἔστι παντάπασιν, οὐδ' ἔστι τούτων παρ' ἀνθρώποις ὡρισμένη τις φύσις, ἀλλ' ὅπῃ τύχοι τούτοις κρινόμενα, ταύτῃ ταῦτ' ἔχειν ἀνάγκη, κρίνεται δὲ ἀποχρώντως οὐδέποτε, τούτοις δὲ πολλοῦ δέω τίθεσθαι· ἦ γὰρ ἂν κόσμος μὲν ἦν οὐδαμοῦ, πᾶσα δὲ ἀκοσμία. ἀλλά φημι καὶ εἶναι χωρὶς τὰ καλά, καὶ οὐκ ἀγνῶτα εἶναι παντάπασι, καὶ πολλοὺς ἐπὶ ταῦτα χωρεῖν, εἰ δὲ δεῖ πείθεσθαι καὶ Σοφοκλεῖ, καὶ πάντας τούτων ἐπιθυμεῖν· φιλεῖ γάρ, φησιν ἐκεῖνος, πρὸς τὰ χρηστὰ πᾶς ὁρᾶν. εἰ δ' οὐ καὶ πᾶς ἐπὶ ταῦτα χωρεῖ, ἕτερος λόγος οὗτος καὶ οὐδὲν τοῦτο πρὸς τὸ καλόν.

Ἆρ' οὖν σε φῶμεν ταυτὶ λεληθέναι, καὶ τίνα μᾶλλον ταῦτα [fol. 226r] φῶμεν εἰδέναι; ἀλλά μοι δοκεῖς τῷ μετριάζειν ἐθέλειν ὑπαχθῆναι πρὸς ταῦτα. ἀλλὰ μὴ σὺ μετριάζων, ἡμῶν ἀναισθησίαν

2: 23–24 cf. Homerum, *Od.*, 12, 39–44 || 30–31 Gregorius Cyprius III, 30 (Leutsch-Schneidewin, II, 89) || 38–39 Sophocles, *Electra*, 972

---

27 post ὁμολογεῖται vocabulum quod legi non potest V[sv]

2

As for you, it is not the birds, nor indeed any other kind of device contrived to show up unwise wisdom, though having nothing of its own which could be called wise; rather it is the beauty and the power of your works which proclaim you great all over the earth, and persuade each man not to honor any of the Hellenes (such as are now Hellenes) above their own author. In just the same way, Homer's works proclaim Homer and Pindar's works Pindar and, if you wish, Demosthenes' works Demosthenes; and, in fact, anyone else from that circle we might name.

In fact, it is not only your works which proclaim you, nor is it just those men who have savored and relished your divine sayings, but now even the celestial bodies, the very sun and the moon and the stars which under your guidance hide from us and appear again, moving as they do. So you do not seem to me justified in being amazed at the way you have found also favor with me, neither does it seem to me at all unreasonable that I should have been so captivated by you. For I am not alone among men in this; I am not so lacking in good taste. Indeed your works naturally overcome all other men who come across them, just as the melodies of the Sirens ⟨overcame⟩ those who sailed through the straits. This is how it happened that I too was spellbound by them.

I must say that I do not think that you spoke after very careful consideration ⟨when you said⟩ that men do not agree on any human matter, one man admiring what the other considers bad, and the other way around. For I am aware that the knowledge of the good is difficult and I do not deny this. How can I, when the proverb proclaims aloud that "It is difficult to learn the nature of the good." But I am far from agreeing with the view that it is altogether impossible to know the good and that the nature of the good is not defined among men, while what is good must of necessity be whatever it is by chance judged to be, there being no satisfactory judgment ⟨on such matters⟩. For, in that case, order could not exist anywhere, only absolute disorder. But I say that the good is distinct and by no means unknown, and many people pursue it, and, if we must trust Sophocles, all men desire it. For he says that "Everybody loves to look to the good". And even if not everybody pursues this, that is a different matter and has nothing to do with the good.

Am I then to say that you have fogotten this, and who am I to say knows this better? But I think that you were led to this by your desire to be modest. However, in your modesty, do not accuse me of obtuseness, alleging lack of judgment about mat-

2

κατηγορῆς, οἷς καλῶς ἐκρίναμεν ἀκρισίαν προφέρων· καίτοι τῇ περὶ τὰ σὰ μανίᾳ, παρά γέ σου καὶ τοῦθ' ἡμῖν ἥδιστον, ὥσπερ καὶ πληγαὶ τοῖς σφόδρ' ἐρῶσι τῶν καλλίστων σωμάτων. ἀλλὰ τίς ἀνθρώπων ἡμῶν σοι τοῦτο συγκαταγνώσεται μέχρι ἂν εἷς σε καὶ τὰ σὰ δήπου βλέπῃ; μᾶλλον μὲν τοὐναντίον πᾶς ἐπιεικῶς ταυτησὶ τῆς κρίσεως ἐπαινέσεται, εἰ καὶ μηδενὸς ἄλλου σχοίη. ὡς γὰρ οὐκ ἐκολακεύσαμεν, ἀλλ' ὑπ' ἀληθείας ἠναγκάσμεθα φρονεῖν τε καὶ λέγειν ταυτὶ περὶ τῆς σῆς σοφίας, κἀκεῖθεν δῆλον· οἱ γὰρ λέγειν ᾑρημένοι πρὸς χάριν, ἤτοι χρημάτων χάριν ἢ δόξης ἢ τοιούτου τινὸς ἄλλου, λέγουσιν ἃ λέγουσι, πρὸς ὅ τι δὴ βούλονται τὸν κολακευόμενον, εἰ χαίρει τούτοις, ὑπάγοντες τοιούτοις λόγοις. ἐγὼ δὲ οὐκ ἔσθ' ὅπως ἕνεκα τοῦ τοιούτου περὶ σοῦ πρὸς σὲ τοὺς λόγους ἐποιούμην ἐκείνους, οὐδ' ἔχεις εἰπεῖν, ὦ γενναῖε· ὥστε λείπεται τἀληθῆ με περὶ τῶν σῶν εἰρηκέναι. ἐγὼ γάρ, ὥσπερ οἶδα πλεῖστα τῶν ἄλλων καὶ ποιεῖν καὶ λέγειν μὴ ἀσφαλέστατος ὤν, οὕτω τὰ ὄντα περὶ τῶν σῶν καὶ δοξάζειν καὶ λέγειν λίαν ὢν ἀσφαλέστατος οἶδα, ὡς καὶ αὐτὰ μαρτυρεῖ μοι τὰ πράγματα. τίνα γὰρ τῶν παρ' ἡμῖν περὶ λόγους ἐχόντων ἣν νῦν ἡμῖν ἐπεπόμφεις ἐπιστολὴν οὐκ ἐδόνησεν (ἵνα τἄλλα παρῶμεν); τί δ', ἐπειδήπερ ἀνεγινώσκετο, μὴ τῶν εὐφημίαν ἐχόντων ἠνέχθη σοι πρὸς τῶν ἀκροωμένων, πολλῶν ἀπαντησάντων καὶ πολλαχῇ; τίς δ' οὐκ ἐπήδησε; τίς δ' οὐκ ἐκρότησεν; ἔνθα πρὸς τὴν ἐπιστολήν, ἐπειδήπερ οὐκ ἦν μοι πρὸς σέ, τουτὶ διελέχθην· "ἆρ' οὖν ἐμὸν μόνου Γρηγορᾶν θαυμάζειν τὸν ἄριστον;" ἡ δὲ μόνον οὐκ ἠφίει φωνήν, ὡς "οὐμενοῦν," εἰπεῖν, "ἔστι τοῦτό γε, ἀλλ' ὁπόσοις ἂν καὶ ὁπωσοῦν πεῖραν τἀνδρὸς εἰληφέναι συμβαίη."

Οὐκοῦν σὺ μὲν οὐκ εἰκότως θαυμάζεις ὅπως εὐδοκιμεῖς παρ' ἡμῖν, ἐγὼ δὲ τοὐναντίον εἰκότως ὅπως τοῦτο θαυμάζεις. οὐδὲ γὰρ οὐδ' ὁ Πλάτων, οὐδ' ἄλλος οὐδεὶς τοῦ κατ' ἐκεῖνον κύκλου, λανθάνειν ᾤετο τοὺς ἀνθρώπους τὴν ἑαυτοῦ σοφίαν, οὐδ' ἂν ἐθαύμαζε διαπορούμενος, εἴ τις τῶν ἀπωτάτω διεξῄει περὶ τῶν αὐτοῦ πρὸς αὐτόν· ἀλλ' εἰδώς, οἶμαι, τὴν ἑαυτοῦ περὶ τὰς Μούσας ἰσχὺν καὶ ἅττα ταύτῃ διβλία δε [fol. 226v] δημιούργηκε, καὶ ὡς π τ ε ρ ό ε ν τ ε ς οἱ λόγοι δοκοῦσί τε εἶναι καὶ λέγονται τοῖς ποιηταῖς, τὸ εἰκὸς ἂν ἐποίει, ἐδέχετ' ἂν τοὺς λόγους. πρὸς ταῦτα πείθου μὴ κολακεύειν ἐμέ, τό γε μὴν ἀληθὲς οὐκ οἴεσθαι δεῖν ἀποκρύπτεσθαι, οὐδὲ σιγᾶν ἀνέχεσθαι.

Πολλὰ δὲ ἡσθείς σου τοῖς γράμμασι, μάλιστα παρὰ τὴν

---

75 cf., e.g., Homerum, *Il.*, 1, 201; 2, 7; 5, 123

---

67 οὔμενουν V

ters which I judged correctly. And yet, with my passion for your works, even this accusation coming from you is most agreeable to me, just as even blows are acceptable to those who are madly in love with the most beautiful bodies. But what man will join you in condemning me for this, so long as he still has his gaze on you and your works? On the contrary, everyone will rightly praise me for this judgment, even if he could not praise me for anything else. It is also evident from the following fact that I did not flatter you, but was compelled by the truth not only to believe but to say this of your wisdom: those who choose to speak for gratification say what they say for money or fame or some other similar favor; by such speech they lead the person they flatter wherever they wish, so long as he is pleased by what they say. But there is no question that I said these things about you to your face for any such reason; and you cannot say this, my noble friend. Therefore, it remains a fact that I spoke the truth about your work. For, just as I know that I do and say many other things without being absolutely correct, so I know that I am quite correct in thinking and saying what is true about your works, as even the facts themselves bear witness. Indeed, what learned man here was not stirred by the letter which you have just sent me, not to mention anything else? And while it was being read, what praise did the listeners not offer you, for many persons were present all over the place! Who did not leap up? Who did not clap? Thereupon, since I could not talk to you, I said this to the letter: "Am I the only one to admire the excellent Gregoras?" And the letter all but cried out, saying: "On the contrary, not only you, but all those who happen to come in contact with the man, however little!"

You are not, therefore, right to wonder how you have found favor with me, while for me, on the contrary, it is reasonable to wonder at your wonder over that. For not even Plato, nor any one else of his circle, thought that his wisdom went undetected by men. Nor was he amazed or quite at a loss, if someone from far away discussed his works with him in detail. But I believe that he knew his power with the Muses and the kind of books he had created with this ⟨power⟩, and that words seem to be, as they are called by the poets, "winged," and he would have done the proper thing: he would have accepted the words ⟨of praise⟩. In view of this, be assured that I am no flatterer: I just do not think that truth must be concealed, or that one must be content to keep it a secret.

Your letter pleased me in many ways, but above all I was moved to celebrate

ὑπόσχεσιν τῆς βεβαίου φιλίας ἑώρτασα, καὶ μάλα εἰκότως. αὐτό τε γοῦν καθ' αὑτὸ τὸ χρῆμα τοῦτο παρὰ πάντα γῆς τὰ λαμπρότατα, τὸ δὲ καὶ παρὰ τοιούτῳ γενέσθαι, τίνα ὑπερβολὴν εὐδαιμονίας ἀφίησι; βασιλέα δὲ τὸν θειότατον ὅταν λέγῃς τούς τε λόγους αὐτοὺς καὶ τοὺς περὶ λόγους θαυμάζοντα περὶ πλείστου ποιεῖσθαι, πιστεύω τε καί—πῶς οἴει;—τῆς αὐτοῦ γνώμης ἄγαμαι, ὅτι θαυμάζειν ἔγνωκε τὰ βασιλεῖ θαυμάζειν προσήκοντα, εἰδὼς ὡς οὐδὲν οὕτως οἰκεῖον ὡς λόγοι τῇ βασιλείας φύσει· ὅταν δὲ ὅτι σου διεξιόντος ἐγκώμια κατ' ἐμοῦ καὶ τῶν ἐμῶν γραμμάτων ἀκούσειε, τοῦτο δέ σοι μικροῦ πιστεύειν, εἴ μοι δίδως εἰπεῖν, οὐκ ἔχω. οὔτε γὰρ οἷα βασιλεῖ γνώριμα εἶναι τἀμά, οὔτ' ἂν ἐκεῖνος παρέσχετο τὰς ἀκοάς. εἰ δ' ἔστι τοῦτο καὶ γέγονε, σόν, ὡς ἔοικε, μόνου καὶ Σειρῆνος τῆς σῆς βασιλέως ἀκοὰς καὶ φαυλοτάτοις αἱρεῖν. ὅθεν συμβάλλομεν μάλιστα, ὅτι σοι λίαν φιλούμεθα· τῷ γάρ τοι διαφερόντως φιλεῖν καὶ βασιλεῖ συστῆσαι τἀμὰ βουληθείς, οὐκ εἰ προσήκοι βασιλέα γνωρίζειν ἐζήτησας, ἀλλ' ὥσπερ ἅττα σὺ στέργεις, πάντα ταῦτα δεῖν εἶναι καὶ βασιλέα γνωρίζειν—μᾶλλον δὲ οὐκ ἄλλως ταῦτ' ἔοικεν ἔχειν—μηδὲν ἐσκεμμένος μηδ' ὑπολογησάμενος, διελέχθης ἃ διελέχθης ὑπὲρ ἡμῶν πρὸς αὐτόν. ἀνθ' ὧν παρὰ μὲν ἡμῖν κείσεταί σοι χάρις ὅση δυνατή, συμμετρουμένη τῷ βίῳ τῷ ἡμετέρῳ, παρὰ δὲ Θεῷ καὶ μισθός.

3. Τῷ Γαβρᾷ

Ἀνέγνων τὸν περὶ τῆς κόμης λόγον καὶ τῶν κακῶς κεχρημένων τῇ κόμῃ καὶ οὐκ ἐκάκισα τούτους τοὐπιτηδεύματος, οὕτως ἠγάπησα τὸν ἐπὶ τούτοις λόγον. ἔδει τοίνυν, ὡς ἔοικεν, αὐτοὺς ἀσελγῶς ἀπολαύειν τῆς κόμης ἕως ὁ λόγος φανῇ, τούτου δὲ ἀνατείλαντος ἀπὸ τῶν σῶν θησαυρῶν, ἐκεῖνο τὸ πονηρὸν ἔθος οἴχεσθαι καὶ τῶν δεσμῶν ἀνεῖσθαι τὸν κόσμον τῆς κεφαλῆς τὸν φυσικόν τε καὶ ἄσκευον καί, ὡς εἰπεῖν, ἀδιάφθορον, καὶ οὕτω τὴν φύσιν ἀπολαβεῖν τὴν οἰκείαν ἐλευθερίαν αὐτῆς καὶ τἀπὶ τούτοις χαριστήρια λύτρα τῷ λόγῳ φέρειν καὶ λαμπρῶς ἑορτάζειν τὰ ἐλευθέρια. εἰ δὲ μὴ τὴν ὅθεν προσήκει συμμαχίαν λαβόντος, ἧττον τῷ σκοπῷ προχωρήσοι καὶ τῇ σπουδῇ, οὐ τοῦ λόγου τὸ ἔγκλημα, τῶν δὲ μὴ συμμαχησάντων· ὃ γὰρ ἦν αὐτοῦ πᾶν ἐξείργασται.

3: Mn 9^r. Ed. Karpozilos, *Letters*, 99–100, no. 13.

2 *τῶν*] *τω* Mn ‖ 12 *τῶ δὲ* Mn

at the promise of steadfast friendship; and with very good reason, since friendship itself is superior to the most splendid blessings on earth. And to be friends with such a man! Is there any greater happiness left? As for the most divine Emperor, when you say that he admires learning and learned men and values them highly, I believe you, and you cannot imagine how much I admire him for his judgment, because he knows how to admire things that befit an emperor's admiration, aware that nothing is as proper to the nature of kingship as learning. But when you say that he listened to you praising my letter, about this, permit me to say, I can hardly believe you. For neither is my letter such as to be presented to the Emperor, nor would he lend an ear to it. But if this did happen, it seems that it was you and your Siren who accomplished it, obtaining an imperial audience for even the most insignificant ⟨work⟩. For this reason, I conclude with certainty that you love me excessively. For out of your exceptional love and desire to recommend my letter to the Emperor, you did not ask if it was fit to be made known to him. But, as if everything that you like should also become known to the Emperor—and it seems that it could not be otherwise—you said to him what you said about me without taking anything into consideration or account. For this you will receive from me a gratitude as great as it can be, my whole life long, and a reward from God as well.

3. To Gabras

I read your discourse about hair and those who do not treat it properly and did not blame them for their practice, thus far I enjoyed your discourse about them. In fact, it seems that they were destined to enjoy their hair in an extravagant style until your discourse appeared; and when it sprang up from your treasure ⟨of wisdom⟩, that wicked habit had to disappear, and the adornment of the head—the natural and plain and pure, so to speak—had to break its fetters; and thus nature was to enjoy its proper freedom and to offer for this a ransom as thanksgiving to your discourse, a brilliant celebration of its deliverance. But if it should attain less than it had in view and sought, because it did not receive assistance from the proper places, it will not be the fault of the discourse, but of those who did not support it. For it did all that it was expected to do.

4. Sine titulo

Πολὺς μὲν κατὰ τῆς σῆς θεοφιλείας φθόνος ἐρρύη τοῦ πονηροῦ, ἔστι δὲ οὐδείς, οἶμαι, ὅτου μὴ τὰ περὶ σὲ γεγονότα καθίκετο· λίθου γάρ, οἶμαι, γέγονεν ὅστις ὡμιληκὼς μέν σοι καὶ πρὸς βραχὺ μὴ καὶ φίλος ὑπῆρξε, φίλος δὲ γενόμενος μὴ συναλγεῖ μὲν ἀλγοῦντι, συγχαίρει δὲ χαίροντι, πάντα δὲ οἰκειοῦται τὰ σὰ καὶ ἀσπάζεται· πάντα γὰρ ἀνδρὸς ἀγαθοῦ καὶ σοφοῦ καὶ γενναίου.

Τὸ μὲν οὖν ῥεῦμα πολὺ τοῦ μισοκάλου φθόνου, πλεῖον δὲ τὸ τῆς φιλοσοφίας τοῦ φθονηθέντος χρῆμα, ᾗ χρώμενος ὑπερέξεις, εὖ οἶδα, τῶν κυμάτων τοῦ φθόνου, οὐδὲ δώσεις ἡσθῆναι τῷ δαίμονι, τῶν βελῶν ἐμπαγέντων καιρίως εἰς τὴν καρδίαν τὴν σήν· ἃ κατὰ σοῦ διὰ τοῦτο τοξεύει καὶ οὐκ ἀνίησιν, ἵνα τυχὼν ἡσθείη. [fol. 8v] τοιοῦτο γὰρ ὁ δαιμόνιος φθόνος κατὰ παντὸς ἀγαθοῦ, ἀλλὰ σὺ τὴν φιλοσοφίαν καὶ τὴν εὐσέβειαν τῆς Ἡρακλέους λεοντῆς ἀσφαλεστέραν ἔχων, ἄτρωτος ἔσῃ μᾶλλον ἐκείνῳ ἢ Ἡρακλῆς σιδήρῳ τὴν λεοντῆν περικείμενος.

5. Γρηγορίῳ ἱερομονάχῳ

Οἵαν ἡμῖν ἡδονὴν διὰ τοῦ πρὸς ἡμᾶς σου θαυμαστοῦ καὶ γενναίου κεχορήγηκας λόγου· καί σου πρότερον τὴν μακρὰν ἐκείνην σιωπὴν δυσχεραίνων, νῦν εὐεργέτιν ἡγοῦμαι, ὡς αὐτήν μοι τεκοῦσαν τὸν θαυμάσιον ἔγγονον. Αἴγυπτος ἄρα ἐμοὶ σύ, κατὰ τὴν παροιμίαν, σπανίως μέν τι τίκτων, γενναῖον δ' ἀεὶ τίκτων. πλὴν οὐκ οἶδ' ὅντινά μοι αἰτιατέον τούτου, πότερόν σε τὸν τεκόντα ἢ τοὺς φιλοσόφου τοῦ ἐκ Σικελίας λόγους, οἵ σε τοῦτον τεκεῖν παρεσκεύασαν· ὃ καὶ αὐτὸς οὐκ ἐσίγησας, ἀλλὰ καὶ σφόδρα δεῖξαι ἡμῖν ἐσπούδασας καὶ διετείνω οὐκ ἂν ἐλθεῖν ἐπὶ τοῦτο, εἰ μὴ διὰ τοὺς εἰρημένους τοῦ φιλοσόφου λόγους. οὕτως ἡμῶν ἧττον δηλοῖς περιφανῶς φροντίζων καί, πλείω λόγους ἀποδείξεως ἢ ἡμᾶς πεποιημένος, οἴει τι πεποιηκέναι δέον. ἐγὼ δὲ οὐκ ἂν φαίην, οὐδ' ἂν αὐτός,

---

5: 5 locum non inveni

4: Mn 8r–8v. Ed. Karpozilos, *Letters*, 96–97, no. 10.
11 *ἀνίνησιν* Mn || 14 *λεοντὴν* Mn
5: A 75v–76v.

4. No Addressee

Much of the devil's malice was poured upon your Reverence, and I think that there is no one who has not been touched by what happened to you. In fact, I believe that a man would have to be made of stone, if after associating with you even briefly he does not become your friend, and having become your friend does not sympathize with your suffering and rejoice at your happiness, taking to himself and loving all your ⟨characteristics⟩, for all are those of a good and wise and noble man.

Mighty, then, is the flow of malice which hates the good, but the philosophy of the maligned man is mightier. I am sure that if you make use of it, you will rise above the waves of malice and will not give the devil the opportunity to delight because his arrows are fatally stuck in your heart. For this purpose he shoots them against you and does not give up, so that he may delight at having succeeded. Such is the devil's malice against everything good. But you who have philosophy and piety as a protection safer than the lion's skin worn by Heracles will be more impervious to the devil's attack than Heracles was to iron when covered by the lion's skin.

5. To the hieromonk Gregory

What a pleasure you have given me with your admirable and excellent letter! And whereas previously I was annoyed at that long silence of yours, now I consider it a benefactor because it produced for me this admirable progeny. You seem to be "Egypt to me," as the saying goes, for you rarely produce something, but what you do produce is always something noble. However, I do not know whom to hold responsible for this ⟨letter⟩: you who wrote it, or the writings of the Sicilian philosopher which made you produce it. This fact you yourself did not hide; you were even extremely anxious to reveal this to me and claimed that you would not have taken this step, if it were not for the aforementioned writings of the philosopher. Thus you make it manifestly clear that your concern is less for me, and you believe that you have done the right thing by valuing demonstrative arguments more than me. But I would not say this and neither, I believe, would you, if you considered what is just.

5

οἶμαι, πρὸς τὸ δίκαιον ἰδών· οὐ γὰρ ἡ ἀπόδειξις καὶ ἡ περὶ ταύτην σπουδὴ φιλίας θεοφιλοῦς καὶ τοῦ ψυχῇ πεινώσῃ τοιαύτης τροφῆς χορηγὸν γεγονέναι θειότερον. ἀλλ' ὅταν τις τὸ ἑαυτῷ μόνῳ διαφέρον διώκῃ, καταφρονεῖ μὲν τῶν ἄλλων, τοῦτο δὲ ποιῶν εὑρίσκει καὶ λόγους εὐπροσώπους, εἴ τις αὐτῷ ἐγκαλέσοι, πρὸς τὴν ἀπάντησιν. τοῦτο δὴ τὸ σόν. ἐγὼ δὲ ἄρα οὕτω σου καὶ τῶν σῶν ἥλων πάλαι, ὡς καὶ τὰς ἐφ' οἷς ἀδικοίμην ἀπολογίας, αὐτὰ νομίζειν πρὸς ἐμαυτὸν παρὰ σοῦ τὰ δίκαια γίγνεσθαι, καὶ τὸν λόγον δὴ τοῦτον οὐκ ἂν πάντως γενόμενον ἄνευ τῶν διά σοι γεγένηται, ὡς ἐμοῦ χάριν δέδεγμαι γεγενημένον.

[fol. 76r] Ἴσθι δέ μοι τοῦτον μετὰ τὸ πολλοῖς ἄλλοις ἐλθεῖν εἰς χεῖρας ἐγχειρισθέντα, ὧν εἷς ἐστι καὶ ὁ δι' ὃν ἐγράφη. ὃς τὸ μὲν ἡ ἐκ τῆς ἀρχῆς ἀρχή, μᾶλλον δὲ τὰς δύο τὰς οὐκ ἀντιδιῃρημένας, ἀλλ' ὑπὸ τὴν ἑτέραν τελοῦσαν τὴν ἑτέραν, ταῦτα ὡς μέν, οὐ πνευματικῶς ἀρχὴν νομίζων τὸν Υἱόν, εἰς τοὺς λόγους εἰσήγαγεν, οὐκ ἔφη δεῖν αὐτῶν ἀπολογίας αὐτῷ· αὐτοὺς γὰρ τοὺς ἑαυτοῦ δήπου λόγους ὑπὲρ τούτου κράτιστα καὶ σαφέστατα ἀπολογεῖσθαι, ὧν γὰρ ὁ πᾶς ἀγὼν καὶ ὅλως ἡ πραγματεία τὴν τοῦ Πνεύματος καὶ ἐκ τοῦ Υἱοῦ παρὰ Λατίνοις ἐκπόρευσιν ἀνελεῖν ὅση δύναμις. πῶς ἂν οὗτοι πάλιν ἀρχὴν τοῦ Πνεύματος τὸν Υἱὸν ὑποτιθεῖντο, καὶ τίς ἂν αὐτὸν ἑαυτῷ τοσοῦτον ἐναντία λάθοι φθεγγόμενος;

Ταῦτα τοῦ μὲν πρὸς ἡμᾶς ἐκ προχείρου, ἡμεῖς δὲ τῇ σῇ θειότητι καὶ σοφίᾳ γεγράφαμεν. ἃ δὲ πρὸς τούτοις ἐπήγαγε, δεικνὺς ὡς οὐκ ἀλόγως καὶ μάτην τοῦτ' ἔδωκε, καὶ τὰ πρὸς ταῦτα ἡμέτερα, καὶ νῦν καὶ πρότερον ὅτε ἀρχὴν αὐτοῦ τοῖς λόγοις περιετύχομεν, οὐ κατ' ἐπιστολὴν ἦν δήπου διεξελθεῖν, ὅθεν αὐτὰ καὶ παρήκαμεν, ἐπεὶ καί σοι τοσοῦτον ἦν τὸ ζητούμενον ὅσον μαθεῖν τὸν φιλόσοφον τίνι γνώμῃ τούτῳ ἐχρήσατο.

Περὶ μέντοι τῆς ἀποδείξεως, "ἐγὼ μέν," ἔφη, "περὶ τῆς κατ' Ἀριστοτέλη καὶ τοὺς τοιούτους τοὺς λόγους πεποίημαι, καθ' ἣν οὐκ ἔστιν εἰς γνῶσιν ἀναβῆναι τοῦ θείου, μᾶλλον δὲ ὑπὸ γνῶσιν τὴν ἡμετέραν τὸ θεῖον ποιήσασθαι, ὃ παῖδες Λατίνων κομπάζουσιν. ἐπεὶ δὲ πολλαχῶς ἐκλαμβάνεσθαι συμβέβηκε τὴν ἀπόδειξιν, καὶ γὰρ ἀπόδειξις ἡ ἐξ ἀνάγκης καὶ πᾶσιν ὁμολογουμένη καὶ ἀναντίρρητος—Ἕλλησι, Λατίνοις, Πέρσαις, Σκύθαις, ποιμέσι, συβώταις, πᾶσιν ἁπλῶς οἷς νοῦς ἐστι καὶ ὁστισοῦν—τῷ ἐξ ἀρχῶν εἶναι πᾶσι γνωρίμων καὶ ὁμολογουμένων, ἀπόδειξις δὲ ἡ διαλεκτικὴ καὶ ἡ

---

26 Greg. Naz., *Or.*45, 9 (PG, 36, 633C)

---

29 *αὐτῶν*] *αὐτὸν* A || 33 *ὑποτίθειντο* A

5

For demonstration and zeal for it are not more sacred than friendship which is beloved of God and the providing of such nourishment for a hungry soul. However, when a person seeks only his own interest, he looks down upon others, and while doing this he finds in turn specious excuses, in case someone should accuse him. This is, of course, what you did. But it seems that long ago I was so captivated by you and everything about you that even when you make excuses for injuring me, I think that you are doing right by me. And so I accept this letter—which really would not have been written without the reasons for which you wrote it—as if it had been written for my sake.

Bear in mind, however, that the letter was handed to me after it had been handed around to many other people, one of these being the man on whose account it was written. He said that there is no need for him to defend the fact that he introduced into his writings the term "The Principle from the Principle"—or rather, the two Principles which are not distinguished as opposites, but are one under the other—because he believes that the Son is not a Principle with respect to the Holy Spirit. For doubtless his own writings themselves speak best and most clearly in defense of this view, since their whole effort and overall task is to refute as best they can the Latin doctrine of the procession of the Holy Spirit from the Son also. How could these ⟨writings⟩, in turn, postulate that the Son is the origin of the Holy Spirit, and what man can so contradict himself without being aware of it?

These things he wrote to me in an offhand manner, and I have written them down for your Sanctity and Wisdom. But as for the arguments he adduced besides, showing that he did not proffer this term without reason or in vain, and my answers to these arguments now and previously when I first came upon his writings, they could not reliably be discussed at length in a letter, hence I disregarded them, since you too desired this much, namely to learn what the philosopher had in mind when he used this term.

Furthermore, as far as demonstration is concerned, he said: "I am writing about the demonstrative syllogism of Aristotle and his followers, in accordance with which it is impossible to ascend to the knowledge of God, or rather to subject God to our knowledge, which is what the Latins boast about. But demonstration happens to have been understood in many ways: for there is demonstration which results from necessity and is admitted and undisputed by all, Greeks, Latins, Persians, Scythians, shepherds, swineherds, in short, by all who have any sense whatsoever, because it is based on principles known to and agreed upon by all; then there is

κατὰ [fol. 76^{v}] ῥητορικὴν πιθανότητα, ἔστι δὲ καὶ ἡ ἀρχαῖς τοῖς λογίοις χρωμένη τοῖς ἱεροῖς, ἣν ἔγωγε οὐκ ἀπόδειξιν, ἀλλ' ὑπὲρ ἀπόδειξιν τίθεμαι, αὐτὸς μὲν περὶ ἐκείνης διείλεγμαι ἣν ᾔδειν ἐξαίρετον λαχοῦσαν τὸ καλεῖσθαι ἀπόδειξιν καὶ ᾗ χρωμένους τοὺς ἡμῖν ἐναντίους ἐπὶ τὴν θείαν περιωπὴν εἰς κατάληψιν· καὶ οἶμαί τι χαρίεν τοῖς τῆς εὐσεβοῦς πεποιηκέναι μοίρας, οἷς τολμηρὸν ὁμοῦ καὶ ἀπαίδευτον ἐπὶ τῇ θείᾳ καὶ πάσης γνώσεως ὑπερκειμένῃ φύσει τὰ τοιαῦτα νεανιεύεσθαι, παρὰ τῶν θεσπεσίων καὶ ὡς ἀληθῶς σοφῶν ἀνδρῶν τῶν εἰς ἡμᾶς ἀπὸ Χριστοῦ ταύτην τὴν εὐλάβειαν πεπαιδευμένοις. εἰ δέ τῳ φίλον τὴν ἐκ τῶν λογίων νομίζειν ἀναγκαιοτάτην καὶ πρώτην ἀπόδειξιν, οὐκ ἀντιλέγω, καὶ τοσοῦτον οὐκ οἶμαι δεῖν τοῦτο ποιεῖν, ὥστε καὶ πλέον αὐτῇ νέμω σεμνότητος, εἶναι νομίζων τὸ ταύτης κράτος ὑπὲρ ἀπόδειξιν."

Ἔδοξεν οὖν ἡμῖν ἁνὴρ ταῦτα εἰπεῖν εὐλόγως καὶ διαιτῆσαι πρὸς ἐπιείκειαν· καί σοι γὰρ ἔδωκεν ἀποδεικνύναι περὶ Θεοῦ ὃν εἶναι τρόπον ᾠήθης ἀποδεικτὰ τὰ θεῖα, καὶ αὐτὸν ἐτήρησεν ἐν εὐλαβείᾳ τῆς ἀποδεικτικῆς περὶ τὰ θεῖα τόλμης, ἀποδεικτικῆς ἐκείνης τῆς κατὰ τὸν πρῶτον τρόπον. ὥσθ' ὑμῖν καὶ ταῦτα εὐσύμβατα καὶ ἡ αὐτὴ φιλίας τοῖς φιλοσόφοις βάσις, ὑπὲρ ἧς ἠγωνίας ὁ σφοδρὸς τῆς εἰρήνης καὶ μανικὸς ἐραστής, δεδιὼς θεοφιλὲς καὶ μακάριον· οὐ γὰρ ἔδει τι φιλοσόφοις ἀνδράσιν ἐμπεσεῖν εἰς τὰς ψυχὰς ἀφιλόσοφον. ἐγὼ δέ, εἰ παντελῶς ἦν ἀστεῖον, εὐξάμην ἄν σοι τοιαῦτα πολλὰ περιίστασθαι, γράφειν ὁμοίως καὶ πολλάκις ἐμοί σε περὶ αὐτῶν ἀναγκάζοντα, εἴ γε χωρὶς τοῦ τοιούτου τῶν τῆς σῆς ἡμᾶς γλώττης παντελῶς εἶναι ἀνάγκη χαρίτων καὶ τῆς ψυχῆς ἀκτίνων ἀνέλπιδας.

6. Sine titulo

Μετὰ τὴν θαυμαστὴν ἐκείνην καὶ λαμπρὰν ἐπιστολήν, λόγον εἶδον ἐξαίσιον, ὃν ἤκουον μὲν καὶ πρότερον γεγονέναι σοι πρὸς τοὺς αἰτιωμένους ὅτι τὴν ἱερωσύνην φεύγεις, καὶ ἐζήτουν ἐπιμελῶς—πῶς γὰρ οὔ;—σαφῶς εἰδὼς ἐξ ὧν προεῖδον ὡς εἴη πλέγμα Μουσῶν ὁ λόγος ἐξαίρετον ἐξ ἀρετῆς καὶ θειότητος καὶ σοφίας ἁπάσης καὶ τῆς

55 *περιοπὴν* A ‖ 64 *ἀνὴρ* A ‖ 66 *αὐτὸν* A ‖ 68 post *κατὰ* scripsit et deinde delevit *πάντα τρόπον* A ‖ *εὐσύμβαντα* A ‖ 71 *τι* A^{sv}

6: M 46^{v}–47^{r}.

demonstration which is dialectic and accords with rhetorical persuasiveness; and there is demonstration which uses the Scriptures as principles, and this I, for my part, regard not as demonstration, but as above and beyond it. I was arguing, therefore, about the one which I knew to have been allotted the name of demonstration par excellence, and which our opponents use for the purpose of studying and apprehending the divinity. And I believe that I have done a favor to pious men, who consider it both bold and ignorant to behave so wantonly with regard to the divine nature which transcends all knowledge, because they have been taught this reverence for God by the divinely inspired and most truly wise men ⟨in a line⟩ from the time of Christ. But if someone likes to think that the first and most indispensable demonstration is from the Scriptures, I do not dispute it and do not think it necessary to do so, inasmuch as I attribute more importance to it by believing that its force is beyond demonstration."

It seemed to me, therefore, that the man said these things with reason and examined them with fairness. For he allowed you to prove, about God, how you thought that theological questions are to be proved, and he took care to avoid the recklessness of proving theological questions ⟨by maintaining⟩ that demonstrative syllogism is of the first type. Therefore, you can readily agree on these questions as well, and the basis remains the same for the philosophers' friendship for which you, the passionate lover of peace, were so anxious, in awe of something blessed and dear to God. For nothing unphilosophical ought to enter the souls of philosophers. So, if it were completely in good taste, I would pray that many such problems beset you, forcing you to write to me often in a similar style, that is, if without such an ⟨excuse⟩ I must not at all hope for the graces of your tongue and the rays of your soul.

6. No Addressee

After that admirable and brilliant letter, I saw an extraordinary discourse. I had, in fact, heard before that you composed it in answer to those who accuse you of avoiding holy orders and was anxiously looking for it. And why not, for I knew clearly from what I had seen before that the discourse would be an exceptional work of the Muses, made up of virtue and godliness and absolute wisdom and all-

6

διὰ πάντων ἀγλαΐας καὶ χάριτος, ἔπεμψε δὲ ὕστερον ἡ διαφερόντως αἰσθανομένη τὰ σὰ καὶ θαυμάζουσα θαυμασία βασίλισσα.

Ὃν διελθεῖν ἐγχειρήσας καὶ ὀφθαλμοῖς ἑκατέροις ἁψάμενος τῆς ἀναγνώσεως, τοῖς τε τοῦ σώματος καὶ τοῖς τῆς διανοίας, οὐκ εἶχον μεταβαίνειν οὐδὲ προέρχεσθαι, τοῦ πρώτου προστυχόντος κατέχοντος θαύματι τῆς διανοίας. τῆς εὐροίας! τῆς καθαρότητος! τῆς γλυκύτητος! τῆς ἐμβριθείας ὁμοῦ καὶ σεμνότητος! τῆς διὰ πάντων ἐλευθερίας καὶ ἱκανότητος! ἀεὶ μὲν οὖν διὰ ταῦτα τὸ πρῶτον κατέχειν ἐβούλετο, εἷλκε δὲ τὰ ἑξῆς καὶ ἀντέσπα ἐλπίδι τῶν ἴσων καὶ καινοτέρων, καὶ ἦν μεταξὺ τῶν λόγων οὐκ ἀγεννὴς ἡ μάχη, τοῦ μὲν κατέχοντος, τοῦ δὲ ἀνθέλκειν σπουδάζοντος. μόλις οὖν ἀποσπώμενος τοῦ κατασχόντος ὑπὸ τοῦ μετ᾽ ἐκεῖνο, ἰσχυροτέρῳ τῷ δευτέρῳ ἐνετύγχανον θαύματι, καὶ κατειχόμην αὖθις περικρατέστερον, καὶ πάλιν ὁ αὐτὸς ἐκεῖνος καὶ καρτερώτερος πόλεμος. καὶ οὕτω μόλις διεξῆλθον τὸν λόγον, ἱδρῶτι περιρρεόμενος ὃν ἤδεις ἀγῶνες ἐξέθλιψαν καὶ συλλογὴ καρπῶν ἱερῶν καὶ σοφῶν ἀφθονίας. ὃ δὲ τοῦ λόγου διαφερόντως ἐθαύμασα, ὅτι τοσαύτῃ μὲν ὑποθέσει ἐπεχείρησεν ὁ λόγος, ὅσην οἱ προηγωνισμένοι ταύτην διὰ πλήθους λόγων κατεσκεύασαν ἀπεριλήπτου, ὁ δὲ τὸν αὐτὸν ἐκείνοις δίαυλον δεδραμηκώς, πολλοστὸς ὢν ἐκείνων εἰς ἀριθμὸν καὶ ποσότητα, ἴσος δοκεῖ τῇ ποιότητι τῷ τῆς ἀπολογίας ἀποχρῶντι καὶ περιττεύοντι, πυκνότητα γὰρ ἐπιχειρημάτων οὔπω τοσαύτην εἶδον ἐν τοσούτῳ τῷ διαστήματι, οὐδὲ δύναμιν τοσαύτην ἐπιχειρήματος, ὅσην ἐν τῷδε τῷ λόγῳ· ἓν ἀντὶ πλήθους ἀπόχρη τῇ χρείᾳ τῆς ὑποθέσεως.

Πρῴην τοίνυν, ἰδὼν τὴν ἐπιστολήν, ἱερὸν ἡγησάμην ἐοικὸς τῷ τῶν νεὼν βελτίστῳ· ἡ δ᾽ ἄρα ἦν λαμπρὰ μὲν ὄντως καὶ τοιαύτη δικαία νομίζεσθαι, προπύλαιον δὲ ὅμως τοῦγε παρόντος λόγου. τὸν δὲ διὰ μὲν αὐτὸν αὖθις νεὼν ἡγοῦμαι τὸν κράτιστον ἐννοιῶν σοφωτάτων, διὰ δὲ τὸν πατέρα δέδοικα τὴν ἀπάτην, [fol. 47r] μὴ καὶ οὗτος ᾖ ἑτέρου λόγου προπύλαιον, κἀκεῖ μοι δοκῶ ταὐτὸ τοῦτο πείσεσθαι, πρὸς τὴν ἔν σοι δύναμιν ἀφορῶν καὶ σοφίαν καὶ ὅ φησιν ὁ ἱερώτατος λόγος, θησαυρὸν μὴ κενούμενον, καινὰ καὶ παλαιὰ χορηγοῦντα φιλοτιμότατα. σὺ μὲν οὖν ἡμᾶς οὕτως ἑστιᾷς οἷς, ὦ σοφώτατε, γράφεις· ἡμᾶς δέ, οὐδὲ θαυμάζειν οἵους τε ὄντας οἷς ἑστιώμεθα, δι᾽ ἐπιείκειαν ἀποδέχου θαυμάζοντας ᾗ δυνάμεως ἔχομεν.

6: 37 cf. Luc. 12:33

---

11 εὔρροίας M ‖ 26 πιότητι M ‖ 31 νεῶν M

6

pervading beauty and grace, but the marvelous Princess, who takes special interest in your work and admires it, sent it to me some time later.

When I attempted to go over it and started to read with both sets of eyes, those of the body and those of the spirit, I could not pass on or go forward because what I hit upon first held me spellbound with admiration. What a fluency of words! What clarity! What sweetness! What gravity together with dignity! What ease and dexterity throughout! For these reasons the beginning tended to hold me forever, but what followed drew me on and pulled me away in the hope of equal and new attractions, and the battle between the parts of the discourse was not ignoble, as one part was holding me back and the other was trying to draw me away. For scarcely would I be torn away from the part which held me spellbound by the part following it, then I would come upon the next with greater admiration and would be again more powerfully captivated, and that same war would begin again more fiercely. And thus I went through the discourse with difficulty, drenched in perspiration brought on by pleasant exertions and the gathering of an abundance of sacred and wise fruits. But what I especially admired about the discourse was that it deals with such a long topic, one upon which previous contenders elaborated with an infinite multitude of words. But, having run the same distance and being much smaller in strength of numbers and size, it appears to match in quality what is sufficient, and more than sufficient, for the defense of the topic. For I have not yet seen such a concentration of arguments in such a short space or such power of argumentation as there is in this discourse; one argument satisfies the demands of the topic in place of a multitude.

A short while ago when I saw your letter, I thought of it as a sanctuary befitting the best temple. It was, of course, brilliant and worthy of being so considered, but it was just the gateway to the present discourse. The latter I consider, in turn, to be on its own account the best shrine of the wisest thoughts, but considering its author, I fear a trick, lest this too be the gateway to another discourse. and in that case too, I suspect that the same thing will happen to me, considering your power and wisdom and, as the Gospel says, your "treasure that is not depleted" but provides an abundance of old and new ⟨treasures⟩ most generously. This is how you feast me with your writings, my most wise friend! But, even though I am not competent to admire what I am feasting on, kindly allow me to admire you as best I can.

7. ⟨Τῷ Βαρλαάμ⟩

Ὁρᾷς τὸν καρπὸν τῆς σιωπῆς τῆς ἐμῆς; σῶν γὰρ ἱερῶν γραμμάτων, εἶθ' ὅπως τούτων τεύξομαι ἀμηχανῶν, ταύτην εἶδον τὴν μηχανήν, ἐπειδή σε τῷ γράψαι οὐχ οἷός τ' ἐγενόμην κεκινηκέναι γράψαι καί, ὡς ἔοικεν, οὐ κακῶς εἶδον ταύτην. ἦλθε γὰρ δή μοι τὰ γράμματα, ἐκεῖνο καὶ μόνον ἀφορμὴν τῆς ἀφίξεως ἐπιδεικνύντα καὶ πρόφασιν, τὴν [fol. 232r] σιωπὴν τὴν ἐμήν. σὺ δέ μοι δοκεῖς ὑπὸ τῆς μεγάλης παρ' Ἰταλοὺς πρεσβείας—ἤ, εἰ βούλει γε, τῆς ὑψηλῆς στιβάδος—ἄνω γενέσθαι πολὺ καὶ τῶν καθ' ἡμᾶς λογισμῶν ἐκδημῆσαι. οἷα γὰρ καὶ συλλογίζῃ καὶ φῄς ἡμᾶς, οἶμαι, τῇ τούτων ἀπροσμάχῳ δυνάμει συμποδίζειν τοσοῦτον, ὁπόσον οὐδ' Ἡρακλῆς ἐκεῖνος τοὺς ὑπ' αὐτοῦ δεθέντας· ἐγκαλεῖν μὲν γὰρ ἐμέ σοι τὸ μὴ γράφειν ἐθέλειν, εἶτα τοῦτο προφέροντα σιωπᾶν αὐτὸν καὶ τῇ σιγῇ σε τὸν ὅτι μὴ γράφειν ἐθέλεις ἡμῖν κακιζόμενον προδήλως ἀμύνεσθαι, τοῦτο δὲ εἶναι ἀνδρὸς αὐτοῖς ἑαυτὸν οἷς ἐγκαλεῖ τινι τῶν ἄλλων ὑποτιθέντος καὶ τοῖς οἰκείοις, φασίν, ἁλισκομένου πτεροῖς, καὶ ἐπὶ τούτοις τὸ ἑκατέρωθεν ἄφυκτον· εἰ μὲν οὐδέν τι φαῦλον παρ' ἡμῖν ἡ σιωπή, τί δή σοι σιωπῶντι μεμφόμεθα; εἰ δὲ τοιοῦτο καὶ ἥκιστα προσῆκον οἷς πάρεστι σύνεσις, πῶς αὐτὸς ἐμαυτόν σοι σιωπῶντα παρέχω, καὶ ταῦτα ὄντι κορυφαίῳ τῶν φίλων, καὶ ὅλως τιμῶ τὸ πρᾶγμα;

Ταῦτά σου τὰ ἰσχυρὰ καθ' ἡμῶν καὶ ἡ ἄμαχος, ὡς αὐτὸς καλεῖς, δύναμις οὐκ οἶδ' ὅπως ἄμαχος, εἰ μὴ τοιαῦτα εἶναι ἀνάγκη τὰ πράγματα ὁποῖά τις ἂν ὀνομάσαι θελήσαι, ἢ λήθης ἐγὼ πόμα πιὼν ἐπιλέλησμαι τῶν πρότερόν μοι πρὸς σὲ γεγενημένων· ὃ σύ μοι δοκεῖς παθὼν Ἰταλικοῖς φαρμάκοις, ἀφωνίαν ἐμοὶ πρὸς σεαυτὸν ἐγκαλεῖν. εἰ μὲν γάρ με πρὸς σὲ σεσιγηκέναι φάσκεις τῇ γε σαρκίνῃ γλώττῃ καὶ τοῖς περὶ τὴν γλῶτταν πρὸς τὸ λέγειν ὀργάνοις καὶ ἔστι τοῦτο ἀδίκημα, εἴ τις ἐκ Βυζαντίου τοῦτον τὸν τρόπον μὴ διαλέγοιτο τοῖς ἐν Θεσσαλονίκῃ, ἀδικεῖν ὁμολογῶ καί, εἴ τις ἔστι τῶν ἀδυνάτων δίκη, λάμβανε παρ' ἐμοῦ τουτὶ μὴ δυνηθέντος· εἰ δὲ τὸ γράφειν λέγειν καλεῖς ἐνταῦθα, τὸ δὲ μὴ γράφειν σιγᾶν, πάλαι παρὰ σοὶ γράμμαθ' ἡμέτερα γέμοντα θαυμαστῆς διαθέσεως, ἅ σοι φέρων κατέπλευσεν ὁ γενναῖος Γεώργιος καὶ ἐνεχείρισέ γε. τοῦτο γὰρ ἡμᾶς ἐδίδαξαν ἕτεροι καὶ [fol. 232v] αὐτὸς ὁ Γεώργιος, σοῦ γε ἡμῖν δηλῶσαι μηδὲ τοῦτο ἐθελήσαντος, καὶ γεγόνασιν ἕτεροι πρὸς

7: 16–17 Aeschylus, *Fragm.* 139, 4

7: S 231v–234r.

7

7. [To Barlaam]

Do you see the fruit of my silence? When I was at a loss as to how I should obtain your divine letter, I hit upon this device, since by writing I was unable to stir you to write; and it seems that my idea was not a bad one, for the letter actually came to me showing one thing only as provocation and reason for its arrival: my silence. But you seem to me to have risen very high as a result of your important mission to the Italians, or, if you prefer, your exalted station, and to have departed from our way of reasoning. For this is how you reason, and you also say, I believe, that by the incontestable power of your reasoning I will be bound even more tightly than those bound by the famous Heracles: you argue that I accuse you of not wanting to write and that, having made this statement, I then keep silent myself, thus by my own silence obviously defending you, though I reproached you of not wanting to write to me. This, you say, is the behavior of a man who undermines himself by the very things of which he accuses others and, as the saying goes, "gets caught by his own wings"; and ⟨you pose⟩ the following questions as inescapable one way or another: if in fact I do not consider silence between us as an evil, why then do I blame you when you keep silent? On the other hand, if I do consider silence evil, and not befitting men of understanding, how can I allow myself to be silent, and towards the foremost friend at that, and actually hold the behavior in honor?

These are your powerful arguments against me, and I do not know how their incontestable power, as you call it, can be incontestable, unless things must of necessity be just as one would like to describe them, or else I have taken the potion of forgetfulness, having forgotten how I acted towards you before! But this, I believe, is what happened to you as a result of the Italian potions, insofar as you accuse me of not speaking to you. For, if you claim that I did not speak to you with my bodily tongue and the other organs of speech connected with it, and if it is a crime for a man from Byzantium not to converse like this with those in Thessalonica, I confess to this crime, and if there is a penalty for the impossible, impose it on me for my inability here. But, if by speech you refer here to writing and by silence to not writing, long ago you received from me a letter full of wonderful sentiments which the noble George, arriving by ship, carried and indeed handed to you. I found this out from others as well as from George himself, for you did not deign to let me know even that, while others, who had not received anything, showed more gratitude to

7

ἡμᾶς ἐφ'οἷς οὐκ εἰλήφασι τοῦ εἰληφότος εὐγνωμονέστεροι. καὶ εἰ μὲν εἰς οὐδενὸς μοῖραν ἐτίθεις, ὦ σοφὴ κεφαλή, τὰ ἡμέτερα, ἡμεῖς μὲν ἂν τοῦτ' ἴσως οὐκ ἀλύπως ἐφέρομεν, ὑπὸ χεῖρα τελοῦντες τῆς ἐν ψυχῇ μοχθηρίας, σὺ δ'ἠκολούθεις ἂν τῇ διανοίᾳ σαυτοῦ, ὃ μηδενὸς ἐποιοῦ, πρὸς τοῦτο μηδὲ φθεγγόμενος· νῦν δὲ ὃ φαίνῃ θέλων ὑπάρχειν σοι καὶ λυπεῖ μὴ λαμβάνων, τοῦτ' αὖθις φαίνῃ τοῦ παντὸς ἀπαξιώσας λόγου. κἀνταῦθα δή σοι τὰ καθ' ἡμῶν ἐπάνεισι δίκτυα μετὰ προσθήκης· εἰ μὲν εὖ ποιῶν ἐσίγας καὶ φιλοσόφως, τί τοῖς ταῦτά σοι δοκοῦσι προῃρῆσθαι φιλοσοφεῖν ἐγκαλεῖς; εἰ δὲ ἀφιλοσόφως καὶ τοῖς φίλοις ἐπιζημίως καὶ οὐδ' ἀνθ' ὧν ἠδικημένος ἔφθης ἀμυνόμενος τὸν προηδικηκότα—ἦν γὰρ ἂν τοῦτο μέτριον καὶ τῶν εἰκότων ἐντός—τί ταῦτα παρρησιάζῃ καὶ προφέρεις ἡμῖν ὡς ἀναίτιος καί, βρύων αὐτὸς ἕλκεσιν, ἄλλους πειρᾷ θεραπεύειν; εἰ δ' ἑτέροις γεγράφαμεν ἄνευ τοῦ καί σοι προγεγραφέναι τούτων, οὐδὲ σὺ φαίνῃ σιγήσας πλὴν ἐμοῦ γε πρότερον πρὸς τοὺς ἐνταῦθα φίλους, οἳ παρὰ σοῦ τι λαβεῖν καὶ αὐτὸν ὑπολαμβάνοντές με, τά τε σφίσιν ἐπεσταλμένα κοινοῦσθαι δεῖν ᾤοντό μοι, καὶ δὴ καὶ ἐδίδοσαν, ὡς τοῦ αὐτοῦ κρατῆρος τῆς σῆς ἑαυτοῖς κοινωνοῦντι φιλίας, καὶ ἃ δὴ λαβὼν εἴην αὐτὸς ἀπῄτουν· τὸ δ'ἀληθὲς ἐγνωκότες, λυπουμένοις ἐῴκεσαν καὶ μεταμελομένοις ὅτι λαβεῖν ὡμολόγησαν, ὡς ἂν ἐμοὶ τοῦ τοιοῦδε λυπηροῦ πεφυκότος.

Ὥσθ' οἷς ἡμᾶς κρίνειν ἔγνως, τούτοις σαυτὸν κατακρίνεις καί, εἴ τινι προσήκει, σοὶ μάλιστα προσήκει τὸ τοῖς οἰκείοις ἑαλωκέναι πτεροῖς. ἐγὼ δέ, ὡς ἔοικεν, εἴτ' ἐσιώπησα, εὖ ποιῶν ἐσιώπησα, θηράσας τῇ σιγῇ τὸ ποθούμενον, εἴτ'οὐκ ἔδει με σιγῆσαι, οὐκ ἐσιώπησα, μᾶλλον δὲ ἑκάτερον, καὶ γράψας καὶ σιωπήσας· ᾗ μὲν ἔδει με γράψαι οὐκ ἐσιώπησα, ᾗ δὲ σιγῆσαι οὐκ ἔγραψα. πρὸς τῆς ἀμάχου δυνάμεως τῶν κομψῶν ἐκείνων καὶ σαθρῶν συλλογισμῶν, [fol. 233ʳ] πρὸς αὐτῆς τῆς ὑψηλῆς στιβάδος ἀφ' ἧς τὰ ὄντα διασκοπεῖς καὶ τῆς καθαρωτάτης ἐμφορῇ θεωρίας ἀναχωρήσας τοῦ σώματος, ἄλυτα ταῦτα καὶ μηδὲν πρὸς ἐμαυτοῦ μοι καταλιπόντα φάναι;

Ἀλλὰ ταῦτα μὲν ἀντεπαίξαμεν παίζοντι καὶ ἀστεϊζομένῳ πρὸς φιλίας ἁπλότητα, ὃ δ'οὐκ ἔθ'ἡμῖν ἐπιτρέπει παίζειν οὐδ' ἀστεΐζεσθαι, τὰ λυπουμένων δὲ λύπῃ κατεσχημένους ἐξαναγκάζει λέγειν, περὶ τούτου δή σοι τὰ εἰκότα καὶ μικρὰ προσοισόμεθα, ἵνα μήθ' ὑπὲρ ὧν ἡμῖν πᾶν ὁτιοῦν κινδυνεύειν προσῆκε, ταῦτα καὶ τῆς

---

49 Euripides, *Fragm.* 1086 || 59–60 Aeschylus, *Fragm.* 139, 4

---

68 *φᾶναι* S || 70–71 *στε ἀΐζεσθαι* S || 73 *τοῖς* S

7

me than he who had received something. And if you thought nothing of my letters, my wise friend, I would not perhaps bear this without a grudge, for I would be under the influence of the resentment in my soul, while you for your part would follow your inclination and not even utter a word concerning something that you thought nothing of. But now you appear anxious to have something and grieve when you do not receive it, yet in turn you have manifestly shown complete disregard for it. And here, exactly, the nets that you cast for me return to you with increase. Indeed, if you were right and wise in keeping silent, why do you bring these charges against those who seem to you to prefer to pursue the course of wisdom? But, if you were not wise and acted enviously towards your friends, not even by reason of an injury for which you were repaying the man who offended you first—that, at least, would have been within ⟨the bounds⟩ of moderation and propriety—why do you have the boldness to say and declare these things to me, as if you were innocent, and "attempt to cure others, while being yourself full of ulcers?" Furthemore, if I have written to others without first writing to you, you certainly do not seem—except, that is, in my case—previously to have kept silent towards your friends here. Assuming that I too had received something from you, they thought it right to inform me about the letters sent to them; in fact, they gave them to me on the assumption that I shared with them the same cup of your friendship, and asked for the letter which, presumably, I had received. But when they found out the truth, they appeared sad and remorseful for having confessed to me that they had heard from you, as if that should have been naturally painful to me.

Thus, by the judgment that you passed on me, you are condemning yourself, and the saying "to be caught by one's own wings" befits you more than anyone else. As for me, it seems that if I kept silent, I did the right thing, since by silence I attained my desire, and insofar as I should not have kept silent, I did not keep silent; rather I did both, since I both wrote and kept silent. Where I was obliged to write, I did not keep silent, and where I was obliged to keep silent, I did not write. In the name of the incontestable power of this subtle and unsound reasoning; in the name of that lofty station from which you observe reality and, having left the body, take your fill of the purest contemplation, are these arguments irrefutable and do they leave nothing for me to say in my defense?

But I was only jesting about this in response to your jests and witticisms, under the liberal spirit of friendship. There is something, however, which does not allow me any longer to make jests or indulge in clever talk; it forces me to say, full of distress, words appropriate to those in distress. On this matter I shall offer you a fitting but small contribution, so that I neither neglect as unworthy even of a few words matters for which I ought to risk anything, nor discuss them far beyond the

7

ἐν ὀλίγοις λόγοις φροντίδος ἀπαξιώσωμεν, μήτε πάνυ πέρα τῶν ἐπιστολιμαίων ὅρων ἐκτείνωμεν, καὶ ταῦτα μέντοι τῆς φιλίας αὐτῆς οὐχ ἧττον παρακαλούσης, ὑπὲρ ἧς πάντα καὶ λέγειν δεῖ καὶ πράττειν ἐξ ὧν ἂν σῴζοιτό τε τοῖς ἔχουσι καὶ προσεπαύξοιτο.

Λυπεῖ με, ὦ βέλτιστε—πῶς δοκεῖς;—καὶ ταράττει τὸ μήπω σε πεπαῦσθαι τῆς κατὰ τῶν θεοφιλῶν ἀνδρῶν βλασφημίας καὶ μάχης· τῶν ἀτέχνως εὐσεβῶν, τῶν ἁπλῶς Χριστιανῶν, τῶν ἀκτημόνων, τῶν ἀπραγμόνων, τῶν ὃ τοῖς αὐτῶν ἡ γῆ σώμασι, τοῦτο ταῖς ψυχαῖς τὸν οὐρανὸν ἐχόντων, τῶν οἵων τε ὄντων λέγειν μετὰ τοῦ θείου Παύλου—ἢ μετ' ἐκεῖνον, ἂν ἐκεῖνο λυπῇ σε— οὐδὲν ἐπιστάμεθα πλὴν Χριστὸν καὶ τοῦτον ἐσταυρωμένον. καὶ οἶμαι δαίμων τις φθονερὸς καὶ πολέμιος ἀρετῇ καὶ καλοκἀγαθίᾳ, μὴ ἐνεγκὼν τὴν ἐν τούτοις ὑπόλοιπον τοῦ Χριστοῦ καὶ τοῦ εὐαγγελίου τῷ βίῳ καθαρωτέραν μοῖραν καθορᾶν ὑπομένουσαν, ταῦτα πάντα κινεῖ τε καὶ πραγματεύεται, ἵνα δὴ καὶ τούτων διαβληθέντων τῇ τῶν πολλῶν ἀκρισίᾳ καὶ μισηθέντων, πρὸς μηδὲν ἔτι βλέπειν ἡμῖν ᾖ καλοῦ τε καὶ σπουδαίου παράδειγμα, καὶ οὕτως, εὑρὼν τὴν πᾶσαν ἐκεῖνος χώραν κενὴν τοῦ βελτίονος, καταπυκνώσῃ τῷ χείρονι καὶ τῆς οἰκείας ἔχῃ τοῦ λοιποῦ πονηρίας ἀπολαύειν ἀνέδην. δοκεῖ δέ μοι τοῦ παντὸς δήπου πεσεῖσθαι σκοποῦ ὁ ἐπίβουλος τῇ τοῦ Χριστοῦ δυνάμει, καὶ ἀντὶ τοῦ τοὺς διαβαλλομένους—ὃ βούλεται—τὸν διαβάλλοντα βλάψειν, ἑαυτὸν προβεβλαφώς.

Ἃ τοίνυν ἔγραψεν ὁ Αἰγύπτιος Ἄ-[fol. 233v]μασις πρὸς Πολυκράτη τὸν Σαμίων μὲν τύραννον, φίλον δὲ αὐτῷ πεφροντισμένον ὄντα, ταῦτα κἀγώ σοι γράφω τῇ φιλτάτῃ κεφαλῇ. ἐκεῖνος ἄγαν ἰδὼν εὐτυχοῦντα τὸν Πολυκράτη καὶ μηδαμοῦ πταίοντα τῶν πραττομένων, καὶ λογισάμενος τὴν ἄκρατον εὐημερίαν, ὥσπερ ἰατρῶν παῖδες τὴν εὐεξίαν, οὐκ εἶναι ἀσφαλεστάτην, καὶ πρὸς λόγον τῆς ἀναβάσεως καταπίπτειν εἰς τὴν ἐναντίαν τύχην πεφυκέναι τὸν ὑψωθέντα, γράφει μὲν πρότερον ἅπαν ποιῆσαι τὸν Πολυκράτην ὅπως αὐτῷ τις ἀπαντήσει καὶ δυσπλοΐα. εἶτα μὴ γενομένου τούτου, καίτοι Πολυκράτους καὶ βουληθέντος καὶ πράξαντος—ἔδει γὰρ αὐτόν, ὡς ἔοικεν, ἀπολωλέναι—ἐπὶ τούτοις Ἄμασις αὐτῷ πέμπει οὐκ ἔτι φίλια γράμματα, τῆς δ' ὑπαρχούσης φιλίας διαλυτήρια πρόφασιν, ἵνα μὴ φίλος ὢν αὐτῷ μεγάλης ἀνάγκην ἔχῃ κοινωνεῖν δυστυχίας, πάντως μὲν γὰρ ἂν δυστυχῆσαι Πολυκράτη τὰ μέγιστα, φίλου δὲ

83–84 I Cor. 2:2

---

93 post παντὸς expunxit ἂν ἐκπεπτωκέναι σκοποῦ et supra versum δήπου πεσεῖσθαι σκοποῦ ὁ ἐπίβουλος scripsit S[1] || 101 post ἀσφαλεστάτην expunxit ἀλλὰ καὶ σφαλερωτάτην S[1] || 104 δύσπλοια S

limits of a letter, especially as friendship itself makes no feeble appeal, and for its sake everything must be said and done so that those who possess it may preserve and increase it.

You cannot imagine, my dear friend, how distressed and troubled I am by the fact that you have not ceased your slander and your battle against God-loving men; the naturally pious, the simple Christians, those who own no property, who are not meddlesome, who think that heaven is for their souls what the earth is for their bodies, who can say together with St. Paul or, if that disturbs you, after him: "We think of nothing but Jesus Christ, Christ nailed to the cross." And I think that a jealous demon, an enemy of virtue and goodness who could not bear to see enduring the purer destiny which remains among these men because of their way of life according to Christ and the Gospel, has set all this in motion and is conducting it so that no example of virtue and excellence will be left for us to contemplate any more, after these men too have been slandered and become hated through want of judgment in the multitude. And thus, finding the whole place empty of the best, he may fill it up with the worst, and be able in the future to enjoy his wickedness without restraint. But it seems to me that with the power of Christ the treacherous demon will fall short of his whole design and, instead of injuring the people he slanders, which is what he wants to do, he will injure the slanderer, having injured himself first.

So, my dearest friend, I am writing you just what the Egyptian Amasis wrote to Polycrates, who was the tyrant of Samos and his highly regarded friend. When Amasis saw that Polycrates was enjoying excessive prosperity and that he nowhere made a false step in anything he did, reasoning, just as physicians do about physical well-being, that absolute prosperity is not the safest thing, and that it is natural for the man who has risen to fall into the opposite lot in a manner proportionate to his rise, he first wrote to Polycrates that he should do everything in order to encounter some adversity as well. Later, when this did not happen, in spite of the wishes and efforts of Polycrates (for he was evidently destined to be destroyed), Amasis thereupon sent him a letter which no longer expressed friendship, but ostensibly dissolved the existing friendship, so that he might not be forced as a friend of his to share in a great misfortune; for Polycrates would inevitably succumb to the greatest unhappiness, and, if he remained his friend, he would have to share equally in his

μένοντος εἶναι μετέχειν ἐξ ἴσης τῶν τῷ φίλῳ παρόντων. ἐκεῖνος μὲν οὖν οὐ πάνυ τί μοι δοκεῖ τὰ φιλικὰ τηρῆσαι πρὸς Πολυκράτην ἐπειδήπερ οὐδὲ πάντῃ Πολυκράτης ἠπείθησε παραινοῦντι τῷ φίλῳ, ἀλλά τις αὐτὸν ἦγεν ἀλάστωρ, ὡς ἔοικε, φιλονείκως εἰς ὄλεθρον· ἐγὼ δέ, ὦ βέλτιστε, οὐχ ἧττον ἐμαυτῷ φίλον ὄντα ἢ Πολυκράτης Ἀμάσιδι—ἂν ἄρα καὶ καταδέχῃ τὸ κοινὸν τοῦτο λέγω—οὐ θαυμαστῇ τύχῃ βλέπων κατ' ἐκεῖνον ἠρμένον, ἀλλὰ μεγάλην περὶ τὰ βέλτιστα καὶ θεοφιλέστατα ἐπιδεικνύμενον ἀγνωμοσύνην, παραινῶ μέν σοι μὴ περαιτέρω χωρεῖν, ἀλλὰ καί, οἷς νῦν εὐγνωμονήσεις, ἀφανίσαι τὰ πρότερα. τούτου δὲ μὴ γεγονότος—οἶμαι μέν σε μέγα ἐπιγελάσειν, εἰ τηλικοῦτος ὢν παρὰ τοιοῦδε τηλικαῦτα ἀκούοις, ἐγὼ δὲ τὸ ἐμαυτοῦ καὶ λέξω καὶ μετὰ ταῦτα δράσω, ὅπως ποτ' ἔχοις αὐτός—ἀποστήσομαί σου τῆς προτέρας φιλίας, μᾶλλον δὲ τοῦ μὲν φιλεῖν οὐδαμῶς, τοῦ δ' ἐπαινεῖν ἃ πράττεις, δεδιὼς μήπου τι πάθῃς Πολυκράτους οὐκ ἔλαττον, κἂν μὴ ταὐτὸ Πολυκράτει, κἀγώ σοι κοινωνεῖν τοῦ πάθους ἀναγκασθῶ· οὐ γὰρ ἐκείνῳ μὲν εἶχε φθονεῖν τὸ διαμόνιον διὰ τὴν μείζω [fol. 234^{r}] *τύχην, σὲ δὲ Θεὸς ἀποδέξεται, τοῖς ἑαυτοῦ τοιαῦτα καὶ δούλοις καὶ φίλοις ἐπηρεάζοντα, ἵνα μὴ λέγω μεῖζον καὶ τῶν ἐκείνου νόμων· ἀλλ' οὐκ ἐρῶ γε τὸ πᾶν, οὕτω γάρ σου τῆς φιλίας ἐξέχομαι, ὡς κισσὸν δρυὸς ἡ τραγῳδία φησίν.*

8. ⟨Τῷ Βαρλαὰμ⟩

Ἃ γέγραφάς μοι περιττά μοι δοκεῖ πρὸς γοῦν ἐμέ σοι γεγράφθαι, ταυτὶ γάρ μοι πρῴην καὶ ἀπὸ στόματος εἶπες καὶ οὐκ ἐπελαθόμην. ὅτι δὲ κἀγώ σοι τὰ περὶ θεολογίας οὐ σφόδρα ἐναντιοῦμαι, ἀλλὰ τῆς ἐξ ἀρχῆς ἐπηρείας ἕνεκα τῶν θείων ἡσυχαστῶν καὶ τῆς περιεργίας ἀκριβῶς ἐπίστασαι. δοκεῖς δέ μοι καὶ αὐτὰ ταῦτα τὰ κατὰ τοῦ Παλαμᾶ περὶ θεολογίας περιεργάζεσθαι· ἀπίθανον γὰρ ἐκεῖνον τὸν ἄνδρα αἱρετικὸν φανῆναι, ὃ σὺ σπουδάζεις αὐτοῦ καταγνῶναι τὴν ἐκκλησίαν πεῖσαι. σὺ δ' οἶμαι, πικρότερον ἐκείνῳ

---

129 Euripides, *Hecuba*, 398

---

111 *πάνυ τοι* S ‖ 112 *Φιλοκράτης* S ‖ 116 *ἡρμένον* S ‖ 125–126 *εἶχε . . . τύχην*] *εἶχε διὰ τὴν μείζω τύχην νεμεσεῖν τὸ δαιμόνιον* S: vocabula *νεμεσεῖν τὸ δαιμόνιον* expunxit et *φθονεῖν τὸ δαιμόνιον* ante *εἶχε* supra versum scripsit S^{1}

8: S 234^{r}–234^{v}. Epistula linea diagonale expuncta S^{1}

friend's fortunes. I do not, of course, believe that Amasis observed the rules of friendship towards Polycrates, since indeed Polycrates did not quite disobey his friend's advice; it seems that an avenging spirit was obstinately leading him to destruction. But, my friend—and you are no less dear to me than Polycrates was to Amasis, provided of course that you accept this association—when I see you exalted not by extraordinary fortune as he was, but displaying great indiscretion about matters which are most important and dear to God, I urge you not only not to proceed any further but also (and you will in fact show good sense by doing this) to destroy what you previously ⟨wrote⟩. And if this does not happen—for I suspect that you will laugh loudly, if you who are so great a man should hear such things from the likes of me, but still I will both express my opinion and later act upon it whatever your feelings—I will break off our former friendship, or rather I will not at all refrain from loving you but only from praising what you do; for I fear that you may suffer a calamity no less than that of Polycrates, if not the same ⟨calamity⟩ as his, and I might be forced to share your suffering. For the deity did not have to be jealous of Polycrates because of his superior luck, while you will be admitted to the presence of God, being an offender of His servants and friends, not to say of something greater, even His laws. But I will not say anything. This is how I cling to your friendship, like "ivy to oak," as the tragedy says.

8. [To Barlaam]

It seems to me that, as far as I am concerned, you did not need to write to me what you have written, for you told me these things recently by word of mouth, and I did not forget. You are precisely aware that I also do not strongly oppose you on the questions of theology, but because of your insulting treatment of the holy hesychasts from the beginning, and your love of meddling. Then you also seem to me to be overdoing things with these very accusations against Palamas regarding theology; for it is unlikely that this man will be proven a heretic, which is what you are anxious to persuade the Church to condemn him for. But I fear lest the more

ἐπιτιθέμενος, μὴ λαμπρότερον αὐτὸν ἐπιδείξῃς οἷς ἔγκεισαι· καὶ ὅσῳ τοιοῦτον ἐπιδείξῃς ἐκεῖνον, τοσούτῳ σεαυτὸν τοὐναντίον. ὁ γὰρ ὀρύσσων, φησί, βόθρον τῷ πλησίον αὐτοῦ ἐμπεσεῖται εἰς αὐτόν. διὰ τοῦτο δή σοι φίλος ὢν πρὸς ἀλήθειαν καὶ οἰκειούμενος τὰ σά, κατὰ τὴν παροιμίαν, συμβουλεύω μὴ οὕτως ἄγαν ἀνδρὸς πολλὴν δόξαν ἔχοντος εἰς εὐσεβείας λόγον καὶ βίου θεοφιλοῦς καταφέρεσθαι, καὶ ταῦτα παρὰ τοὺς θείους νόμους· πρὸ γὰρ ψήφου συνοδικῆς ὀνομάζειν τινὰ φανερῶς αἱρετικὸν καὶ ἀναθεματίζειν οὐ κανονικόν, εἰ καὶ δοκεῖ τοιοῦτος. εἴ τοι δὴ φίλῳ καθαρῷ καὶ ἀδόλῳ μεμάθηκας πείθεσθαι τὰ δέοντα πείθοντι, τὰ μὲν ἐπὶ Παλαμᾶ μετριώτερος γίνου, τὰ δὲ περὶ προσευχῆς καὶ ὅσα τῆς τοιαύτης διδασκαλίας ἐστίν, ἵνα μὴ τῆς ἀωρίας λέγω καὶ ματαιοπονίας, πυρὸς τροφήν σοι καλὸν προθυμηθῆναι θέσθαι· εἰ δὲ μή, τὰ τελευταῖα καὶ ἄκαιρά σοι δοκοῦντα [fol. 234^v] τῆς ἐμῆς ἐπιστολῆς ἐκεῖνα οὐκ ἄκαιρα, οἶμαι, τὸ μέλλον ἀποφανεῖ.

9. ⟨Τῷ Βαρλαὰμ⟩

Τὴν μὲν τοῦ συλλογισμοῦ φύσιν, οὐ παντὸς ἀλλὰ τοῦ ὀρθοῦ καὶ ἀναγκαίου, ἄμαχόν τινα ἔχειν δύναμιν οὐκ ἀπειθῶ· σὲ δέ—πῶς ἂν εἴποιμι εὐλαβῶς;—οὐ πάνυ τι πείθομαι πανταχοῦ τηρεῖν αἱρεῖσθαι τὸ καθαρῶς ἀναγκαῖον καὶ ἀψευδὲς ἐν τῷ λέγειν, καὶ διὰ τοῦτο οὐδ' ἄμαχον. αὐτίκα τοίνυν σοι μὲν δοκεῖ τὸ πείθειν ἀπὸ τῶν δοκούντων ἔχειν τῷ πειθομένῳ μόνον τὴν γένεσιν, ἐγὼ δ' ἂν φαίην, οὐκ ἀπὸ τῆς ἀληθείας οἶμαι, καὶ τὸν ἀποδεικνύντα πείθειν καὶ τὸν διδάσκοντα ὧν οὐδὲν οἶδεν ὁ ἀκροώμενος, ἀλλ' ἅπαν μαθὼν ἀπ' ἀρχῆς τὸ πρὶν ἀγνοούμενον, ἢ γνῶσιν ἔσχεν αὐτοῦ ἧς ἑτέραν οὐκ εἶχεν, ἢ ἀπὸ δόξης εἰς δόξαν μετέπεσε τῆς ψευδοῦς τὴν ἀληθῆ· ὅ μοι κἀγὼ δοκῶ πρὸς σὲ πεποιηκέναι, καὶ σὺ καλῶς πεποιηκὼς ἐπείσθης, εἰ καὶ μὴ ὁμολογεῖν ἐθέλεις. οἰηθεὶς γάρ, ὡς ἔοικε, πρότερον οὐ σοφῶς, ἐμοὶ δοκεῖν, οὐδὲ τῆς ἀληθείας στοχαστικῶς, εἰ πᾶσιν ἐπιχειροίης,

---

8: 12–13 Prov. 26:27 || 14 locum non inveni

---

14 *καὶ* supra versum adiecit S^1 || 18 *εἴ τι* S

9: S 230^r–231^v.

5 *καθαρὸν* S: supra *ον* litteras *ως* superscripsit S^1 || ante *ἐν τῷ λέγειν* scripsit *ἀναγκαῖον καὶ ἀψευδὲς* supra versum S^1 || 5 post *λέγειν* in spatio 7 litterarum lineam habet S || 9 *οὐδὲν οἶδεν ὁ ἀκροώμενος*] *οὐδὲν ὁ πειθόμενος οἶδεν* S: *ὁ πειθόμενος* expunxit et *ὁ ἀκροώμενος* post *οἶδεν* scripsit supra versum S^1

bitterly you attack him, the more you may show up his brilliance to your opponents, and the more you show him as such, so much the more you will do the opposite for yourself. For it is said that "He who digs a pit for his neighbor shall fall into it." For this reason, then, being your true friend and "making your concerns mine," as the saying goes, I advise you not to attack so excessively a man who enjoys a great reputation because of his piety and devout life, and especially when this is in defiance of the sacred laws, for prior to a synodal decision it is uncanonical openly to call someone a heretic or to anathematize him, even though he may appear to be so. If, therefore, you are inclined to pay some heed to a true and sincere friend who is seeking to persuade you to do what is right, be more moderate as far as Palamas is concerned. And as for ⟨your charges⟩ concerning prayer and all that has to do with that doctrine—so that I need not speak of inopportune timing and fruitless labor—it would be good if you made ready to feed them to the fire. Otherwise, I suspect that the future may not prove untimely those recent remarks in my letter which you consider so.

9. [To Barlaam]

I agree that a syllogism, not every syllogism, but any one which is right and ⟨logically⟩ necessary, has by nature a certain incontestable power. But—how can I put it politely?—I do not quite believe that you are inclined to maintain everywhere in your arguments what is purely necessary and true, and for this reason I do not believe that you are incontestable either. For example, now, you think that persuasion is born only from things which appear to be true to the person who is being persuaded, but I would say, not far from the truth, I believe, that he who demonstrates also persuades, and so does the man who teaches things of which his hearer knows nothing; but after the hearer has learnt from the beginning all that he previously did not know, he either acquires knowledge where he did not possess anything similar or else he changes from a false to a true opinion. This is what I also did to you, and you were right to be convinced, even though you do not wish to admit this. For its seems that you thought earlier—neither wisely, I believe, nor with consideration for the truth—that you would appear admirable if you attacked every-

9

θαυμαστός τις φανεῖσθαι καὶ παρὰ πᾶσιν εὐδοκιμήσειν, εἰ ἃ σοι δοκοῦσιν ἕκαστοι φρονεῖν ἡμαρτημένως ἐπανορθοῦσθαι πειρᾷ ὥσπερ τις ὢν Σωκράτης, μᾶλλον δὲ αὐτὸν Σωκράτην ἀτεχνῶς ἐκεῖνον ἀπεργάσασθαι σαυτὸν ἀτόπως ἐπιθυμήσας, καὶ διὰ τοῦτο ἠρεμεῖν οὐ δυνάμενος, ἐπέθου τοῖς Ναζιραίοις μετὰ τοιούτου φρονήματος, μεθ' οἵου περ ἂν ὁ ἐκ Θεοῦ κατελθών. καί πού τι καὶ τοιοῦτο πρὸς ἡμᾶς ἀπεφθέγξω, λέγοντας ἀπὸ φιλίας γνώμης καὶ συμβουλεύοντας τὰ σαυτοῦ σοι δεῖν πράττειν καὶ οἷς οὐδεὶς παρ' οὐδενὸς ἀπαντήσεται ψόγος, καὶ μὴ πάνυ τ' ἀλλότρια σπουδάζειν περιεργάζεσθαι πράγματα, ᾧ δήπου μὴ ψόγον μόνον δοκεῖν ἀλλά που καὶ κίνδυνον ἕψεσθαι καὶ τὰς τούτων αἰτίας. πρὸς σὲ μόνον ἔλεγον οὕτω τό τε προσῆκον, ὁ δ'οὐκ ἐπείθου, καὶ πολλάκις τοῦθ' ἡμῶν εἰργασμένων μετὰ παντὸς τοῦ φιλικοῦ καθήκοντος καὶ φιλανθρώπου, σὺ μᾶλλον ᾤδεις τὸ φρόνημα καὶ τελευτῶν οὕτως ἀκράτως ἔσχες σαυτοῦ καὶ κούφως, ὡς καὶ λόγοις μακροῖς παραδοῦναι προσευχὴν καὶ φόρτον διδασκαλίας ἀήθη [fol. 230v] καὶ παντάπασιν ἄκαιρον τοῖς ἀμαθῶς καὶ ἀτέχνως μετιοῦσι τὰ θεῖα, τοῦτο δ' ἐστὶ πιστῶς τε καὶ τοῖς θείοις ἑπομένως τῆς προσευχῆς κανόσι· σὺ δ' ὥσπερ τινὰ φῂς παρὰ τοὺς τῆς θεολογίας χαρακτῆρας καὶ τύπους θεολογεῖν, οὕτω παρὰ τοὺς χαρακτῆρας καὶ τύπους τῆς ὑπὸ τῶν ἄνωθεν ἱερῶν ἀνδρῶν παραδοθείσης ἡμῖν προσευχῆς, περὶ προσευχῆς καὶ τελειότητος ἀνθρωπίνως διδάσκεις, εἰ καὶ πάνυ σοφῶς καὶ περιττῶς διδάσκεις. ποῦ γάρ ποτε συνέστη προσευχὴ διὰ συλλογισμῶν καὶ συνεχῶν τῶν "ἄρα"; ταυτὶ μὲν οὖν οὐ νῦν μηκύνειν καιρός.

Σὺ δὲ ἐντεῦθεν εἰς πολέμους κατέστης καὶ μῖσος καὶ μῆκος ἐρίδων ἀδιεξόδευτον, ὅπερ ἐγὼ προορώμενος ἐξ ἀρχῆς καὶ φίλος ὢν ἀληθής, ἐπετίμων καὶ συνεβούλευόν σοι τὰ τοιαῦτ' εὐλαβεῖσθαι, εἰ βούλοιο φιλοσοφεῖν, φιλοσοφίας εἶναι καὶ πηγὴν καὶ ταμίαν τὴν εἰρήνην νομίζων. εἰ δέ σοι νῦν ὁ λόγος, ὡς σὺ φῂς, ὑπὲρ τῆς εὐσεβείας, ἀλλ' ἐκεῖνά γε οὐδ' ἂν αὐτὸς εἴποις ὑπὲρ τῆς εὐσεβείας, ἀλλ' οὐκ οἶδ' οὗτινος, εἰ μὴ φιλονεικίας. εἶτα τίς οἶδεν εἰ καὶ τὸ νῦν ἀληθές, μήπω παρόντος τοῦ διαβαλλομένου; ἐγὼ γὰρ ὁρῶν εἰς τὰ πράγματα, ὀκνῶ καὶ δέδοικα περὶ σοὶ μᾶλλον ἢ τῷ καθ' οὗπερ ἧκες. σκόπει γάρ· πρὸς τοὺς ἀναχωροῦντας ἦρξας ἐνταῦθα τοῦδε τοῦ πολέμου καὶ τῆς περιεργίας μεθ' ὑποκρίσεως, πράγματος ἀφιλοσοφωτάτου· εἶτα οὐκ ἔστης μέχρι τῶν τότε σοι κακουργηθέντων, ἀλλὰ καὶ κομψοῖς ταῦτα παραδεδώκεις λόγοις καί τινα αἵρεσιν ἦρας εἰς ὕψος τῷ λόγῳ· τὰς εἰσπνοὰς καὶ τὴν καρδίαν καὶ κλόνον σπλάγχνων καὶ

---

18 post *ἀτόπως* scripsit *ὡς ἐδόκεις* S: quae vocabula expunxit S[1] || 34 *τοὺς* supra versum scripsit S[1] || 46 *οὗτινος* S || 52 *κομψεῖς* S

9

body and would be highly esteemed by all if you attempted to correct what you thought everyone was wrong to believe, just as if you were another Socrates. Or rather, you set your heart absurdly upon becoming simply another Socrates and were therefore unable to keep quiet, and so attacked the monks with the arrogance of someone descended from God. And you even said something like that to me when, inspired by friendship, I spoke up and advised you that you ought to mind your own business and not to act so as to incur any censure from anybody, nor to be too eager to meddle in other people's affairs, because it seemed that such conduct would be followed not only by censure but, perhaps, even danger; and ⟨I explained⟩ why. It was to you alone I spoke thus, saying what was right, but you did not listen, and though I did this many times and with all due friendship and kindness, you swelled even more with pride; and in the end you behaved in such an unrestrained and vain manner that you even wrote long treatises on prayer with a great deal of doctrine that is strange and altogether inappropriate for men who pursue divine matters without learning and with simplicity, that is to say, both with faith and also in accordance with the sacred rules of prayer. But, just as you say that a certain person teaches about God against the standards and rules of theology, so you also teach about prayer and perfection according to the manner of men and against the standards and rules of prayer handed down to us by the holy men of old, even though you teach in a very learned and uncommon manner. For where was prayer ever formed by means of syllogisms and continuous "therefores"? But now is not the occasion to prolong this discussion.

This, then, is how you got into fights with hatred and long disputes from which there was no escape, the very thing that I had foreseen from the beginning; but as a true friend I had rebuked you and advised you to beware of such troubles, if you wished to be a philosopher, because I believed peace to be both the source and the steward of philosophy. But if, as you say, your present argument is for the sake of piety, then even you could not claim that those things were for the sake of piety; indeed, I cannot think of any other purpose they had, aside from contentiousness. Besides, since the accused is not here, who knows whether what you are now saying is true? For when I consider these matters, I hesitate and fear more for you than for the man you have attacked. Indeed, think: it was here that you started this war and your hypocritical meddling against the hesychasts, a thing most unbecoming for a philosopher. Then you did not stop at these evil deeds that you had so far perpetrated, but wrote subtle discourses on these matters and stirred up thereby the question of a heresy. You made fun of the inhalations and the heart, and the agitation and

9

ταραχὴν ἐκωμῴδησας, τὴν ἐκ τοῦ φιλοθέως ταῦτα τῇ ψυχῇ συνδιατίθεσθαι πρὸς τὰ θεῖα διέγερσιν—ἀσυνέτως, οἶμαι, μᾶλλον ἢ συκοφαντικῶς—κλόνον ἀποκαλῶν καὶ πάθος οὐκ ἀγαθόν, καὶ τὴν Μασσαλιανῶν δυσσέβειαν ἀδικώτατα παραλαβών, ταῦτ' ἐκείνῃ συνέπλεξας· εἶτα συνθεὶς πάντας τούτους τοὺς λόγους ἐπὶ τῷ περὶ τοῦ φωτὸς καὶ τῆς θεολογίας, ὃς ἀπὸ τῶν εἰσπνοῶν κακῶς ἀπετέχθη καὶ κλόνων καὶ πανούργως προὐτέθη τῶν τεκόντων τὸ τέκνον, ἤγαγες εἰς τὴν ἁπασῶν ταύτην ἐκκλησιῶν μητέρα.

Εἰ μὲν οὖν οὐ δοκεῖ σοι, τούτων οὕτως ἐχόντων καὶ κατεσκευασμένων, πάντας [fol. 231^r] σχεδὸν ἐκείνῳ κατὰ σοῦ συστήσεσθαι καὶ ἀμαθεῖς καὶ σοφούς—ὥσπερ οὖν οὐδὲ δοκεῖ—οὐ καλῶς, οἶμαι, τοῦτό γε οὐδ' ἀληθῶς σοι δοκεῖ. διατί; ὅτι σὺ μὲν ἦρξας πολέμου τοῦ κατὰ τῶν σπουδαίων, ὁ δέ σοι μὲν ἀντιλέγειν, τοῖς δὲ ἀμύνειν πολεμουμένοις προθυμηθείς, οὐ παροπτέος αὐτοῖς. ἔπειτα εἰ μὲν τὰ πρὸς τὸ δόγμα ἐκείνου μόνον τὸ περὶ τοῦ ὑπὸ τὴν θείαν φύσιν ἀκτίστου καὶ ὑπερουσίου Θεοῦ καὶ ληπτοῦ σωματικοῖς ὀφθαλμοῖς, ἃ φῂς ἐκεῖνον γράφειν, δεῦρ' ἀγαγὼν ἐδείκνυς τοῖς κυρίοις τῶν ψήφων, τἆλλα δὲ ὑπεξῄρεις, μετριώτερον ἂν ἦσθα περὶ σαυτοῦ βεβουλευμένος, οἶμαι, καὶ συνετώτερον, ἤ, ὡς ἂν σὺ φαίης, οἰκονομικώτερον· νῦν δὲ πάντα ὁμοῦ δεδωκώς, τῇ τούτων ἀκαιρίᾳ ἐκνευρίζεις κἀκεῖνα. χωρὶς δὲ τούτων, οὐχ ὁμοίως σοί τε προσέξουσιν ἡ ἐκκλησία κἀκείνῳ, καὶ διὰ τἆλλα πάντα· ἔδει γάρ σε εἰδέναι μὴ μόνον λογογραφεῖν καὶ πλέκειν συλλογισμούς, ἀλλὰ καὶ ὅπῃ δέοι τοῦτο ποιεῖν, καὶ τίνα, καὶ ὅθεν ὡρμημένον, καὶ σκοπεῖν πρὸς τὰ κρατοῦντα ἤθη παρ' οἷς ὢν ταῦτα κινεῖς ἀνέδην.

Ἃ σοι μέν, οἶμαι, ἠγνόητο, ἐγὼ δέ σε ἀδόλως φίλος φίλον ἐδίδασκον ἅ σοι συμφέρειν ἡγούμην, καὶ ἦν τοιαῦτα ὡς ἔοικεν. ἐπεὶ δὲ οὐκ ἤκουες, ἀλλ' ᾤου ληρεῖν μὲν ἐμέ, σαυτὸν δὲ πάντα τῷ "ἄρα" δυνήσεσθαι, ἡσυχίαν ἠγάπων, ἀλλά με ἀμεριμνεῖν οὐ διὰ τέλους εἴα τὸ τῆς φιλίας κέντρον μετὰ τῆς ἀληθείας. πάλιν τοίνυν ἡπτόμην σου καὶ πάλιν ἐπετίμων ἠρέμα· καὶ τοῦτο πολλάκις ἐποίησα,

---

57 *παραλαβὼν*] *παραγαγὼν* S: *γαγών* expunxit et *λαβὼν* scripsit in margine S^1 || 66 post *τῶν* scripsit *μοναχῶν* S: quod vocabulum expunxit S^1 et postea *σπουδαίων* supra versum scripsit || 68 *μόνον* supra versum scripsit S^1 || post *τοῦ* reliquum lineae spatium vacuum in S: in quo spatio *ὑπὸ τὴν θείαν* inseruit S^1 || 68–70 *φύσιν . . . γράφειν* in margine scripsit S^1 || 69 post *Θεοῦ* scripsit et deinde delevit *ὁρατοῦ* S^1 qui postea scripsit *καὶ ληπτοῦ* || post *ὀφθαλμοῖς* scripsit et deinde delevit *ἅ φασιν* S^1 qui postea scripsit *ἃ φῂς* || 70 *δεῦρ'* in margine scripsit S^1 || 72 *οἶμαι* supra versum scripsit S^1 || 73 post *κἀκεῖνα* scripsit *ὁρᾷς ἣν ἐγὼ περὶ σὲ γνώμην ἔχω* S: quae verba expunxit S^1 || 77 post *ἤθη* scripsit *παρὰ τοῖς εὐσεβέσι, τά τε ἔθεσι νόμιμα καὶ τὰ δέλτοις ἱεραῖς παραδοθέντα πλείσταις· οἷς, ὥσπερ ἔφην, ἁπλῶς τε καὶ πεποιθότες νῦν οἱ τῆς ἀρετῆς ἕπονται ζηλωταὶ καὶ μιμηταὶ τῶν πατέρων σὺν τοῖς κατ' ἦθος ἔργοις* S: quae verba expunxit S^1 et postea supra versum *παρ' οἷς ὢν ταῦτα κινεῖς ἀνέδην* adiecit

stirring of the inner organs and—foolishly rather than viciously, I believe—you described as agitation and evil passion the awakening towards the Divine which is aroused by the sympathetic affection of these ⟨organs⟩ along with the soul, through the love of God. And in a most unfair manner you took up the heresy of the Messalians and associated it with these ⟨practices⟩. Then you combined all these discourses with the one about light and theology, ⟨a discourse⟩ which was ill-begotten of the inhalations and agitations, and, though an offspring, it was craftily put ahead of the parents; then you brought them to this Mother of all Churches.

If, therefore, things having been contrived as they are, you do not think (and indeed you do not think this) that almost everybody, both ignorant and learned, will stand with him and against you, then your thinking is neither right nor realistic. Why? Because you started the war against the venerable men, and they will not overlook the man who was eager to answer you and to defend them when they were under attack. Besides, if you had left aside the rest and brought here to show to the judges only his doctrine about a god lower than the divine nature, uncreated, supersubstantial, and perceptible to bodily eyes—which is what you claim that he writes—then I believe that you would have planned your affairs more moderately and sensibly, or, as you would say, more expediently. But now that you have presented everything at once, you weaken the latter ⟨charges⟩ by the inappropriate quality of the former. Apart from this, the Church will not pay as much attention to you as to him, for all the other reasons as well. For you should have known not only how to write discourses and devise syllogisms, but also where to do this and who ought to do it and from what motives; and you should have considered the prevailing customs of the people among whom you live, stirring up trouble in an unrestrained manner.

These things, I believe, escaped you, but I, as one friend to another, indicated to you honestly what in my opinion was to your advantage, and so apparently it was. Then, since you did not listen, but thought that I spoke foolishly, and that you could accomplish everything with your "therefores," I kept my peace; but truth and the goad of friendship did not allow me to remain indifferent to the end. Again I took hold of you and again I rebuked you gently. And I did this many times, just like

9

ὥσπερ οἱ μουσικὴν ἁρμοζόμενοι νῦν μὲν ἐντείνων, νῦν δ' ἀνιείς, τὸ μὲν πάνυ σφοδρὸν ἀεὶ παραιτούμενος, ἠρέμα δὲ καθαπτόμενος, καὶ ὅτε δ' ἐντείναιμι, ὁ τόνος ἐπιεικής. ἦν γὰρ ἔτι ἀκινδυνώτερα καὶ ἧττον τοῦ τε παρὰ σοῦ τὰ τῆς ἱερᾶς ἡσυχίας ἀπολαύοντα κλύδωνος καὶ σὺ τοῦ παρὰ πάντων, ἐμοὶ δοκεῖν, ἐσομένου μακρότερον.

Ἐπεὶ δὲ ἐπὶ ξυροῦ, φασι, τὰ πράγματα ἔστησας, καὶ γαληνῶς ἔχουσαν τὴν ἐκκλησίαν τῇ τοῦ Θεοῦ χάριτι, φθόνῳ τοῦ διαβόλου δεινῷ ταράττετε κλύδωνι καὶ στάσει χαλεπῇ κατασείετε [fol. 231v] οὐκ ἀνεκτὸν ἡγησάμην οὐδὲ καλὸν ἡσυχάζειν, ἀλλὰ πᾶν ὅ τι ἂν οἷός τε ὦ καὶ εἰπεῖν καὶ ποιῆσαι καὶ τοὺς ἄλλους παρακαλέσαι πρὸς τὸ παῦσαι μὲν τὸ θεσπέσιον φῦλον τὸ εἰς ἐμὲ γοῦν ἧκον ὑπὸ σοῦ χειμαζόμενον, παῦσαι δὲ καί σε τῆς οὐκ ἀβλαβοῦς σοι φιλοτιμίας ταύτης καὶ φιλοπραγμοσύνης, διαλῦσαι δὲ τὸ κοινὸν τῆς ὑμετέρας τῶν φιλοσόφων φιλονεικίας νέφος, ἐξ οὗ πάντα φθέγγεσθε καὶ ὅθεν οὐχ ὁρᾶτε οἷ φέρεσθε, κατὰ κρημνῶν που πάντως καὶ βαράθρων φερόμενοι.

Ἆρά σοι καὶ νῦν δοκοῦμεν ἢ πράττειν ἢ λέγειν ἀνοικονόμητα; ἐγὼ μὲν οὐκ οἶμαι. τά γε μὴν ἐν Βερροίᾳ καὶ Θεσσαλονίκῃ καὶ τῇδε ἡμῶν, ὡς φῄς, λελυπηκότα τινὰς τῷ ἀνοικονομήτῳ, κολακεύειν μὲν ἀγαπῶντα καὶ ψεύδεσθαί με, καὶ διὰ τοῦτ' εἰρωνεύεσθαι, ἴσως ἂν ἔρρωσέ τι καὶ φροντίδι παρέδωκε, καθαρᾶς δὲ τῆς ἀληθείας τὰ δυνατὰ προαιρούμενον ἔχεσθαι, καὶ χαίρειν παρασκευάσειε. λόγοι γὰρ σοφῶν ὡς βούκεντρα, σοφός τις εἶπε καὶ εὐδοκίμηκεν.

Ὥστε εἰ ἐκ τῶν ἐμοὶ δοκούντων δεῖ με πείθειν ἐπιχειρεῖν τὸν διαλεκτικῶς ἐπιχειροῦντα πείθειν, οὐ διαλεκτικῶς ἡμᾶς ἐπεχείρησας πείθειν, οὐ γὰρ ὡσαύτως ἐγώ τε καὶ σὺ περὶ τούτων φρονοῦμεν, ἐξ ὧν με πάντως προσεδόκησας πείσειν. ἀλλ', ὦ γενναῖε καὶ μέγα φιλοσοφίας κράτος, δέχου με μόνον τὰ σαυτῷ συμφορώτατα

9: 90 Apostolius VI, 100 (Leutsch-Schneidewin, II, 392 || 99–100 Cf. Greg. Naz., *Or.* 4, 115 (PG, 35, 653C) || Ad apparatum 102 Herodotus, *Hist.*, VI, 127–129; Zenobius, *Centuria*, V, 31 (Leutsch-Schneidewin, I, 132) || 106–107 Eccl. 12:11

---

91 post *φθόνῳ* scripsit *τινὶ τοῦ πονηροῦ πειρᾶσθε ἀναταράττειν καὶ κύματα ἐγείρειν ἁλλόμενα* S: cuius verba expunxit S[1] qui postea in margine scripsit et deinde delevit vocabula *τῆς πονηρίας* et in margine inferiore *τοῦ διαβόλου δεινῷ ταράττετε κλύδωνι καὶ στάσει χαλεπῇ κατασείετε* scripsit || 98 ante *φιλονεικίας* addidit *τῶν φιλοσόφων* supra versum S[1] || 102 post *οἶμαι* scripsit *εἰ δὲ καὶ αὖθις εἴποις, οὐ φροντὶς Ἱπποκλείδῃ, φησὶν ἡ παροιμία· ἕως ἂν οὐχ ὡς ἄν τις εἴποι πάντως οὕτω τὰ πράγματ' ἔχῃ, ἀλλ' ὡς ἂν ἡ φύσις αὐτὰ καταδείξειε* S: cuius verba expunxit S[1] || 106 *παρασκευάσειεν* S: litteram *ν* expunxit S[1] || post *παρασκευάσειε* scripsit *ὡς θιασώτην, οἶμαι, σοφοῖς ἀνδράσιν ἀποδεικνύμενον* S; quae verba expunxit S[1] || 110 post *πείθειν* in margine adiecit et deinde delevit *σοὶ γὰρ οὐκ ἐμοὶ δοκοῦντα πρὸς τὸ πεῖσαί με λέγεις* S[1] qui postea *οὐ γὰρ ὡσαύτως ἐγώ τε καὶ σὺ περὶ τούτων φρονοῦμεν. ἐξ ὧν με πάντως προσεδόκησας πείσειν* in margine superscripsit

those who tune musical instruments, now tightening, now slackening; I always avoided extreme harshness, but accosted you gently, and even when intense, I kept a moderate tone. For at this time hesychasm was still in less danger, and suffered less from the storm you caused, and I believe you too were further from the storm that will be raised by everybody else.

However, you have balanced things on "a razor's edge," as they say, and while the Church has been enjoying serenity by the grace of God, both of you through the devil's envy disturb it with a terrible storm and shake it with dangerous discord. And so I thought it neither tolerable nor right to keep quiet but ⟨I felt I should⟩ say and do everything within my power and appeal to others so as to put an end to your harassment of the holy men as much as I can, and to put a stop to this dangerous conceit of yours and to your love of meddling, and then to disperse the common cloud of the dispute between you philosophers, the cloud from which you make all your pronouncements and whence you do not see whither you are being led as you head, to be sure, for «precipices and pits».

And so, do I appear to you even now to be doing and saying intolerable things? I, for my part, do not think so. As for those deeds of mine which, as you say, annoyed some people in Berroia and in Thessalonica and here by their intolerable character, if someone wanted me to be a flatterer and a liar and therefore insincere, what I did perhaps would have strengthened him and made him ponder; but if a person preferred to cling to the pure truth with all his strength, my deeds could even have made him rejoice. For "the words of the wise are as goads," as a wise man said, and he was held in high esteem.

And so, if the man who attempts to persuade me by the dialectical method has to persuade me on the basis of what appears right to me, you did not attempt to persuade me dialectically, for you and I are not of a like mind regarding the premises from which you evidently expected to convince me. But, O noble and great philosopher, accept from me only what is best for you, and call me the most foolish

καὶ κάλει τὸν ἀφρονέστατον, νομίζων ὡς ἔστι λαθεῖν τι σπουδαῖον πρᾶγμα καὶ τὸν σοφώτατον· ὅπερ ἂν ἴδῃ μετριοφρονοῦσα διάνοια, ἐκτὸς αἰτίας ἐπισκοτούσης οὖσα.

10. Ἐκ τῶν ἐπιστολῶν Γρηγορίου μοναχοῦ τοῦ Ἀκινδύνου πρὸς Βαρλαὰμ τὸν φιλόσοφον ἐπὶ τῇ αὐτοῦ περιεργίᾳ κατὰ τῶν ἡσύχιον καὶ ἀνακεχωρηκότα ἐσπουδακότων βίον

Ἐγὼ νομίζων οὐχ ὕβριν εἶναι οὐδὲ προπηλακισμὸν εἴ τις πρὸς ἄνδρα φίλον, ἢ καὶ ὁντινοῦν ἄλλον, θαρρεῖ τὴν ἀλήθειαν σεμνῶς γε δήπου καὶ ὡς οἷόν τε μετ᾽ εὐφημίας, καὶ εἶπόν τι καὶ λέγω πρὸς τὴν σὴν λογιότητα. λέγω δὲ δὴ ταῦθ᾽ ἅπερ ἡγοῦμαι λέγων οὐ ψεύδεσθαι, οὐδέ σοί πω πείθομαι μὴ ὡς ὑπείληφ᾽ ἔχειν. ὑπείληφα δέ—καὶ ὅπως οἴσεις μετὰ μακροθυμίας τοὺς ἀναγκαίους καί μοί γε λόγους εἰπεῖν, ὥσπερ καὶ σὺ κελεύεις ἡμῖν τοῖς σαυτοῦ τὰς ἀκοὰς παρέχειν, καὶ φερομέν γε οὕτω τοὺς θαυμαστοὺς μυκτῆρας καὶ τὴν πολλὴν ἀφροσύνην ἣν ἐγκαλούμεθά σοι—νομίζω τοίνυν ἤ τοι φιλοδοξίᾳ καὶ φιλονεικίᾳ σε διῳδηκότα τοῖς ἱεροῖς ἀνδράσιν ἐπηρεάζειν, ἢ ἀγνοίᾳ καὶ ἀμαθίᾳ τῶν ἀρετῆς ἀγαθῶν, ἐκεῖνο μὲν σκοπῶν ἐξ ἀρχῆς ἀφ᾽ ὧν εἶδον πολλάκις ἐπιχειρήσαντά σε, ἃ μηδ᾽ αὐτὸς ἀρνήσῃ.

Ὅτε γὰρ πρῶτον ἐλθὼν εἰς τὴν μεγάλην πόλιν πάντα μὲν ἐσπούδασας κενὴν ἁπάσης παιδεύσεως ἀποδεῖξαι τὴν πόλιν, αἰσχρῶς δὲ ἀπήλλαξας καὶ ὡς αὐτὸς ὑπὲρ σοῦ πολλάκις ἐρυθριάσας οἶδα, τίς τότε ἦν ἀνάγκη τῶν ὑπὸ σοῦ πραγμάτων; τί δογμα ἢ ἀρετῆς ἢ θεότητος ἐπλημμελεῖτο; τίς πλάνη τὴν πόλιν κατεῖχε ἢ ἐλυμαίνετο; καίτοι πολλά σοι τῶν ἐν Θεσσαλονίκῃ φίλων ὅτ᾽ ἐξῄεις ἐκεῖθεν ὑποθεμένων ὃν δεῖ σε τρόπον τοῖς τῇδε προσενεχθῆναι, καὶ σὺ δὲ αὐτὸς πάντ᾽ ἐκεῖ διετείνου, [fol. 67v] ὑπερβολήν τινα λέγων, μηδὲ δείξειν ὅλως ἐπιστάμενος γράμματα, εἰ μή σοι συμβαίη γνωσθῆναι κατά τινα ἀνάγκην ἔξω τῆς σῆς προαιρέσεως. ἀλλ᾽ ὅμως ἐνταῦθα γεγενημένου, πάντα ταῦτα ἐξήλασεν ὁ κενῆς δόξης ἔρως, καὶ ζητῶν πάντων φανῆναι σοφώτατος, μᾶλλον δὲ μηδένα μηδὲν εἰδότα ἐξελεγχθῆναι ταῖς ἀποδείξεσί σου, ἀμαθὴς ὢν ἠλέγχθης, ἢ οὐκ οἶδ᾽ ὅπως εἴπω. ὅτε δὲ μετὰ ταῦτα τὰς πρώτας εἰρωνείας τοῦ Παλαμᾶ

10: 4 Demosthenes, *De corona*, 12

113–114 δέχου . . . ἀφρονέστατον non satis perspicio

10: A 67r–73v.

man, considering that even the wisest man may miss something important. A mind that is moderate and free of any cause of blindness would realize this.

10. From the letters of the monk Gregory Akindynos to the philosopher Barlaam with regard to his officious investigation against those who pursue the quiet and anchoritic life.

Thinking that it is neither an "insult nor a slight," if one has the courage to speak the truth to a friend, or to anyone else (respectfully, of course, and in a language as polite as possible) I said and I am still saying something to your Erudition. In fact, I am saying things which I do not think that it is false to say, and I am not yet persuaded by you that they are not as I assume. And I assume—and please bear with patience the words which it is necessary for me to speak, just as you, for your part, bid me to listen to your arguments so that I put up with the extraordinary sneers and your accusations of great folly—hence I think that you speak disparagingly about the holy men either because you are inflated with ambition and contentiousness or because of ignorance and lack of knowledge about the blessings of virtue. For, in fact, I am considering the matter from the beginning, starting with all the things that I often saw you attempting, things even you will not deny.

For when you first came to the great city, you strove in every way to prove that the city was void of all learning, but you came out of this with shame, as I know because I personally blushed many times for your sake. What then was the necessity for the trouble you caused? What doctrine concerned with virtue or the divinity was infringed? What folly came over the city or was causing trouble? And yet our friends in Thessalonica, when you left there, gave you many instructions as to how you ought to behave towards people here, and you personally asserted there everything possible, saying in exaggeration that you would not even show that you were literate at all, unless you should happen to be found out through some contingency outside your choice. But, in spite of this, when you arrived here, your love of empty glory chased all this away, and, in seeking to appear the wisest of all, or rather to prove by your demonstrative syllogisms that nobody knew anything, you were proven to be ignorant, or I do not know how else to put this. And when, after this, you shot from your bow the first mockeries against Palamas, did I not object and

κατετόξευες, οὐκ ἀνθιστάμην καὶ συνεβούλευόν σοι κατέχειν σαυτὸν καὶ μὴ ταῦτ' ἀσχημονεῖν, μηδὲ τοξεύειν ἐπ' ἄνδρα οὐδὲ αὐτὸν ἀμαθῆ παντελῶς τοῦ τοξεύειν; σὺ δὲ μὴ τότε πεισθείς, "ἄφες," λέγων "ταπεινώσω τὸν ἄνθρωπον," ὕστερον ἔγνως ἔτι μᾶλλον κινήσας κατὰ σαυτοῦ τὸν ἀνάγυρον, καὶ ὅπως παύσεις ζητῶν, οὐ ῥᾳδίως ἐτύγχανες· οὕτως αὐτὸν ἐταπείνωσας.

Μετὰ δὲ ταῦτα πάλιν Λαπίθου τοῦ Κυπρίου, ἀνδρὸς εὖ ἥκοντος φιλοσοφίας λόγων ἧς καὶ παρὰ σοῦ πολλάκις μαρτυρίας τετύχηκε, μετὰ σεβασμίου τοῦ σχήματος ἀπορίας τινὰς τῆς Ἀριστοτέλους φιλοσοφίας ἐν γράμμασι προβαλλομένου καὶ ζητοῦντος λύσιν ὥσπερ ἐκ διδασκάλου, ἀντὶ τοῦ εὐγνωμόνως αὐτῷ καὶ μετ' ἐπιεικείας ἀποκεκρίσθαι, μυκτῆρος ἐνέπλησας τοὺς πρὸς ἐκεῖνον λόγους καὶ λίαν ἀσύνετον φανερῶς ἀπεκάλεις. ἐμοῦ τοίνυν καὶ τότε σοι ταῦτα οὐκ ἐπαινοῦντος, οὐδὲν προετίμησας· τοιγαροῦν ἦλθον ἕτεροί σοι παρὰ τοῦ Λαπίθου λόγοι, οὐκέτι μετ' ἐκείνου τοῦ σχήματος, ἀλλ' οὗ σὺ μεστοὺς τοὺς πρὸς ἐκεῖνον πέμψαις. καί σοι συνέβη λαμπρῶς [fol. 68r] τὸ ὁποῖον κ' εἴπησθα, ἡ παροιμία, ὥσπερ ἠχοῦς τὴν φωνὴν ἀντιδούσης ἣν εἴληφεν. οὐ γὰρ μόνον, ὡς ἔοικε, σὺ τοῖς ἑτέρων λόγοις ἀφυῶς ἔχεις πείθεσθαι καὶ ταπεινοῦσθαι, ἀλλὰ κἀκεῖνοι τοῖς σοῖς, καὶ αὐτὸς οὗτος ἐγὼ οὗ σὺ μηδὲν προτιμᾷς.

Ἐντεῦθεν ἐμοὶ πανταχόθεν συνῆκται καὶ τὰ πρὸς τοὺς ἱεροὺς τούτους ἄνδρας ἀπὸ τῆς αὐτῆς πηγῆς, ἧς ἔχεις ἔνδον ἀενάου, ῥυῆναι. οὐκοῦν σὺ μὲν τὰ σαυτοῦ κατὰ τὰ πράγματά με ἀξιοῖς ἐξετάζειν, ἐγὼ δὲ τί ἄλλο πράττων ἂν εἴην παρὰ δικαίῳ κριτῇ, ὅταν ἐκεῖσε βλέπω, ἢ ἐξ αὐτῶν τῶν πραγμάτων ταῦτα συνάγων καὶ συλλογιζόμενος; ὥστ' οὐκ ἂν ἀδικοίην ἐπηρεαστήν σε θεοφιλῶν ἀνθρώπων ἀποκαλῶν καὶ τῆς ἑαυτῶν σωτηρίας μᾶλλον ἢ σύ τε τῆς σαυτοῦ κἀγὼ τῆς ἐμαυτοῦ φροντιζόντων καὶ ἀρετῆς καὶ Θεοῦ. εἰ δὲ αὐτὸς οὐ λέγεις, τίς ἀνάγκη σοι πείθεσθαι; οὐ γάρ τοι μόνον ἐγὼ οἷς ἐπιστέλλω οὐκ ἀποδείκνυμι, ἀλλ' οὐδ' αὐτὸς Βαρλαάμ, ὁ κἂν πτώσει ἀποδεικνύναι νομίζων ἢ διαλέγεσθαί γε. καίτοι τί με συκοφαντεῖς καὶ διαβάλλεις, ὦ τᾶν, οἷς με λέγεις θαυμάζειν τὴν ἀνάγκην τῆς ἀποδείξεως, ὅτι δὴ νομίζοιμι ἀποδεικτικῶς ἐμαυτὸν ἐπιστέλλειν; γελοῖος γὰρ ἂν ἦν τις ἀποδείξει χρώμενος ἐπὶ τοῦ ἐπιστέλλειν, εἰ καὶ ὅ τι μάλιστα ἠπιστάμην ἀποδεικνύναι. ποῦ δὲ αὐτὴν καὶ τεθαύμακα; ἐγὼ γὰρ καὶ τὸ ἀποδεικνύναι εἶπον μὲν ἁπλῶς εἶναι πείθοντι, οὐδὲν εἰς αὐτὸ θαυμαστικὸν προσειπών, ὅτε σὺ μόνον ἔλε-

---

34–35 Gregorius Cyprius I, 22 (Leutsch-Schneidewin, II, 95) || 47 Homerus, *Il.*, 20, 250

---

47 *κ' εἴπησθα* scripsi, cf. Homerum, *Il.*, 20, 250: *οὐκ εἴπησθα* A || 60–61 *ὁ κἂν πτώσει* coni. Ševčenko: *ὃ κἂν πτύσῃ* A

advise you to control yourself and not to do these disgraceful things, nor to aim your arrows at a man who is not himself completely ignorant of archery? But since you did not listen at that time, saying, "let me humiliate the man," you found out later that you had stirred up even more trouble for yourself, and when you sought to put an end to this ⟨trouble⟩, you did not succeed easily. This is how you humiliated him!

Then again, after this, when the Cypriote Lapithes, a man well versed in philosophy, as even you have attested many times, respectfully put forward in his letters some questions about Aristotelian philosophy and asked for their solution as if from a teacher, instead of answering him with consideration and kindness, you filled your letters to him with sneering and you openly called him quite foolish. Even then I did not commend you, but you did not heed me at all. And so, other letters came to you from Lapithes, no longer in the same manner but full of the same kind of things as the letters you would have sent to him. So evidently what happened to you was that, in the words of the proverb, "The sort of thing you say ⟨will be said back to you,⟩" just like an echo which returns the voice it received. For, as it seems, you are not the only one disinclined by nature to listen in humility to the words of others; they ⟨are also disinclined⟩ to listen to your words, and so, in fact, am I, the man for whom you have no respect.

Hence I gathered from all over the place that your conduct towards the holy men originates from the source which you have forever flowing within. Surely you are asking that I examine your conduct according to the facts, and yet, in the opinion of a fair judge, what else could I do whenever I look in your direction, but make these conclusions and inferences from the facts themselves? Therefore, I would not do you an injustice to call you an abuser of men who are dear to God, men who care for their salvation more than you do for yours and I do for mine, as well as caring for virtue and God. And if you do not agree, what need is there to listen to you? For I do not make proofs in my letters, and neither indeed does Barlaam himself, who believes that even by the arrangement of terms ⟨in a syllogism⟩ he does, in fact, produce demonstrative or dialectic syllogisms. And yet, why do you make false accusations and try to discredit me, my friend, by saying that I admire the necessity of a demonstrative syllogism, in fact, that I think that my letters are in the form of demonstrations? For I would have been a ridiculous person, if I had used demonstration in correspondence, even if it was ⟨used⟩ to demonstrate what I knew best. And where have I admired this? For I simply said that it is up to the man who persuades to provide a demonstration as well, that is, without attributing anything admirable to demonstration; meanwhile, you were saying that the man who persuades does so

10

γες πείθειν τὸν ἐκ τῶν δοκούντων πείθοντα τῷ πειθομένῳ· οὐ μὴν ὅτι καὶ ἀποδείκνυμί τι ἐν [fol. 68v] οἷς ἐπιστέλλοιμι, πείθειν μέντοι πρὸς τούτοις καὶ τὸ ἄλλως ὁπωσοῦν τι διδάσκειν τοὺς οὐκ ἐπιστήμονας· τοῦτο δ' ἐμοὶ πεποιῆσθαι πολλάκις πρὸς τὴν σοφίαν τὴν σήν. ἠγνόεις μὲν γὰρ τὸ πρᾶγμα ὅτε ταπεινώσειν Παλαμᾶν ὑπελάμβανες, ἠγνόεις δ' ὅτε Λαπίθην, ἠγνόεις δὲ πρὸς τούτοις καὶ ἀγνοῶν οὐ παύῃ, ὁδὸν δεικνύναι κομπάζων ἀρετῆς, οὐκ εἰδὼς τοῖς εἰδόσιν. ὅταν δὲ ταῦτα λέγω, ἐξαιρῶ μὲν καὶ ἐμαυτὸν τοῦ τῶν εἰδότων κύκλου, ἐπεὶ καὶ τῶν πραγμάτων οὐδ' ὁτιοῦν μετέχω· τοσοῦτο δὲ οὐκ ἐξαιρῶ, ὅσον εἰδέναι οὐκ ἐπιστάμενος, καὶ τοὺς εἰδότας εἰδέναι, καὶ τίνι βίῳ καὶ πολιτείᾳ τὸ εἰδέναι ἁλίσκεται. κἂν τις τοὺς τόνδε τὸν βίον μετιόντας κακίζῃ καὶ διαβάλλῃ καὶ κακῶς φρονεῖν ἀποφαίνηται, οὐκ εἰδέναι τοῦτον τὸ ἀληθὲς διδάσκω, γνώσεσθαι δὲ τὰ τούτων καὶ ἐπαινέσεσθαι ὅταν αὐτοῖς τῆς ζωῆς κοινωνήσῃ καὶ τῆς φιλοσοφίας. κἂν περαιτέρω φιλονεικῇ, ἐπηρεαστὴν ἀποκαλῶ καὶ φιλόνεικον· κἂν ἔτι περαιτέρω, ψυχικὸν ἤδη ἄνθρωπον καὶ νεφέλην ἄνυδρον καὶ φθινοπωρινὸν δένδρον ἄκαρπον καὶ κῦμα θαλάττης ἀνήμερον καὶ ἀστέρα πλάνητα, καὶ τὰ πλείω παρίημι τῶν ὀνομάτων ὧν οἱ τοιοῦτοι παρὰ Παύλῳ καὶ Ἰούδᾳ τοῖς ἱεροῖς ἀποστόλοις ἠξίωνται. ὃν οὐδαμῶς ἀδικεῖν ταῦτ' ὀνομάζων οἶμαι, ταῦθ' ἑαυτὸν ἀκούειν δεξιὴν δεδωκότα. ὁ δεῖνα δὲ εἰ κακῶς θεολογῶν φωρᾶται, ἄλλος οὗτος ὁ λόγος καὶ μετ' ὀλίγον εἰρήσεται.

Καὶ μήν, εἴ με μὴ προαιρέσεως ἔδει τὸ πᾶν καταγινώσκειν τῆς σῆς, ἀγνοίας δὲ εἰ τύχοις ἁμαρτάνων ἐκείνῃ, τοῦτο δὴ [fol. 69r] καὶ πεποίηκα ἐν τοῖς ἐπεσταλμένοις εἰπών, ἀσυνέτως οἶμαί σε μᾶλλον ἢ συκοφαντικῶς πεπλανημένους ἡμῖν τοὺς Ναζιραίους λέγειν. φθόνον δὲ λέγων σὸν ἐμέ σοι προφέρειν αἴτιον τῆς ἐπηρείας τῶν ἀνδρῶν γεγονέναι, οὐκ οἶδας ὑπὸ μικροψυχίας, οἶμαι, ὃ περὶ τούτου γράφω. φθόνῳ γάρ σε κινούμενον ἔφην οὐ τῷ σαυτοῦ, ἀλλὰ τοῦ ἐξ ἀρχῆς τῷ ἀνθρωπείῳ γένει τῆς πρὸς τὸ θεῖον συγγενείας ἧς αὐτὸς ἐμακρύνθη φθονήσαντος, τούτοις ἐπιχειρῆσαι. ὃς ἀεὶ τοῖς ἀγαθοῖς ἐπιβουλεύει φθονῶν, καὶ βούλοιτ' ἂν οὐδένα μὲν φαίνεσθαι θεοφιλῶς βιοῦντα, πάντας δὲ κατ' ἐκεῖνον, καὶ διὰ τοῦτό σε κατὰ τῶν ἐπ' αὐτῷ βιούντων παρασκευάσαι τούτων, ἵνα διαβληθέντες, εἰ μήτοι σφίσιν αὐτοῖς—μὴ γὰρ οὕτω δυνηθείη κατὰ τῶν θεοφρουρήτων ὁ δαιμόνιος φθόνος—τοῖς γε ἄλλοις οἷς νῦν εἰσιν ὠφελείας πνευματικῆς ἀγαπώμενοι πρόξενοι, τότε ἄχρηστοι γένωνται κα-

---

83–84 ψυχικὸν ἄνθρωπον: I Cor. 2:14; Jud. 19 || 84–86 Jud. 12–13

---

75 et 77 ἐξαίρω A || 85 θαλάσσης A || 96 οἶδες A

only from what appears to be right to the person he is persuading. I did not say, however, that I give demonstrations in my letters, rather that I persuade and also instruct somehow those without understanding. In fact, I have done this many times in the case of your Wisdom. For you failed to understand the situation when you assumed that you were going to humiliate Palamas, and you showed lack of understanding in the case of Lapithes; further, you showed the same lack, and you still show this when you boast of pointing at the way of virtue to those who know, when you do not know yourself. And when I say these things, I except myself from the circle of those who are knowledgeable, because I take no part at all in these matters. But I do not except myself insofar as I realize that I lack knowledge; but I know those who have knowledge as well as the mode of life and conduct by which this knowledge is attained. And if someone reproaches those who lead this life and seeks to discredit them and declares that their ideas are wrong, I explain to him that he does not know the truth, and that when he shares their life and philosophy, he will become acquainted with their affairs and praise them. And if he goes on being contentious, I call him an insolent and contentious person; and if he persists any further, "an unspiritual man" as well "and a cloud carried away by the wind without giving rain, and a fierce wave of the sea, and a star that has wandered from its course," and I leave out the greater part of the names of which these men are deemed worthy in the epistles of the holy Apostles Paul and Jude. I do not believe that I do this man an injustice by calling him these names, because he "bargained for it" himself. As for this fellow, if he is discovered to be a bad theologian, that is a different matter and will be discussed shortly.

And besides, if I ought not to blame entirely your intentions, but rather your ignorance, if this should happen to be the cause of your error, this is exactly what I did when I said in my letter that it was folly rather than malice that made you say that the monks are in error. But when you say that I pronounced your envy to be the reason for your abusing these men, you are not aware (because of your pettiness, I believe) of what I am writing about. For I did not say that it was your envy which moved you to attack them, but rather the envy of the one who from the beginning begrudged the human race its kinship with God, from which *he* was alienated. He is always plotting against good men, because he is envious and would like no one to appear to be living in a manner pleasing to God, but would like everyone to follow him; and for this reason he set you up against these men who live for this purpose ⟨of pleasing God⟩, so that after they have been discredited, if not in their own eyes—for may the devil's envy not have such power against men who are under God's protection—at least in the eyes of others, they may become condemned and therefore useless to the people to whom they are a cause of spiritual benefit when

τεγνωσμένοι. τοῦτο καὶ τότε εἴρηταί μοι καὶ νῦν ἰσχυρίζομαι, οὐχὶ νομίζων τἀληθοῦς ἁμαρτάνειν.

Οὐδὲ δή, τὴν ἀρχὴν τοῦ παντὸς πρὸς Παλαμᾶν πολέμου λέγων εἰπεῖν με γενέσθαι σοι ἀπὸ τῶν ἐπὶ τοῖς ἱεροῖς ἀνδράσιν, οἶδας ὃ περὶ τούτου λέγω. εἶπον γὰρ οὐ τοῦτο, ἀλλ' ὅτι σὺ μὲν ἦρξας πολέμου τοῦ κατὰ τούτων, ὁ δέ σοι μὲν ἀντιλέγειν, ἐκείνοις δὲ ἀμύνειν προθυμηθείς, οὐ παροπτέος αὐτοῖς. ταῦτ' ἐπὶ λέξεως ἔγραψα· σὺ δὲ μὴ ἃ γράφοιμί σοι ἀξιῶν ἐπισκέπτεσθαι, ὅ τι τύχοις εὐχερῶς ἀντιγράφεις, καὶ μὴν ὅτε μου τῦφον κατηγορεῖς τοῦ τῶν γραμμάτων ἤθους. ἀτύφως μὲν ἔχειν αὐτὸς οὐκ ἂν διατειναίμην. πῶς γάρ, ὃς ἐμαυτὸν οἶδα [fol. 69v] πᾶσιν ἔτι τοῖς πάθεσι τυραννούμενον; τοῦτο δ' ἐστὶ τῶν παθῶν ἐν τοῖς ὀλίγους ἀθῴους ἑαυτῶν ἀφιεῖσιν. οὐ μὴν οὐδέ σε τύφου χωρὶς θαυμαστοῦ φαίην ἂν ἢ γράφειν ἢ λέγειν ἃ γράφεις τε καὶ λέγεις, ὥστε σοι συμβαίνειν τὸ Διογένους, τύφῳ τῦφον ἐλέγχειν.

Ἀδικεῖν δ' ὅτε λέγεις οὐχ οὓς δοκεῖς ἀδικεῖν, ἀλλ' οὕσπερ διαφθείρεις, εἰ κακῶς εἴης φρονῶν, ὀρθῶς μέν μοι λέγειν δοκεῖς, οὐ μὴν ἃ μὴ γινώσκω. ἐγὼ γάρ σε ὅταν ἐπηρεάζειν λέγω τοῖς ἱεροῖς ἀνδράσιν, ἀδικώτατα κατασκευάζοντα τὰς Μασσαλιανῶν ἐπὶ τούτοις ἐννοίας, καὶ τοὺς ταυτί σοι πειθομένους ἀδικεῖσθαι νομίζω. μὴ τοίνυν σφόδρα τοῦτό γε, ἀμαθῆ με νομίζων, ὑπερσεμνύνου λέγων.

Καὶ μὴν σὺ μὲν ἔοικας ὑπολαμβάνειν σφόδρα με ἡδέως ἔχειν τοῖς πρὸς σὲ τοῖσδε λόγοις, φιλοτιμίᾳ τινὶ καὶ ἀγαπᾶν πολεμεῖν σοι, ἐγὼ δὲ οὐκ' οἶδ' εἴ τι πώποτε τοσοῦτον ἄλλο παρανενόηκας· ὅς, τριῶν ἐτῶν ἢ τεττάρων ὑμῶν ἤδη που ταῦτα νεανιευσαμένων, οὐδὲν τοιοῦτον ἐκίνουν, οὐδὲ συνηρπαζόμην, οὐδ' ἂν ἐπὶ τοῦ παρόντος, εἰ μὴ διὰ τὸ τὴν ὑμετέραν περὶ τὴν ἐκκλησίαν εἰς ἄκρον ὕψος κεκορυφῶσθαι ζάλην.

Ἡγούμενον δέ σε τὰ περὶ τῆς προσευχῆς καὶ τῆς κενῆς τελειότητος ἐξάπλωσιν εἶναι τῶν τοῦ θείου Μαξίμου περὶ τούτων δογμάτων, καὶ διὰ τοῦτο πάντ' ἐκεῖνα παραγαγόντα εἰς πίστιν τοῦ φρονήματος τούτου σοι, οὐ πάντα ἰδεῖν ἡγοῦμαι, ἢ παριδεῖν ἑκόντα τὸ πλεῖστον τῆς τοῦ θείου πραγματείας Μαξίμου. [fol. 70r] εἰ γὰρ κατεῖδες πάντα καὶ τοῦ μαθεῖν τἀληθές, καὶ πρός γε τούτοις μετὰ τοῦ κατ' ἐκεῖνον βίου, θαρρῶν ἀποφαίνομαι οὐκ ἂν ταῦτα εἰπεῖν σε, οὐδ' ἐκεῖνα μέντοι τὴν ἀρχὴν ἐξαπλῶσαι.

Ἔτι λέγοντος ἐμοῦ σε περιεργάζεσθαι οἷς ἐπηρεάζεις τοῖς ἱεροῖς ἀνδράσιν, ἁπλῶς τε καὶ ἀτέχνως τὰ τῆς εὐσεβείας ἀγαθὰ

119–120 Diogenes Laertius. *De clarorum philosophorum vitis*, VI², 26

---

109 εἶδες A ‖ 117 οὐ μὴν οὐ μὴν A ‖ 125 ante μὴ erasit ὑπερσεμνύνου λέγων A

10

loved. This is what I said then, and I am now reaffirming it, and I do not think that I fail to speak the truth.

And when you claim that I said that your whole war with Palamas started because of your attack against the holy men, you do not, in fact, know what I am saying about this either. For I did not say this, rather ⟨I said⟩ that you started the war against them, and because he was eager to contradict you while defending them, he would not be overlooked by them. These are the very words I wrote, but because you do not deem worthy of consideration what I may write to you, you write back carelessly whatever occurs to you and especially when you reproach the tone of my letters with vanity. I could not, naturally, pretend that I am without vanity. How can I do so when I know that I am still under the tyranny of all passions (and this is one of those passions which allow few to escape them)! I would say, however, that you are not without extraordinary vanity when you write and speak what you are writing and speaking, and so it happens that, in the words of Diogenes, you "reproach vanity by vanity."

And when you say that you do not injure those men whom you appear to injure, but those whom you corrupt, if your opinions should be wrong, you seem to me to be saying what is correct, but nothing that I do not know. For, when I say that you insult the holy men, fabricating against them most unjustly the notions of the Messalians, I think that those who believe you about these matters are also injured. Do not, therefore, be so very proud when you say this, in the belief that I am ignorant.

Moreover, you seem to assume that I very much enjoy these arguments with you, out of some ambition and love of fighting with you, but I do not know if there is anything you have ever misunderstood so much. For, though it is now nearly three or four years since you started these things like hotheaded youths, I did not set in motion any such argument, nor was I carried away, nor would I be now, if your commotion concerning the Church had not reached the culminating point.

And when you think that what you write about prayer and empty perfection is a development of the doctrines of the divine Maximos on these doctrines, and for this reason you produced all those works in confirmation of your theory, I think that you did not see everything, or else you purposely overlooked the greatest part of the work of the divine Maximos. For, if you perceived everything along with the truth about learning and, besides this, his life, I say with confidence that you would not say these things, nor indeed would you develop those theories in the first place.

Furthermore, when I say that you show a meddlesome curiosity in your abuse of the holy men, who are simply and artlessly reaping the blessings of piety, you say

καρπουμένοις, σὺ λέγεις τῶν γνωσιμάχων τοῦτον εἶναι τὸν λόγον, παράγων ἡμῖν τὸν μέγαν Ἐπιφάνιον λέγοντα, γνωσίμαχοί εἰσιν οἱ πάσῃ γνώσει τοῦ Χριστιανισμοῦ ἀντιπίπτοντες· τὸ δὲ οὐδὲν πρὸς τὸν ἐμόν γε λόγον. οὐ γὰρ τὸ γνῶσιν ἐγὼ Χριστιανισμοῦ ἢ ζητεῖν ἢ συγγράφειν κωλύω ἀλλὰ τὸ περιέργως καὶ τοῖς ἀπεριέργως καὶ στερρῶς βεβηκόσι ἐπὶ τῆς εὐσεβείας ἐπηρεαστικῶς. εἰ δὲ ᾔδεις εὖ ἃ περὶ πάντων φησὶ καὶ ὁ μέγας Ἐπιφάνιος οὗτος, οὐκ ἂν πάντα εἰς γνῶσιν ἀνθρωπίνην ἀνῆγες, δεδιὼς μὴ τύχῃς τῆς καταδίκης ἧς ἡ γνωστὴ παρ' ἐκείνῳ ἑτέρα αἱρετικῶν φατρία ἐκ τῶν θείων συνόδων. εἰ δὲ καὶ ὅ τι μάλιστά σοι δοκῶ γνωσιμαχεῖν, τελεώτατε, Γρηγόριός με προὔλαβε γνωσιμαχήσας, ὁ σοῦ χείρων θεολόγος, ὡς ἔοικεν, ὅς πού φησιν ἐκεῖνα τῶν ἑαυτοῦ βιβλίων, οὐ τῶν κομψῶν τις ἐγὼ καὶ ἡδέων, οἵους ὁρῶ πολλοὺς τῶν νῦν ἱερατεύειν ἐπιθυμούντων, οἳ τὴν ἁπλῆν καὶ ἄτεχνον ἡμῶν εὐσέβειαν ἔντεχνον πεποιήκασι. καὶ αὖθις ἑτέρωθι· παιδευέτω σοι τῇ συμβουλῇ Σολομὼν καὶ τὸ "κρείσσων ἄπορος πορευόμενος ἐν ἁπλότητι αὐτοῦ," μία καὶ αὕτη τῶν παροιμιῶν σοφῶς ἔχουσα. ὁ πένης ἐν λόγῳ καὶ γνώσει, τοῖς [fol. 70^{v}] ἁπλοῖς ῥήμασιν ἐπερειδόμενος καὶ ἐπὶ τούτων ὥσπερ ἐπὶ λεπτῆς σχεδίας διασῳζόμενος, ὑπὲρ στρεβλόχειλον ἄφρονα τὸν ἀποδείξει λόγου θαρροῦντα σὺν ἀμαθίᾳ καὶ κινοῦντα τὸν σταυρὸν τοῦ Χριστοῦ. καὶ ὁ χρυσοῦς τὴν γλῶτταν, οὐδὲν γὰρ χεῖρόν, φησι, τοῦ λογισμοῖς τὰ πνευματικὰ ἐπιτρέπειν. εἰ ταῦτα γνωσιμαχούντων, ἔστω καὶ τοὐμὸν ἐν τοῖς τῶν γνωσιμάχων, ἀγαπῶ γὰρ πάντα τούτοις τοῖς ἀνδράσι συμφέρεσθαι· εἰ δὲ μὴ ταῦτα, οὐκέτ' ἂν ἔχοις εἰπεῖν ἐκεῖνο, οὐδ', ὡς ἔχεις δι' ἔθους, εἴσω με λαβεῖν τῶν συκοφαντιῶν σου ὥσπερ ἰχθῦν δικτύων.

Τά γε μὴν περὶ πνοῆς καὶ τοῦ περὶ τὴν καρδίαν ἑνοῦσθαι νῷ τὴν ψυχὴν καὶ νεὼν εἶναι Θεοῦ τὴν τοῦ πιστοῦ καρδίαν, ἃ πλάνην ἀποκαλεῖς, ἰσχυρίζεσθαι μὲν οὐκ ἔχω περὶ τούτων ὡς ἔχει· ἓν δ' ἐκεῖνο οἶμαι καλῶς ὑπολαμβάνειν, ἀνδρὸς εἶναι ταῦτά τε καὶ ὁ πᾶς σοι περὶ προσευχῆς ὄχλος λόγων περιέργου—πάλιν ἐρῶ—καὶ κακοσχόλου πάνυ καὶ πρόφασιν ἐκ πολλοῦ λαβεῖν ἐοικότος ἐζητηκέναι κατὰ τοῦ θεσπεσίου βίου, καὶ πρώτου γ' ἄν, εἰ κατὰ τοὺς

145–147 Joannes Damascenus, *De haeresibus*, 88 (PG, 94, 757A) ‖ 156–159 Greg. Naz., *Or.*36, 2 (PG, 36, 265C–268A) ‖ 159–167 Greg. Naz., *Or.*32, 26 (PG, 36, 204C) ‖ 160–161 Prov. 28:6 ‖ 167–168 Joan. Chrys., *In Joannem* 24, 3 (PG, 59, 146) ‖ 174 I Cor. 3:16 ‖ 179 Plato, *Respub.*, 365b

---

171 *ἂν ἔχεις* A ‖ 176 ante *εἶναι* erasit *ταῦτά τε* A

10

that these are the words of the *Gnosimachoi* and you produce the great Epiphanios who says: "*Gnosimachoi* are those who oppose all knowledge of Christianity." But that has nothing to do with what I said, anyway. For I do not hinder the seeking of or the writing about the knowledge of Christianity, but doing it in a manner that is meddlesome and insulting to men who walk the road to piety steadily and without questions. And if you were also well aware of all that the great Epiphanios says on this subject, you would not refer everything to human knowledge, because you would be afraid that you might meet with the same condemnation as that other group of heretics, notable in the writings of Epiphanios, received from the holy synods. But if, my excellent friend, I seem to you to be a primary example of a *Gnosimachos*, Gregory (apparently a worse theologian than you) was a *Gnosimachos* before me. For somewhere in his books he makes the well-known statement: "I am not one of those smart and pleasant men, like many whom I see now desiring to become priests, who have rendered artificial our simple and artless faith." And again somewhere else: "Let Solomon teach you by his advice; and the proverb 'A poor man walking in simplicity is better' is another of those wise proverbs. He who is poor in eloquence and knowledge, leaning on plain words and saved by their support, as if by a light raft, stands above a foolish twister of truth who trusts with ignorance in demonstrative syllogisms and disturbs the cross of Christ." And Chrysostom says: "There is nothing worse than committing spiritual truths to syllogisms." If these are the words of *Gnosimachoi*, let my words also be among those of the *Gnosimachoi*, for I love to agree with these men completely. But if not, you can no longer say that, nor can you catch me in your calumnies like a fish inside the nets, as you are accustomed to do.

As for the question of breathing and of the heart uniting the soul with the mind, and the heart of the faithful being "God's temple," which you call a heretical error, I cannot claim any knowledge of these matters. But I think that I am correct in assuming that ⟨all⟩ this, as well as what constitutes the whole multitude of your writings about prayer, is the ⟨work⟩ of a meddlesome man—I will say this again—and of a man who is very mischievous and seems to have found long ago a pretext for inquiring against the «divine life», and, since this was ⟨a life⟩ according to the

10

ἀποστόλους ἦν, τοὺς ἐνθεούς ἐκείνους καὶ τὰ αὐτῶν μακρὰ κωμῳδήσαντος, ὅτε τὸ Πνεῦμα τὸ ἅγιον ἔλεγον ταῖς τῶν πιστῶν ἐγκατοικεῖν καρδίαις καὶ ταῖς ἡμετέραις ἀσθενείαις συμπάσχειν καὶ ὑπὲρ ἡμῶν ἐντυγχάνειν τῷ Πατρὶ στεναγμοῖς ἀλαλήτοις, αὐτὸ τὸ Πνεῦμα ἐπᾴδοντες, καὶ μυρία τοιαῦτα. ὅταν δὲ ζητῇς λόγους οἵ σε ταῦτα πείσουσιν ἐκ τῶν πραγμάτων, πῶς σοι τὰ πράγματα δείξει τις, ὦ πάντα ὑπ' ἀπόδειξιν ἄγων, ὧν τὴν εὑρετικὴν φεύγεις ὁδόν, ἥτις ἐστὶν ὁ κατ' ἐκεῖνα βίος. [fol. 71r] φασὶ γὰρ πάντες οἱ τῶν θείων ἠμμένοι οὐκ εἶναι ἀποχρῶσαν ἀπόδειξιν πρὸς τοὺς μὴ ἁψαμένους, ὥσπερ οὐδὲ γλυκύτητος μέλιτος πρὸς τοὺς μὴ γευσαμένους.

Ἑταῖρον δὲ πολλάκις ἐμὸν ἀποκαλῶν Παλαμᾶν, ἐνδείκνυσαι μὲν ὅτι διὰ τὴν πρὸς ἐκεῖνον ταῦτα φιλίαν λέγω, ἁμαρτάνεις δὲ τῆς ἐμῆς διανοίας· μᾶλλον δὲ εὐγνωμονεῖν οὐ βούλει, ὃς οἶσθά με ὑπὲρ σαυτοῦ πολλάκις ἀντιταχθέντα ἐκείνῳ καὶ οὐχ ἡδὺν φανέντα. ὁμοίως γὰρ κακίζω καὶ τὰς ἐκείνου κατὰ σοῦ φιλονείκους στρατείας, τάς γε πρὸ τῶν περὶ προσευχῆς καὶ τῶν ἐνταῦθα πλάνων, καὶ τὰς σὰς κατ' ἐκείνου· κἀκείνου τὸν ἄκτιστον θεὸν ἢ θεότητα παρὰ τὴν θείαν φύσιν καὶ καθ' αὑτὸν ὁρατὸν καὶ ὑφειμένον αὐτῆς—εἰ τοῦτ' ἀποφαίνεται—καί σου τὸ κτιστὸν τῆς θεουργοῦ χάριτος—εἰ καὶ σὺ τοῦτο λέγεις—τὴν καινὴν καὶ ἀήθη θεολογίαν ἡμῖν καὶ πλέον ἢ καλῶς ἔχει σοφιζομένην καὶ νεανιευομένην τὰ μὴ προσήκοντα. οὔτοι γὰρ ἡμῖν ἐνθάδε τὰ ὑμέτερα προσκυνητέον, ἀλλὰ τὰς θείας τῶν θεολόγων φωνάς, οὐδ' ὅλως τινὸς ἀνεκτέον περὶ τὴν εὐσέβειαν καινοφωνίας, ἀλλὰ τῆς τῶν πατέρων μόνης ἑκτέον ὁμοφωνίας. τίς οὖν τῶν πώποτε θεολογηκότων ταῦτ' εἰπεῖν ἀπετόλμησεν; ὥστ', εἰ σὺ διὰ τοῦτο Κύριλλος, ὡς ἀπεκόμπασας, πρὸς ἐκεῖνον Νεστόριον, ἢ ὁστισοῦν ὁντινοῦν εὐσεβὴς οὐ τοιοῦτον, κἀκεῖνος πρὸς σὲ διὰ θάτερον, καὶ ἡμεῖς πρὸς ἑκάτερον δι' ἑκάτερον.

Πρόσωπα δὲ μὴ χρῆναι λέγων ἡμᾶς ἐξετάζειν οὐδὲ τὸν ἑκάστου τῶν θεολόγων ἢ διδασκάλων βίον, ἀλλ' ἁπλῶς ἅττα λέγοιεν, οὐκ ὀρθῶς ἡμῖν ὑπολαμβάνῃ λέγειν. διατί; ὅτι καὶ ταῦτα χαρίσματα πνεύματός ἐστί τε δήπου καὶ λέγεται. ὁ δὲ μὴ κατὰ τὸ φρόνημα βιοὺς τὸ τοῦ πνεύματος, [fol. 71v] κατὰ δὲ τὸ τῆς σαρκός, οὐκ ἂν ἔχοι τὸ πνεῦμα ἐν ἑαυτῷ τοῦ Θεοῦ— οὐ μή, γάρ φησι, καταμείνῃ τὸ πνεῦμά μου ἐν τοῖς ἀνθρώποις τούτοις

181–182 I Cor. 3:16 || 182–184 Rom. 8:26 || 212–213 cf. Rom. 8:5–9 || 214–216 Genesis 6:4

204 ἐκτέον A

10

Apostles, he would be the first man indeed to have ridiculed at great length those God-inspired men and their ⟨sayings⟩, when, in praising the Spirit itself, they said that the Holy Spirit "dwells in" the hearts of the faithful and suffers with "our weaknesses" and "through our inarticulate groans pleads for us" with the Father, and innumerable such sayings. But when you seek words that will persuade you from the facts, how can one show you the facts—O my friend, you who subject everything to demonstration!—when you avoid the road that leads to the facts, which is life in accordance with the facts. For all those who engage in divine pursuits say that there is no sufficient demonstration for those who do not engage in them, just as there is no sweetness of honey for those who did not taste it.

And when you often call Palamas a friend of mine, you imply that I say these things because of my friendship for him, but you fail to understand my thinking. Or rather you do not wish to be fair, because you know that I often opposed him for your sake and was unpleasant to him. For I reproach equally his contentious campaigns against you (those preceding the matter of prayer and the errors in question) and yours against him; both his uncreated god or divinity next to the divine nature and lower than it and visible in itself (if that is what he says), and your theory that the divine grace is created (if you, too, say this), which to me are a new and strange theology that devises and insolently attempts what is not fitting, beyond the limits of propriety. For it is not indeed my duty here to venerate your theories, but to venerate the divine pronouncements of the theologians, nor ⟨is it my duty⟩ to tolerate at all any newfangled talk about piety, but to hold to the agreement of the Fathers alone. Really, which one of the theologians ever dared say these things? And so, if for this reason, as you boasted, you are in relation to him as Cyril is to Nestorios, or as any pious man is to an impious one, he too is Cyril to you for the other reason, and I am Cyril to both of you for both reasons.

And when you say that I should examine neither the character nor the life of each theologian or teacher, but simply what they say, I believe that you are not correct. Why? Because, in fact, these too both are and are called gifts of the Spirit. For he "who does not live according to the outlook of the Spirit, but according to that of the flesh" would not have the Spirit of God in him, for He says: "My spirit shall certainly not remain among these men forever because they are flesh"; indeed not

10

διὰ τὸ εἶναι αὐτοὺς σάρκας—οὐδὲ δὴ χρῖσμα πνεύματος, χρῖσμα δὲ λέγω πνεύματος ὃ δίδοται ζωῆς καθαρότητι. πῶς οὖν ἂν εἴποι τὰ περὶ τοῦ πνεύματος ὁ μὴ τοῦ πνεύματος; πῶς ὁ μὴ Θεοῦ τὰ θεῖα; οἱ δὲ τοῦ Θεοῦ τὴν σάρκα ἐσταύρωσαν σὺν τοῖς παθήμασι καὶ ταῖς ἐπιθυμίαις· ἧπου κομιδῇ καὶ αὐτὸς ἐβουλόμην οὕτως ἁλωτὰ εἶναι τοῖς ἀνθρώποις τὰ θεῖα, ἐπείπερ εἰμὶ τῶν χθαμαλῶς βιούντων· ἀλλ' οὔτε τῶν ὑμετέρων οὐδείς πω νοῦν γέ τινα ἔχων ἄνευ καθαρότητος βίου διδασκαλίαν καθαροῦ συνεγράψατο βίου, ἢ περὶ θεολογίας ἐπήρθη καὶ θεωρίας λέγειν. καὶ τάς γε κατὰ τῶν ταῦτα τετολμηκότων ἐπιτιμήσεις τοῖς ἁγίοις κειμένας μακρὸν ἂν εἴη λέγειν καὶ πέρα τῆς παρούσης προθυμίας τοῦ λόγου.

Ὁ σός τε Πλάτων οὐκ ἀσύμφωνα τούτοις φαίνεται νομοθετήσας—ἄλλως τε τίς τῇδε τῶν ἡμετέρων χρεία, ὁπότε Πλάτων φαίνεται τοιαῦτα καὶ νομίζων καὶ λέγων περί γε ἀρετῆς καὶ τοῦ δι' ἔργων βίου, ὁ σπινθὴρ τῆς ἀρετῆς πρὸς τοὺς πυρσοὺς ἐκείνους; οὗ γάρ τις ἧττον ὁρῶν εἶδέ τι καὶ τοῖς ἄλλοις κατέδειξεν, ἐκεῖνον ἔδειξε καὶ μὴ δεικνύντα μᾶλλον ἂν καταδείξαντα, οὗ δῆλός ἐστιν οὗτος ἧττον ὀξυδορκίας ἔχων—Πλάτων τοίνυν τοὺς ποιητὰς τῷ λόγῳ καὶ στρατηγὸν Ὅμηρόν, φησι, τῆς ἑαυτοῦ πολιτείας ἀπήλασε, ἑνὸς δὴ τούτου χάριν, ὅτι μιμηταὶ μόνον εἶεν τῷ λόγῳ καὶ σκηνεργάται, οὐκ ἐπιστήμονες τῶν σπουδαίων πραγμάτων, εὖ μὲν λέγειν δυνάμενοι, πράττοντες δὲ οὐδὲν ὧν λέγοιεν ἄξιον· οὕτω γε δήπου δέον εἰς ἐπιστήμην ἐλθεῖν. καί φησιν ἐν Τιμαίῳ· δοκεῖ δὲ ῥᾷον [fol. 72r] εἶναι μιμεῖσθαι τοὺς λόγους ἢ τὰ ἔργα. σοφιστεύουσι γοῦν οὐκ ὀλίγοι μέν, λόγου τὴν ἀρετὴν ἐπιδεικνύμενοι, ἔργῳ δ' αὐτῆς παντάπασιν ἀπῳκισμένοι. ἔτι καὶ Πρόκλος ὁ τούτου ἐξηγητὴς τῶν λόγων, ἡ μίμησίς, φησι, τῆς τοιαύτης πολιτείας διὰ ζωῆς πρόεισι συμφωνούσης τοῖς παραδείγμασι· τοὺς γὰρ πρέποντας τοῖς σπουδαίοις λόγους οὐ δύναται ἀποδιδόναι ὁ μὴ ζῶν κατ' ἀρετήν. φασὶ δὲ καὶ Διογένην ἰδόντα τινὰ τῶν σπουδαίων ψαλτήριον ἁρμοζόμενον, οὐκ αἰσχύνῃ, φάναι πρὸς αὐτόν, τοὺς μὲν φθόγγους τῷ ξύλῳ προσαρμόττων, τὴν δὲ ψυχὴν εἰς βίον ἐπαινετὸν οὐχ

216–217 I Joan. 2:20 || 219–220 cf. Gal. 5:24 || 225–226 cf. Greg. Naz., *Or.* 27, 3 (PG, 36, 13 C–D) || 234–237 cf. Platonem, *Respub.*, 600e; 606e–608b || 235 Plato, *Theaet.*, 153a || 239–243 Proclus, *Commentarius in Platonis Timaeum*, 20f–21a || 243–247 Proclus, *Commentarius in Platonis Timaeum*, 21c || 248–251 Diogenes Laertius, *De clarorum philosophorum vitis*, VI², 65

---

216 et 217 χρίσμα A || 220 κομιδὴ A || 221 ἁλωτὰ scripsi: ἄωτα A || 222 ἡμετέρων A

10

even the "anointing of the Spirit," and I mean by anointing of the Spirit what is granted by purity of life. How then can a man who is not a man of the Spirit speak of spiritual matters and he who is not a man of God speak of divine matters? "And those who belong to God have crucified the flesh with its passions and desires." Certainly, I too wished altogether that divine things were accessible to men in that manner, since I belong to those who lead a base life. But none of your men who had any intelligence ever wrote any instructions for virtuous life, nor was he roused into speaking of theology or contemplation without a virtuous life. And it would be long and beyond the intent of the letter to mention the censures ordained by the Saints against those who have dared these things.

And your own Plato seems to have enacted laws which are not at variance with these. Besides, why do we need the Fathers here, when Plato, the spark of virtue compared with those torches, seems both to believe and to say such things about virtue and life by deeds? For if a man who sees less than someone else saw something and showed it to others, he proved that the man who is obviously more sharp-sighted than he could have shown the same thing better, even if he does not. Plato, then, expelled from his state the poets and Homer, whom he calls their "leader," for the very reason that they are only imitators by means of words and stage actors, not experts in important matters. They are able to express themselves well, but do nothing worthy of what they say. For, doubtless, this is how one must attain knowledge. And he says in the *Timaeus*: "It seems easier to imitate words than deeds. For instance, not a few men argue like sophists, showing off their excellence of speech, but in fact they are altogether removed from excellence." And Proclus, the commentator on his works, says also: "The imitation of such a way of life proceeds through a life which is in harmony with the examples. For he who does not lead a virtuous life cannot say what becomes excellent men." And they say that when Diogenes too saw one of the important men tune a harp, he said to him: "Are you not ashamed of adjusting the strings to the wood and not the soul to a commend-

10

ἁρμόττων; καὶ πάλιν τοὺς λέγοντας μὲν τὰ σπουδαῖα, μὴ πράττοντας δέ, μηδὲν διαφέρειν κιθάρας, λέγειν, καὶ γὰρ αὐτὴν μήτε ἀκούειν μήτε αἰσθάνεσθαι, φθέγγεσθαι δ' ὅμως πρὸς ἃ κινοῖτο τῷ κιθαρίζοντι· ἐρωτώμενον δὲ διατί βίον μὴ μέτριον ἀλλὰ τραχὺν ἄγαν ἕλοιτο, μιμεῖσθαι τοὺς χοροδιδασκάλους, καὶ γὰρ ἐκείνους ὑπὲρ τὸν τόνον ἐνδιδόναι ἕνεκα τοῦ τοὺς λοιποὺς ἅψασθαι τοῦ προσήκοντος τόνου. τοῦτο τὸ φρόνημα καὶ τόνδε τὸν βίον ἔδει πάντα ἔχειν τὸν ἀρετῆς εἶναι διδάσκαλον ἐπιχειροῦντα. καὶ Πολέμων δὲ ὁ φιλόσοφος ἔλεγε δεῖν ἐν τοῖς πράγμασι γυμνάζεσθαι καὶ μὴ ἐν τοῖς διαλεκτικοῖς θεωρήμασι φάσκειν, καθάπερ ἁρμονικόν τι τεχνίον καταμαθόντα καὶ μελετήσαντα, ὡς κατὰ μὲν τὰς ἐρωτήσεις θαυμάζεσθαι, κατὰ δὲ τὴν διάθεσιν ἑαυτοῖς διαμάχεσθαι.

Ἆρ' οὖν ἡμῖν ⟨ἂν⟩ παρήνεις, εἰ ταῦτα ᾔδεις καλῶς, ὦ πάντων ὑπερφρονῶν ἐπὶ Πλάτωνι καὶ τοῖς ὁμοίοις τῷ Πλάτωνι, μὴ τὸν βίον ἐξετάζειν τῶν εἰς θεολογίαν ἢ λόγους ἀρετῆς ἀφηκότων ἀνέδην καὶ πάντας πειρωμένων τοὺς μὲν ἀρχὴν διδάσκειν, τοὺς δὲ μεταδιδάσκειν ταῦτα [fol. 72ᵛ] δολιχοσκίοις λόγοις, ὡς ἂν Ὅμηρος εἶπε; καὶ πῶς ἂν ἐτίμας, εἰ μὴ τοὺς θείους νόμους, ἀλλὰ τοὺς Πλάτωνος; ἔτι παντὸς πατρὸς βιβλίου τὸν βίον ὁρῶμεν προγεγραμμένον τοῦ πατρὸς τοῦ βιβλίου, καὶ οὗτος ὁ νόμος φαίνεται διὰ πάντων ὁδεύων. τί οὖν ἄν τις προγράφοι τῶν περὶ θείων πραγμάτων καὶ τῶν ἄκρων ἀρετῶν ὑπερφιλοσοφούντων λόγων, ἄνπερ οὐκ ἔχῃ βίον ὁ γεννήσας τοὺς λόγους κατὰ τοὺς παῖδας λόγους; οὐδὲν οὐδαμῶς; ἀλλ' οὐ σύνηθες. ἀλλ' ἃ πεπολίτευται; ἀλλ' οὐκ εὐπρεπές, οὐδὲ πρὸς τοῦ πείθεσθαι τοῖς λόγοις τοὺς τούτοις συνεσομένους· καὶ οὕτω μάτην συμβήσεται τῷ σφᾶς συντεθεικότι πεποιηκέναι τούτους, εἴπερ οὐδεὶς αὐτοῖς πείσεται. οὐκ ἄρα τῶν ἄνευ σπουδαίων ἔργων ὁδὸν δεικνύναι τῆς κατ' ἀρετὴν ὀρθότητος ἀποθρασυνομένων, ἢ Θεοῦ τὰ τοῦ Θεοῦ διδάσκειν, εὐπειθῶς ἀνεκτέον, κἂν πᾶσι δοκῶσι συνᾴδειν τοῖς ἱεροῖς ἀνδράσι, κἂν λέγειν τὰ ἀσφαλέστατα, εἴ γε ταῦτά τε οὕτως ἔχει καὶ διὰ ζωῆς καθαρᾶς περιγίνεται τὸ καθαρῶς περὶ τῶν καθαρῶν τι λέγειν. δεῖ γάρ, οἶμαι, παθεῖν τὰ θεῖα—τοῦτο δὲ διὰ ζωῆς μὲν ἱερᾶς ἀναγκαῖον, ἄλλως δὲ ἀδύνατον φαίνεται—καὶ παθόντα μαθεῖν, τοῦτο δὲ τὸ μάθημα τέλειον, καὶ οὕτω τινὰ θαρρεῖν

251–254 Diogenes Laertius, *ibid.*, 64 || 256–258 Diogenes Laertius, *ibid.*, 35 || 260–265 Diogenes Laertius, *ibid.*, IV³, 18 || 270 Homerus, *Il.*, 3, 346

---

257 λιποὺς A || 260 ἐλέγεσται A || 262 τέχνιον A || 266 ⟨ἂν⟩ addidi || 268 ἀφεικότων A

10

able life?" And again, he said that "Those who say excellent things but do not practice them do not differ at all from a lyre, because it too neither hears nor feels but utters sounds as stirred by the player." And when he was asked why he did not choose a moderate instead of an exceedingly harsh life, he answered that "He imitated the chorus trainers, for they also give the keynote above the key, so that the rest will be in the proper key." Every man who attempts to be a teacher of virtue ought to have this outlook and this way of life. And Polemon the philosopher used to say that "Men ought to be trained in deeds and not in arguing over dialectical propositions, so that they are admired in questioning, while in disposition they fight against one another, just like someone who studied and learned a musical art."

If then you were well aware of these things, O you who scorn everybody because of Plato and men like Plato, would you have urged me not to examine the life of those who have freely arrived at a knowledge of theology or ethics and attempt to teach everybody, some from the beginning and others by conversion, using "long words," as Homer would have said? And how would you have honored, if not the sacred laws, at least those of Plato? Besides, we see the biography of every author of a book written at the beginning of his book, and this law seems to apply to every book. What, then, would one write at the beginning of works which deal above all with divine matters and supreme virtues, if the author of the works does not have a life that accords with the works he fathered? Nothing at all? But that is not normal. What, then, his deeds? But they are neither decent nor will they induce those who will study his works to believe them. And if indeed none will believe them, the author will have composed them in vain. If, in fact, this is so, and if saying something with purity about pure things is the result of a pure life, we must not readily tolerate those who without good works dare to show the way to true virtue or teach the men of God about God, even if they seem to agree with all the holy men and say the most correct things. For, in my opinion, a man must experience things divine—and that, of necessity, is attained through a holy life, otherwise it appears to be impossible—and so, after he has learnt from experience (and this is the perfect lesson), he should have the courage to reveal what he has experienced, not pride him-

ἐκφαίνειν ἃ πέπονθεν, οὐκ ἀφ᾿ ὧν ἄλλοι λέγουσι πεπονθότες ἃ λέγουσι, μὴ παθόντα σεμνύνεσθαι· τοῦτο γάρ ἐστιν ἄλλων νήχεσθαι λόγοις, κατὰ τὸν Σολομῶντα. μήτ᾿ οὖν ἐμὲ δοκεῖ μοι, τὸν ἐν τοῖς φαυλοτάτοις, μήτε σὲ τὸν πολὺ μὲν ἢ κατ᾿ ἐμὲ βελτίω, πλέον δὲ τῶν θείων ἀνδρῶν ἐκείνων ἀπολειπόμενον, οὓς εὖ μιμῇ τῷ περὶ τῶν ἐκείνοις μόνοις καὶ τοῖς αὐτοῖς ὁμοίοις ἐπιβαλλόντων λέγειν, μήτε ἄλλον τοιοῦτον ἐπαινετέον τολμῶντα λέγειν καὶ θρασυνόμενον ἃ μὴ προσῆκεν αὐτῷ, καὶ τοὺς αὐτοῦ θειοτέρους ἐπανορθοῦσθαι πειρώμενον, πρὶν εἰς τὴν ἐκείνων ἀρετὴν ἀφικέσθαι.

[fol. 73r] Εἰ τοίνυν ἐπιθυμεῖς, Βαρλαάμ, κἀνταῦθα εὐδοκιμῆσαι καὶ δόξαι μέγας ἁπανταχοῦ καὶ θαῦμα, ἐπὶ τὸν βίον ἴθι ὧν τοὺς λόγους θαυμάζεις, καὶ τοῖς σαυτοῦ μαρτύρει, κἀμὲ τὸν φίλον συμπαραλάμβανε· κἂν δράμωμεν κατ᾿ ἐκείνους, ἢ ἐκείνων ἐγγύς που, καὶ τὴν ὁμίχλην τῶν παθῶν ὑπερβῶμεν, καὶ ταῖς ἀκτῖσιν ἐντύχωμεν ἐκεῖ που τοῦ ἀκηράτου φωτός, τότ᾿ ἐγὼ μὲν ὀλίγην ὄψιν τῆς διανοίας ἔχων, κατ᾿ ἐκείνην καὶ τεύξομαι τῆς ἐκεῖ φωταυγείας, καὶ οὐδὲν ἔσται μέγα· σὺ δ᾿ ὁ Λυγκεὺς εἰπέ μοι πόσης μὲν ἐμπλησθῆναι, πόσης δ᾿ ἐμπλῆσαι τοὺς ἄλλους, πόσον δὲ καὶ παρὰ πόσοις εὐδοκιμήσειν δοκεῖς, ἃ νῦν σαυτὸν εὖ μὲν νοεῖν, εὖ δὲ καὶ λέγειν πείθεις, τότε καὶ πάντας πείθων, οἷς νῦν ταῦτα οὐ πιθανὸς εἶ λέγων· καὶ τότ᾿ ἂν ἐκείνην εἴης νενικηκὼς τὴν νίκην ἣν σὺ μὲν ἤδη νενικηκέναι λέγεις, ἐμοὶ δὲ οὔπω νενικηκέναι δοκεῖς. οὔτ᾿ ἂν ἴσως ἐμὲ σὺ περιττῆς ἀφροσύνης ἔτι τότε διώκοις, ἐγώ τέ σε τῆς ἐν τῷ στήθει σοφίας ἀγαίμην καὶ τῆς φρονήσεως· ὡς νῦν γε πείθομαι μέν σοι τῶν ἀφρόνων τις εἶναι, οὐ μὴν οὐδέ σε δύναμαί πω πεισθῆναι τῶν φρονίμων ἡγεῖσθαι, ἕως ἄν με μή, τοὺς πολλοὺς ἀφεὶς τοὺς ἐκ γλώττης διαύλους, δι᾿ ὧν ἐργάζῃ πείθῃς, ἐκ τῶν λογίων πεισθεὶς τῶν τε ἄλλων κἀκείνου, εἴ τις σοφὸς καὶ ἐπιστήμων ἐν ὑμῖν δειξάτω ἐκ τῆς καλῆς ἀναστροςῆς αὐτοῦ, τὴν δὲ καλὴν ἐνταῦθα μὴ τὴν παρ᾿ ἡμῖν τοιαύτην, ἀλλὰ τὴν παρ᾿ ἐκείνοις νόει.

Ταῦτα αὖ πάλιν λέγοντες, Ἡράκλεις—εἰ δὲ βούλει, καὶ Ἄπολλον—εἰ μὴ εὐδοκιμοῖμεν παρὰ τῇ σῇ σοφίᾳ, οὐδ᾿ ἡμῖν τοῦτο προὔργου. καίτοι λέγεις μὲν οὐκέτ᾿ ἀξιοῦν πείθεσθαί μοι, πρῴην ὁμολογήσας ὁπωσοῦν μοι πεπεῖσθαι, τοῦτο δὲ ποιεῖν μὴ νομισθῇς τοῖς ἐμοῖς τοῦ μηδαμοῦ μηδενὸς καταπεισθῆναι λόγοις ὁ τελεώτατος, οὐχ ὅτι κακῶς ἐπείσθης. [fol. 73v] οὕτω τοῦ καλοῦ πάντα χάριν

289–290 Job 11:12 ‖ 315–316 Jac. 3:13

---

290 *τῶν ἐν τοῖς* A ‖ 292 *τῷ* coni. Ševčenko: *τὸ περὶ τῶν* A ‖ 299 *μαρτύρῃ* A ‖ 301 *ἀκτίσιν* A ‖ 317 post Ἡράκλεις in margine *ὀνειδιστικῶς κεῖται ἡ λέξις πρὸς τὸν Βαρλαάμ, ἐκεῖνος γὰρ εἶπεν αὐτὴν πρὸς τὸν πατέρα τοῦδε τοῦ λόγου γράφων* scripsit A

10

self, without experience, on what others say who speak from experience. For, as Solomon said, this is "To buoy oneself with words of others." It seems to me, therefore, that neither I who belong among the most common men, nor you who are much better than I (but rather inferior to those divine men whom you imitate well by speaking about matters which are appropriate only to them and their peers) nor is any other such man to be commended who has the boldness and arrogance to say what was inappropriate to him, and attempts to correct those who are holier than he before he achieves their virtue.

If, therefore, you desire, Barlaam, both to succeed here and to appear great and admirable everywhere, follow the life of those whose words you admire and bear witness to your own, and take me, your friend, with you. And if we run towards them or somewhere near them and go beyond the mist of passions, and somewhere over there encounter the rays of the undefiled light, then I who have little intellectual vision will, in accordance with this, of course, attain the brightness of the light there, and this will not be much. But you the ⟨sharpsighted⟩ Lynceus, tell me with how much light you think that you will fill yourself, and how much others, and how much and by how many you will be respected, for then you will persuade everybody about the things which now you persuade yourself that you understand and say correctly, but do not persuade others when you say them now. And then you will have won that victory which you now say that you have won, but which you do not seem to me to have won yet. Neither, perhaps, would you still accuse me then of excessive foolishness, and I would admire you for your wisdom and prudence. For now, of course, I agree with you that I am foolish, but truly I cannot yet be persuaded to consider you sensible, as long as you do not persuade me by your acts, having abandoned all those verbal contests and having ⟨yourself⟩ been persuaded by the scriptural sayings, amongst others the following: "If one is wise and clever among you, let his good conduct give practical proof of it." And do not take "good" here to mean *our* conduct, but theirs.

If, again, when I say this, O Heracles (or Apollo, if you wish), I do not gain the approval of your wisdom, that is not important to me either. And, indeed, you say that you do not consider it worthwhile anymore to be persuaded by me) though you acknowledged recently that you had been somewhat persuaded by me), and that you do this not because you were wrongly persuaded, but lest it be thought that you, the Most-perfect-one, were persuaded by the arguments of mine, I who am a person of no account. This is how my philosopher does and says everything for the sake of

ἡμῖν ὁ φιλόσοφος καὶ φθέγγεται καὶ πράττει. δοκεῖς δὲ τοῦτο τοὔπος ἔρχεσθαι νομίζειν εἰς τὴν ἐμὴν ἀνίαν. ἐμὲ δὲ εἰ ῥᾳδίως τὰ τοιαῦτα ἐλύπει, πάλαι ἂν ἀπολώλειν· οὕτως εἰμὶ συνήθης ἀποτυγχάνειν, πολλοὺς μὲν πολλάκις ἐπιχειρήσας πεῖσαι, ὀλίγους δὲ καταπείσας, καὶ τούτους τῶν οὐκ ἐν λόγῳ, ὥστε μὴ πάνυ τό γ' ἐπὶ τούτῳ θάρρει. ὡς δὲ καὶ ὅταν, ἃ γέγραφά σοι περὶ τοῦ μὴ δεῖν ταῦτα ποιεῖν καὶ γράφειν ἐφ' ὁσίοις ἀνδράσι καὶ πράγματα ἐγείρειν τυφωνικὰ ἐν μέσῃ τῇ ἐκκλησίᾳ γαλήνην ἀγούσῃ θεοχορήγητον, ταῦτα διώκῃς ἀωρίας καὶ τύφου, ὀλίγα λύπῃ χαρίζομαι, ἐκεῖνο σαφῶς εἰδὼς ὅτι πᾶς ὁ στέργειν ἐθέλων τοῖς ἑαυτοῦ λογισμοῖς σκαιοὺς ἡγεῖται τοὺς ἀντιπίπτοντας. οὕτως καὶ Ἄρειος μὲν εἶχε πρὸς τοὺς Ἀθανασίου τοῦ μεγάλου καὶ θείου, Εὐνόμιος δὲ πρὸς τοὺς τοῦ μεγάλου καὶ σοφοῦ Βασιλείου, Νεστόριος δὲ ⟨πρὸς⟩ τοὺς τοῦ θείου Κυρίλλου, καὶ ἄλλοι πρὸς ἄλλους, καὶ πάντες πρὸς ἅπαντας οἱ τῶν οἰκείων περιεχόμενοι τοὺς ἐναντιουμένους. τὸ δὲ κοινὸν οὐ κομιδῇ τοι λυπεῖ, ἄλλως θ' ὅταν τις τὸ κοινόν, αὐτὸς ὢν οἷος ἐγώ, πρὸς τοὺς τοιούτους ἔχῃ. καὶ μὴν εἴ μοι καλῶς ἐπείσθης, κακῶς νῦν μετεπείσθης, καὶ ποῦ τὸ φιλόσοφον; εἰ δὲ μὴ οὕτως, οὐκ ἦσθα χθὲς ὑγιής. πῶς οὖν τἆλλα πάνθ' ἡμῖν ὁ Βαρλαὰμ ὑγιής; ἔστω δὲ ὑγιὴς ἐμοῦ χάριν, κἀγὼ τούτῳ πεισθείην ἐκ τῶν παραγμάτων, οὐκ ἐξ ὧν συλλογίζεται λόγων, εἰ δόξης ἁμαρτάνω.

11. Τῷ Παλαμᾷ

Τὰ μὲν ἐμοὶ σπουδασθέντα ὑπὲρ τῆς σῆς ἱερότητος καὶ πρὸς τοὺς ἀρχιερεῖς καὶ πρὸς τὸν διώκοντα οὐκ ἀναγκαῖον ᾠήθην παρ' ἐμοῦ σε πυθέσθαι, πολλοὶ [fol. 74r] γὰρ ἄλλοι ὧν οἱ μὲν ἤδη ταῦθ' ὑμᾶς ἐδίδαξαν, οἱ δὲ μέλλουσιν. ἔστιν οὖν ἐκείνων τῶν σπουδασμάτων καὶ τὸ παρόν, προλαβόντων τῶν δοκεῖν ἐμοὶ λυπηρῶν πρὸς τὴν θειότητά σου πατριαρχικῶν γραμμάτων, εἰς τὴν σὴν θεραπείαν ἐπιγενόμενον.

Ἣν δέ μοι μεγάλην ἐπιστολὴν καὶ γενναίαν ἀπέστειλας, πάλαι μὲν ἦν ἐνταῦθα, οὐ πρὶν δὲ εἰς τὰς ἐμὰς ἧκε χεῖρας ἢ καὶ τὰ δεύτερα γεγράφθαι πατριαρχικὰ ταῦτα γράμματα. διελθὼν δὴ ταύτην ἐπιστατικῶς καὶ πάνυ θαυμαστικῶς, εἰ μὲν μὴ προσεδόκων ὀφθήσεσθαί μοι μετ' οὐ πολὺ τὴν ἐμὴν κεφαλήν σου, ἀπέδωκα ἂν σοι τὸν δυνατόν μοι λόγον πρὸς τὰ ἐπεσταλμένα· ἐπεὶ δέ σε ἀνάγκη

---

336 ‹*πρὸς*› addidi ‖ 342 *τοῦτο* A

11: A 73v–74r.

7 *θειότητα ραπείαν* scripsit et deinde *ιότητα* delevit A

what is good! And you seem to think that this statement is going to annoy me; but if I were easily distressed by such things, I would have been destroyed long ago. This is how accustomed I am to failure. For I attempted to persuade many men on many occasions, but I persuaded few, and they were not among the important. Therefore, do not be too confident about annoying me at least. Moreover, I feel little annoyance when you accuse of untimeliness and arrogance the things which I wrote to you, namely, that you should not do and write these things against holy men and raise a tempest in the midst of the Church which is enjoying God-given serenity. ⟨I feel little annoyance⟩ because I am clearly aware of the fact that everyone who wishes to favor his own arguments considers those who oppose him inept. This is how Arios felt about the arguments of the great and divine Athanasios, and Eunomios about those of the great and wise Basil, and Nestorios about those of the divine Cyril, and others about others, and all who defend their own about all who oppose them. And certainly the association does not distress me at all, especially when someone like me has something in common with such men. And, besides, if you had been well persuaded by me, you were wrong to change your mind now, and where is your philosophical training! But if not so, you were not well yesterday! How, then, is my Barlaam well in every other way? But let him be well for my sake, and if I am wrong, may he persuade me from facts, not from what he infers syllogistically.

11. To Palamas

I did not think it necessary that you should learn from me about my efforts before the bishops and the prosecutor in the interest of your Holiness. For there are many others, some of whom have already informed you about this, others of whom are about to do so. The present letter, then, is also part of those efforts. It was produced afterwards, as a service to you, because the patriarchal letter to your Holiness, which seems to me distressing, was written previously.

As for the long and excellent letter that you sent me, it has been here for some time; but it did not reach my hands before this second patriarchal letter was also written. I read it with attention and great admiration, and if I did not expect to see your dear face before long, I would have replied to what you write to the best of my ability. But since it is absolutely necessary for you to come here, I shall make clear

πᾶσα παρ' ἡμᾶς ἀφικέσθαι, τότε δή σοι σαφὴς ἡ περὶ τούτων ἡμετέρα καταστήσεται γνώμη. ἴθι δὴ μετὰ τῆς ὑπερφώτου Τριάδος τοῦ ἀπροσίτου φωτός, θεοφιλέστατε πάτερ καὶ σοφώτατε καὶ ἡμῖν ποθεινότατε.

12. Δαυὶδ τῷ Δισυπάτῳ

Ἧκεν εἰς ἡμᾶς φήμη Σκυθῶν θαυμαστὴ καὶ ταῖς πώποτε τῶν ἐκείνων ἐπὶ Ῥωμαίους ἐφόδων ἀνόμοιος, μᾶλλον δὲ οὐδὲ φήμη, ἀλλὰ γράμματα τῆς βασιλέως μὲν θυγατρός, γυναικὸς δὲ τοῦ Σκύθου. λέγει δὴ τὰ γράμματα οὕτω καθ' ἡμῶν παρωξύνθαι καὶ μανῆναι τὸν βάρβαρον, ὡς ἐφ' ἡμᾶς Σκυθῶν ἓξ μυριάδας τὸ παρὸν ἀφιέναι οὓς ἤδη σπεύδειν διαβαίνειν τὸν Ἴστρον, οὐχ ᾗ πρότερον ἐπιόντας τὴν Θρᾴκην, οὐδ' ὃ πρὸ αὐτῶν εὕροιεν ῥᾴδιον λαβεῖν λαβόντας εἶθ' ὑποστρέψοντας οἴκαδε, ἀλλὰ μεθ' ἑλεπόλεων μηχανημάτων κατὰ τῶν ἐρυμάτων· ἃ δὴ πολιορκοῦντας ἐν τριῶν μηνῶν χρόνῳ τοὺς ἑξάκις μυρίους, ἐπελθόντων ἑτέρων τοσούτων ἐπ' ἐκδοχῇ τοῦ ἔργου, τούτους ἀναχωρεῖν μεθ' ὧν αὐτοὶ λαφύρων συλλάβοιεν, κἀκείνους αὖθις ἑτέροις ἐπιοῦσι μετὰ τοσοῦτον χρόνον [fol. 74v] ἐκστῆναι τῆς μάχης καὶ τῆς πολιορκίας, καὶ οὕτω συνεχῶς ποιεῖν παρεσκευάσθαι τὸν βάρβαρον, ἕως ἂν ἐκτρίψῃ καὶ καταστρέψηται καὶ ὅλως ὑφ' ἑαυτῷ ποιήσηται τὰ Ῥωμαίων πράγματα, οὐ πρὶν ἀποστησόμενον ἢ ταῦτα οὕτως ἰδεῖν ἐξειργασμένα. σφόδρα δὲ ταῦτα τὰ γράμματα ἰσχυρίζεται καὶ δείκνυσι δεδοικυῖαν τὴν γράψασαν μή, οὐ πάνυ πιστεύσαντες οἱ Ῥωμαῖοι τοῖς γράμμασιν, ἐξαίφνης ἀναρπασθῶσιν.

Ἡμέτερον οὖν ὃν ταῦτα ὑμῖν μηνῦσαι, ὑμέτερον περὶ ὑμῶν αὐτῶν σὺν Θεῷ τὸ ἀσφαλὲς ἐπισκέψασθαι. Δοκεῖ δὲ ἡμῖν οὐκ εἶναι κρεῖττον ὑμῖν ἢ παρ' ἡμᾶς ἀφῖχθαι, ἔνθα κοινῇ σκεψάμενοι τὸ ποιητέον μετὰ τοῦ κοινοῦ τῆς ἀγάπης συνδέσμου, τῷ παραστάντι ἑψόμεθα, κἂν δόξῃ δὴ μετανίστασθαι, οὐ δυσχερὲς μεταβαίνειν ἐντεῦθεν ὅποιπερ ἂν θελήσαιμεν· ἀεὶ δειλίαν γὰρ ἐγνωκώς, εἰ οὕτω χρὴ φάναι, πρὸς τὴν θάλατταν ἔχειν καὶ πόλεμον ἄσπονδον, ὡς οἶσθα σὺ πάντων μάλιστα, σπείσομαι νῦν πρὸς αὐτήν. ἦ τί πείσομαι, εἴ μέλλοι πάντως τὰ Σκυθικὰ κύματα πέρα ἐλαύνειν Ἴστρου καὶ τοῦ Τανάϊδος, δουλείαν δουλεύοντα ἣν οὐκ ἂν δυνηθείην, εἰ μὴ

12: A 74r–75r. Ed. Laurent, "L'assaut avorté," 157–60.

1 Δαυὶδ τῷ Δισυπάτῳ scripsit et deinde delevit A || 28 ἦ Laurent: ἢ A

to you my opinion on this matter at that time. Come then with the aid of the inaccessible light of the light-transcending Trinity, you who are most dear to God and most wise and a most beloved father to me!

12. To David Dishypatos

An extraordinary rumor reached me about the Scythians, a rumor the like of which has never before been heard, regarding their attacks against the Romans. Or rather, it is not really a rumor, but a letter from the lady who is both the daughter of the Emperor and the wife of the Scythian. In fact, the letter says that the barbarian has become so irritated and infuriated with us that he recently launched against us sixty thousand Scythians, who are already rushing to cross the Istros, not in fact as they did before when they invaded Thrace, ⟨that is⟩, not for the purpose of grabbing whatever they could easily find in their way before returning home, but with siege machines for attacking the fortifications. The sixty thousand men intend to besiege these fortifications for three months and depart for home, with whatever booty they have seized, after an equal number has arrived to succeed them in this task. And then they, too, will leave the siege and battle when replacements arrive after an equal length of time. And the barbarian is prepared to continue doing this until he wipes out and destroys and completely subjugates the Roman empire. For he does not intend to desist before he sees these plans accomplished in this way. The letter strongly emphasizes this and shows that the author fears that the Romans may not quite believe her letter and may be taken suddenly by storm.

It is my duty to relay this information to you, and it is up to you to plan for your own safety with the help of God. And it seems to me that you cannot do better than to come here to me, where with our common bond of affection we shall consider together what is to be done and we shall follow our decision. And if we resolve to emigrate, it is not difficult to go wherever we wish from here. For I admit that I have always been afraid of the sea—if I must say so—and I have waged an implacable war against it, as you know more than anyone else; but now I shall make peace with it. Otherwise, what is to become of me, if perchance the Scythian waves are going to carry me off beyond Istros and Tanais into slavery—something which I would not be able to bear, if I did not have you to share my bondage and lamenta-

12

σοι χρησαίμην συνδούλῳ καὶ συνοιμώζοντι, ἢ ξίφος ἀπαλλάττειν τοῦ βίου, ὃ δέδοικα, πρὸ τῆς τοῦ βίου καθάρσεως, μᾶλλον δὲ οὐδὲ ξίφος ἐμὲ τὸ ζῆν ἀφαιρήσεται, μιᾶς δή τινος πληγῆς εὐτελοῦς προλαβούσης τὸ ξίφος, οὐδ' ἐπὶ τὸν Ἴστρον ἥξω εὐθὺς ἐν ἀρχῇ τῆς ἐκείνων πορείας ἀπειρηκώς, καὶ διὰ τοῦτο πεσών.

Ἄνευ δὲ τούτων ὁ θαυμάσιος Παλαμᾶς *ὅσον ἤδη παρέσται· μεταπέμπεται γὰρ αὐτὸν γράμμασιν ὁ πατριάρχης, λόγον δώσοντα ἐφ' οἷς ἐγκαλεῖται τῷ εὐφυεῖ* Βαρλαάμ· *ἀνάγκη δέ σε παρεῖναι καὶ διὰ τοῦτο μόνον. οὐδὲ γὰρ ὁ* Βαρλαὰμ *εὐκατάβλητος, διὰ τὸ χώραν αὐτῷ τινα δοῦναι τὸν* Παλαμᾶν *ἰσχυρίζεσθαι* [fol. 75r]—*ὅ σοι καὶ πρότερον ἔγραψα—ἣν ἐμοὶ δοκεῖ δεῖν αὐτὸν παρὰ φίλων ἀνδρῶν ἀφελέσθαι πεισθῆναι τὸν ἐναντίον, καὶ οὕτως ἔχειν εὐχείρωτον. ἔστι δὲ τοῦτο φίλων ἀνδρῶν ἰσχῦσαι, καὶ μάλιστα μὲν σοῦ διὰ τὴν σύνεσιν καὶ τὴν φανερὰν εὔνοιαν τὴν πρὸς αὐτόν, ἧττον δὲ ἡμῶν διὰ τό, μὴ πάντα αὐτῷ συναινέσαντας ἐξ ἀρχῆς ἅπερ ἔγραφε, παρασχεῖν ὑποψίαν ἀντιδιακειμένων, εἰ* ⟨*καὶ*⟩ *τὰ σαφεστάτου φίλου νῦν ἐγὼ καὶ εἶπον ὑπὲρ αὐτοῦ καὶ ἔδρασα καὶ δοκεῖ δι' ἐμὲ νῦν ἐνταῦθα κατ' ἄνθρωπον μὴ διθεΐαν νοσεῖν παρὰ τῶν πλείστων νομίζεσθαι. δοκεῖ δὲ σφόδρα ἰσχυρογνώμων εἶναι, ἅπερ αὐτοῦ δοκεῖ μὴ σφόδρα μάτην ὁ διώκων καθάπτεσθαι, ἀφ' ὧν πρὸς ἐμὲ ἄρτι γέγραφε· πέπομφε γάρ μοι πάνυ μακρὰν περὶ τούτων ἐπιστολήν, τὰ ἅπαξ αὐτῷ δεδογμένα ἐν τῇ θεολογίᾳ κρατύνουσαν.*

Δέος οὖν μὴ στάσις καὶ ῥῆγμα τὴν ἐκκλησίαν λάβῃ, τῶν μὲν ἐκείνῳ, τῶν δὲ τούτῳ τιθεμένων καὶ προσχωρούντων, ἢ κατὰ φιλίας λόγον ἢ δόξης τοῦ τὸ κρεῖττον αἱρεῖσθαι ἢ καὶ ἀμφότερα, †*ὡς ἂν δὲ ἡμῖν δοκεῖ ἑκάτερος διορθωθῆναι, μηδ' ἕτερος αἰσχρῶς μηδὲ ἀδόξως, ὅπερ ἴσως αὐτοῖς τι συνεργεῖ πρὸς τὴν ἰσχυρογνωμοσύνην—ἄνθρωποι γάρ—ἐξ ἧς τὸ ῥῆγμα γενήσεται, καὶ μὴ συμβῆναι τοῦτο, ἀλλὰ πᾶν τοὐναντίον ὁμοφροσύνην καὶ ἀγάπην καὶ τῶν τούτοις ἐναντίων καθαίρεσιν.*†

Ἐλθὼν καὶ ἀκούσας, εἰ οὕτως ἔχοι κρινεῖς, καὶ συνδιαπράξῃ καὶ τέλος ἐπιθήσεις χρηστόν, τοῦ Θεοῦ *συνεργοῦντος.* Κἂν *μέν—ὅπερ ἀπείη—καταλάβῃ* Ῥωμαίους *τὰ προσδοκώμενα, οὐ μεταμελον πείσεσθε τοῦ παρ' ἡμᾶς ἀφῖχθαι· εἰ δὲ* Θεὸς *ἡμᾶς ἐλεήσας ἐπίσχοι τὰ ἀπειλούμενα καὶ διαλύσαι τὴν τῶν βαρβάρων ὁρμήν, καὶ πάλιν ὑμῖν ἐξείη τὸν* Αἶμον *καταλαμβάνειν τοῖς ἐρημίας φίλοις (εἴη δὲ καὶ ἡμῖν τοῦ νοσεῖν ἀνεθεῖσι)· τότε ἢ σὺν ἡμῖν ἢ μόνοι πάλιν εἰς τὸν* Αἶμον *ἐπάνιτε καὶ τῶν αὐτῶν ἀπολαύσεσθε. ὅτε τοίνυν τὸ μὲν μένειν ὑμᾶς αὐτόθι πολὺ τὸ δέος ἔχει μή τινι βαρβαρικῷ πε-*

---

36 *παρέσται* Laurent: *πάρεσται* A || 46 *εἰ καὶ*] ‹*καὶ*› add. Laurent || 55–60 *ὡς . . . καθαίρεσιν* non satis perspicio || 63 *ἀπείη* Laurent: *ἀπήει* A

tions—or if I were to die by the sword before I had time to purify my life, which is what I fear? Or rather, a sword will not even be required to deprive me of life, for any slight blow will carry me off before the sword. Nor will I reach Istros, for right away, at the start of the march, I will be exhausted and consequently collapsing.

To leave this aside, the admirable Palamas will be here very shortly. For the Patriarch summoned him by letter to account for the charges brought against him by the clever Barlaam. And it is necessary for you to be here, if only for this reason. For Barlaam is indeed not easy to defeat, because, as I wrote to you before, Palamas has given him some grounds for argument. I think that Palamas' friends must persuade him to deprive his opponent of these grounds and thus render him easy to overcome. It is up to Palamas' friends to influence him in this respect, and above all up to you because of your wisdom and manifest love for him. It is not so much my duty, for he suspects me of opposing him because I did not entirely agree from the beginning with what he wrote; even though now I both spoke and acted in his behalf as the truest friend. And it seems that because of me, as far as men are concerned, the majority of people here believe now that he does not suffer from ditheism. But he seems to be extremely obstinate, just as his opponent seems to accuse him, not altogether without reason, that is, judging from what he wrote to me recently, for he sent me a very long letter concerning these matters which confirms the opinions that he holds in theology once and for all.

There is fear, therefore, lest faction and schism seize the Church, with some men siding and supporting Barlaam and others Palamas, either for reasons of friendship or because of the belief that they made the right choice or both. For it seems to me that each man can be corrected, but neither in a shameful or undignified manner which may contribute to their obstinacy—for they are human—whence schism will be produced. And may this not happen, but quite the contrary, ⟨may there be⟩ concord and love and the destruction of all their opposites.

When you come and hear, you will judge whether this is so and you will assist in the negotiations and, with the help of God, bring the matter to a happy ending. And if—God forbid!—the expected troubles befall the Romans, you will suffer no regrets for having come to us. But if God in his mercy should stop the menace and check the impetus of the barbarians, it would be possible for you, the lover of solitude (and may it be for me also, when I have recovered from illness) to reach Haimos again. Then you will return to Haimos either with me or alone and will enjoy the same advantages. I do not know, therefore, what consideration could stop you from being with me, if your remaining there holds in store the mighty fear of

ριπέσητε, τὸ δὲ παρ’ ἡμᾶς ἀφῖχθαι οὐχ ὕποπτον μὴ τὸ τὴν ἐρημίαν αὖθις ἀπολαβεῖν ἀπολέσητε, οὐκ οἶδ’ ὅστις ἂν ὑμᾶς λογισμὸς κωλύσῃ μὴ παρ’ ἡμῖν γενέσθαι.

13. Sine titulo

Τί ταῦτα, ὦ φίλων ἄριστε καὶ θαυμαστῶν τὴν φύσιν καὶ τὸν Θεὸν φιλούντων καὶ τὸ καλὸν τιμώντων; ἔτι κρατεῖ τὰ χείρω τῆς βελτίονος γνώμης; ἔτι νικήσει παρ’ ἐμοὶ τὰ τῆς λύπης; ἔτι παρὰ σοὶ τὸ φίλον περιορᾶν ἀνιώμενον, καὶ φίλον εἰδότα καλῶς οἷς ἔχοι τὰς εἰς αὐτὸν εὐεργεσίας ἀμείβεσθαι; παρακαλεῖ σε δὴ φιλία· παρακαλεῖ σε Θεὸς ὑπὲρ οὗ παροικοῦμεν ἐνταῦθα καὶ τὴν αἴτησιν ταύτην ποιούμεθα· αὐτὸ τὸ πρᾶγμά σοι προσάγει τὴν παροῦσαν παράκλησιν ὁμοίως ὑπὲρ ἐμοῦ καὶ ὑμῶν, ἀμφοῖν ὂν ἐπωφελὲς ὁμοίως. ὃ παρρησίᾳ δεῖξον, καὶ πάντες ἀκολουθήσουσι, καὶ τὸ ἀντιτεῖνον εἴξει τῇ σοφωτέρᾳ τε καὶ χρηστοτέρᾳ γνώμῃ. ἂν δέ τις μείνῃ τῆς οἰκείας σκληρότητος οὐκ ἀφιστάμενος, νῦν μὲν οὐκ ἂν δυνηθείη τῆς βελτίονος περιγενέσθαι γνώμης, ὕστερον δὲ κἀκεῖνος πεπεισμένος ὑπὸ τοῦ πράγματος ἐπαινέσεται τὴν νικήσασαν κρίσιν καὶ χάριν εἴσεται τῶν ἐντεῦθεν ἐπικερδῶν ἀπηντηκότων αὐτῷ. ὀλίγοι πανταχοῦ τοῖς πολλοῖς τῶν βελτιόνων οἱ σύμβουλοι, ἐν γὰρ τῷ πλήθει σπάνις εὐβουλίας καὶ τοῦ προσήκοντος. σὸν τοῦτο τὸ ἔργον τοῦ σύνεσιν ἔχοντος καὶ τρόπων χρηστότητα κατὰ τὴν σύνεσιν· σὸν καὶ τοῦ δύναμιν κεκτημένου πρὸς ταῦτα· σὸν καὶ γενέσθαι τοίνυν μετὰ πρᾳότητος τοῦτο καὶ τῆς ἄνωθεν ἡμῖν δεδομένης ἀγάπης, ἧς αὐτὸς τῶν καρπῶν ἀπολαύσῃ, ἂν ὑπουργήσῃς τὴν βούλησιν.

14. Νικολάῳ τῷ Καβάσιλᾳ

Εἰ σφόδρα φιλοῦντες, εἰ καὶ μὴ ἔχομεν, σοφίαν καὶ ἀρετήν, οὐ τὸν μάλιστα τούτων τὸ μὲν ἔχοντα, τὸ δὲ μετὰ πάσης ἐπιμελείας

13: S 234^{v}.
10 τις scripsi: τι S ‖ 11 ἀφιστάμενος scripsi: ἀφιστάμενον S ‖ 12 κἀκεῖνο S: litteram ς supra versum adiecit S^{1} ‖ πεπεισμένον S: litteram ν in ς mutavit S^{1}

14: M 40^{v}–41^{r}. Ed. Ševčenko, “Nicolaus Cabasilas’ Correspondence,” 53, n. 4.
2 ἐσφαλμένως ἔχει. χρὴ δὲ οὕτως αὐτὴν λέγεσθαι· + οἱ σφόδρα φιλοῦντες, εἰ καὶ μὴ ἔχομεν, σοφίαν καὶ ἀρετήν, εἰ μὴ τὸν μάλιστα τούτων τὸ μὲν ἔχοντα, τὸ δὲ μετὰ πάσης ἐπιμελείας ἀθροίζοντα φιλοῖμεν τε καὶ θαυμάζοιμεν καὶ τὰ ἑξῆς in margine scripsit manus recentior

encountering some barbarian attack, while your coming here leaves no suspicion that you may not regain your solitude.

13. No Addressee

What is this, O best of friends and best of men, you who are admirable in character, who love God and honor virtue? Does the worse still predominate over the better opinion? Am I still to be vanquished by sorrow? Do you still insist upon disregarding a friend in distress and a friend, at that, who knows well, as far as he can, how to repay the good deeds done to him? Indeed, friendship exhorts you! God, for whose sake I am here making this request, exhorts you! The very matter in hand brings forth to you the present appeal for my sake and yours alike, for it is equally for the good of us both. Show this by speaking openly, and everybody will follow, and the opposition will give way to the wiser and better opinion. And if someone insists upon not retreating from his harsh position, he will not be able to prevail over the better opinion at present, and later he, too, will be persuaded by the facts and will praise the judgment that prevailed and will be grateful for the benefits that came to him thence. Few are the men, everywhere, who offer good counsel to the many, for in the crowd there is dearth of sound and proper judgment. This work is up to you, because you have intelligence and the good character to match it. It is up to you, because you also possess the necessary power. It is up to you, then, also to do this with kindness and the love given to us from Heaven, whose fruits you will enjoy, if you serve its wish.

14. To Nicholas Kabasilas

If I, who love wisdom and virtue excessively, though I do not possess them, ⟨if I⟩ do not both love and admire the man who possesses them more than anyone else and who collects them most diligently, I shall blame myself for unfitting charac-

ἀθροίζοντα φιλοῖμέν τε καὶ θαυμάζοιμεν, ἡμῶν αὐτῶν ἀναρμοστίαν ἤθους καὶ γνώμης κατηγορήσομεν. φιλοῦμεν δὴ καὶ θαυμάζομεν ἐπιεικῶς τὸν ταῦτα κεκτημένον Καβάσιλαν, καὶ τοῦτο οὐδ' αὐτὸς μὲν ἀγνοεῖς ὁ φιλούμενος. ἥκει δὲ ἡμῖν ἔρως καὶ τῶν ἐκ σοῦ γραμμάτων οὕτως εὖ ἡρμοσμένων διὰ παντός, ὥστε λίθους μὲν οὐκ ἂν φαίην τῇ τούτων μουσικῇ τὸ κινεῖσθαι λαμβάνειν—τοῦτο γάρ, οἶμαι, σοφιστικόν—ἀλόγῳ δέ που προσεοικέναι ζῴῳ τὸν τούτων μὴ ἁλισκόμενον [fol. 41r] μηδ' ἐπιστάμενον, ὡς ἔστιν ἐπιεικῶς ἐνταῦθα πρὸς τοῦ ἁλισκομένου τὸ μὴ μένειν ἀνάλωτον.

Γράφομεν τοίνυν ἡμεῖς, ἵνα λάβωμεν γράμματα ὧν τῷ πόθῳ δεδέμεθα· γράφε δὴ καὶ αὐτὸς καὶ μὴ φθόνει τῶν ἐπεράστων ἡμῖν, οὕτως αὐτῶν εὐπορῶν, ὥσπερ ἡμεῖς τοῦ ἐρᾶν· εἰ μή τι ἕτερον, τὸ γοῦν προτέρους ἡμᾶς γεγραφέναι τιμήσας, εἰ καὶ μὴ σὸν ἔρωτα τοῦτο ποιοῦντες πληροῦμεν. τὰ γὰρ ἡμέτερα οὐχὶ τῶν ἐρωμένων· πλὴν οὐδεμία χάρις ἐν τοῖς ἀτίμοις, οἶμαι, κατά γε τὴν δύναμιν τοῦ παρασχόντος οὖσα.

15. Τῷ Στυππῇ

Ἡ π ό ρ ρ ω σ ο φ ί α ς ἢ ἀξίας ἐ λ η λ α κ ὼ ς, οὐκ ἀξιοῖς ἡμᾶς γραμμάτων, ὡς ἔοικεν. εἰ δ' ἔστι τούτου οὐδέτερον, διὰ γραμμάτων δήλου καὶ τὴν αἰτίαν προστίθει δι' ἣν οὐ πρότερον ἔγραφες· οἶμαι δὲ εἶναι ταύτην ὅτι μηδέ σοι παρ' ἡμῶν εἴη γράμματα. εἰ δὲ τοῦτ' ἐστὶ καὶ οὐχ ἥμαρτεν ὁ στοχασμὸς τοῦ σκοποῦ, ἔχω μὲν εἰπεῖν ὡς οὐκ εὔλογος ὁ λόγος οὗτος, σὲ γὰρ ἐχρῆν, οὐκ ἐμὲ γραμμάτων ἄρχειν. σὺ γὰρ γ ε ν ε ῆ φ ι ν ε ώ τ ε ρ ο ς, καὶ ἄλλως ἐμοὶ μᾶλλον ὀφείλεται παρὰ σοῦ ἢ σοι παρ' ἐμοῦ ὁ φόρος οὗτος ἐφ' ὁσονοῦν, κἂν πάντας ὑπερβῇς τῇ σοφίᾳ καὶ τῷ τῆς δόξης ὄγκῳ· εἰ δ' ἐμὲ πάντως ἔδει καὶ τοῦ γράφειν τὴν ἀρχὴν πεποιῆσθαι, ἤδη πεποίημαι. ὡς οὖν οὐκέτ' ἐξόν σοι μηδὲν προφασίσασθαι μὴ ἐπιστέλλοντι, γράφε, εἴ γέ σοι μέλει τοῦ τὰ δίκαια ποιεῖν περί τε ἡμᾶς καὶ σαυτόν, οὗ θαυμασία φήμη διὰ πάντων κηρύττει τὴν περὶ λόγους ἰσχύν, τούς τε ἄλλους καὶ τοὺς ἐκ φιλοσοφίας, ἐξ ὧν οἱ μὲν ἄλλοι σε γνωρίζουσι μετὰ θαύματος, ἐγὼ δὲ καὶ ἀγάλλομαι—πῶς οἴει;—μετὰ θαύματος καὶ

15: 2 Plato, *Euthyphro*, 4b || 7 Homerus, *Il.*, 14, 112

15: M 41r.

ter and judgment. Thus it is that I love and justly admire Kabasilas who possesses these ⟨qualities⟩, and you, the beloved, are not unaware of this either. I am also enamored of your letters which are altogether so well composed that—though I would not say, of course, that their music moves stones, for I fear that this would be contrived—a man seems to be somehow an irrational animal, if he is not captivated by them, or if he does not realize that in this case captivity is quite to the advantage of the captured.

I write, therefore, in order to receive the letter for which I long. Do write yourself also and do not begrudge me ⟨the gifts⟩ I love, since you abound in them as much as I abound in love; if for no other reason, at least to honor me for having written first, even though by writing I do not satisfy your desire. But I believe that no gift is without value, if it is, at least, in accordance with the giver's means.

15. To Styppes

It seems that you consider me unworthy of a letter, because you "have made great strides" either in "wisdom" or dignity. But, if neither of these ⟨alternatives⟩ is true, show this by a letter and add the reason for which you did not write earlier. I suspect that it is because you did not receive a letter from me either. If this is true, and my guess is not amiss, I must say that this is not a good reason. For it is you, not I, who ought to write first. You are "younger by birth," and besides this you owe to me this ever so small courtesy; I do not owe it to you, even if you surpass everybody in wisdom and immensity of glory. At all events, even if I should have written first, I have already made a beginning. Therefore, since you cannot find any more excuse for not writing, do write, if you really care to do what is right by me and yourself, as your literary power both in other subjects and in philosophy has a marvelous reputation everywhere. From these ⟨writings⟩ others make your acquaintance with admiration, but you cannot imagine how I exult with admiration and wish you to use them

βούλομαί σε τούτοις χρήσασθαι ὑπὲρ τῆς εὐσεβείας, ἵν' οὕτως εἴης σοφὸς καὶ πρὸς Θεὸν εὐγνώμων, ὡς ὑπὲρ αὐτοῦ τοῖς παρ' αὐτοῦ κεχρημένος χαρίσμασι.

16. Sine titulo

Ἐπειδή σε ὁ Θεὸς ἀρετῇ καὶ σοφίᾳ καὶ πάσαις ἀγαθαῖς ἐκόσμησε χάρισιν, ὧν ἕνεκα δικαίως καὶ τὰς αὐτοῦ τοῦ δικαίου παρὰ τῆς ἀγαθῆς βασιλείας ἡνίας ἐνεχειρίσθης ὀρθοῦν, οἶμαι δεῖν καὶ ἡμᾶς εἰκότως τῆς σῆς εὐθυδικίας τυχεῖν. εἰ δὲ καὶ περὶ εὐσεβείας ὁ λόγος ἡμῖν ἐστιν, ἐφ' ᾗ σου παρακαλοῦμεν τὴν σοφίαν καὶ τὴν εὐσέβειαν ἡμῖν εἰς ὁμιλίαν ἐλθεῖν, πολλῷ μᾶλλον ἂν εἰκότως ἑτοίμου σου τύχοιμεν, ὥσπερ δὴ καὶ τὸ τὴν ἀμφισβήτησιν πρὸς ἡμᾶς ἔχον μέρος· οὐ γὰρ εἰκὸς τὸν τὸ πᾶσι δικάζειν τὰ πράγματα κεκληρωμένον ἐν τῷ τῆς εὐσεβείας μέρει μᾶλλον αὐτὸν διδόναι θατέρῳ τῶν ἀντιδίκων εἰς τὴν ἀκρόασιν. εἰ γὰρ ἐν τοῖς ἄλλοις τῶν πραγμάτων δέος μὴ κλαπῇ τὸ ἀληθὲς πιθανότητι, καὶ διὰ τοῦτο πολλῆς οἱ νομοθέται τῆς ἀκριβείας προενοήθησαν καὶ περὶ τὰς ἀκροάσεις, πόσην δεῖ τὴν ἀκρίβειαν νέμειν τοῖς ὑπὲρ εὐσεβείας λόγοις τὸν ἀποφαίνεσθαι μέλλοντα, οὐκ ἰδίας οὔσης τῶν γε ἀμφισβητούντων ἀλλὰ κοινῆς πρὸς τὸν κρίνοντα; κἂν οὗτος ἀπατηθῇ πιθανότητι, συνεκινδύνευσε μετὰ τῶν προηπατημένων εἰς τὴν εὐσέβειαν· οὐ γὰρ οἱ δόξαντες ἐνταῦθα κατακεκρίσθαι καὶ κατεκρίθησαν ἢ ἐκινδύνευσαν, πρὸς ἑαυτῶν οὖσαν αὐτὴν τὴν ἀλήθειαν ἔχοντες, κἂν κατατμηθῶσιν ἢ κατακρημνησθῶσιν, ἀλλ' οἱ μάτην δόξαντες νενικηκέναι καὶ τοὺς οὕτως ἡττημένους διώκοντες ἢ διαφθείροντες.

Ἀλλὰ ταῦτα μὲν ἁπλῶς ἡμῖν εἴρηται καί, κατὰ τὸ παρεῖκον, οὐ πρὸς τὴν σὴν ἀπετάθη σοφίαν καὶ μεγαλόνοιαν καὶ πάντων κριτικωτάτην γνώμην. οἰόμεθα γάρ σε παντὸς μὲν [fol. 40^{r}] *μᾶλλον ἅψασθαι τῆς ἀληθείας, ἐπειδὰν ἐν τῷ μέρει καὶ ἡμῶν ἀποχρώντως ἀκούσῃς, ὥσπερ κἀκείνων πολλάκις, παντὸς δὲ μᾶλλον ἔπειτα συνάψειν καὶ διαλλάξειν ἡμᾶς τοὺς ἀντικαθιστῶτας, φίλους μὲν ἀλλήλοις ὑπάρξαντας καὶ ἀδελφοὺς καὶ ὁμόπνους, ὡς οὐκ' οἶδ' εἴ τινες ἀλλήλοις ἐγένοντο πώποτε, νῦν δὲ ἀλγεινότατα διεστηκότας ὑπὲρ τῆς ἀληθείας ἧς οὐδὲν προτιμότερον τῶν μετ' αὐτὴν ἀγαθῶν, οὔτε ἐνεστώτων, οὔτε μελλόντων κατὰ τὸν μέγαν Παῦλον.*

16: M 39^{v}–40^{r}.

for the defense of piety, in order that you may be so wise and grateful to God as to have put His gifts to His service.

16. No Addressee

Since God has adorned you with virtue and wisdom and all good graces, which is why you were justly entrusted by the good Emperor with straightening the reins even of justice itself, I believe that I too must properly obtain your righteous judgment. And if the reason for which I beg your wise and pious Lordship to give me your consideration has to do with piety, I should rightly find you ready, just as indeed does my opponent. For he who has been appointed to judge the affairs of all men must not in questions of piety pay more attention to either of the two opponents. Indeed, if in other matters there is fear that the truth may be concealed by persuasiveness, and if it was for this reason that the legislators provided for so much strictness concerning the hearings as well, how much strictness must the man who will deliver the verdict bestow on questions of piety, since this is not a private concern only of the opponents, but of the judge also? And if he is deceived by persuasiveness, he is in peril along with those who have already been deceived in regard to piety. For in this case it is not those who appeared to have been found guilty who are guilty or in danger—since they have truth itself on their side, even if they are cut to pieces or hurled down a precipice—but those who appeared falsely to have won and who persecute and destroy the men so defeated.

But I have said this simply and in accordance with what is permissible to me; I did not allude to your wisdom and magnanimity or to your most discerning judgment. For I believe that more than anyone you will adhere closely to the truth, when you have, in turn, listened to me sufficiently, just as you have many times listened to them also; and ⟨I believe⟩ that more than anyone you will afterwards bring us together and reconcile us, the adversaries, who have been friends and brothers, who have been in agreement more than anyone else has ever been, to my knowledge. But now we stand most painfully divided for the sake of truth, to which none of the virtues that are next in order, neither present nor future, is to be preferred, according to the great Paul.

17. Τῷ φιλοσόφῳ Γρηγορᾷ

Ἐκείμην ἐν ἀσθενείᾳ καὶ προσηνέχθη μοι λόγος· οὐ λόγος μὲν οὖν ἁπλῶς ὡς ἔοικεν, ἀλλὰ φάρμακον τῆς ἀσθενείας ἀπαλλακτήριον· ὁ δὲ ἦν ποίημα μὲν τῆς σῆς φιλοπόνου σοφίας καὶ τῆς Ἀτθίδος γλώττης ἀπόρροια, κόσμημα δὲ τῆς θείας βασιλίδος Θεοφανοῦς, τῶν ἀρετῶν ἐκείνης καὶ πόνων μόνον ἐπάξιον. τοῦτον διελθὼν καὶ πεπωκὼς καθάπερ τὸ φάρμακον, τὴν ὑγιείαν ἐρράϊσα· ὃν ἀποδίδωμί σοι μετὰ εὐχαριστίας, πάντα μὲν αὐτοῦ ἐπιεικῶς θαυμάσας καὶ πρὸς πάντων ὠφεληθείς, διαφερόντως δὲ ἀπὸ τοῦ τέλους ἐν ᾧ τῆς ἐκκλησιαστικῆς κατεύχῃ τρικυμίας ⟨καὶ⟩ ζάλης· καὶ πρό γε τούτου τὸ πεφυκὸς δέχεσθαι τὰς τυπωτικὰς θεοπτίας καὶ ὄψεις κάλλιστά σοι πεφιλοσοφημένον ὡς ἥδιστά με διέθηκε. τοὺς γὰρ τὴν φυσικὴν τοῦ Θεοῦ καὶ οὐσιώδη μορφὴν καὶ δόξαν ὁρᾶν ὑπεραλαζονευομένους κόμπους σωματικοῖς ὀφθαλμοῖς, διὰ πνεύματος αὐτὴν ἐκείνην ἀπερικάλυπτον, ἀπονοίας γέμοντας ἐξελέγχεις καὶ πλάνης, καὶ οὕτως αὐτῶν ὥσπερ πρεμνόθεν [fol. 46ᵛ] ἀνασπῶν τὴν τῆς πολυθείας ῥίζαν, τῆς ἐντεῦθεν τὴν ἐκκλησίαν τρικυμίας καὶ ζάλης τό γε σὸν ἀπαλλάττεις.

18. Τῷ φιλοσόφῳ Γρηγορᾷ

Βασιλικὸς ὁ λόγος ὡς ἀληθῶς καὶ θεῖος· καὶ ὅσον ὁ μέγας βασιλεὺς Κωνσταντῖνος τῶν ἄλλων βασιλέων προφέρει, τοσοῦτον ὁ τὰ ἐκείνου κἀκεῖνον ἐπαξίως τεθαυμακὼς σὸς λόγος τῶν ἄλλων ἔμοιγε δοκεῖ περιφανῶς πρεσβεύειν. μᾶλλον δὲ τὴν σὴν αὐτοῦ πρὸς τοὺς ἄλλους ὑπεροχήν, ἣν ἔχεις ἐν εἴδει παντὶ καὶ ἐπιστήμῃ λόγων, πρὸς τοὺς ὁμοειδεῖς αὐτῷ τῶν λόγων ἀκριβῶς ἐμιμήσατο· ἔδει γὰρ ὃν ἔχει λόγον ὁ πατὴρ αὐτῷ πρὸς τοὺς ἄλλους πατέρας ἐπιστήμης καὶ λόγων, τὸν αὐτὸν ἔχειν καὶ τοῦτον πρὸς τοὺς τῶν ἄλλων παῖδας, εὐφυῶς ἡρμοσμένον τοῖς ὅλοις καί, ὡς εἰπεῖν, ἀξίως τῆς Κωνσταντίνου θειότητος καὶ μεγαλοπρεπείας. ἔρρωται τὰ νοήματα· χαρίεντα τὰ ὀνόματα· ἡ σύνθεσις εὔρυθμος· ἡ τάξις τῶν μερῶν πρὸς τὴν

17: M 46ʳ–46ᵛ. Ed. Beyer, *Antirrhetika I*, 109, n. 620.
7 *πεποκὼς* M ‖ 10 ‹*καὶ*› addidi ‖ 17 ante *τρικυμίας* lacunam proposuit Beyer sed nihil deesse videtur

18: M 71ʳ–71ᵛ. V 218ᵛ. Huius epistolae partem edidit Mercati, *Notizie*, 12, n. 2.
1 sine titulo V: *αὕτη ἡ ἐπιστολή ἐστι τοῦ Ἀκινδύνου πρὸς τὸν Γρηγορᾶν* in margine V¹

17. To the philosopher Gregoras

I was lying ill and they brought me a discourse; not an ordinary discourse, as it seems, but a medicine to cure the illness. It was the product of your industrious wisdom and the fluency of the Attic tongue, and it was also the adornment of the divine Empress Theophano, the only one worthy of her virtues and accomplishments. When I went over it and drank it, so to speak, as a medicine, I regained my health! I am returning it to you with gratitude. I have generally admired everything in it, and profited from everything, but especially from the end where you denounce the ecclesiastical tempest and turbulence. And even before that, the theory that it is natural to receive representative visions and images of God, which you discuss excellently, gave me the greatest possible pleasure. For you prove that the most pretentious boasts of seeing with the eyes of the body the face and glory of God in its nature and essence, without spiritual cover, are filled with folly and error, and thus you pull up from the bottom, so to speak, the root of their polytheism and, for your part, deliver the Church from the ensuing tempest and turbulence.

18. To the philosopher Gregoras

This is truly an imperial and divine oration! And it seems to me that this oration, which extols the Emperor Constantine and his deeds, excels other orations as notably as Constantine excels other emperors. Or rather, in regard to orations of this type, it imitated exactly the superiority which you yourself possess in all sorts of literary matters and learning. For it too ought to have the same relation to the works of other authors that its author has to other scholars and men of letters, being altogether skillfully composed and in a manner, so to speak, worthy of Constantine's divinity and magnificence. Powerful thoughts; elegant expression; graceful composition; the parts perfectly arranged to make up the whole. Conciseness every-

τοῦ ὅλου συμπλήρωσιν ἠκριβωμένη· τὸ ἱκανὸν πανταχοῦ· τὸ περιττὸν οὐδαμοῦ· τὸ νόθον ἐλήλαται, τὸ γνήσιον ἀντεισῆκται· τὸ μὲν ὡς κίβδηλον ἐληλεγμένον, τὸ δ' ὡς ἀκήρατον δοκιμασθέν· ὧν τὸ μὲν οὐκ οἶδ' ὅπως πρότερον ἐσιωπᾶτο, τὸ δ' ἐν ἐπαίνου μοίρᾳ λεγόμενον εἰς Κωνσταντῖνον, οὐδὲν μᾶλλον ἐσέμνυνεν ἢ καθῄρει τὸν μέγαν τῆς ὑπαρχούσης δόξης.

Περὶ δὲ τοῦ πρὸς Λατίνους καὶ κατὰ τῶν πάντα φθέγγεσθαι περὶ Θεοῦ τολμώντων, ὃν πρῴην ἀνέγνωμεν, τί χρὴ καὶ λέγειν; ὃς τὰ τῶν ἀπονενοημένων οἰδήματα θᾶττον ῥήγνυσι καθάπερ πομφόλυγας, ἢ ἐκεῖνοι φυσῶσι, καὶ τοὺς τυφλοὺς τὴν ψυχήν, οἰομένους γε βλέπειν ἃ βλέπειν οἴεσθαι τυφλώττειν ἐστὶν ὡς ἀληθῶς καθάπαξ, τοὺς μὲν τοῦθ' ὅπερ εἰσὶ δείκνυσι, κἀντεῦθεν εἰς ἐρημίας ἀποπεπλανημένους καὶ βάραθρα καὶ τόπους οὓς οὐκ ἐπισκοπεῖ Κύριος ἀπὸ τῆς ἀληθείας, τῇ δ' εὐσεβείᾳ τὸ εἰκὸς ἀποσῴζει, σοὶ δὲ τὸ ὄντως φιλόσοφον, οὗ τὸ κεφάλαιον ἥ τε περὶ τὸ θεῖον ἐπιστήμων εὐλάβεια καὶ σωφροσύνη καὶ τὸ τῆς ἀμαθίας καὶ πλάνης περὶ αὐτὸ τῶν ταύταις περιπιπτόντων ἐκ δαιμονίας οἰήσεως ἐλεγκτικόν.

Σὰ μὲν οὖν ταῦτα· ἡμεῖς δὲ τούτων ὥσπερ οἱ ἐρωτόληπτοι τῶν ἐρωμένων, διὰ δὲ τούτων καί σοι. ὥστ' οἴκοθεν οἴκαδε πεμπομένους τοὺς λόγους, οἴκοθεν αὖθις οἴκαδε δέχου [fol. 71v] καὶ νῦν ἰόντας, μᾶλλον δὲ τοὺς αὐτοὺς καὶ πεμπομένους καὶ μένοντας, τὸ μὲν τῇ δέλτῳ, τὸ δὲ τῇ ἐπιστήμῃ. σὺ μὲν ἐπανιόντας ἡμῶν ἀπεσταλκότων δέχου, ἡμεῖς δὲ μένοντας ἔχομεν ἐν τῇ ψυχῇ, ὥσπερ ὅθ' ἡμῖν αὐτὸς τούτους ἔπεμπες, ἡμεῖς μὲν ἐδεχόμεθα ἀπεσταλμένους, σὺ δ' εἶχες μένοντας ἐν τῇ ψυχῇ.

19. Sine titulo

Εἰ μὴ πρότερον κατεῖχες τὴν ἡμετέραν γνώμην ἐπὶ σοφίᾳ καὶ μεγαλοφυΐᾳ, νῦν ἐπιεικῶς κατέσχες καὶ τῇ περὶ σαυτὸν φιλίᾳ κατέδησας, ὅτι ἃ σοφῶν ἀνδρῶν ὄντως ἐστὶ καὶ πρός γε φιλοθέων νοήματα, ταῦτα σὺ παρέχῃ περὶ τὰ θεῖα δόγματα καὶ τὴν εὐσέβειαν μετὰ τῆς ἀνδρὶ πρεπούσης παρρησίας τοιούτῳ. νῦν δέ σε καὶ πρότερον μὲν θαυμασίως ἠγάμεθα τῆς μεγαλοφυΐας καὶ τῆς τοσαύτῃ φύσει προσηκούσης σοφίας, προσγέγονε δὲ ἀρτίως καὶ τὸ ἐπὶ τῇ

25–26 cf. Joannis Chrysostomi *Liturgiam* (ed. Brightman), 385, 26 || 32 Pindarus, *Olymp.*, 6.99

15–18 ὧν . . . δόξης om V || 22 φυσσῶσι codd. || 23 οἴονται e corr. V || 29 τῶν ταύταις om V || 31 μὲν om M: ex V supplevi || 32–33 οἴκοθεν . . . λόγους om M: ex V supplevi

19: M 40

where; redundancy nowhere. The spurious has been rejected and the genuine introduced instead. The former because it was proved to be false; the latter because it was scrutinized and approved as true. Of these, I do not know how the latter was previously concealed, while the former, which was recounted as praise for Constantine, did not exalt the great man, but rather deprived him of existing glory.

As for the discourse against the Latins and those who dare say all kinds of things about God, which I have just read, what is there to say? It bursts the bombastic words of the inane men, just as if they were bubbles, faster than they blow them, and shows what exactly is the nature of those who, though blind of soul, claim to see things, when a person who claims to see such things is absolutely blind; and thus it shows that they have strayed away from the truth into deserts and precipices and places not "surveyed by the Lord." For religion it preserves what is right and for you ⟨it preserves⟩ the true philosophy, whose chief characteristic is enlightened reverence and prudence in matters concerning the Divinity and the rebuke of the ignorance and error in such matters of those men who stumble therein because of diabolical conceit.

These discourses belong to you, then, and I belong to them, just as lovers to the beloved, and through them to you. Therefore, since "from home" you sent the discourses "home" to me, accept them now as they return home again from home; rather, they are themselves both in a state of being sent off and of staying, for the book is being sent, but the knowledge stays. So I have sent them, and you will receive them as they return, while I shall keep them in my heart, just as when you sent them I received them because you sent them, but you kept them in your heart.

19. No Addressee

If you did not previously possess my favor as a philosopher and man of noble nature, you possess it now fairly well, and you have bound me with affection for you; for with the boldness suitable to such a man, you express those views about religion and the sacred dogmas which are truly the views of wise as well as God-loving men. Even before this, as a matter of fact, I admired exceedingly your noble nature and your wisdom, which befits so great a nature. But recently there has been

τῶν θειοτάτων δογμάτων ἐπιστήμῃ καὶ τῆς ἀσφαλοῦς θεολογίας θαῦμα, ἣν οὖσαν καρπὸν τῆς ὅλης φιλοσοφίας τὸν ἀνωτάτω εἰκότως ἐδρέψω, τὸ τέλος ἤδη τῶν ἐπ' ἐκείνῃ πόνων καὶ ἧς ἄνευ οὐκ ἔστιν ὄνησις φιλοσοφίας, οὐδὲ μὴν οὖν ὅλως φιλοσοφίας πρᾶγμα, εἰ καί τινες ἄλλως ὀνόματι φιλοσοφίας σεμνύνονται.

Ὡς οὖν οὐ σὸν ὑπάρχον μόνου τὸ τῶν σῶν πόνων τέλος, ἀλλὰ καὶ ἡμῶν οἷς μεταδίδως τούτου τῷ τῶν θείων δογμάτων καὶ τῶν ὅρων τῆς εὐσεβείας ἀντέχεσθαι καὶ ὑπὲρ τούτων νεανικῶς καὶ μάλα θαρραλέως καὶ φιλοσόφως ὄντως ἀνθίστασθαι τοῖς διασπᾶν ἡρημένοις τὴν θειοτάτην ἀμέρειαν ὀνομάτων καινότησιν, ἀγαλλόμεθα ἐπὶ σοὶ καὶ τῇ τριαδικῇ μονάδι τὴν δυνατὴν ἡμῖν αὐτοῖς ὁμολογοῦμεν χάριν, τῇ ἀοράτῳ, τῇ ἀκαταλήπτῳ, τῇ ἀμορφώτῳ καὶ ἀνειδέῳ, τῇ πανταχοῦ παρούσῃ ἑνικῶς καὶ ἀμερῶς καὶ ὑπερηνωμένως· παρ' ἧς σοι καὶ πᾶν ἀγαθὸν αἰτούμενοι διατελοῦμεν, σὺ δὲ ἡμᾶς καὶ γράμμασιν εὔφραινε, φρονῶν μὲν ἃ φρονεῖν ἔδει τὸν φρονιμώτατον ἄνθρωπον καὶ τὸν θεοφιλέστατον, οὐ μᾶλλον δὲ εἰδὼς οὕτω φρονεῖν ἢ γράφειν.

20. Sine titulo

Θαυμαστὴ μέν σε καὶ πρότερον εἰς ἡμᾶς φέρουσα παραδέδωκε φήμη καὶ διεκήρυξεν ἰατρικὴν μὲν ἄριστον καὶ πολλῶν ἄλλων ὡς ἀληθῶς ἀντάξιον, οὐδεμιᾶς δὲ καὶ τῶν ἄλλων ἀμοιροῦντα δυνάμεων αἳ συμπληροῦσι τὴν τῆς σοφίας φύσιν· καὶ νοῦν μὲν [fol. 50^v] ἠσκηκότα γενναῖον, γλῶτταν δὲ ἄγγελον τοιούτῳ νῷ πρέπουσαν, Ἑλλάδος τε παιδείας εἰς ἅπαν ἐληλακότα, καὶ πολλῷ διαφερόντως τῆς θείας καὶ ἡμετέρας· ὅτι καὶ ἀρετὴν μᾶλλον ἢ φιλοτιμίαν μετίοις, τὸ γὰρ εἶναι σοφός, οὐ τὸ δοκεῖν διώκοις, ἀντὶ λιμένος τε σαυτὸν ὅπου τύχοις παρέχοις τοῖς πανταχόθεν ξένοις, καὶ μάλιστα τοῖς ἀφ' ἡμῶν ἐρχομένοις, ἅτε καὶ τρόφιμος ὢν τῆς καθ' ἡμᾶς ἐκκλησίας καὶ τῆς τῶν δογμάτων ἀσφαλείας τῶν ἡμετέρων μύστης.

Ταυτὶ μὲν οὖν καὶ πρότερον κατεῖχε τὰς ἡμετέρας ψυχὰς καὶ ἐξέπληττε, νυνὶ δὲ καὶ ἄλλο προσπαρεγένετο ἓν ἀντὶ πάντων

19: 17 Greg. Naz., *Or.* 22, 12 (PG, 35, 1144C) || 20 Joannis Chrysostomi *Liturgia* (ed. Brightman), 353, 13

20: 2–3 Homerus, *Il.*, II, 514 || 8–9 Aeschylus, *Septem contra Thebas*, 592

20: M 50^r–51^r.

9 παρέχεις M

added the astonishment at your expert knowledge of the sacred dogmas and the correct theology which you have a right to reap, since this is the supreme product of philosophy, in fact the very goal of philosophical pursuits; for without it there is no benefit from philosophy, indeed there is no philosophy at all, even if some men take pride in the name of philosophy for other reasons.

Therefore, since the goal of your labors is not only yours but mine also, because you share it with me when you adhere to the sacred dogmas and the rules of piety, and, in their defense, you resist vigorously and with great courage and true wisdom those who have chosen to tear asunder the most divine indivisibility by "means of strange terms," I exult in you and, to the best of my ability, offer thanks to the Triadic Monad, the invisible, the incomprehensible, Which has no figure and no form, Which "is present everywhere" as one, without division and in perfect unity. I pray continuously that the Holy Trinity may grant you every blessing! For your part, continue to delight me with your letters, thinking what a most wise and God-loving man ought to think, but do not be more proficient at thinking than at writing.

20. No Addressee

Even before now, a marvelous reputation has brought and presented you to me and proclaimed that you are excellent in medicine and truly "worth many men" and not without a share of any of the other faculties which make up the complete nature of wisdom; and that you have trained a noble mind and a tongue which is a suitable messenger for such a mind, and have made great strides in all Hellenic studies and, to a far greater degree, in our own sacred studies; that you pursue virtue rather than ambition, for "your pursuit is to be, not to look wise;" that wherever you happen to be you offer yourself as a haven for visitors from all over the place and above all for those who come from me, because you were nourished by our Church and are well versed in the soundness of our dogmas.

These very things captured and astounded our hearts even before now, but just now something else came up as well, as good as all those others, and extolled to us

20

ἐκείνων καὶ ἐξύμνησέ σου παρ' ἡμῖν τὴν σοφίαν καὶ τὴν εὐσέβειαν. τὴν γὰρ νῦν εἰσκωμάσασαν καὶ τῆς πάλαι φορτικωτέραν πολυθεΐαν, οἶμαι, καὶ τερατωδεστέραν, ἣν Παλαμᾶς τις ἐνόσησε πολυθεωτάτῳ χρησάμενος δαίμονι, φασὶ μὲν ἀφῖχθαι καὶ εἰς τὰς σὰς ἀκοάς, φασὶ δὲ οὕτως μὲν ὀξέως αὐτῆς τὴν σὴν ὀξυδορκίαν αἰσθέσθαι καθάπερ νοσήματος οὗπερ ἂν ἐκ πρώτης εὐστοχήσῃς τῆς πείρας, οὕτω δὲ κατ' αὐτοῦ δριμέως ἀνεγηγέρθαι ὥσπερ Ἀθανάσιος ὁ μέγας κατὰ τῆς Ἀρείου τοῦ κακίστου μανίας. καὶ γὰρ οὐδὲ βελτίω τοῦτον ὑπολαβεῖν ἐκείνου, ἀλλὰ καὶ μάλα χείρω, εἴπερ Ἀρείου μὲν ἦν ἀριθμεῖν τὴν παντουργὸν Τριάδα διαφόροις θεότησι, τὸ δ' αὐτὸ τοῦτο μεθ' ὅσης ὑπερβολῆς καὶ τῆς νῦν ἐστι θεοβλαβείας, διαιρούσης τὴν μίαν καὶ ἄπειρον καὶ ἀμερῆ καὶ ἁπλῆν καὶ ἀόρατον τῆς ἀρρήτου Τριάδος θεότητα εἰς πλῆθος θεοτήτων διαφορώτατον, ἄνισόν τε αὐτῶν καὶ ἀνόμοιον, καὶ τοὐλάχιστον δύο Θεοὺς εἰσαγούσης ἀνίσους καὶ δύο θεότητας, ἵνα μὴ πλῆθος ἀναρίθμητον λέγω, τὴν ὅλην αὐτοῦ καὶ τελείαν ἀσέβειαν· εἰ γὰρ εἷς Θεός, ὅτι μία θεότης, κατὰ τοὺς θείους πατέρας, εἰ πλείους θεότητες ἄνισοι, καὶ πλείους θεοὶ πάντως ἄνισοι καὶ ἀλλήλοις ἀνομοιότατοι.

Ὧν τὴν μὲν ἐνεργεῖν, τὴν δ' ἐνεργεῖσθαι, λέγει, καὶ τὴν μὲν ἀόρατον, τὴν δὲ καὶ σωματικοῖς ὀφθαλμοῖς καθ' αὑτὴν ληπτὴν εἶναι, καὶ τὴν μὲν μεθεκτήν, τὴν δ' ἀμέθεκτον, καὶ τὴν μὲν οὐσίαν, τὴν δ' ἀνούσιον, καὶ τὴν μὲν ὑπερκειμένην, τὴν δ' ὑφειμένην ἀπειράκις ἀπείρως, φῶς θ' ἕτερον ἄκτιστόν τε καὶ ἄναρχον, τοὺς θεοφιλεῖς τῶν ἀνθρώπων φωτίζον παρὰ τὴν φύσιν καὶ παρ' ἐκεῖνο τὸ φῶς ὃ φωτίζει πάντα ἄνθρωπον ἐρχόμενον εἰς τὸν κόσμον, τὸν ὑπερφυᾶ τοῦ Θεοῦ Πατρὸς Λόγον, [fol. 51r] ὡς μήτε Θεὸν εἶναι τοῦτο τὸν ἀνωτάτω, μήτ' ἄγγελον, τοῦ μὲν γὰρ ὑφειμένον ἀπειράκις ἀπείρως, εἰ καὶ αὐτῷ συναΐδιον, τῶν δὲ ὑπερκείμενον, Θεὸς δὲ ὢν καὶ αὐτὸ καὶ τοῦ Θεοῦ θεότης, ἐν ἡμῖν τε διάγων καὶ ἐνεργῶν τὰ κάτω, ἐπείπερ οὐ μεθ' ἡμῶν ὁ πάντων ἐπέκεινα ὡς ἀναφὴς καὶ ἀμέθεκτος κατὰ τοὺς νέους λήρους· ποῦ γὰρ θήσομεν τὸ τὸν οὐρανὸν καὶ τὴν γῆν ἐγὼ πληρῶ λέγει Κύριος, καὶ τὸ ὑμεῖς ἐστε ναοὶ Θεοῦ ζῶντος; ἐφ' ἕτερον Θεὸν καὶ θείαν ἄλλην μεταθήσομεν φύσιν παρὰ

30–31 Greg. Naz., *Or.* 31, 14 (PG, 36, 148D) || 33–45 Ὧν τὴν μέν . . . ἀμέθεκτος cf. Palamam, *Epist. III ad Acindynum*, 1–17, Syngrammata, I, 296–309; *Dialexis*, Syngrammata, II, 164–218 || 36–37 cf. Palamam, *Epist. III ad Acindynum*, 15, Syngrammata, I, 306, 18–20; ed. Nadal, 252, 10–12 || 37 et 42 cf. Maxim. Conf., *Capit. theol.*, 1, 49 (PG, 90, 1101A) = Palamas, *Dialexis*, 24, Syngrammata, II, 186, 26; *Epist. ad Gabram*, 5, Syngrammata, II, 332, 12 || 39–40 Joan. 1:9 || 45 Joan. Dam., *De fide orth.*, 1, 8 (PG, 94, 816A). || 46–47 Jerem. 23:24 || 47 II Cor. 6:16

---

47 ἡμεῖς M

20

your wisdom and piety. For they say that the polytheism which has just burst in and which is, in my opinion, more onerous and more monstrous than the old one—a disease from which somebody by the name of Palamas suffers, the victim of a polytheistic demon—has reached your ears. And they say that your sharp-sightedness saw through it as keenly as if it were a disease which you could diagnose correctly on the first examination, and that you rose up against it as vehemently as did Athanasios the Great against the madness of the wicked Arios. For Palamas, indeed, is not to be considered better than Arios, but even much worse, since it was characteristic of Arios to count different divinities in the all-creating Trinity, and the very same thing, but to an extreme degree, is also characteristic of the present God-inflicted madness, which divides the one and infinite and indivisible and simple and invisible divinity of the inexpressible Trinity into a sundry multitude of divinities, mutually unequal and dissimilar, introducing at least two unequal gods and two divinities, not to say an innumerable multitude, his whole and complete profanity; for if "there is one God because there is one divinity," according to the holy Fathers, if there are many unequal divinities, there are also, no doubt, many gods, unequal and most unlike one another.

Of these two divinities, he says that one is activating, while the other is activated; one is invisible, while the other is apprehensible in itself even by bodily eyes; one is capable of being shared, while the other is incapable of being shared; one is the essence, while the other is not. In fact, one is higher, while the other is "infinitely" lower, a different light, both uncreated and without beginning, which illuminates the men beloved of God; ⟨a light which exists⟩ in addition to the natural light and to that "Light which enlightens every man born into the world," the preternatural Logos of God the Father, so that it is neither the Godhead nor an angel, being infinitely inferior to God, though coeternal with Him, and higher than the angels. Yet this ⟨light⟩ too is God and God's divinity, and it both lives within us and operates this world, because the all-transcendent God is not with us, being impalpable and incapable of being shared, according to the new absurdities. How then are we to regard the sayings: "I fill heaven and earth, saith the Lord," and "you are the temples of a living God"? Are we to refer them instead to another God and to another divine nature in addition to the Highest? For if it is not the ⟨Highest⟩, there

τὴν ἀνωτάτω; εἰ γὰρ οὐκ ἔστιν ἐκείνη, ἄλλη τις ἂν εἴη καὶ Θεὸς ἄλλος ὁ ταῦτα λέγων, οὗ καὶ ναὸς ἡ εὐσεβὴς ἐκκλησία καὶ ἔστι καὶ λέγεται· ἀλλ' ἔστι τοῦτο μανίας εἰπεῖν τῆς ἁπασῶν ἐσχάτης καὶ τῆς νῦν μόνης ἀσεβοῦς τερατείας. τὸ δὲ πάντων τερατωδέστατον ὅτι καὶ τοὺς οἷς ἂν ἐγγένηταί, φησι, τουτὶ τὸ φῶς, ὁ ὑφειμένος θεός, ἀκτίστους ποιεῖ καὶ ἀνάρχους κἀκείνους.

Ταῦτ' ἐκ πολλῶν ὀλίγα τῶν ἐνταῦθα τεράτων. τὰ καιριώτατα μέντοι καὶ τῶν λοιπῶν αἱ ῥίζαι ἦλθον μὲν εἰς αἴσθησιν τῆς σῆς θεοσεβείας, ἦλθον δὲ εἰς πῦρ καυστικὸν τῶν τοιούτων. ἦλθε δ' ἡμῖν ἐκεῖθεν φήμη καὶ ταῦτα κηρύττουσα μετὰ τῶν ἄλλων σου κατορθωμάτων. εἷλε δὲ μᾶλλον ἡμᾶς εἰκότως ἢ πρότερον, καὶ ὥσπερ συνδήσασα δεσμοῖς ἀλύτοις, τῷ σῷ δουλεύειν ἱερῶς παραδέδωκε πόθῳ. ὁ δὲ μάλιστα καὶ ὕστατα πάντων ταῦτ' ἀπαγγείλας ἡμῖν ὁ καλὸς καὶ ἀγαθὸς ἡμῖν ἀδελφός ἐστιν ὁ Μαλαχίας, *ὃν ἀγαπήσαντες διὰ τὸν τρόπον, διὰ ταῦτα μᾶλλον καὶ ἠγαπήκαμεν καὶ ἀγαπῶμεν καὶ τοῦ φιλεῖν οὐ παυσόμεθα.*

Ἴδοιμεν δὲ καὶ τὴν σὴν ὧδε παρ' ἡμῖν ἱερὰν καὶ θαυμαστὴν κεφαλὴν καὶ τὴν ἐπὶ σοὶ τελεωτάτην ἑορτὴν ἑορτάσαιμεν. ὅτι καὶ παρὰ τὸ δέον ἂν εἴη δήπου σέ τε τὸν τρόφιμον τῆς μεγάλης καὶ βασιλίδος τῶν πόλεων, καὶ τῆς μετὰ ταύτην ἀρίστης πόλεως Θεσσαλονίκης, *καὶ τῆς ἱερᾶς τῶν ἱερῶν ἀνδρῶν πόλεως* Ἄθω *τοῦ θαυμασιωτάτου, ὅς σοι καὶ πολλοὺς ἀρετῆς ἕνεκα μαρτυρεῖ τοὺς ἱδρῶτας, ἔξω διάγειν ὑπερόριον τούτων· ταῦτά τε καὶ ἡμᾶς ἀνδρὸς ἐστερῆσθαι τοσούτου, αὐτοῖς διαφέροντος, ἀλλ' οὐ παρ' οἷς διάγει.*

21. Ἱεροθέῳ

Ἀδελφὲ σπουδαιότατε καὶ διὰ τοῦτο θεοφιλέστατε, τὴν μὲν ὑπὲρ τῆς εὐσεβείας σπουδὴν καὶ φροντίδα σου ὑπεραπεδεξάμην· τί γὰρ οὐκ ἔμελλον, ὅτε καὶ πολλῆς δεῖ τῆς συνδρομῆς ἐπὶ τὴν καινὴν ταύτην πλάνην καὶ γάγγραιναν τῆς Χριστοῦ *ἐκκλησίας; τόν γε μὴν περὶ τῆς χάριτος λόγον καὶ τῶν τοῦ* Θεοῦ *χαρισμάτων καὶ δώρων διὰ τὸν ἐκ τούτων ὑφιστάντα πολλὰς συναϊδίους, ὑφειμένας καὶ ὑπερκειμένας θεότητας δεῖ ποιεῖσθαι, ἀλλ' οὐκ ἄλλως*

53–54 cf. Palamam, *Epist. III ad Acindynum*, 16, Syngrammata, I, 308, 14–16 || 48 *ἡμεῖς* M

21: 7–8 et 11 cf. Palamam, *Epist. III ad Acindynum*, 15, Syngrammata, I, 306, 18–20; ed. Nadal, 252, 10–12

---

72 *αὐτοῖς* M

21: Mn 3r–4r. Ed. Karpozilos, *Letters*, 77–78, no. 2.

must be another divine nature and another God who says this and whose temple both is and is called the holy Church. But to say this is characteristic of the worst possible madness and the present impious mythmaking alone. And the most monstrous thing of all is that he says that this very light, the lower God, "renders uncreated and without beginning" even those to whom it may appear.

These are a few of the many affronts in this matter. The most important, of course, and the fundamentals of the others came to the attention of your Piety and to the fire which burns such things. And a marvelous rumor came to me from there proclaiming this together with your other accomplishments. And naturally it captivated me more than before and bound me, so to speak, with unbreakable fetters and delivered me to the sacred bondage of longing for you. And the man who above all was the latest person to report this news to me is our good and noble brother Malachias, whom I loved before for his character, but as a result of this report I have loved him even more, and I love and will not cease loving him.

May I also see you here, near me, my holy and marvelous friend, and celebrate the most perfect feast in your honor! For surely it would not be right for you who were reared in the great Queen of cities and in Thessalonica, the next best city, and in the holy city of the holy men, the most marvelous Mt. Athos, which bears witness to your many virtuous exertions, to live abroad, beyond their boundaries. Not only this, but I am deprived of a man who is so important to me, though not to those amongst whom he lives.

21. To Hierotheos

Most zealous and therefore most beloved brother, I welcomed warmly your zeal and concern for piety. And why should I not, when so much of a concourse, indeed, is needed against this new error and gangrene in the Church of Christ! And so the discourse on the divine grace and God's endowments and gifts must be written on account of the man who created out of them many coeternal, "lower and higher divinities," but not otherwise for reasons of contentiousness. For if "the

21

φιλονεικίας χάριν. ἐπεὶ ἐὰν ἁπλῶς διὰ τῶν ὁμολογουμένων τῆς εὐσεβείας ὅρων ἁπάσῃ τῇ ἁγίᾳ τοῦ Θεοῦ ἐκκλησίᾳ, ὥσπερ εἰκός, ἐκβληθῇ ἡ ὑφειμένη θεότης [fol. 3v] τῆς νέας θεολογίας, μᾶλλον δὲ δυοῖν θάτερον, ἢ τὸ ὑφειμένον τοῦ ἀκτίστου καὶ τὸ πρὸς τὴν θείαν φύσιν ἄνισον καὶ ἀνόμοιον, ἢ τῆς ὑφειμένης καὶ ἐνεργουμένης καὶ σωματικοῖς ὀφθαλμοῖς ὁρωμένης τὸ ἄκτιστον—οὐδὲν γὰρ κοινὸν τῷ ἀκτίστῳ καὶ τούτοις, κἂν πάντα τις ὁρᾷ, κἂν ἓν ὁτιδήποτε· ἀλλ' εἰ μὲν ἄκτιστος, οὐχ ὑφειμένη, οὐδὲ ἐνεργουμένη, οὐδ' ὁρατὴ σωματικοῖς ὀφθαλμοῖς· εἰ δ' ὑφειμένη καὶ ἐνεργουμένη καὶ ὁρατή, οὐκ ἀγένητος—εἰ ταῦτα τοίνυν ἐκποδὼν πάντα γένοιτο καὶ μηδεμία παραδεχθῇ τῆς καινῆς ταύτης τόλμης καὶ ἀτοπωτάτης εἰς τὸ θεῖον ἐγχειρήσεως καὶ καινοπραγμοσύνης ἐπήρεια καὶ πιθανολογία, διαιροῦσα καὶ συνάγουσα καὶ ἐρωτῶσα τὰ ἀτοπώτατα καὶ συλλογιζομένη τὰ ἀφρονέστατα καὶ γράφουσα τὰ τολμηρότατα, ἀλλ' αὐτοὺς ἁπλῶς μόνους τοὺς ὅρους τῶν ἱερῶν διδαγμάτων περὶ τῆς μιᾶς ἀκτίστου καὶ τρισυποστάτου θεότητος ἀπεριέργως καὶ ἀκατασκευάστως καὶ ἀπολυπραγμονήτως καὶ ἀνεξηγήτως ὡς κεῖνται δεξάμενοι πάντες, τὴν καινὴν ταύτην ἀποπέμψωνται πλάνην, μηδεμίαν αὐτῇ χώραν δόντες πλατύνεσθαι καὶ τεχνολογεῖν τὸν ἀπερινόητον Θεόν, τὸν ἀνεξιχνίαστον ἀγγέλοις, τὸν ἀνεξερεύνητον ἀρχαγγέλοις, τὸν ἀθέατον τοῖς Σεραφίμ, τὸν ἀκατανόητον τοῖς Χερουβίμ, τὸν ἀόρατον ἀρχαῖς καὶ ἐξουσίαις καὶ ἁπλῶς πάσῃ τῇ κτίσει, κατὰ τὸν Χρυσορρήμονα· εἰ οὕτω τὰ νέα δόγματα ἐξαιρεθείη καὶ τὰ τοῦ θείου τεχνολογήματα, οὔτε περὶ χάριτος ἐντεῦθεν, οὔτε τῶν χαρισμάτων δεῖν οἶμαι ποιεῖσθαι λόγον τινὰ καὶ διάλεξιν, οὔτε ἄλλου τινὸς τῶν ἁπάντων ὧν νῦν ἐξ ἀνάγκης ἁπτόμεθα πρὸς τοὺς πάντα ἄγοντας ἐπὶ ἀποδείξει δῆθεν καὶ βεβαιώσει τοῦ πλήθους τῶν θεοτήτων· ἀλλὰ σῳζομένης τῆς εἰς τὸν ἕνα τρισυπόστατον Θεὸν καὶ μίαν μόνην θεότητα ἄκτιστον ὁμολογίας καὶ πίστεως, τὴν ἁπλῆν τὴν ἀμερῆ, τὴν ἀόρατον, τὴν ἀνείδεον, τὴν ἄπειρον, τὴν παντουργόν τε μόνην καὶ παντοδύναμον, τὴν μηδενὶ τῶν ὄντων ἐκ φυσικῆς ἐμφάσεως διεγνωσμένην, τὴν μήτε οὐσίαις ἢ φύσεσιν ἢ διαφόροις θεότησιν ἀριθμουμένην, ἀλλ' ὑποστάσεσι μόναις, κατὰ τοὺς θείους πατέρας, πάντα τὰ ἄλλα οὕτως ὡς κεῖται παρὰ τοῖς θείοις πατράσιν, ὥσπερ καὶ

28–31 Joan. Chrys., *De incompr.*, 3, 1 (PG, 48, 720) || 40–41 μηδενί . . . διεγνωσμένην: Maxim. Conf., *Capit. theol.*, 1, 1 (PG, 90, 1084A) || 41–43 Sophronius, *Epistula synodica ad Sergium*, (PG, 87[3], 3156C)

17 εἰ] ἡ Mn || 18 ἐκποδῶν Mn

21

lower divinity" of the new theology is simply driven out by the laws of piety which are accepted by the whole holy Church of God, as is right, or rather, if you take one of two alternatives, either that the lower and unequal and dissimilar to the divine nature is driven out of the uncreated divinity or that the uncreated is driven out of the divinity which is lower and activated and visible to bodily eyes (for there is nothing in common between the uncreated and ⟨bodily eyes⟩, whether one sees all ⟨uncreated beings⟩ or even just one of them; but if it is an uncreated divinity, then it is not lower nor activated nor visible to bodily eyes; and if it is lower and activated and visible, then it is not unbegotten); if, therefore, all these are banished, and one does not accept one single insult or specious argument of this new effrontery or most absurd undertaking or innovation against the Divine, dividing and assembling and asking the most absurd questions and reaching the most foolish conclusions and writing the most brazen things; but if all men, without questions, artifice, officiousness and explications, accept simply only the actual terms of the sacred doctrines about the one uncreated divinity in three hypostases as they are laid down and dismiss this new fallacy without allowing it to grow and to analyze the incomprehensible God "Who is unfathomable to the angels, inscrutable to the archangels, invisible to the Seraphim, inconceivable to the Cherubim, invisible to the principalities and powers and simply to the whole creation," as Chrysostom says; if the new doctrines and systematic analyses of the Divine are thus removed, I do not think that henceforth there will be any need to write any discourse or treatise either about the grace or the gifts of God, or to do any of all the other things that I am forced to undertake now against those who make every effort to give specious proof and confirmation of the multitude of divinities. But, preserving the confession and faith in one God in three hypostases and in one Divinity alone, uncreated, simple, undivided, invisible, formless, infinite, the only all-creating and omnipotent, "Which is not known to any being by means of a natural manifestation and is not numbered according to different essences, natures or divinities, but by hypostases alone," according to the holy Fathers; we must likewise accept everything else as laid down by the holy Fathers and let these things remain simple and immovable and unshake-

ταῦτα στέργοντες, ἁπλῶς καὶ ἀπαρακινήτως καὶ ἀσαλεύτως ἐατέον κεῖσθαι καὶ ὡς κεῖνται νοεῖσθαι καὶ στέργεσθαι· οὐχ ὡς ἐθέλει ὁ τὰς πολλὰς θεότητας ἀκτίστους, ἀνίσους καὶ ἀνομοίους παραδιδοὺς ἡμῖν, τὸν ἀρχαῖον Ἑλληνισμόν, καὶ νῦν μὲν διαιρῶν τὸ θεῖον ἀρειανικῶς εἰς ἐκφύλους ἀλλοτριότητας, νῦν δ' ἐπεισάγων ξένους θεοὺς καὶ θεότητας ἐκ τῶν δημιουργημάτων, οὓς οὔτε ἡμεῖς ἐγνώκαμεν, οὔθ' οἱ πατέρες ἡμῶν, ἀλλ' ὡς ἡ κοινὴ ἔννοια τῆς ἁγίας καθολικῆς καὶ ἀποστολικῆς ἐκκλησίας παρέλαβε καὶ φρονεῖ, καὶ ὡς οὐκ ἂν ἐντεῦθεν τὸ πλῆθος τῶν ἀνίσων καὶ ἀνομοίων θεοτήτων συνάγοιτο κατὰ μηδένα τρόπον, οὐδὲ Θεὸς ληπτὸς μασσαλιανικῶς κατὰ φυσικὸν [fol. 4r] αὐτοῦ καὶ οὐσιῶδες εἶδος σωματικοῖς ὀφθαλμοῖς τισιν, ὧν οὐδὲν ἀσεβέστερον. οὕτως ἐνδεῖ φρονοῦντας ἡμᾶς ἀπολιπεῖν τὸν βίον, ὅπως ἂν ἀπαντήσειεν. ἔρρωσο.

22. Sine titulo

Τὰ σὰ γράμματα πράγματα· οὐ γὰρ πρὶν πράττειν λέγεις, οὐδὲ μᾶλλον τοῦ πράττειν, ἀλλ' ἅτε πράττεις λέγεις, καὶ τοῖς πράγμασι τοὺς λόγους ἑπομένους παρέχῃ. τοιγαροῦν πρότερον ἡμᾶς εὐφράνας οἷς ἔπραξας ὑπὲρ τῶν εὐσεβῶν δογμάτων, νῦν καὶ τοῖς γράμμασιν εὔφρανας οἷς ἔπεμψας ἡμῖν ἐπὶ τοῖς πεπραγμένοις. πεπραγμένα [fol. 70v] δὲ λέγω τὰ γεγραμμένα σοι πρὸς Θεσσαλονικέας, ἐπειδήπερ ἔργων ἐκεῖνα γέγονε συστατικὰ γενναίων· ἔσται δέ, οἶμαι, καὶ νῦν ἑτέρων ἃ πρὸς ἐκείνους γράφεις. ὧν τοίνυν χάριν καὶ πράττων καὶ γράφων ἡμᾶς μετὰ Θεὸν εὐφραίνεις, ἀμοιβὰς ἀντιλάμβανε· γράμματα μὲν παρ' ἡμῶν ἅπερ ἔχομεν, πράγματα δὲ ἐκ Θεοῦ γένοιτό σοι τὰ βέλτιστα καὶ οἷς εὐδαιμονία συνίσταται.

23. Sine titulo

Καὶ πρότερον μεγάλην ᾤμην καὶ ὑπερέχουσαν καὶ διάνοιαν καὶ γνώμην ὑπάρχειν σοι, καὶ ἐπειδήπερ εἶδον καὶ ἐπῆλθον τὰ

51–52 cf. *Fidei symbolum*: Joannis Chrysostomi *Liturgia* (ed. Brightman), 383, 23–24

---

46 ἐθέλοι Mn ‖ 51 ἔνοια Mn ‖ 56 leg. δεῖ?

22: M 70r–70v.

5 εὐφράνας M

23: Mn 9r. Ed. Karpozilos, *Letters*, 99, no. 12.

able, and understand them and accept them as they are, that is, not according to the wishes of the man who has provided us with many uncreated and unequal and dissimilar divinities (the ancient paganism), and who now divides the Divinity after the manner of Arios into strange qualitative differences, and then adds to these strange gods and divinities ⟨arising⟩ from created beings, which neither we nor our fathers have known, but ⟨we should understand them⟩ according to the belief that the "Holy Catholic and Apostolic Church" has received and upholds, and in this way the multitude of divinities unequal and dissimilar cannot be brought in at all, nor a God perceptible to the bodily eyes of certain men, in his natural and essential form, after the fashion of the Messalians. Nothing is more impious than these! With such beliefs we ought to end our lives, no matter how. Farewell.

22. No Addressee

Your letters are deeds! For you do not speak before you act, and neither do you speak beyond what you do, rather you say what you do and you let your words follow your deeds. And so, having previously delighted me with what you did in defense of our pious dogmas, now you have further delighted me with the letter which you sent to follow these deeds. By deeds I mean what you wrote to the Thessalonians, since really that became the cause of noble deeds. And I believe that what you are writing to them now will be the cause of other noble deeds also. Receive, therefore, your rewards for the pleasure that you give me, after God, by your deeds and letters: on the one hand, a letter from me to the best of my ability and, on the other hand, deeds from God: may He grant you all the blessings that make up happiness!

23. No Addressee

Even before now, I thought that you possessed a great and outstanding mind as well as judgment; and, indeed, since I saw and went through the letter in which

γράμματα οἷς ὑπὲρ τοῦ Θεοῦ καὶ τῶν ὅλων πραγμάτων ἐκ σοφῆς μὲν καὶ ἱερᾶς τῆς γνώμης, δι' ὁσίας δὲ τῆς γλώττης ἐξύφηνας, οὐδ' ἔχω λέγειν οἷα μὲν ἥσθην, οἷα δὲ ὠφέλημαι ὥσπερ ἱερᾶς τινος μετεσχηκὼς τελετῆς. τοιούτους ἑαυτῷ στρατηγοὺς ὁ Θεὸς ταμιεύει καί, τοῦ καιροῦ καλοῦντος, ἐξάγει καὶ ἀναδείκνυσιν.

24. Τῷ μεγάλῳ δουκὶ

Ὅπῃ παρείης τί μὴ καλὸν ἐνταῦθα; στρατηγῶν, ἀπαλλάττεις πραγμάτων τὴν βασιλείαν καὶ ἀντιμεθίστης τὰ δεινὰ τοῖς βαρβάροις, ἃ τὸ ἡμέτερον γένος ὑπ' αὐτῶν ἀεὶ πάσχει· ἐπανήκων ἀπὸ τοιούτων ἔργων, τὴν ἐκκλησίαν κρατύνεις οὐκ ἔλαττον, καὶ εἰς καιρὸν τῇ εὐσεβείᾳ γινόμενος, τῇ τ' εὐσεβεῖ σοφίᾳ καὶ τῇ τοιαύτῃ σοφίᾳ προσηκούσῃ δυνάμει ἐκπλεῖς οὐχ ἧττον νικηφόρος ἐπὶ τὰ πρόσθεν ἔργα ἢ καταπλέων τῇδε. ἀνθ' ὧν σε κοσμεῖ τε Θεὸς τοῖς θαυμασίοις ἔργοις, καὶ διὰ σοῦ γε ταῦτα τοὺς ἐν δεινοῖς ὄντας εὐεργετεῖ μεγάλοις, καὶ εἰσέτι κοσμήσειε, καὶ μάλα εἰκότως· οὐδὲν γὰρ [ἂν] ἀνδρὸς γενναίου καὶ εὐσεβείας προμάχου θεοφιλέστερον, οὐκοῦν οὐδὲ συμμαχεῖν [fol. 41v] ἑτέρῳ μᾶλλον τὸ θεῖον βουλήσεται τοῦ οἰκείου προμάχου. ὅθεν ἐσμὲν οἱ τῆς σῆς ἐξηρτημένοι καὶ γνώμης καὶ εὐσεβείας εὐέλπιδες τοῦ πολλὰ μὲν ἂν ἡμῖν ἀγαθὰ διὰ τῆς σῆς περιγενέσθαι σπουδῆς, πολλὰ δέ σοι ἐκ Θεοῦ διὰ τῶν θείων εὐχῶν τῶν ἱερῶν πατέρων.

25. Ἰωάννῃ τῷ ἁγιωτάτῳ πατριάρχῃ

Εἶχον μὲν καὶ πάλαι διὰ φροντίδος, ὁρῶν τὴν λύμην ταύτην τῆς ἐκκλησίας προβαίνουσαν, ὡς ἂν οἷός τε ὦ κατ' αὐτῆς ἀναστῆναι, θαρρεῖν δὲ οὐκ εἶχον, ἰδιώτης ὢν διδασκαλικῆς ἀξίας καὶ τάξεως· φυλάττειν γὰρ ᾤμην δεῖν καὶ τὴν ἐνταῦθα τάξιν οὐχ ἥκιστα τὸν ζῆν [fol. 51v] εὐλαβῶς πρὸς τὰ θεῖα καὶ κατὰ λόγον ἐθέλοντα—θεοφιλὲς δὲ ἄρα τὸ εὐλαβὲς πρὸς ταῦτα καὶ μέτριον—ἕως ἂν ὦσιν ἐνεργεῖς οἷς ἔξεστι κατὰ τοὺς θείους νόμους ἅπτεσθαι τῶν τοιούτων.

---

5 ἤσθην Mn

24: M 41r–41v.

6 εὐσεβῆ M || 11 [ἂν] uncis inclusi

25: M 51r–51v.

you weave your defense of God and the whole matter in question with wise and pious judgment and a hallowed tongue, I cannot even say how delighted I was and how I have profited, as if I had indeed participated in a sacred ceremony. Such generals God preserves for Himself and when the occasion arises brings them out and displays them.

24. To the *Megas Doux*

What blessing fails to appear wherever you are present? When you command the army, you deliver the Empire from trouble and transfer to the barbarians the sufferings which they are forever inflicting upon our nation! When you return home from such deeds, you are no less ⟨eager⟩ to strengthen the Church, and, by supporting piety at the right time with your pious wisdom and the power that befits such wisdom, you sail away to further deeds no less victorious than when you sailed back here! Wherefore God adorns you with marvelous deeds and through you extends these benefits to those who are in great distress. And may He adorn you even more, and quite properly, for nothing is dearer to God than a noble man and defender of piety; nor accordingly, will God choose to ally Himself with another man in preference to His own defender. Therefore I, who depend on your judgment and piety, am hopeful that many blessings will accrue to me through your zeal and to you from God through the prayers of the holy Fathers.

25. To the most holy Patriarch John

Even before this, when I saw this outrage towards the Church making progress, I was anxiously considering how I could rise up against it, but I could not pluck up courage, since I lacked a teacher's dignity and rank. For I thought that the man who wishes to live with reverence for sacred matters and in accordance with the rules should not be less observant of the order here—and it is true that a reverend and modest attitude towards sacred matters is dear to God—until those who are permitted by the sacred laws to handle such matters take action.

Ἐπεὶ δὲ τὴν πονηρὰν ταύτην φορὰν ἰδοῦσα καὶ ἡ σὴ κορυφαία θειότης οὐκ ἀνεκτὸν ᾠήθη μὴ ἀπαντῆσαι ταύτῃ καὶ λόγοις καὶ πράγμασι, καὶ τὰ μὲν ἔργα ἑαυτῇ, τοὺς δὲ λόγους ἡμῖν ἐφῆκε τοὺς ὑπὲρ εὐσεβείας, τὴν ἐπίταξιν ἤδη τελέσας τὴν σὴν εἰς δύναμιν, ἀποδίδωμι· χωρὶς μέν, κατὰ σχῆμα συνεχῶν καὶ τεταγμένων λόγων, χωρὶς δέ, σχολίοις κατὰ ῥῆμα καὶ κῶλον, ἀνῃρηκὼς τὸν Παλαμίτην καὶ παλαμναῖον ὄντως διάλογον, μᾶλλον δὲ οὐκ αὐτὸς ἀνῃρηκώς, ἀλλὰ τοῖς θείοις πατράσιν ἀναιρέταις χρησάμενος, καὶ τοσοῦτ' αὐτῶν τοῖς λόγοις συναράμενος ταῦτα, ὁπόσον που ξίφεσι κατὰ τῶν πολεμίων οἱ ἀμυνόμενοι.

Λάβε δὴ τῆς ἡμετέρας εὐπειθείας τὸν πόνον, τὸν ἐπὶ τοὺς δυσσεβείας ἁπάσης μεστοὺς γεγενημένον λόγους, ἐπὶ τοῖς ἔργοις οἷς αὐτός, ὦ θειότατε, μετὰ παντὸς τοῦ θείου τῶν ἱερῶν κύκλου ἀνεῖλες τὴν Παλαμναίαν λύμην, τοὺς αὐτῆς φυτευτὰς ἐκκηρύκτους ποιήσας καὶ ὡς λοιμοὺς τῆς ἐκκλησίας ἀπωσάμενος τῆς ἐκκλησίας καὶ τῆς ἱερωσύνης, ἱερῶς μάλα κρίνας εἶναι ἀνίερον καὶ τὸ ποσὶ δυσσεβῶν πατεῖσθαι τὰ ἱερώτατα τῶν ἀδύτων τεμένη. καὶ εἰ μὲν ἀνενδεῶς ἐξείργασταί μοι τοὐπίταγμα καὶ κατὰ γνώμην ὑμῖν, τῷ Θεῷ χάρις καὶ τῇ μιᾷ τρισυποστάτῳ θεότητι, ὑπὲρ ἧς πεπονήκαμεν, καί σοι τῷ θειοτάτῳ τόπῳ καὶ κρατῆρι τοῦ Πνεύματος καὶ τοῖς ἄλλοις αὐτοῦ πανιέροις μετόχοις, ὧν ταῖς εὐχαῖς κεχρημένος ἐξετέλεσα τοὔργον· εἰ δ' ἐνδεῶς, καὶ οὕτω μὲν τῷ τε Θεῷ χάρις καὶ ὑμῖν τοῦ γενομένου χάριν, τὸ δ' ἐνδεές, ὑμέτερον προσθῆναι καὶ τὸ πᾶν ἐκτελέσαι διὰ τοῦ Πνεύματος.

26. Sine titulo

Ὁ μὲν τῆς ἀπουσίας χρόνος δεκαετὴς ὢν ἤδη που ἐν ᾧ σου τῇ θαυμαστῇ κεφαλῇ οὔτε αὐτὸς εἰς ὄψιν, οὔτε διὰ γραμμάτων εἰς ὁμιλίαν ἦλθον, προσίστατό μοι καὶ νῦν βουλομένῳ σοι γράψαι· τίκτεται γάρ πως ἐξ ἀργίας ἀργία, καὶ πολλάκις καὶ τὸ εὐκινητότατον ἐν χρονίῳ στάσει γενόμενον, δυσκίνητον γέγονεν· ὥσπερ οὖν καὶ κινηθὲν ῥᾳδίως οὐχ ἵσταται, καὶ μάλισθ' ὅταν κατὰ πρανοῦς τινος φέρηται. οἷον καὶ λόγος καὶ διάθεσις πάσχει, ὅταν εὕρῃ τὸ κινοῦν, ἢ περὶ ὃ κινοῖτο, ἑλκτικὸν ἑαυτοῦ καὶ σφόδρα κινητικόν. ὃ σύ, γενναιότατε, τίνι μὲν οὐκ ἐγένου τῶν αἴσθησιν ἀρετῆς εὐμοιρούντων

26–30 *καὶ εἰ . . . Θεῷ χάρις*: cf. Greg. Naz., *Or.* 42, 18 (PG, 36, 480C)

---

21 post *ἱερῶν* unum verbum, fortasse *ἀνδρῶν*, deest

26: M 38v–39v.

But since, after observing this wicked force, Your Sublime Holiness also thought it unbearable not to oppose it both by the written word and by deeds, and assigned the deeds to yourself and the writing in defense of our piety to me, I have fulfilled your order to the best of my ability and am returning this to you. I have refuted the Palamitic and truly abominable dialogue in separate ways: on the one hand, in the form of continuous and systematic arguments, and on the other, by comments on every phrase and clause. Rather, I did not refute it myself but used the holy Fathers as refuters, and, in this case, I used their words as much as perhaps those who defend themselves against the enemy use swords.

Receive then the fruit of my obedience, which was produced against the writings full of all impiety, in addition to the deeds by which your Holiness and the whole divine circle of holy men destroyed the Palamnaian bane, by excommunicating its progenitors and expelling them from the Church and the priesthood as a plague on the Church; for you decided very piously that it is impious for the most hallowed ground of the sanctuaries to be as much as stepped upon by the feet of the impious men. And if I have performed the assignment without fault and in accordance with your wishes, thanks be to God and to the one divine nature in three hypostases, for whose sake I have labored, and to you, the most divine dwelling place and vessel of the Spirit, and the other most holy men who partake of It, with whose blessings I performed this task. But if I performed it inadequately, even so, thanks be to God and to you for what has been done. And it is up to you, then, to add what is missing and accomplish everything through the Spirit.

26. No Addressee

The period of absence, about ten years already, during which I neither looked upon your marvelous face nor communicated with you by letter, came into my mind even now as I wished to write to you. For somehow idleness breeds idleness, and so often even what is most mobile becomes hard to move when it has stood still for a long time; just as when it has been set in motion it does not stop easily, especially when it is moving downwards. Something similar happens to speech and disposition when they find what stirs them—or that about which they may be stirred—attractive to them and exceedingly stimulating. This, my most noble friend, you have been to every man who has the good fortune to possess a sense of absolute

26

ἁπάσης; καὶ τίνος οὐχ ἕνεκα; δικαιοσύνης; ἀνδρίας; σωφροσύνης; φρονήσεως; εὐσεβείας; φόβου Θεοῦ; ἃ πάντα, καὶ ὅσα τις ἂν εἰπεῖν ἔχοι καλὰ καὶ ἀγαθὰ καὶ θαύματος ἄξια, μετὰ τοσαύτης σπουδῆς ἐπετήδευσας, μεθ' ὅσης οὐδ' οἱ μάλα γενναῖοι τῶν ἐπὶ τούτοις μόνοις καὶ τῷ ταῦτα φιλοσοφεῖν πόρρω πραγμάτων πάντων ἀπαγαγόντων αὐτούς. οὕτω σαυτοῦ τὸν βίον κυβερνᾷς ἀκινδύνως, σοφίας περιουσίᾳ καὶ τῷ Θεῷ προσέχειν.

Ἐμοὶ δὲ αὐτό τε τοῦτο ὃ σιωπᾶν παρήνει, τὸ μῆκος τῆς σιωπῆς, καὶ τὸ πάλαι ἁλῶναι τῆς σῆς μεγάλης ψυχῆς αἴτια γεγένηται τοῦ λῦσαι τὴν σιωπήν, ὥσπερ τινὰ φόρον ἀναγκαῖον καὶ ἀπαραίτητον ἀπητηκότα τοῦτον. συναίτιον δὲ καὶ τὸ ἀεί σε χωρεῖν διὰ γενναίων ἔργων καὶ συνεχῶς ἀκμάζειν ἐν ταῖς τοιαύταις τῶν ἐπιδείξεων μετ'ἀρετῆς ἁπάσης καὶ γνώμης θεοφιλοῦς, ἀνθ' ὧν σε ἡ θεία χάρις τοῖς τοιούτοις ἀμείβεται καὶ διὰ τέλους ἀμείβοιτο ἀεὶ τοῖς βελτίοσι τῶν παρεληλυθότων.

Ἧ σου πράττοντος, χαίρω τε ἐγὼ καὶ σιωπᾶν ἐθέλων οὐ δύναμαι, ἤδη δὲ οὐδὲ βούλομαι· οὐ γὰρ ἀνέχεται ἡ περὶ σέ μοι διάθεσις, τὸ ἐμὸν μέγα θαῦμα, ἑτέραις ὑποθέσεσι τὴν γλῶτταν παρέχοντα, μὴ καὶ τῇδε ἀνεῖναι. εἰ δ' ἀναγκαῖος ὁ πρὸς τ' ἄλλα μοι λόγος, ὑπὲρ γὰρ εὐσεβείας, ἀναγκαῖος καὶ οὗτος· πρὸς γὰρ κανόνα εὐσεβείας καὶ ὅρον καὶ πρὸς τοὺς παρόντας παντοδαποὺς χειμῶνας ἀσφαλῆ κυβερνήτην τῶν ἐγκεχειρισμένων, οὔτοι μὲν ἄξιος ὤν, οὐδ' ἱκανὸς οὐδετέρῳ οὐδέτερος· μὴ καθαρὸν γὰρ καθαροῦ ἐφάπτεσθαι οὐ θεμιτόν τις, εὖ καὶ καλῶς φιλοσοφήσας, εἶπε. πλὴν οὔτε τὸ θεῖον, οὔθ' οἱ τῷ θείῳ προσήκοντες ὑπερορῶσιν οὐδὲ τὴν ἀπὸ κιβδήλου καὶ ῥυπαρᾶς ἁμαρτίαις ψυχῆς τε καὶ γλώττης ἐπ' εὐ[fol. 39r]σεβείᾳ λόγων * * * ᾗ πλησιάζων λόγος καθαίρεται καὶ διὰ λόγου ψυχή· οὗ σύμβολον ἦν, οἶμαι, Ἡσαΐας ὁ μέγας καθαιρόμενος ἄνθρακι.

Ἀλλὰ ταῦτα μὲν εἶπον ὅσον αἰνίξασθαί σου τῇ εὐσεβεστάτῃ καὶ σοφωτάτῃ ψυχῇ, ὁ δὲ πάντων θαυμάσιος Σεναχηρεὶμ καὶ ὄντως σὸς ἀδελφός, ὀξὺς μὲν ὤν, εἴπερ τις, καὶ δεξιώτατος μεγάλων πραγμάτων λόγους ἀναλαβεῖν, οὐδὲν δὲ ἧττον καὶ δυνατῶς ἀπαγγεῖλαι τούτους τῷ βουλομένῳ μαθεῖν, λαμπρῶς μάλα σου δείξει καὶ παραστήσει ταῦτα τῇ σοφωτάτῃ γνώσει· ὅπως μὲν τοὺς θείους τῶν ἁγίων πατέρων τῆς εὐσεβείας ὅρους ἐτόλμησάν τινες κεκινηκέναι καὶ παντοίως λυμαίνεσθαι, ὅπως δὲ οὐ ῥᾳδίως ἡμεῖς ἠνεσχόμεθα τῶν

26: 32–33 Plato, *Phaedo*, 67b; Greg. Naz., *Or*. 27, 3 (PG, 36, 13D) || 37–38 Ἡσαΐας . . . ἄνθρακι cf. Isaiam 6:6–8

---

19 λύσαι M || 36 post λόγων lacunam statui

26

virtue. And for every good reason: justice, bravery, prudence, judgment, piety, fear of God; all these and all the good and noble and admirable virtues that one could name you have pursued with a zeal such as not to be matched even by the most distinguished of the men who devoted themselves to these virtues alone and to their philosophical pursuit beyond all things. This is how safely you conduct your life, with an abundance of wisdom and devotion to God.

Still, both the very thing which urged me to keep silent, the lengthy silence, and the fact that long ago I was captivated by your great soul caused me to break the silence, for they demanded it, so to speak, as a necessary and indispensable tribute. Another reason too was your constant advance through noble deeds and your continuous vigor in such manifestations with all possible virtue and pious inclination, for which the divine grace repays you with such rewards, and may it repay you until the end with rewards better than the previous ones!

I rejoice because you are doing so well, and, though I wish to keep quiet, I cannot, and now, in fact, I do not even want to. For my feelings towards you—my great admiration—do not permit me, when I lend my tongue to other topics, to refrain from speaking in this case also. If my speaking about the other matters is necessary because it is in defense of piety, this too is necessary, for it is about a model and standard of piety and a steadfast helmsman of those entrusted to him in the various impending storms. Although what I say is neither worthy nor adequate in either case. For someone who reflected wisely and well said that the "The impure is not permitted to approach the pure." Except that neither God nor the men of God scorn even * * * from a soul and tongue that are deceitful and filthy with sins * * * for the piety of words at whose contact speech is purged and through speech the soul. I think that the great Isaiah, purged with a coal, was a symbol of this.

But I mentioned these points only just to give a hint to your most pious and wise soul, while that unusually admirable and true brother of yours Senacherim, who is keener than anyone else and most adept in discussing important matters and reporting them just as vigorously to a person who wishes to find out, will present these matters to your Wisdom most brilliantly and show you how certain men dared alter and abuse in every way the sacred laws of piety laid down by the holy Fathers, and how I did not lightly tolerate their newfangled talk, and for this reason until

26

καινοφωνημάτων, καὶ διὰ τοῦτο μέχρι μέν τινος πολλῶν ἡμῖν καὶ λόγων καὶ πραγμάτων πειραθῆναι συμβέβηκεν ὑπὸ τῶν πρῴην φίλων καὶ φιλικῶν οὐκ ὀλίγων ἔργων τε καὶ λόγων παρ' ἡμῶν πειραθέντων, εἶτα μὴ μόνον πᾶσαν διαβολὴν καὶ ὕβριν καθ' ἡμῶν κενωσάντων, ἀλλὰ καὶ ξιφῶν ἀκμὰς καὶ λίθων βολὰς φονίους ἑτοίμως κεκινηκότων, ὅτι μή, τοὺς ὁμολογουμένους ὅρους τῆς εὐσεβείας ἀφέντες, ταῖς κιβδήλοις αὐτῶν καινοφωνίαις ἐπείσθημεν· ὕστερον δέ, φανέντων ἤδη τῶν εἰς τὴν εὐσέβειαν καινῶν πλημμελημάτων αὐτῶν, ἃ τέως ἐκρύπτετο ποικίλοις σοφίσμασι καὶ πιθανότησιν, ἡμεῖς μὲν ὑμνοῦμεν τὸν παντοδύναμον Θεὸν ὅτι παρέσχεν ἡμῖν ὃ διὰ τῆς τοῦ θείου Παύλου γλώττης ὑπέσχετο, οὐκ ἐάσας ἡμᾶς ἐπηρεασθῆναι μᾶλλον ἢ δυνάμεθα φέρειν, οἱ δὲ λυμήνασθαι τοῖς θείοις ὅροις ἐπικεχειρηκότες ἐξ ὑπερηφανίας καὶ ἡμᾶς συναπαχθῆναι σφίσι βεβιασμένοι, ὁ μὲν πρότερον, ὁ δ' ὕστερον ἀπελήλαται τῆς ἐκκλησίας, μᾶλλον δὲ αὐτοὶ τὴν ἐκκλησίαν ἀπέδρον ὥσπερ σκότος οὐκ ἔχον τῷ φωτὶ πλησιάζειν.

Ἡ σὴ δὲ οἶδ' ὅτι σοφία τε καὶ εὐσέβεια ταῦτα ἀκούσασα ἢ πρῶτον νῦν, ἢ καὶ πρότερον, οὔτ' ἄνευ λύπης ᾐσθήσεται, οὔτ' εὐφροσύνης χωρὶς ἀνιάσεται. τοῦτο δὴ τὸ ἡμέτερον· τὸ μὲν ὅτι τοιαῦτα ἔτι περὶ τὴν εὐσέβειαν ἡμῶν ὁ ἀρχέκακος δαίμων ἐπιχειρεῖ κακουργεῖν, καὶ τοὺς τὰ πρῶτα δοκοῦντας εἶναι τῶν εὐσεβῶν σφόδρα κακοήθως αὐτῇ καὶ δεινῶς ἐπανίστησιν, ὅθεν ἀμέλει καὶ πολλοὺς τῶν πρὶν ἀπεριέργως καὶ ἁπλῶς πιστευόντων ταῖς ἱεραῖς παραδόσεσι, τοὺς μέντοι διέσεισε, τοὺς δὲ βαθέως [fol. 39v] κατέσεισε καὶ διχονοίᾳ χαλεπῇ περιέβαλε περὶ τὴν θείαν πίστιν, τοὺς δὲ καὶ παντάπασι τῇ καινοφωνίᾳ προσήλωσε. τούτων μὲν οὖν ἕνεκα οὐκ ἄνευ λύπης ἂν οἶμαί σου τὴν θαυμασίαν ψυχὴν ἀκοῦσαι τοὺς περὶ τούτων λόγους, ὅτι δὲ τὸ δεινὸν οὐκ ἐκράτησε τοῦτο τῆς ἐκκλησίας, οὐδ' ἔλαθε τὴν εὐσέβειαν φθεῖρον, ἀλλ' ἐξελήλεγκται Θεοῦ σοφίᾳ καὶ χάριτι, τοῦτο δέ σου πολλῆς εὐφροσύνης ἐμπλήσει τὴν εὐσεβεστάτην ψυχὴν καὶ φιλοθεωτάτην. λείπεται δὲ πρὸς τὸ τελέως καὶ σὲ και ἡμᾶς εὐφρανθῆναι καὶ πᾶσαν τὴν ἐκκλησίαν εὔχεσθαι πάντας ἡμᾶς εἰς πᾶσαν συμφωνίαν ἀγαγεῖν τῆς εὐσεβείας ἡμῖν τοὺς διενηνεγμένους.

Σὺ δ' ἡμῖν πάντων ἕνεκα χαῖρε, θαυμασιώτατε, καὶ τοῖς μὲν πώποτε γεγενημένοις εὐσεβέσιν ἀνδράσι καὶ ἀγαθοῖς, ὅ τι δή τις ἂν εἴποι, ὁμοιότατε, τοῖς δ' ἐσομένοις τούτων ἁπάντων παράδειγμα.

57–58 I Cor. 10:13 ‖ 60 Gal. 2:13; II Pet. 3:17 ‖ 66 Basil. Caes., *Hexaem.* 6, 1 (PG, 29, 117D)

---

66 ἀρχαίκακος M ‖ 71 διχονεία M

26

recently I happened to suffer much in words and deeds from men who were formerly my friends, having experienced from me not a few deeds and words of friendship; yet later not only did they pour out against me every slander and insult, but also were quick to point swords at me and hurl murderous stones, because I did not forsake the accepted laws of piety to listen to their deceitful and "newfangled talk." Subsequently, now that their new offenses against piety, which were previously concealed under various sophisms and specious arguments, have been exposed, I praise Almighty God because He granted me what He promised through the tongue of the divine Paul, "not allowing me to be tested above my powers," while those who had attempted to destroy the sacred laws from arrogance and had forced me "to be carried away" with them, first one and then the other have been expelled from the Church, or rather they fled the Church themselves, just like darkness which cannot approach the light.

I know that your Wisdom and Piety upon hearing this, whether now for the first time or even earlier, will feel neither pleasure without sorrow nor pain without joy. What I mean, of course, is this: because "the Devil, the initiator of mischief," still attempts such evil doings against piety, and very maliciously and dangerously raises in revolt against it the men who are considered first among the pious, and for this reason, of course, he swayed some of the men who previously believed in the sacred traditions in an artless and simple manner, while others he utterly confounded, involving them in a cruel quarrel about the holy faith, and others he nailed to the "newfangled talk" altogether—for these reasons, then, I thought that your admirable soul would hear the report about these matters not without sorrow. But the fact that this danger did not prevail over the Church and failed to destroy our piety undetected, but was brought to trial through the wisdom and grace of God, will fill your most pious and God-loving soul with much joy. But, in order that you and I and the whole Church may fully rejoice, it remains to pray that all of us will bring to full accord of piety those who have quarrelled with us.

Fare-thee-well, for everyone's sake, my most admirable friend, you who most resemble the pious and noble men who ever existed in any virtue one might mention, as well as those who will be an example of all these virtues to future men!

27. Sine titulo

Ἀφοσιούμεθα μὲν ἡμεῖς ἐπιστέλλοντες πρὸς τὴν σοφίαν τὴν σήν, ὁ δὲ θαυμάσιος Ἴσαρις καὶ ὁ γενναῖος Ἀνδρόνικος βέλτιον ἢ κατ' ἐπιστολήν σοι τὰ ἡμέτερα ἀπαγγέλλουσιν. οἱ μὲν γὰρ οὐχ ἧττον ἡμῶν οἰκεῖα τὰ ἡμέτερα ἄγουσιν, ὁποῖά ποτ' ἂν ᾖ, σέ τε ταῦτα ἀκοῦσαι τῶν ἀναγκαιοτάτων ὂν ἐμοὶ καὶ τούτοις ὁμοίως περισπούδαστον ἔσται· μᾶλλον δὲ καὶ πρὸς σὲ τούτοις οὐδέν ἐστιν ἴδιον, ὅτι σοῦ μηδένα πρότερον ἄγειν ἐοίκασιν ὅ τι δή τις ἂν εἴποι. ἀλλ' εἴ γε παρ' αὐτοῖς ⟨οὐκ⟩ ἔσται ἄλλο τι προὔργου ἢ τὰ ἡμέτερά σε, τὸ δ' ἐστὶ τὰ ἑαυτῶν διδάξαι, οὔτε σὺ τῶν οὐ τῆς αὐτῶν εἶ περὶ ἡμᾶς κοινωνούντων φιλίας—εὖ καὶ πολὺ πρὸ τούτων ἴσμεν ἀπολελαυκότες τῆς καλοκἀγαθίας—ὥστε πανταχόθεν καὶ διὰ πάντα εἰκότως ἂν ἐθελήσαις ἀκοῦσαι ὥσπερ οἰκεῖα σαυτοῦ τὰ ἡμέτερα.

Ἐπεὶ δὲ καὶ ὑπὲρ τοῦ Θεοῦ ταῦτ' ἐστὶ καὶ τῶν θείων πραγμάτων, ἔτι σοι μᾶλλον ἀναγκαῖα πάντως μαθεῖν ὑπάρξει, ὡς ἂν καὶ αὐτός τι τοῖς θείοις τῆς εὐσεβείας ὅροις ἐπικουρήσῃς, ἐπηρεαζομένοις ἀλλοκότῳ τινὶ τερατείᾳ καὶ πλάνῃ, ἐκ δυοῖν συντεθείσῃ τῶν οὐ μετρίων κακῶν, ἀμαθίας καὶ αὐθαδείας περὶ τὸ θεῖον ὕψος. μᾶλλον δὲ οὐχ ἁπλῶς τι, ἀλλὰ καὶ τὸ μέγιστον ἐπικουρήσῃς τῇ εὐσεβείᾳ μέρος, κατὰ τὸν λόγον ἧς εὐμοιρεῖς σοφίας καὶ τῆς τῶν θείων ἐπιστήμης δογμάτων. οὕτω γὰρ ὁ σὸς ἐμπεσεῖται λόγος τῇ ψυχῇ τοῦ ἀκροασαμένου, ὥσπερ ἐξ αὐτῆς ἀληθείας αὐτόχρημα, τῆς οὔσης ἕνεκα δόξης ἧς παρὰ πάντων ἔχεις εἰκότως ἐπί τε σοφίᾳ καὶ ἀκριβεῖ συνέσει. κἂν διὰ βάθους ἠπατημένος ὤν τις ὑπὸ τῆς ἐναντίας δόξης εἶτα προσίῃ σοι, αὐτοῦ τὴν πλάνην μὲν καταθέμενος, τὸν θεοειδῆ δὲ χιτῶνα τῆς ἀληθείας μεταλαβών, ἄπεισιν ἀπαστράπτων εὐσέβειαν.

Ἤδη μὲν οὖν σε καὶ πράττειν τοῦτο πρῴην μὲν ᾤμην, ἀποσκοπῶν πρὸς τὴν σὴν σοφίαν καὶ σύνεσιν ᾗ συνοικεῖς μετὰ τῆς εὐσεβείας—εἰ γὰρ ἀνδρός ἐστι σοφοῦ ὀρθῶς καὶ τῶν οὔπω πεφηνότων στοχάζεσθαι, πολλῷ γ' ἂν μᾶλλον τὰ παρόντα ἤδη καὶ κηρυττόμενα, ὧν οὐ παντελῶς ἀνήκοος ἔμεινεν, ὅ γε τοιοῦτος γνοίη, καὶ τοῖς [fol. 36ᵛ] ἄλλοις αὐτὸς διδάσκαλος γένοιτο, καὶ τοῦ μὲν ἀσφαλοῦς προστάτης, τῷ δ' ἐναντίῳ πρηστήρ τις ἢ καταιγὶς ἢ ξίφος—νῦν δὲ καὶ ἤκουσα παρὰ τῶν σῶν τε καὶ ἡμετέρων τοῦτο, καὶ ἐνέπλησα θαύματος καὶ ἱερᾶς ἡδονῆς τοὺς εὐσεβείᾳ φίλους, καὶ πολλή σοι παρὰ πάντων εὐχαριστία μετὰ τοῦ θαύματος, οὐχ ὧν μόνον καὶ λέγεις καὶ εἴρηκας, ἀλλὰ καὶ ὧν ἐρεῖς, καὶ τῆς σαυτοῦ

27: M 36ʳ–38ʳ.

8 οὐκ addidi

27

27. No Addressee

I am fulfilling a sacred obligation in writing to your Wisdom, but the admirable Isaris and the noble Andronikos will report my news to you better than the letter. For they consider my concerns, whatever they may be, on a par with their own, and they will be just as anxious that you hear about them, and this is of the utmost necessity to me. Moreover, they have no secrets from you either, for they seem to honor no one above you in every respect. But if perhaps they have nothing more important to do than to inform you of my concerns—their own, that is—neither are you one of those who do not share their love for me. I am well aware of having enjoyed this kindness long before they did. Therefore, in every way and for every reason it is to be expected that you would be willing to hear about my concerns as if they were your very own.

And since they also concern God and sacred matters, it will be even more necessary for you to know about them, so that you may yourself give some assistance to the sacred rules of piety which are being threatened by some strange mythmaking and delusion composed of two great evils: ignorance and insolence to the divine sublimity. Rather, you will not simply give some assistance, you will do piety the greatest service, considering the wisdom and knowledge of the sacred dogmas which you have the good fortune to possess. For your words will fall on the soul of your listeners just exactly as if ⟨they fell⟩ from truth itself, because of the reputation for learning and accurate insight which you rightfully enjoy amongst all men. And if someone who has been profoundly deceived by the opposite view approaches you later, he will lay down his deception and taking instead the godly cloak of truth, he will go off shining with piety.

Actually I thought that you were already doing this, considering your wisdom and insight which dwell with you along with piety. For, if a wise man is wont to form a correct opinion even of future events, much rather would this man show knowledge of current events which are publicly proclaimed and of which he is not entirely uninformed. In fact he would become a teacher to others and a protector of those who do not stray, while to the opposite side he would be a hurricane or tempest or sword. But now I have also heard this from your friends and mine, and I filled the lovers of piety with wonder and pious pleasure, and there is for you much gratitude as well as admiration from everybody not only for what you are saying and have said, but also for what you will say and consider in a manner worthy of your

27

σοφίας καὶ γνώμης καὶ θεοσεβείας ἀξίως φιλοσοφήσεις. σοφίᾳ μὲν οὖν καὶ μεγαλοφυΐᾳ ὅστις οἴεταί σε μὴ προέχειν τῶν ἄλλων οἷς νῦν ἐστιν ὄνομα ἐπὶ τούτοις, οὗτός ἐστιν ἀμαθής, κρίσεως ἀμοιρῶν, ἢ σοῦ καὶ τῶν σῶν τοῖς ὅλοις ἀπείρατος. εἰ δέ τις τῇδε μὲν εἴη τὸ ἀληθὲς περὶ σοῦ, ἧττω δέ σέ τινος νομίσοι περὶ τὴν τῶν θείων τῆς εὐσεβείας ἡμῖν ἐπιστήμην δογμάτων, ἐνταῦθα αὖ οὐκ εἰδώς ἐστι καὶ κομιδῇ σε ἀγνοῶν κατὰ τοῦτο. οὐ μὴν οὐδ' ἐκεῖνό τινι γένοιτ' ἂν εἰπεῖν, οἶμαι, ἢ φήσαντι μὴ τ' ἀληθοῦς ἐκπεσεῖν, ὡς ἄρα σὺ σοφὸς μὲν εἴης πάντα, καὶ μάλιστα τὰ πρὸς εὐσέβειαν, χάριν δὲ τῶν ἀνθρωπίνων τινός, δι' ἀνανδρίαν ψυχῆς τὸ ἀληθὲς προήσῃ καὶ σιωπῇ κατακρύψεις· ὅπερ δὴ πολλοὶ πάσχουσιν, εἰπεῖν μὲν οὐκ ἔχοντες ὡς οὐ Θεὸς βλασφημεῖται καὶ πλάνη πάλιν πρεσβεύεται καὶ δυσσέβεια παρρησιάζεται καὶ τὸ πάλαι πᾶν, ὡς εἰπεῖν, τῶν πονηροτάτων αἱρέσεων δι' ἑνὸς ἀνδρὸς τὰ νῦν εἰς τὴν ἐκκλησίαν ἐκώμασεν, ἃς αἱμάτων πλῆθος μαρτυρικῶν καὶ μυρία δὴ πάθη τῶν ἀθλητῶν τῆς εὐσεβείας ἐξήλασε, καὶ πρὸ πάντων τοῦ πρώτου ἀρχιερέως Χριστοῦ τοῦ Θεοῦ ἡμῶν, ἀγεννῶς δὲ καὶ λίαν ἀφιλοσόφως, ἵνα μηδὲν στυφὸν εἴπω, τὴν ἀλήθειαν ἐν ἀδικίᾳ κατέχοντες, οἷς οὐκ ἔστι σύνεσις τοῦ ἀποφαινομένου ὅστις ὁμολογήσει ἐν ἐμοὶ ἔμπροσθεν τῶν ἀνθρώπων, ὁμολογήσω κἀγὼ ἐν αὐτῷ ἔμπροσθεν τοῦ πατρός μου τοῦ ἐν οὐρανοῖς· ὅστις δέ με ἀρνήσεται, κἀγὼ αὐτὸν ἐπ' ἐκείνου ἀρνήσομαι. ὅτι δὲ μὴ μόνον ὁ πρὸς τὴν ἐναντίαν δόξαν μεταπίπτων ἀπὸ τῆς εὐσεβείας, οὗτός ἐστιν ὁ τὸ θεῖον ἀρνούμενος, ἀλλὰ καὶ ὁ σιωπῶν ἀσεβουμένου Θεοῦ, καὶ ταῦτα παρὰ τῶν εὐσεβεῖν ἔτι νομιζομένων τοῖς γε ἀφελεστέροις, τίς ἀγνοεῖ νοῦν ἔχων; τὸ γὰρ μὴ ἀντιλέγειν ὅτῳ δή τινι λόγῳ συνηγορία πως γίνεται· καὶ τοῦτο ἐδήλωσεν ἡ τοῦ Θεοῦ σοφία καὶ δύναμις, ὅς οὐκ ἔστι καθ' ἡμῶν, ὑπὲρ ἡμῶν ἐστι λέγουσα.

Ἐπιστάμενοι καὶ ἀκριβῆ παρὰ πάντας ἐν ἅπασι, καὶ μάλιστα τοῖς δόγμασι τῆς εὐσεβείας, οὐκ ἀνέξεσθαι οὐδὲ περιόψεσθαι ὑπο-[fol. 37ʳ]λαμβάνομεν, εἴ τίς τι περὶ ταύτην πεπλάνηται ἢ κινδυνεύει τοῦτο παθεῖν, ὥσπερ λοιμοῦ τινος σπάσας—τοιοῦτο γὰρ ἡ πρὸς ἀσέβειαν πλάνη, διὸ καὶ ὁ θεσπέσιος Παῦλος Τιμοθέῳ γράφων, τὰς βεβήλους, φησί, καινοφωνίας περιίστασο· ἐπὶ πλεῖον γὰρ προκόψουσιν ἀσεβείας καὶ ὁ λόγος αὐτῶν ὡς γάγγραινα νομὴν ἕξει—ἀλλὰ κἀνταῦθα τῶν ἄλ-

---

27: 53–54 cf. Hebr. 2:17, 3:1, 4:14, 5:5 ‖ 56–59 Matt. 10:32; Luc. 12:8 ‖ 64–65 ἡ . . . δύναμις I Cor. 1:24–25 ‖ 65–66 Marc. 9:40 ‖ 72–74 II Tim. 2:16–17

---

41 εἴῃ M ‖ 55 στύφον M

27

learning and judgment and piety. For whoever does not believe that you surpass in learning and talent the other men who are now famous for these ⟨qualities⟩ is himself an ignorant man and lacking in judgment, or one who does not know you and your accomplishments at all. If, on the other hand, someone speaks the truth about you in this matter, yet considers you inferior to another man as far as knowledge of the sacred dogmas of piety is concerned, here again he is mistaken and quite ignorant about you in this respect. Indeed, I believe that one could not say this either, in fact one could not fail to lie by saying it: namely, that you are wise in all matters and especially in things to do with piety, but for some material interest, due to lack of moral courage, you will betray the truth and will conceal this in silence. This actually happens to many men who cannot deny that God is blasphemed and that error is honored again and impiety finds free expression, while all the most wicked heresies of old, so to speak, are thriving in the Church, and this because of one man—heresies which were driven out by a great deal of shedding of the martyrs' blood as well as innumerable sufferings of the champions of piety, and above all by those of the first Archpriest, Christ our God—but they unjustly suppress truth in an ignoble and altogether unphilosophical manner, to put it politely, because they do not understand Him Who said: "Whoever will acknowledge me before men, I will acknowledge him before my Father in heaven; and whoever disowns me, I will disown him before my Father." And what sensible man does not know that it is not only the man who changes from the true to the opposite belief who denies God, but it is also the man who keeps silent while God is being insulted, especially, that is, by those who are still considered pious, at least by the more simple people. For not to contradict a statement at all becomes in a way an act of support. And this was made clear by the "Wisdom and Power of God" when He said: "He who is not with us is against us."

Since I know that you are indeed stricter than any man in every way, and above all concerning the doctrines of piety, I think that you will be neither tolerant nor negligent, if a person has somehow gone astray in this respect, or if he runs the risk of being afflicted thus, just as if he had contracted some sort of pestilence; for that is what straying into impiety is, and for this reason the divinely-inspired Paul says, in writing to Timothy: "Avoid the profane newfangled talk; those who indulge in it will stray further and further into godless courses, and the infection of their teaching will spread like gangrene." But I believe that in this case also you will

27

λων πάντων διενεγκεῖν σπουδάσειν. ὅθεν οὐδὲ δεῖν ἡμῖν πλειόνων λόγων πρὸς σὲ περὶ τούτων οἰόμεθα, οὐδὲ τῶν τίς ἡ παροῦσα καινότης περὶ τὴν θείαν πίστιν καὶ τὴν εὐσέβειαν σαφές σοι καταστησόντων. τί γὰρ ἀσφαλοῦς διανοίας καὶ σοφῆς περὶ τὸν θεῖον κλῆρον ὀξυδερκέστερον; οὐδὲν δὲ ἴσως σκαιὸν τοσοῦτον εἰπεῖν πρὸς ταύτην, οἷς ὑπῆρξεν ἀνάγκη διαφερόντως, ὥς ἔοικεν, ἐνταυθοῖ διατρῖψαι. ὅτι τοῦ καινοῦ θεολόγου δύο θεότητας ἀκτίστους κηρύττοντος, ἵνα μὴ λέγω νῦν καὶ πλείστας, καὶ λόγοις μακροῖς ἐγγράφως καὶ τοῖς ἐκ στόματος, τὴν μὲν ὑπερκειμένην, τὴν δ' ὑφειμένην ἀπειράκις ἀπείρως, καὶ τὴν μὲν ἀόρατον, τὴν δὲ καὶ σωματικοῖς ὀφθαλμοῖς ἔστιν ὧν ὁρωμένην, καὶ τὴν μὲν ἐνεργοῦσαν, τὴν δὲ ἐνεργουμένην, καὶ τὴν μὲν ἀνώνυμον, τὴν δὲ ὀνομαζομένην, καὶ τὴν μὲν οὐσίαν, τὴν δὲ ἀνούσιον, καὶ τὴν μὲν ἀμέθεκτον, τὴν δὲ μετεχομένην, ἣν καὶ θέωσιν ὀνομάζει καὶ δύναμιν καὶ ἐνέργειαν καὶ χάριν καὶ ἔλλαμψιν καὶ μορφὴν καὶ δόξαν τὴν οὐσιώδη καὶ φυσικὴν τοῦ θεοῦ, ἑτέραν οὖσαν, ὥς φησι, τῆς οὐσίας αὐτοῦ καὶ τῆς φύσεως, καὶ οὕτως οὐ τοῖς προσώποις μόνον, ἀλλὰ καὶ διαφόροις θεότησιν ἀριθμοῦντος τὴν μακαρίαν Τριάδα καὶ ὑπερούσιον, καὶ ὅλως ἕτερα μὲν τιθέντος τὰ οὐσιώδη καὶ φυσικὰ τοῦ Θεοῦ—τὴν δύναμιν, τὴν σοφίαν, τὴν ζωήν, τὴν ἐνέργειαν, τὴν ἀγαθότητα, τὴν ἁγιότητα—ἑτέραν δὲ τὴν οὐσίαν, καὶ ταύτην ἐκείνων ἀπείρως ὑπερτιθέντος, καὶ τὸ μὲν καλοῦντος ὑπερκειμένην θεότητα, τὰ δὲ ὑφειμένας καὶ ὀνομαζομένας καὶ νοουμένας καὶ ὁρωμένας ἐνίων πνευματικῶς σωματικοῖς ὀφθαλμοῖς, καὶ οὕτω διασπῶντος ἐκθέσμως τὴν ὑπερηνωμένην ἑνάδα, ὥσπερ ὁ μέγας φησὶ Διονύσιος.

Ἡμεῖς δὲ ταῦτα ὑπ' αὐτοῦ τοῦ διδασκάλου τούτων ἀναγκαζόμενοι δέξασθαι, οὐκ ἠνεσχόμεθα, ὥσπερ οὖν οὐδὲ τὴν τοῦ Βαρλαὰμ ἐκείνου τρόπον ἕτερον περιεργίαν, τήν τε κοινὴν τῆς θείας ἐκκλησίας δόξαν καὶ παράδοσιν εἰδότες παραδιδοῦσαν ἡμῖν ἕνα Θεὸν τρισυπόστατον καὶ μίαν ταύτην τρισυπόστατον θεότητα, ἄκτιστον, ἁπλῆν, ἀμερῆ, ἀνείδεον, ἀόρατον, ἀναφῆ, ἀπρόσιτον, ἀνείκαστον, ἀκατανόητον, μονάδα μονάδων καὶ ἀνερεύνητον κρυφιότητα· φῶς

---

81 cf. Greg. Naz., *Or.* 29, 10 (PG, 36, 88A) || 83–84 ὑπερκειμένην . . . ὑφειμένην: cf. Palamam, *Epist. III ad Acindynum*, 15, Syngrammata, I, 306, 18–20; ed. Nadal, 252, 10–12 || 84 cf. Maxim. Conf., *Capit. theol.*, 1, 49 (PG, 90, 1101A) = Palamas, *Dialexis*, 24, Syngrammata, II, 186, 26; *Epist. ad Gabram*, 5, Syngrammata, II, 332, 12 || 92 cf. Sophronium, *Epist. syn. ad Sergium* (PG, 87[3], 3156C) || 96–97 cf. Palamam, *Epist. III ad Acindynum*, 15, Syngrammata, I, 306, 18–20; ed. Nadal, 252, 10–12 || 99 Dion. Areop., *De div. nom.*, 2, 1 (PG, 3, 637A)

80–81 διατρίψαι M

strive to surpass everybody else. I do not think, therefore, that I need say any more to you about these matters, nor about the things which will make clear to you the nature of the present newfangled doctrine which concerns our sacred faith and piety. For what is more sharpsighted than a mind which is sound and well versed in the sacred legacy? And nothing is so awkward as to say so much to such a man about the subject upon which, as it seems, it was especially necessary for me to dwell here. Namely, that the "new theologian" not only in long written discourses but also by word of mouth has been proclaiming two uncreated divinities, not to say actually a great many, "one higher and the other infinitely lower;" one invisible and the other visible even to the bodily eyes of certain men; one activating and the other activated; one nameless and the other having a name; one being the essence and the other not; one capable of being shared and the other incapable of being shared. The latter he calls deification and power and energy and grace and illumination and form and essential and natural glory of God, being separate, as he says, from His essence and nature. And thus he not only numbers different persons but also different divinities in the blessed supersubstantial Trinity, and considers entirely separate the essential and the natural attributes of God—the power, the wisdom, the life, the energy, the goodness, the holiness—from the essence which he places far above them; this he calls a "higher divinity," while he calls the ⟨attributes⟩ lower and expressible and intelligible and spiritually visible to the bodily eyes of some men, and thus he "unlawfully" tears apart the "supremely united Monad," in the words of the great Dionysios.

When I was forced to accept these doctrines by the very man who is their teacher, I did not tolerate this, just as I could not tolerate the somewhat different officiousness of the notorious Barlaam; for I know that the common belief and tradition of the holy Church has taught us of one God in three hypostases, and that is, a single divinity in three hypostases, uncreated, simple, indivisible, formless, invisible, intangible, inaccessible, unimaginable, incomprehensible, monad of monads, and inscrutable mystery; invisible light, creator of all lights under it—visible as

27

ἀόρατον, φώτων ἁπάντων τῶν ὑπ' αὐτὸ [fol. 37v] καὶ ὁρατῶν καὶ ἀοράτων δημιουργόν, δύναμιν, σοφίαν, ζωήν, ἐνέργειαν τὴν πάντων δημιουργόν, οὐσίαν, βασιλείαν, μακαριότητα· ἓν ἀμερὲς αὐτὸ τοῦτο πολλοῖς ὀνόμασιν ἀπὸ τῶν ὄντων ὀνομαζόμενον καὶ ὑποστάσεσιν ἀκινήτοις τρισὶ διαιρούμενον, Πατέρα, Υἱόν, Πνεῦμα ἅγιον· Πατέρα σοφόν, δυνατόν, ἀγαθόν· Χριστὸν Θεοῦ δύναμιν καὶ Θεοῦ σοφίαν, λόγον καὶ ἐνέργειαν οὐσιώδη καὶ φυσικὴν τοῦ Πατρός· καὶ τὸ Πνεῦμα τὸ ἅγιον, οὐσιώδη δύναμιν καὶ φυσικὴν τοῦ Πατρὸς ἐξ οὗ ἐκπορεύεται· τὰ τρία ἓν τῇ θεότητι, καὶ τρία τὸ ἓν ὑποστάσεσιν.

Εἰ οὖν αὗται δυνάμεις ἐν τῷ Θεῷ ἐνυπόστατοι, παντουργοὶ καὶ ἐνέργειαι καὶ ζωαὶ καὶ σοφία καὶ λόγος καὶ ἁγιότης, καὶ μία δύναμις ταῦτα καὶ ζωὴ καὶ οὐσία καὶ φῶς καὶ ἐνέργεια καὶ μορφὴ καὶ δόξα καὶ ἀγαθότης, τίν' ἔχει χώραν ἢ χρείαν ἐν τούτῳ τὰ ἀνυπόστατα; ὥσπερ ἀθέμιτον ὂν μὴ καθ' ἡμᾶς εἶναι τὸν δημιουργὸν ἡμῶν καὶ τοῦ παντὸς ποιητὴν κατὰ φύσιν, σύνθετον ἐξ οὐσίας καὶ πολλῶν ποιοτήτων καὶ διαφόρων ἀλλήλων, καθ' αὑτὰς μὲν οὐ δυναμένων εἶναι καὶ ὑπόστασιν ἔχειν, ἐν ἑτέρῳ δὲ ὥσπερ ἐποχουμένων, καὶ οὐ τῷ εἶναι οὐσῶν, τῷ δὲ φέρεσθαι· καὶ τὸ παράδοξον, εἶναι μὲν οὐ δυναμένων καθ' ἑαυτάς, εἶναι δὲ δυναμένων θεοτήτων ἀκτίστων καὶ δὴ καὶ ὁρᾶσθαι σωματικοῖς ὀφθαλμοῖς.

Τούτων δὲ καίπερ ὄντων πᾶσι τοῖς ὁπουδὴ γῆς εὐσεβέσιν ἐκ τοῦ εὐθέως, ἁπλῶς καὶ θαρραλέως ἀνομολογουμένων ὡς εἴη τῆς πολυθέου πλάνης ἐπανανέωσις, ἡμεῖς καὶ πάντων τῶν πώποτε θεολήπτων γεγενημένων ἀνδρῶν καὶ θεολόγων λόγοις καὶ βιβλίοις ἐγκύψαντες, πάντα τἀναντία τοῖς νέοις τούτοις εὑρήκαμεν δόγμασι, μᾶλλον δὲ παλαιοῖς τὴν ἀσέβειαν, ὥστ' εἴτ' ἐκεῖνοι πρὸς ταῦτα μόνα τὸν πόλεμον ἐσπούδασαν ἄρασθαι, εἴτε ταῦτα τῆς πρὸς ἐκείνους μάχης ἕνεκα παρέστη μελετῆσαι τῷ πλάσαντι, οὐκ ἂν εἰπεῖν εἶναι γενέσθαι περιφανέστερον, οὐδὲ ἐπιμελέστερον· οὕτως ἐστὶν ἀλλήλοις ἐκ διαμέτρου καὶ ἀκριβῶς ἀντικείμενα, καὶ οὕτω σφόδρα ἐπ' ἀλλήλοις ἠκόνηται.

Ἐφ' ὧν ἡμεῖς πρὸς τῇ κοινῇ τῆς ἐκκλησίας δόξῃ περὶ τοῦ θείου καὶ ὁμολογίᾳ τῆς πίστεως ἐρηρεισμένοι, παρ' ἡμῶν μὲν αὐτῶν οὐδὲν τέως εἰπεῖν ἐβουλήθημεν συντρέχον μὲν καὶ ἀμῦνον ἐπηρεα-

---

113–114 I Cor. 1:24–25 || 116 cf. *Fidei symbolum*: Joannis Chrysostomi *Liturgia* (ed. Brightman), 383, 21

121–123 ἀγαθότης . . . κατὰ φύσιν scripsi: ἀγαθότης εἶναι τὸν δημιουργὸν ἡμῶν καὶ τοῦ παντὸς ποιητήν. τίν' ἔχει χώραν ἢ χρείαν ἐν τούτῳ τὰ ἀνυπόστατα, ὥσπερ ἀθέμιτον ὂν μὴ καθ' ἡμᾶς κατὰ φύσιν M || 136 πλάσσαντι M

27 well as invisible—power, wisdom, life, all-creating energy, essence, majesty, beatitude; One, itself indivisible, acquiring many names from the world of ⟨created⟩ beings and divided into three immovable hypostases: Father, Son, and Holy Spirit. The Father: wise, mighty, and good; "Christ: the Power and Wisdom of God," the Logos and the essential and natural energy of the Father; and the Holy Spirit: the essential and natural power of the "Father from Whom It proceeds." The three are one with respect to divinity, and the one is three with respect to hypostases.

If, therefore, these are all-creating powers, having hypostatic existence in God, as well as energies and lives and wisdom and word and holiness, and if all of these are one power, life, essence, light, energy, form, glory, and goodness, what place or purpose do the non-hypostatic ⟨powers⟩ have in Him? It is just as if it were unlawful for our creator and the maker of all not to be like us in nature, a composite of essence and many qualities which differ from one another, and ⟨which⟩ can have neither being nor hypostasis of their own, but use others as a vehicle, so to speak, and exist not by their being, but by virtue of their carriage. And, paradoxically, while they cannot exist by themselves, they can be uncreated divinities, and, moreover, they can be seen by the eyes of the body.

Although all pious men the world over agree immediately, simply and confidently, that this is a revival of the polytheistic delusion, I studied closely the discourses and books of all the God-inspired men and theologians who ever lived, and found that everything was quite contrary to these new doctrines (or rather, old doctrines with respect to impiety), so that if, on the one hand, those ⟨theologians⟩ had been eager to start a war against these doctrines alone, or, on the other hand, if it had occurred to their author to devise them because of his battle against the theologians, it is impossible to say that it could have been done in a more conspicuous or diligent manner. This is how diametrically and exactly and acutely opposed they are to each other.

Concerning this matter, supported though I was by the common doctrine of the Church about God and the confession of faith, I did not previously wish to say anything on my own initiative that would come to the rescue and defense of the laws

27

ζομένοις—ἵνα μὴ λέγω καταλυομένοις παντάπασι—τοῖς τῶν θείων πατέρων περὶ τῆς εὐσεβείας καὶ τῆς θεολογίας ὅροις, ἀνατρέπον δὲ τὰς μακρὰς ἀδολεσχίας καὶ τὴν ὅλην ἀπόνοιαν τῶν γε τοσαύτην τετολμηκότων τόλμαν, τὴν περὶ τὸ θεῖον εὐλάβειαν σῴζοντες καὶ τὸ μὴ παθεῖν ταὐτὸν οἷς ἐγκαλοῦμεν περὶ ἐκεῖνο αὐθάδειαν φυλαττόμενοι· αὐτοὺς δὲ τούτους τοὺς τῶν ἱερῶν ἀνδρῶν λόγους παραλλήλους θέμενοι τοῖς ἀρτιφύτοις, κελεύσαντος ἡμῖν [fol. 38^r] *τοῦτο ποιῆσαι τοῦ θειοτάτου ἡμῶν δεσπότου τοῦ οἰκουμενικοῦ πατριάρχου, καί που καὶ τὰ καινὰ ταῦτα καὶ πρὸς τὴν κοινὴν ἡμῶν ὁμολογίαν τῆς εὐσεβείας ἀσύμβατα παντελῶς οἷον ἀπορρητικῶς καὶ εὐλαβῶς ἐξετάσαντες καὶ πᾶσαν ἐναντιότητα εὑρόντες πρὸς τὰ ὁμολογούμενα δόγματα τῆς εὐσεβείας, τῷ τε θειοτάτῳ ἡμῶν δεσπότῃ τῷ οἰκουμενικῷ πατριάρχῃ καὶ τῇ θείᾳ συνόδῳ εὐλαβῶς προσηγάγομεν, καὶ τῶν πολλῶν ὀλίγα παρ' ὑμᾶς κατεπέμψαμεν, περιττῶς μέν, τί γὰρ ἂν ἡμεῖς ἴδοιμεν τὴν σὴν νοερὰν ὀξυδορκίαν διαφυγὸν ἢ τοῦτο δρᾶσαι δυνάμενον; πλὴν ἐπειδήπερ ἡμῖν ἐπέπεσεν ἀνάγκῃ τινὶ τοῦτο τὸ μέρος, διαφερόντως ἐπεμελήθημεν ὅσα εἰκὸς ἦν, ἡγουμένου Θεοῦ καὶ καταδεικνύντος ἡμῖν τοὺς περὶ εὐσεβείας εὖ πεποιηκότας ὅρους, ἐξ ὧν ἀνατέτραπται μὲν τὰ νέα καὶ σφαλερά, καὶ θείᾳ συνοδικῇ ψήφῳ δὶς κατεκρίθη καὶ ἐκκεκήρυκται καὶ τὸ πῦρ ἐκληρώθη πρὸς καῦσιν· ἔστη δὲ πᾶς ἐν τῇ πρώτῃ τῆς εὐσεβείας βάσει, τῇ μόνῃ ἀσφαλεῖ καὶ ἀτρεμεῖ καὶ βεβαίᾳ καὶ σωτηρίῳ· οὐδεὶς γάρ, φησι, δύναται θεῖναι ἄλλον θεμέλιον παρὰ τὸν κείμενον.*

Ἡμεῖς δὲ τὸν Θεὸν ἐπὶ τούτοις ὑμνοῦντες καὶ μεγαλύνοντες, οὐχ ἡδέως ἐκεῖνο τὸ μέρος διατιθέμεθα, ὅτι μὴ εὐπειθής ἐστι τῇ ἐκκλησίᾳ μεθ' ὧν ἐξηπάτησεν ὁ τῶν καινῶν τούτων δημιουργὸς δογμάτων, ἀδελφὸς ὢν ἡμῶν καὶ φίλος καὶ οὗτος καὶ οἱ τὰ τούτου πρεσβεύοντες· ἀλλ' ἔτι φεύγει καὶ κρύπτεται καὶ δοκεῖ τῇ φυγῇ τοὺς ἐλέγχους διαδιδράσκειν καὶ περιέπειν τὰ ἅπαξ αὐτῷ δεδογμένα καὶ σῴζειν, οὐκ εἰδὼς ὡς νῦν μὲν μετρίως αὐτοῦ τὸ πρᾶγμα τοῦτο καθάπτεται, ὕστερον δέ ποτε, ἂν φιλονείκως στέρξῃ τούτοις τοῖς δόγμασιν, εἷς ἔσται τῇ ἐκκλησίᾳ τῶν ἤδη περιεργάσθαι τὸ θεῖον ἐπικεχειρηκότων καὶ διὰ τοῦτο ἀποκεκηρυγμένων, κἂν εἴσω τῶν ἑαυτοῦ δικτύων ὥσπερ κἀκεῖνοι πᾶσαν ποιήσηται τὴν οἰκουμένην. ὃ καὶ θρηνῶ ἐνθυμούμενος καὶ λογιζόμενος στένω καὶ οὐδὲν ἔχω πρᾶξαι πλὴν τοῦ φανερῶς ὁμολογεῖν τὴν ἀλήθειαν· εἰ φίλος μὲν

165–166 I Cor. 3:11 || 179–180 Georgides, *Gnomologion*, ed. Boissonade, *Anecdota graeca*, I, 6

---

149 *ἀρτιφοίτοις* M || 158 *δράσαι* M

of the holy Fathers concerning piety and theology, ⟨laws⟩ which are being outraged, not to say completely abolished, and ⟨which⟩ would refute the long prattle and the complete folly of those who attempted such an insolent act, for I was preserving the reverence due to God and taking care that I do not suffer the same punishment as those whom I accuse of insolence to God. But when, at the command of our most divine Lord, the Ecumenical Patriarch, I compared the very words of the holy Fathers with those that have just arisen and examined covertly, so to speak, and cautiously these newfangled ⟨doctrines⟩ which are completely irreconcilable with our common confession of faith, and ⟨when⟩ I found all possible disagreement with the accepted doctrines of piety, I submitted this respectfully to our most divine Lord, the Ecumenical Patriarch, and the holy Synod, and sent you a few of my many ⟨refutations⟩. This was, of course, unnecessary for what could I perceive that has escaped your keen perception or might do so? Yet, since this role was assigned to me by necessity, I took special care to do what was proper, with God guiding me and showing me the right authors in regard to our pious laws, through whom the new and false doctrines were refuted, and twice condemned by vote of the holy Synod and banished and assigned to the fire for burning. And everybody stood firm on the original foundation of piety, which is the only secure and unshakable and steady and redeeming one, "For there can be no other foundation," he says, "beyond that which is already laid."

As for me, I praise and magnify God for this, but I am unhappy about one thing, namely, that the author of these new doctrines together with those whom he deceived—for he is a brother and friend of mine, both he and those who maintain his views—is not ready to obey the Church, but is still running away and hiding, and thinks that by running away he will escape judgment and that he will cherish and preserve what he believes to be right once and for all. For he does not realize that this thing has a moderate hold on him already, but if he cherishes these doctrines contentiously, then some time later he will be for the Church one of those men who have already attempted to tamper with God and for this reason have been publicly renounced, even if he ensnares the whole inhabited world, as they also did. I lament this when I think about it, and groan when I consider it, and can do nothing but confess the truth openly, for "If the man is dear to me, truth is even dearer." And

ἄνθρωπος, φιλτέρα δὲ ἡ ἀλήθεια, καὶ δεῖ τῷ λέγοντι πείθεσθαι, ὅστις εὐαγγελίσηται ὑμῖν παρ' ὃ παρελάβετε, εἴτε ἄγγελος ἐξ οὐρανοῦ, εἴτε αὐτὸς ἐγὼ Παῦλος εἴην, ἀνάθεμα.

Σὺ δέ, ὦ σοφώτατε καὶ πάντων θεοφιλέστατε, λυπῶν ἡμᾶς ὅτι μὴ καὶ ἄνευ τούτων ἡμῖν ἐπιστέλλειν ἐθέλεις, μάλιστα ἂν λυπήσαις, εἰ μὴ νῦν ἐπιστέλλοις ῥωννύς τε πρὸς τοὺς ἀγῶνας τούσδε καὶ διδάσκων τὰ δέοντα.

28. Sine titulo

Ἔδει τὴν μὲν σὴν σοφίαν καὶ τῶν θείων ἀκριβεστάτην ἐπιστήμην δογμάτων, τὰ ἑαυτῆς ποιοῦσαν, τοὺς ἐκπίπτοντας ἀεὶ τοῦ ἀσφαλοῦς ἐπανάγειν, καὶ μετὰ πολλοῦ τοῦ κρείττονος τοῖς εὐσεβείας ὅροις περιποιεῖσθαι τὸ ἀπαράτρεπτον, ἡμᾶς δὲ πυνθανομένους ταῦτα τῶν ἐκεῖθεν ἀφικνουμένων οὐδεμιᾶς ἀπολείπειν ὑπερβολὴν εὐφροσύνης, ᾗ τοὺς εὐσεβείᾳ φίλους εὐδοκιμούσης τῆς εὐσεβείας τέρπει. τοιαῦτα δεῦρο περὶ τῆς σῆς σοφίας ὑπὸ πολλῶν ἀπαγγέλλεται· οὔτοι μόνον ἀνθρώπων ἐνταῦθα παρ' ὑμῶν ἐρχομένων, ἀλλὰ καὶ γραμμάτων πεμπομένων ἡμῖν παρὰ τῶν αὐτόθι καταμενόντων φίλων. ἔστι δὲ τῶν μὲν ὁ μάλισθ' ἡμῖν ἐνεγκὼν τὰ φαιδρότατα πρωτονοτάριος ὅδε, ὁ κομιδῇ μὲν ἐμοὶ πεφιλημένος ἀεί, μᾶλλον δὲ νῦν φιληθεὶς διὰ τὸ ταῦτά τε ἡμῖν παρὰ σοῦ τὰ δῶρα κεκομικέναι καὶ τὸ τῆς σῆς ἀμηχάνως ἐξηρτῆσθαι σοφίας· τῶν δὲ ἐπεσταλκότων Ἀνδρόνικός ἐστιν ὁ Τζυμισκῆς καὶ τὴν ἑταιρειάρχου προσειληφὼς ἀξίαν, ὃν οὐχ ἧττον ἀπὸ τοῦ σε θαυμάζειν εὐδοκιμεῖν ἢ τῶν ἄλλων ἁπάντων ὧν πολλῶν ἔχει προτερημάτων συμβέβηκε· [fol. 42v] ἡ γὰρ τοῦ θαυμαζομένου καὶ φιλουμένου φύσις παραπλησίαν ἑαυτῇ τὴν τοῦ φιλοῦντος αὐτὴν καὶ θαυμάζοντος δείκνυσι, τὰ γὰρ ὅμοιά, φασι, τῶν ὁμοίων ἐξῆφθαι.

Σὺ μὲν οὖν, εἰ καὶ μηδὲν ἡμῖν προὐχώρει, τὰ δὲ τῶν ἀντιλεγόν-

---

181–183 cf. Gal. 1:8–9

28: 19 Cf. Homerum, *Od.*, 17, 218; Platonem *Lysis*, 214a; *Phaedrus*, 240c; Aristot., *Ethic. Nicom.*, 1155a, 32–35

---

185 ἐθέλοις M

28: M 42r–43r.

8 ἡμῶν M || 20 προχώρει M

we must obey him who says: "Whoever preaches to you a gospel at variance with the gospel which you received, whether he should be an angel from heaven or I, Paul, myself, let him be outcast."

But as for you, O most wise and beloved of God amongst men, though you distress me because you are not willing to send me a letter even without these reasons, you would distress me even more, if you failed to send a letter now, providing encouragement for these struggles as well as proper instructions.

28. No Addressee

You with your wisdom and your most accurate knowledge of the sacred dogmas ought to do your part and lead back those who happen to digress from the safe road, and with much vigor secure the immutability of the rules of piety, while I, upon learning this from the men who come here from those parts, ought to be filled to excess with every joy that delights the lovers of piety when piety is flourishing. Many bring here such reports about your Wisdom, not only messengers who come from you, but also letters sent to me by friends who live there. One of the former is our friend the *Protonotarios*, who certainly brought me the most cheerful news. He has always been quite a favorite of mine, but now he is even more so, both because he brought me this gift from you and because he is sincerely devoted to your Wisdom. One of those who wrote to me is Andronikos Tzimiskes, who has been appointed to the office of hetaeriarch. As it happens, he is highly esteemed no less for admiring you than for all his other numerous accomplishments. For the character of the man whom one admires and loves is shown to be similar to the character of the one who loves and admires him, for they say that "like follows like."

I am, of course, clearly aware that even if nothing went well with me, and if

28

των τοῖς εὐσεβείας ὅροις ἐκ παντὸς εὐδοκίμει, ὡς οὐδὲν ἂν ἧττον μετὰ τῆς ἀληθείας ἐτέταξο καὶ γνώμῃ καὶ γλώττῃ καὶ παρρησίᾳ, σαφῶς ἐπιστάμεθα. ὁ γὰρ σοφὸς τοῦ τῆς ἀληθείας λόγου προεστηκὼς οὐ φρίττει τὴν τοῦ δοκοῦντος πλήθους ὀχλοκρατίαν ἐπὶ ψεύδους ὀχουμένην, ὃ κἂν πρὸς βραχὺ κρατήσῃ, μᾶλλον δὲ κρατῆσαι δόξῃ τῇ τῶν πολλῶν εὐχερείᾳ, μετ' ὀλίγον ἐλέγχεται· ἀδρανὲς γὰρ ὂν καὶ ἄστατον καὶ ἀνίδρυτον, μᾶλλον δὲ οὐδὲ ὂν τὸ παράπαν, πῶς ἂν εἰς ἅπαν σταίη;

Ὅτι δὲ καὶ πάσῃ τῇ ἐκκλησίᾳ Θεοῦ καὶ τοῖς ἐν βασιλείοις, μάλιστα μέντοι πάντων τῇ δεσποίνῃ, πεφώραται τὸ κακὸν ἤδη τοῦτο τῆς ἄρτι περὶ τὴν εὐσέβειαν καινοτομίας, καὶ ὁ ταῦτα τολμήσας ἀπήτηται μὲν πρὸς πάντων ἀποβαλέσθαι ταῦτα πάντως ὄντα κακόδοξα, ὁ δὲ καὶ νῦν ἀπειθῶν, εἰς τὸν θειότατον ναὸν τῆς τοῦ Θεοῦ Σοφίας κατέφυγε, καὶ τὰ ἐντεῦθεν συμβάντα πάντα περὶ αὐτὸν ἐμοὶ μὲν οὐ σχολὴ διεξέρχεσθαι, πρωτονοτάριος δὲ ὁ καλός, συνετὸς ὤν, εἴπερ τις, καὶ ἱκανὸς πᾶν ὁτιοῦν ἀπαγγεῖλαι, πάντα δι' ἀκριβείας ὑπ' ὄψιν θήσει τῆς διανοίας ὑμῖν. καὶ μετὰ πάντων, ὡς οὐδ' ἡμεῖς ἐν μετρίᾳ ὑπὲρ τῶν ἀνδρῶν τούτων λύπῃ—πῶς γάρ;—φίλων ἡμῖν καὶ συνήθων σφόδρα γεγενημένων πάλαι· ὅθεν καὶ προὐκαλεσάμεθα πολλάκις αὐτοὺς ἐπὶ τῷ ταῦτα ἀφέντας καὶ ἀποβαλομένους οὕτως εἰς τὴν προτέραν ἡμῖν αὖθις ἀποκαταστῆναι φιλίαν τε καὶ ὁμόνοιαν, τῆς κοινῆς καὶ γνωρίμου πάσῃ τῇ ἐκκλησίᾳ περὶ τῆς εὐσεβείας ἐχομένους συνθήκης· τῶν δὲ μὴ τούτοις πεπεισμένων τοῖς λόγοις, ἡμεῖς τῷ μεγάλῳ Παύλῳ ἀδυνατοῦντες μὴ πείθεσθαι λέγοντι, κἂν ἄγγελος ἐξ οὐρανοῦ εὐαγγελίζηται ὑμῖν παρ' ὃ παρελάβετε, κἂν ἐγὼ Παῦλος, ἀνάθεμα ἔστω· καὶ πάλιν, τὰς βεβήλους καινοφωνίας περιίστασο, ἐπὶ πλεῖον γὰρ προκόψουσιν ἀσεβείας καὶ ὁ λόγος αὐτῶν ὡς γάγγραινα νομὴν ἕξει, ἀπεσχόμεθα τούτων μετὰ τῆς ὅλης τοῦ Θεοῦ ἐκκλησίας, ἣ τούτους ἀπείργουσα τῶν ἱερῶν περιβόλων, οὐ μεταδίδωσι σφίσιν ἱεροτελεστίας.

Ἐν τούτοις μὲν οὖν τὰ τῇδε· σὺ δ' ὅπως ἀεὶ τοῖς αὐτοῖς οἷς καὶ [fol. 43r] πρῴην τέρψεις τε ἡμᾶς καὶ πρὸ ἡμῶν τὸ θεῖον, φιλοθεώτατε καὶ σοφώτατε καὶ χαρίτων ἁπασῶν ἐνδιαίτημα.

46–47 Gal. 1:8–9 || 47–49 II Tim. 2:16–17 || 50–51 II Mac. 6:4

---

22 ἐτετάξατο M || 40 ἀποβαλλομένους M

the cause of those who defy the rules of piety were highly popular, you would have ranged yourself just as much on the side of truth deliberately, eloquently, and frankly. For when the wise man defends the word of truth, he does not tremble at the power of the mob of an apparent majority riding on falsehood, which, even if it prevails for a while—or rather, appears to prevail due to the indifference of the many—is exposed shortly afterwards. For since it is weak and unstable and without foundation, indeed since it does not exist at all, how can it remain forever?

As for the fact that this evil of the recent novel doctrine regarding piety has already been detected by the whole Church and those in the Palace, indeed most of all by the Empress, and that he who dared ⟨proclaim⟩ these ⟨doctrines⟩ was called upon by all to renounce them because they are completely wrong—in fact, he has just defied them and taken refuge in the most holy Church of St. Sophia—as well as everything else about him that occurred thereafter, I do not have time to discuss this in detail, but the good *Protonotarios* who, more than anyone else, is wise and capable of reporting to you anything whatsoever, will present everything to you accurately. And, moreover, he will ⟨explain⟩ how I too, grieve considerably for these men—how can I help this?—since we were friends and very intimate before now, and for this reason I invited them many times to forsake and reject this and to return again to our earlier friendship and concord, adhering to the agreement about piety that is common and known to all the Church. But, since they did not listen to these words, I together with the whole Church which excommunicated them and does not allow them within "the ambit of the holy places," I have kept away from them, because I am unable to disobey the great Paul who says: "If an angel from heaven, if I Paul should preach to you a gospel at variance with the gospel which you received, let him be outcast!" And again: "Avoid the profane newfangled talk; those who indulge in it will stray further and further into godless courses and the infection of their teaching will spread like gangrene."

This is all the news from here. But you who are most God-loving and wise and the dwelling place of all graces shall continue to delight me, and God before me, with the same things as before!

29. Τῷ Καβαλλαροπούλῳ

Τὸν ἄοκνον πρὸς τοὺς ὑπὲρ τῆς εὐσεβείας ἄθλους ὀκνεῖν ἐπαινεῖν οὐκ ἄμεμπτον. σοῦ δὲ οὐδεὶς πρὸς ἀγῶνας τουτουσὶ προθυμότερος· ὁ τοίνυν ἐθέλων ἐκτὸς εἶναι μέμψεως ἐπαινείτω τὸν γενναῖον Καβαλλαρόπουλον καὶ κομιδῇ θαυμαζέτω, ὃν πολλῶν καὶ ἀγαθῶν προτερημάτων παρὰ πᾶσιν εὐδοκιμεῖν ποιούντων, οὐδὲν οὕτω κηρύττει ὡς τὸ τῆς εὐσεβείας προκινδυνεύειν καὶ ἴσα τῷ ἀναπνεῖν ἔχειν τοῦτό γε. καὶ μάλα εἰκότως· εἰ γὰρ οὐδὲν τἄλλα πάντα πρὸς τὴν εὐσέβειαν τοῖς ὄντως εὐσεβέσι, κατὰ λόγον δὲ τούτοις ἀξίας αὐτῇ καὶ αὐτὸς τὴν σπουδὴν ἀποδίδωσι, πῶς οὐκ εὐλόγως μάλιστα πάντα διὰ ταύτην εὐδοκιμεῖ καὶ κροτεῖται Καβαλλαρόπουλος, γνήσιον αὐτῇ παῖδα παρέχων αὐτόν, ἧς ὡς μητρὸς εὐγενοῦς καὶ φιλόπαιδος προκινδυνεύει πρὸς τὰς ἀναιδεῖς ἐπ' αὐτῇ τῶν δυσσεβῶν ἐφόδους; ἤδη μὲν οὖν τις ὡς εὐδαίμονας ὕμνησε τὴν πρώτην εὐδαιμονίαν τοὺς ἐφ' ἁμάξης εἰς θεωρίαν κομίσαντας παῖδας μητέρα, κατὰ νόμον βοεικὸν ὑπ' αὐτῶν εἱλκυσμένης. εἰ τοῦτο τοίνυν ἦν εὔδαιμον καὶ ἄκρας εὐδαιμονίας, καὶ διὰ τοῦτο τῆς Ἡροδότου γλώττης εἰς εὐφημίαν ἀπέλαυσε, πόσον εἰκὸς χρὴ νομίζειν τοὺς ἀθανάτου μητρός, τῆς εὐσεβείας ἡμῶν, καὶ ἅρματα γινομένους καὶ ἵππους ἱεροὺς καὶ ἱππεῖς καὶ ὁπλίτας ἐφ' ὧν τε ὀχεῖται καὶ δι' ὧν τοὺς ἑαυτῇ πολεμίους ἀμύνεται;

Συμβέβηκε δέ, οἶμαι, σὲ μὲν τῶν ἄλλων τοῖς τοιούτοις ἀγωνίσμασι προὔχειν, ἐμὲ δὲ τό σε θαυμάζειν· ὅθεν οὐ μόνον πρὸς ἀπόντα δεῖν ἐπιστέλλειν οἶμαι, ἀλλὰ καὶ πρὸς παρόντα· οὕτως ἀκορέστως ἔχω τῶν περὶ σὲ θαυμάτων. ἀλλὰ σὺ μὲν βάλλε τοὺς καταράτους ἐκείνους καὶ σύντριβε, παρὼν τε τοὺς παρόντας ἐνθάδε, καὶ ἀπὼν τοὺς ἀπόντας, μήτε τὸ πλῆθος, μήτε τὸ ἰταμὸν αὐτῶν εὐλαβούμενος, κρείσσων γάρ, φησιν, εἷς ποιῶν τὸ θέλημα τοῦ Θεοῦ ἢ μυρίοι παράνομοι, τοῦτο δ' ἐστὶν ἰσχυρότερος, [fol. 71r] ἐπικρατέστερος. ἡμῖν δὲ νῦν μέν σε δίδου τὰ πλεῖστα βλέπειν αὐτοπροσώπως, ἀπόντι δ' ἡμεῖς ἐπιστελοῦμεν μακρότερα.

29: 14–16 cf. Herodotum, *Hist.* 1, 31 || 28–29 Sirac. 16:3

29: M 70v–71r.

17 Ἡρωδότου M || 27 ἱταμὸν M

29

29. To Kaballaropoulos

It is not beyond reproach to hesitate to praise the man who refuses to hesitate before laboring on behalf of piety. And there is no one more eager for these very struggles than you. He who wishes, therefore, to be above reproach must praise the noble Kaballaropoulos and wholly admire him. For, though he is highly esteemed by all for his many and noble accomplishments, nothing proclaims his ⟨name⟩ as much as his risking his life for piety and considering this equal indeed to breathing. And very properly! For, if to truly pious men all other things are nothing compared with piety, and if he, too, shows a zeal for piety to compare with the esteem in which it is held by pious men, surely it is for exceedingly good reasons that he distinguishes himself in everything and is applauded because of his piety. For he shows himself as its true offspring, and, as if it were a noble and loving mother, he braves danger for it in the face of the insolent attacks of impious men against it. Indeed, someone has already extolled as supremely happy the sons who brought their mother to the festival in a wagon which they themselves drew after the manner of oxen. If this, then, was true happiness and, in fact, happiness of the highest degree, and if it was for this reason that it enjoyed the praise of Herodotus' tongue, how highly must we think of men who become chariots and sacred horses and horsemen and soldiers of the immortal mother, our piety, which rides on their backs and finds through them a defense against its enemies?

It is, I believe, your fate to surpass others in such contests, and mine to admire you. I think, therefore, that I ought to write to you not only when you are away, but also when you are here. This is how much I long for your marvelous accomplishments. But keep on smiting and crushing those accursed men—when you are here, those who are here, and when you are abroad, those who are abroad—and fear neither their great number nor their insolence, "for," he says, "one that does the will of God is better than a thousand lawless," and this means that they are mightier and more victorious. But now grant me the favor of seeing you often in person, and while you are away I will write to you at great length.

30. Sine titulo

Ὄντως ἐστὶν ἀληθὴς ὁ νομὴν ὡς γάγγραιναν τὰς βεβήλους καινοφωνίας ἕξειν καὶ ἐπὶ πλέον ἀσεβείας προκόψειν, εἰ μὴ παρὰ τὴν πρώτην ἔκφυσιν εὐθὺς ἐκριζωθεῖεν, λέγων. σκόπει γάρ, ὦ θαυμάσιε· πρῶτον τοῖς Παλαμᾶ περιπεσὼν φαρμάκοις καὶ τὰς ἀκοὰς φαρμαχθεὶς ἀφυλάκτως, ἔπειτα καὶ παρ' ἡμᾶς ἀφίκου βουλόμενος ἀκοῦσαι καὶ παρ' ἡμῶν ἃ παρ' ἐκείνου καθ' ἡμῶν ἠκηκόεις. εὖγε ποιῶν, ὦ βέλτιστε, τὸ γοῦν ἐρήμην ἡμᾶς παντάπασι καταδικάσαι φεύγων· οὐ γὰρ ἁπλῶς ὑπὲρ τῆς αὐτοῦ καινοφωνίας ἀπολογεῖται καὶ πείθει τοὺς ἀγνοοῦντας τὸ ὑψηλὸν καὶ λεπτὸν καὶ δυσθεώρητον δόγμα, καὶ διὰ τοῦτο καινόν τε καὶ ἄηθες τῇ ἐκκλησίᾳ τοῦ Θεοῦ καὶ τοῖς πολλοῖς ἡμῖν καὶ χθαμαλοῖς, ὥς αὐτός φησιν ὁ σεμνὸς καὶ μέγας—τί μέγας; ὁ ἄκτιστος καὶ ἄναρχος τῇ μετοχῇ τῶν καινῶν ἑαυτοῦ θεοτήτων γεγενημένος—ἦν γὰρ ἂν τοῦτο μέτριον, εἰ διδάσκων παρ' ὃ παρελάβομεν οἷς Παῦλος ὁ μέγας προανεφώνησε κἂν ἄγγελος ἐξ οὐρανοῦ εὐαγγελίζηται ὑμῖν, παρ' ὃ παρελάβετε, ἀνάθεμα ἔστω, οὔπω δυσσεβεῖν ἀπεφαίνετο Παύλῳ πειθομένους, οὐ Παλαμᾷ, ἐπειδήπερ ἀμφοτέροις οὐκ ἔξεστι· νῦν δὲ τὰς ὑπὲρ ὧν ἠσέβησεν ἀπολογίας, ἐγκλήματα ποιεῖται καθ' ἡμῶν ἀσεβείας, ταὐτὸν εἶναι λέγων ἀσεβεῖν καὶ τὴν αὐτοῦ θεογονίαν μὴ παραδέχεσθαι, οὕτω γὰρ εἰπεῖν οἰκειότερον.

Ἐλθὼν τοίνυν καὶ παρ' ἡμᾶς, ὡς ἔφην, καὶ τοὺς περὶ τούτων λόγους ἡμᾶς ὡς εἰκὸς ἀπαιτήσας, ἀκήκοας ἃ Παλαμᾶς διδάσκει λόγοις πολλοῖς καὶ ἰταμοῖς οὓς [fol. 56r] ἐπὶ τούτῳ συντέθεικε· καὶ πρὶν ἡμῶν τι κατὰ τούτων ἀκοῦσαι, παρ' αὐτὴν τὴν ἀνάγνωσιν, "ὢ τῆς ἀσεβείας!" ἀνέκραγες, "ὢ τῆς πολυθεΐας καὶ τῆς ὑπὲρ πᾶσαν δυσσέβειαν καινοτομίας, ὅπως αὐτῷ λάθοι τὰ δυσσεβήματα πραγματευθείσης, ταῖς ἐκ τῶν θείων πατέρων δῆθεν μαρτυρίαις ἐπαλειφέντα!" ἀλλ' οὐδὲν τοῦτο γέγονεν ἐμποδὼν σοι πρὸς τὸ κατιδεῖν εὐθέως τὰ δυσσεβήματα, τοιοῦτο γὰρ σύνεσις καθαρὰ καὶ διάνοια, ὥσπερ ὄμμα καθαρὸν καὶ ὄψις ὀξυδερκής, διορᾷ καὶ τὰ μὴ καθαρῶς πρὸς θεωρίαν ἐκκείμενα. λαβὼν τοίνυν ταῦτα τῇ διανοίᾳ, ἦλθες πρὸς τὸν αὐτῶν πατέρα καὶ ἐπειρῶ διορθοῦσθαι τὸν ἄνθρωπον, προφέρων τὴν τῶν δογμάτων αὐτῷ φανερὰν μοχθηρίαν. ὁ δέ, ὡς ἀπηγ-

---

30: 1–3 II Tim. 2:16–17 ‖ 14 Gal. 1:9 ‖ 15–16 Gal. 1:8–9

30: M 55v–58r.

1 ὄντως] οὕτως M ‖ 4 ἐκριζωθείη M ‖ 17 ἀνεφαίνετο M ‖ 24 ἱταμοῖς M

30

30. No Addressee

Truly he speaks the truth who says that "The profane newfangled talk will spread like gangrene and those who indulge in it will stray further and further into godless courses," unless it is eradicated as soon as it arises! For think, my admirable friend: first you fell under the spell of Palamas, and, lacking protection, your ears were poisoned. Then you came to me wishing to hear from me what you had heard from him against me. You did very well, my excellent friend, to avoid condemning me altogether by default. For he does not speak simply in defense of his own "newfangled-talk," nor does he ⟨simply⟩ convince those who do not know his lofty and subtle doctrine which is so hard to perceive and therefore strange and novel to the Church of God and to us, the many and lowly, as he himself says, the august and great. (Why great? He who has become uncreated and eternal through the participation of his own new divinities!) For it would have been tolerable, if, preaching a doctrine "at variance with that which we received"—though the great Paul forewarned us: "If an angel from heaven, if I, Paul, should preach to you a gospel at variance with the gospel which you received, let him be outcast!"—he did not declare that those who obey Paul and not Palamas are impious, for certainly it is not possible to obey both. But now he turns the defense of his own impious deeds into accusations of impiety against me, saying that being impious and not accepting his own theogony are the same thing, to put it in more appropriate terms.

Well then, when you came to me, as I said, and rightly asked for my writings on these matters, you heard what Palamas teaches in many arrogant works which he has composed for this purpose. And before even hearing anything from me against them, during the reading itself, you cried out: "What impiety! What polytheism and innovation beyond all impiety, which contrived that his profanities, daubed presumably with the testimony of the holy Fathers, should escape detection." But this did not prevent you from at once perceiving his profanities, for such is genuine intelligence and understanding, just like a clear eye and sharp vision which distinguishes even those things that are not clearly exposed to view. Having, therefore, apprehended these, you went to their author and you tried to correct the man, showing him the obvious wickedness of his doctrines. But he, as you reported, denied that

30

γειλας, ἀπηρνεῖτο μηδὲν τοιοῦτο μήτε φρονεῖν, μήτε γράφειν, ἀλλ' ἡμῶν εἶναι ταῦτα συκοφαντούντων αὐτὸν καὶ τὰ μὴ αὐτῷ γεγραμμένα παραγραφόντων. τοιαῦτα γὰρ ὁ δαιμόνιος ἐπιτετήδευκεν· ὅταν ἴδῃ τινὰ τῶν οὐ λίαν εὐκόλων ἀποδέξασθαι γυμνὴν αὐτοῦ τὴν ἀσέβειαν, οὐ γυμνὴν αὐτῷ ταύτην προβάλλεται, ἀλλὰ δυσχεραίνοντος μὲν πρὸς τὴν φήμην, εὐθὺς ἔξαρνος γίνεται καὶ συκοφαντεῖσθαι διισχυρίζεται, προσαναγκάζοντος δὲ δὴ τὴν αἰτίαν ὡς εἰκὸς ἀποτίθεσθαι, ἐλεγχόμενος ἤδη, οὐκ ἔτ' ἀρνεῖται ὥσπερ προτοῦ τὰ ἐγκλήματα, ἐπιχειρεῖ δὲ ἄλλως, σοφιστικοῖς δικτύοις ἀπαγαγεῖν τῆς εὐσεβείας τὸν ἄνθρωπον καὶ τοῖς ἑαυτοῦ παραπέμψαι βαράθροις.

Εἶτ' αὖθις ὡς ἡμᾶς ἐπανῆκες καὶ διηγοῦ τὴν ἀπάρνησιν. καὶ ἡμεῖς αὖθις ὅτι μὲν ἄλογος ὁ λόγος οὗτος καὶ ὡς, εἰ ταῦτα ἠλήθευεν, οὐκ ⟨ἂν⟩ ἦν πόρρω τὸ ἀπηλλάχθαι ταύτης αὐτὸν τῆς αἰτίας, δείξαντα ἑαυτὸν τῇ θείᾳ καὶ ἱερᾷ συνόδῳ συκοφαντούμενον, οὐδ' ἂν αὐτὸς ἐφρουρεῖτο ἐπὶ ταύτῃ τῇ αἰτίᾳ προδήλως, οὐδ' ἂν ὁ Ἰσίδωρος τῶν τῆς ἀρχιερωσύνης ψήφων ἐξέπιπτε καὶ αὐτῆς τῆς ἱερωσύνης καθῄρητο, ταῦτ' ἐγκαλούμενος καὶ τὸ ταῦθ' ὁμολογῆσαι μὴ φρονεῖν ἀπαιτούμενος, εἰ βούλοιτο μὴ καθηρῆσθαι τοῦ ἀξιώματος· νῦν δὲ πᾶν τοὐναντίον· ὁμολογήσας ταῦτα τῷ Παλαμᾷ συμφρονεῖν, οὐκ ἐκείνων μόνον ἀλλὰ καὶ τῆς ἐκκλησιαστικῆς κοινωνίας ἐξέπεσε— ταῦτα μὲν οὐκ εἴ-[fol. 56v]πομέν σοι, ἀλλ' ἔτι τούτων ἁπλούστερά τε καὶ δικαιότερα· ὡς ἄρα, εἰ λέγει συκοφαντεῖσθαι, ταῦθ' ἃ συκοφαντεῖσθαί φησι καὶ νῦν ἐξομοσάμενος καὶ ἀναθεματίσας, ὡς ἔθος τοῖς περιπίπτουσι ταῖς τοιαύταις αἰτίαις, καὶ τὴν κοινὴν ὁμολογίαν τῆς ἐκκλησίας ἀκριβῶς ἐκφωνήσας καὶ ἀνομολογήσας, ὡς ὁμογνώμων ἤδη τῇ ἐκκλησίᾳ τοῦ Θεοῦ καὶ ἀδελφὸς ἡμῖν καὶ φίλος ἀγαπηθήσεταί τε καὶ τιμηθήσεται, καὶ οὕτως αὐτός τε τῶν παρόντων πραγμάτων ἀπαλλαγήσεται καὶ ἡμᾶς ἀπαλλάξει, χάριν αὐτῷ πολλὴν ἐπὶ τούτῳ καὶ μεγάλην ὁμολογοῦντας.

Ἐκθέμενοι τοίνυν τά τε ὑπαίτια δόγματα καὶ τὴν τῆς ἐκκλησιαστικῆς πίστεως ὁμολογίαν, ὧν κοινῇ πάντες ἐγώ τε καὶ σὺ καὶ οἱ συνόντες ἡμῖν τῇ μὲν συμφρονεῖν αὐτόθεν ὡμολογοῦμεν ἐξότου φρονεῖν ἐδεξάμεθα, τὰ δὲ εἶναι προφανῶς δυσσεβήματα, σοὶ ταῦτα ἐπαινοῦντι τὴν δοκιμασίαν καὶ προσαναγκάσαντι δίδομεν. ἀγαθὸς γὰρ ὢν καὶ τὰ τοιαῦτα θέλων, ᾤου τὸν ἄνθρωπον ἀληθεύειν φάσκοντα συκοφαντεῖσθαι, καὶ αὐτίκα μάλα ἡμῖν καὶ πάσῃ τῇ ἐκκλησίᾳ τὸ πρῴην μὲν φίλον, ὕστερον δὲ ἀπερρωγὸς συνάψειν, ὁμολογῆσαν πᾶσι τὰ πᾶσι δεδογμένα περὶ τοῦ θείου· νῦν δέ μοι Γαβρᾶς ὁ θαυμάσιος, τὸ μέγα χρῆμα τῆς φιλίας, ἀπήγγειλεν ὡς ἐπειδὴ σὺ ταῦτα αὐτῷ προσαγάγοις καὶ δείξαις τὴν σὴν καὶ κοινὴν

---

47 ⟨ἂν⟩ addidi || 66 τῇ] τὴν M

30

he either thought or had written any such thing, and claimed that these are my calumnies and forgeries of things he did not write. For this diabolical man has contrived such things: when he sees one of the people who do not accept very easily his undisguised impiety, he does not present it to him undisguised; but if the man is displeased with the rumors, he ⟨Palamas⟩ immediately denies them and claims that he has been falsely accused; and if the man also compels him, as is fitting, to clear himself of the charge, seeing that he is now put to the test, he does not any more deny his crimes as before, but attempts in other ways by a sophist's snares to lead the man away from piety and to send him to his own pits of death.

Afterward, you came back to me and described his denial in detail, and I again ⟨might have replied⟩ that what he says does not make sense, and that, if he were speaking the truth, it would have been within his power to free himself of this charge by proving to the divine and holy Synod that he was being falsely accused, and then he would not have been in custody manifestly because of this charge, nor would Isidore have been deprived of his episcopal appointment and banished from the priesthood. For the same charges were brought against him, and he was asked to confess that he did not hold these beliefs, if he did not wish to be deposed from office. But now things have turned out quite otherwise. For he has confessed that he holds the same beliefs as Palamas, and not only was he deprived of that appointment, but he was also excommunicated. But it was not this that I said to you, but even simpler and more just things than these: namely, that if he claims to be falsely accused, after renouncing and anathematizing even now those doctrines of which he claims to be falsely accused—as is customary for those who are caught in such accusations—and after proclaiming exactly and admitting the common confession of the Church, he will be loved and honored as being actually in agreement with the Church of God and a brother and friend of mine. And thus he will be free of the present troubles, and he will also free me, so that I will be very grateful to him for this.

After explaining, therefore, the reprehensible doctrines and the confession of faith of the Church and agreeing—myself as well as you and our companions all together—that we were of one mind with the latter from the moment we had a mind, while the former are obviously profanities, I gave you these writings, because you praised my scrutiny and also pressed me. For, being good and desiring what is good, you thought that the man was speaking the truth when he said that he was falsely accused, and that presently you would unite him, having been a friend once and having later broken away, with me and the whole Church after he had confessed before all the commonly accepted doctrines about God. But now the admirable Gabras, a great friend, reported that when you brought these writings to him and showed him the common confession of faith, both yours and that of the Church of

τῆς τοῦ Θεοῦ ἐκκλησίας ὁμολογίαν τῆς πίστεως καὶ τὰς βεβήλους καινοφωνίας αὐτοῦ, τὴν μὲν Ἀρείου καὶ Εὐνομίου καὶ Σαβελλίου καὶ ὅ τι ἕτερον ἀσεβὲς ὀνομάζει, τὰς δὲ τὸ πλήρωμα καὶ τὸ κεφάλαιον τῆς εὐσεβείας.

Τὸ μὲν γὰρ μίαν καὶ μόνην θεότητα ἐν τρισὶ προσώποις καὶ ὑποστάσεσιν ὁμολογεῖν, ἁπλῆν, ἀόρατον, ἀπερινόητον, ἀμέριστον, ἀδιαίρετον, ἐνεργῆ, παντοδύναμον, καὶ οὕτως ἕνα Θεὸν τρισυπόστατον, ἄκτιστον, παρ' ᾧ οὐκ ἔστι παραλλαγή, ἐν μονάδι τριάδα καὶ τριάδι μονάδα, ἕτερον δὲ οὐδὲν ἄκτιστον, οὐ θεόν, οὐ θεότητα, οὐδ' ὁτιοῦν, οὐδ' ἐν τῇ μονάδι ταύτῃ διαφορὰς καὶ βαθμοὺς θεοτήτων ἀνίσους ἢ ἀριθμῶν καθάπαξ, εἰ μὴ προσώπων καὶ ὑποστάσεων ἐν μιᾷ τῇ θεότητι—τοῦτο μὲν οὖν τῆς ἀσεβεστάτης ἔφη σοι μοίρας εἶναι· τὸ δὲ πλῆθος θεοτήτων πρεσβεύειν ἀνίσων ἀλλήλαις καὶ ἀνομοιοτάτων, καὶ τὸ εἰς τοῦτο τὸ πλῆθος κατατέμνειν τὴν μίαν, ὑπερκειμένων καὶ ὑφειμένων ἀπειράκις ἀπείρως, καὶ ὁρατῶν καὶ ἀοράτων, [fol. 57r] καὶ ἐνεργουμένων καὶ ἐνεργούσης, εἶτα συναϊδίων, τοῦτ' εἶναι τὸ εὐσεβέστατον καὶ θαυμαστῶς εὐαπόδεικτον (οὐκ οἶδα ἐκ τίνων βαράθρων καὶ τίνος Ὠκεανοῦ καὶ Τηθύος ἀποδεικνύμενον).

Ἤδη τοίνυν ἔγνως πείρᾳ μαθὼν ἐν σεαυτῷ τὸ κακόν· ἣν γὰρ ἐκ παιδὸς ὡμολόγεις εὐσέβειαν, ταύτην ὡς ἀσέβειαν εὑρέθης τῷ Παλαμᾷ πρεσβεύων, καὶ ἣν ᾔδεις ἀσέβειαν καὶ ἧς κατεβόας εὐθὺς ὡς ἀκήκοας, ταύτην εἶναι τὴν ὄντως εὐσέβειαν ἤκουσας τοῦ Παλαμᾶ δισχυριζομένου καί, ὅ φησι, τὰ ἄνω κάτω ποιοῦντος καὶ τοὔμπαλιν. οὐ γὰρ ἐγὼ τὸ ἐμὸν ἤδη λέγω, ἀλλὰ τὸ σὸν καὶ κοινόν, εἰ μὴ νῦν τὰ ἐκ παιδὸς εἰς τόδε τῆς ἡλικίας ἐντυπωθέντα σου τῇ ψυχῇ τῆς εὐσεβείας μαθήματα καὶ τὴν πατρῴαν καὶ παππώαν εὐσέβειαν μεταμαθήσῃ μὴ εὐσέβειαν οὖσαν ἀλλὰ δυσσέβειαν, οὐκ ἐννοήσας, ὅταν σοί ποθέν τινα ἐκ τῶν πατέρων παράγῃ ῥῆσιν συστατικήν, ὡς οἴεται, τῶν δυσσεβῶν δογμάτων, εἰ μήπω συνίῃς, τῆς κακουργίας αὐτοῦ, ἢ μηδὲν ὧν ἄγει ῥῆμα ὑγιὲς καὶ ὁλόκληρον δείκνυσιν ἐν τοῖς οἰκείοις λόγοις, ἀλλ' ἐξεστραμμένα πάντα καὶ περικεκομμένα τὰ καιριώτατα καὶ καθαρὰ δείγματα τῆς ἀληθείας. ἐκεῖνό γε πρόδηλον ὡς οὐδὲ τῶν πώποτε δυσσεβησάντων οὐδεὶς ἀμάρτυρον παρὰ τῆς θείας Γραφῆς τὴν αἵρεσιν ἔφερεν, ἀλλ' εἶχε λέγειν οὐκ ὀλίγα ἐκεῖθεν, οἷς τοὺς πολλοὺς παρῆγε, δοκοῦντα μᾶλλον τὰ ἐκείνου κρα-

---

75–76 II Tim. 2:16 ‖ 82 *παρ' . . . παραλλαγή*: cf. Jac. 1:17 ‖ 82–83 Greg. Naz., *Or.* 25, 17 (PG, 35, 1221C) ‖ 89–90 Palamas, *Epist. III ad Acindynum*, 15, Syngrammata, I, 306, 18–20; ed. Nadal, 252, 10–12 ‖ 90 *ἀπειράκις ἀπείρως* cf. Maxim. Conf., *Capit. theol.*, 1, 49 (PG, 90, 1101A) = Palamas, *Dialexis*, 24, Syngrammata, II, 186, 26; *Epist. ad Gabram*, 5, Syngrammata, II, 332, 12 ‖ 93 cf. Greg. Naz., *Or.*31, 16 (PG, 36, 152A) ‖ 98 Gregorius Cyprius I, 61 (Leutsch-Schneidewin, II, 61)

30
God, as well as his "profane newfangled talk," he called the former the heresy of Arios and Eunomios and Sabellios and every other impious name, and the latter the fulfillment and sum total of piety.

For he told you that it is the worst sort of impiety to acknowledge one and only one divinity in three persons and hypostases, simple, invisible, incomprehensible, admitting of no partition or division, active, omnipotent; and thus one God in three hypostases, uncreated, "with whom there is no variation," "one in three and three in one"; and nothing else uncreated, neither god nor divinity nor anything whatsoever, nor differences in this Monad nor degrees of unequal divinities, nor of numbers absolutely, ⟨that is⟩, except for ⟨differences of⟩ persons and hypostases in a single divinity. But to believe in a multitude of divinities which are mutually unequal and most dissimilar, and to cut up the one divinity into this multitude of divinities "higher and infinitely lower," and visible and invisible, and passive and active, and then coeternal, this he said is most pious and wonderfully easy to prove (I know not from what chaos and Ocean and Tethys it is proven)!

Already, therefore, you know, having learnt from experience, that the evil is in you. For you were found by Palamas to hold impious beliefs, because you believe in what you acknowledged as piety since childhood; and what you knew to be impious and inveighed against as soon as you heard it, this you heard Palamas claim to be piety and, as they say, turn things "upside down" and vice versa. For it is not actually my own beliefs which I express, but yours and those of everybody else in general. Unless you are now going to learn differently that the lessons of piety which have been imprinted on your soul from childhood up to this age and your paternal and ancestral faith are not pious but impious, having failed to notice, if you do not know it yet, Palamas' wickedness by which, whenever he presents to you some patristic quotation or other, in confirmation, as he believes, of his impious doctrines, he does not present any of the sayings that he adduces sound and whole in their own words, but all of them are distorted and with the principal and genuine proofs of truth missing. For it is certainly known to all that none of the impious men who ever lived produced a heresy unsupported by evidence from the Holy Scripture or without being able to quote from there not a few passages with which to mislead many people, since they appeared rather to confirm his views. Hence many of those

τύνειν· ὅθεν καὶ πολλὰς ἐκείνων ἐπὶ πολὺ κρατῆσαι τῆς πλείστης ἐκκλησίας συμβέβηκε, τῶν πολλῶν ἀεὶ πρὸς τὰ καινὰ κεχηνότων. τοιγαροῦν Παῦλος μὲν Τιμοθέῳ, καὶ δι' ἐκείνου πᾶσι, τὰς βεβήλους καινοφωνίας περιίστασο, γράφει, ἐπὶ πλεῖον γάρ, φησιν, ἀσεβείας προκόψουσι καὶ ὁ λόγος αὐτῶν ὡς γάγγραινα νομὴν ἕξει· ὁ δὲ μέγας Βασίλειος φυλάττειν ἡμῖν ἡμᾶς αὐτοὺς παραινεῖ, μήτε ὑπὸ τῶν παθῶν σαλευομένους, μήτε ὑπὸ τῶν ψευδῶν δογμάτων διὰ πιθανότητος εἰς συγκατάθεσιν περιελκομένους· ὁ δὲ ἑταῖρος αὐτοῦ καὶ τῆς θεολογίας ἐπώνυμος, ἕν, φησι, δίδασκε φοβεῖσθαι μόνον τὸ λύειν τὴν πίστιν ἐν τοῖς σοφίσμασι.

Πῶς οὖν δυσσεβοῦντες ἠλέγχθησαν, εἰ πίστιν ἦγον ἐκ τῶν ἱερῶν γραφῶν οἷς δυσσεβῶς ἐφρόνουν; πρῶτον μὲν ἐπειδὴ παρὰ τὰ τοῖς πᾶσι φρονούμενα καὶ ὁμολογούμενα ἐφαίνοντο λέγοντες, τοῦτο γὰρ δὴ τὸ καινόν· τοῦ δὲ κρατοῦντος τὸ νεωστὶ παρελθὸν οὐκ ἀνθαιρετέον τοῖς πατράσιν ἐδόκει, ἦσαν γὰρ [fol. 57v] τοῦ λέγοντος ἀκροαταί, μὴ μέταιρε ὅρια αἰώνια, ἃ ἔθετον οἱ πατέρες σου· ἦσαν τοῦ κεκραγότος, κἂν ἄγγελος ἐξ οὐρανοῦ εὐαγγελίζηται ὑμῖν παρ' ὃ παρελάβετε, ἀνάθεμα ἔστω· καὶ τῶν τοιούτων πάντων. ἔπειτα πρὸς τούτοις οἱ τῆς εὐσεβείας ἀντιποιούμενοι, πρὸς τῷ τὰ πάλαι πρεσβευόμενα τῇ ἐκκλησίᾳ στέργειν, εἶχον ἀπὸ τῆς αὐτῆς θείας Γραφῆς φανερὰν τὴν ἀλήθειαν ἐπιδεικνύναι κἀκείνους ἠπατημένους καὶ μὴ νοοῦντας, ἀλλὰ παρανοοῦντας ἃ νοεῖν δοκοῦσι, καὶ ὅθεν εἰς τὴν ἀσέβειαν πίπτουσιν.

Εἰ μὲν οὖν καὶ Παλαμᾶς οὐδὲν καινὸν κηρύττει, οὐδὲ ἀνόμοιον τῇ κοινῇ συμφωνίᾳ τῆς ἐκκλησίας περὶ τῆς πίστεως, τί δεῖ πολλῶν λόγων καὶ ἀποδείξεων; δειξάτω τοῦτο μόνον, αὐτὴν ὁμολογήσας τὴν κοινὴν ὁμολογίαν τῆς πίστεως, καὶ ἡμεῖς ἀσπαζόμεθα. εἰ δ' οὐδεὶς μὲν ἂν φαίη τὴν ἀρχήν, ἀκούσας αὐτοῦ τὸ πλῆθος τῶν θεοτήτων, ὡς ἐκεῖνα λέγει καὶ διατείνεται οἷς ἐντεθράμμεθα καὶ μεθ' ὧν εἰς τοῦθ' ἧκεν ἡλικίας ἕκαστος ὁμολογῶν ᾗ νῦν ἕστηκεν, ὁ δὲ τὰ μὲν κρατοῦντα λύειν, εἰς τὰ καινὰ δὲ καὶ τοῖς κειμένοις ἐναντία μεθέλκειν ἐσπούδακε τοὺς ἐντυγχάνοντας, τί δεῖ καὶ οὕτω τῶν πολλῶν αὐτοῦ λόγων καὶ σοφισμάτων; πάντως γὰρ ὁποῖά ποτ' ἂν εἴη καὶ ὁποθενδήποτε αὐτῷ τὰ μαρτύρια, τό γε τὰ ἐναντία δόγματα τοῖς ὁμολογουμένοις καὶ ξένα τῆς συνηθείας ἡμῖν κρατῆσαι οὐκ εὐσεβές, οὐδὲ ὅσιον ἄλλην μαθόντας πίστιν, ἄλλην μεταμανθάνειν ἄρτι, πρὸς αὐτοῖς τοῖς ὅροις, ὡς λέγεται, τοῦ παντὸς τοῦδε κόσμου καὶ τῇ μετα-

---

114–116 II Tim. 2:16–17 ‖ 117–119 Basil. Caes., locum non inveni ‖ 120–121 Greg. Naz., *Or.* 25, 18 (PG, 35, 1224B) ‖ 127–128 Prov. 22:28 ‖ 128–130 Gal. 1:8–9

30

heresies happened to prevail over most of the Church for a long time, for always the many are all agape at things new. Therefore, Paul writes to Timothy and through him to all men: "Avoid the profane newfangled talk, for," he says, "those who indulge in it will stray further and further into godless courses, and the infection of their teaching will spread like gangrene." And Basil the Great urges us to watch ourselves and "be neither shaken by passions nor dragged into assent by the persuasiveness of false doctrines." And his friend, who is named the Theologian, says: "Teach only the fear of destroying the faith through sophistry."

How then were they ⟨the heretics⟩ proven impious, if they brought confirmation of their impious beliefs from the Holy Scriptures? First, it was because they appeared to be saying things which were at variance with what everybody believed and confessed, for this indeed is innovation, and the Fathers did not think that what had just appeared ought to be preferred to the prevailing dogma. For they listened to him who says: "Remove not the old landmarks which thy fathers placed;" and to him who cried out: "Even if an angel from heaven should preach to you a gospel at variance with the gospel which you received, let him be outcast!" and to all such men. Then, in addition to this, those who fought for the pious beliefs of the Church were able to show from the same Scriptures the manifest truth and that the others had been deceived, and did not understand but misunderstood what they thought they understood, and for that reason they fell into impiety.

If, therefore, Palamas also proclaims nothing new or dissimilar to the common agreement of the Church about the faith, what need is there for many arguments and proofs? Let him prove this alone by acknowledging the common confession of faith itself, and I will be delighted. But if, on the one hand, no one from the beginning who heard his doctrine about a multitude of divinities could claim that he says and maintains the things on which we were brought up and which each one reached his present age confessing, while, on the other hand, Palamas has sought to destroy the prevailing beliefs and to draw, instead, those who converse with him to beliefs that are new and contrary to the accepted doctrines, what need is there in this case also for his many arguments and sophistries? At any rate, no matter what and from where his evidence may be, the prevalence of doctrines which are contrary to those we confess and foreign to our custom is impious, and it is certainly not sanctioned by divine law that, having learned one faith, we should forget it now and learn another which alters the very laws of the universe, as they say, and its shape.

θέσει τοῦ σχήματος. ἀλλὰ δεῖ τοὺς μέν, οἷς ἀπορία τῶν πρὸς ταῦτα ἐλέγχων, οὐδὲ λόγων κοινωνεῖν, οὐδ᾽ ἀκοὰς ὑπέχειν τοῖς λειτουργοῖς τοῦ ψεύδους καὶ διὰ τοῦτο ἀποτμηθεῖσι τῆς Χριστοῦ ἐκκλησίας, ἵνα μὴ τῇ κοινωνίᾳ λυμαίνωνται τῷ Χριστοῦ τούτῳ σώματι· τοὺς δὲ μὴ ἀδυνάτους καὶ ἀνατρέπειν αὐτοὺς καὶ τὰς πηγὰς συνορᾶν ὅθεν ἀπορρεῖ τὸ κακὸν τοῦτο ῥεῦμα, μὴ συγχωρεῖν προϊὸν τὰς ψυχὰς κατασύρειν, ἀλλ᾽ ὡς οἷόν τε τέμνειν καὶ διαιρεῖν καὶ πάντα τρόπον ἐκδαπανᾶν τὴν λύμην καὶ τῶν τῆς ἐκκλησίας περιβόλων ἀπάγειν· βλέπετε, γάρ φησι, τοὺς κύνας, βλέπετε τοὺς κακοὺς ἐργάτας, βλέπετε τὴν κατατομήν· καὶ ἕτερος τῶν Ἀποστόλων ἐπαγωνίζεσθαι κελεύει τῇ ἅπαξ παραδοθείσῃ πίστει τοῖς ἁγίοις.

Ἀλλ᾽ οὔτε τὸ φῶς τὴν τοῦ σκότους μεταλήψεται [fol. 58ʳ] φύσιν, οὔτε σὺ τῆς ἐκ παιδὸς εὐσεβείας ἀνταλλάξῃ τὰ νέα καὶ τοῖς ἐκείνης ὅροις ἀντίθετα. πρὸς μὲν οὖν ἐκείνους, ὡς ἔοικεν, οὐκ ἔτ᾽ ἔστι σοι λόγος, ἐν τῷ ἀσφαλεῖ μένειν ἐθέλοντι τῆς εὐσεβείας· αἱρετικόν, γάρ φησιν, ἄνθρωπον μετὰ μίαν καὶ δευτέραν νουθεσίαν παραιτοῦ, εἰδὼς ὅτι ἐξέστραπται ὁ τοιοῦτος· καί, σκοπεῖτε τοὺς τὰ σκάνδαλα καὶ τὰς διχοστασίας ποιοῦντας παρὰ τὴν διδαχὴν ἣν ὑμεῖς ἐμάθετε καὶ ἐκκλίνατε ἀπ᾽ αὐτῶν. τῶν δὲ ἠπατημένων ὑπ᾽ αὐτῶν καὶ νῦν διαφθειρομένων καὶ διαφθαρησομένων δεῖ μὲν παντὶ μέλειν ᾧ μέλει τῶν τοῦ Κυρίου μελῶν, δεῖ δέ σοι πάντων μάλιστα, ὅσῳ καὶ λόγων ἀπολαύεις δυνάμεως καὶ θεογνωσίας εὐτυχεῖς τὴν ἀκρότητα, οἱ γὰρ τοιοῦτοι τῆς σιωπῆς λόγον δώσουσιν ἐκκλησίας σπαραττομένης αἱρετικοῖς θηρίοις, καὶ λόγον οὐ πάνυ πόρρω κείμενον τῶν σπαραττόντων αὐτῶν, ὡς ἐκ τῶν θείων πατέρων πολλαχοῦ μεμαθήκαμεν.

31. Sine titulo

Οὐκ ἄρα ἔμελλε κατ᾽ ἐρημίαν τοῦ κατ᾽ ἀξίαν ἀνταίροντος παρρησιάζεσθαι τὰ Παλαμναῖα κηρύγματα, οὐδ᾽ ἀπαλλάξειν ἀθῷα τοῦ δοῦναι δίκας ἀνδρὶ ῥώμην ἔχοντι μεγάλην καὶ σθένος ἀδηρι-

153 *τῷ Χριστοῦ τούτῳ σώματι* cf. Eph. 1:23 ‖ 158–159 Phil. 3:2 ‖ 160–161 Jud. 3 ‖ 165–167 Tit. 3:11 ‖ 168–170 Rom. 16:17 ‖ 172 I Cor. 12:28

31: M 43ʳ–43ᵛ.

But those who do not possess the means of refuting these doctrines must neither converse with nor listen to the ministers of falsehood who, for that reason also, were cut off from the Church, that they may not by association inflict injury upon this body of Christ. And those who are able not only to overthrow these ⟨doctrines⟩, but also to perceive at once the sources from which this evil current flows, must not allow it to sweep away the souls as it advances; they must as far as possible cut and divide ⟨the current⟩ and in every way destroy the corruption and remove it from the precincts of the Church. For he says: "Beware of those dogs and their malpractices. Beware of those who insist on mutilation!" And another Apostle enjoins ⟨us⟩ "to join the struggle in defense of the faith which God entrusted to His people once and for all."

But neither will light exchange its nature for that of darkness nor will you exchange the pious faith you learnt from childhood for doctrines that are new and contrary to its laws. Therefore, as it seems, you have nothing more to discuss with the ⟨Palamites⟩, if you wish to remain in the safety of piety. For he says: "A heretic should be warned once and once again; after that, have done with him, recognizing that a man of that sort has a distorted mind;" and "Keep your eye on those who stir up quarrels and lead others astray, contrary to the teaching you received, and avoid them." But everyone who cares about the "limbs of Christ" must care about those who have been deceived by them and who are now being corrupted and will be in the future, and this is especially necessary for you, inasmuch as you enjoy the power of eloquence and have the good fortune to possess an extensive knowledge of theology. For such men will be held accountable for their silence when the Church is being torn to pieces by heretical beasts, and not much less accountable than those who are doing the tearing, as we have often learnt from the holy Fathers.

31. No Addressee

Palamnaian doctrines were not destined, as it seems, to find free expression without ⟨finding⟩ a worthy opponent, nor to escape punishment from a man who has great vigor and, as the saying goes, "irresistible force" of eloquence in his tongue

31

τον, κατὰ τὸ ἔπος, ἔν τε τῇ γλώττῃ λόγων, ἔν τε ψυχῇ εὐσεβείας. καὶ μάτην ἤλπισεν ὁ πονηρὸς γεννήτωρ τῶν πονηρῶν ἐγγόνων τὴν παροῦσαν δυσσέβειαν τῇ τῆς εὐσεβείας ἐνιδρύσασθαι μοίρᾳ· σοῦ γὰρ τὴν πονηρὰν ἀνατρέποντος οἰκοδομήν, καμεῖται πάντως ὁ ταύτην ἀναστῆσαι σπουδάζων καὶ τῆς ἀπονοίας ἀφέξεται, ὁρῶν αὐτῷ πλέον οὐδὲν ἀνυόμενον, ἀλλά τοι καὶ πρὸς πᾶν τοὐναντίον χωροῦντα τὰ πράγματα, εἰ καὶ λίαν ἐστὶν ἰταμὸς καὶ ἀναίσχυντος.

Ἔστι μὲν γὰρ καὶ τὸ σὸν μόνον—οὕτω μὲν ὂν ἔνθεον, οὕτω δὲ ἠσκημένον τὴν περὶ λόγους ἕξιν—ἱκανώτατον αἰσχῦναι καὶ καθελεῖν τὸν ὑπὲρ τὰς νεφέλας αἰρόμενον καὶ τὸ ἀντίθεον ἐκεῖνο καὶ ὑπερήφανον λέγοντα, θήσω τὸν θρόνον μου ἐπὶ νεφελῶν καὶ ἔσομαι ὅμοιος τῷ Ὑψίστῳ, ἔσται δέ τι καὶ πλέον παρὰ τοῦτο ἐντεῦθεν εἰς τὴν τῆς ἀσεβείας καθαίρεσιν· σοῦ γὰρ ἡγουμένου, πολλοὺς ὁ σὸς παρακαλέσει ζῆλος ἐπὶ τὸν αὐτὸν ἀγῶνα τὸν ὑπὲρ εὐσεβείας, τοὺς ἀρετῇ μὲν ζῶντας διὰ τὴν σὴν ἀρετήν, τοὺς δὲ λόγων τροφίμους διὰ τὸ τούτων κράτος ὃ κεκτημένος φαίνῃ, οἷς δ' ἀμφοῖν τούτων μέτεστι δι' ἀμφότερα ταῦτα, ὅτι περίεστί σοι.

Εἶτ', οἶμαι, τούτων οὕτω χωρούντων, τῆς κοινῆς παρὰ πάντων εὐσεβείας ἀνομολογουμένης καὶ τῆς μιᾶς ἐν τῇ θείᾳ καὶ ἀπορρήτῳ τριάδι θεότητος, οἰχήσεται τὸ τῆς πολυθεΐας ἄρτι φυόμενον νόσημα, καὶ καθαρεύσει πάλιν ἡ ἐπώνυμος τοῦ Χριστοῦ ἐκκλησία παντὸς ἐναντίου τῇ εὐσεβείᾳ φρονήματος, καὶ οὕτως ἑνὶ στόματι καὶ μιᾷ καρδίᾳ, κατὰ τὸ λόγιον, τὴν μίαν ἐν τῇ Τριάδι θεότητά τε καὶ δύναμιν ἀνυμνοῦντες διατελέσομεν, μηδὲν ὑπερσέβοντες, μηδ' ὑποσέβοντες (τὸ μὲν γὰρ ἀδύνατον, τὸ δὲ ἀσεβές), μηδὲ μέγεθος ἓν ὀνομάτων καινότησι διακόπτοντες (οὐδὲν γὰρ ἑαυτοῦ μείζων ἢ ἔλαττον), τὰς δὲ περιττὰς καὶ ἀχρήστους παραφυάδας καὶ παραδόξους τῶν ζητημάτων ἀποτρεπόμενοι. τοῦτον γὰρ τὸν ὅρον τῆς εὐσεβείας ἐδίδαξεν ὁ ἀψευδὴς θεολόγος Γρηγόριος, καὶ τὰ τῶν θεολόγων περὶ Θεοῦ προσήκει λέγειν ἡμῖν, οὐ τὰ ἡμέτερα αὐτῶν· ἃ παραβαίνειν οὐ χρή, οὐδ' ἄλλους ἑαυτοῖς ὅρους εὐσεβείας πηγνύναι, οὓς οὔτε ἡμεῖς ἔγνωμεν, οὔτε οἱ πατέρες ἡμῶν, καὶ τοῖς τὰ ὅρια τῶν πατέρων ἡμῶν κινοῦσιν [fol. 43v] οὐκ ἐπιτρέπειν. οὔκουν

31: 3–4 Aeschylus, *Prometheus Vinctus*, 105 || 13 cf. Isaiam 14:14 || 14–15 Isaias, 14:13–15 || 26–27 Rom. 15:6; Act. Apost. 4:32; Joannis Chrysostomi *Liturgia* (ed. Brightman), 390, 1–2 || 28–33 Greg. Naz., *Or.* 22, 12 (PG, 35, 1144C)

---

10 ἱταμὸς M

31

and piety in his soul. Indeed, the wicked progenitor of wicked offspring hoped in vain to establish as pious the present impious beliefs. For when you overturn the wicked edifice, the man who strives to set it up will undoubtedly become weary and desist from rebellion, for he will perceive, even though he is extremely bold and shameless, that nothing is working to his advantage, but that things are in fact working out quite the opposite way.

For, being so inspired by God and so experienced in the art of writing, you are alone fully able to put to shame and bring down the man who raises himself "above the clouds" and says those ungodly and arrogant words: "I will set my throne upon the clouds and will be like the most High!" On the other hand, in addition to this, something more will be contributed thereby to the downfall of impiety, for if you are the leader, your zeal will exhort many men to ⟨join⟩ the same struggle for piety: those who lead a virtuous life will be induced by your virtues; those who cultivate letters, because of the mastery of this art which you obviously possess; and those who have a claim to both, for both of these reasons, since you possess them in abundance.

Then, I believe that as things progress in this way, as the common faith and the one God in the holy and ineffable Trinity find again agreement from everyone, the sickness of polytheism which has recently arisen will disappear, and the Christian Church will be free of every presumptuous idea contrary to piety, and thus, as the saying goes, we will "with one mouth and one heart praise" continuously the one God and power in the Holy Trinity, "without honoring anything more or less (for the former would be impossible and the latter impious), and without cutting up the single Sublimity with novel terms—for nothing is greater or smaller than itself—but shunning the superfluous and useless and strange offshoots of the present inquiries." For Gregory the true theologian taught us this rule of piety, and we must say what the theologians said about God, not our own words. We must neither violate their word nor establish other rules of piety unknown to ourselves or to our fathers, nor must we put up with those who disturb the boundaries set by our fa-

οὐδ' ἐπιτρέπομεν. μάρτυς ἀσφαλὴς ἡ γλῶττα τοῦ καθ' ἡμᾶς θείου ῥήτορος, ἧς τῶν κατὰ τῆς καινοφωνίας λόγων δίκαιοι καὶ ἡμεῖς ἀπολαῦσαι· τοιγαροῦν πέμψας ἡμῖν τοὺς λόγους, τὰ δίκαια ποιήσεις.

32. Τῷ Γαβρᾷ

Δεξάμενος τὴν ἐπιστολὴν ἀμφοῖν ὁμοῦ τῶν ἐναντίων, ἡδονῆς καὶ λύπης ἀπέλαυσα· τῆς μὲν ὅτι τοιοῦτον ἄνδρα ἐτόλμησεν ὑβρίσαι καθάρματα ταῦτα μόνον εἰδότα εἴς τε θεὸν ἀσεβεῖν εἴς τ' ἀνθρώπους ὑβρίζειν οἷς εὐσεβείας μέλει καὶ τοῦ μὴ σφίσι συμφέρεσθαι, τὴν δ' εὐφροσύνην ἐποίησε τὸ τοιοῦτον ἄνδρα τῆς παρ' ἐκείνων ἀπανθρωπίας γενέσθαι μοι μάρτυρα, ἣν ἤδη δυοῖν ἐτῶν οἱ μὲν ἐπαντλοῦσί μοι, ἐγὼ δὲ ὑφίσταμαι. μᾶλλον δὲ οὐχὶ ταύτην, ἀλλ' ἔστιν αὕτη σκιά τις τῶν ἐπ' ἐμὲ φερομένων καὶ εἴδωλον, ὅπερ ἂν μοι συμφήσαις ὡδὶ λογισάμενος· εἰ γὰρ ἀνδρὸς οὐδενὸς λειπομένου μήτε δυνάμει λόγου, μήτε γένους φιλοτιμίᾳ, μητ' ἀρετῆς εὐσθενείᾳ, μητ' εὐπορίᾳ δόξης, γήρᾳ τε λαμπρῷ πρὸς τούτοις κεκοσμημένου καὶ πανταχόθεν αἰδουμένου, οὕτω προπετῶς ἐτόλμησαν ἅψασθαι, τίνα δοκεῖς παρ' αὐτῶν ἐπὶ τὸν πάντων ἐνδεᾶ τῶν εἰρημένων ἐμὲ παρὰ τοσοῦτον χρόνον ἐνεχθῆναι τὰ βέλη;

Τὸ τοίνυν ἐμοὶ ταῦτά σε συνειδέναι καὶ κοινωνῆσαι τούτων οὐ μέτριον εἰς εὐφροσύνην· τὸ γὰρ κακῶς πάσχειν, σχέτλιον ὄν, κουφότερον τῷ πάσχοντι γίνεται ὅταν οἱ κοινωνοῦντες ὦσι, καὶ τότε μᾶλλον κουφότερον ὅταν βελτίους οἱ κοινωνοῦντες ὦσι. ποιεῖ δὲ ἄρα κἀκεῖνο μόνον δριμύτερα τἀδικήματα, ὅταν κακῶς τις παρὰ δίκην ἢ ἀκούων ἢ πάσχων οὐκ ἔχῃ τὸν συνειδότα ὡς παρὰ δίκην πάσχοι, καὶ διὰ τοῦτο δοκεῖ μὴ παρὰ δίκην πάσχειν, αὐτὸς ὑπὸ τῶν ἀδικούντων ἀδικεῖν φημιζόμενος. ὅπερ ἐμοὶ πολύ τι πάσχειν συνέβαινε, νυνὶ δὲ ἀνδρὸς τοσούτου ἐπιστολαῖς καὶ λόγοις, ὧν οὐδὲν ἀκοῦσαι τοῖς εὐσεβείᾳ φίλοις καὶ γλώττῃ ῥήτορος ἀγαθῇ καὶ ἀρετῇ χαριέστερον, διὰ πάσης τῆς πόλεως, ἤδη δὲ καὶ τῶν πόλεων, ἡμᾶς εὐσεβοῦντας κηρύττοντος καὶ διὰ τοῦτο κακῶς καὶ πάσχοντας καὶ ἀκούοντας ὑπὸ τῶν δυσσεβούντων, ὅτι μὴ συνδυσσεβεῖν αὐτοῖς ὑπακούομεν, ἐκείνους δὲ ἀδικοῦντας ὅτι ταῦτα ποιοῦντες ἐπίπαν ἀναισχυντοῦσι— τούτων οὕτως ἐχόντων, πῶς οὐκ ἐν ἑορτῇ θαυμαστῇ τὰ ἡμέτερα ὑπὸ χορηγῷ τῷ θαυμασίῳ Γαβρᾷ; καὶ οὐχ ἡ πᾶσα σὴ καὶ τῆς σῆς νίκη

32: M 43v–44v. Mn 13r–14r. Ed. Karpozilos, *Letters*, 114–115, no. 17. 1 titulus deest in Mn ‖ 5 *μέλλει* M ‖ 11–12 *εὐσθενία* Mn ‖ 13 *αἰδούμενος* M: *αἰδέσιμον* Mn ‖ 16 *σοι* M ‖ 21 *ἔχει* codd. ‖ 23 post *συνέβαινε* scr. *πρότερον* Mn ‖ 31 *Γαυρᾷ* Mn

thers. That is why we do not put up with them either! As an infallible witness, ⟨take⟩ the tongue of our divine orator, whose discourses against the "newfangled talk" I, too, have a right to enjoy. Therefore, you will be doing what is right, if you send me the discourses.

32. To Gabras

When I received your letter, I experienced at once two contrasting ⟨sensations⟩: pleasure and sorrow. Sorrow, because outcasts who know only this: how to sin against God and insult men who care for piety and who will not associate with them, dared to insult such a great man; pleasure, on the other hand, arose from the fact that such a man became a witness of their inhumanity to me, which for two years already they have been pouring upon me like a flood, while I stood my ground. Or rather, this is not quite the case; this is, in fact, just a shadow and a mere ghost of what is being brought against me. On this you will certainly agree with me, if you reason like this: if indeed they so rashly dared touch a man who does not lag behind anyone either in eloquence or distinction of birth or strength of virtue or abundance of fame, who is, moreover, adorned with splendid old age and respected everywhere, what darts do you think they have hurled, over such a long period, at me, deprived as I am of all the above-mentioned ⟨advantages⟩?

The fact that you can testify to these for me and share them with me is a great cause for joy. For, though suffering is hard, it becomes lighter for the sufferer when there are people with whom he can share it, and even more so when those who share it are his betters. Indeed, what makes the injustice even harsher is this fact alone, that a man does not have anyone to testify that he is suffering unjustly, when he is unjustly accused or treated, and for this reason he does not appear to suffer unjustly, since he is publicly called a wrong-doer by the wrong-doers. This, as it happens, is exactly what I suffered before now to a considerable degree; now, however, when such an important man proclaims through the whole city, indeed already throughout various cities, by letters and discourses which are more pleasing than anything else to the lovers of piety and to the capable tongue of an orator and to virtue, that I am pious, and that for this reason I am ill-treated and accused by the impious men, because I refuse to obey them and join in their impiety; and that they are in the wrong in that, besides doing these things, they behave shamelessly—this being the case, how can I refrain from extraordinary celebration, under the direction of the extraordinary Gabras? Does not the entire victory belong to you and your Muse

32

μούσης, ἢ τοὺς ἔτι μὲν ἀπατωμένους καὶ τῇ πλάνῃ προσέχοντας, τἀληθὲς ἐπιδείξασα, τῆς ἀπάτης ἀπέσπασε, τοὺς δὲ τὴν πλάνην ταύτην [fol. 44[r]] *φωράσαντας μέν, ἀμύνασθαι δὲ ῥαθυμότερον ἔχοντας, ἐπὶ τὴν μάχην ἐξώρμησε καθάπερ* Ἀλέξανδρον τὸν Μακεδόνα Τιμόθεος *τὸ μάχιμον ἀναβαλόμενος; εἰ δέ τι καὶ τὸ ἡμέτερον ἦν, σὺ καὶ τοῦτο κλονούμενον ἔστησας, καὶ* λόγον *σπινθῆρος ἔχον, πυρσὸν ἀέριον ἔδειξας. τοιγαροῦν εἰκότως εἰς τοσοῦτον ἦλθες εὐδοκιμήσεως, ὥστ' αὐτὸν τὸν θειότατον τῆς οἰκουμενικῆς ἐκκλησίας τοῦ* Χριστοῦ *κυβερνήτην καὶ τῆς εὐσεβείας διδάσκαλον τοῖς σοι κατὰ τῆς* Παλαμναίας *ταυτησὶ* δυσσεβείας *γεγονόσι φιλοτιμεῖσθαι* λόγοις *καὶ ἐπιδείκνυσθαι. ἡ* δὲ *θειοτάτη βασιλὶς ἡμῶν καὶ βασιλέως καθαρωτάτη μήτηρ, τοσοῦτον ἐνδεικνυμένη κράτος κατὰ τῆς* δυσσεβείας *ταύτης, ὁπόσον ὑπερανέχει πάντων καὶ τἀξιώματι, πῶς δοκεῖς ἥσθη τοῖς ταύτην σοῖς ἀνατρέπουσι* λόγοις. *τί* δ' *ἂν εἴποι τις περὶ τοῦ τῶν ἄλλων κύκλου θείων τε ἀρχιερέων, θεοφιλῶν τε ἀρχόντων, καὶ πάντων ἁπλῶς ὅσοι τε κοινῶς καὶ ὅσοι μοναδικῶς βιοῦσιν, οἷς εὐθὺς καὶ τοὔνομα φρικτὸν τὸ πολύθεον, ἅτε μίαν ἐν τῇ παντουργῷ* Τριάδι *θεότητά τε καὶ* δύναμιν *δοξάζειν πεπαιδευμένοις καὶ τῷ μαθήματι τούτῳ ἐκ παίδων ἐντεθραμμένοις;*

Τὰ *μὲν οὖν τοῦ χάριν τῆς εὐσεβείας εἰργασμένου σοι* λόγου *τοιαῦτα καὶ οὕτω* λαμπρὰ *καὶ τῇδε, παρὰ* Θεῷ *δὲ οἷα* *ὅ σ τ ι ς ὁ μ ο λ ο γ ή σ ε ι ἐ ν ἐ μ ο ί, φησιν, ἔ μ π ρ ο σ θ ε ν τ ῶ ν ἀ ν θ ρ ώ π ω ν, ὁ μ ο λ ο γ ή σ ω κ ἀ γ ὼ ἐ ν α ὐ τ ῷ ἔ μ π ρ ο σ θ ε ν τ ο ῦ π α τ ρ ό ς μ ο υ τ ο ῦ ἐ ν τ ο ῖ ς ο ὐ ρ α ν ο ῖ ς· αἱ* δὲ τῶν δυσσεβῶν *τούτων κατὰ τῶν εὐσεβούντων ὕβρεις πρὸς τῷ μὴ* δύνασθαι *βλάπτειν οὓς κακῶς ἀγορεύουσι, καὶ ὠφελοῦσι τὰ μέγιστα· ἥ τε γὰρ* δόξα *μείζων παρὰ τῷ ἀθλοθέτῃ* Θεῷ *τοῖς καὶ* βλασφημουμένοις *ὑπὲρ τῆς εὐσεβείας ὑπὸ τῶν* δυσσεβούντων, *τοῖς τε ἀπατωμένοις διὰ τῶν ἐν τοῖς* λόγοις *πιθανοτήτων αὐτῶν ἐντεῦθεν* δυσσεβεῖς *ὄντες, ὅπερ εἰσί, καταφωρῶνται. ἰδίωμα γὰρ παλαιόν τε καὶ γνώριμον τῶν μὲν οὐκ εὐσεβούντων τὸ καὶ κακῶς* λέγειν *τε καὶ* δρᾶν *ὅπῃ* δύνωνται *τοὺς ἀπειθοῦντας αὐτοῖς, τῶν* δὲ *τῆς εὐσεβείας τὸ πάσχειν τε καὶ ἀκούειν παρὰ τῶν ἀντιδόξων ἃ παρὰ τῶν ἀσεβῶν τοὺς εὐσεβοῦντας εἰκός,*

32: 41–42 *φιλοτιμεῖσθαι καὶ ἐπιδείκνυσθαι*: cf. Platonem, *Phaedrus*, 232a || 52–55 cf. Matt. 10:32; Luc. 12:8

---

36 post Τιμόθεος scr. *ὁ αὐλητὴς* Mn || *ἀναβαλλόμενος* Mn || 38–39 *εὐδοκημήσεως* Mn || 39 *ὥστ'*] *ὡς* Mn || 42 *θειοτάτη* om. Mn || 43 *καθαρωτάτη* om. Mn || 53 *φησιν* post *ἀνθρώπων* scr. Mn || 60 *πιθανοτάτων* Mn || 62 *ούκ εὐσεβούτων*] *κακοδοξούντων* Mn || 62 *δύνονται* M || 63–64 *τῶν δὲ . . . εἰκὸς*] *τῶν δ' εὐσεβείᾳ κεκοσμημένων τὸ πάσχειν μὲν καὶ ἀκούειν τὰ παρὰ τῶν ἀντιδόξων* Mn

32

which, after showing the truth to those who were still deceived and clinging on to error, tore them away from deceit, then urged on to battle those who had detected that error but were rather slow to resist, just as the ⟨flute player⟩ Timotheos did Alexander of Macedon, striking up martial music? If, then, my ⟨stand⟩ was of any importance, it was in fact you who made it firm when it was tottering, and, where it was like a spark, you turned it into a lofty beacon. And so it was with good reason that you acquired so much respect that the most divine leader of the Ecumenical Church of Christ and teacher of piety takes pride in the discourses that you wrote against this Palamnaian impiety and puts them on display. Then again our most divine Empress, the most virtuous mother of the Emperor, whose vigor against this impiety equals her exalted dignity of office, was certainly delighted at the arguments of your refutation. Then what can one say about other circles, the holy bishops and the God-loving dignitaries, and simply all laymen and monks, to whom even that polytheistic name is awful, in that they have been taught to honor one divinity and power in the all-creating Trinity and have been brought up on that lesson since childhood?

The accomplishments, then, of the discourse that you composed in defense of piety are so great and so illustrious here too as well as before God; just as He says: "Whoever will acknowledge me before men, I will acknowledge him before my Father in heaven." As for the insults of these profane men against the pious, while being unable to hurt those whom they slander, in fact they are the greatest help. For not only is there greater glory before God the Arbiter for those who are cursed even for the sake of piety by profane men, but also the latter are shown to be exactly what they are, profane, to those who are deceived by the persuasiveness of their arguments. For it is an old and well-known trait of the impious both to insult and abuse in every possible way those who do not listen to them; and of the pious to suffer and hear from their opponents what the pious expect to suffer and hear from the profane,

καὶ πάντα φέρειν ἐθέλειν ὥστε μὴ κοινωνῆσαι τῆς δυσσεβείας αὐτοῖς, αὐτοὺς δὲ μηδὲν μήτε κακουργεῖν, μήτε κακηγορεῖν ἑτέρως πλὴν τοῦ τὴν δυσσέβειαν τὴν αὐτῶν ὅση δύναμις ἐξελέγχειν σπουδάζειν, κατὰ τὸ μὴ συγκοινωνεῖν τοῖς ἔργοις τοῦ σκότοθς τοῦ αἰῶνος τούτου, μᾶλλον δὲ καὶ ἐλέγχειν καὶ τὰς βεβήλους καινοφωνίας περιίστασθαι κελεῦον στόμα Χριστοῦ, τὸν Παῦλον, καὶ [fol. 44^{v}] τὴν αἰτίαν ἐπάγον τοῦ περιίστασθαι, ἐπὶ πλέον γὰρ προκόψουσιν ἀσεβείας καὶ ὁ λόγος αὐτῶν ὡς γάγγραινα νομὴν ἕξει.

Εὐσεβῶς τοίνυν δράσας καὶ κακῶς διὰ τοῦτο ἀκούσας παρὰ τῶν οὐκ εὐσεβῶς φρονούντων, εὖ καὶ καλῶς ἀκούσεις πρὸς τοῦ εὐσεβουμένου καὶ ὑπὲρ οὗ πεπαρρησιασμένος λοιδορίας ἀπέλαυσας. οἶσθα δ' ὅπερ ἀκούσεις μετὰ τῶν ἀκουσάντων χαίρετε καὶ ἀγαλλιᾶσθε ὅτι ὁ μισθὸς ὑμῶν πολὺς ἐν τοῖς οὐρανοῖς.

33. Sine titulo

Τί τις ἂν πάθοι; μὴ δεχόμενοι γράμματα τῆς σῆς ἱερότητος, ἀνιώμεθα δι' αὐτὸ δὴ τοῦθ' ὅτι τούτων στερούμεθα, πράγματος ἀντὶ πάντων καθεστηκότος ἡμῖν οἷς χαίρουσιν ἄνθρωποι, καὶ δεχόμενοι οὐδὲν ἧττον λυπούμεθα ὅτι μὴ καθάπερ ῥεῦμα ἡμῖν συνεχὲς ἐπιρρέοι ἄληκτα, τῶν σῶν τῶνδε ναμάτων καὶ κομιδῇ διψῶσι, καὶ τοσοῦτο μᾶλλον ὅσον καὶ ῥᾷστα ταῦτα προχεῖς ἐθέλων καὶ ποτιμώτατα, τοῦ Ὀλυμπίου μὲν οὖν οὐ δεύτερα νέκταρος εἰς εὐφροσύνης λόγον. καίτοι—πῶς οἴει;—πρῴην ὅθ' ἡμῖν ἧκε ὁ Καλλιόπης πέπλος, τὴν θαυμασίαν ἐπιστολήν σου λέγω, ἡδεῖς ἀμφοῖν ἕνεκεν ὤφθημεν, ὧν τ' ἐλάβομεν ἤδη καὶ ὧν ἠλπίκαμεν λήψεσθαι· νυνὶ δὲ κατὰ μικρὸν εἰς ἀμαυρόν τι καὶ ἀδρανὲς κατέστη τὸ πάνυ φαιδρὸν ἐκεῖνο καὶ χαρίεν, ὥσπερ ἐν μουσικῇ τις φθόγγος ἅπαξ κρουσθείσης, εἶτ' ἀφεθείσης χορδῆς. ἐνδοῦναι δή σε δεῖ πάλιν ἡμῖν τῶν παρὰ σοὶ χαρίτων, μουσόληπτε, εἴ γε μὴ τῶν ἡμῖν φθονούντων βούλει ταυτησὶ τῆς ἡδονῆς ὑπάρχειν, μηδὲ λυπεῖν ἐθέλεις ἡμᾶς λύπην ἑτέρως ἀπαραμύθητον, εἰ μὴ διὰ τοῦ γράφειν.

68–70 Eph. 5:11–12 || 70–73 II Tim. 2:16–17 || 70–71 *στόμα . . . Παῦλον* cf. *Menaion Junii* (ed. Saliveros), 153 || 75 Matt. 25:21, 23 || 77–79 Matt. 5:12

---

77 *δ'* om Mn || 78 *τοῖς*]*τοι* M

33: Mn 8^{v}–9^{r}. Ed. Karpozilos, *Letters*, 97–98, no. 11.

8 *Καλλιώπης* Mn || 12 *χάριεν* Mn

while bearing everything willingly in order not to share their profanity, neither doing nor saying anything evil, apart from seeking to refute the profanity of these people as far as they can, in accordance with Paul, the mouthpiece of Christ, who enjoins ⟨us⟩ "to take no part in the deeds of darkness" of this age, "but to show them up for what they are" and "to avoid the profane newfangled talk," adding the reason for avoiding it: "for those ⟨who indulge in it⟩ will stray further and further into godless courses, and the infection of their teaching will spread like gangrene."

Therefore, since you have acted piously, and for this reason you have been insulted by men who do not think piously, you will hear "Well done!" and "Well said!" from the One Whom you honor and for Whose bold defense you suffered abuses. And you know precisely what you will hear, together with those who heard "Rejoice and be exceedingly glad, for great is your reward in heaven!"

33. No Addressee

What could happen to a man! When I do not receive letters from your Holiness, I am distressed by the very fact that I am deprived of them, of the thing, that is, which for me has taken the place of everything which makes men rejoice. And when I do receive them, I grieve no less because they do not keep on flowing incessantly as a continuous stream towards me, as I simply thirst indeed for these spring waters of yours; in fact, all the more so since, when you wish, you pour them forth, most easy and pleasant to drink, nay, rather, as far as pleasure is concerned, they are not second to the Olympian nectar. And so, when the robe of Calliope—I mean your admirable letter—reached me recently, you cannot imagine how happy I was observed to be for what I had already received as well as for what I hoped to receive in the future. But now, little by little, that very joyous and beautiful feeling became something dim and feeble, just like the sound of the chord of a musical instrument that has been struck and then let go. You must, then, grant me again some of your favors, O you who are inspired by the Muses, if, that is, you do not wish to be one of those who begrudge me this particular pleasure, or to cause me a grief that cannot be consoled in any other way except by your writing.

33

Κορυφαῖος δὲ ἡμῖν καὶ ὢν καὶ δοκῶν τὴν μουσικὴν τῶν λόγων, οὐδὲν ἧττον κορυφαῖος ἡμῖν καὶ εἶ καὶ δοκεῖς τὰ θεῖα καὶ τὴν εὐσέβειαν· ἧς νῦν πλημμεληθείσης ἀνοήτοις ἀνδράσι καὶ ἀπονοηθεῖσι, καὶ τοὺς μὲν ἡμῖν πάλαι κειμένους ὅρους καὶ νόμους περὶ αὐτῆς καταλῦσαι σπουδάσασιν, ἀντεισαγαγεῖν δὲ τούτων καινά τινα καὶ νόθα καὶ ἀφροσύνης πλέα καὶ πλάνης καὶ ἀπονοίας, τῶν μὲν οὐκ ἀνήκοός ἐστιν ἡ σὴ σοφία καὶ ἱερὰ τελειότης, οὐδὲ ἡμεῖς γε τῆς σῆς πρὸς μὲν ἐκείνους καὶ τὰς αὐτῶν βεβήλους καινοφωνίας θαυμαστῆς ἀηδίας, τοῖς δὲ πατρῴοις ἡμῖν περὶ τῆς εὐσεβείας νόμοις λαμπρᾶς συνηγορίας. ὧν δὲ ἡμῖν ὑπὲρ τῆς κοινῆς εὐσεβείας δεῖν ἔδοξε συνεισενεγκεῖν τῇ θείᾳ τοῦ Χριστοῦ ἐκκλησίᾳ, τοῦ θειοτάτου καὶ οἰκουμενικοῦ πατριάρχου κελεύσαντος καὶ τοῦ λοιποῦ τῶν θείων ἀρχιερέων κόσμου—καὶ δοκοῦμεν αὐτῇ ταῦτα προσενεγκεῖν οἰκείως καὶ ὁμοφρόνως—καὶ τούτων σοι τῇ θειότητι μικρ' ἄττα πεπόμφαμεν, ἅτε ἡμῖν οὔσῃ διδασκάλῳ καὶ τούτων. γέγραπται δὲ καὶ κοινότατα, ἵνα μηδεὶς ἀποροίη περί τε τῆς ἡμετέρας δόξης καὶ τῆς τῶν ἐναντίων, οἳ μὴ μόνον ἔγνωσαν πολεμεῖν τοῖς εὐσεβείας ὅροις, ἀλλὰ καὶ ἡμᾶς τοὺς ἀπειθοῦντας σφίσι, κατὰ τὰς θείας παραγγελίας ἡμῖν, διαβάλλειν καὶ συκοφαντεῖν ἀθεώτατα, εἰ καὶ τούτων οὐδὲν ἀδρανέστερον τῶν συκοφαντημάτων, ψεύδους γὰρ οὐδὲν ἀδρανέστερον †ὅ τι μηδὲ τοῦ μὴ ὄντος,† τὸ γὰρ ψεῦδος μόνον τοῦ ὄντος ἐστέρηται.

Καίτοι ταῦτα μὲν ἐγώ σοι πλείονος ἕνεκα τῆς ἀσφαλείας πέμπω, σὲ δὲ ἡμῖν καὶ τὰ πρὸς ἡμᾶς γράμματά σου καὶ πᾶς ὁ παρ' ὑμῶν ἐκεῖθεν ἐρχόμενος καὶ πρὸς τούτων τὸ συνειδὸς τῆς διὰ πάντων σου σοφίας καὶ τελειότητος μηνύουσιν ἐπιεικῶς ἐπαινεῖν τὰ ἡμέτερα· τὴν μὲν γὰρ εὐσέβειαν ἀναπνεῖς ὡς ἀέρα καὶ τὰς βε-[fol. 9r]βήλους καινοφωνίας θαυμαστῶς περιίστασαι, κατὰ τὸν θεῖον Παῦλον, καὶ οὐδὲν οὐ μήποτε παρηλλαγμένον καὶ ἄνισον καὶ ἀνόμοιον τῶν οὐσιωδῶς ἐν τῷ Θεῷ φῂς εἶναι τῇ μακαρίᾳ Τριάδι, οὐδὲ τοὺς εἰς δῆμον θεοτήτων τοιούτων ὑπερκειμένων καὶ ὑφειμένων καὶ πάντα διαφόρων ἀλλήλων κατατέμνοντας τὴν ὑπερηνωμένην ἑνάδα βλασφήμως καὶ ἀθέως ἀνάσχῃ. ἄλλο δὲ οὐδὲν ἢ τουτὶ τὸ ἡμέτερον, ἐπὶ γὰρ τούτοις ἡμεῖς ἐσπουδάκαμεν, τὰς Παλαμναίας ταύτας καινοφωνίας ἀποτρεπόμενοι.

33: 24 et 43–44 II Tim. 2:16 || 47–48 cf. Palamam, *Epist. III ad Acindynum*, 15, Syngrammata, I, 306, 18–20; ed. Nadal, 252, 10–12 || 49 Dion. Areop., *De divin. nomin.*, 2, 1, (PG, 3, 637A)

---

37 ἀδρενέστερον Mn || ὅ τι μηδὲ τοῦ μὴ ὄντος: non satis perspicio

33

But, though you both are and are considered to be our leader in the art of rhetoric, you are and are considered to be no less our leader in matters concerning piety and the Divinity. That piety was of late insulted by foolish men who have lost their senses and have sought to destroy our long established rules and laws about piety, and to introduce instead some new and spurious doctrines filled with folly and deceit and madness; this your Wisdom and holy Perfection has heard, just as I have heard about your admirable disgust with them and their "profane newfangled talk" and your brilliant defense of our ancestral laws of piety. But I have sent to your Grace (because in these matters, too, you are my teacher) a little of what I thought fit to contribute to the Church of Christ in defense of the common faith, at the behest of the most divine and Ecumenical Patriarch and the rest of the holy bishops, and I seem to have made my contribution to the Church properly and in accordance with its views. It is written in very ordinary language, so that no one may have any doubts about my views or about those of my opponents, who are not only determined to wage war against the laws of piety, but also to discredit me in a most ungodly manner and to calumniate me, because I disobey them in accordance with the divine injunctions to us; though there is nothing more impotent than falsehood, except the non-existent (?), for falsehood alone is deprived of existence.

And yet, I am sending you these as an added precaution, while your letter to me and everyone who comes from you and, besides this, the knowledge of your wisdom and perfection in general indicate that you approve of my views. For you breathe piety like air and admirably "avoid the profane newfangled talk," in accordance with the divine Paul, and you never say that any of the essential properties of God is different and unequal and dissimilar to the blessed Trinity, and neither do you tolerate those who in a blasphemous and ungodly manner cut up "the supremely united Monad" into a multitude of such "higher and lower" and altogether different divinities. These, and no others, are my beliefs, and on their basis I have sought to refute this Palamnaian "newfangled talk."

34. Τῷ Λαγαρᾷ Σάββᾳ

Πολλῶν λεγόντων ὡς ἄρα, εἰ νῦν ἀληθὴς ἐπιστήμη καὶ σοφία παρ' ἡμῖν διῃτᾶτο μετὰ τῆς κατ' ἦθος ἀρετῆς καὶ φροντίδος τῶν θείων, οὐκ ἂν αἱ βέβηλοι καινοφωνίαι χώραν παρ' ἡμῖν καὶ παρρησίαν εἶχον, ἐγώ, "τὸν δεῖνα δέ," (τὴν σὴν λέγων σοφίαν καὶ μεγαλόνοιαν) "τίνα δοκεῖτε εἶναι; τῷ τῶν πώποτε καὶ σοφῶν καὶ σπουδαίων καὶ μεγαλοφυῶν ἀνδρῶν ἢ τῆς ἕνεκα σοφίας ἢ τῆς κατ' ἦθος ἀρετῆς οἴεσθε δικαίως ἂν ἐκστῆναι φιλοτιμίας, εἴ γε τοῦτο ἐβούλετο, ὥστε πᾶν μᾶλλον ἂν ἢ καινοφωνία περὶ τὴν ἡμετέραν εὐσέβειαν προὔκοψε, μὴ ὅ τι γε ἡ τοσαύτη καὶ φανερῶς Ἑλληνὶς καὶ πολύθεος καὶ ἔτι τῆς Ἀρείου καὶ Εὐνομίου μοίρας καὶ τῆς Μασσαλιανῶν οὐκ ἀπολειπομένη, ἀλλ' οὐδὲ ἡ τυχοῦσα καὶ τοὐλάχιστον παρακινοῦσα τῶν ὡμολογημένων καὶ εἰλικρινῶν τῆς εὐσεβείας ὅρων; μεγάλην γάρ τοι φύσιν, φιλοσοφίας ἅμα καὶ ἀρετῆς εὐπορήσασαν, ὥσπερ ὀμμάτων καθαρῶν καὶ ὀξυδερκεστάτων, οὐδὲν ἂν λάθοι κακόηθες καὶ τῶν λίαν ἀμυδρῶν εἰς δυσσέβειαν ἐφέρπον τῇ ἐκκλησίᾳ."

Καὶ μὴν εἰωθός ἐστι τοῖς καινοῖς θεολόγοις τοὺς μὲν ἀρετῇ μόνῃ καὶ ἀγαθῇ πολιτείᾳ κομῶντας, μὴ προσιεμένους δὲ τὰ τούτων καινοφωνήματα, παραγράφεσθαι ὅτι μὴ καὶ λόγων εἰσὶ καὶ παιδεύσεως ἔμπειροι· τοὺς δὲ περὶ ταῦτα εὐδοκιμοῦντας ἐν ἀρετῆς μετριότητι, ὅτι μὴ καὶ ταύτης τὰ πρῶτα φέρουσιν, οὐκ ἄγουσιν ἐν λόγῳ· τῶν δὲ περὶ λόγους πάλιν οἳ γραμματικῆς μὲν μόνης εὖ καὶ ἀκριβῶς εἰσιν ἔχοντες, ὅτι μὴ καὶ τῆς φιλοσοφίας· τοὺς δὲ φιλοσοφίας, ὅτι μηδὲ κἀκείνης. καὶ οὕτω διὰ πάντων πάντας ἀτιμάζουσί τε καὶ παραγράφονται, οὕτως οἰόμενοι τοὺς τῆς καινοτομίας ἐλέγχους διαδιδράσκειν, καίτοι γε αὐτοὶ μήτε τῶν ἐπὶ γραμματικῇ, μήτε τῶν ἐπὶ φιλοσοφίᾳ εὐδοκιμούντων ὄντες, εἰ δὲ μηδὲ τῶν ἐπ' ἀρετῇ καθαρᾷ καὶ ἀδόλῳ, ἄλλοι λεγέτωσαν.

Οὐκοῦν εἰ [fol. 46r] τῆς σῆς διὰ πάντων τελειότητος εἰς πεῖραν ἧκον, ἀντιπιπτούσης αὐτῶν ταῖς δυσσεβέσι τόλμαις, αὐτίκ' ἄν, οἶμαι, μᾶλλον δὲ οἶδα σαφῶς, ὥσπερ πυρὸς πειραθεῖσαι ἀκρίδες, ἀπήλλαξαν. ὥστε εἰ ἕνα ἄνδρα τοιοῦτον ἑκάστοτε, Δημοσθένης ἂν εἶπεν, εἶχεν ἡ πόλις αὕτη, καὶ ἕνα Θεσσαλονίκη

34: 4 II Tim. 2:16 || 9–10 II Tim. 2:16 || 18 Greg. Naz., *Or.*29, 10 (PG, 36, 88A) || 33–34 Demosthenes, *De corona*, 304

34: M 45v–46r.
14–15 *ἀρετὴν* M || 32 *πειραθέντας* M

34

34. To Sabbas Logaras

When many people say that perhaps if true learning and wisdom existed among us, together with moral virtue and concern for divine matters, the "profane newfangled talk would not have found room and free expression here, I answer: "Who do you think So-and-so is?" (meaning your Wisdom and Magnanimity). "To which of the wise and important and talented men who ever lived do you think that he should justly cede the distinction for wisdom and moral virtue—that is, if he wished this—so that anything but a 'newfangled talk' about our faith would have spread, not indeed ⟨a talk⟩ as great as this one, obviously pagan and polytheistic and not at all different from the heresy of Arios and Eunomios and the Messalians, but not even an insignificant one that does not in the least disturb the accepted and true rules of piety? For a man of superior character who abounds in love of both wisdom and virtue, just as if he had an abundance of most clear and sharp-sighted eyes, does not miss any wickedness that creeps upon the Church, even if it be very hard to distinguish with regard to impiety."

Indeed, these "new theologians" are wont to reject those who pride themselves on virtue alone and good conduct, while not accepting their "newfangled talk"; this on the pretext that they are not trained in learning and education as well. On the other hand, they do not think highly of those who excel in these pursuits while possessing a modest measure of virtue, on the ground that they do not hold the first prize in this, too. Again, when it comes to men of letters, they do not think highly of those who have a good and precise knowledge of grammar alone, on the ground that they do not also know philosophy, and of those who know philosophy, on the ground that they do not also know grammar. And thus they dishonor and reject all men by all standards, thinking that in this manner their own strange doctrines will escape detection. And yet they are not really famous for either grammar or philosophy; as for pure and unadulterated virtue, it is up to others to say.

And so, if you, accomplished as you are in everything, gave them a taste of your opposition to their daring acts of impiety, I believe, or rather I know clearly, that they would give up immediately, just like locusts which have come in contact with fire. And so, as Demosthenes would have said, "if this city had one such man" at any given time and Thessalonica another and any other big city anywhere another,

καὶ ἄλλη δή τις ἄλλον τῶν ἀρχουσῶν ὁπουδήποτε, οὔτ' ἂν ὅλως ἀνέφυ, οὔτε εἰ καὶ ἀνέφυ δυσσέβεια, οὑτωσὶ προεχώρησεν ὥσπερ ἡ νῦν, φῦσα μὲν ἐν τῇ Θεσσαλονίκῃ, αὐξηθεῖσα δὲ ἐνταῦθα καὶ παρρησιασαμένη κἂν τοῦ πλείστου τῆς ἐκκλησίας ἐγκρατὴς γενομένη, εἰ μὴ διὰ τῆς σῆς ἀπὸ τῆς ἡσυχίας, ὥσπερ τινὸς ἐπιβλέψεως, τῆς φορᾶς ἀνεκόπη. οὐ γὰρ ἄνευ τῆς σῆς διεγέρσεως, μήτε τὴν τῆς δεσποίνης, μήτε τὴν τοῦ θειοτάτου δεσπότου μου τοῦ οἰκουμενικοῦ πατριάρχου, μήτε τὴν τοῦ γενναιοτάτου πρωτοσεβαστοῦ, μήτε πρὸς τούτων τὴν τοῦ πάντα ἀρίστου μεγαλοδουκὸς κίνησιν γενέσθαι κατὰ τῆς παρούσης ἀναισχυντίας περὶ τὸ θεῖον οἶμαι.

Ταῦτα ἐμοῦ λέγοντος πρὸς τοὺς περιουσίαν ἀρετῆς καὶ σοφίας * * *, ἅπαντες ἐπευφημοῦσιν ὡς ἀληθεύοντι καὶ παρ' ἑαυτῶν προσπορίζουσι τὸ "εἴπερ ἤθελεν ἔτι" καὶ "εἰ προεθυμήθη" καὶ τὰ τοιαῦτα· οἱ δὲ καὶ "εἰ ἐκκλησιαστικῆς παρακλήσεως ἔτυχεν" ἐπιτιθέασιν. ἐγὼ δὲ ὡς μὲν ἀληθῆ ταῦτα καὶ τῇ σῇ προσήκοντα ἐπιστήμῃ καὶ ἀρετῇ πάντων μάλιστα οἶδα, ὡς δ' ἂν τῇ δυνάμει χρήσαιο κατὰ τῆς πλάνης ταύτης καὶ λύμης τῆς ἀληθείας, οὐκ οἶδ' ὅτου ποτ' ἂν ἔργον γένοιτο πλὴν τῆς θείας κινήσεως.

35. Τῷ Λογαρᾷ κῦρ Σάββᾳ

Ὅπερ ἡ σὴ τεθεώρηκεν ἐνταῦθα τῶν Παλαμναίων λόγων ἀκρίβεια, [fol. 49ᵛ] παρὰ φρονίμοις κριταῖς ἀκριβῶς τεθεώρηκε καὶ οὐκ ἂν ἄλλως ἔχοι. οὐ τοῦτο μέντοι σε οἶμαι μόνον ἄτεχνον αὐτοῦ καὶ ἀμαθὲς συνιδεῖν, ἀλλ' ἓν τῶν πλείστων τοῦτο, τῷ δὲ μὴ μακρηγορεῖν ἐθέλειν, περὶ τούτου μοι δεδηλωκέναι μόνου. δοκῶ δέ μοι καὶ αὐτὸς αὐτοῦ πολλὰ τοιαῦτα ἰδεῖν, ὑπὸ δὲ τῶν κατὰ νοῦν ἁμαρτημάτων αὐτοῦ καὶ σολοικισμῶν καὶ βαρβαρισμῶν τοιούτων περί τε αὐτὸ τὸ θεῖον καὶ τὴν τῶν ὄντων φύσιν, οὐκ ἐκείνοις προσέχειν ἔχειν, ἀλλὰ τούτοις κατέχεσθαι· ὅπερ οἶμαι καὶ τὴν σὴν διὰ πάντων ὀξυδορκίαν ὧν ἥμαρτε περὶ ταῦτα βραχυλογεῖν ποιῆσαι.

Πολλὰ δὲ ἐγὼ θαυμάσας τῆς σῆς θεοφιλοῦς σοφίας, οὐχ ἧττον ἁπάντων τοῦτο τεθαύμακα, καὶ ἥσθην μετὰ τοῦ θαύματος, ὅτι μηδὲ τὸ σμικρότατον παριδεῖν ἠνέσχου τῆς ἀμαθίας τοῦ ἀνδρός. ὁ γὰρ οὕτω καὶ τοῦ βραχυτάτου πεποιημένος λόγον καὶ οὐκ ἀφεὶς ἀνεξέλεγκτον, τίνα ποτὲ δεῖ τοῦτον ὑπολαμβάνειν εἶναι περὶ τὰ μέγι-

---

46 post *σοφίας* lacunam statui

35: M 49ʳ–49ᵛ.

impiety would not have sprung up at all; and if impiety had sprung up, it would not have advanced as much as the present impiety, which arose in Thessalonica, but developed here and found free expression, and it would have conquered most of the Church, if you had not restrained it with a look, so to speak, from solitude. For I believe that without your prompting neither the Empress nor my most divine lord the Ecumenical Patriarch nor the most noble *Protosebastos* nor, in addition to them, the most excellent *Megas Doux* would have made a move against the present insolence regarding the Divinity.

When I say this to men who ⟨have⟩ an abundance of virtue and wisdom, they all applaud me for speaking the truth and offer of their own accord the additional remark: "If he were still willing and eager," and so on; while others add: "If he happened to be encouraged by the Church also." As for me, I know better than anybody else that all this is true and fitting for your learning and virtue, but as to how you should use your power against this deception and corruption of the truth, I do not know whose task it should be to induce you, except God's.

35. To master Sabbas Logaras

The observation you made here, after a careful scrutiny of the Palamnaian treatise, is accurate by the standards of discerning judges, and there could be no doubt about it. Of course, I do not think that you picked out this as a single instance of ineptitude and ignorance but as one of many; and because you did not wish to prolong this discussion, you pointed out only this to me. I believe that I too saw many similar mistakes of his, but due to his mental errors, solecisms, and barbarities regarding God Himself and the nature of beings, I was unable to pay attention to the former, but was detained by the latter. It is exactly this, I suspect, that caused you, sharp-sighted as you are regarding all his errors, to discuss this briefly.

While I admired many things about your wisdom which is dear to God, I was nonetheless full of admiration as well as delight that you did not forbear to overlook even the minutest detail of the man's ignorance. For if a man mentions even the smallest detail and does not let it go unscrutinized, what do you think he must be

στα; περὶ τοίνυν ἑνὸς καὶ τοῦ βραχυτάτου σφάλματος τῶν Παλαμναίων κρίσιν ἀρίστην δεξάμενος, ὡς περὶ πάντων οὖσαν ἐθαύμασα καὶ πρὸς τούτῳ εὐφράνθην καὶ χάριν τοῦ παντὸς ὡμολόγησα τῷ τοῦ παντὸς ἀληθεῖ τε καὶ ἀκριβεῖ κανόνι.

36. Σάββᾳ τῷ Λογαρᾷ

Οὐ καλῶς ἔλεγον ἐγώ σε θεοκίνητον λαβεῖν κατὰ τῆς παρούσης καινοφωνίας χάριν; νῦν γὰρ ἤδη δεύτερον ὁρῶ τουτονὶ πρηστῆρα τῶν ἀτόπων δογμάτων ἐκ τῆς σῆς ἐνθέου κατενεχθέντα γλώττης καὶ τὴν πλάνην καταπιμπράντα ταύτην, θεοφιλέστατε. οὐδὲν γὰρ οὕτω τῷ Θεῷ φίλον ὡς ἡ εὐσέβεια καὶ ὁ πρὸς τοὺς ἐπηρεαστὰς ταύτης πόλεμος, δι᾽ ὃν τὸ μέγα ὄνομα τῶν θειοτάτων μαρτύρων μετὰ Θεὸν ἀνυμνεῖται πανταχοῦ γῆς ἐν ταῖς θείαις τοῦ Χριστοῦ ἐκκλησίαις.

Ὢ ψυχῆς πῦρ πνεούσης ὑπὲρ τῆς εὐσεβείας· ὢ γλώττης ὁμοῦ μὲν εὐλαβοῦς περὶ τὸ θεῖον ὕψος καὶ τὰ ἀπόρρητα, ὁμοῦ δὲ εὐτόλμου κατὰ τῶν τὴν ὑπερηνωμένην τῆς τριλαμποῦς θεότητος μονάδα διασπάσαι τετολμηκότων εἰς ἀλλοκότους ἀλλοτριότητας. εἰ ταῦτα εὐλαβουμένου λέγειν καὶ διὰ πλειόνων ἐξελέγχειν τὸ τῆς παρούσης καινοτομίας ψεῦδος, τίνα ἂν εἴη τὰ τῆς τελεωτάτης παρρησίας τοξεύματα, ἣν ἐξ ἀνάγκης κατ᾽ αὐτοῦ προκαλεῖται ἡ ἄμετρος αὐτοῦ κατὰ τῶν ἀπορρήτων τόλμα; ἣν μέχρι μὲν νῦν ἐδεδίειν μὴ ἄρα, οὐδενὸς ἀνδρὸς ἀξιολόγου τὴν εὐσεβῆ λόγου ῥώμην ἀντιτάττειν ἐθέλοντος, πλεονάσοι τὸ χεῖρον καὶ τὰ πάντα κατάσχοι, νῦν δὲ ὁρῶν κινηθεῖσαν καὶ προχωροῦσαν ἀεὶ τὴν σὴν ὑπὲρ τῆς εὐσεβείας ἰσχυρογνωμοσύνην ἐθάρσησα, καὶ ἀνέθαλεν ὁ νοῦς μου καὶ ἥλατο καὶ τῶν λογικῶν ὅπλων ἥψατο ἐπὶ τοὺς ἐπιόντας, τοσοῦτον ὁρῶν ἀλείπτην καὶ πρόμαχον ἐφεστηκότα, καὶ τοῦτον παρὰ Θεοῦ πεμφθέντα, οὐ γὰρ ἐξ ἡμῶν ὡς ἀληθῶς ἀλλὰ Θεοῦ τὸ δῶρον.

36: 12–13 *ὑπερηνωμένην μονάδα*: cf. Dion. Areop., *De div. nom*, 2, 1 (PG, 3, 637A) || 12 *τῆς τριλαμποῦς θεότητος*: cf. *Horologion* (ed. Saliveros), 79 || 14 cf. Platonem, *Phaedo*, 101c

---

36: M 44ᵛ.

like when it comes to the most important matters? Therefore, since I received a perfect judgment on one, and the smallest, of the Palamnaian errors, I admired it as if it applied to all, and, besides, I rejoiced and gave thanks for everything to the true and accurate standard of everything.

36. To Sabbas Logaras

Was I not right in saying that you received your inspiration from God against the present "newfangled talk"? For now, my friend most dear to God, I see already this second flash of lightning against the absurd doctrines; it has been hurled by your God-inspired tongue and has burnt up this deceit. For nothing is as dear to God as piety and the war against its offenders, on account of which the great name of the most holy martyrs is praised after God in the holy churches of Christ the world over.

O soul that breathes fire for the sake of piety! O tongue that is at once pious regarding divine sublimity and ineffable matters and bold against those who have dared to break up the "supremely united Monad" of the "three-splendored divinity" into strange qualitative differences! If these are the words of a man who is "cautious of speaking" and who is putting to further test the falsehood of the present innovation, what would be the arrows of his complete denunciation, which this falsehood necessarily provokes against itself by its immeasurable audacity against ineffable matters! Up to now I feared that this audacity, in the absence of any remarkable man willing to set against it the pious vigor of his reasoning, might increase severely and conquer everything. However, now when I see that your resolution about piety has been roused and is constantly gathering momentum, I feel confident, and my spirit has revived and leapt up and reached out for intellectual weapons against the attackers, seeing so great a trainer and champion standing by, and sent by God, at that, for truly this gift is not from us but from God.

37. Τῷ πατριάρχῃ κῦρ Ἰωάννῃ

Οἷα γίνεται καὶ οὔπω κωλύεται! ῥᾷστα μὲν ὄντα τῇ σῇ μεγάλῃ κεκωλῦσθαι δυνάμει, ἀναγκαίως δὲ τοῦτο γενέσθαι δέον, εἴπερ, θειότατε δέσποτα, ἀνάγκη τῆς εὐσεβείας μέλειν εὐσεβέσιν ἀνθρώποις, καὶ μάλιστα τοῖς κατ' ἀξίαν προεστηκόσι ταύτης.

Μᾶρκος ἐκεῖνος, τὸ βδέλυγμα τῆς εὐσεβείας, τὸ θερσίτειον εἴδωλον ἢ καὶ Θερσίτης αὐτὸς ἀτεχνῶς, ἀκριτόμυθος, καὶ τῶν ἐκείνου πληγῶν καὶ Ὀδυσσέως δεόμενος, οὗ πέρι λόγος, εἰπεῖν καὶ φιλεῖν ἐκεῖνον τὸν στιχουργὸν εὐθὺς ὡς εἶδεν αὐτόν, "βραχὺς μοναχός, τοῦ Σατὰν δίφρος μέγας"—καὶ ταῦτα οὐχ ἡδόμενος λέγω, οὐδ' ὀνειδίζων τύχας, ὥς φησιν ἡ τραγῳδία, κρείσσω γὰρ εὐσεβῆ ψυχὴν οἶδα ἐν πεπηρωμένῳ τῷ σώματι τῆς ἐν ὑγιεῖ σώματι πεπηρωμένης, ἀλλ' ὅτι συνέδραμε σώματος εἰς ταὐτὸ καὶ ψυχῆς ὁμοῦ πήρωσις, καὶ μείζων ἡ τῆς ψυχῆς τῆς τοῦ σώματος, ἀσέβεια γὰρ οὐχ ἁπλῶς ἁμαρτία, τοῦτο τοῦ Μάρκου τὸ νόσημα καὶ Παλαμᾶ καὶ τῶν ὁμοίων αὐτοῖς, διὰ τοῦτο ἐμνήσθην καὶ τῆς τοῦ σώματος, ὡς τῆς ἔνδον συμβόλου πηρώσεως, ἣν ὁ Χριστὸς προειδὼς καὶ τὸ ταύτης ἀνίατον οὐ μετέδωκε τῆς θεραπείας αὐτῷ ἧς τῇ συγκυπτούσῃ μετέδωκεν, ἐπειδὴ πεπίστευκε μὲν ἐκείνη Θεοῦ σοφίαν εἶναι μόνην ἐκεῖνον καὶ δύναμιν, Μᾶρκος δὲ οὐκ ἀνέκυψεν ἐπὶ τὴν πίστιν ταύτην, μᾶλλον δὲ ἀφεὶς ταύτην τὴν ὑψηλήν τε καὶ θειοτάτην πίστιν, συνέκυψε καὶ κατεκλάσθη, μᾶλλον ἢ φαίνεται κατὰ τὸ σῶμα, ἐπὶ πίστιν ἑτέρας θεότητος, σοφίας τε καὶ δυνάμεως ἀνυποστάτου ἀντὶ τῆς ἐνυποστάτου, καὶ ἀνουσίου ἀντὶ τῆς ὄντως οὔσης, καὶ ἀνθ' ὁμοτίμου καὶ ἴσης τῷ δυνατῷ καὶ σοφῷ καὶ διὰ τοῦτο Πατρί, ἀπειράκις ἀπείρως τῆς αὐτοῦ θείας οὐσίας ὑφειμένην καὶ φύσεως, καὶ ἀντὶ τῆς πάντ' ἐνεργούσης καὶ δεδημιουργηκυίας ἀλλ' οὐκ ἐνεργηθείσης, ἐνεργουμένην, καὶ πρός γε τούτοις ἀντὶ τῆς καθάπερ ὁ Πατὴρ ἀοράτου καὶ ἀνειδέου καὶ ἀναφοῦς καὶ πᾶσι τοῖς οὖσι παντάπασιν ἀκαταλήπτου καθ' ἑαυτήν, ὀφθαλμοῖς σωματικοῖς καθ' αὑτὴν ὁρωμένην αὐτῷ τε καὶ [fol. 12^{r}] τοῖς ὁμοίοις αὐτῷ—οὗτος τοίνυν ὁ Μᾶρκος μόλις διαφυγὼν τὰς Θεσσαλονικέων χεῖρας, ἐπεὶ καὶ περὶ τὸ θεῖον καὶ τὸ βασίλειον

37: 6–7 Appendix proverbiorum, III, 19 (Leutsch-Schneidewin, I, 419) ‖ 11 Euripides, *Orestes*, 4 ‖ 18–19 Luc. 13:11 ‖ 19–20 I Cor. 1:25 ‖ 26 Maxim. Conf., *Capit. theol.*, 1, 49 (PG, 90, 1101A) = Palamas, *Dialexis*, 24, Syngrammata, II, 186, 26; *Epist. ad Gabram*, 5, Syngrammata, II, 332, 12

37: Mn 11^{v}–13^{r}. Ed. Uspenskij, *Synodikon*, 80–84; ed. Karpozilos, *Letters*, 109–113, no. 16.
3 *κεκωλύσθαι* Mn ‖ 6 *Μάρκος* Mn ‖ 9 *φιλῆν* Mn ‖ 20 *Μάρκος* Mn ‖ 32 *Μάρκος* Mn

37

37. To the Patriarch lord John

What a situation this is, and still going on without hindrance! Yet it could have been easily prevented by your great authority. And this, your Holiness, must of necessity be done, since indeed it is a necessity for pious men to take an interest in piety, and especially those who are officially in charge of it.

The notorious Mark, the abomination of piety, the image of Thersites or quite simply Thersites in person, the confused babbler who needs both an Odysseus and the thrashing of Thersites, Mark, about whom the story goes that as soon as that well-known versifier saw him, he said—and liked to do so (?)—"a small monk, yet Satan's great chariot"—and I do not delight in saying this, nor do I "reproach ill fortune," as the tragedy says, for I know that a pious soul in a maimed body is better than a maimed soul in a healthy body, but because the maiming of both body and soul coincided in the same person, and the soul's maiming is worse than that of the body (for the sickness of Mark and Palamas and their like is impiety, not simply sin); for this reason I thought of the body's maiming as a symbol of the internal maiming. Christ foresaw this ⟨harm⟩ as well as its incurability, and did not give him a share of the cure that he gave to the "woman who was bent double," for she believed that He is the only "wisdom and power of God," whereas Mark did not lift up his head to this belief, but rather forsook this lofty and most divine belief and bent double and bowed down, more than his physical appearance, before a belief in another divinity, wisdom, and power, without hypostasis instead of with hypostasis; a ⟨divinity⟩ deprived of essence, in place of the one which really exists. And instead of the divinity which is held in equal honor and is equal with the Father Who is mighty and wise for this reason also (?), ⟨he bowed before a divinity⟩ "infinitely" lower than the Father's divine essence and nature. And instead of the divinity which has created and activates everything but is not acted upon, ⟨he bowed⟩ before one which is acted upon. And, moreover, instead of the divinity which is, just like the Father, invisible and formless and intangible and, in itself, completely incomprehensible to all beings, ⟨he bowed⟩ before one visible in itself to the bodily eyes of himself and those like him. This Mark, then, having just escaped the hands of the Thessalonians, because he was shown there to be impious and disloyal regarding both the divine and the imperial authority, has now wretchedly arrived at Chios,

37

κράτος δυσσεβὴς ὢν ἐν αὐτοῖς ἐφάνη καὶ ἄπιστος, νῦν κακῶς τὴν Χῖον καταλαβὼν οὐ μετρίως ταράττει καὶ συγκυκᾷ τὴν νῆσον, ὡς εἴωθεν (ἠρεμεῖν γὰρ οὐκ οἶδεν οὐδ᾽ ἡσυχάζειν ἡ πλάνη, ὅτι μηδ᾽ ὁ διδάσκαλος αὐτῆς καὶ τῇ ἀληθείᾳ πρῶτος ἐχθρὸς καὶ πολέμιος). ὢν οὖν τοιοῦτος, δυσσεβὴς μὲν περὶ Θεόν, ἄπιστος δὲ περὶ τὸν βασιλέα, τοὺς ἀμφότερα ἡμᾶς θαρρῶ καὶ λέγω καθαροὺς καὶ ἀντιπάλους ἑκατέρᾳ κακίᾳ, κατὰ πολλὴν τὴν ἄδειαν ἀποκηρύττει, ὁ δυσσεβὴς τοὺς τῆς εὐσεβείας προκινδυνεύοντας, καὶ πρό γε ἡμῶν τὴν ἀκηλίδωτον τοῦ Χριστοῦ ἐκκλησίαν ᾗ κοινωνοῦμεν ἡμεῖς, καὶ τὴν σὴν πάντως τῆς εὐσεβείας ῥίζαν ἣ πάντων ἡμῶν ἀρχὴ καὶ κρηπίς ἐστιν.

Ἐνταῦθα δὲ ἑώρων ἐκεῖνον ἐγὼ προχωρήσοντα τῆς ἀναιδείας καὶ πάλαι μὲν ἐξ ὅτουπερ ἔγνων τὴν πονηρὰν αὐτοῦ φύσιν καὶ πρὸς τὴν πλάνην εὐχέρειαν, μάλιστα δὲ ἀφ᾽ οὗπερ αὐτὸν ἤκουσα γεγραφέναι πρὸς τὸ σὸν θεῖον ὕψος μετ᾽ ἰταμότητος ἐγκλημάτων γέμον κατὰ τῆς εὐσεβείας γράμμα καὶ τῆς σῆς θείας ψήφου καὶ κρίσεως, καθ᾽ ἣν περιίστασαι τὰς βεβήλους καινοφωνίας, κατὰ τὸν μέγαν Παῦλον, καὶ οὐκ ἐᾷς αὐτὰς ἐπὶ πλεῖον ἀσεβείας προκόπτειν καὶ τὸν λόγον αὐτῶν ὡς γάγγραιναν νέμεσθαι τὸ θεῖον τῆς ἐκκλησίας σῶμα οὗ ὁ Χριστὸς κεφαλὴ καὶ ὑπὲρ οὗ τὸ ἴδιον αἷμα φιλανθρώπως ἐξέχεεν.

Ἆρ᾽ ἀνεκτὰ ταῦτα ἡμῖν, ὦ θειότατε; ἆρα σιωπητέα; καὶ τίς οὕτως ἠμέλησε τῆς εὐσεβείας καὶ ἐπιλέλησται; ἆρ᾽ εἰ μὴ νῦν γοῦν τοῦτο τὸ κακόν, ἡ πολυκέφαλος ὕδρα, τομῆς τινος πειραθείη καὶ καύσεως παρὰ τῆς σῆς μαχαίρας τοῦ πνεύματος καὶ τοῦ πῦρ πνέοντος ὑπὲρ τῆς εὐσεβείας λόγου, φείσεται τῆς οἰκουμένης, ὥστε μὴ διὰ πάσης πειραθῆναι χωρῆσαι καὶ πᾶσαν ταῖς βεβήλοις καινοφωνίαις διαλυμήνασθαι; πολλή γέ τις ἀνάγκη. ἀλλὰ μὴ τοιαύτης εὐημερίας ἡ ἀσέβεια τύχοι, σοῦ, θειότατε, τῆς οἰκουμενικῆς ἐκκλησίας ἡγεμονεύοντος, μηδὲ προΐοι τὸ δεινὸν περαιτέρω, μηδὲ δυστήνων καὶ πονηρῶν ἀνθρωπίων ἀπόνοια κρείττων γένοιτο τῆς ἐκκλησιαστικῆς καὶ τῆς σῆς τοῦ θαυμασίου τῆς οἰκουμενικῆς ἐκκλησίας ἡνιόχου δυνάμεως· μὴ τὰ καινὰ καὶ ἀρτίφυτα, τῶν πάλαι κεκρατηκότων τῆς εὐσεβείας ὅρων· μὴ τὰ αἰσθητὰ καὶ κηλοῦντα τὴν αἴσθησιν, οὐ μόνον τῶν νοητῶν, ἀλλὰ καὶ τῶν ὑπὲρ νοῦν καὶ λόγον καὶ τῶν ἐν ταῖς μετὰ τὸ θεῖον ἀνωτάτω δυνάμεσι· καί, ὡς ἔπος εἰπεῖν, μὴ τὸ ψεῦδος τῆς ἀληθείας, μηδὲ ἡ πλάνη καὶ

49–52 II Tim. 2:16–17 ‖ 52–53 cf. Eph. 1:23; Col. 1:18 ‖ 53 cf. Matt. 26:28; Marc. 14:24; Luc. 22:21 ‖ 56 cf. Method. Olymp., *De lepra*, 6 (GCS, 27, 458); Niceph. Patr., *Adversus Mamonam*, 1, 5 (PG, 100, 209C) ‖ 57 Eph. 6:17 ‖ 59–60 II Tim. 2:16

---

47 *μεθ᾽ ἰταμότητος* Mn ‖ 51 *γάγραιναν* Mn ‖ 67 *τὸν ὑπὲρ* Mn ‖ 68 *τὸν ἐν* Mn

and, as he is wont to do, he is causing considerable trouble and confusion in the island (deceit does not know how to be still or quiet, for neither does its mentor and first enemy and opponent of truth). So, in fact, as he is such a man, impious with regard to God and disloyal with regard to the Emperor, he renounces me publicly with great licence, though I can say confidently, I am innocent of both ⟨crimes⟩ and opposed to either vice. The impious one renounces me, though I bear the brunt of the battle for piety, and even more than me, ⟨he renounces⟩ the unblemished Church of Christ, of which I am a communicant, and especially you who are the root of piety and the head and foundation of us all.

It was, in fact, a long time ago that I saw that he was going to proceed to this point of insolence, that is, ever since I discerned his wicked nature and aptitude for deceit, and especially since I heard that he wrote to your Sublimity, with effrontery, a letter replete with accusations against piety and your divine decision and judgment, by which you "avoid the profane newfangled talk," in accordance with the great Paul, and do not allow it "to stray further and further into godless courses and the infection of its teaching to spread like gangrene" in the divine "body of the Church whose head Christ is" and for which "He shed His own blood" out of love for men.

Must we, indeed, tolerate these things, your Holiness? Must we pass them over in silence? And who has so neglected or forgotten piety? If this evil, the "many-headed serpent," does not now, at least, experience some cutting and burning from the "sword given you by the Spirit" and from your tongue which breathes fire on behalf of piety, will it spare the inhabited world so as not to attempt to advance through all of it and corrupt it all with the "profane newfangled talk"? Certainly not! But may the impiety not attain such prosperity while your Holiness is ruling the Ecumenical Church; may the evil not advance further; nor the madness of despicable and wicked wretches prevail over the authority of the Church and over you, the marvelous charioteer of the Ecumenical Church! May the fresh and newborn not prevail over the laws of piety which have prevailed since the days of old! May that which can be perceived and appeals to the senses not ⟨prevail⟩ either over the intelligible or, indeed, over what is above intelligence and expression and among the highest powers next to God! And, in short, may falsehood not ⟨prevail⟩ over truth, nor deceit and desolation and pits not admitting God's visitation, along

37

ἐρημία καὶ βάραθρα τὰ τῆς θείας ἐπισκοπῆς ἀνεπίδεκτα, τῆς λεωφόρου καὶ τετριμμένης καὶ ἀπλανοῦς πορείας καὶ διὰ τῶν ἡμερωτάτων καὶ φωτεινῶν καὶ συνήθων ἀγούσης ἐπὶ τὴν ἀλήθειαν τῆς εὐσεβοῦς τελειότητος τῆς εἷς θεὸς κηρυττούσης, ὅτι μία θεότης τρισυπόστατος, ἁπλῆ, ἀδιαίρετος, ἀμερὴς καὶ ἀνείδεος· ἄπειρος, ἄποιος, ἀναφής, ἀνείκαστος, ἀπαράλλακτος καὶ μηδενὶ τῶν ὄντων ἐκ φυσικῆς ἐμφάσεως διεγνωσμένη· πανταχοῦ καὶ τοῖς πᾶσι παροῦσα καὶ ὑπὲρ πάντα οὖσα, παντουργός τε καὶ παντοδύναμος· ὑπέρσοφος σοφία, ὑπεράγαθος ἀγαθότης, ὑπερούσιος οὐσία, [fol. 12v] ὑπέρζωος ζωή, ὑπερδύναμος δύναμις, ὑπερφαὲς φῶς, ὑπερήλιος ἔλλαμψις, πάντα καταφωτίζουσα καὶ μηδενὶ καθ' αὑτὴν ὁρωμένη· πάντα περιέχουσα καὶ οὐδενὸς ἁπτομένη, τῷ μήτε ἐπαφὴν αὐτῆς εἶναι μήτε ἄλλην τινὰ πρὸς τὰ μετέχοντα συμμιγῆ κοινωνίαν, ὁρωμένη τῷ μὴ ὁρᾶσθαι καὶ γινωσκομένη τῷ μὴ γινώσκεσθαι, ὑπερουράνιος βασιλεία, ἓν κράτος ἀμερές τε καὶ ἀδιαίρετον, μία τῶν πάντων ὑπερκειμένη ἐξουσία καὶ δύναμις· μονὰς μονάδων καὶ ἑνὰς ἑνάδων, δημιουργὸς ἁπασῶν, προσώποις ἀριθμουμένη τρισὶν οὐ διαφόροις θεότησιν, οὐ βαθμοῖς μετρουμένη καὶ ὑποβάσεσιν, οὐχ ὑπερβολαῖς καὶ ὑφέσεσιν ἑαυτῇ μαχομένη, οὐ τὰ μὲν ὑπερσεβομένη, τὰ δ' ὑποσεβομένη, οὐδ' ὀνομάτων καινότησι διασπωμένη παρὰ τῶν αὐτὴν εὐσεβῶς θρησκευόντων.

Ταύτης ἡμῶν τῆς ἐκκλησιαστικῆς καὶ πατρῴας καὶ συνήθους ὁμολογίας τῆς πίστεως μὴ περιείη, θειότατε, ἡ τἀναντία πάντα κηρύττουσα καινοφωνία, πλῆθος ἀριθμὸν ὑπερβαῖνον οὐσιωδῶν τῷ Θεῷ θεοτήτων, τῶν μὲν ὑφειμένων, τῶν δὲ ὑπερκειμένων, καὶ τῆς μὲν ἐνεργούσης τὰς ἄλλας, τῶν δὲ ἐνεργουμένων, καὶ τῆς μὲν ἀμεθέκτου παντάπασι, τῶν δὲ μετεχομένων, ὃ μόνων τῶν τὴν πολύθεον πλάνην νενοσηκότων ἐστί, μᾶλλον

73–74 cf. Maxim. Conf., *Capit. theol.*, 2, 1 (PG, 90, 1124D–1125A) || 76–77 Maxim. Conf., *ibid.*, 1 (PG, 1084A) || 77 cf. Joannis Chrysostomi *Liturgia* (ed. Brightman), 353, 13 || 78 Dion. Areop., *De div. nom*, 7, 2 (PG, 3, 868C) || 79 *ὑπεράγαθος ἀαθότης*: *ibid.*, 2, 4 (PG, 3, 641A) || *ὑπερούσιος οὐσία*: *ibid.*, 1, 1 (PG, 3, 588B) || 80 *ibid.*, 6, 3 (PG, 3, 857B) || 87–88 cf. Sophronium, *Epist. syn. ad Sergium* (PG, 87³, 3152D, 3156C) || 88–89 cf. Greg. Naz., *Or.* 18, 16 (PG, 35, 1005B || 90–91 cf. Greg. Naz., *Or.* 22, 12 (PG, 35, 1144C) || 95 cf. Palamam, *De divinis operationibus*, 13. Syngrammata, II, 106, 24, 96–97 cf. Palamam, *Epist. III ad Acindynum*, 15 Syngrammata, I, 306, 18–20; ed. Nadal, 252, 10–12 || 98–99 cf. Basil. Caes., *Epist.* 189, 4 (PG, 32, 688D)

---

71 ἀπλανοῦς Mn

37

the main and constantly used and safe course which leads through the smoothest and bright and familiar places to the truth of pious perfection which proclaims that "there is one God because there is one divinity" in three hypostases, "simple, admitting of no division or partition" and formless; infinite, without qualities, intangible, unrepresentable, unchanging, and "not known to any being by means of a natural manifestation"; "present everywhere" and in everything; and superior to all and all-creating and almighty; "wisdom which transcends wisdom"; "goodness which transcends goodness"; "essence which transcends essence"; "life which transcends life"; power which transcends power; light which transcends light; brilliance which transcends the sun and illuminates everything and is not, in itself, visible to anyone; all-encompassing and not touching anything, having neither contact nor any other common association with what participates in it; visible by being invisible and known by being unknown; a super-celestial kingdom; one dominion admitting of no partition or division; one authority and power superior to all; a monad and henad, creator of all monads and henads, "numbering three persons, not different divinities"; not "measured by degrees and successive diminutions"; not in conflict with itself on account of superiorities and subordinations; not "reverenced partly more and partly less," nor torn asunder "with novel terms" by those who piously worship it.

Over this, our ecclesiastical and ancestral and familiar confession of faith, your Holiness, let not the newfangled talk which teaches all the opposite prevail: an "innumerable" multitude of divinities essential to God, some of which are "lower" and others "higher"; while one activates the others and the others are activated; while one is absolutely incapable of participation and the others are capable of participation—"which is the belief only of those who suffer from the delusion of polytheism," rather it surpasses pagan polytheism—and, moreover, some are invisible

37

δὲ καὶ τῆς Ἑλλήνων πολυθεΐας ἐπέκεινα· καὶ πρὸς τούτοις τῶν μὲν ἀοράτων, τῶν δὲ σωματικοῖς ὀφθαλμοῖς καθ' αὑτὰς ὁρωμένων, οὐ πνευματικῶς, ὡς φυσᾷ καὶ κομπάζει, ἀλλὰ δαιμονιωδῶς, * * * αὐτῆς, ὥς φησι, τῆς φυσικῆς καὶ οὐσιώδους μορφῆς καὶ δόξης τοῦ ἀοράτου Θεοῦ. φρῖξον ἥλιε! φρῖξον ἀγγέλων φύσις, ἡ τῶν Χερουβὶμ καὶ Σεραφὶμ ἀκρότης ἡ μηδὲ τὸν θεῖον θρόνον (ὅστις ποθ' οὗτός ἐστι) δυναμένη προσβλέπειν καὶ διὰ τοῦτο τὰς ὄψεις περικαλύπτουσα! εἶτα εἷς αὖθις θεὸς καὶ μία, φησί, θεότης ἐξ ἀπείρων τὸ πλῆθος καὶ τοσοῦτο διαφόρων ἀλλήλων καὶ ἀνίσων καὶ ἀνομοιοτάτων, ἐνεργουμένων καὶ ἐνεργοῦντος, μεθεκτῶν καὶ ἀμεθέκτου, ὁρατῶν καὶ ἀοράτου, ὑπερκειμένου καὶ ὑφειμένων ἀπειράκις ἀπείρως, ὧν τί ἂν ἀσεβέστερον γένοιτο, τί δὲ τῇ ἐκκλησιαστικῇ καὶ κοινῇ πάντων ὁμολογίᾳ τῆς εὐσεβείας ἐναντιώτερον;

Εἰ δὴ ταῦτα διδάσκων ὁ Μᾶρκος καὶ ὁ Κουρᾶς—καὶ ὃν ἄν τις ἄλλον εἴποι, μετὰ τοῦ πατρὸς αὐτῶν τε καὶ τῶν αἱρέσεων—κατὰ τῆς εὐσεβείας καὶ τοὺς τῶν θείων ἀντεχομένους ὅρων ἀποκηρύττοντες, ταῦτ' ἀδεῶς πράττειν ἕξουσι, σοῦ τῆς μεγάλης μετὰ Θεὸν ἐξουσίας καὶ δυνάμεως ἡγουμένης ἁπάσης τῆς Χριστοῦ ἐκκλησίας, ἡ σὴ κρινάτω παραχωρεῖν τοῖς λύκοις τὸν καλὸν ποιμένα καὶ Χριστομίμητον καὶ μὴ μόνον τὴν ποίμνην, ἀλλὰ καὶ ἑαυτὸν προδιδόναι τοῖς λύκοις, ἢ προσέχειν ἑαυτῷ τε καὶ παντὶ τῷ ποιμνίῳ, κατὰ τὸν θεῖον Παῦλον ταῦτα προειρηκότα σαφῶς, ἃ νῦν ὁρῶμεν τελούμενα· ἀναστήσονται, γάρ φησιν, ἄνδρες λαλοῦντες διεστραμμένα τοῦ ἀποσπᾶν τοὺς μαθητὰς ὀπίσω αὐτῶν, διὸ γρηγορεῖτε· ἃ καὶ Χριστὸς πρὸ αὐτοῦ, ἐφ' οἷς καὶ προασφαλίζεται τοὺς ἐπιγενομένους καὶ παραινεῖ, ἐὰν ὑμῖν εἴπωσιν ''ἰδοὺ ὧδε Χριστός,'' ἢ ''ἰδοὺ ἐκεῖ,'' λέγων, μὴ πιστεύσητε αὐτοῖς· ἐγερθήσονται γὰρ ψευδόχριστοι καὶ ψευδοπροφῆται καὶ δώσουσι σημεῖα καὶ τέρατα ἐν τῷ λαῷ ὥστε πλανῆσαι, εἰ δυνατόν, καὶ τοὺς ἐκλεκτούς. τί τούτοις ἀνόμοιον τῶν ἐν τοῖς καινοῖς πλάνοις τούτοις; [fol. 13r] οὐ λαλοῦσι διεστραμμένα;

---

104 cf. *Triodion*, 385 ‖ 104–106 cf. Isaiam 6:2–3 ‖ 110 cf. Palamam, *Epist. III ad Acindynum*, 15, Syngrammata, I, 306, 18–20; ed. Nadal, 252, 10–12 ‖ 110–111 Maxim. Conf., *Capit. theol.*, 1, 49 (PG, 90, 1101A) = Palamas, *Dialexis*, 24, Syngrammata, II, 186, 26; *Epist. ad Gabram*, 5, Syngrammata, II, 332, 12 ‖ 119 cf. Joan. 10:11–12 ‖ 121–122 cf. Act. Ap. 20:28 ‖ 123–125 Act. Ap. 20:30–31 ‖ 127–131 Matt. 24:23–25; Luc. 17:21 ‖ 132 Act. Ap. 20:30

---

102 *φυσσᾶ* Mn ‖ ante *αὐτῆς* lacunam statui ‖ 104 *φρίξον* Mn ‖ 108–109 *ἀνομοιώτατα* Mn ‖ 113 *Μάρκος* Mn

while others are, in themselves, visible to bodily eyes, not spiritually, as he ⟨Palamas⟩ boasts and brags, but in a diabolical way * * * of the very natural and essential form and glory of the invisible God, as he claims. "Shudder thou, O sun!" Shudder thou, O nature of the angels; the sublimity of the Cherubim and the Seraphim who are not even able to look at God's throne, whatever that is, and who therefore cover up their faces! Then again, he says that there is one god and one divinity consisting of an innumerable multitude of divinities so far different from one another and unequal and dissimilar; of which one is active and the others acted upon; one incapable of being shared and the others capable of being shared; one invisible and the others visible; one "higher" and the others "infinitely lower". What can be more impious than these and what is more opposed to the common confession of piety of the Church and of all men?

If, therefore, Mark and Kouras (and anyone else we might mention, together with their spiritual father and father of heresies) who teach these ⟨doctrines⟩ against piety and publicly renounce the men who cling to the divine laws, ⟨if they⟩ are to be allowed to do so without fear, while you, the great authority and power, after God, are the head of the whole Church of Christ, it is for you to decide: whether you will deliver the "good shepherd" and Christ's imitator to the "wolves" and betray not only the flock but yourself also to the wolves, or will "keep watch over yourself and over the whole flock," in accordance with St. Paul, who foretold clearly what we now see happening. "There will be men coming forward," he says, "who will distort the truth to induce the disciples to break away and follow them. So be on the alert!" ⟨This is⟩ exactly what Christ said before him, to secure posterity in advance, when He admonished: "If they say to you, 'Look, here is the Messiah' or 'There he is,' do not believe them. Impostors will come claiming to be Messiahs or prophets and they will produce great signs and wonders among the people, to mislead even the chosen, if such a thing were possible." Is anything in these sayings different

37

οὐ τὴν θείαν Γραφὴν διαστρέφουσιν; οὐ τὴν πίστιν μετατιθέασιν ἐφ' ἑτέραν, ἣν οὐχ ᾔδειμεν οὔτε ἡμεῖς, οὔθ' οἱ πατέρες ἡμῶν; οὐκ ἰδοὺ ὧδε ὁ Χριστὸς καὶ ἰδοὺ ἐκεῖ λέγουσι—Μᾶρκος μὲν ἐν ἑαυτῷ καὶ Παλαμᾷ καὶ Κουρᾷ, Κουρᾶς δὲ ἐν ἑαυτῷ καὶ Παλαμᾷ καὶ Μάρκῳ, ὁ δ' ἐν ἑαυτῷ καὶ τῷ Δαυὶδ καὶ ἄλλῳ—τὴν φυσικὴν καὶ οὐσιώδη μορφὴν καὶ δόξαν τῆς ἀρρήτου θεότητος ὁρᾶν διά πάντων κηρύττοντες τοῖς ἑαυτῶν σωματικοῖς ὀφθαλμοῖς, καὶ οὕτω πιστεύεσθαι ἀξιοῦντες περὶ τῆς πολυθεΐας καὶ τῆς τοῦ ἑνὸς ἁπλοῦ τε καὶ ἀμεροῦς διαιρέσεως εἰς θεοτήτων ὑπερκειμένων καὶ ὑφειμένων καὶ σφόδρα ἐξηλλαγμένων πλῆθος; οὐ σημεῖα καὶ τέρατα διὰ πάντων θρυλοῦσι θαυματουργεῖν, εἰ καὶ μηδενὸς μᾶλλον δύνανται; εἰκότως ἄρα αὐτοῖς ἀπιστοῦμεν καὶ ἀπιστήσομεν, εἴ γε πιστεύσομεν τῷ, μὴ πιστεύσητε αὐτοῖς, ἡμῖν παρακελευομένῳ· καὶ ἀναγκαίως αὐτοὺς ἀναθεματιοῦμεν, εἴ γε πειθοίμεθα τῷ, κἂν ἄγγελος ὑμῖν ἐξ οὐρανοῦ εὐαγγελίσηται παρ' ὃ παρελάβετε, ἀνάθεμα ἔστω, ἰσχυρῶς ἐπιτάττοντι.

Εἰ μὲν οὖν τι πλημμελοῦμεν ἐν τούτοις καὶ τῶν τῆς εὐσεβείας ὅρων ἐκβαίνομεν, ὦ κορυφαῖον τῆς εὐσεβείας κράτος, τί μὴ τὸ ἀληθὲς διδασκόμεθα, κἂν μὴ πειθώμεθα, ὡς εἰκὸς κολαζόμεθα; εἰ δὲ ταῦθ' οὕτως ἔχοι καὶ οὐδὲν παρὰ τὸν τῆς εὐσεβείας σκοπὸν καὶ τὸν σὸν ἡμῖν λέγεται, μηκέτι Μᾶρκος καὶ κατ' ἐκεῖνον ἄλλος, μηδ' εἴ τις ἄγγελος ἐξ οὐρανοῦ καὶ ἄλλος Παῦλος εἶναι δοκοίη, κινείτω τὰ ἅπαξ ἐσφραγισμένα τῇ σφραγίδι τοῦ πνεύματος, μηδὲ παρρησιαζέσθω κατὰ τῆς εὐσεβείας ἢ διδάσκων ἢ γράφων ἃ τῇ τῆς ἐκκλησιαστικῆς ὁμολογίᾳ πίστεως ἐναντιοῦται καὶ τὰς ἀξιολόγους ὑπολήψεις περὶ τοῦ θείου καὶ τοὺς κοινοὺς τῆς ἐκκλησίας περὶ αὐτοῦ κανόνας ἰταμῶς ἀνατρέπει καὶ διαρρήδην κηρύττει καὶ ἀποφαίνεται ὡς ὥσπερ ἡ ἐπὶ τὴν οἰκονομίαν ἀπὸ τοῦ νόμου μετάστασις γέγονε, κεκρυμμένη τοῖς πολλοῖς καὶ ἀφανὴς οὖσα πρότερον, οὕτω καὶ ἀπὸ τῆς νῦν κοινῇ κρατούσης ὁμολογίας περὶ τῆς εὐσεβείας καὶ γνώσεως ἐν πάσῃ τῇ ἐκκλησίᾳ, ἐφ' ἑτέραν δεῖ μετατίθεσθαι πίστιν τὴν παρ' αὐτοῖς, φασιν, ἐν μυστηρίῳ κειμένην.

Εἰ δὲ ταῦτα δεῖ ἐπ' ἀδείας κηρύττεσθαι καὶ ἡμᾶς τοὺς τούτοις μὴ πειθομένους ὑπὸ τῶν ἐκεῖνα κηρυττόντων ἀποκηρύττεσθαι κατὰ πολλὴν τοῦ κωλύσοντος τὴν ἐρημίαν, ἐν εὐεργεσίας μέρει

134–135 Matt. 24:23; Luc. 17:21 || 141–142 cf. Palamam, *Epist. III ad Acindynum*, 15, Syngrammata, I, 306, 18–20; ed. Nadal, 252, 10–12 || 142–143 Matt. 24:24 || 145 Matt. 24:24 || 147–148 Gal. 1:8–9 || 154 Gal. 1:8–9 || 155 *ἐσφραγισμένα . . . πνεύματος* cf. Eph. 1: 13 || 167 cf. Demosthenem, *Philip.* 1, 49

---

143 *θρυλλοῦσιν* littera *ν* expuncta Mn || 154–155 *κινήτω* Mn || 159 *ἱταμῶς* Mn

37

from what is happening with these new impostors? Do they not "distort the truth"? Do they not distort the Holy Scripture? Do they not change the faith to a different one, which neither we nor our fathers before us knew? Do they not say, "Look, here is the Messiah" and "There he is"—Mark to himself and Palamas and Kouras, and Kouras to himself and Palamas and Mark, and Palamas to himself and David and somebody else—when they proclaim in every way that they see with their own bodily eyes the natural and essential form and glory of the ineffable Divinity, and thus demand to be believed concerning polytheism and the division of the simple and indivisible One into a multitude of "higher" and "lower" and exceedingly varied divinities? Do they not keep talking of miraculously producing "signs and wonders," though they can do no more than anyone else? And so I am right not to believe them, and I shall not believe them, so long as I believe Him Who admonishes us: "Do not believe them." And I shall perforce anathematize them, so long as I obey him who strongly enjoins: "Even if an angel from heaven should preach a gospel at variance with the gospel which you received, let him be anathematized!"

Therefore, O leading pious Authority, if I make an error in these matters and digress from the standards of piety, why am I not taught the truth, and if I do not obey, why am I not rightly punished? If, on the other hand, things are so, and if I say nothing contrary to your objectives and to those of piety, let no longer Mark or anyone like him, even if he should seem to be "an angel from heaven" or another Paul, disturb what has been sealed once and for all with the seal of the Spirit; let him not speak freely against piety by either teaching or writing that which contradicts the confession of faith of the Church and which insolently overthrows the important beliefs about God and the common rules of the Church about Him, and ⟨which⟩ expressly proclaims and declares that just as the change from the Mosaic law to the economy of salvation occurred, being previously concealed and invisible to the many, so too, they say, it is necessary to change from the confession and knowledge of piety which now prevails in the whole Church to another, their own, which is wrapped in mystery.

But, if these things must be proclaimed without fear, and I, who do not listen to them, must be publicly renounced by those who proclaim them, because "there is no one to prevent it," I consider it a great benefaction to have learnt this too, so that,

μεγάλης καὶ τοῦτο μεμαθηκέναι τιθέμεθα, ἵν' ὡς μηδεμίαν ἐντεῦθεν ἐλπίδα τῆς τούτων διορθώσεως ἔχοντες, ἀλλ' ἀπογνόντες τὰς ἀμείνους ἐλπίδας, ἠρεμῶμεν παντάπασι πρὸς μόνον τὸν Θεὸν ἀφορῶντες κἀκεῖθεν μόνον τὴν τῆς νόσου ταύτης ἀναίρεσιν ἀναμένοντες.

38. Ἰωάννῃ τῷ θειοτάτῳ πατριάρχῃ

Ἔδει μὲν ἡμᾶς παρόντας ἀπολαύειν παρούσης τῆς σῆς θαυμαστῆς καὶ θεαυγοῦς ἀκτῖνος, ἀλλὰ μὴ διὰ γραμμάτων ἀσθενῶς αὐτῆς καὶ ἀμυδρῶς τυγχάνειν. γράφοντες μὲν γὰρ μόνον, ἡμῖν δὲ οὐκ ἀντιγραφομένου, τίνος ἂν καὶ τυγχάνοιμεν; ἢ καὶ αὐτὸ τὸ γοῦν ἐξεῖναι ἡμῖν ἐπιστέλλειν τῷ τῆς σῆς ὕψει κορυφαίας θειότητος, τυγχάνειν ἡμᾶς ἐστιν οὐκ ἀγεννοῦς ἀγαθοῦ, κἂν μὴ τῶν θείων αὐτῆς καμάτων καὶ ἱερῶν ἀξιώμεθα. ἔχει γὰρ οὕτω τοῦτο· μήτε δὲ τὴν σὴν ὑπερφυᾶ κεφαλὴν οἴκοι μένειν ἀφείσης τῆς ὑπὲρ τῶν θείων νόμων ἐνστάσεως, μήθ' ἡμᾶς ἀφείσης ἀκολουθεῖν σοι τῆς ἀσθενείας ἡμῶν, εἰκότως ἡμῖν, μᾶλλον δὲ ἀναγκαίως ἐδέησε τοῦ γε διὰ γραμμάτων φανῆναί σου τῇ θειότητι καὶ δεῖξαι τὸν πρὸς αὐτὴν ἡμῖν ἐμπεφυκότα πόθον, καίτοι πρὸς ἀγνοοῦντα δεῖ δείκνυσθαι ὧν ἐστιν ἐν ἀγνοίᾳ, ὁ δὲ μάλιστα πάντων εὖ εἰδὼς τὰ ἡμέτερα πρὸς ἑαυτὸν ὡς ἔχει, αὐτός ἐστιν ὁ μέγας νοῦς καὶ θεόληπτος ᾧ ταῦτα παρ' ἡμῶν ἐπιστέλλεται· ὃς κἂν ἄλλους πείσειε περὶ ἡμῶν, οἶμαι δ' ὅτι καὶ πέπεικεν, ὁποῖον πρός τε αὐτὸν τὸ ἡμέτερον καὶ τὴν ἀγαθὴν ἐκ Θεοῦ βασιλείαν καὶ ὑπὲρ τῆς εὐσεβείας. [fol. 50r] ἀλλὰ καὶ οὕτως ἐπιστέλλειν προσῆκε, καὶ δὴ καὶ ἐπέσταλται καὶ τυχεῖν αἰτεῖται τόπου τὰ γράμματα παρὰ τῷ σῷ μεγέθει, ὃν τοῖς εὔνοις προσήκει παρὰ τοῖς οὕτω τιμωμένοις ὑπάρχειν. εἰ δέ τι καὶ ἀμαθὲς οἷς τῇ σῇ μεγαλειότητι γράφομεν λάθοι ποι παρεμπεσόν, συγγινωσκέτω ἡμῖν ὁ κοινὸς πάντων πατὴρ καὶ τῶν πατέρων πατήρ, ἐκεῖνο σαφῶς εἰδὼς ὡς ἄρα πολλῶν ἡμᾶς ἀγαθῶν τῆς ἐκδημίας τῆς αὐτοῦ στερησάσης, δι' ἃ λύπης ἡμῖν ἀπολαύειν ἐκείνοις ἀντιπάλου περίεστιν, ἕν ἐστι τῶν ἡμᾶς ἀνιώντων καὶ μέγιστον ἡ τοῦ λοιμοῦ παρρησία τῶν εὐσεβῶν δογμάτων. ἡ γὰρ ὑπὲρ τῆς εὐσεβείας κακουργουμένης λύπη τῶν εὐσεβείᾳ φίλων πολλὴν ἂν ἔχοι καὶ δικαίαν συγγνώμην ἐκ τῶν αὐτῆς προμάχων, ἂν ἄρα που προπετὲς ὑπὸ τοῦ θείου ζήλου πρὸς αὐτοὺς φθέγξωνταί τι.

168–169 ἐντεῦθεν Mn[mg]

38: M 49v–50r.

5 ἀντιγραφουμένου M || 8 καμμάτων M

having no hope that these matters would be corrected from here and having given up better expectations, I may remain completely quiet and turn my eyes to God, expecting the removal of this disease from there alone.

38. To his Holiness Patriarch John

I should have been present to enjoy the presence of your marvelous rays and not attain them feebly and dimly through letters. For, if I only write without receiving an answer, what do I attain? Except that for me, even to be allowed to write to your sublime Holiness, is to attain a not insignificant blessing, even if I am not deemed worthy of your divine and sacred labors. For this is how the matter stands: since your intervention on behalf of the divine laws did not permit your Holiness to remain at home, nor did my unworthiness permit me to follow you, rightly or rather necessarily, I had to communicate with your Holiness, at least by letter, and to express my natural yearning for you; although it is only to someone ignorant that we must point out the things that he does not know, while the man who above all others is well aware of my feelings towards him is the great and God-inspired man to whom I am sending this letter. He could even convince others about me, and I believe that he has convinced them as to what my feelings are towards him and towards his gracious and divine Majesty as well as towards piety. But it was proper to write even so, and I have written, and the letter begs to find by your Sublimity the place that friends ought to have with those whom they honor. And, if something unlearned has found its way into the things I write to your Holiness, let the common father of all and father of ⟨spiritual⟩ fathers forgive me, since he knows distinctly that, although his departure has deprived me of many blessings, as a result of which I suffer a sorrow equal to these blessings, my one and biggest sorrow is the license that the bane of the pious doctrines is enjoying. For if, perhaps, out of sacred zeal the lovers of piety say somewhere something rash to its defenders, their grieving for the ill-suffering piety should be greatly and justly excused by its defenders.

Τί οὖν ἐστιν ὃ καὶ νῦν δεῖν ᾠήθην ἀνενεγκεῖν σου τῷ θείῳ καὶ κορυφαίῳ κράτει περὶ τῆς εὐσεβείας; τοῦτο ἐκεῖνο δήπου τὸ εἰωθὸς ἀεί μοι καὶ ἀναγκαῖον πράττειν· ἡ γὰρ κακὴ κεφαλὴ τῆς παλαμναίας ὕδρας συντριβεῖσα μὲν τῇ σῇ πολυδυνάμῳ χειρί, παντελῶς δὲ ἀποκοπεῖσα δήπου, καὶ νῦν ἀδείας τινὸς διὰ τὴν ἀπουσίαν τῆς ἐνθέου κεφαλῆς λαβομένη, πάνθ' ὁμοῦ μηχανᾶται καὶ σπεύδει τὸ πονηρὸν εἰς πλείστους καταβαλέσθαι σπέρμα, ὥσπερ καθεύδοντος τοῦ γεωργοῦ διὰ τὴν ἀπουσίαν. καὶ δὴ κακὰ κακῶς ἀπολέσθον τὰ πονηρὰ ταῦτα σπέρματα· τῷ γεωργῷ μελήσαι τῆς σιτοφθόρου λύμης, ὃς αὐτῶν τὰ τοιαῦτα βλαστήματα, πρόρριζα ἀνεσπακὼς καὶ πάντα συναγαγών, τῷ πυρὶ παραδώσει τοῦ μακαρίου ζήλου καὶ κατακαύσεται, τὸν σῖτον μόνον καὶ καθαρὸν ἀποδοὺς αὐτῷ τε καὶ ἡμῖν τὸν ἐξ ἀρχῆς σπαρέντα. ἀλλὰ καὶ ὁ δίκαιος καὶ ἀληθινὸς βασιλεὺς ὃν οὐκ ἠθέλησαν ἐπ' αὐτοὺς βασιλεύειν, ἄλλην ἑαυτοῖς ἀντ' αὐτοῦ βασιλείαν ἑλόμενοι, ἐπεὶ καὶ θεότητα, μέτεισι τῆς ἀπειθείας ταύτης αὐτοὺς καὶ σκαιότητος.

39. Sine titulo

Ἔλεγχε σοφὸν καὶ ἀγαπήσει σέ φησιν ἡ σοφὴ παροιμία, ᾗ καὶ αὐτὸς πειθόμενος, πρὸς ταύτῃ δέ τι θαρρῶν καὶ τῇ πρὸς σὲ παρρησίᾳ τῆς παλαιᾶς φιλίας, δεῖν ᾠήθην ἐλέγξαι σε, οὐκ ἀνθρώπῳ προσκρού-[fol. 48r]οντα, τῷ δὲ τῶν ὅλων Θεῷ· νομίζων ἔτι σε σοφὸν εἶναι καὶ τῆς πάλαι καλοκἀγαθίας ἐκείνης ἀντιποιεῖσθαι, εἰ καὶ μὴ τῆς πρὸς ἡμᾶς φιλίας ὁπόσον ἡμῖν ἀνῆκεν· οὐκ οἶδα τί πλημμελήσαντας ἄξιον τῆς νῦν ὑπεροψίας, εἰ μὴ πλημμέλημα ἐμὸν εἶναί τις εἴποι τὸ μὴ θελῆσαι ἀλλοτρίοις δόγμασι τῆς εὐσεβείας ἀκολουθῆσαι, καταλιπόντα τὴν καλὴν καὶ κοινὴν τῶν εὐσεβῶν ὁμολογίαν τῆς πίστεως, ἣν ἐκ παιδὸς εἰς δεῦρο πεπρέσβευκα.

Σὺ τοίνυν, ὦ βέλτιστε, τῷ μὲν λόγῳ δοκεῖς ἡμῖν συναινεῖν τὴν καλὴν ταύτην ἕξιν, τοῖς δὲ πράγμασι τἀναντία πρεσβεύειν καὶ τοῖς ἡμῖν ἀντικειμένοις συνηγορεῖν, μᾶλλον δὲ τοῖς ἀντικειμένοις τῇ κα-

---

38: 38–39 cf. Matt. 21:41; Aristophanes, *Plut.*, 65 ‖ 40–43 cf. Matt. 13:24–31 ‖ 44–45 cf. Luc. 19:14, 27

39: 1 Prov. 9:9

38–40 *καὶ δὴ . . . σιτοφθόρου λύμης* scripsi: *καὶ δεῖ κακὰ κακῶς ἀπολέσθον τὰ πονηρὰ ταῦτα σπέρματα τῷ γεωργῷ μελήσαις τῆς σιτοφθόρου λύμης* M ‖ 42 *σίτον* M

39: M 47v–49r.

What is this, then, that I thought necessary, even now, to bring to the attention of your Holiness concerning piety? It is, indeed, that which is forever customary and necessary for me to do, because the wicked head of the murderous serpent, which was crushed by your mighty hand and almost cut off, now has acquired some freedom due to the absence of your Holiness and is devising all sorts of intrigue and is anxiously seeking to sow the wicked seed in a great many men, as if the farmer were asleep because he is absent. And so, let this bad seed "come to a bad end!" May the farmer take care of the disease that is destroying the wheat! For he will first pull out by the roots such offshoots as will spring forth from this seed, and he will gather them all and deliver them to the fire of sacred zeal and burn them up, and give back to himself and to us only the pure wheat which has been sown in the first place. But, in fact, the just and real Emperor "whom they did not wish to reign over them," having instead chosen for themselves another emperor since they chose another God, will punish them for this disobedience and iniquity.

39. No Addressee

"Rebuke a wise man and he will love thee," says the wise proverb. Trusting in this, too, and emboldened a little by it as well as by the courage of our old friendship, I thought it necessary to rebuke you, because you are offending not man but the God of all. Besides, I think that you are wise and aspire to that old nobleness of character, though not to my friendship as much as I deserve. I do not know what offense I committed worthy of the present disdain, unless one could say that my offense is my unwillingness to follow doctrines alien to piety, abandoning the good and common confession of faith of the pious, which I have honored from childhood until now.

You, then, my excellent friend, appear to join in approving by words this good conduct, but by your acts you appear to believe the opposite and to agree with my opponents or, rather, with the opponents of the pure and holy Church of Christ

39

θαρᾷ καὶ θείᾳ τοῦ Χριστοῦ ἐκκλησίᾳ καὶ τοῖς θείοις τῆς εὐσεβείας ὅροις. δῆλον δέ· ἡμῖν μὲν γὰρ μόλις που καὶ σὺν ὄκνῳ καὶ ῥαθυμίᾳ καὶ δυσχερείᾳ πάσῃ πρὸς ὁμιλίαν ἔρχῃ, καὶ μετὰ πολλά τε καὶ πολλάκις τοῦτο ἡμᾶς ζητῆσαι, τοῖς δὲ αὐτόματος καὶ ἡδὺς καὶ χαρίεις προσφέρῃ καὶ πάντα προσφυῶς καὶ συνεχῶς ὁμιλεῖς· καὶ ὅλως λαβὼν τὸ ἡμέτερον ἐκείνοις ἀπένειμας οὕτω δὴ φανερῶς καὶ πεπαρρησιασμένως, ὥστε κἀκείνοις τοῦτο φρόνημα καὶ πρόβλημα καθ' ἡμῶν εἶναι μέγα, καὶ πολλοὺς αὐτοῖς ἐντεῦθεν συναπάγεσθαι καὶ ὀνειδίζειν ἡμῖν, ἡμῶν μὲν κατάγνωσιν εἶναι παρὰ σοῦ, τῶν ἐκείνων δὲ δογμάτων ἀποδοχήν, τὸ πρὸς μὲν ἐκείνοις εὐόμιλον, πρὸς δὲ ἡμᾶς δυσχερές σου.

Καὶ τοσοῦτ' ἐστὶ τοῦτ' ἀληθὲς καὶ σαφές, ὥστε μοι καὶ ἡ σὴ τοῦτο πρῴην ἀπήγγειλε σύνεσις, ὅτι δή σοί τις εἴποι καταγνῶναι μὲν ἡμῶν, συνθέσθαι δὲ ἐκείνοις. εἰ μὲν οὕτως εἶχε, καὶ καταγνοὺς τῆς μιᾶς τρισυποστάτου θεότητος καὶ τῆς αὐτοῦ τοῦ Θεοῦ πανταχοῦ παρουσίας, καὶ παρ' ἡμῖν τὰ ἐκείνων ἐπῄνεις, καὶ θεὸν ἄλλον ἢ θεότητας ἐλάττους τῆς θείας φύσεως καὶ ὑφειμένας ἀπειράκις ἀπείρως ἐνόμιζες ἐνεργεῖν τὰ ἡμέτερα—τό γε ἐκείνων δόγμα—καὶ μὴ αὐτὸν δι' αὐτοῦ τὸν ἕνα καὶ τριλαμπῆ δημιουργὸν τοῦ παντός, οὐκ ἂν ἴσως ἦν τοσοῦτον ἀνιαρόν, καίπερ ἀνιαρόν· ὁ γὰρ ἄκων τι πλημμελῶν, δι' ἄγνοιαν καὶ πλάνην τῆς διανοίας, συγγνωστότερος τοῦ μετὰ γνώσεως ἑκόντος τὸ κακὸν αἱρουμένου. νῦν δὲ καὶ εἰδὼς ἀσφαλῶς τὴν τῆς εὐσεβείας ἀσφάλειαν, καὶ μηδένα μήτε θεὸν ἄλλον μήτε θεότητα παρὰ τὸν ἕνα καὶ μόνον τὸν ἐν Τριάδι Θεὸν καὶ εἰδὼς καὶ ὁμολογῶν παρεῖναι πᾶσι καὶ πανταχοῦ, καὶ ζωογονεῖν καὶ φωτίζειν καὶ ἁγιάζειν πάντας, καὶ πάντα δι' ἑαυτοῦ ποιεῖν τε καὶ [fol. 48v] ἐνεργεῖν, τὸν ἐν ἀρρήτῳ Τριάδι θεολογούμενον, μίαν θεότητα, τὴν θείαν φύσιν αὐτήν, ἄκτιστον καὶ ὑπερούσιον, τὴν καὶ μόνην προσκυνητήν, ὡς ἂν ὁ μέγας εἴποι Βασίλειος, εἶτα τοῖς τἀναντία πάντα κηρύττουσι, καὶ ἡμᾶς διὰ τὴν εὐσέβειαν μισοῦσι καὶ ἀποστρεφομένοις, ἐπιμελῶς καὶ οἷον συμφυῶς καὶ θαυμαστῶς προσέχων, ἡμῶν δὲ ὑπερορῶν, πῶς οὐ σχέτλια ποιεῖς καὶ ἐναντία σαυτῷ τε καὶ τῷ τῆς εὐσεβείας λόγῳ; ἐῶ γάρ σου τὴν πάλαι σφοδρὰν ἐκείνην περὶ ἡμᾶς φιλίαν, ἣν νῦν περιφρονήσας ἄλλας καινὰς προτιμᾷς καὶ ἀντιθεραπεύεις. καὶ ταῦτα λέγω μὴ φθονῶν ἑτέροις τῆς σῆς περὶ αὐτοὺς φιλίας, οὐδὲ δόξης ἐπι-

---

30 ὑφειμένας cf. Palamam, *Epist. III ad Acindynum*, 15, Syngrammata, I, 306, 18–20; ed. Nadal, 252, 10–12 ‖ 30–31 Maxim. Conf., *Capit. theol.*, 1, 49 (PG, 90, 1101A) = Palamas, *Dialexis*, 24, Syngrammata, II, 186, 26; *Epist. ad Gabram*, 5, Syngrammata, II, 332, 12 ‖ 38 Joannis Chrysostomi *Liturgia* (ed. Brightman), 353, 13 ‖ 39 cf. *Horologion* (ed. Saliveros), 45 ‖ 42 Basil. Caes., *Adv. Eunom.* V (PG, 29, 733C)

and the holy rules of piety. And it is obvious that you associate with me hardly ever, and with hesitation and indifference and total discontent and after many and frequent requests from me, while you approach them willingly and pleasantly and graciously and converse with them always naturally and continually. And, generally, you have taken what belonged to me and have given it to them so conspicuously and openly, indeed, that even to them this is a matter of great pride and a pretext against me, and hence many have joined them, and they are reproaching me with the fact that your familiarity with them and your annoyance at me is a condemnation of me on your part and an acceptance of their doctrines.

And this is so true and clear that even your Wisdom announced to me recently that in fact someone told you to condemn me and to agree with them. If, then, things were so and you condemned the one divinity in three hypostases and God's own ubiquitous presence, and if you expressed praise of their doctrine to me and believed that another god or divinities lesser and "infinitely lower" than the divine nature operate our world—the doctrine of these men—and not alone the Creator of all Who shines with triple brightness, distressing though this is, it would not have been so distressing. For he who commits an offense unwillingly because of ignorance and mental error is more to be forgiven than the man who chooses evil willingly and knowingly. But now, although you know with certainty the infallible faith and know and confess that no other god nor divinity except the one and only God in the Trinity "is present" in everything and "everywhere" and gives life and "illuminates and sanctifies" all men and alone creates and operates all, the God Who is spoken of as God in ineffable Trinity, one divinity, the divine nature itself, uncreated and supersubstantial, "the only one, in fact, to be worshipped," as Basil the Great would say—do you not act offensively and contrary both to yourself and to the word of piety, when afterwards you neglect me and attach yourself with care and solidarity, as it were, and admiration to those men who preach all the contrary ⟨doctrines⟩ and hate me because of my piety and turn away from me? For I do not mention your old ardent friendship for me, which you have now scorned, preferring and cultivating instead other new ones. And I do not say this because I am jealous of your friendship for others, nor because I desire the honor that you would do me

39

θυμῶν ἧς ἂν με ἐδόξαζες τῶν ἄλλων διαφερόντως στέργων. οἶσθα γὰρ ἐκ τῶν πάλαι ὡς οὐκ ἦν πάνυ σφοδρὸς ἐγὼ ζητητὴς τῶν τοιούτων, εἰ καὶ ἄλλως φιλαμαρτήμων, μᾶλλον μὲν οὖν με τοὺς φιλικοὺς θορύβους οἶσθα κατὰ κράτος ἀναχωροῦντα καὶ παραιτούμενον. ἀλλὰ διὰ τὸν τῆς εὐσεβείας λόγον σπαράσσομαι τὰ σπλάγχνα καὶ διαπίμπραμαι, ὅτι μὴ μόνον ἄλλως ἡ πλάνη λαμβάνει χώραν ἐν τῇ τῆς εὐσεβείας μοίρᾳ, ἀλλὰ καὶ οἱ συνιέντες ταύτης ἀπ' ἄλλης καταφρονήσεως καὶ τῆς πρὸς τοὺς καιροὺς ταπεινότητος εἰς ἴσα τοῖς τῇ πλάνῃ κεκρατημένοις καθίστανται.

Ὢ οἷα παίζεται Θεός· καὶ τοῖς μὲν ἀσεβεῖται, τοῖς δὲ ἀσεβούμενος περιορᾶται, οἳ πότε ἂν πρὸς τύραννόν τινα πνέοντα δεινὸν κατὰ τῆς εὐσεβείας ἀντέστησαν, τοὺς πάλαι μάρτυρας τῆς ἀληθείας μιμούμενοι; ὁπότε ἀκινδύνως ἐξὸν εὐσεβεῖν καὶ ἀπωθεῖσθαι τὴν πλάνην, πάντων συντρεχόντων εἰς τοῦτο τῶν ἰσχυρῶν—τῆς τοῦ Χριστοῦ ἐκκλησίας, τῆς ἐκ Θεοῦ βασιλείας—οἵδ' ἑκόντες ὄντες τὴν ἑαυτῶν εὐσέβειαν προδιδόασιν οὐδενὸς κέρδους χάριν. οὐκ ἔμαθες ὡς κρείσσων ἐμπαθοῦς ὁμονοίας ἡ ὑπὲρ εὐσεβείας διάστασις παρὰ τοῦ θεολόγου καὶ τῶν ἄλλων πατέρων; οὐ παρ' αὐτοῦ τοῦ Χριστοῦ ὡς ὅστις ὁμολογήσει ἐν αὐτῷ ἔμπροσθεν τῶν ἀνθρώπων, ὁμολογήσει καὶ αὐτὸν αὐτὸς ἔμπροσθεν τοῦ πατρὸς αὐτοῦ τοῦ ἐν τοῖς οὐρανοῖς, ὅστις δὲ ἀρνήσεται ἢ παρασιωπήσεται τὴν ὑγιᾶ τῆς πίστεως ὁμολογίαν, ὁ Χριστὸς καὶ αὐτὸν ἐν τῷ παγκοίνῳ θεάτρῳ τῆς κτίσεως, ἔμπροσθεν τοῦ πατρὸς αὐτῷ κρινομένης, ἢ ἀρνήσεται ἢ παρασιωπήσεται; ἀγνοεῖς ὅτι τελευταῖός ἐστιν ὁ παρὼν ἤδη χρόνος καὶ αὐτὸς ὁ πάλαι θρυλούμενος τοῦ ἀντιχρίστου ἐν ᾧπερ ἀναστήσεσθαί τινας ψευδοχρίστους καὶ ψευδοπροφήτας τὰ θεῖα προανεφώνησε λόγια καὶ λέγειν ἰδοὺ ὧδε ὁ Χριστὸς καὶ ἰδοὺ ἐκεῖ, καὶ τὰ καὶ τά, οἷα νῦν [fol. 49^{r}] ἀκούεις ἀσεβῶς κηρυττόμενα; ἐν ᾧ πλανηθήσεσθαι, εἰ δυνατόν, καὶ τοὺς ἐκλεκτοὺς προηγόρευται; οὐ φοβηθήσῃ τὰς ἀκολάστους γλώττας καὶ τὸν καιρὸν τῆς πλάνης καί, συσταλεὶς ἀπ' αὐτῶν, πάσῃ δυνάμει φρουρήσεις σου τὴν εὐσέβειαν, μεθ' ἧς καὶ ζῶν μακάριος ἄνθρωπος καὶ ἀπελθὼν ἐνθένδε μακαριώτερος, καὶ ἧς χωρὶς ἄθλιος κἀκεῖ κἀνταῦθα, κἂν ὅλον τὸν παρόντα κόσμον κέρδος οἰκεῖον ποιήσηται; μὴ τοίνυν οὐδενὸς χάριν ζημιοῦ

66–67 Greg. Naz., *Or.*6, 11 (PG, 35, 736B) ‖ 68–71 cf. Matt. 10:32–33 ‖ 74–75 τελευταῖος . . . ἀντιχρίστου cf. I Joan. 2:18 ‖ 76–80 cf. Matt. 24:24–25; Luc. 17:23 ‖ 84–85 cf. Matt. 16:26; Luc. 9:25

---

75 θρυλλούμενος M

by loving me above all others. For you know from before that, although I am otherwise prompt to sin, I did not seek such things very eagerly; rather, you know that I avoid completely and decline the acclamations of friends. But my heart is rent to pieces and burnt up for the sake of piety, because not only does the deceit otherwise find acceptance as if it were piety, but also those who perceived it become just like those who have been conquered by it, because of a different form of neglect and opportunism (?).

O what sport is made of God! And while some insult Him, others neglect Him while He is being insulted! When would these men imitate the old martyrs of truth and rise up against a tyrant who breathes forth terror against piety? When it is possible to be pious and repel deceit with no risk, since all the powerful concur in this—the Church of Christ; the divine Emperor—these men willingly betray their piety for no profit at all! Did you not learn from the Theologian and the other Fathers that "discord for the sake of piety is better than fervent concord"? Did you not learn from Christ Himself that "Whoever will acknowledge Him before men, He too will acknowledge him before His Father in heaven"; and "whoever will disown Him" or keep silent about the sound confession of faith, Christ will also disown him or pass him over in silence when judgment is made before His Father on the common stage of the creation? Are you not aware that this is the end of time, the very age of anti-Christ, of which they spoke long ago, when, as the gospel predicted, "Some impostors will come claiming to be Messiahs or prophets, and they will say, 'Look, here is Christ,' or 'There He is,' " and such things as you hear now impiously proclaimed? At which time it was prophesied that even "God's chosen will be misled, if such a thing were possible"? Will you not fear the dissolute tongues and the age of deceit and draw away from them and guard, with all your strength, your piety, with which a man is blessed not only when he is alive, but even more blessed when he has left this world, and without which he is miserable both there and here, even if he "should win for himself the entire world"? Do not, therefore, lose the important

τὰ μεγάλα, μηδὲ δεινὸς ὢν τἄλλα καὶ δεξιός, εἴπερ τις, οὐχ ὅμοιος τὰ πρὸς τὸ θεῖον ἴσθι· ἀλλ'ὅτε αὐτὸ μὴ μᾶλλον, μηδὲ γοῦν ἧττον τῶν ἀνθρωπίνων ἄγε—μᾶλλον δὲ ὅτε σοι μὴ θάνατος ἀνθαιρετέος ἐστὶ τοῦ τῆς εἰς τὸ θεῖον παροινίας ἀκούειν—ἀλλὰ μηδὲ συνὼν συνήδου τοῖς ὑβρισταῖς τοῦ Θεοῦ.

Ἐβουλόμην καὶ λόγον ὅλον σοι περὶ τούτων ὑφῆναι, καὶ διὰ σοῦ τοῖς ἄλλοις οἷς ἐμπίπτειν ἀπροόπτως συμβαίνει τοῖς παροῦσι βαράθροις. ἐκεῖνο δὲ λογισάμενος τῶν πλειόνων ἀπέσχον, ὡς εἰ μὲν ἡμῶν τι καὶ ὁπωσοῦν φροντίσοις καὶ μὴ ἀπαξιώσοις τὴν ἡμετέραν παραίνεσιν, φίλου νομίσας αὐτὴν καὶ συμφέρουσαν εἶναι, ἀλλ'οὐκ ἐχθροῦ καὶ φαύλην, ἀρκέσει καὶ ταῦτα· εἰ δὲ ἀφροντιστήσοις ὡς ἀκαίρως ληρούντων, κἂν πλεῖστα συνείρω καὶ δεξιώτατα, μάτην πονήσω δήπου. προστίθημι δὲ καὶ τοῦτο τοῖς εἰρημένοις, ὡς εἰ μὲν ἐμέ τις ἐβλασφήμει καὶ οὐκ ἠγανάκτεις κατὰ τοῦ λοιδοροῦντος, εἰ μὲν ἀπαθέστερος ἔμενον ἐγὼ καὶ οὕτως ὑπερεώρων τῶν εἰς ἐμὲ γινομένων, οὐκ ἂν πρὸς σὲ διὰ τοῦτο πολὺν ἐποιούμην τὸν λόγον· εἰ δὲ ἐμικροψύχουν, τότε ἄν σε ἠνώχλουν ἀναμιμνήσκων τῶν χρόνων τῶν παλαιῶν ἐκείνων ἐν οἷς τι πλέον πρὸς ἐμὲ τῶν ἄλλων ἔπασχες τὰ εἰς φιλίαν, οὐχ ἧττον αὐτὸς οὗ παρεῖχες λαμβάνων, ἅπερ οὐκ ἦν καλὸν περιφρονεῖν ἐνταῦθα, οὐδὲ πρὸς ἀνδρὸς ἀγαθοῦ καὶ βεβαίου. ἐπεὶ δὲ περὶ τὸ θεῖον ἡ βλασφημία καὶ τὰ παρόντα δεινά, εἰ μὲν μηδὲν τῆς δόξης τοῦ Θεοῦ προτιμήσεις, ἀντιδοξασθῇ σοι παρ' αὐτοῦ τὰ γιγνόμενα καὶ νῦν καὶ μετὰ ταῦτα· εἰ δὲ τοῦ Θεοῦ τὰ ἀνθρώπινα προθήσῃ καθ' οἱονδήποτε τρόπον, ἐ γ ὼ π ρ ᾶ γ μ α ο ὐ κ ἔ χ ω, τῶν πατέρων τις ἔφη, διαμαρτυράμενός σοι καὶ ἅπαξ καὶ δὶς καὶ πλειονάκις ἤδη, καὶ νῦν ἀναθεὶς αὐτῷ τῷ Θεῷ τῶν ἑαυτοῦ φροντίσαι.

40. Sine titulo

Ἧκεν εἰς ἡμᾶς ψευδὴς μέν, ὡς ἐγῷμαι, καὶ συκοφάντης λόγος, ἧκε δ' οὖν ὡς ἄρα σύ τῳ πεισθείης, ὃς Χαρατζᾶς ὀναμάζεται, ἀσφαλῶς ἔχειν καὶ ὁμοφώνως τοῖς πάλαι κειμένοις ἡμῖν τῆς εὐσε-

---

109 cf. *Vita Danielis* (ed. Clugnet, *Revue de l'orient chrétien*, 5 [1900]), 259 (?)

---

107 ἀντιδοξασθήσῃ M

40: Mn 9ʳ–11ᵛ. Ed. Karpozilos, *Letters*, 102–107, no. 15. Huius epistolae partem edidit Uspenskij, *Synodikon*, 80.

3 τῆς] τοῖς Mn

things for the sake of anything else, nor while you, more than anyone else, are marvelous and skillful in all else, be different where God is concerned. But if you do not value God above human matters, at least do not value Him less, especially when death is not the alternative to listening to the abuse of God, nor keep company and rejoice with those who insult Him.

I even wanted to write a whole discourse about this for you and through you for the others who happen to fall unwarily into the present pits. But I refrained from writing more, because I thought that even this would be sufficient for you, if you should pay ever so little attention to me and not scorn my advice, considering it to be friendly and profitable and not hostile and malevolent. But if you should pay no heed to me, as if I were talking inopportune nonsense, even if I argue a great deal and most skillfully, I will certainly labor in vain. And I add this to what I have already said, that if someone spoke ill of me and you were not annoyed at him, if I remained unaffected and thus overlooked what was happening to me, I would not talk to you much about it; but if I were petty, then I would bother you by reminding you of those bygone years when you cared a little more for me than for others, receiving no less than you gave—things which it was not right to disregard now, nor befitting a good and steadfast man. But since the blasphemy and the present evils have to do with God, if you will prefer nothing to the glory of God, you will be in return glorified by Him for your deeds now and hereafter. But if you, in any way whatsoever, put the affairs of men before God, "I have nothing to do with it," as one of the Fathers said, for I have protested to you once and twice and many times already, and now I have left it up to God Himself to look after His own.

40. No Addressee

A rumor reached me—false and slanderous, as I believe—but it did reach me, namely, that someone by the name of Charatzas persuaded you that Palamas' "newfangled talk" is sound and in agreement with the traditional laws of piety,

40

βείας ὅροις τὰς Παλαμίτιδας καινοφωνίας, ᾧπερ ἔγωγε παντὸς μᾶλλον ἠπίστησα. πῶς γὰρ ὁ σοφὸς τὰ θεῖα τῷ γε μηδὲν εἰδότι καὶ ὁ τῷ μεγάλῳ Παύλῳ πειθόμενος, κἂν ἄγγελος ἐξ οὐρανοῦ εὐαγγελίσηται ὑμῖν παρ' ὃ παρελάβετε, κἂν ἐγὼ Παῦλος, ἀνάθεμα ἔστω, τοῖς εὐσεβεῖν ἐθέλουσιν ἐπι-[fol. 9v]τάττοντι, τῷ σφόδρα δυσσεβῶς καινοφωνοῦντι πεισθήσεται; τίς γὰρ πώποτε καὶ παρὰ τίνι τῶν τῆς εὐσεβείας τροφίμων ἐκκλησιῶν δύο θεοὺς ἢ θεότητας ἤκουσε συναϊδίους, καὶ τὴν μὲν ὑπερκειμένην ἀπειράκις ἀπείρως, τὴν δ' ὑφειμένην, ἢ τὴν μὲν ἐνεργοῦσαν, τὴν δ' ἐνεργουμένην, ἢ τὴν μὲν οὐσίαν οὖσαν, τὴν δὲ ἀνούσιον, καὶ τὴν μὲν ἀόρατον, τὴν δὲ καὶ σωματικοῖς ὀφθαλμοῖς τινων καθ' αὐτὴν ὁρωμένην, μᾶλλον δὲ μὴ μόνον οὕτως ἀνίσους ἀλλήλαις καὶ ἀνομοίους καί, ὡς εἰπεῖν, ἐναντίας, ἀλλὰ καὶ ἴσας καὶ ὁμοτίμους, καὶ ὡσαύτως καὶ οὔσας καὶ ἐνεργούσας καὶ ἀοράτους, πλείους δὲ μιᾶς οὔσας; ἢ τίς τὴν μίαν ἐν τῇ παντουργῷ Τριάδι θεότητα εἰς ἀπείρους διεῖλεν ἀνίσους, ὡς εἴρηται, καὶ ἀνομοίους, καθάπερ ὁ Παλαμᾶς; ἢ τὰ οὐσιώδη καὶ φυσικὰ τοῦ Θεοῦ εἰς τὴν τῶν ἐνεργουμένων μοῖραν ὑπὸ Θεοῦ κατεβίβασε καὶ διεῖλε καὶ ὑπεβίβασε τῆς θείας φύσεως ἀπειράκις ἀπείρως, ἢ ἐξ ἐνεργούσης οὐσίας καὶ πλήθους θεοτήτων ἐνεργουμένων, καὶ οὕτως ἀνίσων καὶ ἀνομοίων καὶ παντάπασι διαφόρων ἀλλήλων καὶ τῆς θείας ὑφειμένων ἀξίας ἀπειράκις ἀπείρως, μίαν ἐδίδαξεν εἶναι θεότητα σύνθετον;

Οὐ μονάδα θεότητος ἐν ὑποστάσεων τριάδι προσκυνεῖν μεμαθήκαμεν; οὐ πολὺ μᾶλλον ἡμεῖς εὐσεβέστερον λέγομεν τῆς πολυειδοῦς καὶ πολυμεροῦς τῶν αἱρετικῶν θεότητος ὅτι τὴν μίαν ἐν τῇ Τριάδι θεότητα φρονοῦμεν, κατὰ τὸν μέγαν εἰπεῖν καὶ σοφὸν Ἀθανάσιον; οὐ κατὰ τὸν πρὸ τούτου θαυμαστὸν Διονύσιον τὸν Ἀρεοπαγίτην, χρὴ καὶ ἡμᾶς ἀπὸ τῶν πολλῶν ἐπὶ τὸ ἓν τῇ δυνάμει τῆς θεϊκῆς ἑνότητος ἐπιστρεφομένους ἑνιαίως ὑμνεῖν τὴν ὅλην καὶ μίαν θεότητα, τὸ πάντων αἴτιον ἕν, τὸ πρὸ παντὸς ἑνὸς καὶ πλήθους;

40: 6–8 Gal. 1:8–9 || 11–12 *ὑπερκειμένην, ὑφειμένην*: cf. Palamam, *Epist. III ad Acindynum*, 15, Syngrammata, I, 306, 18–20; ed. Nadal, 252, 10–12 || *ἀπειράκις ἀπείρως*: cf. Maxim. Conf., *Capit. theol.*, 1, 49 (PG, 90, 1101A) = Palamas, *Dialexis*, 24, Syngrammata, II, 186, 26; *Epist. ad Gabram*, 5, Syngrammata, II, 332, 12 || 22 et 25 Maxim. Conf., *Capit. theol.*, 1, 49 (PG, 90, 1101A) = Palamas, *Dialexis*, 24, Syngrammata, II, 186, 26; *Epist. ad Gabram*, 5, Syngrammata, II, 332, 12 || 29–30 Athanasius, *Contra Arrianos* III, 15 (PG, 26, 353B) || 32–35 Dion. Areop., *De divin. nomin.*, 13, 3 (PG, 3, 980C)

---

8 *εὐσεβεῖν* scripsi: *εὐσεβέσιν* Mn || 27 *τριάδι ἄδι* Mn || 30 *θεότητι* Mn

which I, of course, believe less than anyone else. For how will a man who is wise about divine matters and who listens to the great Paul enjoining those who wish to be pious: "If an angel from heaven, if I, Paul, should preach to you a gospel at variance with the gospel which you received, let him be outcast!"—how will he be convinced by a man who is ignorant and preaches newfangled doctrines most profanely? For what man, nourished by piety at any of the churches, ever heard of two coeternal Gods or divinities, "one infinitely higher and the other lower," or one activating and the other activated, or one being the essence and the other not; and one invisible, while the other is perceived in itself even by the bodily eyes of some; rather, not only unequal to each other in this manner and dissimilar and, so to speak, opposed, but also equal and held in equal honor, and both being and acting in like manner, and being invisible and more than one? Or who was it who divided the single divinity in the all-creating Trinity into innumerable unequal and dissimilar ones, as I mentioned, just as Palamas did? Or who reduced the essential and natural attributes of God to the lot of that which is activated by God, and distinguished them from, and subordinated them "infinitely" to the divine nature; or taught that there is one divinity composed of an activating essence and a multitude of activated divinities, and thus unequal and dissimilar and altogether different from one another and "infinitely" lower than the divine sublimity?

Have we not learnt to worship a single divinity in three hypostases? Do we not say much more piously than the multiform and manifold divinity of the heretics that "we believe in one divinity in the Trinity," to use the words of the great and wise Athanasios? "Must we not," in accordance with his predecessor, the admirable Dionysios the Areopagite, "turn our attention, with the strength of the divine unity, from the many to the one, and praise without division the one and whole divinity, the one cause of all, which existed before every monad and multitude"? Is there not

40

οὐχ εἷς Θεὸς ἡμῖν ὅτι μία θεότης, κατὰ τὸν θεολόγον; οὐχ ἕνα μὲν ὅρον εὐσεβείας νομίζειν παρ' αὐτοῦ μεμαθήκαμεν, προσκυνεῖν τὸν Πατέρα καὶ τὸν Υἱὸν καὶ τὸ ἅγιον Πνεῦμα, τὴν μίαν ἐν τοῖς τρισὶ θεότητα καὶ δύναμιν, μηδὲν ὑπερσέβοντες, μηδ' ὑποσέβοντες (τὸ μὲν γὰρ ἀδύνατον, τὸ δὲ ἀσεβές), μηδὲ μέγεθος ἓν ὀνομάτων καινότησι διακόπτοντες (ὅτι μηδὲν ἑαυτοῦ μεῖζον ἢ ἔλαττον), τὰς δὲ περιττὰς καὶ ἀχρήστους παραφυάδας καὶ παρεξόδους ἐκκόπτειν; οὐ τὴν εἰς Πατέρα καὶ Υἱὸν καὶ ἅγιον Πνεῦμα, κατ' αὐτόν, ὁμολογίαν ἀκλινῆ καὶ βεβαίαν φυλάξομεν, μηδὲν προστιθέντες, μηδ' ἀφαιροῦντες, μηδὲ σμικρύνοντες τῆς μιᾶς θεότητος (τὸ γὰρ ἐλαττωθὲν τοῦ παντός ἐστιν ἐλάττωσις), τοὺς δ' ἄλλο τι φρονοῦντας ἢ λέγοντας ὡς λύμην τῆς ἐκκλησίας καὶ τῆς ἀληθείας ἰὸν ἀπωσόμεθα, οὐ μισοῦντες, ἀλλ' ἐλεοῦντες τοῦ πτώματος; οὐ πῶς δὲ μετρεῖται τὸ ἄπειρον, ἵν' ὃ τῶν περατουμένων ἐστί, τοῦτο πάθοι θεότης βαθμοῖς μετρουμένη καὶ ὑποβάσεσι, πρὸς τοῦ αὐτοῦ ἀκηκόαμεν; οὐ πρὸς τοῦ θείου τῆς Νύσσης Γρηγορίου ὅτι μία τίς ἐστιν ἐξουσία καὶ δύναμις ἡ τοῦ παντὸς ἀναδεδεγμένη τὸ κράτος καὶ βασιλεύουσα; οὐχ ὥσπερ ἕνα Θεὸν φρονεῖν ἐδιδάχθημεν, οὕτω καὶ μίαν θεότητα ὁμολογεῖν παρειλήφαμεν, κατὰ τὸν μέγαν Σωφρόνιον; οὐχ οὗτός ἐσθ' ὁ κηρύττων, ἀριθμεῖται ἡ παναγία Τριὰς οὐκ οὐσίαις ἢ φύσεσιν ἢ διαφόροις θεότησιν, ἀλλ' ὑποστάσεσι μόνον; καὶ πάλιν, ἥ τε γὰρ ἁγία Τριὰς ἀριθμεῖται προσώποις [fol. 10r] καὶ ὑποστάσεσιν, ἥ τε παναγία μονὰς πάσης ἐκτός ἐστιν ἀριθμήσεως; οὐχ ὁ θεσπέσιος Μάξιμος, ἕν ἐστί, φησι, τὸ ὑπερούσιον ἀγαθόν, ἡ ἁγία τρισυπόστατος μονάς; καὶ πάλιν, αὐτὸ κατ' οὐσίαν νόησίς ἐστιν ὁ Θεὸς καὶ ὅλος νόησις καὶ μόνον, καὶ αὐτὸ κατὰ τὴν νόησιν οὐσία καὶ μόνον, διότι μονὰς ἀδιαίρετος καὶ ἀμερὴς καὶ ἁπλῆ; οὐ συνοδικὸς τῆς εὐσε-

---

36 Greg. Naz., *Or.* 31, 14 (PG, 36, 148D) || 37–44 Greg. Naz., *Or.*22, 12 (PG, 35, 1144C) || 45–52 *idem*, *Or.*36, 10 (PG, 36, 277B) || 52–54 *idem*, *Or.*18, 16 (PG, 35, 1005A) || 55–57 Greg. Nys., locum non inveni || 57–59 Sophronius, *Epist. syn. ad Sergium*, (PG, 87^3, 3156A || 60–62 *ibid.*, 3156C || 62–64 *ibid.*, 3152D || 65–66 Maxim. Conf., *Capit. quinq.*, I, 1 (PG 90, 1177A) || 66–69 Maxim. Conf., *Capit. theol.*, 1, 82 (PG, 90, 1116C–1117A)

---

46 ἀκλινεῖ Mn

for us, according to the Theologian, "only one God, because there is only one divinity"? Have we not learnt from him "to believe in one pious rule: to worship the Father and the Son and the Holy Spirit, the one divinity and power in three ⟨hypostases⟩, without honoring anything more or less (for the former would be impossible and the latter impious), nor cutting up the single sublimity with novel terms (for nothing is greater or smaller than itself), but ⟨have we not learnt⟩ to cut off the superfluous and useless offshoots and deviations"? "Shall we not," according to him, "preserve our confession ⟨of faith⟩ in the Father and the Son and the Holy Spirit unswerving and steadfast, without adding or taking away anything, and without diminishing the one divinity (for any diminution is a diminution of the whole), and shall we not push away those who think or speak otherwise as a bane of the Church and poison of the truth, not hating them but pitying them for their fall"? Have we not heard from the same man: "How is the infinite to be measured, so that what applies to finite beings should apply to divinity when it is measured by degrees and successive diminutions"? Did we not hear from the divine Gregory of Nyssa that "There is only one authority and power: ⟨namely⟩, that which reigns and possesses the overall power"? "Have we not been taught by tradition to acknowledge one divinity, just as we were taught to believe in one God," according to the great Sophronios? Is it not he who proclaims: "The All-holy Trinity is not numbered according to essences or natures or different divinities, but according to hypostases alone"? And again: "For the Holy Trinity is numbered according to persons and hypostases and the All-holy Monad transcends all numbering"? Does not the divine Maximos say: "The supersubstantial Good is one, the Holy Monad in three hypostases"? And again: "This is what God is with respect to essence: intelligence. He is all intelligence and only intelligence; and that is, with respect to intelligence He is essence and only essence. For He is a simple monad, admitting of no division or partition"? Is it not a synodal rule of piety that "He is a Christian who believes that

40

βείας ὅρος, Χριστιανός ἐστιν ὁ πιστεύων μίαν εἶναι θεότητα ἐν ἴσῃ ἐξουσίᾳ Πατρὸς καὶ Υἱοῦ καὶ ἁγίου Πνεύματος, ὁ δὲ παρὰ ταῦτα δοξάζων αἱρετικός ἐστι; καὶ ἁπλῶς, ἵνα μὴ πάντα λέγων οὐδαμῇ λήγω λέγων, ἄπειρα γὰρ τὸ πλῆθος τὰ τοιάδ' ἄν τις εὕροι, οὐ παρὰ πάντων ταύτην τῶν ἱερῶν πατέρων καθαρὰν καὶ εὐσύνοπτον ἔχομεν τὴν εὐσέβειαν παρειληφότες;

Πῶς οὖν ἡ σὴ σοφία καὶ ἀσφαλὴς ἐπιστήμη καὶ θεοσέβεια, ὁτῳδήτινι πεισθεῖσα, ἕτερόν τι παρὰ ταῦτα ἐφρόνησεν; ἢ πῶς εὐσεβείας τὸ παράπαν μετεῖναι νενόμικε τοῖς Παλαμναίοις κηρύγμασιν; ἔστιν ἄρα θεότης ὑφειμένη καὶ ἄκτιστος, δῶρον οὖσα τῆς ὑπερκειμένης καὶ ὑπὲρ ταύτην τὴν θεότητά ἐστιν ὁ Θεός; καὶ πάλιν, ἔστιν ἄρα θεότης ἄλλη παρὰ τὴν οὐσίαν τοῦ Θεοῦ, συναΐδιος αὐτῇ καὶ ὑφειμένη αὐτῆς ὡς ἐνεργουμένη γε ὑπ' αὐτῆς καὶ ἀνούσιος; ἀεὶ γὰρ τὸ ἐνεργοῦν τῶν ἐνεργουμένων ὑπερέχει, καὶ τῶν ἀνουσίων ἡ οὐσία, καὶ τῶν ὀνομαζομένων τὸ ὑπερώνυμον. τίς γὰρ οὕτω τὴν παντουργὸν ἐνέργειαν τῆς θείας διέστησε φύσεως καὶ δύναμιν, ὥστε ἀνίσους καὶ ἀνομοίους καὶ ὅλως διαφόρους ἀλλήλων παραδοῦναι θεότητας, τὴν μὲν ὑπὲρ νόησιν, τὴν δὲ νοητήν, τὴν δὲ καὶ ληπτὴν σωματικοῖς ὀφθαλμοῖς τῶν οἷος ὁ Παλαμᾶς—καὶ λέγειν οὐδὲν ξένον, οὐδ' ἄτοπον—καὶ πολλὰς εἶναι καὶ μίαν ἀκτίστους θεότητας; πολλῶν γὰρ οὐσῶν εἶναι καὶ μίαν, μία μὲν γάρ φησιν ἡ ὑπερούσιός ἐστιν οὐσία τοῦ Θεοῦ, αἱ δὲ ἄλλαι, εἴτε μία εἴτε δύο εἴτε πλείους, καὶ οὕτως εἰς ἄπειρον ἀριθμὸν προάγει τὸ πλῆθος τῶν θεοτήτων. ὅλως δὲ τίς ἄκτιστα πολλὰ τῶν τροφίμων ἐξεφώνησεν εἶναι τῆς εὐσεβείας ἀνδρῶν καὶ τούτων ἄνω καὶ ὑψηλότερον οὐσιωδῶς τὸ θεῖον, καθάπερ ὁ Παλαμᾶς ἀρτίως; φησὶ γὰρ ὁρᾷς πολλὰ ἄκτιστά τε καὶ ἄναρχα περὶ Θεὸν οὐσιωδῶς θεωρούμενα, καὶ τούτων ἄνω καὶ ὑψηλότερον τὸ θεῖον, καὶ εὐσεβὴς οὐ νενόμισται τοῖς εὐσεβέσιν, ἐπιμένων τῷ δόγματι· ἓν εἶναι καὶ ἀμερὲς τὸ θεῖον καὶ ἀδιαίρετον καὶ παντελῶς ἀδιάφορον ἑαυτοῦ, πλὴν τῶν κατὰ πρόσωπα ἰδιωμάτων, πρὸς πάντων τῶν θείων ἡμῶν πατέρων καὶ θεολόγων παραδοθέν, καὶ οὐδὲν τῶν ἄλλων ὅλως αὐτῷ συναΐδιον, οὐ μεῖζον, οὐκ ἴσον, οὐκ ἔλαττον.

Πῶς δ' ἂν ὁ γράφων ἐμοὶ καὶ τὸ πάλαι κείμενον ἐν αὐτῷ μυ-

70–73 Photius, *Nomocanon*, I, 1 (PG, 104, 980A) ‖ 80–81 Palamas, *Epist. III ad Acindynum*, 15, Syngrammata, I, 306, 18–20; ed. Nadal, 252, 10–12 ‖ 93 Palamas, *Dialexis*, 27, Syngrammata, II, 189, 23 ‖ 97–99 cf. Palamam, *De divinis operationibus*, 29, Syngrammata, II, 117, 14–16

---

98 οὐσιωδῶς οὐσιωδῶς Mn

40

there is one divinity with equal authority of Father, Son, and Holy Spirit, and whoever entertains other beliefs than these is a heretic"? And in short—in order that I shall not mention everything and in no way stop talking, for one can find an infinite number of such sayings—have we not inherited from all the holy Fathers this piety pure and easy to perceive?

How, then, did your wisdom and sound learning and piety trust in someone or other and have other thoughts than these? Or how could you believe that the Palamnaian doctrines have a claim to piety at all? "Is there, then, a lower" and uncreated "divinity which is the gift of a higher one," and is God above this divinity? And again, is there another divinity besides the essence of God, which is coeternal with and lower than the essence, because it is activated by it and is itself no essence? For the activating ⟨principle⟩ is always superior to things activated, and essence ⟨is superior⟩ to things without essence, and that which is above every name ⟨is superior⟩ to things that can be designated by name. For who was the man who separated the all-creating energy and power from the divine nature so as to teach unequal and dissimilar divinities, altogether different from one another, one incomprehensible and one comprehensible, and another even to be apprehended by the bodily eyes of such men as Palamas, and ⟨so as⟩ to say that it is not strange or absurd for many as well as one uncreated divinity to exist? For while there are many, there is also one, because the supersubstantial essence of God is one, so he says, and the others are "either one or two or more," and thus he raises the multitude of divinities to an infinite number. And, generally, who was the man who, nourished by the pious faith, proclaimed that there are many uncreated beings and that God is above them and higher in essence, just as Palamas did recently? For he says: "You see around God many uncreated and eternal beings visible in their essence, and God stands above them and higher." And when he insists on this doctrine, he is not considered pious by pious men, for all our holy Fathers and theologians have taught that God is one and admits of no partition or division or absolutely any differences in Himself, except the characteristic properties of the persons, and nothing else at all is coeternal with Him or greater or equal or smaller.

How is it, then, that a man writes to me, revealing the secret that lay heavily

στήριον ἀποκαλύπτων καὶ λέγων τὸν ἀρχαῖον αὐτοῦ πυρσὸν ἠλαττῶσθαι τῆς πρὸς ἐμὲ φιλίας ἐκ τῆς αἰτίας ταύτης ὅτι τὸν ταῦτα φρονοῦντα καὶ γράφοντα πεφωρακὼς οὐ πάλαι ἀπεπεμπόμην, ἀλλ' ἔστεργον, νῦν δέ με θαυμάζων καὶ μακάριον ἀποκαλῶν καὶ πάλιν εἰς ὕψος αἴρων τὸν πυρσὸν ἐκεῖνον τῆς πρὸς ἐμὲ φιλίας, ἐπειδὴ ταύτην τὴν ἀσέβειαν τοὺς πολλοὺς λεληθυῖαν ἥπερ ἐστὶν οὖσαν ἐξήλεγξα καὶ προὐκινδύνευσα τῆς εὐσεβείας, [fol. 10v] *πῶς οὗτος αὖθις μετέγνω καὶ μεθῆκε τὰ πρότερα, μεταμαθὼν τὴν τέως εὐσέβειαν, καὶ ὧν μὲν τρόφιμος ἦν ἐκ παιδὸς καὶ συνήθης, πρὸς τῶν θείων αὐτὰ παρειληφὼς πατέρων καὶ τῆς τοῦ Χριστοῦ θαυμαστῆς ἐκκλησίας ὡς διαθήκην καὶ κλῆρον αἰώνιον, ταῦτα νῦν ἀγνοήσας, οἷς δ' ἐπολέμει πρότερον ὑπὲρ τῶν καθεστώτων τῆς εὐσεβείας ὅρων ὡς ἀσεβέσι καὶ νῦν καινουργηθεῖσι, τούτοις ἀρτίως κατ' ἐκείνων πεισάμενος, καὶ ἀντὶ τοῦ πείθειν ἐπιχειρεῖν τοὺς ἄλλους καὶ ἀνορθοῦν μὲν τοὺς πεπτωκότας ἤδη, προασφαλίζεσθαι δὲ ὥστε μὴ τοῦτο παθεῖν τοὺς μήπω νενοσηκότας, αὐτὸς πεπτωκὼς εἰς ὅπερ ἀπετρέπετο πρῴην καὶ τοὺς ἄλλους ἀπέτρεπε νόσημα, καὶ ταῦτα πεισθεὶς ἀνθρώποις οὐδ' ἑαυτοὺς εἰδόσιν, οὐδὲ δὴ τὰ ἐν ποσὶ καὶ πᾶσιν ὁρώμενα μὴ ὅ τι τὰ ὑπὲρ ἔννοιαν; οὐκ ἔστι ταῦτα· οὐκ ἔστιν.*

Οὐ *ταῦθ' ἡμᾶς ἡ σὴ σοφία καὶ ἀρετὴ πείθει δέξασθαι, καὶ ταῦθ' ἡνίκα ὑπὸ τῆς θείας ἐκκλησίας ἡ καινότης κατέγνωσται καὶ ἀσεβῶν χώραν ἔλαβε, καὶ τῆς ἐκ* Θεοῦ *καθεστώσης εὐσεβοῦς βασιλείας, τῆς θειοτάτης δεσποίνης ἡμῶν καὶ τοῦ εὐσεβεστάτου παιδὸς μὲν αὐτῆς, ἡμῶν δὲ βασιλέως, καὶ τῆς συγκλήτου πάσης, τοῦ τε θειοτάτου καὶ οἰκουμενικοῦ πατριάρχου μετὰ τῶν περὶ αὐτὸν ἁπάντων θείων τε ἀρχιερέων καὶ τῶν οἳ τὸν θεσπέσιον κλῆρον τῆς ἱερᾶς καὶ μεγάλης ἐκκλησίας κοσμοῦσι, καὶ τῶν ἐν τοῖς καὶ θείοις φροντιστηρίοις τῶν τε κατὰ κοινὸν συννενευκότων βίον καὶ τῶν ἰδιώτατα φιλοσοφούντων, καὶ πάντων ἁπλῶς, πλὴν ὧν ἥδε ἡ πλάνη βαθέως καθήψατο, οὐδὲ αὐτῶν ἀντιλέγειν τολμώντων. τί γὰρ ἂν ἀντιλέγοιεν πρὸς οὕτω φανερὰν τὴν ἀλήθειαν; ἀλλ' ἤτοι φιλίας οὐκ ὠφελίμου πάθη πρὸς τοὺς καινοφωνοῦντας, ἢ τῆς πρὸς ἐμὲ δυσμενείας προκατασχούσης τινάς, ἢ τῆς πολλῆς ἀγνοίας καὶ ἅμα οἰήσεως περὶ αὐτοῦ ὅτι* Θεὸν *ὁρῴη, ὃν οὐδεὶς εἶδεν οὐδὲ ἰδεῖν δύναται, κατὰ τοὺς διδασκάλους τῆς εὐσεβείας ἡμῶν καὶ αὐτὸ τοῦτο καλῶς ἰδόντας τὸ θέαμα ὡς ἀληθῶς τὸ θειότατον, ὅτι* Θεὸν *ἰδεῖν καὶ* Θεοῦ *μορφὴν φυσικήν, ἥτις ποτ' ἐστίν, ὡς ἔχει, τῶν ἀδυ-*

139–140 I Tim. 6:16

---

106 *ἀποκαλύπτ*[ω]*ον* Mn ‖ 110 *αἴρων* Mn ‖ *πρὸς* Mn[sv] ‖ 128 post *ἡμῶν* scripsit *καὶ ὄντως καὶ* et deinde *ὄντως* delevit Mn ‖ 133 *συνενευκότων* Mn ‖ 137 *πάθοι* Mn

on him for such a long time and saying that his old torch of friendship has weakened for this reason, namely that, though I had detected the man who thought and wrote these things, I did not send him away long ago, but continued to love him; and that now he admires me and calls me blessed and again raises high that torch of friendship for me because, although that impiety had escaped most men, I showed it up for what it was and bore the brunt of the battle for piety—how did this man, in turn, change his mind and give up his previous beliefs and unlearn his former piety? And how has he now come to ignore the doctrines with which he was nourished and was familiar since childhood, having received them from the holy Fathers and the marvelous Church of Christ as a testament and eternal legacy; and how has he gone against them, trusting now in those doctrines which previously he fought as impious and newfangled, while supporting the established rules of piety? And instead of attempting to persuade others and set right those who had already fallen and make sure that those who were not yet sick did not suffer the same thing, he has himself fallen into that very disease from which he shrank before and turned others away! And that, because he trusted in men who know neither themselves nor indeed what lies in front of their feet for all to see, let alone the incomprehensible! It is not possible! It is not!

Your wisdom and virtue do not allow me to accept this, especially when this innovation has been condemned and placed in the category of the impious by the Holy Church and by the divinely established pious rulers, our most divine Empress and her most pious son and Emperor of ours; also by the whole senate and the most divine and Ecumenical Patriarch together with all the holy bishops around him, and those who adorn the divine clergy of the Holy and Great Church, and also by the monks in the holy monasteries, both those who have agreed to live in coenobitic communities and those who pursue asceticism in solitude, and in short by everybody, except those on whom this deception has a strong hold; in fact, even they do not dare to speak in opposition. For what could they say against such an obvious truth, except to mention the unfortunate accidents of either a harmful friendship with the innovators or of some men's hostility that has prejudiced them against me, or ⟨Palamas'⟩ great ignorance and, at the same time, conceit about himself, in claiming that he sees God "Whom no man has ever seen or ever can see," according to the teachers of our faith who also have seen clearly this most truly divine spectacle as it is, because it is impossible for a created being to see God and His natural form as it is, whatever that form may be. And for this reason God Himself spoke in

40

νάτων ἐστὶ πεποιημένη φύσει. καὶ διὰ τοῦτο Μωσεῖ τῷ μεγάλῳ καὶ θεοφιλεστάτῳ ποθοῦντι Θεὸν ἰδεῖν τὸν ποθούμενον, οὐδεὶς ὄψεταί μου τὸ πρόσωπον καὶ ζήσεται, αὐτὸς ὁ Θεὸς διὰ συμβόλων εἶπε· καὶ ὁ μονογενὴς υἱὸς αὐτοῦ ὁ ὢν ἐν τοῖς κόλποις τοῦ Πατρός, τῷ ἠγαπημένῳ μὲν ὑπ' αὐτοῦ, βροντῆς δὲ υἱῷ κληθέντι διὰ τὴν ἄρρητον καὶ ὑψηλὴν τῆς θεολογίας ἐκφώνησιν, Θεὸν οὐδεὶς ἑώρακε πώποτε· ὁ δὲ ἡμᾶς τοὺς ἄλλους ὡς ἀναγκαῖον ὂν μάθημα καὶ αὐτὸ τὸ κεφάλαιον τῆς εὐσεβείας ἐδίδαξε. καὶ ὁ μετ' αὐτὸν διαφερόντως τῆς θεολογικῆς αὐτοῦ χάριτος κληρονομήσας καὶ τῆς ἐπωνυμίας, θεότης, φησί, καθ' ἑαυτὴν ἀόρατος· τί γάρ; τὸ ὁρατὸν τοῦ ὁρῶντος; καὶ πόσον ἐστὶν ὑψηλότερόν τε καὶ θεοειδέστερον, ἵν' ᾖ τὸ μὲν προσκυνοῦν, τὸ δὲ προσκυνούμενον;

Ἃ νῦν ἀναιδῶς ἀνατρέπειν ἐσπούδακεν ὁ σφόδρ' ἀναιδὴς τῆς εὐσεβείας Τελχίν. εἰ δὲ τέμνων καὶ διαιρῶν τὴν μίαν τοῦ Θεοῦ φύσιν εἰς οὐσίαν καὶ οὐσιώδη—δύναμιν, χάριν, ἐνέργειαν, ζωήν, σοφίαν, ἀγαθότητα, δόξαν, μορφήν, καὶ ἁπλῶς ὅσα οὐσιωδῶς ὁ Θεὸς καὶ ὑπερφυῶς εἶναι λέγεται τοῖς ἱεροῖς πατράσι—καὶ τὴν μὲν οὐσίαν ὑπερτιθεὶς τῶν [fol. 11r] οὐσιωδῶν ἑαυτῆς, τὰ δ' ὑποτιθεὶς ἀπειράκις ἀπείρως, οὐ τὴν οὐσίαν ὁρᾶν τοῦ Θεοῦ προφασίζεται, ἀλλὰ τὴν οὐσιώδη καὶ φυσικὴν δόξαν αὐτῆς καὶ μορφήν, * * * ὅτι μὲν ἕν ἐστι διὰ πάντων τὸ θεῖον καὶ ἀδιάφορον, καὶ οὐκ ἄλλο μὲν τἀγαθόν, ἄλλο δὲ τὸ ὄν, ἄλλο δὲ ἡ ζωὴ καὶ ἕτερον ἡ σοφία, οὔκουν οὐδ' ἡ μορφὴ καὶ δόξα, οὐδὲ πολλαὶ θεότητες ὑπερέχουσαι καὶ ὑφειμέναι, ὡς διαρρήδην ὁ μέγας φησὶ Διονύσιος· ἀλλ' ἔστι τοῦτο τῆς Ἑλλήνων ἀγνοίας, αὐτός τε, οἶμαι, παντὸς μᾶλλον ἐπίστασαι κἂν ἄλλοις τούτων διδάσκαλος γένοιο, τοῦθ' ὁμοφώνως [τῶν] κηρυττόντων ἁπάντων τῶν ἱερῶν πατέρων ὅτι μορφὴ καὶ φύσις ἐπὶ Θεοῦ καὶ οὐσία ταὐτόν τι καὶ ἕν ἐστι.

Τίς δὲ οὐκ οἶδεν ὅτι καὶ τὰ τῶν κτισμάτων ἄϋλα καὶ νοητὰ καὶ ἀσώματα, καὶ ταῦτα παντάπασίν ἐστ' ἀπρόσιτα καὶ ἀνάλωτα σωματικοῖς ὀφθαλμοῖς, ἡ τῶν ψυχῶν λέγω καὶ πολὺ μᾶλλον ἡ

144–145 Exodus 33:20 || 146–147 Joan. 1:18 || 147–148 Marc. 3:17 || 149 Joan. 1:18 || 152–153 *θεότης . . . ἀόρατος* Greg. Naz., Epist. 101 (PG, 37, 181A) || 153–155 *idem*, *Or.* 28, 13 (PG, 36, 44B) || 162 *ἀπειράκις ἀπείρως* Maxim. Conf., *Capit. theol.*, 1, 49 (PG, 90, 1101A) = Palamas, *Dialexis*, 24, Syngrammata, II, 186, 26; *Epist. ad Gabram*, 5, Syngrammata, II, 332, 12 || 162–163 cf. Ps.-Athanasius, *Quaest. ad Antiochum ducem*, 28 (PG, 28, 616A) || 165–167 Dion. Areop., *De div. nom.*, 5, 2 (PG, 3, 816C) || 171–172 Joan. Dam., *Dialectica*, 41 (PG, 94, 608B) || 173–174 Plato, *Soph.*, 246B

---

146 *μονογεννὴς* Mn || 164 post *μορφὴν* lacunam statui || 170 [*τῶν*] uncis inclusi

40

symbols to Moses, the great and most dear to God, who was longing to see the longed-for God, saying: "No man shall see my face and live!" And "His only Son, He who is nearest to the Father's heart," said to the man who was dear to Him and has been called "Son of thunder" because of his ineffable and sublime expression of theology: "No one has ever seen God." And he taught the rest of us that this was a necessary lesson and the sum total of piety. And after him, the one who especially inherited his theological charisma and title said: "Divinity is invisible in itself." "For, surely, how can that which is perceived be the ⟨object of worship⟩ of that which perceives it? And how much higher and more divine is it in order to be the object of worship, while the other is the worshipper?"

A Telchin, so exceedingly shameless in regard to piety, has now shamelessly sought to overthrow these. And if, when he cuts and divides the single nature of God into essence and essential ⟨properties⟩—power, grace, energy, life, wisdom, goodness, glory, form, and, simply, all the things that the holy Fathers say that God essentially and supernaturally is—and if, when he places the essence above its own essential properties, while he lowers them "infinitely," he pretends that he "does not see the essence of God but" its essential and natural "glory" and form * * * because God is one and without difference throughout; and "goodness is not one thing, and being another, and life another, and wisdom another," therefore neither is form nor glory "nor many higher and lower divinities," as the great Dionysios explicitly states. But I believe that you know better than anyone else that this is a trait of pagan ignorance, and you could even instruct others about this, because all the holy Fathers with one voice proclaim that "form and nature and essence are one and the same thing with regard to God."

And who does not know that even those created beings which are immaterial and "intelligible and incorporeal" are also completely inaccessible and unattainable to bodily eyes—I mean the nature of souls and, much more, the nature of angels?

40

τῶν ἀγγέλων φύσις; διὸ καὶ ταῦτα συμβολικῶς ὁρᾶται, ὅτε καὶ οἷς ὀφθείη, ἀλλ᾽ οὐχὶ κατ᾽ οὐσίαν, ὡς ὁ μέγας φησὶν Ἀθανάσιος, διὰ τοῦτο, λέγων, πολλαὶ αὐτῶν αἱ μορφαί, μία δὲ ἡ οὐσία ἡ ἀθεώρητος· μορφὰς λέγων αὐτῶν ἃς ἄλλοτε ἄλλας συμβολικῶς ὑποδύονται, σχηματιζόμενοι πρὸς τὴν δύναμιν τῶν θεωμένων. καὶ ὁ μέγας Διονύσιος, οὐ δυνατόν ἐστι τῷ καθ᾽ ἡμᾶς νῷ, φησι, πρὸς τὴν ἄϋλον ἐκείνην ἀναταθῆναι τῶν οὐρανίων ἱεραρχιῶν μίμησίν τε καὶ θεωρίαν, εἰ μὴ τῇ κατ᾽ αὐτὸν ὑλαίᾳ χειραγωγίᾳ χρήσαιτο. καὶ ὁ θεολόγος, ἀγγελικὸν δὲ ἡ λαμπροφορία καὶ ἡ φαιδρότης, φησίν, ὅταν τυπῶνται σωματικῶς· σύμβολον, οἶμαι, τοῦτο τῆς κατὰ φύσιν αὐτῶν καθαρότητος. καὶ ὁ χρυσοῦς τὴν γλῶτταν περὶ ψυχῆς, διὰ τοῦτο καὶ τὴν ταύτης γνῶσιν ἀπέκλεισεν ὁ Θεὸς ἐκ πολλῆς περιουσίας ἐπιστομίζων ἡμᾶς καὶ κατέχων καὶ μένειν κάτω πείθων καὶ τὰ ὑπὲρ ἡμᾶς μὴ περιεργάζεσθαι μηδὲ πολυπραγμονεῖν. εἰ τοίνυν τὴν γνῶσιν ἡμῖν αὐτῆς ἀπέκλεισεν ὁ Θεός, πολλῷ μᾶλλον τὴν αἴσθησιν, ἡ γὰρ γνῶσις οἰκειοτέρα τοῖς ἀΰλοις καὶ ἀσωμάτοις καθ᾽ αὑτὴν τῆς αἰσθήσεως. καὶ εἰ κτίσμα ὄντα ἡ ψυχὴ καὶ ὁ ἄγγελος συμβολικὴν ἔχει τὴν αἰσθητὴν θεωρίαν ὡς ἄληπτα καθ᾽ αὑτὰ σωματικοῖς ὀφθαλμοῖς ὁτουδήποτε, πῶς ἡ θεία καὶ ἄκτιστος τοῦ Θεοῦ μορφὴ καὶ δόξα ληπτὴ καὶ ὁρατὴ καθ᾽ αὑτὴν τοῖς καινοῖς τούτοις ἐστὶ θεόπταις σωματικοῖς ὀφθαλμοῖς, ὁπότε καὶ διῃρημένη γε ἦν καὶ ὑφειμένη τῆς ἑαυτῆς οὐσίας, κατὰ τὴν οὐχ ὑφειμένην τινὸς ἀλλὰ πασῶν ὑπερκειμένην ἀσέβειαν;

Ταῦτα μὲν οὖν ἐστιν, οἶμαι, πᾶσι καὶ αὐτόθεν κατάδηλα, εἰ καί τινας ἐξηπάτησαν στροφαῖς δειναῖς πιθανότητος καὶ εἰς τὸ οἰκεῖον αὐτῶν κατέσπασαν βάραθρον· οὐ γάρ ἐστιν ἐκφυγεῖν πάντας παντάπασι τὴν τῆς καινοφωνίας λύμην ἐμπεσούσης εἰς ἐκκλησίαν ἅπαξ, ὥσπερ οὐδὲ νόσου λοιμώδους ἀθῴους ἀπαλλαγῆναι πάντας ἐμπεσούσης εἰς πόλιν· συχνοὺς μὲν οὖν ἐστιν ἀπαλλαγῆναι βίου ὡς ἔδειξαν αἱ πώποτε πρότερον αἱρέσεις ἑαυτὰς ταῖς ἐκκλησίαις εἰσφρήσασαι, διὸ καὶ ὁ μὲν θεῖος ἀπόστολος παραινεῖ Τιμοθέῳ, τὰς βεβήλους καινοφωνίας περιίστασο, λέγων, ἐπὶ πλεῖον γὰρ προκόψουσιν ἀσεβείας, καὶ ὁ λόγος αὐτῶν ὡς γάγγραινα νομὴν ἕξει· ὁ δὲ θεολόγος,

---

176–179 Ps.-Athan., *Quaest. ad Antiochum ducem*, 29 (PG, 28, 616B) || 181–185 Dion. Areop., *De coel. hier.*, 1, 3 (PG, 3, 121C–D) || 185–188 Greg. Naz., *Or.*25, 2 (PG, 35, 1200B) || 188–192 Joan. Chrys., *De incompr.*, 5, 4 (PG, 48, 741) || 199 cf. Palamam, *Epist. III ad Acindynum*, 15, Syngrammata, I, 306, 18–20; ed. Nadal, 252, 10–12 || 210–212 II Tim. 2:16–17

40

Wherefore, as the great Athanasios states, "these, too, are seen symbolically, but not in essence, whenever and by whomsoever they are seen," saying that "for this reason their forms are many, but their essence is one," that which is invisible. By forms he means the different forms they assume at different times symbolically, as they vary their appearance in accordance with the strength of the beholders. And the great Dionysios says: "It is not possible for our intellect to reach up to that immaterial imitation and contemplation of the celestial hierarchies unless it makes use of its own material guidance." And the Theologian says: "Brilliance and joy are a characteristic of the angels whenever they receive a bodily form; they are a symbol, I believe, of their natural purity." And John Chrysostom says about the soul: "For this reason God barred its knowledge, curbing us exceedingly and restraining and persuading us to remain below and not to be curious about things that are beyond us nor to busy ourselves about them." If, therefore, God barred the knowledge of the soul to us, much more the soul's sense perception, for knowledge is in itself more akin to the immaterial and incorporeal than sense perception. And if the soul and the angel, which are created beings, are symbolically perceived because they cannot be apprehended in themselves by the bodily eyes of any man whatsoever, how can the divine and uncreated form and glory of God be apprehended and seen in itself by these new God-seeing bodily eyes, when not only was it divided from but also placed lower than its own essence, not according to the lower, but to the highest impiety of all?

These things, then, in my opinion, are self-evident to all; although they deceived some by skillful tricks of persuasion and dragged them down with themselves to their own pit of death. For not everybody can escape completely the bane of the "newfangled talk" once it has fallen upon the Church, just as not everybody can escape the plague unscathed when it falls upon a city. Indeed, it is possible for many men to lose their lives, as the previous heresies have shown up till now, whenever they slipped into the Church. Wherefore the divine Apostle advised Timothy, saying: "Avoid the profane newfangled talk; those who indulge in it will stray further and further into godless courses, and the infection of their teaching will spread like gangrene." And the Theologian says: "Teach one thing only: the fear of de-

ἓν δίδασκέ, φησι, φοβεῖσθαι μόνον τὸ λύειν τὴν πίστιν ἐν τοῖς σοφίσμασι. [fol. 11v]

Πέπομφα δέ σοι κἀγὼ ἃ πρὸς τὴν θείαν καὶ ἱερὰν ἀνήνεγκα σύνοδον ἀπὸ κοινῆς τῆς γνώμης τῶν τὴν ἀρχὴν ἐνστάντων πρὸς τὰς βεβήλους καινοφωνίας ταύτας, ἐν οἷς εἰσι τούτων σαφέστατοι καὶ ἀναντίρρητοι ὡς ἀσεβῶν οὐσῶν ἔλεγχοι πρὸς τῶν θείων ἁπάντων καὶ ἱερῶν πατέρων. ἅπερ ἐπιεικῶς ἀναγνῶναι δεῖ σου τὴν ἱερότητα, οὐχ ὡς ἀγνοοῦσαν, ἀλλ' ὡς οἷς ἐπίσταται συνηγοροῦντα. σὺ μὲν οὖν καὶ εἶ καὶ εἴης ἐκεῖνος ὃν ἡμεῖς ἴσμεν καὶ ὁ εὐσεβέστατός τε καὶ τῆς εὐσεβείας ὑπέρμαχος καὶ ἡμέτερος ἀλείπτης πρὸς τοὺς ὑπὲρ αὐτῆς ἀγῶνας καὶ κατὰ τῆς νῦν φυείσης ἰταμωτάτης πλάνης, ὡς ταύτης τε προκαταγνοὺς καὶ ἐμοῦ, τῆς μὲν ὡς ἀσεβείας, ἐμοῦ δὲ ὡς ἀργοῦ γεγονότος πρὸς τοὺς ἐλέγχους αὐτῆς. ἐγὼ δέ σοι δεῖν ὑπείληφα τὴν ὁτουδήποτε περὶ σὲ βλασφημίαν δηλῶσαι, ὃν ἐγὼ δῆλός εἰμι πρὸ παντὸς ἄγων ἄλλου καὶ οὐδὲν ἧττον τῆς ἐμαυτοῦ κεφαλῆς, ἵν' εἰδὼς οὐκ ἀμελοίης τοῦ πᾶσιν ἀεὶ δεικνύναι ὡς ἔστιν οὐδενὸς ἧττον ἀπηχθημένη σοι καὶ ἀπόβλητος ἡ τοῦ Παλαμᾶ πονηροτάτη νόσος.

41. Τῷ Βρανᾷ

Ὃν ἡ Θεσσαλονικέων πόλις ἐπ' ἀρετῇ τε λόγων καὶ ζήλῳ εὐσεβείας τεθαύμακεν ἀδικοῖμεν ἂν ἡμεῖς μὴ θαυμάζοντες, παρ' οἷς καὶ οἷς ἐστι παραστάτης καὶ σύμμαχος κατὰ τῶν ἀσεβούντων ὁ καὶ Θεσσαλονικεῦσι θαυμαστὸς ἐπὶ τούτοις. πᾶν γὰρ ὁτιοῦν ἢ ἀποδεχομένης ἢ μὴ τῆς φύσεως τῆς ἡμετέρας, καὶ φαύλων ⟨μὲν ὄντων τῶν⟩ τὰ φαῦλα τιμώντων, ἀγαθῶν δὲ τῶν τὰ βελτίω τεθαυμακότων κατὰ τὸ ἐν τούτοις διάφορον, οὐ τοῦ κακοῦ πρὸς τἀγαθ⟨ὰ⟩ λέ⟨γομεν⟩ οὐδὲ πρὸς τοὺς ἀγαθοὺς τῶν φαύλων, ἀλλὰ καὶ πρὸς φαύλους φαύλων ⟨καὶ⟩ ἀγαθοὺς ἀγαθῶν, οὓς τὸ μᾶλλον καὶ ἧττον εἶναι πεφυκέναι τοιούτους οὐχ ἧττον ἐπλήθυνε ἢ Παλαμᾶς τὰς θεότητας σὸν τὸ μάλιστα εὐδοκιμεῖν περὶ τὴν κρείττω μοῖραν, ὅθεν εἰκότως καὶ τὸ θαυμάζεσθαι.

213–214 Greg. Naz., *Or.* 25, 18 (PG, 35, 1224B) || 217 II Tim. 2:16

41: Mn 1r–3r. Afflictum folium 1r edidit P. Wirth ("Ultraviolett-photostudien zu spätbyzantinischen Theologen," *Byzantion*, 34 [1964], 117–118) cujus editionem sequor. Ed. Karpozilos, *Letters*, 70–75, no. 1.

1 Αἱ ἐπιστολαὶ Mn: Τῷ Βρανᾷ scr. Wirth, cf. lineam 204 *infra*

stroying the faith through sophistries."

I have sent you also what I presented to the divine and holy Synod with the common consent of those who objected to this "profane newfangled talk" from the beginning. In these works there are most clear and irrefutable proofs that in the eyes of all the divine and holy Fathers this ⟨newfangled talk⟩ is impious. Your Holiness must read these with tolerance, not as if you did not know them, but as if they advocated what you know for certain. You, indeed, are and may you continue to be the man whom I know, the most pious and the defender of piety and my trainer for the contests in its behalf and against the most bold deception which has just sprung up; for you condemned that and me beforehand: that for being impious and me for having been too slow in exposing it. But I assumed that I ought to reveal to you the slander of someone or other against you, whom it is clear that I honor before anyone else and no less than myself, that you may know and not neglect to show everybody always that you despise and reject Palamas' most wicked disease more than anything else.

41. ⟨To Branas⟩

I would be unjust if I did not honor the man whom the city of Thessalonica honors both for his distinction in learning and his zealous piety, especially since he is my supporter and ally against the impious and is admired for this also by the Thessalonians. For our nature either approves of anything whatsoever or does not; and those who honor the bad are bad, while those who admire the better things are good, according to the difference among them. I do not mean just the difference between evil and good things or bad and good men, but also the difference between bad men and bad men, and between good men and good men whose natural tendency to be more or less so you increased by your extraordinary distinction in virtue no less than Palamas increased the divinities. You are, therefore, rightly honored.

41

Τοῦ γὰρ Παλαμᾶ καὶ τῆς αὐτοῦ φατρίας οὕτω πᾶσαν ἀσέβειαν παριόντων τοῖς δόγμασι, καὶ τῶν τῆς εὐσεβείας οὐκ ἐθελόντων ἀφίστασθαι, τῶν μὲν μᾶλλον, τῶν δ' ἧττον ἀγανακτούντων ⟨ἐπὶ ταῖς βεβήλοις καινο⟩φ⟨ων⟩ίαις αὐτοῦ, ⟨τοῖς⟩ δ' οὐδὲ μέλον, εἰ οἱ μὲν ἀσεβοῖ⟨εν καὶ τοῦ Χριστοῦ τὴν ἐκκλησίαν σ⟩παράττοιεν, οἱ δὲ πάσχοιεν κακῶς ἐπὶ τῷ τούτους ἀμύνεσθαι, οὐ δυσσεβ⟨έσι⟩ μέν, ψυχροῖς δὲ τὴν εὐσέβει⟨αν⟩ οὖσι, σὺ φα⟨ί⟩νῃ μηδενὶ τῶν πρώτων ἄ⟨θλ⟩ων παραχωρῶν καὶ τοσαύτῃ χρώ⟨μεν⟩ος περιουσίᾳ, ὥστε μὴ τοὺς ἐν ταῦθα μόνον κλονεῖ⟨ν⟩ καὶ καταβάλλειν φαινόμενος, ἀλλά τοι μηδὲ τοὺς ἀπωτάτ⟨ω τού⟩των ταῖς ἐκείνῃ πόλεσι λυμαινομένους ἐᾶν ἀ⟨θῴους τῶν⟩ σῶν β⟨ελ⟩ῶν περαίνειν τὰ ἑαυτῶν, οἷς καὶ τῶν ὧδε δήπου εὐσεβείᾳ συνόντων ἐγείρεις μὲν τοὺς ῥαθύμους, τοὺς δ' εὐψύχους εὐψυχοτέρους δείκνυς ἐπὶ ⟨τὴ⟩ν λύμην ταύτην· ⟨καὶ τὸ⟩ ἑτέροις παρακαλεῖσθαι πρὸς τὴν εὐσέβειαν γενναίως ἐκπέφευγας, μ⟨εγαλο⟩φυοῦς ἀνδρὸς εἶναι νομίσας οὐ τὴν παρ' ἑτέρων ἀναμένειν παράκλησιν, οὐδὲ παραδεί⟨γμασ⟩ιν ἑτέροις χρῆσθαι πρὸς τὰ τοιαῦτα—καίτοι καὶ τοῦτο καλόν—ἀλλ' αὐτὸν ἑαυτῷ τε καὶ τοῖς ἄλλοις ἀκόνην τὴν ἀρίστην ὑπάρχειν, ὥστε μηδ' ἐμοὶ ⟨νῦν⟩ μέλειν τῆς πρὸς σὲ παρακλήσεως, ἀλλ' ὅπως ἂν ἀξίως θαυμάσαιμί σου ⟨τήν τε⟩ παροῦσαν γνώμην ⟨καὶ τὴν πρὸς τὰ μέλλοντα⟩ παρασκευήν, καὶ πᾶν ἀγαθὸν εὖ ⟨χοίμην παρὰ⟩ Θεοῦ γενέσθαι καὶ δ⟨ύναμιν ἄμαχον κατὰ τῶν⟩ δυσσεβούντων σοί ⟨τε καὶ τοῖς σε μι⟩μουμένοις, δι' οὓς ἐλπίδες ⟨ἐμοὶ γενναῖαι τοῦ μὴ⟩ ἂν δυνηθῆν ⟨αι τὸ κακὸν⟩ προχωρῆσαι, καὶ κοῦφος ⟨ὁ διωγμὸς οὑτοσὶ καί, εἴ⟩ τῳ μὴ ἀπιστοίμην, ⟨αἱρε⟩τώτερος οὕτως ὑμῶν ἐχόντων τῆς ἄνευ ὑμῶν ῥᾳστώνης. οὕτως ἐγὼ χαίρω, πάντως δὲ καὶ ⟨ὁ Θεός—πῶς γὰρ⟩ οὔ;—τοῖς ὑμετέρ⟨οις⟩ ἀγῶσιν ὑπὲρ αὐτοῦ πρὸς τοὺς αὐτῷ δυσμ⟨ενεῖς. τοῦτο⟩ γενναίων ψυχῶν. τοῦτο παιδείας καὶ λόγων. τοῦτο φιλοσοφίας καρ⟨πὸς τῆς ἐν βίῳ⟩ [fol. 1ᵛ] καὶ λόγοις ἀληθής τε καὶ τρόφιμος, ὃν οἱ πολλοὶ πόνοι φέρουσιν, ὡς ἄνευ γε τούτου μάτην ἐμοὶ δοκοῦσιν ἑκατέροις ἀσκεῖσθαι καὶ λόγοι καὶ ἀρεταί, καθάπερ ἀγροὶ μηδὲν φέροντες μετὰ πολλὴν γεωργίαν καὶ πολὺν κάματον.

Ἐκεῖνο δέ σε καὶ αὐτὸν οἶμαι μὲν ἂν συνιδεῖν ᾧ τοσαύτη φροντίς ἐστιν ὑπὲρ τῆς εὐσεβείας σὺν ἀγχινοίᾳ τοσαύτῃ, οὐδὲν δὲ σκαιὸν εἰ κἀγὼ τοῦτο φαίην· ὁ θαυμάσιος Τρικανᾶς οἷς μὲν τοῦ δυσσεβοῦς Χαρατζᾶ ὡς δυσσεβοῦς καταφέρεται καλῶς ποιεῖ καὶ πρὸς

41: 16 II Tim. 2:16

---

17 βεβήλοις scripsi: ἐκείναις Wirth ‖ 21 χρώ⟨μεν⟩ος scripsi: χρώ ⟨ματ⟩ ος Wirth ‖ 24 ἀ⟨θῴους⟩ scripsi: ἀ⟨γεύστους⟩ Wirth ‖ 25 μὲν scripsi: μετὰ Wirth ‖ 28 μ⟨εγαλο⟩φυοῦς scripsi: μ⟨ετ' εὐ⟩φυοῦς Wirth ‖ 45 πολὺ κάματον Mπ

41

For when Palamas and his faction greatly surpass all impiety with their doctrines, and amongst the men who do not want to forsake piety some are more and others less vexed at his "profane newfangled talk," and others—not because they are impious, but because they are rather indifferent as far as piety is concerned—do not even care if the Palamites are impious and tear apart the Church of Christ while the others suffer for warding them off, you appear not to concede to anyone the first prizes ⟨for pious contests⟩; in fact, ⟨you appear⟩ to possess such superiority that when you show up, you not only shake and strike down those present, but you do not even allow to accomplish their ends safe from your arrows those who in the most distant parts ruin the cities with that ⟨impiety⟩. With these arrows, surely, you arouse the indolent among the pious here, and you render the courageous more courageous towards this outrage; and you have gallantly avoided being exhorted to piety by others, because you consider it characteristic of a noble man neither to await the exhortation of others nor to use other examples for such things, though this is also good, but to be the whetstone for yourself and for others. So that even I am not concerned with appealing to you now, but with properly admiring both your present views and your preparation for future ⟨contests⟩; and I wish that every blessing and invincible power against the profane will accrue to you from God and to those who imitate you, because of whom I have strong hopes that the evil will not be able to advance. And this persecution is light and—if I do not sound incredible—preferable, because you are so disposed, to a carefree existence without you. This is how much I rejoice, and undoubtedly God rejoices too—how could He not?—at your struggles on His behalf against His enemies. This is the mark of education and learning! This is the true and nourishing fruit of philosophy in theory and practice which is brought forth with much labor! For without it, indeed, I believe that both learning and virtue are pursued by either group of men in vain, just like fields which bear nothing after much farming and much toil.

And I think that you must know the following too, since you have such concern for piety and such discernment, but it is not an awkward thing if I also say this to you: when the admirable Trikanas inveighs against the impious Charatzas for being impious, he does well and piously; but when he says, out of fear of their in-

41

τῆς εὐσεβείας, οἷς δέ φησι, δεδοικὼς τὰς ἐξ ἐκείνων ὕβρεις, μήτε μετὰ Κλεοβούλου, μήτε μετὰ Καλλιάδου τετάχθαι—τῷ μὲν τοὺς Παλαμίτας, τῷ δὲ ἡμᾶς αἰνιττόμενος—οὔτ' εὐσεβεῖν μοι δοκεῖ λέγειν, οὔτ' ἀσεβεῖν, καὶ μήτε μετὰ τῆς Χριστοῦ ἐκκλησίας ἑστάναι, μήτε μετὰ τῶν ἀντικειμένων αὐτῇ καὶ τἀναντία φρονούντων. τὸ γάρ τοι λέγειν ἡμᾶς, αὐτήν ἐστι πάντως τὴν ἐκκλησίαν λέγειν, τὸ δ' οἷς ἡμεῖς ἀντιπίπτομεν, τοὺς οἷσπερ ἡ ἐκκλησία μεθ' ἧς ἡμεῖς τετάγμεθά τε καὶ τοὺς κοινοὺς ἐχθροὺς ἀμυνόμεθα, οὓς ἑαυτῆς ἀποκόψασα λελογισμένῃ καὶ πανιέρῳ ψήφῳ, ἀπέρριψεν ὡς μέλη διεφθαρμένα, καὶ τῶν ἄλλων ὅπως μὴ τῇ πρὸς αὐτοὺς ὁμιλίᾳ τῆς λύμης μετασχήσουσι τῆς αὐτῶν προὐνοήθη. καίτοι προσῆκεν αὐτὸν πεπαιδευμένον ὄντα καὶ πρὸς αὐτὰ τὰ πράγματα βλέποντα ἢ μετ' ἐκείνων λέγειν ἢ μεθ' ἡμῶν τετάχθαι· οὐ γάρ ἐστιν ᾗ παρὰ ταῦτα στῇ τις, ἐναντιώτατα γὰρ κἀκ διαμέτρου ταῦτα, εἴπερ ἡμεῖς μὲν μετὰ τῆς πάντων τῶν θείων καὶ ἱερῶν εὐσεβείας πατέρων μονάδα ἐν τριάδι καὶ τριάδα ἐν μονάδι τὸ θεῖον ὁμολογοῦμεν· τρεῖς μὲν ὑποστάσεις, θεότητα δὲ μίαν, ἁπλῆν, ἀμερῆ, ἀδιαίρετον, ἀπλήθυντον, ἀναφῆ καὶ ἀόρατον καὶ μηδενὶ τῶν ὄντων ἐκ φυσικῆς ἐμφάσεως γινωσκομένην, ἀλλ' ἀοράτως πᾶσι καὶ πανταχοῦ παροῦσαν καὶ πάντα καθ' αὐτὴν ἐνεργοῦσαν, καὶ μήτε τὸ πλῆθος τῶν ἐν αὐτῇ προσώπων ἐπέκεινα τῶν τριῶν ἐκτεινόμενον, μηδ' ἔνδον αὐτῶν συστελλόμενον· ἁπλοῦν γὰρ ὅτι μὴ τῇ ἐξ αὐτοῦ παραγωγῇ τῶν πολλῶν ὄντων, ὡς λέγεται, πολλαπλασιαζόμενον, μηδ' εἰς διαφόρους θεότητας διαιρούμενον, ἀδιαίρετον γὰρ καὶ αὐτὸ ἑαυτοῦ ἀδιάφορον, μηδὲ μεριζόμενον ἐν τῷ παρεῖναι πᾶσιν, ἀμερὲς γάρ, μηδ' ἑτέρας ἐξ ἀϊδίου θεότητας ἐφελκόμενον καὶ ὑφειμένας αὐτοῦ, δημιουργοὺς τῶν ὄντων—αὐτὸ γὰρ τὸ ἓν καθ' αὑτὸ καὶ δι' αὑτοῦ ἡ πάντων ἐστὶ δημιουργὸς ἑνικῶς καὶ οὐσιοποιὸς καὶ συνεκτικὴ καὶ περιεκτικὴ καὶ προνοητικὴ καὶ ὑπερούσιος θεότης καὶ δύναμις—οὐδ' ὁρατὴν μορφὴν περικείμενον οὐσιώδη καὶ φυσικὴν ἑαυτῷ, αὐτὸ γὰρ τοῦτο ἔστιν ἡ ὑπέρφωτος μορφὴ καὶ ὑπερούσιος φύσις καὶ τὸ φῶς ὃ φωτίζει πάντα ἄνθρωπον ἐρχόμενον εἰς τὸν κόσμον. ἀόρατος μέντοι πᾶσι καὶ ἀναφὴς καὶ ἀ-

64–65 Greg. Naz., *Or.* 25, 17 (PG, 35, 1221C) ‖ 66–67 cf. Maxim. Conf., *Capit. theol.*, 2, 1 (PG, 90, 1124D–1125A) ‖ 67–68 Maxim. Conf., *ibid.*, 1, 1 (PG, 90, 1084A) ‖ 69 Joannis Chrysostomi *Liturgia* (ed. Brightman), 353, 13 ‖ 72–73 Dion. Areop., *De divin. nomin.*, 2, 11 (PG, 3, 649B) ‖ 76 cf. Palamam, *Epist. III ad Acindynum*, 15, Syngrammata, I, 306, 18–20; ed. Nadal, 252, 10–12 ‖ 78–80 Dion. Areop., *De coel. hier.*, 14, 1 (PG, 3, 321A) ‖ 82–83 Joan. 1:9

63 *ἐναντιώτα* Mn

41

sults, that he sides neither with Kleoboulos nor with Kalliades—meaning the Palamites on one hand and myself on the other—he seems to me to say that he is neither pious nor impious, and ⟨he seems⟩ to stand neither with the Church of Christ nor with those who oppose it and who believe what is hostile to it. For, surely, to speak of me is in fact to mean the Church, and those whom I oppose are exactly those whom the Church opposes; it is on the side of the Church that I stand warding off the common enemies, people whom the Church, by a calculated and all-sacred vote cut off from itself and cast away as corrupt members, taking care that others would not partake of their iniquity by associating with them. Though being educated and looking at the facts themselves, he ought to say that he is either with them or with me. For there is no other stand that one could take except this; for these are quite contrary and diametrically opposed positions, since I, together with all the divine and holy Fathers of the faith, confess that God is "one in three and three in one"; three hypostases but one divinity, "simple, without partition or division," without plurality, intangible and invisible and "not known to any being by means of a natural manifestation," but "present" in everything and "everywhere" invisibly, and operating everything alone. And ⟨we confess⟩ that neither the number of persons in the divinity extends beyond three nor does it contract within the persons, for it is simple, because, as they say, "it does not multiply by producing of itself many beings"; nor is it divided in different divinities, for it is indivisible and without distinctions in itself; nor is it divided into parts by being present in all, for it does not admit of partition; nor does it draw after it other eternal divinities, "lower" than itself, creators of beings, for the One by itself and through itself is singly the all-creating and "substance-giving and connecting and encompassing" and provident and supersubstantial divinity and power; nor does it bear a visible form which is essential and natural to it, for it is itself the light-transcending form and the supersubstantial nature and the "light which enlightens every man born into the world." Of course, He is invisible to all and intangible and inaccessible, for the God of all

41

πρόσιτος, ὅτι μηδενὸς ἂν ἦν βελτίων ὁ τῶν ἁπάντων Θεός, εἰ ἐξ ὁρατοῦ καὶ ἀοράτου, δύο πραγμάτων τοσοῦτο διαφόρων ἀλλήλων, συνέκειτο.

Οἱ δὲ περὶ Παλαμᾶν πᾶσι καταφανεῖς εἰσι τἀναντία [fol. 2r] φωνοῦντες· ἀντὶ μὲν τῆς μιᾶς ἐν τῇ τῶν ὅλων δημιουργῷ Τριάδι θεότητος, πλῆθος ἀριθμὸν ὑπερβαῖνον θεοτήτων ἀκτίστων, ἀντὶ δὲ ἁπλῆς καὶ ἴσης ἑαυτῇ καὶ ὁμοίας—εἴ γε καὶ τοῦτο χρὴ λέγειν ἐπὶ τοῦ πάσης ἑνάδος ἑνοποιοῦ καὶ ὑπὲρ πᾶν ἓν ἑνός—ἐκ τοσούτων συγκειμένην πραγμάτων ἀνίσων καὶ ἀνομοίων καὶ ἀλλήλοις καὶ αὐτῇ τῇ ὁλότητι τῆς ὑπερθέου θεότητος, καὶ οὕτω διαφερόντων αὐτῆς, φησιν, ὡς τῶν ἐνεργούντων τὰ ἐνεργούμενα καὶ τῶν οὐσιῶν τὰ ἀνούσια καὶ τῶν ἀμεθέκτων τὰ μεθεκτὰ καὶ τῶν ὑπὲρ νόησιν τὰ νοητὰ καὶ τῶν ἀοράτων τὰ ὁρατὰ καὶ τὰ ῥητὰ τῶν ἀρρήτων καὶ τῶν ὑπερωνύμων τὰ κυρίως ὀνομαζόμενα καὶ τῶν ἀμερῶν καὶ ἁπλῶν τὰ ποικίλα καὶ μεριστά, καὶ τὸ τῶν ὅλων ἄθροισμα, τῶν ὑπερκειμένων ἀπειράκις ἀπείρως τὰ ὑφειμένα· ὅπερ ἐστὶν ὡς τοῦ ποιητοῦ τῶν ὅλων τὰ κτίσματα, κἂν ἄλλως λόγῳ χαρίζηται τοῖς ἐνεργουμένοις καὶ ὁρατοῖς σωματικοῖς ὀφθαλμοῖς καὶ οὕτως ὑφειμένοις τοῦ θείου τὸ ἄκτιστον, οὐδέν τι δήπου διαφερόντως λέγων ἢ εἰ διαρρήδην τὰ κτίσματα ὠνόμαζεν ἄκτιστα, ἢ τὰ ἄκτιστα κτίσματα. τίς γὰρ οὕτως οὐ μόνον τῆς εὐσεβείας ἀλλὰ καὶ ὅλως τοῦ φρονοῦντος ἐκπέπτωκεν, ὥστε τὸ ἐνεργούμενον καὶ ὁρατὸν καθ' αὐτὸ σωματικοῖς ὀφθαλμοῖς τινων καὶ ἀπειράκις ὑφειμένον ἀπείρως Θεοῦ τοῦ πάντων ἐπέκεινα, θεὸν ἢ θεότητα νομίσαι ἀγένητον καὶ ἄναρχον καὶ τῷ Θεῷ συναΐδιον; οὕτω γὰρ ἂν εἴη πάντα, καὶ τὰ χείριστα πάντων, θεοὶ καὶ θεότητες ἄκτιστοι· πάντων γὰρ ὑπερέχει τὸ θεῖον τῶν ποιημάτων, ὥσπερ φησὶ Παλαμᾶς τοῦ πλήθους τῶν θεοτήτων τὸν Θεὸν ὑπερκεῖσθαι, ὡς τῶν ἐνεργουμένων τὸ ἐνεργοῦν καὶ τῶν ὀνομαζομένων τὸ ὑπερώνυμον καὶ—τί δεῖ πάντα λέγειν—ἀπειράκις ἀπείρως. τὰ δὲ ὡσαύτως ὑφειμένα τινὸς ὑπερέχον-

---

89 cf. Palamam, *De divinis operationibus*, 13, Syngrammata, II, 106, 24 || 91 *πάσης . . . ἑνοποιοῦ*: Dion. Areop., *De divin. nomin.*, 1, 1 (PG, 3, 588B) || 91–92 *ibid.*, 13, 3 (PG, 3, 980C) || 93 *ibid.*, 2, 4 (PG, 3, 641A) || 95–98 cf. Palamam, *De divinis operationibus*, 47, Syngrammata, II, 132, 25–30 || 99–100 et 107 cf. Maxim. Conf., *Capit. theol.*, 1, 49 (PG, 90, 1101A) = Palamas, *Dialexis*, 24, Syngrammata, II, 186, 26; *Epist. ad Gabram*, 5, Syngrammata, II, 332, 12 || 107–108 cf. Joan. Dam., *De fide orth.*, 1, 8 (PG, 94, 816A) || 112–113 cf. Dion. Areop., *De divin. nomin.*, 12, 4 (PG, 3, 972B); Palamam, *De divinis operationibus*, 47, Syngrammata, II, 132, 25–30 || 114 et 117 Maxim. Conf., *Capit. theol.*, 1, 49 (PG, 90, 1101A) = Palamas, *Dialexis*, 24, Syngrammata, II, 186, 26; *Epist. ad Gabram*, 5, Syngrammata, II, 332, 12

---

93 ὁλότιτι Mn

41

would have been better than none, if He were composed of visible and invisible, two properties so different from one another.

But it is obvious to all men that those around Palamas say the opposite, for instead of the one divinity in the all-creating Trinity, ⟨they speak of⟩ a "countless multitude" of uncreated divinities, and instead of the simple and in itself equal divinity without variations—if, indeed, we should say this about the "One which unifies every monad and transcends every one"—they ⟨speak of⟩ a divinity composed of so many ⟨divinities⟩, unequal and different from each other and from the very total of the "superdivine divinity" and as different from it, Palamas says, as the activating from the activated, and the essences from those which lack essence, and "those incapable of being shared from those capable of being shared," and the incomprehensible from the comprehensible, and the invisible from the visible, and the expressible from the inexpressible, and "that which is above every name from those which have a proper name," and the indivisible and simple from the complex and divisible, and in sum total, the "infinitely" higher from the lower, which is exactly how the Creator of all differs from created things, even if ⟨Palamas⟩, in a different way, grants by his words uncreatedness to that which is activated and visible to the bodily eyes and thus lower than God, saying indeed nothing different than if he expressly called the created uncreated, or the uncreated created. For who has taken leave not only of piety but also of his senses so completely as to believe that what is activated and visible in itself to the bodily eyes of certain men and "infinitely" lower than the "all-transcending God" is a god or divinity uncreated, without beginning and coeternal with God? For in this way all things, even the worst of all, could be uncreated gods and divinities. For the divine "infinitely" surpasses all created things, exactly as Palamas says that God surpasses the multitude of divinities, as the activating surpasses the activated and "that which is above every name those that have a name," and what need is there to mention everything? Indeed, any sensible man would say that those things which are in like manner inferior to something that

41

τος πᾶς τις ἂν εἴποι δήπου, μὴ ἀναισθήτως ἔχων, ἴσα ἀλλήλοις εἶναι καὶ ὅμοια ᾗ γ' αὐτῷ ὑπερέχεται.

Ἢ τί περαιτέρω τῆς ἀπειράκις ἀπείρως ἐστὶ τοῦ Θεοῦ διεστηκυίας χώρας, ἵν' ἐκεῖ μὲν τὰ ποιήματα θῶμεν, ἐνταῦθα δὲ κεῖσθαι τὰς τούτων καὶ τοῦ Θεοῦ μεταξὺ φυείσας οἰηθῶμεν θεότητας; ἢ γὰρ ἔγγιον πάντως, ἢ πορρωτέρω ταύτης εἶναι τῆς χώρας πρός γε τὸ θεῖον οἰητέον τὰ κτίσματα, ἢ κατ' αὐτήν γε μετὰ τῶν καινῶν τουτωνὶ θεοτήτων. καὶ πορρωτέρω μὲν οὐκ ἔνι· τί γὰρ ἐπέκεινα τοῦ πάντων ἐπέκεινα; ἔγγιον δὲ εἰ ἔσται, τιμιώτερα τῶν θεοτήτων ἔσται τὰ κτίσματα· μετ' αὐτῶν δέ, ὁμότιμα. πόθεν οὖν ἄκτιστοι καὶ τῷ Θεῷ συναΐδιοι καὶ φυσικαὶ καὶ οὐσιώδεις αὐτῷ αἱ ὑφειμέναι θεότητες, ἢ πόθεν τὰ οὐσιώδη καὶ φυσικὰ τοῦ Θεοῦ μετὰ τῶν ἀπειράκις ὑφειμένων ἀπείρως καὶ φανερῶς κτισμάτων; εἰ μὲν γὰρ οὐχ ὑπερέξουσι τῶν κτισμάτων αὐτῷ αἱ θεότητες διὰ τὰ εἰρημένα, πῶς ἔσονται ἄκτιστοι καὶ τῷ Θεῷ συναΐδιοι καὶ οὐσιώδεις αὐτῷ; εἰ δ' ὑπερέξουσι, πῶς τούτων ἐκείνας ὑπερέχειν ἐροῦσιν, ὡς ἐνεργουμένων ἐνεργουμένας καὶ ὀνομαζομένων [fol. 2ᵛ] ὀνομαστὰς καὶ ὁρατῶν ὁρατὰς καὶ νοητῶν νοητάς; εἰ δὲ ἄλλως, καὶ ἄλλως ὁρᾶσθαί τε καὶ νοεῖσθαι φήσουσι τὰ εἰρημένα, τὸ γοῦν ὑφεῖσθαι Θεοῦ ἀπειράκις ἀπείρως αὐτοῖς ἀπαράλλακτον. πῶς οὖν ἐστι τούτων τὰ μὲν θεότητες ἄκτιστοι καὶ κοσμουργοί, κατ' αὐτούς, τὰ δὲ τούτων ποιήματα, καὶ ταῦτα ἔστιν ἃ καὶ αὐτῶν τιμιώτερα, τὰ γὰρ πᾶσιν ἀόρατα καὶ νοῦ κρείττω, μὴ ὅτι σωματικῆς τινων ὄψεως—εἰσὶ δὲ τοιαῦται τῶν ἀγγέλων αἱ φύσεις καὶ τῶν ψυχῶν—τῶν ληπτῶν σωματικοῖς ὀφθαλμοῖς τοῦ Παλαμᾶ θεοτήτων τίς οὐκ ἂν φαίη κρείττω, ὑγιοῦς νοῦ μετέχων; ἃς εἶναι λέγων οὐσιώδεις καὶ φυσικὰς τοῦ Θεοῦ, εἶτα ἐνεργουμένας καὶ ὑφειμένας αὐτοῦ, κατὰ τὰ εἰρημένα, δυοῖν πάντως θάτερον· ἢ κτιστὸν αὐτόν, καὶ τῶν κατωτάτω κτιστῶν, ἀποφαίνεται εἶναι—οὗ γὰρ τὰ οὐσιώδη κτιστά, τοῦτ' αὐτὸ δήπου κτίσμα—ἢ τὰ κτίσματα θεοποιεῖ τῷ ἀκτίστῳ Θεῷ ταῦτα συντάττων ὡς ἄκτιστα, μᾶλλον δὲ ἄμφω ποιεῖ καί, ὅ φασι, τὰ ἄνω κάτω καὶ τοὔμπαλιν, καὶ ὧν οὐδὲν ἂν εἴη τερατωδέστερον, οὐδ' ἕτερον ἑτέρῳ ἐναντιώτερον τῷ γε τοῖς εὐσεβέσι δόγμασι ἐντεθραμμένῳ τῶν ἱερῶν πατέρων ὧν τὸ πρῶτον καὶ τὸ κεφάλαιον, ἄκτιστον ἀκτίστου καὶ ἄπειρον ἀπείρου μηδαμῶς ὑπερέχειν, μηδ'

---

123 cf. Joan. Dam., *De fide orth.*, 1, 8 (PG, 94, 816A) || 126 cf. Palamam, *Epist. III ad Acindynum*, 15, Syngrammata, I, 306, 18–20; ed. Nadal, 252, 10–12 || 134 Maxim. Conf., *Capit. theol.*, 1, 49 (PG, 90, 1101A) = Palamas, *Dialexis*, 24, Syngrammata, II, 186, 26; *Epist. ad Gabram*, 5, Syngrammata, II, 332, 12 || 146 Gregorius Cyprius, I, 61 (Leutsch-Schneidewin, II, 61)

---

116 ᾗ] ἡ Mn || 117 ἢ] ἡ Mn || 120 ἔγγυον Mn || 123 ἔγγυοι Mn || 137 σωματικοῖς Mn

41

surpasses them are mutually equal and alike, insofar as they are inferior to that which surpasses them.

Truly, what is further than the place which is "infinitely" distant from God, that we may place there the created things, while we assume that the divinities which sprang between them and God remain here? For, surely, we must assume that, in relation to God, created things are either closer to or further than this place, ⟨or they are⟩ within it together with these new divinities. And to be further is, of course, impossible. For what is beyond "Him Who is beyond everything?" On the other hand, if they are closer, then the created things are held in higher honor than the divinities; and if they are together with the divinities, they are held in equal honor. How can it be, then, that the "lower divinities" are uncreated and coeternal with God and natural and essential to Him, or how can that which is essential and natural to God be placed together with the "infinitely" and manifestly lower created things? For if, for the reasons stated above, Palamas' divinities are not superior to created things, how will they be uncreated and coeternal with God and essential to Him? And if they are superior, how will ⟨the Palamites⟩ say that they are superior to created things? As activated to activated, and that which has a name to that which has a name, and visible to visible, and comprehensible to comprehensible? On the other hand, if they are superior in a different manner, they must say that the aforementioned are also seen and comprehended in a different manner, for their "infinite" inferiority to God is, of course, exactly the same. How, then, are some of them, according to the Palamites, divinities uncreated and creators of the world, while the others are their creations, and, in fact, there are certain of them which are held in even higher honor than the divinities? For what sane man would not say that those things which are invisible to all and superior to intelligence, let alone to the bodily eyes of certain men—and such are the natures of angels and souls—are superior to the divinities of Palamas which can be apprehended by bodily eyes? For, by saying that these divinities are essential and natural to God, then that they are activated and lower than He, according to what was said, he is certainly saying one of two things: either he declares that God is created and one of the lowest creatures—for something whose essential elements are created is itself certainly created—or he deifies the created things, putting them as uncreated together with the uncreated God. Rather, he does both, and, as they say, he turns things "upside down" and vice versa. And nothing could be more monstrous than these ⟨ideas⟩ nor anything more opposed to another for a man brought up in the pious doctrines of the holy Fathers, whose primary and principal doctrine is that the uncreated is not superior to the uncreated and the infinite to the infinite in any way, nor do they differ at all, except

41

ὅλως διαφέρειν ὅτι μὴ προσωπικῶς—ὅπερ ἡ θεία Τριὰς ἡ καὶ μονὰς ἀμερὴς τῇ θεότητι—μηδ' ἐν βαθμοῖς ἀνίσοις ὅλως εἶναι τὸ ἄκτιστον, καὶ ταῦτα οὐσιωδῶς.

'Αλλὰ ταῦτα μὲν οὐκ ἐν καιρῷ νῦν λέγω, ὑπὲρ γὰρ ἐπιστολήν, μᾶλλον δὲ καὶ περιττῶς πρός γε τὴν σὴν ἐπιστήμην καὶ τὴν ἀκρίβειαν τῶν ἱερῶν δογμάτων. τὸν Τρικανᾶν μέντοι δίδαξον καὶ τοὺς ὁμοίους αὐτῷ μὴ ταὐτὰ περὶ τῶν ἐναντίων φρονεῖν, μηδ' ἐναντία περὶ ταὐτοῦ, καὶ παῦσον ζημιουμένους περὶ τὸ μέγιστον, τὴν γνῶσιν τῆς ἀληθείας. ὃ γὰρ οὐκ ἔμαθον πρὸς τῶν θείων πατέρων—ἢ μαθόντες παρεῖδον διὰ δειλίαν, δυσσεβείας μητέρα καὶ ἄλλως ἀνόητον—ὡς ὁ καταγινώσκων τῶν μίαν λεγόντων θεότητα ἢ τῷ πολλὰς λέγοντι ἢ τῷ μηδεμίαν συνθήσεται, καὶ τὸ εἰς πλῆθος ἐκτείνειν τὸν ἀριθμὸν τῶν θεοτήτων μόνων τῶν τὴν πολύθεον πλάνην νενοσηκότων ἐστί, τὸ δὲ μίαν νομίζειν μόνην καὶ ἀπαράλλακτον τῆς εὐσεβείας. τοῦτο σὺ τούτους φώτισον διὰ γραμμάτων (οἷς σε πάντας ἐκπλῆξαί φησιν, εὖ λέγων, ὁ Τρικανᾶς τοὺς ἐν Θεσσαλονίκῃ), ἐξ ὧν μαθήτω μηδὲν ἧττον Παλαμίζων ὁ φίλος ὅταν λέγῃ μηδετέροις προσκεῖσθαι. τὸ γὰρ ἡμῖν μὴ προσκεῖσθαι, αὐτομάτως ἐκείνῳ ἐστὶ προσκεῖσθαι, ὅτι τοῖς μίαν ὁμολογοῦσι μὴ προσέχειν θεότητα, τοῖς πολλάς ἐστι δήπου προσέχειν ὁμολογοῦσι· τοῦτο δέ φησι τῶν τὴν πολύθεον πλάνην νενοσηκότων εἶναι ὁ θεῖος Γρηγόριος ὁ Νυσσαέων. οὐ μὴν ἀλλὰ καὶ ἡμῖν αὐτομάτως προσέχει ὁ μὴ προσέχειν ὁμολογῶν ἐκείνοις· εἰ γὰρ μὴ πολλὰς ἐκείνοις πείθεται [fol. 3r] δοξάζειν θεότητας ἀνίσους καὶ ἀνομοίους, τοῖς μίαν πάντως καὶ μόνην καὶ ἀπαράλλακτον ἡμῖν ὁμολογοῦσι πεισθήσεται, μᾶλλον δέ, οἶμαι, καὶ πάλαι πεπεισμένος πρὸς τῆς ἐκκλησιαστικῆς ὁμολογίας ἐστὶ καὶ σύμφωνος οἷς μὴ προσκεῖσθαί φησιν. ὥσθ' ὅταν λέγῃ τετάχθαι μετ' οὐδετέρων, οὐδὲν μᾶλλον λέγει μετ' οὐδετέρων τετάχθαι ἢ καὶ μεθ' ἑκατέρων, καὶ οὕτω τὸν αὐτὸν κατὰ ταὐτὰ καὶ μετὰ μηδετέρων συμβήσεται· εἰ μὴ ἄρα τίς ἐστιν ἐραστὴς ἀθεΐας, τὸ γὰρ μήτε μίαν, μήτε πολλὰς νομίζειν θεότητας ἄθεον, ὡς ὅ τε θεῖος Γρηγόριος εἴρηκεν καὶ αὐτόθεν κατάδηλον.

Ταύτης ἀπάλλαξον τῆς ἀπορίας τοὺς πάνυ μὲν συνετοὺς καὶ σοφοὺς καὶ λογίους ἐκείνους, οὐκ οἶδα δ' ὅπως ἀπορουμένους τῆδε, μᾶλλον δὲ ἀγνοοῦντας μὲν δίδαξον, πέμψας καὶ τὸν ἱερὸν αὐτοῖς λόγον, ᾧ τούτους ὡς μέλος σεσηπὸς ἀποκόψας ἀπέρριψε τοῦ σώμα-

---

160–164 Basil. Caes., *Epist.* 189, 4 (PG, 32, 688 C–D) || 171 Basil. Caes., *ibid.*, (PG, 32, 688D)

---

162 ἐκτίνειν Mn

as to persons—that is precisely the Holy Trinity Which is indeed an undivided monad as to divinity—nor does the uncreated exist at all in unequal grades and, especially, as far as the essence is concerned.

But I say these things inopportunely, for they are beyond the limits of a letter, and rather superfluously to a man of your learning and precise knowledge of the sacred doctrines. Instruct, therefore, Trikanas and those like him not to hold the same opinions about opposite matters, nor opposite ⟨opinions⟩ about the same ⟨matters⟩, and stop them from suffering the loss of the most important thing, the knowledge of truth. For what they did not learn from the holy Fathers—or if they learned, they forgot it because of cowardice, which is the mother of impiety and otherwise senseless—is that "He who condemns those who proclaim one divinity will agree either with the man who proclaims many or with the man who proclaims none. And to extend the number of divinities to a multitude is a characteristic of those who suffer from the delusion of polytheism." But to believe in one and only one ⟨divinity⟩ without distinctions is to be pious. Enlighten them as to this with your writings with which, Trikanas says, putting it well, you have astonished all the Thessalonians. Let our friend learn from them that he is no less a follower of Palamas when he says that he is attached to neither party. For not to be attached to me is, inevitably, to be attached to him, because not to follow those who acknowledge one divinity is certainly to follow those who acknowledge many. And "this," says St. Gregory of Nyssa, "is characteristic of those who suffer from the delusion of polytheism." Not just that, but also he who admits that he does not follow them has no choice but to follow me; for if he is not persuaded by them to believe in many unequal and dissimilar divinities, he will, of course, listen to me who believes in one and only one ⟨divinity⟩ without distinctions. Rather, I think that he has been convinced even long ago by the confession of the Church and agrees with those to whom he says that he is not attached. When he says, therefore, that he sides with neither ⟨party⟩, he says no more that he sides with neither than ⟨that he sides⟩ both with one and the other, and in this way only it will happen that the same man will side equally with neither ⟨party⟩; unless, perhaps, he is a worshiper of atheism, because to believe neither in one nor in many divinities is atheism, as St. Gregory says and as is also self-evident.

Deliver these very intelligent and wise and learned men from this perplexity—I know not how they are perplexed in this case—rather, instruct them, if they do not know, sending them also the sacred encyclical by which the most divine

τος τῆς Χριστοῦ ἐκκλησίας ὁ θειότατος αὐτῆς φύλαξ καὶ πρόβολος ὁ πατριάρχης ἡμῖν, ὁ ποιμὴν ὁ καλὸς ὁ τιθεὶς τὴν ψυχὴν αὐτοῦ ὑπὲρ τῶν προβάτων. εἰ δὲ εἰδότες, ἑκόντες ἑαυτοὺς παρακρούονται, ἀνθρωπίνως οἰκονομοῦντες τὰ καθ' αὐτοὺς ἀλλ' οὐ θείως, ἔλεγξον οὐκ εὐθυποροῦντας πρὸς τὴν ἀλήθειαν καὶ ἀξίωσον μηδὲν περὶ πλείονος ποιεῖσθαι τῆς εὐσεβείας, ἀλλὰ μιμεῖσθαι Παῦλον εἰς δύναμιν, λέγοντας τίς ἡμᾶς χωρίσει ἀπὸ τῆς ἀγάπης τοῦ Θεοῦ; θλῖψις ἢ στενοχωρία καὶ τὰ λοιπά; μὴ δὴ κακοὺς οἰκονόμους εἶναι περὶ τὸ θεῖον, ὡς εὐθύτης οἰκεῖον, ἀλλ' οὐχ ὑπόκρισις—οὐ δύνασθε γὰρ μου μαθηταί, φησιν, εἶναι δόξαν παρ' ἀνθρώπων λαμβάνοντες—μηδὲ μάτην παρὰ Θεοῦ τὴν χάριν ἔχειν εἰληφότας τῶν λόγων, μὴ τὸ τοῦ τάλαντον κρύψαντος καὶ τοῦ μὴ ἔμπροσθεν τῶν ἀνθρώπων τὸν Χριστὸν ὁμολογήσαντος Θεὸν εἶναι πάθωσιν, ὡς τοῖς τοιούτοις ἠπείληται κατὰ τὸ δικαστήριον ἐκεῖνο τὸ παγκόσμιον καὶ τελευταῖον.

Χάρις δὲ καὶ τῷ γενναίῳ Βρανᾷ πρὸς ὃν ἡ ἐπιστολή, ὅτι καὶ οὗτος καὶ ἀδελφὸς αὐτῷ τοῖς δυσσεβέσι τούτοις εἰσὶν ὅπερ εἰκὸς εἶναι δυσσεβέσιν ἀνδράσι τοὺς γνησιωτάτους τῆς εὐσεβείας παῖδας.

42. Τῷ σοφῷ Λαπίθη

Εἰ τοιαῦτα ἦν παρ' ἡμῖν τῆς εὐσεβείας ξίφη, οὐκ ἂν ἡ μία θεότης ἡμῖν εἰς πλῆθος θεοτήτων ἐτέμνετο, ἀλλ' οἱ τοῦτο ποιοῦντες τούτοις ἂν εὐλόγως διῃροῦντο τοῖς ξίφεσιν. εἰ τοιαύταις ἀκτῖσιν ἐχρώμεθα, οὐκ ἂν ὑπὸ τοῦ τῆς ἀσεβείας ἠνωχλούμεθα σκότους, ἀλλ' ἦν ἂν ἡμῖν τὸ φῶς τῆς εὐσεβείας ἀνεπηρέαστον, πᾶσαν ὁμίχλην ἀσεβῆ διακρῖνον ἢ μηδὲ τὴν ἀρχὴν ἐῶν καὶ ὁπωσοῦν συστῆναι. εἰ δέ σε καὶ κυβερνήτην δεξιώτατον φαίην, οὐκ ἂν ἀφέντα, παρ' ἡμῖν εἰ παρῆσθα, τουτὶ τὸ σκάφος—τὴν ἐκκλησίαν τοῦ Χριστοῦ—κινδυνεύειν καὶ καταδύεσθαι τῷ τῶν ἀσεβῶν κλυδωνίῳ δογμάτων, οὐκ

189–190 Joan. 10:11 ‖ 194–195 Rom. 8:35 ‖ 196 *οἰκονόμους*: cf. Luc. 12:42; I Cor. 4:2; I Pet. 4:10–11 ‖ 198–199 cf. Joan. 5:44 ‖ 199–200 *τάλαντον κρύψαντος*: cf. Matt. 25:23–24 ‖ 200–201 cf. Matt. 10:32–33

---

205 leg. *ἀδελφός*?

42: M 52v–55v.

4 *ἀκτίσιν* M

guardian and bulwark of the Church, our Patriarch, the "good shepherd who laid down his life for the sheep," cut off the Palamites as a rotten member and cast them out of the Church of Christ. But if they do know and lead themselves astray willingly, because they manage their affairs after the manner of man and not God, prove to them that they are not following a straight course to truth and ask them to honor nothing more than piety, but to imitate Paul as much as possible, saying: "What can separate us from the love of God? Can affliction or hardship?" etc. ⟨Ask them⟩ not to be bad stewards concerning God, for righteousness is befitting, not hypocrisy; for He says: "You cannot be my disciples so long as you receive honor from men." ⟨Ask them⟩ not to have received from God in vain the literary gift, lest they suffer the punishment of the man who hid the talent and the man who did not acknowledge before men that Christ is God, as has been threatened against such men at that world-wide and final judgment.

But thanks be to the gallant Branas to whom this letter is addressed, because both he and his brother are to the impious men exactly what the most genuine sons of piety must be to impious men.

42. To the sage Lapithes

If we had here such pious swords, our single Divinity would not be cut into a multitude of divinities, but the men who do this would with justice be cut to pieces by these swords. If we made use of such rays, we would not be disturbed by the darkness of impiety, but our light of piety would be undisturbed, detecting every impious mist or not allowing it even to start at all. And I believe that I would not fail to speak the truth if I called you a most skillful captain, one who, if here with us, would not have let this very ship—I mean the Church of Christ—run the risk of being sunk by the tempest of the impious doctrines. For you are a wise man and not

42

ἂν ἁμαρτεῖν τῆς ἀληθείας οἶμαι· σοφὸς γὰρ εἶ, καὶ σοφὸς οὐ τῶν δοκούντων, ἀλλὰ τῶν ὄντως ὄντων, οὐ γὰρ δοκεῖν ἄριστος ἀλλ' εἶναι θέλεις, κατὰ τὸν εἰρηκότα, βαθεῖαν αὔλακα διὰ φρενὸς καρπούμενος, ἐξ ἧς τὰ κεδνὰ βλαστάνει βουλεύματα. σοφοῦ δὲ ἀνδρὸς ἡ εὐσέβεια τῆς θεωρίας τέλος καὶ τῶν ὅλων, οἶμαι, προτάσεων τὸ συμπέρασμα, μᾶλλον δὲ τῶν συμπερασμάτων αὐτῶν τὸ συμπέρασμα καὶ ὑπὲρ τοῦτο· οὗ χάριν καὶ τὴν ὅλην φιλοσοφίαν ἐπιτετήδευκε, καὶ πάντα αὐτῷ διὰ τοῦτο ἐσπούδασται. ἡ γὰρ πρώτη καὶ κορυφαία φιλοσοφίας ἕξις, μᾶλλον δὲ τῆς σοφίας ἧς χάριν ὑμεῖς πᾶν ὁτιοῦν πονεῖτε καὶ πραγματεύεσθε, ἡ τῆς θεολογίας ἐστὶν ἀσφαλὴς ἐπιστήμη, ὥστ' ἄνευ ταύτης οὐδεὶς ἂν εἴη σοφός, κἂν δοκῇ γε εἶναι σοφώτατος.

Ὁ συνείς, ὡς ἔοικεν, ἐξ ἀρχῆς, ὦ σοφώτατε, οὕτως ἀξίως φιλοσοφίας ἐφιλοσόφησας, ὥστε νῦν οὐκέτ' εἶναί τις φιλόσοφος, ἀλλὰ σοφὸς ἕνεκα τῆς θεολογικῆς ἐπιστήμης τε καὶ δυνάμεως καὶ τῆς κατὰ τῶν εἰς ταύτην παρανομούντων ἐνστάσεως· ἐνστάσεως καθ' ἣν οὐ μόνον σαυτὸν ἐπὶ τοὺς ἀσεβοῦντας παρώξυνας, ἀλλὰ καὶ τοὺς παρ' ἡμῖν καὶ σοφοὺς καὶ σπουδαίους, ὥσπερ ἀγαθὸς καὶ θαυμαστὸς στρατηγός, ἐπὶ τοῦτον ἐγείρεις τὸν πόλεμον, τοιούτους μὲν ὄντας δήπου καὶ τὸ κακὸν ᾐσθημένους—καὶ μάλιστα τὸν σόν τε καὶ ἡμέτερον ἥρω καὶ τῆς νίκης ἐπώνυμον—πῶς γὰρ οὔ; μαλθακώτερον δὲ (δότωσαν γὰρ εἰπεῖν μοι τοῦτό γε) διατεθέντας ἢ ὡς αὐτοὺς ἐσχηκέναι πρὸς τὰ τοιαῦτα, ὑπεριδόντας τῶνδε ὧν ἥκισθ' ὑπεριδεῖν προσῆκε τούς γε μεμαθηκότας τὰς βεβήλους περιίστασθαι καινοφωνίας, ὅτι φησὶν ὁ ταῦτα γράφων καὶ παραγγέλλων Παῦλος, ἐπὶ πλεῖον προκόψουσι [fol. 53r] καὶ ὁ λόγος αὐτῶν ὡς γάγγραινα νομὴν ἕξει.

Ἐμοὶ δέ, ὦ βέλτιστε, ὃν φῂς τοῦ δέοντος μαλθακώτερον ἀντιλέγειν τῷ δόγματι—καὶ χαίρω θαυμαστῶς διὰ τοῦτο, τὴν ὑπερβάλλουσαν ὁρῶν ἐμαυτῷ συμμαχίαν παροῦσαν κατὰ τῶν ἀσεβούντων—ἐμοὶ τοίνυν συμβέβηκεν εἶναι μὲν εὐτελεῖ τινι καὶ μηδὲν μέγα μηδ' ἀξιόχρεων ἔχειν οὔτε σοφίας, οὔτ' ἀρετῆς, καὶ διὰ τοῦτο παρορᾶσθαι τοῖς τῇδε καὶ λόγου μηδενὸς ἀξιοῦσθαι—ὅπερ ἦν καὶ πρὸς ἐμοῦ πρίν γε φανῆναι τὰ δυσσεβῆ ταῦτα δόγματα, μονάζοντι γὰρ οὐδὲν οὕτως οἰκεῖον, οὐδὲ ὠφέλιμον ὡς τὸ λανθάνειν ζῶντα, οὐδ' ἐπιζήμιον ὡς τὸ πολλοῖς τιμᾶσθαι καὶ τοῖς ἐν τέλει γνωρίζεσθαι· χλιαρὸν γὰρ ἡ τιμὴ καὶ διαχυτικὸν ἡ παρρησία ψυχῆς καὶ τὸ πάνυ

42: 12–15 cf. Aeschylum, *Septem contra Thebas*, 592–594 ‖ 34–37 II Tim. 2:16–17

---

13 *βαθείαν* M ‖ 32–33 *ἢ . . . τοιαῦτα* non satis perspicio

42

one of those who appear to be wise, but ⟨one of those⟩ who are truly so. For your "resolve is not to seem the best, but to be," as someone said, and "you reap the harvest of your mind's deep furrowing, whence your sage counsels spring." And I believe that piety is the goal of a wise man's contemplative pursuits and the conclusion of all premises, or rather, the conclusion of conclusions themselves and above that. For the sake of this, indeed, he pursues all philosophy, and for this purpose he zealously studies everything. For the first and principal attainment of philosophy, or rather of wisdom, for which you take all sorts of trouble and work systematically, is the correct knowledge of theology, so that without it nobody would be wise, even though he should seem to be most wise.

It seems, my most wise friend, that you realized this from the beginning, and you pursued philosophy in a manner so worthy of philosophy that you are no longer just a philosopher but a wise man, on account of your theological learning and strength as well as your resistance against those who offend theology. A resistance by which you not only roused yourself against the impious, but like a good and admirable general you are also rousing to this war both our wise and prominent men here, ⟨men⟩ who are of this nature, indeed, and have sensed the evil—for how could they not?—and especially your hero and mine, the man who is named after victory. But—and they must allow me to say this at least—they have taken a softer stand towards this evil than they should have done, because they overlooked what they ought least to overlook, since they have learnt to "avoid the profane newfangled talk," because Paul, who wrote and enjoined this, says that "those who indulge in it will stray further and further into godless courses and the infection of their teaching will spread like gangrene."

As for me, on the other hand, my most excellent friend, you say that I speak up against this doctrine more feebly than I ought to, and I am wonderfully delighted at your saying so, for I see that I have here an overpowering alliance against the impious. As for me, then, I happened to be an insignificant person, having nothing great or worthy as far as either wisdom or virtue is concerned, and for this reason I am disregarded by people here and deemed unworthy of consideration. This, of course, was actually to my advantage, at least before the appearance of these impious doctrines, for nothing is so suitable or so profitable for a monk as to live in oblivion nor so damaging as to be honored by many and acquainted with those in power. For honor softens, while spiritual license and too much esteem enervate.

42

τιμᾶσθαι—τοιούτῳ δὲ ὄντι συμπλακῆναι τοῖς καινοῖς θεολόγοις, μεγάλοις ὀνόμασι καὶ σφόδρα περιβοήτοις ἐπ' ἀρετῇ καὶ σοφίᾳ, οἷς γε καὶ τὸ τὸν Βαρλαὰμ ἐκεῖνον, ὃς αὐτοῖς ἦν διάφορος, ἀποδεδοκιμάσθαι προσγέγονε παρὰ τῇ ἐκκλησίᾳ, ἐπεί τινα κἀκεῖνος ἐκαινοφώνει, ἃ νῦν οὐκ ἔμοι γε διεξιέναι καιρός. τοῦτο ἐξῆρε τὸν Παλαμᾶν ἐκτόπως καὶ διεφύσησε, καὶ λαβόμενος οὐ μόνον τῆς φυγῆς ἐκείνου καὶ καταδίκης, ἀλλὰ καὶ γράμματος ἐκκλησιαστικοῦ κατ' ἐκείνου γεγενημένου, κατεχρῆτο τούτοις ἀσεβέστατα τῆς εὐσεβείας καὶ τῶν αὐτοῦ τὴν δυσσέβειαν πεφωρακότων ἡμῶν, ὥσπερ ὁ Ἄρειος τοῖς κατὰ Σαβελλίου· ἧς εἶναι συστατικὰ τὰ γεγονότα ἐκήρυττε, καὶ ἡμᾶς ὡς πάντῃ ταὐτὰ τῷ Βαρλαὰμ φρονοῦντας ἐκκηρύκτους ἐτίθετο τῆς ἐκκλησίας, καὶ πάντα καθ' ἡμῶν συνεκρότει. καὶ ἀκινάκαι εἱλκύσθησαν, καὶ αἷμα ἡμῶν ἐρρύη κατὰ τοῦ τῆς εὐσεβείας ἐδάφους—ὢ γῆ καὶ ἥλιε!—ὅτι μὴ φωνῶν ἀσεβῶν ἠνεσχόμεθα * * * τῶν μίαν ἡμῖν τρισυπόστατον παραδόντων θεότητα, ἐν τριάδι μονάδα καὶ μονάδι τριάδα, καὶ τοῦτο μόνον ἄκτιστόν τε καὶ προαιώνιον, ἁπλοῦν, ἀμερές, ἀδιαίρετον, ἀόρατον, ἀναφές, ἀνείδεον, ἀκατάληπτον, ἄποιον· τούτῳ δὲ μηδὲν συναΐδιον κατὰ μηδένα τρόπον, οὔτε ὄν, οὔτ' ἀνούσιον, οὐ ζωήν, οὐ σοφίαν, οὐκ ἀγαθότητα, οὐχ ὁρατόν, οὐκ ἀόρατον· ἀλλ' εἴτε ζωήν, εἴτε σοφίαν, εἴτ' ἐνέργειαν, εἴτε δύναμιν, εἴτ' ἀγαθότητα, εἴτε δόξαν, εἴτε βασιλείαν, εἴθ' ὅ τι δή τις ἂν ἄκτιστον ὀνομάζῃ καὶ ἄναρχον καὶ ἀγένητον [fol. 53^v] καὶ ὑπερούσιον, τοῦτ' εἶναι τὴν θείαν φύσιν αὐτήν, τὴν τριάδα μὲν τοῖς προσώποις, μονάδα δὲ τῇ θεότητι, ἀλλ' οὐ πολλὰ καὶ ἄνισα καὶ ἀνόμοια καὶ πάντῃ διάφορα πράγματα, καὶ θεότητας ἀκτίστους καὶ ἀγενήτους ταῦτα, οὐσιώδεις τε καὶ φυσικὰς τοῦ Θεοῦ, τὰς δὲ αὐτὰς καὶ ἐνεργουμένας καὶ ὑφειμένας αὐτοῦ ἀπειράκις ἀπείρως, καὶ τὰς μὲν καθ' ἑαυτὰς νοητάς, τὰς δὲ καὶ ληπτὰς σωματικοῖς ὀφθαλμοῖς, καὶ οὕτω καὶ τούτων αὐτῶν τῶν ὑφειμένων αὖθις τὰς μὲν ὑπερεχούσας, τὰς δ' ὑφειμένας δήπου, κατὰ τοὺς ἄρτι λήρους οἵ, κατὰ τὸν θείων ἀριθμὸν ὀνομάτων, ἀριθμὸν ἀκτίστων καὶ ἀνίσων καὶ διαφορωτάτων θεοτήτων γεννῶσι· μᾶλλον δὲ νῦν μὲν τοῦτο, νῦν δὲ ἀριθμὸν ὑπερβαίνειν τὸ πλῆθος τῶν θεοτήτων φασί, μακρῷ καὶ τῶν

48–49 cf. Greg. Naz., *Or.*29, 10 (PG, 36, 88A) ‖ 63 *idem*, *Or.*25, 17 (PG, 35, 1221C) ‖ 64–65 cf. Maxim. Conf., *Capit. theol.*, 2, 1 (PG, 90, 1124D–1125A) ‖ 75 *ὑφειμένας*: cf. Palamam, *Epist. III ad Acindynum*, 15, Syngrammata, I, 306, 18–20; ed. Nadal, 252, 10–12 ‖ 75 cf. Maxim. Conf., *Capit. theol.*, 1, 49 (PG, 90, 1101A) = Palamas, *Dialexis*, 24, Syngrammata, II, 332, 12 ‖ 80–81 *idem*, *De divinis operationibus*, 13, Syngrammata, II, 106, 24

62 post *ἠνεσχόμεθα* lacunam statui

42

Being such a man, then, I came to be entangled with the "new theologians" who are big names and extremely famous for virtue and wisdom, the men, in fact, who were responsible for the rejection by the Church of the notorious Barlaam—who was their opponent—because he too was saying some strange things, but it is not the time to discuss these now. This elated Palamas no end, and inflated his pride, and, having seized the opportunity of Barlaam's departure and condemnation, but also of an ecclesiastical tome against him, he made full use of them, in a most impious fashion, against piety and against myself who had detected the impiety of his doctrines, just as Arios made full use of the decisions against Sabellios. And he proclaimed that what had happened confirmed his ⟨impious doctrine⟩, and he regarded me as banished from the Church because I, allegedly, held altogether the same beliefs as Barlaam, and he organized everything against me. And swords were drawn against me, and my blood fell on the ground of piety—O earth and sun!—because I did not tolerate the impious sayings * * * who taught us that there is one divinity in three hypostases, "one in three and three in one," and that this is the only uncreated and eternal, simple, without partition or division, invisible, intangible, formless, incomprehensible, without qualities; and that nothing is coeternal with it in any way, neither being, nor nonbeing, nor life, nor wisdom, nor goodness, nor visible, nor invisible. On the other hand, anything that one might call uncreated and without beginning and unbegotten and supersubstantial, whether life or wisdom or energy or power or goodness or glory or kingdom, this ⟨they taught us⟩ is the divine nature itself, a triad with respect to persons and a monad with respect to divinity. ⟨They did not teach us⟩ that there are many things unequal and dissimilar and altogether different, which are uncreated and unbegotten divinities, of the nature and essence of God, ⟨divinities⟩ which are activated and "infinitely lower" than God and of which some are comprehensible in themselves while others can be apprehended even by bodily eyes; so that even amongst these lower divinities, some are higher while others are lower, as the present humbug ⟨proclaims⟩, which produces a number of uncreated and unequal and most varied divinities at the rate of the number of divine names. Or rather, at one time they ⟨the Palamites⟩ do this, and at another they say, in a manner far more polytheistic even than that of the pagans, that the multitude of

Ἑλλήνων πολυθεώτερον, τίνος μὲν οὐ καὶ συνθετώτερόν τε καὶ πολυειδέστερον, τίνος δὲ οὐ πολυμερέστερον καὶ ἀνομοιώτερον καὶ ἀνισώτερον αὐτὸ ἑαυτῷ τὸ θεῖον τιθέμενοι; τὸ ἄρρητον καὶ ὑπερούσιον καὶ πάντων αἴτιον ἕν, τὸ πρὸ παντὸς ἑνὸς καὶ πλήθους καὶ ὅλου καὶ μέρους καὶ ὅρου καὶ ἀοριστίας καὶ πέρατος καὶ ἀπειρίας, κατὰ τοὺς θείους τῆς εὐσεβείας ὅρους· ἐφ' ὃ δεῖν καὶ ἡμᾶς, ὁ μέγας φησὶ Διονύσιος, ἀπὸ τῶν πολλῶν τῇ δυνάμει τῆς θεϊκῆς ἑνότητος ἐπιστρεφομένους ἑνιαίως ὑμνεῖν τὴν ὅλην καὶ μίαν θεότητα, τοῦτο δὴ τὸ πρὸ πάντων καὶ πάντων αἴτιον ἕν. καθ' ὧν ἀτέχνως κἀκεῖνον ἐκτεθεικὼς τὸν ὅρον φαίνεται τῆς εὐσεβείας ὁ τοῦτον ἐκτεθεικώς, ἢ καθ' οὗ μάλιστα πάντων ὅρου τῆς εὐσεβείας οὗτοι διὰ πάντων ἐχώρησαν, ὃν ὁ μέγας μετὰ τὸν πρῶτον θεολόγος συντέθεικεν, οὐχ ἕνα μὲν ὅρον εὐσεβείας ἡγησόμεθα, λέγων, προσκυνεῖν τὸν Πατέρα καὶ τὸν Υἱὸν καὶ τὸ ἅγιον Πνεῦμα, τὴν μίαν ἐν τοῖς τρισὶ θεότητα καὶ δύναμιν, μηδὲν ὑπερσέβοντες, μηδ' ὑποσέβοντες (τὸ μὲν γὰρ ἀδύνατον, τὸ δὲ ἀσεβές), μηδὲ μέγεθος ἓν ὀνομάτων καινότησι διακόπτοντες, οὐδὲν γὰρ ἑαυτοῦ μεῖζον ἢ ἔλαττον; ἢ πῶς μετρεῖται τὸ ἄπειρον, ἵν' ὃ τῶν περατουμένων ἐστί, τοῦτο πάθοι θεότης βαθμοῖς τε μετρουμένη καὶ ὑποβάσεσι;

Τούτων οὕτως ἐχόντων, οἱ μὲν ἔγραφον ὑπὲρ τῆς ἀσεβείας τῆς ἑαυτῶν παμπληθεῖς καὶ πολυτρόπους λόγους καὶ οὐδὲν οὔτ' ἀσεβείας, οὔτ' ἀμαθίας ἐλλείποντας, [fol. 54r] ὡς καὶ αὐτὸς συνεῖδες σοφώτατά γε καὶ ἀκριβέστατα, ἡμῖν δὲ οὐδὲ γρύζειν ἐξῆν πρὶν εἰς πληγὰς ἐμπίπτειν καὶ δεινὴν ἀτιμίαν· καὶ οἷς γὰρ εὐσεβεῖν ἐδοκοῦμεν, οὐδὲ τούτοις ἡμᾶς ἐδόκει δεῖν ἀντιγράφειν πρὸς τὰς καινοφωνίας, ἵνα μὴ καὶ αὐτοὶ θορυβῶμεν τοῖς λόγοις τὴν ἐκκλησίαν, ὡς ἔλεγον, καὶ τὸ πῦρ προσανάπτωμεν. καὶ ἦσαν τῶν ἀσεβῶν οἱ εὐσεβεῖς ἀδιάκριτοι, ἁμαρτάνειν καὶ οὗτοι σὺν ἐκείνοις δοκοῦντες, μᾶλλον δὲ τοῖς μὲν καθάπαξ πεπεισμένοις ἐκείνοις—οὐκ ὀλίγοι δὲ ἦσαν—ἀσεβεῖς ἐκρινόμεθα παρ' εὐσεβοῦντας αὐτούς, τοῖς δὲ μέσοις ἀμφοῖν γενομένοις, ὥσπερ ἐπὶ τρυτάνης, καὶ συνιδεῖν οὐ δυναμένοις τὸ ψεῦδος ἢ τἀληθές—καὶ γὰρ καὶ εἰς τοιαύτην οὐκ ὀλίγοι

84–87 Dion. Areop., *De divin. nomin.*, 13, 3 (PG, 3, 980C) || 88–92 Dion. Areop., *De div. nom.*, 13, 3 (PG, 3, 980C) || 95–101 Greg. Naz., *Or.* 22, 12 (PG, 35, 1114C) || 101–104 *ἢ . . . ὑποβάσεσι idem*, *Or.*18, 16 (PG, 35, 1005A)

---

116 *τριτάνης* M

42 divinities is "beyond counting." For do they not consider God to be unto Himself more composite and multiform and multiple and dissimilar and unequal than anything else? "The ineffable and supersubstantial One, the cause of all; which existed before any monad and multitude and whole and part and limit and illimitability and finite and infinite," according to the divine laws of piety. "Turning from the many towards this, with the power of the divine unity," the great Dionysios says, "we too must praise as a unit the whole and single Divinity, the One itself, that is, the cause which precedes all and all!" He who set forth the following rule of piety, also, seems to have done so simply against the Palamites, or they in every way have gone especially against this rule of piety which the second great theologian composed, saying: "Shall we not hold one rule of piety: to worship the Father and the Son and the Holy Spirit, the one divinity and power in three hypostases, honoring nothing more or less (for the former is impossible and the latter impious) without breaking up the single majesty with newfangled terms, for nothing is bigger or smaller than itself?" "Or how is the infinite to be measured, so that what is characteristic of finite beings may happen to divinity when it is measured by degrees and successive diminutions?"

Things being so, they wrote in defense of their impieties a multitude of wily discourses which lacked nothing either in impiety or ignorance, as you too perceived most wisely and accurately indeed, but I was not permitted even to make a sound before being subjected to beatings and terrible disgrace. And even those who thought that I was pious did not think that I ought to write an answer to the "newfangled talk," lest I disturb the Church with my writings, as they said, and kindle the fire. And the pious were indistinguishable from the impious, since these too appeared to be at fault together with them. Or rather, those who were absolutely persuaded by the Palamites—and they were not few—decided that I was impious in comparison with the ⟨Palamites⟩, who were pious. And those who stood in the middle, as if on a balance, and were unable to perceive the falsehood or the truth—for many also fell into that state because of them, being pulled in this direction by their

42

διάθεσιν ὑπὸ τούτων ἐνέπεσον, τῇδε μὲν ἐκ τῆς ἐθάδος αὐτοῖς περὶ τοῦ θείου δόξης ἑλκόμενοι, ἐκεῖσε δὲ ἀνθελκόμενοι ταῖς καιναῖς πιθανότησι—τοῖς δὴ τοιούτοις καὶ αὐτοὶ πλημμελεῖν ἐδοκοῦμεν. οἱ δὲ συνήδεσαν μὲν ἡμῖν καθαρὰν τὴν εὐσέβειαν, οὔτε δὲ συνηγόρουν, οὔτ' εἴων ἡμᾶς ἐλευθέρως μάχεσθαι τῇ δυσσεβείᾳ διὰ τὰ προειρημένα, παρορᾶν δὲ ὡς οὐδὲν ὂν ἠξίουν οὐδὲ οἷον τὴν ἐκκλησίαν βλάψαι, καὶ ταῦτα πολλῶν φανερῶς καὶ σφόδρα πολλῶν ἡμμένον καὶ διαφθεῖραν αὐτοὺς καὶ πρόσω χωροῦν ἀεί· τοῖς δ' ὡς ἰδιώταις ἡμῖν ἀρχιερατικῆς ἀξίας οὐκ ἐξεῖναι τοῖς τοιούτοις ἐπιχειρεῖν ἐδόκει, κἂν πάνυ σαφῶς ὑπὲρ τῆς εὐσεβείας καὶ κατὰ δυσσεβείας ἐσχάτης ἀγωνιζώμεθα· καὶ ταῦτα μυρίων ὄντων οἳ πρὸς ἀρχιερέας, καὶ τούτων τοὺς κορυφαίους, καὶ συνόδους ὅλας αἱρετικῶν, αὐτοὶ μηδ' ἱερεῖς ὄντες ὅλως, ἀντέστησαν ὑπὲρ τῆς εὐσεβείας καὶ προὐκινδύνευσαν.

Διὰ ταῦτα τότε ἡμεῖς εἰς τοὐμφανὲς οὐκ ἐγράφομεν, ἀλλ' ἀνῃροῦμεν μὲν τὸ κακὸν διὰ λόγων, αὐτοὺς δὲ τοὺς λόγους οὐκ ἐπεδείκνυμεν, κρύφα γὰρ τοῦτο ἐποιοῦμεν καί, ὡς εἰπεῖν, ὑπ' ὀδόντα, τὸ δὲ τῶν λόγων εἶδος οὐκ ἐκ παρασκευῆς καὶ τάξεως, οὐδ' ἀναλόγου τόνου ταῖς ὑποθέσεσιν, ἀλλ' ὡς ἐν μεθημερινοῖς ἀγῶσι καὶ πράγμασι, τρεχόντων ἡμῶν ἀεὶ πανταχόσε τῆς πόλεως καὶ νύκτωρ καὶ μεθ' ἡμέραν, ὥσπερ ἐπὶ πυρκαϊὰν (τὸ δόγμα τῆς ἀσεβείας τόδε ἅπαν σχεδὸν ἐμπιπρῶν οὗπερ ἅψαιτο), καὶ τούτοις οὐδ' ἀναπνεῖν ἐχόντων. ἐπεὶ δ' ὁ τῆς εὐσεβείας Θεὸς ἐπεῖδε τὸ κακὸν ὅποι πρόεισι καὶ [fol. 54v] ἠλέησε τὴν θ' ἡμετέραν ἀσθένειαν καὶ τὴν ἱερὰν αὐτοῦ ἐκκλησίαν, ὁ μὲν θειότατος ἡμῶν δεσπότης ὁ οἰκουμενικὸς πατριάρχης, στραφεὶς ἀπὸ τῶν ἄλλων αὐτοῦ φροντίδων ἃς ἑαυτῷ δεινὰς καὶ μεγάλας ἐπικειμένας εἶχεν ὑπὲρ τῆς εὐσεβοῦς ἐκ Θεοῦ βασιλείας τυραννουμένης, ἀντέστη καὶ πρὸς τὴν Παλαμναίαν πλάνην, ἀκολουθούσης αὐτῷ προθύμως καὶ τῆς ἡμῶν εὐσεβοῦς τε καὶ θείας καὶ κρατίστης δεσποίνης μετὰ τοῦ θειοτάτου παιδὸς μὲν αὐτῆς, Ῥωμαίων δὲ βασιλέως, καὶ τῆς φιλευσεβοῦς αὐτῶν καὶ γενναίας συγκλήτου, οἳ σύνοδον ἱερὰν συγκροτήσαντες μετεκαλέσαντο μὲν τὸν καινὸν θεολόγον ἐπὶ τοῖς δόγμασιν, ὁ δὲ ἀπέδρα καὶ ᾤχετο προκαταγνοὺς ἑαυτοῦ·. οἱ δὲ αὐτοῦ τῶν λόγων δυσσέβειαν, ὡς ἔδει, κατέγνωσαν καὶ πυρὸς τροφὴν γενέσθαι δεῖν αὐτοὺς ἐψηφίσαντο. ὕστερον δὲ φωραθεὶς ἐν Ἡρακλείᾳ τῆς Θρᾴκης

134–135 cf. Basil. Caes., *Adv. Eunom.* I, 1 (PG, 29, 501A); *Epist.* 204, 4 (PG, 32, 794B) || 150 cf. Greg. Naz., *Or.*29, 10 (PG, 36, 88A)

---

121 *συνείδεσαν* M || 137 *ἀγῶσι ἀγῶσι* M || 139 *ἐμπιπρᾶν* M

42

customary belief about God, and in that direction by the newfangled persuasion—of course the latter thought that I as well was at fault. Others were well aware that my piety was genuine, but neither pleaded my cause nor allowed me to fight freely against this impiety for the aforementioned reasons, and demanded that I disregard it as being insignificant and unable to hurt the Church; this despite the fact that it had openly attacked many, in fact a great many, and had destroyed them and was forever advancing. Others thought that I, lacking the rank of bishop, was not permitted to attempt such things, even though I was very clearly fighting for piety and against extreme impiety. And that, when there are innumerable men who fought against bishops, even those at the top, and against whole synods of heretics; without being themselves priests at all, they resisted and were the first to risk their lives in defense of piety.

For this reason, I did not write openly at that time, but refuted the evil by means of discourses; yet I did not show these discourses, for I was doing that secretly and, so to speak, surreptitiously. And the form of the discourses was not the outcome of preparation and orderly arrangement, nor was their tenor suitable to the topics, but like my daily struggles and troubles, for I was forever running all over the city night and day, as if combating a fire. (I mean this doctrine of impiety which burns almost anything that it would touch), and so I did not have the time even to breathe. And when the God of piety, seeing how far the evil had advanced, showed His mercy towards my infirmity as well as towards His Holy Church, our most divine lord the Ecumenical Patriarch, turned from the other cares which he had pressing upon him greatly and terribly, ⟨cares⟩ for the safety of the pious and divine Empire which was under the sway of tyranny, and rose against the Palamnaian deception also, and our pious and divine and excellent Empress followed him eagerly, together with her most divine son, the Emperor of the Romans, and their pious and noble senate. They convoked a holy synod and summoned the "new theologian" to account for his doctrines, but he fled and was gone, condemning himself in advance. And they condemned his writings for impiety, as was fitting, and voted that they should be fed to the fire. Later, when he was caught hiding in Heracleia in Thrace

κρυπτόμενος καὶ ταῦτα τοὺς συνόντας διδάσκων, εἰς τὴν Πόλιν ἀνήχθη καὶ ἀπῃτήθη παραίτησιν τῶν ἑαυτοῦ δογμάτων, ἀλλ' οὐ παρέσχε, καὶ διὰ τοῦτο εἱρκτῇ παραδέδοται, ἣ καὶ νῦν αὐτὸν ἔχει, ὡς ἂν μὴ λυμαίνηται τῇ τοῦ Θεοῦ ἐκκλησίᾳ, τὰ γὰρ ἐν μέσῳ παρίημι, μὴ σφόδρα πολὺ τῆς ἐπιστολῆς ὑπερβαίην τὸ μέτρον. ἐνταῦθά τινος παρρησίας ἧπται ἡμῶν ὁ λόγος καὶ προὔκοψέ τι τοῦ πολλοῦ πρῴην σκότους, αὐτοῦ τοι τοῦ θειοτάτου πατριάρχου γράψαι ἡμῖν ἐπιτρέψαντος, καὶ τοῦτο μετὰ στενοῦ τοῦ θάρρους καὶ σχολιαστικῶς, ἀλλ' οὐκ ἐλευθέρου παντάπασιν, οὐδὲ ἀξίως ἀποδυομένου πρὸς τὸν ἀγῶνα τῆς ὑποθέσεως, εἴ τίς ἐστιν ἱκανὸς εἰς τοσοῦτον, ὡς ἔγωγε οὔκ εἰμι· καὶ τοῦτο ποιεῖ δέει τοῦ μή τι καὶ αὐτοὺς ἡμᾶς, ὥς φησι, παρενεχθῆναι φιλοτιμίᾳ τινί.

Τῶν δὴ γεγενημένων ἡμῖν προχείρως καὶ σχολιαστικῶς, ὡς ἔφην, κατὰ τῆς ἀσεβείας λόγων τῇ σῇ σοφίᾳ πεπόμφαμεν, εἰργασμένοι μὲν καί τινας σπουδαιοτέρους, οὔπω δὲ καιρὸν εἰληφότες τῆς αὐτῶν παρρησίας διὰ τὰ εἰρημένα. σὺ δὲ καὶ ταῦτα λαβών, ὦ σοφώτατε, τὸ πᾶν μὲν τῆς ἀσεβείας διὰ τούτων συνήσεις, ὅς γε καὶ τούτων ἄνευ αὐτὴν ἀπὸ βραχέων τινῶν ὀξέως μάλα πεφώρακας καὶ ὡς ἔδει σε πεφωρακέναι ταύτην, ἀγωνιῇ δὲ κατ' αὐτῆς ἀξίως τῆς εὐσεβείας καὶ τῆς σαυτοῦ σοφίας, καὶ ἡμῖν ἀποστελεῖς τοὺς λόγους ἐπ' αἰσχύνῃ μὲν καὶ πτώσει τῆς ἀσεβείας αὐτῆς [fol. 55r] καὶ τοῦ πατρὸς τοῦ ταύτης, δόξῃ δὲ Θεοῦ, κράτει δὲ τῆς εὐσεβείας, παροξυσμῷ δὲ καὶ τῶν ὁμοίων ζήλῳ, τῶν γε νῦν ἐπὶ τούτοις ἐγνωκότων κοιμᾶσθαι, τὴν μὲν αὐτὴν ἡμῖν εὐσέβειαν πεπρεσβευκότων, μεῖζον δὲ δυναμένων κατὰ τῆς ἀσεβείας περιουσίᾳ λόγων. εἰ γὰρ ὀλίγαι σου συλλαβαὶ μεγάλην ῥοπὴν καὶ τροπὴν ἐνεποίησαν τῇδε, τὴν μὲν τοῖς εὐσεβέσι καθάπερ ἐκβακχευθεῖσι, τὴν δὲ τοῖς ἐναντίοις ὥσπερ κεραυνωθεῖσι, τί γένοιτ' ἄν, εἰ λόγους ἐναγωνίους δεῦρο; τί ἔτι; οὕτως ἡμᾶς ἴσθι σοι τεθαρρηκότας καὶ οὕτω μόνον ἱκανὸν ἡγουμένους δικαίως εἶναι προστάτην τῆς εὐσεβείας καὶ πρόμαχον, ὥστε σε καὶ ἀξιοῦμεν χώραν ἡμῖν ἑτοιμάσαι ἀποστροφῆς αὐτόθι, καὶ πρὸ πολλοῦ γε τοῦτο διενοήθημεν, εἴ τι συμβαίη τῇδε ἀντίξουν ἡμῖν ἀπὸ τῆς δυσσεβείας καὶ βιαζόμενον. γράψαι δὲ ἡμῖν δίκαιος ἂν εἴης ἐκ τῆς σαυτοῦ σοφίας καὶ περὶ τῶν ἡμετέρων λόγων, εἴτε πάντ' ἀσφαλεῖς σοι δοκοῦσιν εἶναι, εἴτε τι καὶ τ' ἀκριβοῦς ἐκπίπτειν, ὡς ἡμεῖς γέ σε νόμον ἀξιοῦμεν ἤδη κἀν τοῖς τοιούτοις ἔχειν, καὶ μάλιστα ἐν τοῖς τοιούτοις, τῆς τε σοφίας ἧς ἔχεις χάριν, τῆς τε περὶ τὴν εὐσέβειαν εὐγνωμοσύνης.

Τήν γε μὴν ἐπιστολὴν ἔγραψέ μοι—δεῖ γάρ σε καὶ τοῦτ'

---

172 πεφωρακέναι] περιωρακέναι M || 181 εἰ . . . δεῦρο non satis perspicio

42

and teaching these things to those who kept company with him, he was brought back to the city and a rejection of his doctrines was demanded of him, but he did not submit it, and for this reason he was sent to prison, which still holds him that he may not disgrace the Church of God (for I am not mentioning what happened in between, in order not to exceed too much the limits of the letter). At this point, I attained some freedom of speech and made a little progress after the previous great darkness, for the most holy Patriarch himself allowed me to write, and that with limited audacity and in the style of commentaries, not altogether freely and in the manner of a man stripping for a fight worthy of the topic—if anyone is equal to such a great task, as I certainly am not—and this he does, as he says, from the fear that I too may be carried away by some ambitious rivalry.

I have, therefore, sent to your Wisdom ⟨one⟩ of the discourses against this impiety which, as I said, I wrote hurriedly and in commentary style. For I have written some others which are more important, but I have had no opportunity to bring them into the open for the reasons that I have already mentioned. But when you receive even this, my most wise friend, you will comprehend from them the whole impiety, for even without them, from some brief examples, you detected it very acutely and exactly as you ought to; and you will fight against this in a manner worthy of your piety and wisdom, and will send me your writings to the disgrace and downfall of this impiety and of its author, but to the glory of God and the victory of piety and to the provocation and envy of your peers who are determined, at least for the moment, to close their eyes to these things, though they hold the same pious beliefs as I do and are able to do more against the impiety due to their superior learning. For, if a few syllables from you produced here such a great change and such a turn in the state of affairs, on the one hand, amongst the pious, just as if they had been filled with Bacchic enthusiasm, and, on the other hand, amongst their opponents, just as if they had been struck by a bolt, what would happen if ⟨you should send⟩ here polemical tracts? What then? Be assured that I have such confidence in you and such regard for you, as the only person able to be justly the protector and defender of piety, that not only do I ask you to prepare for me over there a place of refuge, but I thought of it long ago, in case something adverse or violent should happen to me here as a result of this impiety. You have a right, on account of your own wisdom, to write to me also about my discourses, whether they seem to you to be entirely correct or, in fact, to fall somewhat short of perfection, because I already expect to have you as a law in these matters also, and especially in these, both on account of your wisdom and your good judgment regarding piety.

εἰδέναι—ὁ Παλαμᾶς ἀπὸ Θεσσαλονίκης, φθάσαντος μὲν αὐτὸν τοῦ Βαρλαὰμ καὶ παραγενομένου τῇδε καὶ ἐγκαλοῦντος αὐτῷ πρὸς τὴν σύνοδον Μασσαλιανισμὸν καὶ παραδογματισμόν, ἐμοῦ δὲ ἀντιπεσόντος αὐτῷ ἐφ' ᾧ μὴ ἑλεῖν ἐρήμην τὸν ἄνθρωπον, ἀλλὰ περιμένειν αὐτὸν ἀφῖχθαι καὶ δοῦναι περὶ τῶν ἐγκλημάτων λόγον· τοῦτό τε οὖν λέγων, καὶ τὸ κοινῇ κατὰ τῶν παρ' ἡμῖν Ναζιραίων ἁπάντων φέρεσθαι τὸν Βαρλαὰμ ὡς Μασσαλιανῶν, ἀλλ' οὐχὶ μόνον τὸν Παλαμᾶν κακίζων, καὶ τὸ μηδ' αὐτὸν ὀρθῶς πάντῃ, μηδ' ἀνεπιλήπτως ταῦτα μετέρχεσθαι δοκεῖν μοι τὸν Βαρλαάμ, ἐπεῖχον τὸν κατὰ τοῦ Παλαμᾶ παροξυσμὸν τῆς ἱερᾶς συνόδου. ἀνθ' ὧν μοι ταῦτα ἔγραψεν ἅπερ ἐγὼ νῦν σοι πέπομφα μετρίως ἀνασκευάσας, ὡς ἂν τά θ' ἡμέτερα κρίνῃς, εἰ μηδαμοῦ τῆς ἀληθείας ἀφέστηκε, τά τε τῆς ἐπιστολῆς, εἰ μηδαμοῦ τῆς πλάνης· ὡς γὰρ οὐκ ἔρρωται τοῖς δόγμασιν ὁ Παλαμᾶς εἰς εὐσέβειαν, καὶ προὔμαθες εὖ ποιῶν καὶ ἔφθης ἀποφηνάμενος. ταῦτα δὲ οὕτω κρίνας, κατὰ τὴν τελεωτάτην ἐπιστήμην ἣν ἔχεις, ἀξίως ταύτης τε καὶ σαυτοῦ τοῖς πᾶσι δείξῃς [fol. 55v] αὐτὰ τοῖς οἰκείοις ἀγῶσιν ἅπερ ἐστί, καὶ στήσῃς τῆς Παλαμναίας πλάνης τὸν ἐπὶ πλέον δρόμον, μᾶλλον δὲ ἀπελάσῃς καθάπαξ τῆς ἐκκλησίας Χριστοῦ. καίτοι σε οἶμαι δήπου μηδ' ἀξιώσειν σφοδροῦ ταῦτα ἀγῶνος, εὐκαταγέλαστα ὄντα καθάπερ τὰ πάνυ γερόντων παραληρήματα, καὶ αὐτὰ ἑαυτοῖς ὅπερ αὐτοὶ ἑαυτοῖς οἱ αὐθένται γινόμενα· οὕτω δεινῶς ἑαυτοῖς ἀντιπίπτει καὶ μάχεται. τὸ δ' οὖν πλῆθος καὶ τοῖς τοιούτοις ἁλίσκεται, κατ' ἐρημίαν ἐλέγχων ἐρρωμένων τῆς πλάνης. ὅπερ οὖν εὖ συνιδὼν καὶ αὐτὸς ἀποφαίνῃ· δεῖ δὴ πρὸς ταῦτα λόγων, ὡς ἔφης, ἐμβριθεστέρων, εἰ μέλλοι τῆς τῶν πολλῶν λύμης παύσεσθαι, καὶ κλεινῶν ἀνδρῶν ὧν ἂν εἶεν οἱ λόγοι· τοιοῦτος δὲ σὺ καὶ τὰ σὰ καὶ τῶν τοιούτων τὰ πρῶτα καὶ τὸ κεφάλαιον.

43. Τῷ φιλοσόφῳ Γρηγορᾷ

Νύττω σε τὸν κοινὸν Ἡρακλέα ἐφ' ἅ σε νύττειν παρακαλεῖ Λαπίθης ὁ Κύπριος, ὃν οὐ δεύτερον εἶναί σου στρατηγόν, ἀλλὰ πρῶτον, οὐ πρὸς τῆς σῆς σοφίας· τὸν ἐκ τῆς ὑπερορίας τοῦ τὴν πόλιν οἰκοῦντος παρ' ᾗ τὰ κατὰ τῆς εὐσεβείας ὀρχεῖται τολμήματα καὶ τὰ πρῶτα παρ' αὐτῇ φερομένου τῆς ἐπὶ λόγοις δόξης. δεινὸν δὲ καὶ τὴν μεγάλην πόλιν Κύπρου δευτέραν ἐν τούτῳ τὸ κατὰ σὲ φανῆναι.

---

193 οὐ Παλαμᾶς M || 213 παραλυρήματα M

43: M 47r.

As for the letter—for you must know this, too—Palamas wrote it to me from Thessalonica, because Barlaam had arrived here first and was accusing him, before the Synod, of Messalianism and of teaching false doctrines; whereas I opposed Barlaam in such a way that they would not condemn the man by default, but would wait for him to arrive and answer the charges. By saying this, then, as well as by criticizing the fact that Barlaam brought the charge of Messalianism against all our monks in general and did not blame Palamas alone, while he himself did not seem to me either to pursue these matters in an altogether correct and irreproachable manner, I restrained the Holy Synod's acute annoyance with Palamas. Wherefore he wrote to me what I have now sent you after refuting them moderately, so that you may judge both of my views, and ⟨decide⟩ whether they diverge from truth anywhere, and from those of the letter, if they diverge anywhere from error. For not only did you find out correctly beforehand that Palamas' doctrines with regard to piety are not sound, but you also declared this first. When you have so judged these doctrines, according to the excellent learning that you possess, you will show everybody what they are by your own arguments, in a manner worthy of your learning and yourself, and you will stop the further progress of the Palamnaian deceit; rather, you will drive it out of the Church once and for all. Though in fact I do not think that you will deem them worthy of vehement arguments, because they are easily exposed to ridicule, just like the ravings of the senile; and they become so of their own accord, just as their authors do. This is how terribly they contradict and fight themselves. But the multitude, of course, is won over even by such ⟨arguments⟩, in the absence of vigorous refutations of the deceit. This is exactly what you have well perceived and declared. If these doctrines are to stop causing damage to most people, there is need of more serious writings against them, as you said, and of famous men who would be their authors. You are such a man, and your writings are such, and among men of this caliber you are the first and foremost.

43. To the philosopher Gregoras

I am goading you on to the deeds to which the Cypriote Lapithes urges me to goad you, our common Heracles! It does not befit your wisdom that he should be first and not second to you in command of the fight for piety; for he comes from beyond the frontiers, while you live in the city where insolent acts against piety are being perpetrated, and you have the fame of being the city's foremost scholar. Besides, it is awful for the great City to appear in this respect second to Cyprus on account of you.

Ὥστ' οὐχ ὑπὲρ τῆς εὐσεβείας μόνον, ἀλλὰ καὶ τῆς πόλεως καὶ τῆς σῆς σοφίας πρεσβεύομεν, ὡς καὶ τοῦ Θεοῦ καὶ τῆς πόλεως καὶ τῆς σῆς ἐπιστήμης καὶ ὅλως τῶν λόγων αὐτῶν παρακαλούντων δι' ἡμῶν ἐπὶ τὰς βεβήλους καινοφωνίας τὴν θαυμαστήν σου γλῶτταν. γενοῦ δὴ στρατηγός, ὦ γενναῖε· οὐ Παυσανίας ἐπὶ τοὺς Μήδους τοῖς Ἕλλησιν, οὐδὲ Φίλιππος Θηβαίοις ἐπὶ τὰς πύλας, ἀλλ' ὃ πολλῷ τούτων ἐστὶν ἐνδοξότερον, τοῖς εὐσεβέσιν ἐπὶ τοὺς ἀσεβοῦντας.

44. Τῷ φιλοσόφῳ Γρηγορᾷ

Τῆς ἀναισθησίας! τῆς ἰταμότητος! οὐ μᾶλλον δεῖγμα τοῦτο τῆς μὲν Ἀκινδύνου περὶ τὴν εὐσέβειαν εὐπορίας καὶ ἀσφαλείας, τῆς δὲ Παλαμᾶ θαυμαστῆς ἀσεβείας καὶ ἀπορίας, ἀλλὰ πᾶν τοὐναντίον; τὸ μὴ μόνον τὴν τῆς οἰκουμένης προϊσταμένην τοῦ Θεοῦ ἐκκλησίαν ὑπὲρ τῶν κοινῶν δογμάτων συμμαχεῖν Ἀκινδύνῳ καὶ τὸν Παλαμᾶν ἀποβάλλεσθαι καὶ ἀναθεματίζειν, ἀλλὰ καὶ τὰς πορρωτάτω, καὶ μὴ μόνον τοὺς ἐν τῇ τῆς ἐκ Θεοῦ βασιλείας Ῥωμαίων ἐπικρατείᾳ, ἀλλὰ καὶ τοὺς ὑφ' ἑτέροις μὲν ἡγεμόσι τελοῦντας, εὐσεβεῖς δὲ ὁμοίως, παντὶ τῷ θυμῷ τῆς ἀσεβείας ταύτης συγκαταφέρεσθαι; Παλαμᾶς δέ, ὡς ἔοικε, τὴν μὲν παροῦσαν ἐκκλησίαν ἀσεβεῖν ὑπείληφεν, ἧς δὴ καὶ ἀπέρρηκται, ὅτι ταῖς αὐτοῦ δυσσεβείαις οὐ τίθεται, ταῖς πόρρω δὲ κατ' αὐτό τε τοῦτο καὶ ὅτι πόρρω αὐτοῦ διεστήκασι, καὶ τοὺς ὑφ' ἑτέρας δὲ ἡγεμονίας τελοῦντας μετ' εὐσεβείας αὐτὸ τοῦθ' ὅτιπερ ὑφ' ἑτέραις ἡγεμονίαις οὐκ εὐσεβέσιν εἰσί. τὸ δ' εὐσεβὲς οὐκ οἶδα ποῖον αὐτῷ ὑπολέλειπται. τῶν γὰρ εὐσεβῶν οἱ μέν εἰσιν ὧδε, οἱ δ' ἑτέρωθι καὶ πανταχοῦ τῆς οἰκουμένης, ἄλλοι κατ' ἄλλα μέρη καὶ δυναστείας ἄλλας, οὓς πάντας οὗτος ἀσεβεῖς ἀποφαίνεται, ὅτι πάντες αὐτοῦ [fol. 78ᵛ] τὴν ἀσέβειαν ᾔσθηνται καὶ οὐδὲ τοῖς πέρασι δύναται τῆς οἰκουμένης λαθεῖν· ἀλλὰ μεστὴ μὲν Ἀντιόχεια καὶ Κύπρος, ἐῶ γὰρ τὰ καθ' ἡμᾶς, μεστὴ δὲ Ἀλεξάνδρεια, μεστὴ δὲ καὶ αὐτὴ Ῥώμη τῆς τῶν ἀσεβημάτων ὑπερβολῆς τῶν τούτου, μεστὰ δὲ πάντα. πάντων δὲ καταβοώντων ταύτης, ὀλίγοι κομιδῇ τῇδε ὑπὸ τούτου πεπλάνηνται, μεθ' ὧν πρὸς τοῖς ἄλλοις κακοῖς οὑτοσὶ καὶ ἀκέφαλος· οὐκ Ἀκινδύνῳ πεπεισμένων—πόθεν;—ἀλλ' ὑφ' ἑτέρων ζηλωτῶν εὐσεβείας, πανταχόσε τῆς ἀσεβείας τῆς αὐτοῦ βοηθείσης,

---

43: 11 II Tim. 2:16

44: M 78ʳ–79ʳ. Ed. Tsolakes, Γεώργιος Λαπίθης, 88–90.

I am, therefore, making an appeal not only on behalf of piety, but also on behalf of the City and your wisdom, because God and the City and your learning, in short, scholarship itself, through me exhort your marvelous tongue ⟨to fight⟩ against the "profane newfangled talk." Become, then, a general, my noble friend! Not as Pausanias was to the Greeks in the war against the Persians or Philip to the Thebans against their city gates, but, what is much more glorious than this, a leader of the pious against the impious!

44. To the philosopher Gregoras

What callousness! What insolence! Is this not, rather, evidence of Akindynos' abundance of piety and sound thinking and of the astonishing impiety and perplexity of Palamas, but quite the opposite? ⟨I mean⟩ the fact that not only the Church of God which presides over the inhabited world is allied with Akindynos in defending the sacred dogmas and in rejecting and anathematizing Palamas, but also the most distant churches, and that pious men, not only those under the rule of the divine emperor of the Romans, but also those who live under other rulers and are equally pious, wholeheartedly condemn this impiety? As it seems, then, Palamas assumes that the Church here, from which, in fact, he has broken away, is impious because it does not confirm his profanities; the churches abroad for the very same reason and because they are greatly at variance with him; and those who live under foreign rule because of the very fact that they are under foreign, not pious, rule. But I do not know what sort of piety is left for him! Since some pious men are here and others elsewhere and all over the inhabited world, while others are in different parts and kingdoms, all of these he denounces as impious, because they have all detected his impiety, and he cannot escape being found out, even at the end of the world; but Antioch has had enough, and so has Cyprus (for I shall not mention us here), and Alexandria and even Rome have had enough of this man's extravagance in impiety; everything has had enough! Here just a few people have been deceived by him (along with these men, in addition to other evils, he also has no bishop), since everybody inveighs against him, not because they were persuaded by Akindynos—how can it be?—but by other admirers of piety, seeing that his profanity was proclaimed everywhere, or rather, even by its own author, Palamas and his disciples.

44

μᾶλλον δὲ καὶ ὑπ' αὐτοῦ τοῦ ταύτης πατρὸς Παλαμᾶ καὶ τῶν αὐτοῦ σπουδαστῶν· διασπαρέντων αὐτοῦ τῶν πονηρῶν σπερμάτων ἐπὶ τῷ ῥιζωθῆναι καὶ φυῆναι καὶ αὐξηθῆναι καὶ καρπὸν ἐνεγκεῖν τὸν παμπόνηρον, τὰ δὲ ἀντὶ τοῦ ἐπιδοῦναι καὶ θαυμασθῆναι, κατέγνωσται ἁπανταχοῦ καὶ κεκίνηκε δεῦρο καθ' ἑαυτῶν ἐπιστολὰς οἵας προσῆκε καὶ λόγους εὐσεβῶν καὶ σοφῶν ἀνδρῶν φέρεσθαι κατ' ἀσεβῶν δογμάτων. ὧν οὐ φέρων τὸν ἔλεγχον, ἐπὶ τὸν 'Ακίνδυνον τρέπεται καὶ βλασφημεῖ τηνάλλως ὁ τοιοῦτος ἄνθρωπος, οἷον ἐκεῖνοι φημίζουσιν—οὐ γὰρ ἄλλο γε οὐδὲν ἐρῶ—τὸν οὐχ οὕτως αἴτιον αὐτῷ γεγονότα ὡς αὐτὸς αὐτῷ τῶν καθ' αὑτοῦ γραμμάτων. μάρτυς γὰρ ἡ σὴ σοφία καὶ αὐτὰ παρόντα τοῦ Λαπίθου τὰ πρῶτα πρὸς τὸν ἱερὸν Ὑάκινθον γράμματα ὡς οὐ παρ' 'Ακινδύνου μαθὼν ἐκεῖνος ἢ γράψαντος ἢ ἄλλως μεμηνυκότος αὐτῷ τὴν Παλαμναίαν πολυθεΐαν, ἀλλ' οὐκ οἶδ' ὅθεν ἑτέρωθεν τῷ ἀνδρὶ ταῦτα γράψειεν, ὅθεν ἐν τούτοις καταβοῶν μὲν τῆς ἀσεβείας ταύτης, θαυμάζων δὲ καὶ τῆς σῆς ἡρωϊκῆς ὑπεροχῆς τῶν λόγων ὡς πρὸς τοσαύτην σιωπώσης ἀσέβειαν, δέον μηδένα εἶναι πρὸ σοῦ τὸν ἀναιρέτην ταύτης, οὕτω μέμνηται τοῦ 'Ακινδύνου ὡς ἀμυδρότατα διακούσας περὶ αὐτοῦ καὶ τοσοῦτο μόνον ὡς εἴη τις ὁ τοῦ κακοῦ τούτου μὴ ἀνασχόμενος, μηδὲ τοὔνομα εἰδώς· καὶ αὐτῷ μέντοι τούτῳ μαλακίαν ἐξονειδίζει πρὸς τὸν ἀγῶνα τοῦτον.

Ἆρ' οὖν γένοιτ' ἂν τοῦ Παλαμᾶ πικρότερος συκοφάντης καὶ ἰταμώτερος, ὃς ὑπὸ παντὸς ἀνδρὸς εὐσεβοῦς ἀσεβῶν ἐλεγχόμενος αὐθορμήτοις ἐλέγχοις ἐπ' 'Ακίνδυνον μάλιστα τὴν κακίαν τρέπει τὴν ἑαυτοῦ, τοῦτον τὸν τρόπον οἰόμενος ἐκφυγεῖν τοὺς ἐλέγχους; κακῶς εἰδώς· ἕως γὰρ ἂν ἀσεβῇ, οὐκ ἔστιν αὐτὸν ἀπαλλαγῆναι τῶν εὐσεβῶν ἐλέγχων, κἂν μηδεὶς ᾖ 'Ακίνδυνος, μᾶλλον δὲ μυρίοις 'Ακιν-[fol. 79r]δύνοις καὶ πολλῷ σφοδροτέροις 'Ακινδύνου περιπεσεῖται, οἷς εὐσεβείας ὡς ἀληθῶς μελήσει.

Σὺ δέ, ὦ βέλτιστε, εἰ φίλον ἦγες εἰς τὸ παρὸν δυσσεβῆ τὸν Λαπίθην, ὡς Παλαμᾶς ἀποφαίνεται, καί σε τοῦτ' ἐλελήθει, σκόπει· ἢ γὰρ Παλαμᾶν ἢ Λαπίθην εὐσεβῆ νομίζειν ἀνάγκη σοι, τὸν δ' ἕτερον δυσσεβῆ. ἀλλ', οἶμαι, Λαπίθου μόνος ἂν καταγνοίη δυσσέβειαν ὁ δυσσεβέστατος· σὺ δὲ κἀγὼ καὶ πᾶς ὅστις ἐστὶν εὐσεβὴς οὐ τολμήσει. πῶς γὰρ τὸν οὐ μόνον εὐσεβείας περιφανέστατα τρόφιμον, ἀλλὰ καὶ ἧς τρόφιμός ἐστιν εὐσεβείας ὑπέρμαχον, οὐ μόνον ὡς τῇ τοῦ Παλαμᾶ πολυθεΐᾳ μαχόμενον, ἀλλὰ καὶ τῇ τῶν Λατίνων βεβήλῳ καινοφωνίᾳ παρ' ὁντινοῦν; καὶ μαρτυροῦσιν

---

64 II Tim. 2:16

---

34 τηνάλως M

44

For his wicked seeds were scattered so as to take root and spring up and grow and bear the most wicked fruit; however, instead of waxing strong and being admired, they have been condemned everywhere, and they have stirred here against themselves the kind of letters and writings from pious and wise men which should be brought against impious doctrines. Not bearing the scrutiny, since he is such a man as they say he is—for I shall not for my part mention anything else—he turns against Akindynos and curses in vain the man who is not responsible for the letters against him as he is himself. For both your Wisdom and the first letter of Lapithes to his holiness Hyakinthos, which is at hand, testify that Lapithes did not find out from Akindynos, either because he wrote to him or otherwise informed him of the Palamnaian polytheism, but from elsewhere, I do not know from where they wrote this to him. Whatever the source, while he inveighs in this letter against this impiety and wonders how your prodigious literary eminence remains silent in the face of such impiety, whereas no one in preference to you should be the one to confute it, he mentions Akindynos just as if he had very dimly heard about him from someone else and only to the extent that there was a man who did not tolerate this wickedness—he does not even know his name—and in fact he reproaches this very man for weakness in respect of this struggle.

Could there be, then, a meaner and more insolent slanderer than Palamas? This man who, while he is automatically exposed as impious by every pious man, turns his own malice against Akindynos more than anyone, thinking that in this way he will escape scrutiny? He is wrong, for as long as he is impious, it is impossible for him to be rid of pious scrutiny, even if there be no Akindynos; rather he will encounter innumerable Akindynoi who will be much more vehement than Akindynos and will care most truly for piety!

But if you, my excellent friend, considered your friend Lapithes to be impious in this case, as Palamas claims, and the following had escaped you, think carefully: you must of necessity consider either Palamas or Lapithes to be pious and the other impious. But I think that only that most impious man would accuse Lapithes of impiety, while you and I and anyone who is pious will not have the effrontery. How is this possible? Since not only has he been nourished by piety most notably, but he also defends the piety that nourished him, not only because he fights against the polytheism of Palamas, but also against the "profane newfangled talk" of the Latins more than any other man whatsoever. And this is attested by the discourses which

οἱ κατὰ ταύτης αὐτῷ γεγενημένοι λόγοι, οὐ τῆς τοῦ Παλαμᾶ γε ὄντες ἀτονίας καὶ ἀθεΐας μεστοί, ἀλλὰ ἀνδρὸς σοφοῦ τε καὶ γενναίου δυνάμεως καὶ τῆς κατὰ τοῦ πατρὸς ἑαυτῶν συκοφαντίας, ἣν αὐτὸν ὡς Λατινόφρονα συκοφαντεῖ Παλαμᾶς, ὑπερτιθέντες τὸν ἑαυτῶν πατέρα.

Σκέψασθαι δὲ ἄξιον καὶ τὴν τοῦ ἤθους τοῦ ἀνδρὸς μοχθηρίαν· ὁ γὰρ παρὰ τοὺς Γαλατηνοὺς τούσδε οὐκ ὀλιγάκις πέμψας τοὺς πείσοντας τὰ ἑαυτοῦ καὶ εἰς Ῥόδον τοὺς λόγους τοὺς ἑαυτοῦ τῷ μαΐστορι καὶ τοῖς ἐκεῖ Λατίνοις, νῦν ἐπειδήπερ οὐδένα πέπεικε Λατίνων ὡς εὐσεβεῖ ταῦτα λέγων, οἷα συκοφαντεῖ καὶ διαβάλλει καὶ βλασφημεῖ τοὺς παρ' ἐκείνοις μὲν διαιτᾶσθαι λαχόντας, πολέμῳ κατασχεθείσης αὐτοῖς τῆς πατρίδος ὑπὸ Λατίνων, οὕτω δὲ ἐκείνοις οὐ πανταχῇ συμφρονοῦντας, ὡς καὶ γενναίοις λόγοις αὐτοῖς ἀντιτάττεσθαι καὶ διελέγχειν ἐλευθέροις ἐλέγχοις ὅποι σφάλλοιντο τῆς εὐσεβείας.

Οὕτως ἐστὶ μιαρὸν καὶ πάντολμον καὶ ἄλογον ἡ ἀπόνοια καὶ τῆς εὐσεβείας ἀπόπτωσις, ἥτις ἀρχὴν λαβοῦσα τῷ Παλαμᾷ, τῷ γενέσθαι Θεὸν ἄκτιστον καὶ ἄναρχον ἑαυτὸν οἰηθῆναι, ὡς φανερῶς ἀποφαίνεται, καὶ τὸ θεῖον οὕτως ὁρᾶν ἐναργῶς, ὥστε αὐτοῦ καὶ τοῖς σαρκικοῖς ὀφθαλμοῖς ἀκριβῶς ὑποπίπτειν τὴν φυσικὴν τοῦ Θεοῦ καὶ οὐσιώδη μορφὴν καὶ θεότητα, οὕτω προῆλθεν ἐπὶ τὸ διασπᾶσαι τοῦτον εἰς ἀνομοίους ἀλλοτριότητας καὶ θεοτήτων πλῆθος ἀριθμὸν ὑπερβαῖνον ἀνίσων καὶ ἀνομοίων καί, ὡς εἰπεῖν, ὁμωνύμων. διόπερ αὐτὸν οὐ μόνος Ἀκίνδυνος, ἀλλὰ καὶ πάντες Χριστιανοὶ οἱ μίαν θεότητα τρισυπόστατον ὁμολογοῦντες, ἄκτιστον, ἀόρατον, ἁπλῆν, ἀδιαίρετον καὶ ἀπαράλλακτον, ὡς τῆς ἐσχάτης ἀσεβείας μετὰ τοῦ πατρὸς αὐτῷ τοῦ Σατανᾶ πατέρα εἰκότως ἀποστρεφόμεθα.

45. Sine titulo

Ἓν ἀγαθὸν ἡ τοῦ Λαπίθου γραμμάτων ἀποστολή· δεύτερον καὶ τούτου μεῖζον ἡ τῆς σῆς αὐτοῦ μετ' ἐκεῖνα παρουσία σοφίας ἐζητηκυίας ἡμᾶς, ἧς ἡμῖν οὐδὲν χαριέστερον. ἀλλὰ τῶν μὲν ἀπελαύσαμεν, σοῦ δ' ἀπετύχομεν, ὥσθ' ὧν ἀπελαύσαμεν οὐχ οὕτως εὐτυ-

---

81–82 τῷ . . . οἰηθῆναι cf. Palamam, *De divinis operationibus*, 37, Syngrammata, II, 122, 27–30 ‖ 86–87 Palamas, *ibid.*, 13, Syngrammata, II, 106, 24

---

81 ante ἀπόπτωσις add. ἡ Tsolakes ‖ 81–82 τῷ γενέσθαι scripsi] τὸ γενέσθαι M

45: Mn 4ʳ. Ed. Karpozilos, *Letters*, 79–80, no. 4.

he composed against it which are, indeed, full not of Palamas' weakness and atheism but of the vigor of a wise and noble man, and they set their author above the false charge against him whereby Palamas charges him falsely with being a Latin sympathizer.

It is also worthwhile considering Palamas' moral depravity. For after sending his men to these Latins in Galata, not a few times, to convince them about his doctrines, and ⟨after sending⟩ his writings to the Master ⟨of the Hospitallers⟩ of Rhodes and to the other Latins there, now that he has failed to convince any of the Latins that he is pious when he says these things, ⟨consider⟩ how he falsely accuses and discredits and slanders those whose lot was to live with them; for their country was seized by the Latins in war, while they disagree with the ⟨Latins⟩ so completely as to oppose them in courageous discourses and to refute them openly wherever they stray from piety.

This is how abominable and shameless and irrational are madness and lapsing from piety; these started with Palamas, with his imagining that he became himself uncreated and eternal God, as he openly declares, and that he sees God so clearly that the natural and essential form and divinity of God are exactly apprehended by his bodily eyes; and in this way he proceeded to tear God up into dissimilar qualitative differences, into an "innumerable" multitude of divinities unequal, dissimilar, and homonymous, so to speak. Wherefore not only Akindynos but all Christians who confess one divinity in three hypostases, uncreated, invisible, simple, indivisible and invariable, rightly turn away from him as the father of the worst impiety, along with his father Satan.

45. No Addressee

The first good thing ⟨that happened to me⟩ was that Lapithes sent me a letter. The second thing, even more important than this, was that after that letter you came here in person, my learned friend, seeking me out, and this pleases me above everything else! But, whereas I enjoyed the letter, I missed you. Since, therefore, I have not so much been fortunate in what I enjoyed as unfortunate in what I missed, I was

χηκότες ὡς δεδυστυχηκότες οἷς οὐκ ἐτύχομεν, μᾶλλον ὡς εἰκὸς ἠνιάθημεν τοῖς δευτέροις ἢ τοῖς προτέροις εὐφράνθημεν. ἀλλ᾽ ὧν μὲν ζητῶν ἡμᾶς ἐπόνησας, ἄριστε, χάριν ὁμολογοῦμεν· ἀντιπονήσομεν δὲ καὶ αὐτοὶ μετ᾽ οὐ πολύ—πῶς γὰρ οὔ;—τὴν παρὰ σὲ πορείαν.

46. Τῷ Λαπίθῃ

Λιμοῦ πρῴην μεγάλου παραμυθίαν τὴν προτέραν ἐπιστολὴν ἰδόντες, νῦν ἤδη πλουτοῦμεν καὶ κορεννύμεθα τῶν σῶν γραμμάτων, σοφώτατε, καὶ θαυμαστῆς ἰσχύος ἐπειλημμένοι συναισθανόμεθα. οὐ γὰρ οὕτω τὰ Ἀχιλλέως ὅπλα τοὺς μὲν οἰκείους ἐθάρσυνε, τοὺς δὲ Τρῶας κατέσειε λάμποντα, ὡς τὰ σὰ γράμματα νευροῖ μὲν τοὺς εὐσεβεῖς, ἐκνευροῖ δὲ τὴν ἀσε-[fol. 68ʳ]βοῦσαν μοῖραν φαινόμενα, καὶ τοὺς μὲν ἠπατημένους ἤδη τῇ πονηρᾷ γοητείᾳ ἐπανάγει τῆς πλάνης, τοὺς δὲ μέλλοντας πεσεῖσθαι προασφαλίζεται. οὐχ ἅπερ ἐμοὶ μόνον γράφεις, ἀλλὰ καὶ ἃ τοῖς ἄλλοις, οἷς τοὺς κορυφαίους τῶν περὶ λόγους ἐνταῦθα ἐσπουδακότων ἐπὶ τὴν τῶν καινῶν καθαίρεσιν παρακαλεῖς δογμάτων, πῦρ ἐπὶ ταῦτα πνέων ἁπανταχοῦ τῶν λόγων καὶ μόνος, οἶμαι, σχεδόν, ἀξίως τῆς τε εὐσεβείας φρονῶν καὶ ἱκανῶς κατὰ τῆς κειμένης αὐτῇ δυσσεβείας φερόμενος.

Ἡμᾶς δὲ τοῖς ἐπαίνοις οὕτω περιφανῶς ἐξῆρας, ὥστ᾽, εἴ μή τι συντελεῖν ἡγούμεθα καὶ τοῦτο τῇ εὐσεβείᾳ, οὐκ ἂν ἠνεσχόμεθα· μακρῷ γὰρ ἡμᾶς ὑπερέθηκας τῆς καθ᾽ ἡμᾶς ἀξίας, τὸ δὲ τοῖς παρ᾽ ἀξίαν ἐπαίνοις ἐνήδεσθαι τὸν ἐπαινούμενον αἰσχρόν τι καὶ ἀφιλόσοφον· ἀλλὰ φέρομεν καὶ ταῦτα τέως ὑπὲρ τῆς εὐσεβείας, ἕως ἂν ἀφαιρεθῶμεν αὖθις ὑπὸ σοῦ τοῦ θαυμάζοντος. ἄλλῳ μὲν οὖν ἄν τῳ τάχα αἰνίγματι παραπλήσιον τὸ λεγόμενον δόξαι, σοὶ δ᾽ εὐθὺς ἄρα δῆλον, ὡς ἐπειδὰν τοὺς λόγους οὓς ἔτι δημιουργεῖν ἐδήλους δεῦρ᾽ ἐκτελέσας πέμψῃς ἐπὶ τήνδε τὴν πλάνην, τοὐμὸν οὐ φανήσεται, ὥσπερ ἐν θρυαλλίδι φέγγος ἐν καθαρᾷ μεσημβρίᾳ γενόμενον ὑπὸ παντὶ τῷ φωτὶ τοῦ τῆς ἡμέρας λύχνου. ὡς δὲ οὐκ ἔστιν ὅπερ ἡμᾶς εὐφρανεῖ τούτου μᾶλλον παντί που δῆλον, εἴπερ ὅτι καὶ τὸ παρὰ τῶν οἰκείων ἐπικούρων ἡττᾶσθαι τοῖς κατὰ τῶν πολεμίων ἀνδραγαθήμασι, τοῦ παρ᾽ αὐτῶν τῶν πολεμίων αἱρετώτερον τοῖς γε πολεμουμένοις. τοιγαροῦν ταύτην ἐγὼ τὴν ἧτταν ἀναμένω παρὰ τῆς σῆς δεξιᾶς ὡς οὐδεὶς μεγάλην νίκην καὶ θαυμαστῶν τροπαίων ἀνά-

46: M 67ᵛ–69ᵛ.

4 ἐπειλλημμένοι M ‖ 6 Τρώας M

naturally more annoyed at the latter than pleased with the former. But I am grateful to you, my excellent friend, for the effort you made to visit me, and before long I too will, of course, repay your visit.

46. To Lapithes

Until recently I regarded your previous letter as a relief from a great famine, but now I already have a wealth and an abundance of your letters, my most wise friend, and I feel possessed of a marvelous strength. For when Achilles' arms shone, they did not embolden his kinsmen and shake down the Trojans in the way that your letters give nerve to the pious and unnerve the impious when they appear. And they lead back from error those who have already been deceived by the wicked witchcraft and secure in advance those who are likely to fall. ⟨I mean⟩ not only what you write to me alone, but what you write to others also, in which you urge our leading men of letters here to refute the new doctrines, breathing fire against them in all your letters and being the only one, I believe, who thinks in a way worthy of piety as well as moving sufficiently against the impiety that opposes it.

And you exalted me so conspicuously with your praises that I would not have tolerated it, if I had not thought that this too contributes something to piety. For you set me far above my own merit, and it is something shameful and unphilosophical for the man who is praised to delight in undeserved praises; but I bear even with these for a while for the sake of piety until you, in turn, my admirer, deprive me of them. To anyone else this saying would seem perhaps almost like a riddle, but to you it is at once obvious that, whenever you complete the discourses which you indicated that you were still writing, and send them here against this deceit, mine will fail to shine, just like the light of a wick when at noon, on a clear day, it comes under the full light of the sun. That nothing will please me more than this is obvious to almost everyone, if, that is, it is also obvious that for embattled men it is preferable to be defeated by their own allies as a result of manly deeds against the enemy rather than by their enemies themselves. So it is that I await this defeat by your right hand in a way that a man awaits a great victory and the setting up of admirable

46

στασιν ἀπὸ τῶν πολεμίων. ἴτωσαν οὖν οἱ λόγοι καὶ δι' ἀμφοτέρων ἐλαυνόντων, ὥς ἔφη τις τῶν ἐχθρῶν συμπλακέντων πρὸς τὸν ὄπισθεν φίλον, μὴ διαφύγῃ δείσας ὁ τύραννος· καίτοι τὸ μὲν ἦν ἀνελεῖν ἀμφοτέρους καὶ τὸν φίλον καὶ τὸν πολέμιον, μὴ τὸν ἐχθρὸν διαδρᾶναι συμβαίη, τὸ δὲ σὸν τὸν μὲν ἐχθρὸν ἀναιρήσει προδήλως, τὸν δὲ φίλον, τῆς αὐτῷ μὴ προσηκούσης δόξης καθηρηκός, οὐδὲν ἧττον ἀνάξει ἐπὶ τὴν ἧς προκινδυνεύει δόξης ἀσφάλειαν. τὸ γὰρ καθελεῖν αὐτὸν τοῦ δοκεῖν εἶναι πρῶτον ἐν τοῖς ἀναιρετικοῖς ἀγῶσι τῶν πονηρῶν δογμάτων, βεβαίωσις αὐτῷ τοῦ δοκεῖν [fol. 68ᵛ] ἀληθεύειν ἐν τοῖς κατὰ τούτων λόγοις ὁποιοισδήποτ' ἔσται.

Ἀπαιτῶν δ' ἡμᾶς ἔτι λόγους τοῦ τε Παλαμᾶ πλείους πρὸς ἀκριβεστέραν ὧν δυσσεβοίη γνῶσιν, τοῦ τε Βαρλαὰμ πρὸς τὸ εἰ ὅλως ἁμαρτάνοι τι περὶ τὰ τῆς εὐσεβείας δόγματα καταμαθεῖν, καί τι τῶν ἡμετέρων ἄλλο, ἴσθι τὸν καιρὸν ἡμᾶς τέως τὴν τούτων ἀφῃρημένον δόσιν καὶ βραχὺν γεγονότα πρός γε τὴν παρασκευὴν καὶ τῶν ἐγχωρίων θορύβων εἴπερ ποτ' ἀνάμεστον. πλὴν οὐδὲ οὕτως ἧττον εἰδέναι σου δεῖ τὴν θαυμαστὴν κεφαλὴν ὅτι τῆς μὲν τῷ Παλαμᾷ δυσσεβείας ἁπάσης καὶ ἀφροσύνης οἱ καρποὶ φανεροὶ πάρεισί σοι, καὶ ὅθεν ὁρμηθεὶς εἰς ταῦτα ἐλήλυθεν, ὅπερ ἡ πρὸς ἐμὲ τοῦ ἀνδρὸς ἐπιστολὴ πάνυ σαφῶς διδάσκει ἡ καὶ συνεχὴς ἑξῆς παρ' ἡμῶν σοι πεμφθεῖσα. τὰ δ' ἄλλα λῆρος πλατὺς καὶ οὐδὲν ἄλλο σαφῶς ἢ νηπιώδης ἕξις, μᾶλλον δὲ μανιώδης, οἷς οὐδ' ἂν ἀξιώσειας ὅλως ἀντιλέγων φανῆναι. ἐξολισθὼν γὰρ ἅπαξ εἰς τὴν ἀσέβειαν, εἶτα φωραθεὶς καὶ τῆς δεούσης ἀπολαύων αἰτίας παρὰ τῆς ἐκκλησίας, ἀντὶ τοῦ ἑαυτοῦ συναισθόμενος ἡμαρτηκότος ἵλεω ζητῆσαι τῆς ἐκκλησιαστικῆς φιλανθρωπίας τυχεῖν ὁμολογίᾳ τοῦ πλημμελήματος, ὁ δὲ ἀπονοηθεὶς ἐπειράθη μὲν εὐσεβὲς ὂν ἀποδεῖξαι τὸ δόγμα, ἀποτυγχάνων δὲ ὡς εἰκὸς ἀποδείξεως, πανταχόσε ἠνέχθη καὶ τυφλοῦ δίκην πανταχοῦ παραπαίει καὶ περιπίπτειν ἀεὶ τοῖς δευτέροις αὐτῷ συμβέβηκε χείροσι τῶν ἐφθακότων. τοῦτο δ' αὐτὸν ἤδη τελέως ἐξέμηνε, καὶ οὕτω τρισὶ θηρσὶ γίγασι, θυμῷ καὶ ἀπαιδευσίᾳ καὶ ἀσεβείᾳ κατασχεθείς—θυμοῦ γὰρ τροφὴ τοῖς ἀπαιδεύτοις ὁ ἔλεγχος—οὐδὲν ὧν λέγει λογίζεται.

Ὅθεν αὐτὸς ἑαυτὸν παντὸς μᾶλλον οἷς γράφει προκαταβάλλει καί, εἰ μὴ διὰ τοὺς ἀφελεστέρους, οὐδ' ἂν τὴν ἀρχήν τις ἐσπούδασεν, ὡς οἶμαι, τοῦτον ἀποσκευάζειν, αὐτὸν ὑφ' αὐτοῦ συντριβόμενον, καθάπερ στόλον ἀπειροθάλαττον ἐν ἀλιμένῳ στενῷ τῆς θαλάττης ἀπειλημμένον, πολεμίων ἐμπείρων ἢ κλύδωνος ἐπι-

---

46: 31–32 cf. Herodotum, *Hist*. 3, 78, 9–10

---

35 διαδράναι M

46

trophies from the enemy. Let your discourses, then, "strike through both" as they charge forward, as someone said to his friend behind him while he was locked in combat with the enemy, for fear that the tyrant might escape; and yet that meant killing both friend and enemy so that the enemy would not escape, whereas your achievement will obviously do away with the enemy, and, after divesting the friend of the glory which did not belong to him, you will no less raise him to the security of belief for which he risks his life. To deprive him of the reputation of being first in the contests for the refutation of the wicked doctrines will be, in fact, a confirmation of his reputation for speaking the truth in whatever he says against them.

But since you demand of me more writings both of Palamas, for a more accurate knowledge of his impieties, and of Barlaam, in order to find out whether he is actually somewhat at fault regarding the doctrines of piety, as well as any other work of mine, be assured that circumstances prevented me recently from giving you these, and the time even for preparing them was short, and more than ever filled with local disturbances. But even so, my most admirable friend, you must know nonetheless that you have there manifest before you the products of Palamas' complete impiety and folly and the basis from which he arrived at them; this, in fact, is made very clear in the man's letter to me, which I, in turn, sent to you in its entirety. The rest is so much nonsense and clearly nothing else but childishness or rather madness, such as you would not even deign to appear to contradict at all. For having once slipped into impiety, and then having been found out, and enjoying the benefit of being properly charged by the Church, instead of being conscious of having sinned and asking to obtain the merciful clemency of the Church by admitting his fault, he lost all sense and attempted to prove his doctrine right. But when he failed, naturally, to furnish proof, he was carried in every direction, and like a blind man he stumbles everywhere and happens to fall every time into worse errors than before. This has driven him completely mad, and thus, being possessed by three giant beasts—anger, ignorance, and impiety—because rebuke is food for anger to the ignorant, he does not reflect upon anything that he says.

Hence, he, more than anyone else, is the first to refute what he writes, and were it not for the more naive, one would not even have attempted to confute him, as I think, since he smashes himself to pieces like a fleet unused to the sea which is caught in a harborless strait while an experienced enemy or a storm is imminent.

46

κειμένου. τὸ δὲ ἀλόγιστον, ὅτι μὴ μόνῳ ἀτοπωτέραις ἀπολογίαις ἐχρήσατο τῶν πρώτων ἀσεβημάτων ὧν ἔγνωκεν ὑπεραπολογεῖσθαι, ἀλλὰ καὶ τὴν ὑπὸ τοῦ εὐσεβεῖν ἐθέλειν μὴ βουλομένην αὐτῷ κοινωνεῖν τῶν δογμάτων ἱερὰν ἐκκλησίαν ἀσεβεῖν ἀποφαίνεται, πάντας [fol. 69ʳ] ἀσεβεῖν νομίζων τοὺς αὐτῷ μὴ τὰ αὐτὰ φρονοῦντας, ὥσπερ οἱ μέθῃ κλονούμενοι ἑαυτοὺς μὲν ἑστάναι, κινεῖσθαι δὲ τὰ πεπηγότα φαντάζονται καὶ τὴν γῆν ἄνω φέρεσθαι. τί γὰρ τοῦ δυσσεβεῖς ἡγεῖσθαι καὶ ἀποφαίνεσθαι τοὺς μὴ θεῶν ἀκτίστων ἢ θεοτήτων πλῆθος ἀνίσων καὶ ἀνομοίων βουλομένους νομίζειν, ἀλλὰ μίαν καὶ τρισυπόστατον, καὶ τοὺς μὴ τὸ θεῖον ὅλως εἰς ἀνίσους καὶ ἀνομοίους θεότητας διῃρημένον, ἀλλ' ἀμερές τε καὶ ἀδιαίρετον, καὶ τοὺς μὴ ληπτὸν σωματικοῖς ὀφθαλμοῖς ἐν ἑαυτοῦ φυσικῇ καὶ οὐσιώδει μορφῇ, μηδ' ἄλλο μὲν μορφὴν Θεοῦ φυσικὴν τὸ παράπαν, ἕτερον δὲ οὐσίαν, ἀλλ' ἓν καὶ ταὐτὸ καὶ ἄληπτον καὶ ἀόρατον καθάπαξ σωματικοῖς ὀφθαλμοῖς, τὰ πρότερα δὲ καθαρὰν ἀσέβειαν ὑπολαμβάνειν, πάντας δὲ τοῖς δευτέροις ῥηθεῖσι δόγμασιν ἐνειθισμένους μετασκευάζειν ἐπὶ τὰ πρότερα, σαφῶς ἀπὸ τῆς Χριστοῦ διδασκαλίας καὶ τῆς προφητικῆς μυσταγωγίας ἐπὶ τὸ πάλαι πολύθεον καὶ περαιτέρω—τί τούτων ἄν τις εὖ φρονῶν ἀλογώτερον εἴποι πρός γε τὴν ἐκκλησιαστικὴν ἡμῖν ἀποβλέπων εὐσέβειαν; τί δὲ τοῖς ταύτης ἀκραιφνεστάτοις ὅροις καὶ δόγμασιν ἐναντιώτερον; ἃ βούλεται στέργειν δοκεῖν ὁ κηρύττων ἐκεῖνα, ὥσπερ ἐν ταὐτῷ σκότος καὶ φῶς ἡγουμένοις διαλεγόμενος.

Ὅ γε μὴν Βαρλαὰμ ὅτι μὲν ἥμαρτέ τι περὶ τὴν εὐαγγελικὴν καὶ θείαν θεσμοθεσίαν καθ' ἣν ἐν ψυχαῖς ἀνάγκη τὴν μακαριωτάτην ἀποτελεῖσθαι ζωήν, καὶ πολυπραγμονικῶς εἶχε περὶ τὴν ἁπλότητα τῶν παραδεδομένων μᾶλλον τοῦ δέοντος, ἐφ' οἷς ἐστι καὶ συνοδικῶς ἐνταῦθα κατεγνωσμένος, πρὸς τῷ νῦν Λατινισμῷ δῆλον· οὐχ ὅσον δὲ Παλαμᾶς εἰς τὰ δόγματα. ὁ δὲ αὐτὸς καιρὸς καὶ τοῦτ' ἀφείλετό με δηλῶσαί σοι.

Σὺ μὲν οὖν, ὦ γενναῖε, τῶν καλῶν καὶ γενναίων μὴ ἀφίστασο πόνων τῶν ὑπὲρ εὐσεβείας, ὧν εἴπερ ποτε δεῖ νῦν ἡμῖν καὶ τῇ πάσῃ τῆς εὐσεβείας μοίρᾳ. ἡ δ' ὑπὲρ ἧς ἀγωνίζῃ θεότης, ἡ μία καὶ μόνη ἄκτιστος, ἄναρχος, ἁπλῆ, ἀμερής, ἀδιαίρετος, ἀναφὴς καὶ ἀόρατος, ἡ μονὰς ἐν τριάδι προσώπων καὶ τριὰς ὑποστάσεων ἐν μονάδι θεότητος, ἀμείψεταί σου [fol. 69ᵛ] τοὺς πόνους τοῖς ἑαυτῆς ἀγαθοῖς.

---

102 cf. Maxim. Conf., *Capit. theol.* 2, 1 (PG, 90, 1124D–1125A) || 103–104 cf. Greg. Naz., *Or.*25, 17 (PG, 35, 1221C)

---

80 λεπτὸν M

46

And the irrational thing is that he not only used arguments of defense more absurd than his original errors of impiety, which he is determined to defend excessively, but he also declares that the holy Church is impious because it does not wish to share his doctrines, wanting to remain pious. For he thinks that those who do not have the same views as he does are impious, just as those who sway from drunkenness imagine that they are standing, while what is firmly fixed is moving and the ground is rising. For what could a sensible man call more absurd from the point of view of our ecclesiastical laws of piety than to consider and declare impious those who wish to believe not in a multitude of uncreated gods or divinities unequal and dissimilar, but in one divinity in three hypostases; and ⟨who do not wish to believe⟩ that it is to be apprehended by bodily eyes in its natural and essential form, nor that the natural form of God is altogether one thing and essence another, but ⟨that He is⟩ one and the same and incomprehensible and invisible to bodily eyes once and for all, and who consider the former ⟨beliefs⟩ to be pure impiety? And ⟨what could one call more absurd⟩ than to change all men, though they are accustomed to the doctrines I stated second, to those stated first, ⟨leading them away⟩, clearly, from the teaching of Christ and the instruction of the Prophets to the ancient polytheism and even further? And what ⟨could one call⟩ more opposed to the purest terms and doctrines of piety? Yet the man who proclaims those doctrines wishes to appear fond of the ⟨purest terms and doctrines of piety⟩, just as if he were speaking to people who believe that darkness and light are the same thing!

As for Barlaam, it is clear that, in addition to his present conversion to the Latin Church, he was wrong, to a degree, regarding the precepts enjoined by God and the New Testament, in accordance with which the most blessed life must of necessity be attained spiritually, and that he meddled more than he ought to with the simplicity of the traditions, and for this he has been condemned here by a synod. But he did not err so much as Palamas regarding the dogmas. However, the same circumstances prevented me from explaining this to you also.

Do not, then, my noble friend, shrink from your good and noble labors in defense of piety, which ⟨labors⟩ I along with all the pious need now more than ever. And the Divinity for Which you are fighting—the one and only uncreated, "without beginning, simple, admitting of no partition or division," intangible and invisible, the "monad in three" persons and the "triad" of hypostases in "a single" divinity—will reward your labors with Its blessings.

47. Τῷ σοφῷ Λαπίθῃ

Δοκοῦντες τὰ γράμματα κομισθήσεσθαί σοι τῷ προτέρῳ τῶν πλοίων, τὰ τότε εἰκότα ἐγράφομεν· ἐπεὶ δὲ ἀπελείφθη ἐκείνου, ἅ σοι τότε μὴ δύνασθαι πέμψαι ἐγράφομεν, ταῦθ' ὕστερον πέμψαι δυνηθέντες καὶ πέμπομεν δὴ διάλογον τοῦ Παλαμᾶ συνεχῆ, πάντων αὐτοῦ περιεκτικὸν τῶν μοχθηρῶν δογμάτων καὶ ὧν εὐπορεῖν ἀποδείξεων οἴεται πασῶν εἰς ταῦτα, καὶ τῆς ἀπαιδευσίας ἐλεγκτικὸν ἱκανῶς, καίτοι γε οὐχ ἅπερ ἂν ἡμεῖς ἀπεκρινάμεθα, τοιαῦτα ποιεῖ τὸν Βαρλααμίτην ἀποκρινόμενον αὐτῷ πρὸς τὰς ἐρωτήσεις τὰς ἐν τῷ διαλόγῳ, ἀλλ' ἅπερ αὐτὸς ἐθέλει, τὸ δὲ ἐθέλειν αὐτῷ διαβολῆς καὶ συκοφαντίας ἰταμωτάτης γέμει. ὅθεν οὐ μόνον αὐτοὺς ἡμᾶς πολλαχοῦ, ἀλλὰ καὶ τοὺς θείους πατέρας συκοφαντεῖ, νῦν μὲν ἃ μὴ λέγουσιν ἐκεῖνοι ὡς λεγόντων εἰσάγων, νῦν δὲ ἃ λέγουσι περικόπτων· ὑφ' ὧν ἐλέγχεται δυσσεβῶν περιφανῶς, καὶ τοῖς οἰκείοις πτεροῖς, ὡς ἀληθῶς, ἁλίσκεται, κατὰ τὴν παροιμίαν. τὸ δὲ ἀνοητότατον, [fol. 77^{v}] ὅτι λήσειν ἤλπισε τοὺς συνετοὺς καὶ σπουδαίους, μᾶλλον δὲ οὐδ' ᾠήθη, ὡς ἔοικεν, εἶναί τινα τοιοῦτον ἐν τῷ παντὶ τῆς ἐκκλησίας πλήθει, καὶ διὰ τοῦτο τοῦθ' οὕτω μετεχειρίσατο. ἐφ' οἷς ἔστι καὶ ἡμέτερα σχόλια ἀντιρρητικὰ πρὸς ταῦτα κατὰ τὸ σχέδιον, λόγους γὰρ οὐκ ἦν εὐχερὲς ἀποστεῖλαι, ἀλλ' ἐν τοῖς σχεδίοις τούτοις ἐντελές πως καὶ τὸ ἡμέτερον βούλημα.

Σὺ δ' ἤδη τέρπε μὲν ἡμᾶς καὶ Θεὸν καὶ πᾶσαν τὴν ἐκκλησίαν αὐτοῦ, κατάπληττε δὲ τελέως τὴν δυσσεβῆ φατρίαν καὶ τὸν στρατηγὸν αὐτῶν δαίμονα τοῖς πυρίπνοις σου λόγοις, οὓς οὐκ ἂν στήσειαν τῆς θεοφορήτου φορᾶς, εὖ οἶδ' ὅτι, οἱ τοῦτο ἐπιχειρήσαντες ἠλογημένως· πυνθάνομαι γάρ τινας τῶν ἀπὸ τῆς φατρίας ταύτης, οὐ φέροντας τὸν τῶν ἐλέγχων ὄγκον τόν τε ἤδη φανέντα καὶ μάλιστα τὸν προσδοκώμενον, πλῆθος συμπλάσαι γραμμάτων, ὡς δὴ πολλῶν λογίων, ὑπὲρ τῶν πονηρῶν τοῦ Παλαμᾶ δογμάτων πρὸς τὴν σὴν κορυφαίαν σοφίαν, ὡς καταπλήξοντες αὐτὴν καὶ τῆς καθ' ἑαυτῶν φορᾶς ἀνακόψοντες. ὅπερ ἀκούσας ἥσθην, ὅτι κινοῦσι, μᾶλλον δὲ ὅτι κεκινημένον προσεπικινοῦσι καθ' ἑαυτῶν τὸν ἀνάγυρον. ὅτι δὲ ταῦθ' οὕτως ἔχει αὐτίκα δὴ πειραθήσονται, οὐ γὰρ δὴ οὔτ' ἀπατηθῆναι οἷός τέ ἐστι ψεύδεσιν, οὔτε δεῖσαι μὴ ὅτι γε ἀνθρώπων

47: 14–15 Aeschylus, *Fragm.* 139, 4 || 31–32 Greg. Cyp. I, 22 (Leutsch-Schneidewin, II, 95)

47: M 77^{r}–78^{r}.

9–10 *πρὸς τάς . . . ἐθέλειν αὐτῷ* M^{mg} || 11 *ἱταμωτάτης* M || 25 *οἱ*] *οὐ* M

47

47. To the sage Lapithes

Thinking that my letter would have been brought to you by an earlier ship, I wrote what was appropriate at the time. But, since it missed that ⟨ship⟩, I am now able to send you what I wrote then that I could not send. I am, in fact, sending you a continuous dialogue of Palamas containing all his wicked doctrines and all their proofs (of which he believes that he has an abundance) and furnishing adequate proof of his ignorance. This, though he does not make the Barlaamite give to his questions in the dialogue the answers which I would have given, but those indeed that he wants, and what he wants is full of slander and most insolent calumny. Therefore, not only does he falsely accuse me personally in many places, but also the holy Fathers, now introducing as their sayings things that they do not say, and then cutting off what they say; by this he is shown to be manifestly impious and is most truly "caught by his own wings," as the proverb goes. And what is most foolish, he hoped to escape the detection of wise and good men; or rather, he did not even think, as it seems, that there was any such man in the whole multitude of Church members, and for this reason he treated the matter thus. There are also my comments on these ⟨doctrines⟩, refuting them in an offhand manner, for it was not easy to send discourses, but even in these offhand comments my purpose is accomplished to a degree.

But now do delight me, as well as God and His whole Church, and completely confound the impious faction and their leader, the Devil, with your fire-breathing discourses which they cannot stop from their divinely-directed drive (I know it well), those who tried it foolishly. For I am informed that certain members of this faction would not tolerate the great number of rebukes which have already appeared, and especially those which are expected; and they fabricated a multitude of letters, as if indeed by many learned men, in defense of Palamas' wicked doctrines, and addressed them to your eminent Wisdom for the purpose of confounding you and checking your drive against them. When I heard this I was delighted, because they are "stirring up trouble" for themselves, or rather they are stirring up more the trouble which has already started for them. And they will certainly find out immediately that this is how the matter stands. For obviously my hero cannot be deceived by lies, nor can he fear the threats of pitiable men at all, not even of the most sophis-

οἰκτρῶν ἀπειλάς, ἀλλ' οὐδὲ τῶν κομψοτάτων, καὶ οὕτω τι προδοῦναι τῆς ἀληθείας ὁ ἡμέτερος ἥρως, ὁ μόνος ἄξιος, οἶμαι, τῆς ἀληθείας προστάτης, κἂν δάκνῃ τινὰς ὁ λόγος. οὐδὲ γὰρ οὐδ' ἐγὼ προδότης φανῆναι τῆς ἀληθείας ἀνέχομαι, ὥσπερ εἰς τὰ περὶ Θεοῦ, οὕτως οὐδ' εἰς τὰ περὶ τοῦ θεοφιλεστάτου καὶ τῆς εἰς αὐτὸν εὐσεβείας ἀθλητοῦ καὶ προστάτου τοιούτου, οἷον αὐτὸς ἐθέλει ὁ εὐσεβούμενος, ὃν οὐδ' ἐκεῖνο λέληθε—πῶς γὰρ τόν γε σοφώτατον καὶ ἀγχινούστατον;—ὡς οὐκ ἔστι μὴ διαρρήγνυσθαι τὸ τῶν αἱρετικῶν καὶ δυσσεβούντων γένος τοῖς τῶν σοφῶν ἐλέγχοις, ἅπαξ ταῖς ἀσεβείαις, εἰς ἃς ἀφρόνως ἐνέπεσον, ἐγνωκότας ἐμμένειν ἀπονενοημένως καὶ μηδαμόθεν θεραπείαν προσίεσθαι. τοιοῦτο γὰρ ἀεὶ δέδεικται τὸ φῦλον ἀνίατον καὶ δέον σοφοῖς ἐλέγχοις πρὸς τὴν ἧς ἐκπέ [fol. 78r] σειεν ἕξιν ἀγαπητῶς ἐπανέρχεσθαι· οἱ δὲ μαίνονται κατὰ τῶν ἐπανάγειν αὐτοὺς ἐπιχειρούντων καὶ θεραπεύειν, οὕτως ἀθλίως ἐσκότωνται.

Ἐπεὶ δέ σοι ἔδει καὶ τοὺς πατριαρχικοὺς ἀποσταλῆναι τόμους τοὺς κατὰ τῆς κακοφροσύνης τοῦ Παλαμᾶ καὶ ἀποκόπτοντας αὐτόν τε καὶ τοὺς ὁμόφρονας αὐτῷ τῆς ἐκκλησίας τοῦ Χριστοῦ τῆς αὐτοῦ πολυειδοῦς αἱρέσεως ἕνεκα, τόν τε τοῦ οἰκουμενικοῦ, ἐν ᾧ μετρίως διείληπται καὶ τὰ κατὰ τὸν Βαρλαάμ, καὶ τὸν τοῦ Ἀντιοχείας, αὐτοῦ τοῦ θειοτάτου ἡμῶν δεσπότου τοῦ οἰκουμενικοῦ πατριάρχου κελεύσαντος ἀπεστάλησαν. σὺ δ', ὦ πάντων ἄριστε καὶ σοφώτατε καὶ στῦλε τῆς εὐσεβείας ἀκράδαντε, γράφοις ἂν ἡμῖν συνεχῶς καὶ περὶ τούτων τὰ δοκοῦντα διδάσκων, οὐκ ἄνευ τῶν γενναίων ἐγγόνων πρὸς οὓς ἀεὶ καθάπερ οἱ νεοττοὶ πρὸς τὴν μητέρα κεχήναμεν, πότε ἀφίξονται καὶ θρέψουσι τοὺς οὕτω κεχηνότας ἐκεῖσε καὶ κατέδονται τοὺς ἐπιβούλους ὄφεις.

48. Τῷ Φιλαδελφείας

Ὅσον ἐστὶ γλῶττα ἀγαθὴ καὶ γνώμη σοφὴ καὶ ἀξιώματος ὕψος συνελθόντα εἰς ἀντικειμένης μοίρας τῇ ἀληθείᾳ καθαίρεσιν· σὺ γὰρ δὴ θείων ἀνδρῶν καὶ σοφῶν ὅ τι κράτιστον καὶ ῥεῦμα προχέων ἀπὸ τῆς γλώττης θαυμάσιον, ὑπὲρ τῶν πατρικῶν δογμάτων καὶ κατὰ τῆς νῦν πολυθεΐας τῆτες ἀφεὶς τὴν γλῶτταν, ὥσπερ βροντήσας, τὴν ἐκκλησίαν ἐπέστρεψας· καὶ πανταχοῦ νῦν ᾄδεται Φιλαδελφείας, οἷον ἐχρῆν αὐτὸν ὑμνεῖσθαι, προστάτης τῶν εὐσεβῶν δογμάτων καὶ

---

56 στύλε M

48: M 65r. Ed. Passarelli, *Macario*, 32, n. 28

ticated; he ⟨cannot⟩ thus betray any part of truth, for, in my opinion, he is the only worthy defender of truth, even if my saying so vexes certain people; for I cannot bear to be a traitor to truth either, whether it be in matters concerning God or else in regard to a man most dear to God, who is such a champion and protector of His piety as He Himself Whom he reveres wishes. And the following fact certainly did not escape this man—for how could it escape a man who is indeed most wise and astute?—namely, that it is impossible for the heretic and impious species not to burst with passion against the rebukes of wise men, once they are determined to persist hopelessly in the profanities into which they fell foolishly and not accept a cure from anywhere. For this race was always shown to be like this, incurable and in need of wise rebukes in order to return amiably to the state from which they fell. And they rave against those who attempt to bring them back and cure them, and thus they are pitiably confounded.

And since it was necessary to send you also the patriarchal tomes which oppose this foolishness of Palamas and cut both him and his followers off from the Church of Christ on account of his multiform heresy, I sent to you, at the command of my most divine lord the Ecumenical Patriarch, both the tome of the Ecumenical Patriarch, in which the doctrines of Barlaam are also moderately defined, and the tome of the Patriarch of Antioch. But you, O most excellent and most wise of all men and unshakable pillar of piety, do write to me continuously, teaching me also what in your opinion is right about these matters, but not without the noble offspring for which I am forever hungrily waiting, just as young birds ⟨wait⟩ for their mother, as I wonder when they will come and not only feed those who are thus eagerly waiting hungrily, but will also devour that insidious snake.

48. To the metropolitan of Philadelphia

How important are a good tongue and wise judgment and exalted rank when they combine to destroy those who oppose truth! For certainly when you—who represent all that is best in holy and wise men and pour out from your tongue a marvelous stream—spoke out this year in defense of the ancestral dogmas and against the present polytheism, you turned the Church around as if you had hurled a thunderbolt. And now the Metropolitan of Philadelphia is hailed everywhere, just as he ought to be praised, as the protector of the pious dogmas and the most powerful

ἀριστεὺς κατὰ τῶν ἐναντίων ὁ κράτιστος, καὶ πρότερόν γε μέγας ὢν ὑπέρμαχος τῆς ἀληθείας.

Ἐφ' οἷς ἡμεῖς ἡσθέντες οἱ τῆς μὲν κακοδοξίας τῆς νῦν αἰσθανόμενοι, ἀδυνατοῦντες δὲ βοηθεῖν τοῖς πατρικοῖς δόγμασι ἐπηρεαζομένοις ἀπὸ τῆς εὐτελείας ἐφ' ἧς ἐσμεν, χάριν ὁμολογοῦμεν Θεῷ τῷ προπαρασκευαζομένῳ στρατηγοὺς αὐτοῦ τοιούτους τῇ ἐκκλησίᾳ, μελλουσῶν αἱρέσεων φύεσθαι, κατὰ τὸν Παύλου λόγον, ἵνα οἱ δόκιμοι ἀναφανῶσι. βάλλε δὴ οὕτως, ἄριστε, ὅπως τοι φάος γένοιο τῇ ἐκκλησίᾳ τὸ μέγιστον, οἱ γάρ τοι Παλαμῆται οὐ παύονται τὸ σῶμα τοῦ Χριστοῦ διασπῶντες· οἷς, οἶμαι, σὺ μόνος ἀντιφθεγγόμενος ὥσπερ πνεῦμα ἰσχυρὸν τοῖς κουφοτάτοις ἔσῃ, ἢ πῦρ φρυγάνοις, ἢ ἀκτὶς καθαρωτάτη πάχνῃ. συνῆμεν οὖν σοι καὶ πάλαι διὰ τὴν ἀρετὴν καὶ σοφίαν αἷς σύνει, ὧν ἐραστὴς εἴπερ τις ὁ ἐμὸς πατὴρ καὶ τῆς μονῆς τῆς καθ' ἡμᾶς προστάτης, νῦν δὲ καὶ μεθ' ἑορτῆς σύνεσμέν σοι καὶ πανηγύρεως, χάριν τοῦ πῦρ πνέοντος ὑπὲρ τῆς εὐσεβείας λόγου, ὃν πολλοὶ μὲν καὶ ἄλλοι πανταχοῦ τῆς πόλεως διακηρύττουσιν, ἡμῖν δὲ πρὸ πάντων ὁ θειότατος καὶ σὸς ἀδελφὸς ὁ Βιζύης ἐμήνυσε μετὰ θαύματος.

49. Τῷ Τζακονοπούλῳ

Οὐκ οἶδα ὅ τι μᾶλλον θαυμάσαιμ' ἂν ἕτερον, εἰ μὴ τὴν σὴν πρὸς ἐμαυτὸν σιωπήν· οὐδὲ γὰρ εὑρεῖν ἔχω τὸν ἐμαυτοῦ φίλτερον, μέμνημαι δὲ καὶ τῶν καιρῶν ἐκείνων εἴπερ τινός, καὶ τῶν κοινῶν μουσείων, καὶ τῶν περὶ ἐμέ σου, θερμότατε, φροντίδων, καὶ ὧν μετ' ἐκεῖνα περὶ ἀλλήλους ἐπεδεικνύμεθα· ὧν τί σοι τὸ τὴν οὕτω μακρὰν σιωπὴν ἐμποιῆσαν; καὶ ταῦτα ὅτε καὶ οἱ πρὸς τοῖς ἐσχάτοις που τῆς οἰκουμένης οἰκοῦντες, οὐδέ τι πάνυ σαφὲς ἀκούσαντες περὶ ἡμῶν, ἐπιστολαῖς ἡμᾶς καὶ λόγοις φιλοφρονοῦνται κατ' εὐσεβείας χρείαν, ᾗ καὶ συνέστησεν ἐκείνοις ἡμᾶς ὡς ἐν καιροῖς πονηροῖς οὐ προδιδόντας αὐτήν· καὶ γράφουσί γε ἡμῖν τῶν πρῴην ἀγώνων οὐ μόνον ἀποδεχόμενοι, ἀλλὰ καὶ πρὸς μείζους παρακαλοῦντες. ὧν πόσῳ μᾶλλον ἐχρῆν σε, τὸν ὅ τι τίμιον ἡμῖν ἐκ τοσούτου καὶ ὄνομα

48: 15–16 I Cor. 11:19 18 *σῶμα Χριστοῦ*: cf. Eph. 1:22–23; 4:12

---

21 *ὧν*] ὃν M

49: M 64ʳ–65ʳ.

champion against the enemy, being a great defender of truth even before now.

This delighted me, as I detect the present heresy, but because of my insignificance I cannot come to the assistance of the ancestral dogmas which are being threatened, and I am grateful to God Who prepares for the Church such generals of His when "heresies are to appear, if only to show which members are sound," according to the words of Paul. Therefore, keep on hitting out, most excellent Father, that you may become the greatest illumination of the Church, for the Palamites do not cease tearing up the body of Christ. But I believe that if you alone speak out against them, you will be exactly as a strong wind is to the lightest things, or as fire is to dry sticks, or as the clearest ray of sunshine to frost. I was your follower before now, because you are the follower of virtue and wisdom, which my spiritual father and head of our monastery admires more than anyone else. But now I follow you, indeed, feasting and celebrating because of your discourse which breathes fire in defense of piety. It has been acclaimed by many different men all over the city, but above all it was your brother the most holy Metropolitan of Bizye who told me about it with admiration.

49. To Tzakonopoulos

I do not know what else to marvel at more than your silence towards me. For I cannot find a man dearer to me, and I remember those times more than anything else when we were fellow students, and your care for me, my most ardent friend, and the concern we showed for each other afterwards. Which of those things is the cause of such a long silence on your part? And especially when even those who live somewhere at the end of the world and have not even heard anything very clear about me compliment me with letters and discourses, according to the dictates of piety which, in fact, recommended me to them, because I did not betray it in evil times. And they write to me not only approving my former struggles, but even urging me on to greater ones. How much more than these men ought you to be doing this, you who are for me all that is precious in name and deed! Besides, you would be acting in

49

καὶ πρᾶγμα, τοῦτο ποιεῖν, ἄλλως τε καὶ τὸ σαυτοῦ γ' ἂν ποιοῦντα, ὅ σοι σύνοιδα συνοικοῦν ὥσπερ αὐτὴν τὴν ψυχήν, τὴν ὑπὲρ τῶν καλῶν λέγειν καὶ ἀληθῶν παρρησίαν, ἥπερ ἂν ἴδοις ὑπὸ τῶν ἐναντίων ταῦτα κακούμενα. τὸν δ' ὑπὲρ τῶν ἐν τοῖς οὖσι τῇδε καλῶν τοιοῦτον, οἷον ἐχρῆν εἶναι ὑπὲρ τοῦ πάντων ἀνωτάτου τῶν ὄντων καὶ ποιητοῦ τῶν ὅλων βλασφημουμένου καὶ εἰς πλῆθος θεοτήτων ἀλλόκοτον διαιρουμένου καὶ συναριθμουμένου πάλιν τοῖς κτίσμασιν ὡς θεοῖς καὶ θεότησι συναϊδίοις αὐτοῦ κομιδῇ πολυθέως καὶ ἀρειομανικῶς καὶ μασσαλιανικῶς; ὅτε καὶ ὁρατὸν ἑαυτοῖς θεὸν ὑπεστήσαντο ἄναρχόν τε καὶ ἄκτιστον, πλὴν ὑφειμένον καὶ ἐνεργούμενον, οἱ πρόδρομοι τῆς τελευταίας πλάνης, καθ' ὃ πάλιν αὖ κτιστὸν αὐτοῖς εἶναι συμβαίνει τοῦτον, κἂν μυριάκις ἄκτιστον αὐτὸν ἀποφαίνωνται· τὸ γὰρ ἐνεργούμενον καὶ ὁρατὸν καὶ ὑφειμένον τῆς θείας [fol. 64[v]] φύσεως ἀπειράκις ἀπείρως πῶς ἄκτιστον; βοῶσι δ' οὖν "ἰδοὺ ὧδε ὁ Χριστὸς παρ' ἡμῖν ὁρατὸς τῇ θεότητι," κἂν πιστευθῶσί τῳ, τοῦτον ποιοῦσι πολυθεώτατόν τε καὶ δυσσεβέστατον· ὁ γὰρ ἅπαξ πιστεύσας αὐτοῖς ὅτι Θεὸν ὁρῷεν καὶ Θεοῦ μορφὴν ἄκτιστον σωματικοῖς ὀφθαλμοῖς πᾶν ἀξιοῖ σφίσι πείθεσθαι. οἱ δὲ Χριστοῦ μαθηταὶ παρ' ἐκείνου μαθόντες ἕνα Θεὸν πρεσβεύειν τριαδικὸν ὑποστάσεσι, μοναδικὸν τῇ θεότητι, ἁπλοῦν, ἀμερῆ, ἀδιαίρετον, ἀόρατον, ἀκατάληπτον, ἀνείδεον, ἄποιον, ἀνείκαστον, ἄρρητον, δημιουργικὸν ἁπάντων τε, πειθόμενοι λέγοντι ἐὰν ὑμῖν εἴπωσί τινες· ἰδοὺ ὧδε ὁ Χριστὸς ἢ ἐκεῖ, μὴ πιστεύσητε αὐτοῖς, καταγελῶσιν αὐτῶν, μᾶλλον δὲ ἐλεοῦσι τῆς πλάνης καὶ προσυπεραλγοῦσι τούτων τμηθέντων καὶ ἀπερριμμένων τῆς Χριστοῦ ἐκκλησίας ὡς ἐφθαρμένων καὶ ἀνιάτων μελῶν.

Ἡμεῖς μέντοι καὶ παντὸς μᾶλλον ἐπ' αὐτοῖς ἀλγοῦμεν οὕτω παραφρονήσασι, διὰ τὴν πάλαι φιλίαν ἣν ἡμῖν πρὸς αὐτούς, ὡς οἶσθα, πάλαι γεγενῆσθαι συνέβη· ἀλλ' ἀνιώμενοί γε κοινωνεῖν οὐ τολμῶμεν, οὐδὲ δὴ ψαύειν ὅλως, ἐκκλησιαστικοῖς αὐτῶν διῃρημένοι θριγγοῖς τοῖς ἐρρωμενεστάτοις· δεινὴ γὰρ ἡ νόσος ἀνθάψασθαι τοῦ προσιόντος, ἀπόνοια γάρ, ἣν ὁ τοῦ Θεοῦ πρῶτος ἀποστάτης νοσήσας, ἑωσφόρος ὤν, σκότος γέγονε σὺν ἀμυθήτῳ πλήθει, καὶ ἧς μεταδοὺς καὶ τῷ προπάτορι τῷ ἡμετέρῳ ἀντὶ τῆς θαυμαστῆς ἐλπίδος ἐκείνης ἧπερ αὐτὸν ἐπῆρε, δηλαδὴ τῆς θεότητος, καὶ τῆς ἀθανασίας ἧς εἶχε κατὰ χάριν ἐκ τοῦ ποιήσαντος αὐτὸν ἀπεστέρησεν· ὡς οὐχ

49: 23–24 *οἱ . . . πλάνης* cf. Matt. 24:11–12 || 26 cf. Palamam, *Epist. III ad Acindynum*, 15, Syngrammata, I, 306, 18; ed. Nadal, 252, 10–12 || 27 cf. Maxim. Conf., *Capit. theol.*, 1, 49 (PG, 90, 1101A) = Palamas, *Dialexis*, 24, Syngrammata, II, 186, 26; *Epist. ad Gabram*, 5, Syngrammata, II, 332, 12 || 27–28 Matt. 24:23; Luc. 17:23 || 33–34 cf. Maxim. Conf. *Capit. theol.*, 2, 1 (PG, 90, 1124D–1125A) || 35–37 cf. Matt. 24:23; Luc. 17:23

49

accordance with the principle which I know well to dwell with you just like your very soul, I mean your courage to speak up on behalf of goodness and truth, however you might see them abused by their enemies. And when a man is like this with regard to the values of this world, what should he be like with regard to the Supreme Being and Maker of all when He is blasphemed and divided into a strange multitude of divinities and, in turn, counted with created things, in the belief that they are gods and divinities coeternal with Him, in a manner altogether polytheistic and Arian and Messalian? When the forerunners of the final deceit even created a god visible to themselves, without beginning as well as uncreated, yet lower and activated? Wherefore their god turns out again to be created, even if they declare him uncreated ten thousand times! For how can that which is activated and visible and "infinitely lower" than the divine nature be uncreated? Then they cry: "Look here! Christ is seen by us in His divinity!" And if someone believes them, they make him most impious and a believer in polytheism. For once a man has accepted their belief that they see God and the uncreated form of God with their bodily eyes, he expects the whole world to believe them. But the disciples of Christ, because they learned from Him to believe in one God Who is a triad with respect to hypostases and a monad with respect to divinity—simple, admitting of no partition or division, invisible, incomprehensible, without form, without qualities, unrepresentable, ineffable, the creator of all—and because they obey Him when He says: "If some say to you, 'Look, here is Christ!' or 'There He is!', do not believe them," they laugh at them, or rather, they pity their delusion and grieve excessively for them as well, because they have been cut off and thrown out of the Church of Christ as corrupt and incurable members.

I, of course, on account of my old friendship for them which, as you know, dates from long ago, grieve for them more than anyone else, because they have become so deranged. But, though I am distressed, I do not dare to associate with them, not even to touch them at all, for I am separated from them by the strongest ecclesiastical barriers. For the disease has a strange power for attacking the man who comes close, since it is the madness from which the first apostate from God suffered, and though he was the morning star, he became darkness along with an untold multitude. And he transmitted it to our Forefather in return for that wondrous hope by which he excited him—the hope of divinity, that is—and deprived him even of immortality, which he had by the grace of his maker. Just as the present

ἧττω ποιοῦσι τοὺς πειθομένους αὐτοῖς καὶ οἱ νῦν ἀποστάται, θεοὺς ἀκτίστους καὶ ἀνάρχους αὐτούς τε γεγονέναι κομπάζοντες καὶ τοὺς αὐτοῖς εὐπειθεῖς ποιήσειν ἐπαγγελλόμενοι.

Ἀλλ' εἰς τὸ πλέον μηκύνειν οὔτε κατ' ἐπιστολήν, καὶ ὁ θαυμάσιος ἡμῖν ἀδελφὸς Ἀτουέμης, γέμων ἁπάσης σοφίας καὶ νοῦ καὶ φρονήσεως ὑπὲρ τὴν ἡλικίαν καθ' ἥν ἐστι καὶ τῶν οὐκ ὀλιγάκις συμπλακέντων ὧν τοῖς ἀτοπωτάτοις τούτοις αἱρετικοῖς ⟨καὶ⟩ τρεψαμένων τούτους μετὰ ῥαθυμίας καὶ παιδιᾶς, πάντα σοι διασαφήσει τὰ κατ' αὐτοὺς ἀκριβέστατα. ἀκούων δὲ καὶ Μακρηνὸν ἀδελφόν σοι συνεῖναι, ἄνδρα πολλῆς ἀρετῆς καὶ παιδεύσεως ἔμπλεων, τοῖς αὐτοῖς τούτοις αὐτὸν [fol. 65r] γράμμασι δεξιοῦσθαι* * *οὐ γὰρ ἦν ἀπεικὸς τοὺς τοῖς αὐτοῖς κεκοσμημένους τρόποις καὶ ἀλλήλοις συμπνέοντας καὶ τοῖς αὐτοῖς παρ' ἡμῶν γράμμασι προσηγορεῦσθαι.

50. ⟨Ματθαίῳ τῷ ἱερωτάτῳ⟩

Πάντα χρὴ προσδοκᾶν, εἴ γε καὶ σὺ διασέσεισαι ταῖς βεβήλοις καινοφωνίαις καὶ κακοπράγμοσιν, ὁ μὴ μόνον μεθ' ἡμῶν ὕστερον τετρανωμέναις ταύταις, ἀλλὰ καὶ πολὺ πρὸ ἡμῶν ἐν ἀμυδρῷ κειμέναις μεμαχημένος. ὁ γὰρ Μασσαλιανοὺς καὶ πλάνης διδασκάλους ἐσχάτης καὶ τὰ τοιαῦτα πάλαι πολλάκις βοῶν τε καὶ κεκραγὼς τοὺς νῦν καὶ πολυθέους τούτους [fol. 65v] τίς ἦν; οὐ σὺ μετὰ φορᾶς πυρίπνου καὶ ἀληθῶς ἐνθέου; τί λέγοντας; οὐχ ὅτι φῶς ὁρῶσιν ὁπότε βουληθεῖεν καθήμενοι; καὶ ἐπὶ τούτῳ οὕτως οἰδοῦσι τὰς ψυχὰς καὶ ὀγκοῦνται ὥστε τοὺς οὐχ ὁρῶντας τοῦτο, κἂν τἄλλα ὦσι θεοειδέστατοι, τὴν ἀγάπην, τὴν χαράν, τὴν εἰρήνην, τὴν ἐγκράτειαν, τὴν μακροθυμίαν, τὴν χρηστότητα, τὴν ἐπιείκειαν, τὴν ἀπάθειαν, τοὺς καρποὺς τοῦ Πνεύματος ἅπαντας, ἀκάρπους εἶναι παρ' αὐτοῖς καὶ δυστυχεῖς τὰ θεῖα, καὶ τηνάλλως ἀνθρώπους ἐλεεινοὺς τῶν πόνων, ἐλεεινοτέρους τῆς τοῦ φωτὸς τοῦ παρ' αὐτοῖς δυστυχίας.

50–51 cf. Palamam, *De divinis operationibus*, 37, Syngrammata, II, 122, 29–39; *Epist. III ad Acindynum*, 16, Syngrammata, I, 308, 11–15

50: 1–2 II Tim. 2:16 ‖ 5–6 Matt. 27:65 ‖ 6–7 Joannis Chrysostomi *Liturgia* (ed. Brightman), 385, 6

---

51 *αὐτούς* M ‖ 56 ⟨*καὶ*⟩ addidi ‖ 60 post *δεξιοῦσθαι* lacunam statui

50: M 65r–67r. Ed. Loenertz, *Epistulae*, 97–101, no. 5.

1 titulum ex linea 105 *infra* supplevi: sine titulo M: *Ματθαίῳ μοναχῷ* scr. Loenertz

apostates do, no less, to those who trust in them, both boasting that they have themselves become uncreated gods without beginning and promising that they will make such those who are obedient to them.

But it is not fitting for a letter to prolong this discussion, and, moreover, our wonderful brother Atouemes, who is filled with all wisdom and intelligence and prudence beyond his age, and who is among those who engaged in a dispute with these absurd heretics not a few times and defeated them with ease and amusement, will tell you all about them clearly and precisely. And, since I hear that brother Makrenos is with you, a man full of great virtue and learning * * * to send him my greetings by the same letter. For it was not unfitting to address by the same letter those who are adorned with the same manners and who are of the same opinion.

50. ⟨To the most holy Matthew⟩

Everything is to be expected if even you, indeed, have been shaken by the malignant "profane newfangled talk"! You who fought with me against it not only afterwards when it was made clear, but even long before I did, when it was still indistinct. For who was the man who many times, long ago, "cried and called aloud" ⟨describing as⟩ Messalians and teachers of the "final deception" these men who now believe even in many gods? Was it not you, with a fire-breathing and truly God-inspired force? What were they saying? ⟨Were they not saying⟩ that while sitting, they see light whenever they wish? And for this reason, they become so swollen and inflated spiritually that to them those who do not see this light are barren and unfortunate so far as divine matters are concerned and, generally, men who are to be pitied for their labors and more so for their failure to see this light which they see, even though they may be most God-like in everything else: love, joy, peace, self-control, forebearance, honesty, clemency, freedom from passions, all the fruits of the Spirit!

50

Διὰ μὲν οὖν ταῦτα ὁποῖος ἦσθα πρὸς τούτους τὸν ἀνωτέρω χρόνον οὐκ ἀγνοεῖς. καίτοι τό γε φῶς ὁρᾶν οἴεσθαί τε καὶ θεοφανειῶν ἀξιοῦσθαι ποικίλων παρὰ Θεοῦ τούς γε τούτων ἀξίους κατά τινα θείαν οἰκονομίαν καὶ χρείαν ὡμολόγηται τοῖς εὐσεβέσι καὶ γέγραπται παρὰ τοῖς θείοις λογίοις, εἰ καὶ μή, ὡς ἔδοξε τοῖς Παλαμήταις, οὐσιῶδες καὶ φυσικὸν τοῦ Θεοῦ. τὸ δὲ θεοὺς ἑτέρους ἢ θεότητας πλάττειν ἐκ τῶν τοιούτων, συναϊδίους τῷ ἐπὶ πάντων τρισυποστάτῳ Θεῷ, ἢ τὸν ἕνα τοῦτον Θεὸν ἐν ᾧ μία θεότης καὶ παρ' ᾧ, κατὰ τοὺς θείους λόγους, οὐκ ἔστι παραλλαγή, κατατέμνειν ἀθέως εἰς πλῆθος θεοτήτων ἀνίσων καὶ ἀνομοιοτάτων, οὐσιωδῶν τοῦ Θεοῦ, τίνων ἔγνως ἑτέρων παρὰ τοὺς Ἕλληνας ὄν; μᾶλλον δὲ οὐ μόνον ἐστὶ τῆς Ἑλλήνων πολυθεΐας τοῦτο, ἀλλὰ καὶ τῆς Ἀρείου μανίας καὶ τῆς Μακεδονίου. τὸ γὰρ ἄλλο μὲν τὴν ἄκτιστον τοῦ Θεοῦ μορφὴν καὶ δόξαν εἶναι καὶ δύναμιν καὶ ζωὴν καὶ σοφίαν δισχυρίζεσθαι, ἄλλο δὲ τὴν οὐσίαν καὶ ταύτην μὲν ὑπερκειμένην, ἐκείνας δὲ ὑφειμένας, καὶ τὴν μὲν ἐνεργοῦσαν, τὰς δὲ ἐνεργουμένας, οὐχὶ σαφῶς ἐκείνων; τίς γὰρ Θεοῦ σοφία καὶ δύναμις; οὐχ ὁ Υἱὸς καὶ Λόγος; τίς δόξα ἧς Πατὴρ ὁ Θεοῦ Λόγου Πατήρ; οὐχ οὗτος; τίς ἐπαγγελία τοῖς ἀποστόλοις καὶ δύναμις ἐξ ὕψους; οὐ τὸ Πνεῦμα τὸ παντουργόν; διὰ τίνων δὲ ἄλλων τὴν κτίσιν ἐδημιούργησεν ἀκτίστων δυνάμεων; οὐ διὰ τοῦ Υἱοῦ ἐν τῷ Πνεύματι πάντα ἐγένετο καὶ νῦν ἔτι τὰ γινόμενα γίνεται κατ' αὐτὸν τὸν δι' οὗ τὰ πάντα γεγένηται καὶ τοὺς αὐτοῦ μαθητάς; οὐκ ἴσος δὲ ὁ Υἱὸς τῷ Πατρὶ καὶ τὸ Πνεῦμα, καὶ μία δὴ θεότης, μονὰς ἀδιαίρετος καὶ ἀμερὴς καὶ ἁπλῆ καὶ παντελῶς ἀπαράλλακτος; οὐχ ἓν φῶς ἀληθινὸν ὁ Θεὸς καὶ τρισήλιον, ὃ [fol. 66r] φωτίζει πάντα ἄνθρωπον ἐρχόμενον εἰς τὸν κόσμον; διό φησιν ἡ θεολόγος τοῦ Γρηγορίου φωνὴ ἑπομένως τῷ τῆς βροντῆς Ἰωάννῃ καὶ τῷ μεγάλῳ Δαυίδ, ἐκ φωτὸς τοῦ Πατρὸς φῶς τὸν Υἱὸν ἐν φωτὶ τῷ Πνεύματι θέασαι τὸ τρισσὸν φῶς καὶ ἀμέριστον. καὶ πάλιν, ἑνὶ φωτὶ περιαστράφθητε καὶ τρισί, τρισὶ μὲν κατὰ τὰς ὑποστάσεις, ἑνὶ δὲ κατὰ τὸν τῆς οὐσίας λόγον, εἴτ' οὖν θεότητος.

Πῶς οὖν ἂν τῷ Παλαμᾷ πεισθείημεν νῦν, ἢ πλῆθος θεοτήτων

---

24 cf. Greg. Naz., *Or.* 31, 14 (PG, 36, 148D) || 25 Jac. 1:17 || 31–32 cf. Palaman, *Epist. III ad Acindynum*, 15, Syngrammata, I, 306, 18–20; ed. Nadal, 252, 10–12 || 33–34 I Cor. 1:25 || 34–35 cf. Eph. 1:17; Greg. Naz., *Or.* 30, 8 (PG, 36, 113B) || 37–38 cf. Joan. 1:3; I Cor. 8:6 || 39 I Cor. 8:6 || 40–41 Maxim. Conf., *Capit. theol.*, 2, 1 (PG, 90, 1124D–1125A) || 42 Joan. 1:9 || 42–43 *φῶς . . . τρισήλιον*: cf. Athan., *De communi essentia*, 49 (PG, 28, 76B) || 43–44 Joan. 1:9 || 45 cf. Marc. 3:17 || 46–47 cf. Ps. 35(36):9; Greg. Naz., *Or.*31, 3 (PG, 36, 136C) || 47–50 Greg. Naz., *Or.*39, 11 (PG, 36, 345C)

50

You know, therefore, how you were previously disposed towards them on account of this. Though, of course, pious men agree and it is written in the Holy Scriptures that, by some divine dispensation and intent, those men, at least, who are worthy of this believe that they see light and are deemed by God worthy of various visions of God, though not of the essence and nature of God, as the Palamites thought. But do you know of any people, other than the pagans, who would habitually fabricate out of such ⟨visions⟩ other gods or divinities coeternal with the all-transcendent God in three hypostases, or who would cut up impiously this "one God in Whom there is one divinity" and "with Whom there is no variation," according to the Holy Scripture, into a multitude of unequal and most dissimilar divinities, pertaining to the essence of God? Or rather, this is not only characteristic of pagan polytheism, but also of the madness of Arios and Macedonios. For is it not clearly their doctrine to affirm that the uncreated form and glory and power and life and wisdom of God are one thing and the essence another, and that the latter is "higher" while the former are "lower," and the essence activates whereas the others are activated? For who is the "Wisdom and Power of God"? Is it not the Son and Logos? Who is the "Glory Whose father is the Father of God the Logos"? Is it not He? Who is the promise and power for the Apostles from above? Is it not the all-creating Spirit? And through what other uncreated powers did He create the Universe? Did not "all things come to be," as they still do, "through the Son" in the Holy Spirit, according to Him "through Whom all came to be" as well as His Apostles? And are not the Son and the Holy Spirit coequal with the Father and indeed "one Divinity, a simple Monad, admitting of no division or partition" and absolutely invariable? Is not God one "light, real" and "shining through three suns," "which enlightens every man born into the world"? For this reason Gregory the Theologian, following John the "Son of Thunder" and the great David, says: "Behold 'in the light which is the Holy Spirit the light which is the Son proceeding from the light which is the Father,' the threefold and indivisible light!" and again: "Be dazzled by one as well as three lights! Three with respect to hypostases and one with respect to essence, that is, to divinity."

How, then, can we now listen to Palamas teaching a multitude of divinities

50

συναϊδίων μέν, ἀνίσων δὲ καὶ ἀνομοίων, ὡς εἴρηται, παραδιδόντι καὶ μὴ φανερῶς αὐτὸν τὴν Ἑλλήνων πολυθεΐαν παραδιδόναι νομίσαιμεν, ἢ μὴ ἀρειανίζειν ἕτερον φῶς ἄκτιστον παρὰ τὴν θείαν φύσιν εἰσάγοντι, "δι' οὗ φωτίζονταί," φησιν, "οἱ ἅγιοι καὶ φῶς γίνονται καὶ ἑνοῦνται τῷ Θεῷ," ἐκεῖνο δὲ ἀθετήσαντι δι' οὗ τὴν πρὸς τὸν ἀρχίφωτον πατέρα προσαγωγὴν ἐσχήκαμεν. εἰ γὰρ ἐκεῖνο δι' οὗ τὴν πρὸς τὸν πατέρα προσαγωγὴν ἐσχήκαμεν καὶ ὃ φωτίζει πάντα ἄνθρωπον ἐρχόμενον εἰς τὸν κόσμον, οὐκ ἔχει χώραν ἕτερον παρὰ τὴν τούτου φύσιν ὂν καὶ ὑφειμένον τούτου δι' οὗ ταῦτα γίνοιτ' ἄν. τοῦτο γὰρ δι' οὗ ταῦτα γίνεται, κατὰ τὰ θειότατα λόγια, οὐχ ὁρατὸν ὂν οὐδ' ἐκ φυσικῆς ἐμφάσεως διεγνωσμένον οὐδενὶ τῶν ἁπάντων, ὡς οἱ θεῖοι πατέρες διδάσκουσιν, ἀοράτῳ δὲ καὶ νοερᾷ φωτοφανείᾳ τοῖς οἰκείοις ἐρασταῖς ἐναστράπτον, παντὸς ὁρατοῦ φωτὸς φωτεινότερον. εἰ δ' οὐδὲν ἕτερον φῶς ἐκτὸς τοῦ Θεοῦ Λόγου μετὰ Πατρὸς καὶ τοῦ Πνεύματος τὸ φωτίζον θεϊκῶς τοὺς ἁγίους καὶ πάντα ἄνθρωπον ἐρχόμενον εἰς τὸν κόσμον, τὸ δὲ ταῦτα ποιοῦν ἕτερον εἶναι τῆς θείας φύσεως Παλαμᾶς ἀποφαίνεται καὶ ἐνεργούμενον καὶ ὑφειμένον αὐτῆς ἀπειράκις ἀπείρως καὶ ὁρατὸν καθ' αὑτὸ σωματικοῖς ὀφθαλμοῖς, ἆρ' οὐ ταῦτα κατὰ τοῦ Θεοῦ Λόγου καὶ τοῦ Πνεύματος λέγει καὶ χεῖρον Ἀρείου περὶ ταῦτα βλασφημεῖ; καὶ γὰρ ἐκεῖνος ἐλάττω μὲν εἶναι καὶ ὑφειμένον τῆς οὐσίας τοῦ Θεοῦ τὸν Υἱὸν τοῦ Θεοῦ καὶ Θεὸν ἐβλασφήμει καὶ ἔργον τοῦ Παντοκράτορος, ὁρατὸν δὲ καθ' αὑτὸν σωματικοῖς ὀφθαλμοῖς εἰπεῖν οὐκ ἐτόλμησεν· ἀλλὰ τοῦτό γε τοῦ Παλαμᾶ συνετώτερος ὑπῆρξε καὶ εὐγνωμονέστερος Ἄρειος. τὸ γὰρ οἴεσθαι μὲν εἶναι τὸ προαιώνιον φῶς καὶ τῶν ἀοράτων δυνάμεων ποιητικόν, αὐτὸ δὲ τοῦτο θεατὸν σωματικοῖς ὀφθαλμοῖς, οὐκ ἀσεβείας μόνον ἦν ἁπάσης ἐπέκεινα, ἀλλὰ [fol. 66ᵛ] καὶ ἀφροσύνης καὶ τελείας μανίας.

Οὐ μόνον μέντοι καὶ πρὸ ἡμῶν, ὦ βέλτιστε, σὺ τὰς τούτων ἀφορμὰς καὶ προεώρας ἐν τούτοις καὶ προὔλεγες καὶ ἀντέλεγες αὐτοῖς καὶ τοὺς ἄλλους ἀπέτρεπες αὐτῶν ἀκούειν, Μασσαλιανοὺς καὶ πλάνους ἀποφαινόμενος, ἀλλὰ καὶ ὕστερον αὐτὸς τῆς αἱρετικοῖς οἰκείας θρασύτητος καὶ λῃστείας παρ' αὐτῶν ἐπειράθης. καὶ δεῦρο

55–56 cf. Palaman, *Trias* 3, 1, 6, Syngrammata, I, 620, 14–22; *Dialexis*, 11, Syngrammata, II, 173, 12–20 ‖ 56–57 Dion. Areop., *Coel. hier.*, 1, 2 (PG, 3, 121A) ‖ 58–59 Dion. Areop., *ibid.* ‖ 59–60 Joan. 1:9 ‖ 62–64 Maxim. Conf., *Capit. theol.*, 1, 1, (PG, 90, 1084A) ‖ 68 Joan, 1:9 ‖ 70–71 cf. Palamam, *Epist. III ad Acindynum*, 15, Syngrammata, I, 306, 18–20; ed. Nadal, 252, 10–12; *Dialexis*, 24, Syngrammata, II, 186, 26; *Epist. ad Gabram*, 5, Syngrammata, II, 332, 12

---

56 *ἀθετίσαντι* M

50

which are coeternal, but unequal and dissimilar, as it was said, and not think that he is openly teaching pagan polytheism, or that he is a follower of Arios when he introduces another uncreated light besides the divine nature, "by which," he says, "the Saints are enlightened and become light and are united with God," while he rejects that light "through which we were introduced to the leading light, the Father"? For if it is that light "through which we were introduced to the Father" and "which enlightens every man born into the world," there is no place for one different in nature and lower than that through which these could be accomplished. For that light through which these are accomplished is not visible, according to the most Holy Scripture, nor "known to anyone at all by means of a physical manifestation," as the holy Fathers teach, but flashes on its beloved in an invisible and spiritual illumination and is brighter than any visible light. But, if there is no other light except God the Logos, together with the Father and the Holy Spirit, which divinely enlightens the Saints and "every man born into the world," and if Palamas declares this to be different from the divine nature and activated and "infinitely lower" and visible in itself to bodily eyes, does he not say these things against God the Logos and the Holy Spirit, and does he not speak, concerning these matters, worse blasphemy than Arios? For he said, with irreverence, that God the Son of God is inferior to and lower than the essence of God and a creature of the Almighty, but he did not dare say that he was visible in Himself to bodily eyes. In this respect, at least, Arios was wiser and more prudent than Palamas. For to believe that the light which exists before time is the creator of even the invisible powers and yet that it is itself visible to bodily eyes was not only beyond all impiety, but also beyond folly and utter madness.

Therefore, my excellent friend, not only did you foresee before me their inclinations in these matters and speak in advance in opposition to them and dissuade others from listening to them, calling them Messalians and impostors, but you also later yourself experienced their insolence and assault proper to heretics. And you

50

παραγενόμενος ἐπὶ τοῦ θειοτάτου καὶ οἰκουμενικοῦ πατριάρχου καὶ τὴν ἀσέβειαν καὶ τὴν θρασύτητα τὴν αὐτῶν διεξῄεις, κἀνταῦθα τοιαῦθ' ἕτερα καὶ πολλῷ χείρω τῶν ὑπὸ σοῦ λεγομένων αὐτοῖς τετολμημένα μεμάθηκας—ἔκ τε πολλῶν ἑτέρων καὶ παρ' αὐτοῦ τοῦ κορυφαίου τῆς ἐκκλησίας κράτους, οὗ καὶ λόγους ἐκ στόματος καὶ γράμμα ἐπὶ τούτοις ἐδέξω καὶ διεκόμισας τῷ μακαρίτῃ Θεσσαλονίκης ἐκείνῳ μητροπολίτῃ—καὶ αὐτὰ τοῦ Παλαμᾶ τὰ κίβδηλα δόγματα καθαρῶς πολυθεΐαν διδάσκοντα, καὶ παρὰ ταῦτα τῶν ἱερῶν πατέρων ἀντίθετα καὶ δόγματα καὶ διδάγματα· ἐφ' οἷς ἡμῖν καὶ γράμματα πολλάκις ἀπέστειλας, μηνύων ὅτι τε πᾶσι ταῦτα ἐπέδειξας καὶ ὡς ἅπαντες τῶν μὲν τοῦ Παλαμᾶ κατέγνωσαν ὡς δυσσεβῶν δογμάτων, τὴν δ' ἡμετέραν περὶ τῆς εὐσεβείας γνώμην καὶ πρὸς αὐτὸν ἐναντίωσιν ὡς κοινὴν τῆς ἐκκλησίας καὶ τῶν θείων πατέρων ἠσπάσαντο, καὶ ὡς ἄριστα καὶ ἀκριβέστατα ἐγὼ τὰ δόγματα ἐκτίθεμαι τῆς ἐκκλησίας καὶ ὁμολογουμένως τοῖς κειμένοις τῆς εὐσεβείας ὅροις· οὐκ ἐμοὶ μέντοι μόνῳ, ἀλλὰ καὶ τῇ θεοφιλεστάτῃ καὶ θαυμαστῇ βασιλίσσῃ γράφων ἀνωμολόγεις.

Εἶτα μετὰ τοσαύτην ἀπόδειξιν καὶ μαρτυρίαν τῆς τε τοῦ Παλαμᾶ δυσσεβείας καὶ ἡμετέρας ὀρθότητος, ἕτερος αὐτὸς ἑαυτοῦ Ματθαῖος ὁ ἱερώτατος; καὶ τίνος ὀστράκου μεταπεσόντος; ὅτι με τῆς τοῦ Θεοῦ ἐκκλησίας ἐπὶ τὴν τῆς ἱερωσύνης χάριν ἑλκυσαμένης ἐμάνησαν οἱ πολέμιοι καὶ ἀπόβλητοι τῆς ἐκκλησίας οὗτοι, καὶ ἐπανέστησαν τῇ ἐκκλησίᾳ κἀμοί; διὸ δὴ καὶ τελέως αὐτοὺς ἀπέρρηξεν ἑαυτῆς, συνόδῳ κατ' αὐτῶν παντελεῖ χρησαμένη, παρόντος αὐτῇ καὶ τοῦ Ἀντιοχείας καὶ ἄλλων Ἀσιανῶν ἐπισκόπων; ἀλλὰ τοῦτό γε ἦν ὁ σαφέστατος ἔλεγχος τῆς τε ἡμετέρας εὐσεβείας καὶ τῆς τοῦ Παλαμᾶ δυσσεβείας καὶ τῆς αἱρετικοῖς συνυπαρχούσης σκαιότητος. καὶ ὁ καιρὸς ἐκεῖνος ἔνστασιν μᾶλλον ἀπῄτει παρ' ὑμῶν ὑπὲρ τῆς εὐσεβείας, ἀλλ' οὐ κλίσιν τῆς γνώμης ἧς πρότερον εἴχομεν περὶ αὐτὴν καὶ τῆς ὁμολογίας. κἄν τι πάσχωμεν χαλεπὸν ὑπὲρ αὐτῆς μετὰ τῆς ἐκκλησίας, αὐτὸ τοῦθ' ὅτι [fol. 67r] πάσχομεν ὑπὲρ αὐτῆς καὶ μετὰ τῆς ἐκκλησίας εἰς εὐφροσύνης ἔχει ἐφόδιον, ἀλλ' οὐ δειλίας· οὐ γὰρ ἐλάβομέν, φησι, πνεῦμα δειλίας, ἀλλὰ δυνάμεως.

Νῦν δὲ οὐδὲ οὕτως ἀνῃρέθημεν ἢ κατεπόθημεν ὑπὸ τῆς μανίας τῶν ἐπιβεβουλευκότων, οὐδ' ὁ τῆς εὐσεβείας προστάτης πατριάρχης καθῄρηται ἀντὶ τοῦ ἐμοὶ μεταδοῦναι ἱερωσύνης, ὡς αὐτοὶ δι-

---

105 Diogenianus, III, 54 (Leutsch-Schneidewin, II, 45) || 118–119 II Tim. 1:7

---

117 ἔχει scripsi: ἔχειν M

50

came here before the most holy and Ecumenical Patriarch and related in detail their impiety and insolence, and learned from many others, as well as the Supreme Authority of the Church, that here too they attempted other similar deeds and much worse than what you were reporting. And you received from the Patriarch oral instructions as well as a letter concerning these matters, and you conveyed them to the late metropolitan of Thessalonica of blessed memory. And you ⟨learned⟩ that Palamas' fraudulent doctrines themselves purely teach polytheism and, in addition to this, beliefs and doctrines opposite to those of the Fathers. Wherefore, many times you sent me letters informing me both that you showed these to everybody and that everybody condemned Palamas' doctrines as impious, whereas they hailed my views on piety and my opposition to him as the common ⟨position⟩ of the Church and the holy Fathers, and the fact that I expound the dogmas of the Church in the most excellent and accurate way and in accordance with the established rules of piety. You admitted these things not only when you wrote to me, but also ⟨when you wrote⟩ to the admirable Princess most dear to God.

And then, after such proof and evidence of both Palamas' impiety as well as my rightness, did the most holy Matthew become different from himself? And why did "heads become tails"? Because the Church of God admitted me to the grace of the priesthood, and these enemies and outcasts of the Church became enraged and rebelled against the Church and me? Wherefore, in fact, she severed them completely from herself, having made use of a full synod against them, at which the Patriarch of Antioch and other Asiatic prelates were present? But this, indeed, was the clearest proof of both my piety and Palamas' impiety and the distortion that accompanies heretics. That time, in fact, demanded from you resistance in defense of piety rather than a change of the opinion and agreement that we had previously come to about it. And if I suffer some hardship on its behalf together with the Church, the very fact that I suffer on behalf of piety and together with the Church provides an incentive for rejoicing, not for cowardice. For he says: "The Spirit that God gave us is no craven spirit, but one to inspire strength."

As a matter of fact, I was neither destroyed nor swallowed up by the frenzy of those who plotted against me, nor was the defender of piety, the Patriarch, deposed for having ordained me, as they publicly announced. For by what synod of bishops

ἐφήμισαν. τίνι γὰρ ἂν συνόδῳ ἐπισκόπων καθῄρητο—ὑπὸ γὰρ ἐπισκόπων ἐπ' αἰτίᾳ καθαιρεῖται τοιαύτῃ—πάντων συμπεπνευκότων αὐτῷ, καὶ τῶν ἄλλων πατριαρχῶν, τοῦ τε 'Αντιοχείας λέγω καὶ τοῦ Ἱεροσολύμων, καὶ τῶν μητροπολιτῶν ἁπάντων, εἴς τε τὴν κοινὴν ἡμῖν ὁμολογίαν τῆς πίστεως καὶ τὴν ἐμὴν ἱερωσύνην; καὶ τίς ἦν οὕτως ἐκτὸς τοῦ λογίζεσθαι, ὥστε τοῦθ' ὑποπτεῦσαι; οὐδὲ γὰρ τοὺς Παλαμήτας κριτὰς τῆς ἐκκλησίας ἐκάθισαν· ὧν τοὺς προστάτας, τὸν μὲν ἐξελόντες τῶν ψήφων τῶν ἐφ' ἱεραρχίᾳ καὶ αὐτῆς καθελόντες καθάπαξ ἱερωσύνης ὡς τὰ αὐτὰ τῷ Παλαμᾷ φρονοῦντα, ἕτερον ἀντεισήγαγον τοῖς ἐκείνου πολέμιον δόγμασι, κατ' αὐτὸ δήπου τοῦθ' ὅτι τοῖς ἐκείνου πολέμιον δόγμασι· τὸν δὲ καὶ εἱρκτῇ παραδόντες ἐφρούρουν καὶ νῦν οὐδὲν ἧττον φρουροῦσι. καὶ πέμπει δὴ βασιλεὺς ὁ θειότατος μετὰ τῆς μητρὸς αὐτῷ τῆς θείας καὶ ἡμετέρας δεσποίνης καὶ συνόδου τῆς θείας ἐπιστολὰς εἰς Ὄρος τὸ ἱερόν, βεβαιοῦντες τὴν αἰτίαν ἐφ' ᾗ φρουροῖτο, καὶ δυσσέβειαν ὁμολογοῦντες εἶναι, ἐφ' οἷς δὴ καὶ πάσαις ψήφοις ἐκκήρυκτοι γίνονται τῆς ἐκκλησίας οἱ Παλαμῆται πάντες, ὡς οἱ κατ' αὐτῶν ἐκτεθειμένοι λόγοι καὶ γνῶμαι τοῖς θειοτάτοις πατριάρχαις πρὸς ὑμᾶς ἐνεχθέντες ἢ ἐδίδαξαν, ἢ νῦν διὰ τοῦ θεσπεσιωτάτου δικαιοφύλακος ἢ σακελλίου τοῦ Βρυεννίου διδάξουσιν, ὃς τοῦτο παρὰ τῆς καθ' ἡμᾶς μεγάλης τοῦ Θεοῦ ἐκκλησίας πρὸς τὴν καθ' ὑμᾶς διακονῆσαι παρέλαβεν. ὑφ' οὗ καὶ περὶ τῆς σῆς ὁσιότητος ὅτι συκοφαντοῖτο τὴν μεταβολὴν ἐδιδάχθημεν καὶ τῆς ἐπὶ ταύτῃ προτέρας ἀνίας ἀνείθημεν· εἰ δὲ καὶ σοῖς τοῦ νῦν καταμάθοιμεν γράμμασι, βεβαιοτέρας ἀπολελαύκαμεν τῆς εὐφροσύνης.

51. Τῷ Λογαρᾷ κῦρ Σάββᾳ

Ὅτε τοῦ μεγάλου χειμῶνος καταλαβόντος ἡμᾶς τελέως τὴν γαλήνην ἀπέγνωμεν, τότε ἡ σὴ κυβερνητικὴ πρόνοια καὶ ἐπιστήμη τὴν ἑαυτῆς εἰκότως ἐπεδείξατο δύναμιν, δι' ἣν μετὰ Θεὸν τοῦ μὲν χειμῶνος εὐθὺς ὑπερέσχομεν, γαλήνην δὲ αὖθις εἴδομεν· σὸν δ' ἄρα καὶ τοῦ λοιποῦ ταύτης ἡμᾶς ἀπολαύειν, ἐκείνῳ μὴ περιπίπτοντας. τὸν δὴ τοιοῦτον ὡς ἄγομεν τί χρὴ καὶ λέγειν; τὰ γάρ, οἶμαι, ἀφανῆ

---

137 *φρουροῖτο* scripsit Loenertz: *φρονοῖτο* M

51: M 69v–70r.

5 *ἴδομεν* M

was he deposed? Because in case of such a charge, he is deposed by ⟨a synod⟩ of bishops; whereas they have all agreed with him, both the other patriarchs—I mean those of Antioch and Jerusalem—and all the metropolitans, on the matter of our common confession of faith as well as on my ordination. And who was so out of his mind as to suspect that? For they did not set up the Palamites as judges of the Church. Of their leaders, one they deposed from the episcopal office to which he had been elected and once for all banished from the priesthood itself, because he held the same beliefs as Palamas, and in his place they brought in another man who opposes Palamas' doctrines (for the very reason, indeed, that he opposes his doctrines), while the other ⟨leader⟩ they kept in jail under guard, and they are still guarding him now. And the most divine Emperor, together with his divine mother, our Empress, and the Holy Synod, in fact, sent letters to the Holy Mountain confirming the reason for which he is kept under guard and agreeing that it is impiety. For these reasons, indeed, all the Palamites are also by unanimous vote banished from the Church. Just as the writings and judgments against them set forth by the most holy patriarchs either informed you when they were brought to you, or will inform you now through the most divine *dikaiophylax* or *sakelliou* Bryennios, who undertook to perform this service to your Church on behalf of our Great Church of God here. From him I learned that your Piety was falsely accused of a change of position, and I was relieved of the distress that I suffered previously on this account. And if I should also learn it now from your letter, I would experience a surer joy.

51. To master Sabbas Logaras

When the great storm overtook me completely and I gave up all hope of calmness, then your navigating foresight and skill properly showed its strength. Thanks to this, after God, I rose immediately above the storm and saw calmness again. It is up to you, then, ⟨to ensure that⟩ I enjoy it in the future as well and that I do not fall into the storm. What is the use, therefore, of saying how I regard such a man? Only

51

δεῖται λόγων εἰς πίστιν, τὰ δ' αὐτόπιστα πείθειν ἀπαίδευτον· φανεροῦ γὰρ ὄντος ὅτι διὰ τὴν σὴν ἀρετὴν καὶ σοφίαν καὶ τὸ περὶ τὴν εὐσέβειαν ἐπιεικῶς ἰσχυρὸν ἔστη μὲν ὁ καθ' ἡμῶν ἐγηγερμένος κλύδων, ἔστη δὲ ἡ μανία τῶν ἐκεῖνον ἐγειράντων πνευμάτων, ἐξ ὧν οὐ μᾶλλον ἡμεῖς ἢ τὸ τῆς εὐσεβείας χρῆμα ἐκλυδωνίζετο, ἐπανήκει δὲ ἡμῖν αὖθις καὶ ἐπανήξει δὴ τελεώτερον τὸ εὐσεβεῖν ἀφόβως, πῶς οὐ σαφὲς ὁμοίως καὶ τὸ ἑπόμενον; ἔστι δὲ τοῦτο δήπου τό σε σωτῆρα μετὰ Θεὸν νομίζειν καὶ πρόμαχον [fol. 70^{r}] *τῆς εὐσεβείας ἡμῶν, εἰ μὴ ἀναισθητοῖμεν, καί, ὡς ἔπος εἰπεῖν, πᾶν ὅπερ ἂν ἄγοιεν εὐγνώμονες ἄνθρωποι τὸν ἐφ' ᾧπερ αὐτοῖς κεῖται μετὰ Θεὸν τῆς πάσης σωτηρίας τὰ πράγματα.*

Τὴν μὲν δὴ σὴν σοφίαν οὕτως ἡμῖν ἀνάγκη τοῦ πλείονος καὶ τοῦ παντὸς τιμᾶσθαι· ὅτι δὲ καὶ τὸν μεγέθει τῆς φύσεως καὶ διανοίας ὀξύτητι τῶν πώποτε τούτοις ἐνευδοκιμηκότων εἰς τοὺς πρώτους τελοῦντα, τὸ μέγα δήπου καὶ πρᾶγμα καὶ ὄνομα, πολλή τις ἡμῖν ἀνάγκη φιλεῖν ὑπὲρ τοὺς ἄλλους πάντας, πολλῶν ἕνεκα καὶ τῶν ἀναγκαιοτάτων, εἰ μὴ τοῖς ἄλλοις, τῇ γε σῇ τελειότητι δῆλον· * * * *ἀλλ' ὅμως ἥκιστα πάντων ταύτης ὄντες ἄξιοι τῆς ὑποψίας καὶ τῆς ἐπιτιμήσεως τῷ γε καὶ ὁπωσοῦν τὰ ἡμέτερα λογιζομένῳ. Θεὸς δέ, ὡς ἔοικεν, οὐκ εἰς μακρὸν ἀφῆκε τἀληθὲς κακῶς πάσχειν· οὐκ ἀφῆκε δὲ διὰ τῆς σῆς σοφίας, ἣ τῆς ἀδίκου καὶ πονηρᾶς καθ' ἡμῶν ὑποψίας ἀπαγαγοῦσα τὸν ὑπ' αὐτῆς ὀργιζόμενον, αὐτήν τε τὴν ὀργὴν κατεκοίμησε καὶ ἡμᾶς ἔπαυσε τοῦ διὰ ταύτην διώκεσθαι. καὶ νῦν διὰ τῆς σῆς ἀγαθότητος τὸ μὲν κινούσης, Θεῷ δὲ κινουμένης, εὐμενής τ' ἐστι πάλιν, εὔνοις αὐτῷ καθαρῶς καὶ γενομένοις καὶ οὖσι καὶ ἐσομένοις γε· οὐ λημμάτων οὐδὲ βρωμάτων χάριν, ὥσπερ τινὲς οἷς καθ' ἡμῶν τὰς ἀκοὰς ὑπέσχε, τοῦ δὲ ἀδεῶς ἡμῖν εὐσεβεῖν ἐξεῖναι δι' αὐτοῦ καὶ μὴ ἀναγκάζεσθαι τῆς πατρῴας εὐσεβείας ἐξίστασθαι, ἢ τὰ τῶν δυσσεβῶν καὶ κακούργων ὑπομένειν τιμήματα. δυοῖν γὰρ τούτων ἡμῖν ἐξ ἀνάγκης προκειμένου θατέρου, ἢ ζῆν μετ' εὐσεβείας ἢ προαποθνῄσκειν αὐτῆς, ἥν τις ἡμῖν αὐτὴν διορύττειν πειρᾶται, ὁ θατέρου διδοὺς ἀδεῶς ἀπολαύειν καὶ θάτερον δίδωσι, καὶ ὅλου μέντοι τούτου, ζωῆς εὐσεβοῦς, βραβευτὴς καὶ πρύτανις γίνεται· τὸν δὲ τοιοῦτον οὐκ ἔστιν ἧττον φιλεῖν ἑαυτῶν τοὺς οὕτω πρὸς εὐσέβειαν ἔχοντας. οὔτε τοίνυν ἕτερον ἡμῖν μετὰ Θεὸν ἄγειν δεῖ πρὸ σοῦ καὶ τοῦ μεγάλου δουκός, οὔθ' ἕτερον ἡμῖν εἶναι παρ' ὑμᾶς ἢ πρὸ ὑμῶν τὸν ἐλευθέρως βιοῦν εὐσεβείᾳ προσέχοντα.*

51: 22 Cf. Greg. Naz., *Or.* 43, 21 (PG, 36, 524B)

---

24 post *δῆλον* lacunam statui

51

obscure things require words of proof, but it is foolish to prove what is self-evident. For since it is obvious that due to your virtue and wisdom and suitably strong ⟨convictions⟩ about piety, the billows that had risen against me and the frenzy of the winds that raised them—by which the cause of piety was shaken more than I was—stood still, and the right to be pious without fear is returning to me and will return, indeed, more complete, is not what follows also equally clear? And this is, of course, the fact that, unless I am insensitive, I consider you as my savior, after God, and the defender of our piety, and, in short ⟨I regard you as⟩ everything that sensible men would consider appropriate to the man with whom rests, after God, the matter of their whole salvation.

This is how necessary it is for me, then, to value your Wisdom as the greatest and ultimate blessing. That it is also very necessary for me, for many most urgent reasons, to love above all others the man who by the stature of his character and keeness of intelligence belongs to the first class of those who have ever been famous for such accomplishments, the great man both "in name and deed," this is obvious to your Excellence, if not to others * * * but still being least of all worthy of such suspicions and reproach, however one considers my conduct. But, as it seems, God did not allow truth to suffer for long. He prevented this through your Wisdom who removed the unjust and wicked suspicion against me on the part of the man who was angered by it, and both lulled to sleep the anger itself and stopped me from being persecuted because of it. And now through your kindness, which stirred him while being itself stirred by God, he is again favorably disposed toward me—I who have been and am and will be sincerely friendly to him indeed. Not for the sake of profit or food, as in the case of certain men to whom he lent his ear against me, but in order to be allowed through him to live piously without fear and not be forced to give up my ancestral piety or suffer punishment from impious and criminal men. For if by necessity one of two choices lies before me, either to live with piety or die for it, if one attempts to undermine it, the man who allows me to enjoy either without fear grants me the other also and becomes, of course, the arbiter and curator of it all—of the pious life, that is. Men who are so disposed towards piety cannot love such a man less than themselves. Neither should I, therefore, honor anyone else, after God, above you and the *Megas Doux*, nor should the man who devotes himself to living in piety with freedom be for me different from or better than you.

52

52. Τῷ Μονεμβασίας

Οὐκ ἄρα δύναται ταὐτὸ λόγος ἀνδρὸς ὁ αὐτὸς ἀρχομένου τε καὶ ἀρχὴν μεταχειριζομένου, καὶ δὴ σοφῶς εἴρηται τῇ τραγῳδίᾳ λόγος γὰρ ἔκ τ' ἀδοξούντων κἀκ τῶν δοκούντων ἰὼν αὐτὸς οὐ ταὐτὸ σθένει. ἂν δὲ καὶ ἱερὰν ἀρχὴν ἄρχῃ τις, ἡλίκον τὸ τῆς δυνάμεως· ἂν δὲ καὶ μετὰ τοῦ ἀληθοῦς ᾖ τεταγμένος καὶ δικαιοσύνης προεστηκὼς καὶ τῆς εὐσεβείας ὑπερμαχῶν, ἐνταῦθα τὸ ἄμαχον. σὺ γάρ, ὦ θειότατε, ἠγώνισαι μὲν λόγοις λαμπροῖς καὶ γενναίοις ἐνταῦθα κατὰ τῆς Παλαμᾶ *δυσσεβεστάτης πλάνης, εὐδοκίμηκας δὲ παρὰ τῇ ἐκκλησίᾳ τοῦ* Θεοῦ *κατὰ τὸν τοῦ δικαίου λόγον, ἐπέβης δὲ τοῦ θείου τῆς ἀρχιερωσύνης ὕψους, οὐ προῖκα κατά τινας οὐδὲ πρὶν παρασχέσθαι τὸν ἄξιον τοῦ ἀξιώματος ἐκ τῶν ὑπὲρ τῆς ἐκκλησίας ἀγώνων καὶ τῶν θείων δογμάτων, ἀλλ' ἆθλον ἔλαβες τὸν θρόνον ἀντὶ τῶν ὑπὲρ τῆς εὐσεβείας ἄθλων, καὶ κινδυνεύοντα τὸν τῆς* Πελοποννήσου *προεστηκότα θρόνον τὸ* Παλαμναῖον *ἀναδεδέχθαι κακόν, ἀντιπαραταξάμενος καθεῖλες μὲν ἐκεῖνο μετὰ τῆς ἐκκλησίας, ἐξήρπασας δὲ τὸν θρόνον κακοῦ τοσούτου τῆς* Ἰσιδώρου *πλάνης, ἠξίωσαι δὲ καὶ τούτου δικαίως παρὰ τοῦ* Πνεύματος, *μᾶλλον δὲ τῆς σῆς σοφίας καὶ ἀρετῆς καὶ θειότητος ὁ θρόνος ἠξίωται. καὶ κοσμεῖται νῦν ἀνδρὶ τοσούτῳ τὸ* Δωριέων *γένος, οὐ καλοῦ κάλλιον, ἀλλ' ἀντ' ἐσχάτου κακοῦ, δυσσεβείας, τὸ κάλλιστον ἀντειληφότες, εὐσέβειαν, δι' ἀνδρὸς* ποιμένος *καὶ τἆλλα μὲν τελείου, ἀθλητοῦ δ' εὐσεβείας καὶ πρὶν ἐπιστῆναι τῇ ποίμνῃ τοὺς ἐπιόντας αὐτῇ διεφθαρκότος λύκους.*

Ἐκεῖνα δή σου τοιαῦτα ὄντα καὶ λόγους οὐ βραχεῖς ὑπὲρ τῆς εὐσεβείας, νῦν οὐ μακραῖς ἐπιστολαῖς, ὥσπερ ἥλιος ἐπιφανεὶς ἀκτῖσιν ὑπερφαέσιν, ἠφάνισας περιουσίᾳ *δυνάμεως τῆς ἐκ τοῦ* Πνεύματος *τοῦ χρίσαντός σε κἀπὶ τὸν θρόνον τῆς ἀρχιερωσύνης καθίσαντος. ἢ μᾶλλον κἀκείνους ἀνῆψας τοὺς λόγους τούτοις εἰς τὸ* λαμπρότερον· *καὶ γὰρ ἐκεῖνοι τοῦ* Μονεμβασίας *εἶναι φημίζονται, οἷς τότε βληθεῖσα κἀπὶ* [fol. 72r] *γόνυ πεσοῦσα ἡ* Παλαμναία *πλάνη, νῦν τοῖς αὐτοῖς ἐκείνοις σὺν τούτοις ἐπιοῦσιν, ὡς εἰκὸς καταπίπτει τελέως διὰ τὴν ἐκ τοῦ χρίσματος ἐπικουρίαν, οἷς ὧδε γράφεις ἡμῖν, οἷς τῷ* Κορινθίων *ποιμένι πέμπεις ἐκεῖσέ πῃ, οἷς εἰς* Κύπρον *Λαπίθῃ· οἷς οἱ δεχόμενοι καὶ ψυχροί γ' ἄν τινες ὄντες ἀνήφθησαν, ὄντες*

52: 4–5 Euripides, *Hecuba*, 294–295

52: 71v–72v. Ed. Loenertz, *Epistulae*, 89–92, no. 1.

5 *αὐτὸς* Loenertz: *αὐτὸς* M

52

52. To the metropolitan of Monemvasia

Certainly the same words do not have the same influence when coming from the ruled as from the rulers. And the tragedy says wisely indeed that "The same word does not have the same power when coming from unimportant as from important men." And if one is ruling in a sacred capacity, how great is the power! And if he sides with truth and protects justice and defends piety, right is indisputably there! For you fought here, your Holiness, against the most impious deceit of Palamas with brilliant and noble discourses, and became justly famous in the Church of God, and you rose to the divine sublimity of the episcopal office, not freely as some do, nor before showing yourself worthy of the office by your struggles in defense of the Church and the sacred dogmas, but you received the throne as a prize for your labors in defense of piety; and while the throne which is at the head of the Church of the Peloponnesos was in danger of accepting the Palamnaian evil, you set yourself against it, and, together with the Church, you destroyed that evil and rescued the throne from such a great disaster, Isidore's deceit, and you were justly deemed worthy of the throne by the Holy Spirit. Or rather, the throne was deemed worthy of your wisdom and virtue and holiness. And now the Dorian people are adorned with such a great man, having exchanged not good for better, but the extreme evil, impiety, for the greatest blessing, piety, through a man who is a perfect pastor in all other respects, as well as a champion of piety who, even before becoming the head of the flock, destroyed the wolves who attacked it.

Yet those deeds of yours, which are so ⟨illustrious⟩, and your long discourses in defense of piety you eclipsed now by your brief letters—appearing just as the sun with exceedingly bright rays—with abundant power from the Holy Spirit Which anointed you and set you on the episcopal throne. Or, rather, by these letters you made even those discourses shine brighter, for they too are reputed to be the work of the Metropolitan of Monemvasia. By them was the Palamnaian deceit struck at that time, collapsing to its knees. Now, as those same discourses together with these letters—the ones you write to us here and to the pastor of the Corinthians there, somewhere, and to Lapithes in Cyprus—⟨as these⟩ proceed against it, it is collapsing completely, as is right, because of the assistance of the ⟨episcopal⟩ anointment. By such letters the recipients would have been inflamed, even if they were a cold

52

δὲ ὅπερ εἰσὶ πρὸς τὸν παρόντα τῆς αἱρέσεως θῆρα πῶς—οἴει;—προσαναφλέγονται, καὶ πάσχουσιν ὑπὸ τούτων ὅ γέ φασιν Ἀλέξανδρον τὸν Μακεδόνα ὑπὸ τῆς Ἀντιγενίδου μούσης· ᾄσαντος γὰρ ἐνυάλιον ἐκείνου οὐκ ἐγκρατὴς ἦν Ἀλέξανδρος ἑαυτοῦ κἂν εἰ δειπνῶν εὑρέθη, ἀλλ' ὥρμα εὐθὺς ἐφ' ὅπλα καὶ τὴν παράταξιν.

Ἃ μὲν οὖν πρὸς τὸν γενναῖον καὶ ἱερὸν Κορίνθου, καὶ ἃ πρὸς Λαπίθην τὸν σοφώτατον γράφεις θαυμάζων αὐτοὺς τοῦ κατὰ τῆς Παλαμήτιδος πολυθεΐας μένους, καὶ ἀνέγνωμεν καὶ ἐθαυμάσαμεν, καὶ ὅσους ταῦτα—πολλοὺς δέ—ἀναγνῶναι συνέβη, τοὺς μὲν τῆς ἐκκλησίας ἐφαίδρυνε, τοὺς δὲ τῆς ἐναντίας μοίρας κατῄσχυνεν, ἢ τῶν μὲν τὴν προτέραν φαιδρότητα, τῶν δὲ τὴν αἰσχύνην ἐδιπλασίασε. γράφε δ' ἀεὶ ταῦτα ταῖς ἐκκλησίαις πάσαις καὶ μάλιστα τοῖς Θεσσαλονικεῦσι καὶ τῷ τούτων ποιμένι. ἔστι δὲ οὗτος Ὑάκινθος ὁ θαυμάσιος ὁ τῆς μονῆς οἰκήτωρ Ὁδηγητρίας τῆς παναγοῦς Θεομήτορος· οὗτος γὰρ νῦν ἀρχιερεὺς Θεσσαλονίκης κεχειροτόνηται. ᾧ γράφε δή, καὶ τοῖς ἄλλοις οὓς ὠφελήσεις γράφων, καὶ βοηθήσεις τοῖς σεαυτοῦ πολίταις οἷς οὐκ ὀλίγον ἐνέσπαρται τὸ Παλαμναῖον κακὸν παρὰ τὸ χρονίους ἐκεῖ διατετριφέναι τὸν Παλαμᾶν τε καὶ τὸν Ἰσίδωρον.

Οἶσθα δὲ ὅτι καὶ Μασσαλιανισμὸς μέρος ἐστὶ τῆς ὅλης αἱρέσεως τοῦ Παλαμᾶ· ᾗ γὰρ ὁρᾶν φασι σωματικοῖς ὀφθαλμοῖς μορφὴν Θεοῦ φυσικὴν καὶ θεότητα, καὶ Πνεῦμα ἅγιον καὶ ἄναρχον αἰσθητῶς ὑποδέχεσθαι, σαφὴς Μασσαλιανισμός ἐστι πρὸς τῇ πολυθεΐᾳ. αὕτη τοίνυν ἡ αἵρεσις νῦν ἀνεφάνη μετ' αἰσχίστων ἔργων ἑτέρων καὶ εἰκονομαχίας ἐν Ὄρει τῷ ἱερῷ καὶ τῇδε κἀν τῇ Θεσσαλονίκῃ. καὶ πρώτη τῆς πλάνης ταύτης τῆς μετ' αἰσχρότητος ⟨αἰτία⟩ Γεώργιος ἐκεῖνος ὁ Ἰσιδώρῳ χρόνον συνῳκηκὼς ἱκανὸν ἐν τῇ Θεσσαλονίκῃ. ὃς φωραθεὶς ἐκεῖ τότε βλασφημῶν εἰς τὰ θεῖα, ἐξώρμησε μὲν καθ' αὑτοῦ τὸν Θεσσαλο-[fol. 72v]νικέων δῆμον, διέφυγε δὲ μόλις τὰς ἐκείνων χεῖρας ἀπ' αὐτῆς τῆς κοινῆς οἰκίας αὐτοῦ τε καὶ Ἰσιδώρου. ὃς αὖθις νῦν φωραθεὶς καὶ φρονῶν καὶ πράττων ἃ μηδ' ἔξεστι λέγειν, σταυροειδῶς ἐστίχθη καυτηρίαις τὸ πρόσωπον καὶ ἀπηλάθη τοῦ θείου Ὄρους ὡς β δ έ λ υ γ μ α τ ῆ ς ἐ ρ η μ ώ σ ε ω ς, καὶ πολλοὶ σὺν αὐτῷ σατυρικοὶ καὶ μονάζοντες· ὧν ἄρχουσα ἡ Πορινὴ καὶ θεά τις εὑρέθη, πάσης αὐτοῖς ὑπουργὸς αἰσχρότητος καὶ βδελυρίας, ἧς φοιτητὴς παρ' ὁντινοῦν Ἰσίδωρος γέγονε, καὶ πρὸς ἣν ὁρῶν ὡς πρὸς κανόνα θεῖον πᾶν ὁτιοῦν λέγουσαν καὶ πράττουσαν

---

68 Dan. 9:27; 12:11; Matt. 24:15

---

60 οἰκονομαχίας M ‖ 6 Post αἰσχρότητος unum verbum deest: αἰτία scr. Loenertz ‖ 69 σατυρικοὶ coni. Loenertz: σατηρικοὶ M

52

kind of men; but disposed as they are towards the present beast of heresy, you cannot imagine how much more they are incensed! And these letters have on them the same effect which they claim that the music of Antigonides had on Alexander of Macedon. For whenever that man sang a warlike song, Alexander could not restrain himself, even if he happened to be dining, but immediately made a dash for his armor and the line of battle.

I read and admired what you write to the noble and holy Metropolitan of Corinth and to the most wise Lapithes in admiration of their ardor against Palamas' polytheism. And among those who happened to read them—and there are many—your letters filled with joy the followers of the Church, whereas they put to shame its opponents, or they doubled the earlier joy of the former and the shame of the latter. Keep on writing such things to all the churches and especially to the Thessalonians and their pastor, the admirable Hyakinthos, the resident of the monastery of Hodegetria, for he has now been ordained metropolitan of Thessalonica. Write to him, then, and to others whom you will succor by your writing, and ⟨hence⟩ you will assist your fellow-citizens in whom the Palamnaian evil has been sown not a little, because of the long sojourn there of both Palamas and Isidore.

You know, moreover, that Messalianism is part of Palamas' whole heresy. For when they say that they see with bodily eyes the natural form and divinity of God and that they receive by means of the senses the Holy and eternal Spirit, this is manifest Messalianism as well as polytheism. This heresy, indeed, together with iconoclasm and other more shameful deeds, has appeared now on the Holy Mountain and here and in Thessalonica. And the primary cause of this delusion as well as infamy is the notorious George, who resided with Isidore in Thessalonica for a considerable time. When he was at that time found out there speaking blasphemy against God, he incited against himself the people of Thessalonica and barely escaped from their hands from the very house that he shared with Isidore. Soon afterwards, because he was again detected both believing and doing things that are inconceivable even to speak of, he was branded crosswise on the face with an iron and banished from the Holy Mountain as "the abomination of desolation," and together with him many wanton men and monks. Their leader and goddess, as it were, was found to be Porine, a minister to them of all infamy and abomination. Isidore visited her more than anyone else and spent his time watching her, as if she were a divine rule, while she was saying and doing everything possible and nodding and dancing

καὶ νεύουσαν καὶ σχηματιζομένην καὶ πίνουσάν γε καὶ μέθῃ συνοῦσαν διηνεκεῖ διῆγεν οὗτος, ἐξυμνῶν ὡς προφῆτιν, σὺν Παλαμᾷ τῷ σοφῷ. καὶ νῦν αὐτῆς οὕτως ἔχονται καθάπερ τῆς ὑφειμένης θεότητος, μᾶλλον δὲ καθάπερ τῆς πάντων ὑπερκειμένης οἱ εὐσεβεῖς.

Ταῦτα μὲν οὕτως ἔχει. σὺ δὲ δὴ τὸν διάλογον δέξαι τὸν ἐχιδναῖον, καὶ ὅπως αὐτὸν οὐ μόνον ἐπιδεικνὺς τοῖς ὅτι συκοφαντοῦμεν τὸν Παλαμᾶν συκοφαντοῦσιν ἡμᾶς συκοφάντας αὐτοὺς ἡμῶν ἐναργῶς ἀποδείξεις, ἀλλὰ καὶ λόγους δημιουργήσας τοὺς τῇ σῇ δυνάμει προσήκοντας, πρὸς τοῖς προτέροις, ἀντιτάξεις τῇ πλάνῃ καὶ διὰ τούτων τοῖς ἁπανταχοῦ γῆς ὁμιλῶν ἀπαλλάξεις τῆς νόσου τοὺς ἐντεῦθεν νοσήσαντας, καὶ τοὺς ἐμπεσουμένους ταύτῃ ἐμπεσεῖν οὐκ ἐάσεις καί, ὡς εἰπεῖν, θησαυρὸν καταλείψεις τῇ ἐκκλησίᾳ τοῦ Θεοῦ τιμιώτατον.

53. Sine titulo

Οἶμαί σου λυπηθῆναι τὴν θαυμαστὴν κεφαλὴν ἀκούσασαν τὰ καθ' ἡμᾶς λυπηρά. ἔστι δὲ τοῦ αὐτοῦ πάντως ἀνδρὸς καὶ χαίρειν εὖ πράττοντος ἐφ' ᾧπερ ἀσχάλλοι δυσημεροῦντι· δεῖ δή σε ἡμῖν συνευφραίνεσθαι νῦν ἐφ' οἷς ἐσκυθρώπαζες πρότερον διωκομένοις, τὰ γὰρ σκυθρωπὰ πάντ' ἐκεῖνα Θεοῦ νεύσει λέλυται· οἷς μὲν ἧττον ἠσχάλλομεν οἵ γε καὶ ἐντρυφῶντες τοῖς πάθεσιν, οἱ δ' ἐπανιστάμενοί μοι καὶ πρὸς ἀλλήλους διαλεχθέντες δεῦτε καὶ ἐξολοθρεύσωμεν αὐτὸν ἐξ ἔθνους καὶ μὴ μνησθῇ τὸ ὄνομα αὐτοῦ ἔτι, τότε μὲν ἑώρταζον ὡς ἤδη με καταπιόντες, καὶ οὐδὲν αὐτοὺς ἐχώρει φλεγμαίνοντας τῷ τῆς ἡδονῆς ἐκτόπῳ καὶ ἀκρατεῖ, νυνὶ δὲ αὖθις οἰμώζουσιν, ἐπειδήπερ πρὸς τῷ μηδέν τι βλάψαι καὶ λαμπρότερον ἔδειξε τὸ καθ' ἡμᾶς ἡ ἐπήρεια, οὐκ ἀνασχομένων τῶν ἀγαθῶν ἀρχόντων ἐπὶ μακρὸν ἀσελγαίνειν ἐᾶν τὸ ψεῦδος εἰς τὴν ἀλήθειαν καὶ τὴν ἱερὰν τοῦ Θεοῦ ἐκκλησίαν. διὰ δὴ ταῦτα σαυτὸν λῦε τῆς ἐφ' ἡμῖν ἀνίας, ὦ βέλτιστε, καὶ τοὺς ἄλλους οἵ σοι τῆς αὐτῆς ἀλγηδόνος ὑπὲρ ἡμῶν μετέσχον.

75–76 cf. Palamam, *Epist. III ad Acindynum*, 15, Syngrammata, I, 306, 18–20; ed. Nadal, 252, 10–12

53: 6–7 ἐπανιστάμενοι: cf. Ps. 58(59):1; 91(92):11 ‖ 7 πρὸς . . . διαλεχθέντες: cf. Marc. 9:34 ‖ 7–9 Ps. 82(83):4

53: M 69ᵛ.

3 δυσσημεροῦντι M ‖ 8 ἐξολοθρεύσομεν M ‖ 15 λύε M

and drinking and being constantly intoxicated, and he praised her as a prophetess together with the sage Palamas. And now they are so attached to her, just as to the "lower divinity," or rather, just as the pious to the "all-transcendent" divinity.

This is how the matter stands. Receive, therefore, the venomous dialogue, and not only so that you may show it to those who accuse me falsely of accusing Palamas falsely and prove distinctly that they are my false accusers, but also so that you may produce discourses befitting your power and set them together with the previous ones against this deceit and, speaking through them to men the world over, you may rid of the disease those who suffer from it and not allow those in danger of this to fall ill and, in a word, to bequeath to the Church of God a most valuable treasure.

53. No Addressee

I believe, my admirable friend, that you were sorry to hear my sorrowful news. But it is also entirely natural for the same man to rejoice at the good fortune of the man for whose misery he would grieve; and so you must indeed rejoice now with me for whose sake you were previously sad when I was persecuted. For, by the command of God, all those sad things have disappeared. I, who even find pleasure in suffering, was less annoyed at these things, but "those who rose up against me" and "said among themselves, 'Come, let us utterly destroy him out of the nation and let his name be remembered no more' " were celebrating at that time, as if they had already swallowed me up, and there was nothing containing them, swollen as they were with extraordinary and uncontrolled pleasure. But now, after this, they are lamenting, because the abuse, while not hurting my cause at all, in fact made it even more illustrious, since the good rulers could not bear to let falsehood insult truth and the holy Church of God for long. For this reason, my excellent friend, set yourself and the others who shared the same grief for me free of sorrow on my account.

54. Μυστικῷ τῷ Κινάμῳ

Τὸ μὴ θαρρεῖν ἐγκαλούμενος, ἔγνων θαρρήσας τῆς ἐνταῦθα αἰτίας ἐμαυτὸν ἐξελέσθαι· καίτοι ὅτῳ που εὐεργέτημα μέν τὸ αἰτίαμα, εὐεργέτης δ' ὁ τὴν αἰτίαν ἐπάγων, ὥσπερ ἐμοὶ σὺ καὶ τὸ ἔγκλημα [fol. 76ʳ] *τὸ σόν, ὦ θαυμάσιε, πῶς οὐκ ἂν τούτῳ χαίροντι περαίνοιτο τὸ ἐπίταγμα; ᾐσθεὶς οὖν τῷ ἐγκλήματι τῷ παρὰ σοῦ ὅτι σε μὴ θαρροίην, δέον θαρρεῖν ὡς ἀσέμνου μὴ δεξομένου τὴν παρρησίαν, θαρρῶ μὲν ἤδη καὶ εἰς καιρόν γε, οἶμαι, παρρησιάζομαι· τὸ γάρ, οἶμαι, πρὶν ταύτην λαβεῖν τὴν μέμψιν θαρρεῖν τοὺς μεγάλους οὐκ εὐλαβὲς οὐδὲ προσῆκον ἀνδράσιν ἀνακεχωρηκόσι.*

Συναίτιος δὲ τοῦ θάρρους φίλος ἀνὴρ οὐκ ἐμοὶ μέντοι μόνῳ, ἀλλὰ καί σοι πρὸ ἐμοῦ, καὶ σφόδρα ἐπιεικής, Εὐφημιανὸς οὑτοσίν, *ὃς ᾐσθημένος τὴν σὴν περὶ ἡμᾶς ἐρρωμένην οὖσαν φιλοφροσύνην, καὶ ταῦτα ἐν ἀρχῇ τῆς ἐντεύξεως, καὶ πρὸς τὸ μέλλον ἐπίδοσιν, ἰσχυροτέραν ἐνόμισεν εἶναι τῶν ὑπαρχόντων αὐτῷ πρός γε τὸ ταύτῃ χρήσασθαι ὑπὲρ αὐτοῦ. τοιγαροῦν ὁ μὲν ἐμὲ παρεκάλεσεν ἐπὶ τὸ τὴν σήν τι δύναμιν γράμμασι παρακαλέσαι ὑπὲρ αὐτοῦ, ἐγὼ δὲ ταύτην ἐπὶ τὸ τοῦτο αὐτῷ παρασχεῖν τοῖς παροῦσι γράμμασι παρακαλῶ. ἔστι δὲ δήπου τόδε· εἷς τῶν ὑπὸ σοὶ τελούντων ἐθέλει βασιλικῶν γραμματέων γενέσθαι, τοῦτο μὲν ἀεὶ τῇ σῇ συνεῖναι χρηστότητι ἐπιθυμῶν ἧς ἡττημένος ἐστί, τοῦτο δὲ καί τινα πόρον οὐκ ἄδικον τῷ βίῳ τῷ ἑαυτοῦ μηχανώμενος· ἔστι δὲ αὐτῷ δεύτερον μὲν τοῦτο, πρότερον δὲ ἐκεῖνο. καὶ θαυμαστὸν οὐδέν· τοῖς γὰρ ἀγαθοῖς ἀνδράσι καὶ σώφροσιν οἱ φίλοι πρὸ τῶν χρημάτων, κἂν πένωνται.*

Ἐμοὶ μὲν οὖν οὔπω καιρὸς ἐδόκει τοσαύτης εἶναι τῆς παρρησίας πρὸς τὴν ἀξίαν τὴν σήν, κἂν σφόδρα ἧς ἐπιεικής τε καὶ μεγαλόφρων, ὥστε σε ἀπὸ γραμμῆς φασι τῆς φιλίας αἰτεῖν τι. Εὐφημιανὸς *δὲ ὁ βέλτιστος καὶ* Μανασῆς *ὁ θαυμάσιος, ὁ πάνυ δή σε καὶ φιλῶν καὶ θαυμάζων, εἰς τόδε με ἤγαγον, ἰσχυρισάμενοι ὡς ἂν σὺ παρ' ἐμοῦ λάβῃς γράμματα ὑπὲρ* Εὐφημιανοῦ, Εὐφημιανὸς *αὐτίκα μάλα παρὰ τῆς σῆς ἐπιεικείας ἡδομένης τὴν αἴτησιν λήψεται, ἡμᾶς μὲν γὰρ εἶναί σοι φίλους πάντας καὶ αὐτὸν τὸν δεόμενον, τὸ δὲ ῥᾴδιον τοῦ δοῦναι παρεῖναι τῇ σῇ δυνάμει παντάπασιν, εἰ βουληθείης, πῶς δὲ οὐκ ἂν βουληθείης, οὕτω μὲν ὢν τῇ φύσει χρηστὸς καὶ φιλάνθρωπος, οὕτω δέ σε φιλοῦντας μέλλων εὐεργετήσειν, ὥστε πάντως ἂν ἑτοίμως ἀκολουθῆσαι τὴν χάριν ἣν αἰτούμεθά σου τὴν γενναιότητα.*

54: M 75ᵛ–76ᵛ.

25 *τοσαύτην* M

54

54. To Kinamos, the Imperial Private Secretary

Since I have been accused of shyness, I decided to make bold and to free myself of this present charge. And yet, if someone finds the accusation a favor and the accuser a benefactor, as you, your Excellency, and your charge are to me, how could he not fulfill the command gladly? And so, as I was pleased with your accusation that I am reserved with you—and it is necessary not to be reserved, for the man who will not take the liberty will be rude—I have already become bold, and I think that I am taking this liberty at the proper time. For I believe that to be bold with important people before receiving this rebuke is neither discreet nor becoming to men who have withdrawn from the world.

There is a man who is partner in my crime of boldness—⟨a man⟩ who is not only a friend of mine but also before me a friend of yours and an exceedingly good man, our friend Euphemianos. He has sensed that your friendliness towards me was conspicuous even at the beginning of our meeting and that it was capable of growing even more so in the future, and he thought that, at least, for the purpose of using it in his favor it is stronger than anything he possesses. He asked me, therefore, to make an appeal by letter to your Authority on his behalf, and I am appealing to you in this letter to grant him his request. This is, indeed, what he asks: he wants to become one of the imperial secretaries under you, partly because he is anxious to be always near your Worthiness by whom he is captivated, and partly to procure for himself an honest means of livelihood. But to him the latter is second in importance and the former first. And no wonder, since good and wise men, even if they are poor, prefer friends to money.

I did not think that it was time for me yet to be so bold with your Worthiness, even though you are extremely kind as well as generous, so that they say that one can ask you for a favor from the very beginning of friendship. But the excellent Euphemianos and the admirable Manasses, who loves and admires you very much indeed, led me to this, claiming that if you received a letter from me in behalf of Euphemianos, Your Clemency will be pleased and grant Euphemianos his request immediately, because all of us, as well as the petitioner himself, are your friends, and it is quite easy for you with your power to grant the request, if you should be willing—and how could you not, since you are naturally so kind and humane and will be doing a favor to people who love you so much—so that the favor we ask from your Excellency would, no doubt, follow most readily.

Ἐμοὶ μὲν δὴ γέγραπται ὅπερ ἐμὸν ἦν ὑπὲρ Εὐφημιανοῦ, ἀνδρὸς καλοῦ κἀγαθοῦ, τὸ δὲ μὴ μάτην μοι γεγράφθαι ταῦτα ὑπὲρ αὐτοῦ σὸν ἤδη, καὶ τὸ μὴ λαβεῖν ἐξ ἀπάτης [fol. 76ᵛ] αἰτίαν τούς γε ἰσχυρισμένους ἡδέως τοῖς γράμμασι τὴν χάριν ἀκολουθήσειν καὶ διὰ τοῦτό με ταῦτα ἐναγαγοῦσι γράψαι τῇ σῇ δυνάμει· τὸ γὰρ ἀντὶ τοῦ λαβεῖν ἅπερ ἤλπισαν ἄνδρες φίλοι σοι, ῥᾴδιον ὄν, καὶ προσζημιώθῆναι τούτους εἰς ἀληθείας δόξαν οὐ δίκαιον.

55. Sine titulo

Ἔοικας, θεοφιλέστατε δέσποτα, μηνίειν ἡμῖν ἐφ' οἷς οὐκ ἦμεν κύριοι χαρίσασθαί σοι. τί γάρ σε λίαν ἐσπουδακότας ἰδεῖν καὶ τοῦτό σοι μεμηνυκότας, τῆς σαυτοῦ παρουσίας ἡμᾶς οὐκ ἠξίωσας, ἀλλ' ἀφῆκας φθινύθειν ἦτορ ὡς ἀδικήσαντας καὶ πάνυ μέντοι μέγα ἠδικηκότας σε; σκόπει μή, μηνίων ἡμῖν †ἀδικήσαντος†, φανῇς ἡμᾶς ἀδικῶν ὁμοῦ καὶ σαυτὸν οὐκ ἐλάχιστα τοὺς οὐδὲν ἀδικοῦντας. οὐ γὰρ ἁπλῶς φιλίαν, ἀλλ' ἣν ἡμῖν ὁ τῆς εὐσεβείας ἐνεφύτευσε λόγος πρὸς σὲ παρωθούμενος, οὐ μόνους ἡμᾶς, ἀλλὰ καὶ σαυτὸν εἰς τοσοῦτο πρᾶγμα ζημιώσας ὀφθήσει διὰ τέλους μηνίσας. ὅπερ ἵνα μὴ γένηται, ἀπορρίψας τὴν λύπην, φάνηθι τοῖς ὡς οἶσθα ποθοῦσί σε μετὰ τῆς συνήθους φαιδρότητος.

56. Τῷ Μαγίστρῳ

Τὴν τοῦ φοίνικος ἡμῖν ἐμιμήσατο φύσιν, ὡς ἔοικεν, ὁ σοφώτατος Μάγιστρος διὰ χρόνου φαινόμενος τῷ ἐπιστέλλειν, ὥσπερ Ἰνδοῖς ἐκεῖνος καὶ Αἰγυπτίοις ἐπιδημῶν. ἀλλ' ἡμεῖς γε τὴν γοῦν τοῦ Νείλου φύσιν αὐτὸν μεμιμῆσθαι ἠθέλομεν, ἐπετείως ἡμᾶς τοῖς γράμμασιν ἄρδοντα, ἐπειδήπερ οὐκ ἐθέλει πολλάκις ἐνιαυτοῦ. ὁ δ', οἶμαι, γράφειν ἡμῖν καὶ παντελῶς ἀπεῖπεν, οὕτω βαθείᾳ σιγῇ πρὸς ἡμᾶς ἐκ πολλοῦ πάνυ χρῆται, αὐτοὺς ἀεὶ γράφοντας. καίτοι τὰ ὕστατα ἐπιστέλλων ἡβῶντί τινι πρὸς τοῦτο τοὖργον ἐῴκει καὶ πάνυ

55: Mn 9ʳ. Ed. Karpozilos, *Letters*, 101, no. 14.
4 φθινίθειν Mn || 5 leg. ἀδίκως?

56: M 73ᵛ–75ʳ. W 199ʳ–200ᵛ. Ed. Loenertz, *Epistulae*, 95–97, no. 4.
1 ante τῷ scr. ἐπιστολὴ Γρηγορίου τοῦ Ἀκινδύνου W || 4 ἐπιδυμῶν W || 5 μιμῆσθαι W || 7 βαθεῖα W || 9 τοῦργον W

I have written, then, what I was obliged to write for Euphemianos, who is a good and noble man, and it is now up to you to see that I did not write this for him in vain, and that those who claimed that the favor will gladly follow the letter and therefore persuaded me to write to your Authority, will not be blamed for deceit. For it is unfair for men who are your friends, instead of receiving what they expected (a favor which is easy to grant), to suffer the loss of their reputation for truthfulness.

55. No Addressee

You seem, my lord Bishop, most beloved of God, to be angry with me over something which it was not in my power to grant you. Why, indeed, when I was very anxious to see you and sent you a message to that effect, did you, deeming me unworthy of your presence, leave me to pine away, as if I had done you wrong, nay, a very great wrong? Take care lest by being angry at me without cause (?) you be shown to do considerable wrong both to yourself and to me who do nothing wrong. For by pushing away not simply friendship, but one that was planted in me by the cause of piety, you will be shown injuring not only me but yourself also in a very important matter, if you remain angry to the end. To avoid this, cast away your grievance and appear with your usual beaming countenance to those who love you, as you know.

56. To Magistros

In my case, as it seems, the most wise Magistros imitated the nature of the phoenix, making an appearance through his letters at long intervals, just like the phoenix visiting the Hindus and Egyptians. Yet I wish that he had imitated at least the nature of the Nile, refreshing me annually with his letters, since he does not wish to do so many times a year. But I suspect that he even gave up entirely writing to me, this is how profound a silence he has retained towards me for a long time, though I always write. Yet, the last time he wrote, he appeared to be as vigorous as a youth for this task and quite eager to perform it in the future, both for the sake of

56

προθυμουμένῳ τοῦ λοιποῦ τοῦτο πράττειν, τῶν τε ἄλλων ἕνεκεν ὧν ἡμῖν ἐκ πολλοῦ πρότερον πρὸς ἀλλήλους ὑπῆρχε καὶ ὅτι τοῦ [fol. 74^{r}] κοινοῦ τῆς εὐσεβείας λόγου, παρ' ἀνδρὸς καινοτόμου πολεμουμένου ὃν αὐτὸς πολλάκις ληροῦντα πρότερον καὶ σαφῶς πεπλανημένον ἀπέδειξας, ἀντιποιούμεθα καὶ τῆς ἐκκλησιαστικῆς ὁμολογίας καὶ θεογνωσίας οὐκ ἀφιστάμεθα.

Νῦν δ' οὐκ οἶδα ὅπως αὖθις ἐσίγησας· δέον τὴν γοῦν αἰτίαν σημᾶναι τῆς σιωπῆς, ἵν' εἰ μέν τι πλημμέλημα εἴη, διορθωθῇ, εἰ δὲ συκοφαντία, λυθῇ· εἰ δὲ δειλία τῶν πονηρῶν στομάτων ἃ ῥεῖ χειμάρρων δίκην ἐπὶ τοὺς οὐ τῇ καινῇ πίστει ταύτῃ προσρέοντας, ἀλλὰ τοῦτό γε οὐ σοὶ προσῆκεν, ἀνδρῶν ἱερῶν ἱερώτατε, ὃν καὶ τοῖς ἄλλοις προσῆκεν ἐπιτιμᾶν τοῦτο πάσχουσι καὶ παντὸς ὑπερκειμένην ἔχειν τὴν γνώμην· ὃ τούτους ποιεῖ τῶν ⟨εἰς⟩ ὑπερκειμένας καὶ ὑφειμένας θεότητας κατατεμνόντων τὸ θεῖον ἀνέχεσθαι καὶ ἐπὶ τούτῳ τὴν τοῦ Θεοῦ διαιρούντων ἀφειδῶς ἐκκλησίαν ἀποστασίᾳ καὶ ὕβρει τῆς ἐκκλησίας αὐτῆς ἣν αἷμα Θεοῦ σαρκωθέντος αὐτῷ συστῆσαν ἐφύλαττεν, οὐκ ἀνεπηρέαστον μὲν πάλαι πονηρῶν αἱρέσεων ἀναισχυντίᾳ, μετ' ἐκείνας δ' οὖν εἰς τόδε πολὺν ἤδη χρόνον ἀνεπηρέαστον.

Νῦν δὲ αὖ πάλιν, οὐκ οἶδ' ὅπως, ἀνῆκε πειραθῆναι κακοῦ μηδενὸς τῶν πώποτε μείονος, ἤ, τό γε ἀκριβὲς εἰπεῖν, περιεκτικωτάτου· τίνα γὰρ τῶν φανεισῶν αἱρέσεων οὐ περιέχει; οὐ τὴν Ἑλλήνων πολυθεΐαν; ἀλλὰ πλῆθος θεοτήτων συναϊδίων ἀνίσων καὶ ἀνομοίων κηρύττει· τοῦτο δὲ ὅστις οὐ νενόμικεν Ἑλληνισμόν, ὅ τι ποτέ ἐστιν Ἑλληνισμὸς οὐκ οἶδεν. οὐ τὴν Ἀρείου μανίαν καὶ τὴν Μακεδονίου; ἀλλὰ τὴν φυσικὴν τοῦ Θεοῦ καὶ παντουργὸν ἐνέργειαν καὶ σοφίαν καὶ δύναμιν ἐνεργουμένην καὶ ὑφειμένην ἀπειράκις ἀπείρως τῆς θείας ἀποφαίνεται φύσεως· τοῦτο δ' ἦν ἡ τοῦ Ἀρείου νόσος καὶ τοῦ Μακεδονίου. Χριστὸς γὰρ Θεοῦ δύναμις καὶ Θεοῦ σοφία, δι' οὗ τὰ πάντα γεγένηται, καὶ δύναμις αὐτοῦ φυσικὴ τὸ Πνεῦμα τὸ παντουργόν. τί δ' οὐχὶ καὶ Σαβελλίου; ἀλλ' οἷς ἀνούσιον εἶναι καὶ ἀνυπόστατον τὴν ἄκτιστον καὶ δημιουργικὴν τοῦ Θεοῦ λέγει δύναμιν—ἡ δέ ἐστιν ὁ Υἱός—σαβελλίζει,

---

56: 22–23 cf. Palamam, *Epist. III ad Acindynum*, 15, Syngrammata, I, 306, 18–20; ed. Nadal, 252, 10–12 || 25–26 *αἷμα . . . συστῆσαν*: cf. Act. Ap. 20:28 || 36–37 cf. Maxim. Conf., *Capit. theol.*, 1, 49 (PG, 90, 1101A) = Palamas, *Dialexis, 24, Syngrammata, II, 186, 26; Epist. ad Gabram*, 5, Syngrammata, II, 332, 12 || 38–39 I Cor. 1:25 || 39 *δι' . . . γεγένηται*: Joan. 1:3

---

11 *πρώτερον* W || 22 post *τῶν* add. *εἰς* Loenertz || 27 *ἤδει* W || 30 *πόποτε* W || 31 *ἐμφανεισῶν* W || 32 *ἑλλήνην* W || post *ἀλλὰ* scripsit et deinde delevit *διὰ τὴν* W || 38 *ἀνομίων* W || *κηρύττη* W

56

what existed between us before, for a long time, and because I exerted myself about the common cause of piety, which is attacked by a rebellious man—whom, many a time before, you personally proved to be talking nonsense and to be clearly in error—and because I did not relinquish the Church's confession of faith and knowledge of God.

But now I do not know how you, in turn, kept silent! You ought, at least, to declare the cause of your silence, so that should there be any offense, it may be corrected; should there be calumny, it may be cleared; and should there be fear of the wicked mouths which flow like a torrent against those who do not rush up to this new faith—but this did not become you, O holiest of the holy, you who ought to reprove even those others who suffer from this fear and to have judgment superior to that of all others. This fear makes them tolerate those who cut up God into "higher and lower divinities" and thereupon freely divide the Church of God by desertion from and insolence against the Church itself, which the blood of the incarnated God won for Him and guarded, not unmolested, of course, by the impudence of the wicked heresies of old (although it was, in fact, unmolested for a long time after them).

But now I do not know how He allowed it again to experience such an evil, which is no smaller than those that ever existed; or, to put it more accurately, it fully encompasses all of them. For which of the known heresies does it not contain? Perhaps the polytheism of the pagans? But it proclaims a multitude of coeternal, unequal, and dissimilar divinities. And whoever does not consider this to be paganism, he does not know what paganism really is. What of the madness of Arios and Macedonios? But it declares that the natural and all-creating energy and wisdom and power of God is activated and "infinitely" lower than the divine nature. And this was the sickness of Arios and Macedonios. For Christ is the "power of God" and "the wisdom of God" through Whom everything was created" and the all-creating Spirit is His natural power. What, then, does it not also contain the heresy of Sabellios? But, by what he says about the uncreated and creative power of God (and that is the Son) being without essence and hypostasis, he is guilty of Sabellianism,

56

τἆλλα γε ὑπεραρειανίζων καὶ ὑπερελληνίζων. τί δὲ οὐχὶ καὶ Μασσαλιανός; [fol. 74v] ἀλλὰ τοῦτό γε καὶ λίαν περιφανές· ὁρᾶν γάρ φησι τὴν ἄκτιστον τοῦ Θεοῦ μορφὴν καὶ δόξαν καθ' ἑαυτὴν σωματικοῖς ὀφθαλμοῖς· μορφὴ γὰρ καὶ οὐσία καὶ φύσις ἐπὶ Θεοῦ ταὐτὸ καὶ οὐκ ἄλλο καὶ ἄλλο, ἵνα μὴ σύνθετος ᾖ, κατὰ τοὺς ὅρους τῆς εὐσεβείας τῶν ἱερῶν πατέρων. εἰ δ' ἄλλη μὲν ἐκείνη, ἄλλη δ' αὕτη κατὰ τοῦτον θεότης, ἡ μὲν ὡς ἀόρατος ὑπερκειμένη, ἡ δὲ ἐλάττων, ἐπειδήπερ ὁρᾶται τοῖς θεόπταις ἀνθρώποις καὶ ἐνεργεῖται πρὸς τῆς ὑπερκειμένης, πρῶτον μὲν πῶς ἄκτιστος ἡ ὑφειμένη, ἐνεργουμένη οὖσα καὶ ὁρατὴ καθ' αὑτὴν σωματικοῖς ὀφθαλμοῖς καὶ ὑφειμένη τῆς θείας φύσεως ἀπειράκις ἀπείρως; τοιαῦτα γὰρ τὰ ποιήματα. κἂν τις αὐτὸν ἔρηται, "ἆρ' οὐχ ὑπερέχει τὸ θεῖον τῶν ἑαυτοῦ κτισμάτων ὡς ἐνεργῶν ἐνεργουμένων καὶ ὑπερκείμενος ὑφειμένων ἀπειράκις ἀπείρως;" οὐχ ἕξει ἀρνήσασθαι. ὥσθ' ὑπὲρ ὧν ὁ γεννάδας ἐσπούδακε, ταῦτ' ἐστὶν ὁ καταβάλλων αὐτός. ἐσπούδακε μὲν γάρ τινας δογματίσαι θεότητας ἀκτίστους καὶ ἀνάρχους καὶ τῷ πάντων ὑπερκειμένῳ συναϊδίους Θεῷ· ὁ δὲ ταύτας ἀποφαίνεται δημιουργήματα. εἰ δὲ πάντως αὐτῷ τις ἀκολουθήσειε καὶ πεισθείη τὸ δόγμα συναϊδίους εἶναι Θεῷ πλῆθος θεοτήτων ἀνίσων καὶ ἀνομοίων οὕτω, πῶς Ἑλλήνων ἑστήξει τῶν πολυθέων ἔξω; εἰ δ' ἕνα πάλιν ἐκ τοῦ πλήθους τῶν οὕτω διαφόρων θεοτήτων νομίσοι, πῶς ἁπλοῦν καὶ ἀσύνθετον; τὸ γὰρ ἐξ ὁρατοῦ καὶ ἀοράτου καὶ ἀμεθέκτου καὶ μεθεκτοῦ καὶ ἐνεργοῦντος καὶ ἐνεργουμένου καὶ ὑπερκειμένου καὶ ὑφειμένου ἀπειράκις ἀπείρως συγκείμενον πῶς ἀμερὲς καὶ ἁπλοῦν;

Ταῦτα μὲν οὖν οὐ καιρὸς ἐμοὶ νῦν γράφειν, οὐδὲ κατ' ἐπιστολήν, ἄλλως τε καὶ πρὸς τὴν σὴν ἀκρίβειαν ἐπιστέλλοντι, καὶ ταῦτα καὶ τοῦ θείου ποιμένος, καὶ εἴπερ τις ἐπισταμένου ταῦτα, τὴν ἑαυτοῦ μὲν ποίμνην, ὑμετέραν δὲ πατρίδα καταλαμβάνοντος· ᾧ πρῶτον ἔργον ἔσται καὶ μέγιστον τὸ τὴν Παλαμῆτιν ἀπελάσαι τῆς ἑαυτοῦ ποίμνης ὡς πορρωτάτω νόσον· σοὶ δ' ἡμᾶς, ὦ θαυμάσιε, εἰ

44–46 ὁρᾶν . . . ὀφθαλμοῖς cf. Palamam, *Trias* 1, 3, 36–40, Syngrammata, I, 447–450; *Trias* 3, 2, 3, Syngrammata, I, 657–658 || 46–47 cf. Joan. Dam., *Dialect.*, 41 (PG, 94, 608B) || 47 ἵνα . . . ᾖ cf. Basil. Caes., *Adv. Eunom.* IV, 1 (PG, 29, 673B) || 49 cf. Palamam, *Epist. III ad Acindynum*, 15, Syngrammata, I, 306, 20; ed. Nadal, 252, 10–12 || 51–52 *ibid.*, 306, 18 || 53, 56 et 66–67 cf. Maxim. Conf., *Capit. theol.*, 1, 49 (PG, 90, 1101A) = Palamas, *Dialexis*, 24, Syngrammata, II, 186, 26; *Epist. ad Gabram*, 5, Syngrammata, II, 332, 12

---

58 post *γὰρ* scr. *αὐτὸς* W || 59 post *ἀνάρχους* scripsit et deinde delevit *θεότητας* W || 68 *οὐ*] *ὁ* W || 73 *σὺ* Loenertz

being in other ways extremely guilty of Arianism and paganism. What, then, is he not also a Messalian? But this is, indeed, too obvious! For he says that he sees with his bodily eyes the uncreated proper form and glory of God. For "with respect to God, form and essence and nature are the same thing" and not one thing and another, so that God "may not be composite," according to the laws of the holy Fathers about piety. And if, according to Palamas, that is one and this another divinity, and if the former is "higher" because it is invisible, while the other is "lower" (since, indeed, it is seen by the God-seeing men and activated by the higher divinity), how, in the first place, can the "lower divinity" be uncreated, since it is activated and visible in itself to bodily eyes and "infinitely" lower than the divine nature? For such are created things. And if one asks him: "Does not God excel His own creatures, as the activating the activated and the higher the 'infinitely' lower?", he will be unable to deny it. Of himself, therefore, this noble man refutes the very things he has sought to prove. For he has sought to proclaim certain divinities which are uncreated and without beginning and coeternal with the all-transcendent God. Yet he declares that they are created. And, in fact, if one should follow him and believe his doctrine that a multitude of such unequal and dissimilar divinities are coeternal with God, how will he be distinguished from the polytheistic pagans? If, on the other hand, he should believe in one God consisting of a multitude of such diverse divinities, how can this God be simple and uncompounded? For how can that which consists of visible and invisible, incapable of being shared and capable of being shared, activating and activated, higher and "infinitely" lower, be indivisible and simple?

But now is not the time for me to write these things, nor is it appropriate for a letter, especially since I am writing to your Accuracy, and, in fact, the holy pastor who knows these things better than anyone else is about to reach his flock and your native city. For him the first and most important task will be to drive as far as possible from his flock the Palamite sickness. As for your Excellence, if it still pleases

τυραννεῖν ἔτι φίλον, τυράννων ἁπάντων ἔσῃ τυραννικώτατος ὁ πάντων ἐπιεικέστατος, καὶ παῖδά γε τυραννῶν καὶ μαθητὴν οὐ κακὸν ὁ πατὴρ καὶ δι-[fol. 75[r]]*δάσκαλος.*

Τῷ δὲ καλῷ ποιμένι πολλὰ διελέχθημεν περὶ τῆς σῆς σοφίας, ἐρευνωμένῳ τίνας ἂν αὐτόθι γενόμενος ἔχοι συνεργοὺς πρὸς τὴν ὑπὲρ τῆς εὐσεβείας σπουδὴν καὶ ἀνακάθαρσιν τῶν πονηρῶν δογμάτων, καὶ τὰς πρώτας ἐλπίδας εἰς αὐτὴν κατεθέμεθα. ἃς μὴ κενὰς μηδ' ἀκάρπους ποιήσῃς, μηδ' αὐτὸν ἡμῖν ἠπατημένον δείξῃς.

57. Sine titulo

Ἄλλοις μὲν ἄλλοθεν ὑπάρχει γνωρίζεσθαι, σὺ δ' ἐμοὶ καὶ πρὶν ὀφθῆναι φίλος καὶ γνώριμος ἀπὸ τῆς εὐσεβείας. ἆρ' οὖν ἠγνόησα τἄλλα; τὴν ἐν τοῖς λόγοις ῥώμην, τὴν ἐν τῇ γλώττῃ χάριν, τὸ ἐπιεικὲς τῶν τρόπων, τὸ τῆς φύσεως μέγεθος; οὔκ, ὦ γενναῖε καὶ χαρίτων ἀνάμεστε. ἀλλ' ὅτε ταῦτα προῄει, καὶ τοὺς πόρρω λαμπρὰ κατελάμβανε φήμη, συνέβαινε καὶ τοὺς τῆς εὐσεβείας ὅρους παρακινεῖσθαι β ε β ή λ ο ι ς κ α ι ν ο φ ω ν ί α ι ς καί σε τούτων ὑπερμαχεῖν ἐκείναις ἀντιταττόμενον, καὶ δεῦρο πέμπειν ἐπιστολὰς ἐν αἷς Χαβάρων ἡμῖν ὁ θαυμαστὸς ἐθαυμάζετο ἀνθ' ὧν τῆς εὐσεβείας ὑπερεμάχει καὶ Χαρατζᾶς ὁ πάντολμος ἐκακίζετο ἀνθ' ὧν τοῖς εὐσεβέσιν ὑμῖν θηριωδῶς ἐπετίθετο μὴ πειθομένοις αὐτοῦ τοῖς ληρήμασι. τότε τοίνυν ἅμα πάντα καθάπερ ἐν ἐσόπτρῳ τοῖς γράμμασιν ἐνεωρῶμεν, καὶ πάντα θαυμάζοντες ἐπιεικῶς—οὐ γὰρ ἠναισθητοῦμεν—διαφερόντως τὸ τῆς γνώμης θεοσεβὲς καὶ πρὸς τὰς αἱρετικὰς τῶν [fol. 73[v]] *δυσσεβῶν ἐκβολὰς ἐρρωμένον εἴχομεν δι' εὐφημίας, σοφοῦ γὰρ ἀνδρὸς καὶ γενναίου διάνοια οὐχ ὅταν οὐδὲν ᾖ τοῖς δόγμασιν ἐπηρεάζον γίνεται καταφανής, ἀλλ' ὅταν πόλεμος ᾖ καὶ κρίσις περὶ ψεύδους καὶ ἀληθείας, καὶ μάλιστα τῆς κατ' εὐσέβειαν, καὶ πλείους μὲν ἐκείνου ἧττους δὲ ταύτης οἱ πρόμαχοι, καὶ νόμῳ χειρῶν κρατῶσιν οἱ χείρους περὶ τὰ δόγματα. ἃ πάντα, οἶμαι, τότε συνέπιπτε παρ' ὑμῖν· ἐκράτει γὰρ Χαρατζᾶς, ὡς ἐπέστελλες, μᾶλλον δὲ κρατεῖν ἐδόκει, οὐ λόγοις νοῦν ἔχουσιν ἀλλ' ὕβρει καὶ λοιδορίαις καὶ συκοφαντίαις καὶ χειρῶν αὐτῶν ἔργοις, ὑμῶν τῶν*

57: 7 II Tim. 2:16

---

78 *ἔχει* W || 80 *καταθέμεθα* W

57: M 73[r]–73[v]. Ed. Loenertz, *Epistulae*, 93–94, no. 3.

you to torture me, you will be the most tyrannical of all tyrants, you the fairest of all men; torturing both a son and a student who is not bad, you who are the father and teacher.

I said many things about your Wisdom to the good pastor and set highest hopes in you when he was asking whom he should have upon his arrival there to assist him in his endeavor for piety and the clearing away of the wicked doctrines. Do not render these hopes vain or fruitless, and do not show him up as deceived by me.

57. No Addressee

It is possible for other men to be known for other reasons, but you are dear to me and I know you because of your piety, even before I have seen you. Did I, then, forget your other virtues? The literary prowess, the grace of the tongue, the gentleness of manner, the magnanimity of character? No, my noble friend, filled full of virtues! But when these progressed and an illustrious reputation reached those far away, it so happened that the laws of piety were also disturbed by a "profane newfangled talk," and you defended them, resisting this talk, and sent here letters in which you extolled to us the admirable Chabaron for defending piety, and reproached the impudent Charatzas for attacking brutally your pious men, who did not obey his nonsense. At that time, therefore, I observed everything at once in your letters, as if in a mirror, and while I admired everything appropriately, for I am not insensitive, I acclaimed especially the piety and vigor of your judgment regarding the impious outpourings of the heretics. For the intelligence of a wise and noble man is fully revealed not when there is nothing threatening the doctrines, but when there is a war and dispute about falsehood and truth, and especially about truth concerning piety, and the defenders of falsehood are more numerous, while those of truth are fewer, and those who are inferior as far as doctrines are concerned prevail by the law of force. All these things, I believe, happened at that time in your city. For Charatzas prevailed, as you wrote, over you who were pious and did not heed his impious sayings, or rather, he thought he prevailed, not by meaningful words but by insolence and abuse and calumnies and deeds of sheer violence. But, in fact, you

φιλευσεβῶν καὶ τοῖς Χαρατζᾶ *δυσσεβέσι μὴ προσεχόντων λόγοις. οἳ δ' ὄντως ἐκρατεῖτε τῷ μὴ προσέχειν αὐτῷ, καὶ τὴν ἐκείνου νίκην καὶ τὴν θρασύτητα ἧτταν ἐκείνου καὶ θαυμαστὴν αἰσχύνην* * * * *τότε μὲν ὑμεῖς, νῦν δὲ καὶ* Θεός· *καὶ τότε μέντοι* Θεός, *ἀλλὰ νῦν περιφανῶς ἀποδείκνυσιν οὖσαν.*

Ὁ *δὲ πανίερος ἡμῶν μὲν δεσπότης, ὑμέτερος δὲ ποιμήν, φανεὶς παρ' ὑμῖν καὶ τοῦτο δείξει καλῶς, ἢ τοῦτό γε πρὸ πάντων· καί σε κατὰ τὸ εἰκὸς ἀγάσεται μὲν τῶν ἄλλων, ἀγάσεται δὲ διαφερόντως τῆς εὐσεβείας αὐτῆς, τὸν ἕνεκα πάντων ἀξιοθαύμαστον. εὐδοκιμήσεις δὲ σὺ μὲν παρ' αὐτῷ διὰ τὰ εἰρημένα, ὁ δὲ παρὰ τῇ πόλει καὶ διὰ τό σε τιμᾶν.*

Ἐ*μὲ δὲ σὺ ταῖς πρὸς ἑτέρους ἐπιστολαῖς ᾑρηκώς, αἵρει καὶ ταῖς πρὸς ἐμέ· ἡδὺ γὰρ ἐμοὶ τούτοις βεβλῆσθαι τοῖς βέλεσιν ἐνεργεστέροις.*

58. Τῷ *ἀρχιδιακόνῳ* Βρυεννίῳ

Οὐ*κ ἀνήκοοι, σοφώτατε δέσποτά μου, τῆς σῆς γενναίας ἐνστάσεως πρὸς τὴν τῆς πίστεως καινοτομίαν ἐμείναμεν· καὶ τοῦτ' ἀκηκόαμεν ἐν τῷ καιρῷ τῆς ἀκμῆς ἐκείνης τῶν ἀλαστόρων παρρησιάσασθαί σου τὴν τελειότητα, ὅτε* Χαρατζᾶς *ἔπνει σφοδρῶς ὁ δεινὸς* Παλαμίτης *κατὰ τῆς εὐσεβείας. νῦν δ', οἶμαι, καὶ ἄλλως τῆς* Χαρατζᾶ *μανίας λελωφηκυίας, ἧκε θαυμαστὸς ὑμῖν τῆς ἐκκλησίας τῆς ὑμετέρας ποιμήν—ἵν' αὐτὸν αὐτοῖς προσείπω τοῖς ῥήμασιν οἷς ὁ ποιμένων ποιμὴν ἁπάντων καὶ ἀρχιερέων ἀρχιερεὺς πρῶτον ἑαυτὸν προσηγόρευσε, προσήκων γὰρ οὗτος ἐκείνῳ εἴπερ τις ἄλλος ἀνήρ—ἧκε δὲ ποιμανῶν μὲν εὖ καὶ καλῶς καὶ τἄλλα τὴν* [fol. 73^{r}]*ποίμνην τὴν ἑαυτοῦ, τὸ δὲ κεφάλαιον, ἐξελῶν αὐτῆς τὴν* Παλαμῆτιν *νόσον, ἣν ἀγαθοῦ ποιμένος ἐρημίᾳ νενόσηκεν. ᾧπερ, οἶμαι, κεχαρισμένος ἔσῃ καὶ περισπούδαστος, καὶ ὧν αὐτῇ πεπολέμηκας καὶ ὧν τοῦ λοιποῦ συμπολεμήσεις αὐτῷ καὶ συνεξαλᾷς γε τὴν εἰρημένην νόσον. ἡμῖν δέ, οἶμαι, κατὰ πρόνοιαν* Θεοῦ *κἀνταῦθα συνῆλθε τὰ πράγματα, ἵν' ὥσπερ οἰκείως ἀλλήλοις ἐξ*

58: 9–10 cf. Joan. 10:11 || 9 *ἀρχιερέων ἀρχιερεὺς*: cf. Hebr. 4:14

---

26 post *αἰσχύνην* lacunam statui: *αἰσχύνην κρίνοντες* coni. Loenertz

58: M 72^{v}–73^{r} Ed. Loenertz, *Epistulae*, 92–93, no. 2.

7 *θαυμαστὸς* scripsi: *θαυμαστῶς* MLoenertz || 9 *ποιμένων* scripsi: *ποιμαίνων* MLoenertz || 12 *ἐξελῶν* scripsi: *ἐξελὼν* MLoenertz || 13 *ᾧπερ* scripsit Loenertz: *ὦνπερ* M

prevailed by not heeding him and ⟨by proving⟩ his victory and insolence to be his defeat and astonishing shame * * * You ⟨proved it⟩ then, and now God proves this also. Of course, God proved this even then, but now He proves it conspicuously.

And when my all-holy lord and your pastor makes his appearance among you, he will also prove this well or this, at any rate, before anything else. And he will rightly admire you for your other virtues, but he will admire you especially for your very piety, you who are worthy of admiration on all accounts. And you will be highly esteemed by him for the aforementioned reasons, and he by the city and for honoring you.

But since you captivated me with the letters you addressed to others, captivate me also with letters addressed to me, for it pleases me to be struck more effectively by these arrows.

58. To the archdeacon Bryennios

I did not remain ignorant, my most wise lord, of your brave resistance against the innovation in the faith. And this is what I heard: that at the time of the highest power of the evil demons your Excellence spoke up with courage when Charatzas, the terrible Palamite, was blowing vehemently against piety. But now, I believe, Charatzas' fury has subsided in other ways, and to you there has come a marvelous shepherd of your Church (to call him by the same words by which the shepherd of all shepherds and first archpriest called Himself, for more than any other man he comes close to that shepherd). He came to tend his flock well and wisely in other respects also, but primarily to drive out of it the Palamite sickness from which it has suffered because of the absence of a good shepherd. He will welcome you and seek you out, because of the war that you waged against this sickness, and because of the war that you will wage with him in the future, to drive out together the aforementioned sickness. And I believe that here also things worked out for us in accordance with divine providence, so that we may be in the struggles for piety just as we were from the beginning, affectionately disposed towards each other. This is how we

ἀρχῆς διεκείμεθα, οὕτως ἔχωμεν κἀν τοῖς ἀγῶσι τοῖς ὑπὲρ εὐσεβείας, ἐν οἷς ἡμᾶς οὕτω προσῆκεν ἔχειν, εἰ καὶ τἄλλα διεφερόμεθα. οὐ γὰρ Θεμιστοκλεῖ μὲν καὶ Ἀριστείδῃ τῷ κατ' αὐτὸν καλῶς εἶχεν ἐπιόντος τοῦ Μήδου διαλελύσθαι τὰ πρῴην πρὸς ἀλλήλους διάφορα ἵνα τοὺς Ἕλληνας σώσωσιν, ἀνδράσι δ' εὐσεβέσιν ἑτέρως, ἐπιόντος αἱρετικοῦ καὶ δυσσεβοῦς πολέμου ἐπὶ τὴν ἐκκλησίαν.

Ἀλλὰ ταῦτα μὲν πρὸς ἄλλους ἡμῖν ἴσως ὑπάρχει λέγειν· σὺ δ' ἡμῖν, ἱερώτατε, καὶ πάλαι καὶ μετὰ ταῦτα καὶ νῦν καί, ὡς εἰπεῖν, ἐκ παιδὸς ἄχρι τοῦδε, καὶ φίλος καὶ διδάσκαλος καὶ κομιδῇ περισπούδαστος, καὶ ἔσῃ γε διὰ τέλους, καὶ ζῶσι καὶ μετὰ βίον, οἶμαι, εἴ γέ τις αἴσθησις τοιάδε μετὰ τὸν ὧδε βίον.

59. Τῷ Ἴσαρι

Τοιαῦτα δή τοι τοῦ τοῦδε βίου τὰ παίγνια· τοιαύταις ἐλπίσι μετεωρίζει τοὺς κουφογνώμονας· ὑπὸ τοιούτων ἐξίστανται τῶν ἀσφαλῶν ἀγαθῶν—πίστεως εἰς φίλους, εἰς Θεὸν εὐσεβείας, γνώμης βεβαίας περὶ τὰ κάλλιστα—ψευδόμενοι, ἐπιορκοῦντες, ἀλλήλοις ἐπιβουλεύοντες, παρανομοῦντες, ὑποκρινόμενοι, ταχέως μεταρριπτούμενοι ἀπὸ τούτων εἰς τάδε καὶ τούτων ἐφ' ἕτερα τῆς τύχης νεανιεύματα καὶ τέλος εἰς βάραθρα· οὔτ' ἀγαθοὶ βουληθέντες εἶναι διὰ τοιαύτην κτῆσιν καὶ μανίαν ἐρωτικὴν δόξης κενῆς καὶ χρημάτων, οὔτ', ἐπειδήπερ τῶν ἀληθῶς ἀγαθῶν διὰ ταῦτα ἐξέπεσον, ταῦτά γε κερδάναντες, ἀλλ' αἰσχύνης διπλῆς ἀπολαύσαντες καὶ διπλῆν ζημίαν ὑπομεμενηκότες, πρώτην μὲν τὴν ἐκ τῆς τῶν κρειττόνων ἀρνήσεως διὰ τὰ χείρω, δευτέραν δὲ τὴν ἐκ τοῦ καὶ τούτων ἐκπεπτωκέναι ἢ καὶ διαφθαρῆναι παντάπασι, μετὰ τῶν ὄντως καλῶν οἷσπερ ἐξῆν ἐμμένειν, καὶ τῶν δοκούντων ἃ τῶν ὄντων ἠλλάξαντο, καὶ τοῦ ζῆν ἐκπεσόντες. ὅπερ ὁρῶν ὁ Δαυὶδ προανεφώνει, παραινῶν τοῖς τοιούτοις, μὴ παραζήλου ἐν πονηρευομένοις, μηδὲ ζήλου τοὺς ποιοῦντας τὴν ἀνομίαν, ὅτι ὡσεὶ χόρτος ταχὺ ἀποξηρανθήσονται, καὶ ὡσεὶ λάχανα χλόης ταχὺ ἀποπεσοῦνται. ἔλπισον ἐπὶ Κύριον καὶ ποίει

59: 17–21 Ps. 36(37):1–3

59: M 75r–75v.
15 ἠλλάξατο M

ought to be in these struggles, even if we differed in other matters. For it was not well for Themistocles and Aristeides, his contemporary, to have solved their former differences in order to save the Greeks when the Persians were approaching, while pious men do otherwise when a heretical and impious war is threatening the Church.

But, perhaps, I can say these things to other men, whereas, your Holiness, long ago as well as after this and at present and, so to speak, from childhood up to this moment you have been both friend and teacher, and in every way most cherished, and so you will be until the end, both in life and after life, if indeed there is any feeling like this after this life.

59. To Isaris

Such indeed are the tricks of this life! With such hopes it buoys up the thoughtless! Such are the things which turn them away from the unfailing blessings: loyalty to friends, piety towards God, steadfast convictions regarding the most important matters. And they lie; they commit perjury; they plot against one another; they disobey the law; they act deceitfully; they swiftly turn from these to other wanton, random acts, and finally to ruin. For they did not want to be good, on account of such mad love and acquisition of empty glory and money, and neither did they, in fact, win these after renouncing the real blessings for their sake. But they enjoyed the benefit of twofold disgrace and suffered twofold injury—the first resulting from their denial of better things for the sake of worse, and the second from the loss of these also—or even total ruin, and thus together with the real blessings by which, of course, it was possible to abide, they lost the specious blessings and exchanged for them the real blessings as well as their lives. Seeing this clearly, David proclaimed as he exhorted such men: "Fret not because of evildoers, nor envy them who commit iniquity. For like grass, they shall quickly wither, and like the tender herb, they shall quickly fall. Trust in the Lord and exercise kindness." Apparently, these

59

χρηστότητα. ἀλλ' οὐ πᾶσιν ἄρα ταῦτα ἐλέγετο, τοῖς δὲ ἀκουσαμένοις· οἷς γὰρ οὐκ ἐμέλησε τῶν διδαγμάτων, τούτοις οὐδ' ἐρρήθησαν αἱ παραινέσεις.

Ἐγὼ δὲ λύπης ἐπὶ σὲ πληρωθεὶς τὴν καρδίαν συμφορᾷ κεχρημένῳ τοσαύτῃ, κενοῦμαι πάλιν αὐτῆς διὰ τῆς ἐκ τοῦ φυγεῖν σε τὸν τῶν συμμάχων ὄλεθρον παραμυθίας. οὐκ αὐτὸ τοῦτο μόνον ὅτι τὰ ξίφη διέφυγες, ἀλλ' ὅτι καὶ τοῦ λοιποῦ βουλεύσῃ πῶς βιοτέον σοι, ἀνδρὶ φρονίμῳ καὶ οὐκ ἀξίῳ δουλεύειν πονηρίᾳ πραγμάτων ὧν καρπὸς ἃ πεπόνθατε. καίτοι τὸ κακῶς πάσχειν οὐχ ὅτι πάθος κακόν· τὸ γὰρ ἀδικούμενον πάσχειν καὶ ὑπὲρ εὐσεβείας ἀγαθὸν καὶ μακάριον, ἀλλὰ τὸ κακῶς [fol. 75ᵛ] ποιοῦντα ταύτῃ καὶ πάσχειν διδόντα δίκας αἰσχρόν. γίνεται δὲ καὶ τοῦτ' ἀγαθόν, ὁπόταν ὁ πάσχων βελτιωθῇ ἐφ' ᾧ καὶ νόμοι καὶ δίκαι καὶ πρὸς Θεοῦ καὶ πρὸς ἀνθρώπων προβέβληνται, φαρμάκων λόγον ἔχοντα πρὸς τοὺς ψυχῇ νενοσηκότας καὶ διὰ τοῦτο τῇδε κολαζομένους ἐπ' ἀναιρέσει μὲν τῶν νόσων, ἀναλήψει δέ τῆς ψυχικῆς ὑγείας ἥτις ἐστὶν ἀρετὴ καὶ εὐσέβεια. ἡ γὰρ αὐτοαγαθότης ἀεὶ μὲν ἀγαθύνει καὶ οὓς δοκεῖ κολάζειν, ποιεῖ δὲ κακῶς ὡς ἀληθῶς οὐδαμοῦ· αὐτὸς δ' ἑαυτὸν ἕκαστος κακοποιεῖ, πρῶτον μὲν ἁμαρτάνων, εἶτα μηδ' ἐκ τοῦ δίκας ὑπέχειν σωφρονιζόμενος· ὃς ἄν, μετὰ τὸ κολασθεὶς πολλάκις μὴ κατεστάλθαι, ὀλέθρῳ παραδοθῇ τελείῳ, οὐχ ὁ Θεὸς οὐδ' ἄλλος οὐδεὶς αὐτῷ, ἀλλ' αὐτὸς αὐτῷ δήπου τὸ πάθος ἐπήνεγκε. τίς σοφὸς καὶ φυλάξει ταῦτα; καὶ τίς νοῦν ἔχων ἑτέραν χάριν αἰτήσεται παρὰ Θεοῦ πλὴν ταύτης; νοεῖν μὲν τὰ δέοντα, μὴ μάτην δὲ νοεῖν ἄνευ τοῦ πράττειν ταῦτα, φοβεῖσθαι δὲ τὸν Θεόν, προσκεῖσθαι δὲ τοῖς καλοῖς, μισεῖν δὲ τὰ πονηρά, καὶ οὕτω διανύσαι τὸν βίον μετ' ἀγαθοῦ συνειδότος μᾶλλον ἢ τῶν Κροίσου χρημάτων καὶ τῆς Ἀλεξάνδρου τοῦ Μακεδόνος δόξης· ἃ καὶ σύ ποτ' ἐφρόνεις, ὡς ταῦτα φιλοσοφήσων διὰ βίου παρεσκευάζου, καὶ διὰ τοῦτο τῶν ἀληθῶν ἐπαίνων ἐτύγχανες καὶ τῆς μὴ ψευδομένης δόξης, γέρων ἐν νέοις ὑπὸ πάντων ὀνομαζόμενος καὶ σοφὸς αὐτοφυῶς. πλήν, εἴ τί σοι, καὶ ἡμεῖς πρὸς τοῦτο συνετελέσαμεν παλαιῶν ἀνδρῶν καὶ σοφῶν—ὡς ἐπίστασαι—λόγοις, εἰ ἄρα καὶ τούτων τὴν μνήμην τῆς ψυχῆς οὐ μεθ' ἡμῶν ἐξεῖλες. ἀλλ' ὁ μὲν σωτὴρ καὶ Θεός σε τοῦ θανάτου καὶ τῶν ξιφῶν μέσον ἐκείνων ἐξήρπασε, σὺ δὲ αὐτῷ καὶ ἡμῖν ἀπόδος τὸν Ἴσαριν ἐκεῖνον τὸν μεγαλόφρονα, οἷόν ποτ' εἴχομεν καὶ οὐχ οἷον ἑωράκαμεν ὕστερον, καὶ ταύτῃ δώσεις ἀρκοῦντα τῷ σώσαντί σε Θεῷ τὰ

---

37 cf. Dion. Areop., *De div. nom.*, 2, 1 (PG, 3, 636C); 11, 6 (PG, 3, 956A) ‖ 42–43 Ps. 106(107):43

---

55 μέσων M

59

⟨words⟩ were not addressed to everybody, but to those who would listen. For the exhortations were not addressed to those who did not care for the lessons.

But I, whose heart was filled with sorrow at your experiencing such a great misfortune, I am in turn relieved of it with the consolation that you escaped the disastrous fate of your allies. There is not only the fact that you escaped the swords, but also the fact that you will reflect how you must live in the future, since you are a prudent man and not worthy of becoming a slave to the wickedness of the times; the result of this is what you have suffered, although suffering is not a bad experience. For to suffer unjustly and for the sake of piety is noble and blessed, but to suffer because you have offended piety and are being punished is disgraceful. But even this becomes noble whenever the sufferer improves his lot; and for this reason both laws and penalties are set forth by God and men, in place of medicines, for those whose souls are not healthy and who, on this account, are so punished to get rid of the disease and regain moral health, which is virtue and piety. For the "Absolute Goodness" always renders good even those whom He appears to punish and truly does no harm anywhere, while each person hurts himself, first by sinning and then by failing to become disciplined through punishment either. He who is delivered to total perdition after having been punished many times and not chastened surely has inflicted his own suffering on himself; it is not God or anyone else who ⟨has inflicted it⟩ upon him. "Who is wise and will observe these things?" And what sensible man will ask for any other favor from God except this? To perceive what is right, but not to perceive it in vain without practicing it; to fear God; to abide by the good; to hate evil; and thus to go through life with a good conscience rather than with the wealth of Croesus or the glory of Alexander of Macedon. You too thought so once, and you were preparing to make this your philosophy of life, and for this reason you won genuine praise and true glory, being called by everyone an old man among the young and naturally wise. Except that, if anything, I also contributed to this, as you know, with the works of the wise men of old, if indeed you did not remove from your heart their memory together with me. But our Savior and God snatched you away from death and from the midst of those swords. Give back to Him, then, and to me that high-minded Isaris, such as he was once and not as I saw him later, and thus you will give sufficient ransom and thank-offerings to God Who saved you;

λύτρα καὶ χαριστήρια· εἰ δὲ μή, οὐ διέφυγες. ἀλλ' εἴης ἡμῖν, ὦ μέλημα παλαιόν, τελέως διαφυγὼν τὰ κακὰ καὶ τοῦ λοιποῦ τοῖς ὅλοις εὐημερήσων, ἀρέσκων Θεῷ καὶ ἀγαθοῖς ἀνδράσι ἐπὶ τῇ πολιτείᾳ.

60. Λαπίθῃ

Μόλις ἐλαβόμεθα τῆς ἱερᾶς ἀγκύρας τῶν παρὰ σοῦ γραμμάτων. τί δ' ἡμᾶς περιεῖδες τοσοῦτον χειμαζομένους χρόνον οὐδὲ πυρσῷ θαρρύνας; καὶ τοῦτ' εἰδὼς ἀκριβῶς ὅτι τὸ κεφάλαιον τῆς βοηθείας ἡμῖν ἐπὶ τοὺς ἐχθροὺς τῇ ἀληθείᾳ παρὰ σοὶ κεῖται καὶ σόν ἐστι περιφανῶς καὶ συστρατηγεῖς τοῖς ἄλλοις ἐπὶ τὴν αἵρεσιν σοφίας περιουσίᾳ. εἶτα γράμματα μὲν λαβόντες περὶ τῶν λόγων, αὐτοὺς δὲ τοὺς λόγους οὔπω δεξάμενοι, ἀλλ' εἰς ἐλπίδας ἐξ ἐλπίδων αὖθις παραπεμπόμενοι, πῶς δοκεῖς ἠθυμήσαμεν, ὁπότε ἀναπνεύσειν ἠλπίκαμεν, τότ' εἰς ἑτέρας ἐλπίδας παρατεινόμενοι καί, ὥσπερ ἢ λιμῷ μακρῷ τε καὶ συνεχεῖ ἤ, τὸ μετριώτερον, ἔρωτος ἀναβολῇ σφοδροτάτου πολυμήκει, κατατεινόμενοι.

Ἡ δ' αἰτία τῆς ἀτυχίας ἡμῖν κυκεῶνες πραγμάτων, ἣν μᾶλλον αἰτίαν εἶναι προσῆκε τοῦ παρεῖναι τοὺς λόγους ἡμῖν καὶ προμαχεῖν εὐτόλμως· διὰ γὰρ τοὺς κλύδωνας οἱ κυβερνῆται καὶ στρατηγῶν ἐπιστήμη περὶ τὰς μάχας. ἔνθα δέ τις καὶ πόρρω χειμῶνος καὶ τῶν κινδύνων ἑστώς, ἀλλ' οὐχ ὥσπερ ἐκεῖνοι συγκινδυνεύων, ἔχει τι πράττειν ὠφέλιμον τοῖς κινδυνεύουσι, τί μὴ βοηθητέον αὐτοῖς τὸν τοῦτο δυνάμενον; ὥσπερ ἡ σὴ σοφία νυνὶ ἀκινδυνότατα πάντων ῥοπὴν μὲν παρέχειν ἔχει μεγίστην τῇ ἐκκλησίᾳ τοῦ Θεοῦ, βλάπτειν δὲ οὐ τὰ τυχόντα τοὺς πολεμίους αὐτῇ. εἰ δὲ δεῖ μὴ ταῖς τῶν ἐχθρῶν χερσὶν ἐμπεσεῖν σοι τοὺς λόγους, οὐκ ἐμπεσοῦνται· καὶ εἰ τοῖς μετὰ τὸν θειότατον ἀρχιερέων [fol. 5r] Ὑάκινθον φίλοις αὐτοὺς ἐντυχεῖν, τοῖς ὁμοίοις ἐντεύξονται. τίς γὰρ ἡμῶν τοῖς λόγοις τοῖς σοῖς οἰκειότερος καὶ τῷ περὶ πλείονος τὸ τούτους εὐδοκιμεῖν; ὥστε κατὰ καιρὸν καὶ δείξομεν ἡμεῖς τοὺς λόγους παντὸς μᾶλλον, καὶ πάλιν οὐ δείξομεν, εἰ τοῦτο λυσιτελέστερον. εἰ δέ σοι δῆλον ἦν τὸ καθ' ἡμᾶς περὶ σὲ καὶ τὴν σὴν ἀρετὴν καὶ σοφίαν, οὐκ ἂν ταῦτα ἐπέστελλες. ἀλλ' ἴσως σοφώτατος· σοὶ μηδένα ὄντα πρὸ ἡμῶν οἰκειότερον * * * οὐδ'

58–59 cf. Aeschylum, *Choeph.*, 235

60: Mn 4v–5v. Ed. Uspenskij, *Synodikon*, 75–77; ed. Karpozilos, *Letters*, 82–85, no. 6.
21 *ταῖς*] *τοῖς* Mn ‖ 24 *τίς* scripsi: *τί* Mn ‖ 29 post *οἰκειότερον* lacunam statui

otherwise you have not escaped. But may you escape trouble completely, my old friend, and prosper altogether in the future, pleasing God and good men by your conduct!

60. To Lapithes

With difficulty I grasped the sacred anchor of your letter. Why did you neglect me while I was being tossed by the tempest for such a long time, without even encouraging me with a signal light? And this, when you know full well that with you rests and yours is the sum total of my assistance against the enemies of truth, and that with your abundance of wisdom you are to others a fellow-general against heresy! And then, when I received the letter about your discourses, without having in fact yet received the discourses themselves, but being led from expectations back to expectations, you can imagine how despondent I was. When I had hoped to revive, I was further put off with different hopes, and constrained to the utmost, as if by a long and continuous famine or, to put it more moderately, by a long delay of an ardent love.

And the cause of my misfortune is a host of troubles, which ought rather to be a reason for your discourses to be here with me, fighting bravely like champions. For skippers are for storms and generalship has to do with battles. And when a man is far away from both storm and danger and can be of some assistance to those who are in danger without running the same risks as they do, why should he not help them so long as he is able to do so? Just as now your Wisdom can, most safely of all, have the most decisive influence for the Church of God and cause no ordinary harm to its enemies. And if your discourses ought not to fall into the hands of the enemy, they will not. And if they ought to be read by the men who are next in the line of friendship after the most holy Metropolitan Hyakinthos, they will be read by the same. For who is fonder than I of your discourses and to whom is their success more important? So, according to the circumstances, I shall display your discourses more than anyone else, and then again, if this is not the more advantageous course, I shall not display them. But if my feelings for you and your virtue and wisdom were clear to you, you would not have written these instructions. But, perhaps, you are most wise * * * that no one is closer to you than I * * * who do not even value my own

60

ἡμῖν μᾶλλον αὐτοῖς τι τῆς σῆς σοφίας ἡμᾶς φιλίας καὶ οἰκειότητος νέμοντας, οὐδὲ Πλάτωνι θαύματος εἵς γε σοφίας λόγον, οὐδὲ τοῖς ἄκροις εὐσέβειαν εἰς εὐσεβείας, οὐδὲ καλοκἀγαθίας εἰς ταύτην.

Εἰ δὲ ἡμῖν οὐ θαρρεῖς, ἐνθυμοῦ τοὺς Κυπρίους. οὐχ ὁ θεῖος Βαρθολομαῖος ὧδε; οὐ Κοσμᾶς ὁ θαυμάσιος; οὐχ ὁ θεσπέσιος Βλάσιος; ποῦ δὲ Λέων ὁ λογιώτατος; οἳ πάντες σε μὲν πνέουσιν οὐχ ἧττον ἢ τὸν ἀέρα καὶ τὴν σὴν αὐχοῦσι σοφίαν οὐχ ἧττον ἢ τὸν δακτύλιον Γύγης, Παλαμήταις δὲ ἀντιπνέουσιν οὐδενὸς ἧττον ἄλλου. πέμπε δὴ θαρρῶν τοὺς λόγους εἴς γε τοιούτων χεῖρας καὶ ψυχὰς καὶ φροντίδας, καὶ μὴ κρύπτε τὸν ἱερὸν θησαυρόν, ἀλλὰ τὸ τάλαντον αὐτὸ τοῖς τραπεζίταις δίδου—σιωπῶ δὲ τὸ σκυθρωπόν—μηδὲ τὸν τῆς ἐκκλησίας λύχνον ὑπὸ τὸν μόδιον τῆς ἄλλως εὐλαβείας, ἀλλ' ἐπὶ τὴν λυχνίαν τίθει, τὴν ἐκκλησίαν αὐτήν, ἵνα φωτίζοι μὲν αὐτήν, δεικνύοι δὲ τοὺς φῶρας, φαίνοι δὲ καὶ τὸν ἅψαντα, ὑμνοίη δὲ τὸν Θεὸν ὑπὲρ οὗ καὶ ὑφ' οὗ πρωτουργικῶς ἀνῆπται. κρατεῖ γὰρ ἡ ἐκκλησία, κἂν κολοιοὶ θορυβῶσιν, οἵ μέγαν αἰγυπιὸν ὑποδείσαντες πτήξουσί σου φανέντος διὰ τῶν λόγων, οἵ γε καὶ δι' ἐπιστολῶν φαινομένου συντρίβονται, ὥσπερ οἱ Τρῶες καὶ τοῖς τυχοῦσι τῶν Ἀχιλλέως ὅπλων, εἰ μὴ ἐλάνθανον.

Ἐμὲ μὲν δὴ τὸ θαρρεῖν ἤδη καὶ ὁ τῆς εὐσεβείας λόγος ταῦτα σοι γράφειν πείθει, σοφώτατε, μᾶλλον δὲ καὶ βιάζεται. εἰ δὲ προάγομαι, συγγνώμης ἂν ἀξιοίμην εἰκότως τῇ θαυμαστῇ κεφαλῇ, ἡ γὰρ ἀνάγκη δήλη, ἔρως καὶ χρεία περὶ εὐσέβειαν χειμαζομένην τὰ βιαιότατα.

Βουλόμενος δέ σοι καὶ περὶ τοῦ θειοτάτου Ὑακίνθου τοῦ γενομένου Θεσσαλονικέων ἀρχιερέως γράφειν ὀκνῶ· τοιαύτης γάρ σοι φήμης οὐκ ἐβουλόμην ὑπηρέτης γενέσθαι. ἀνὴρ γὰρ ἐκεῖνος γεγονὼς ἀρχιερεὺς ἀξιώτατος τῆς ἐκκλησιαστικῆς ἀξίας καὶ ὑποθέσεως κἂν τῇ παρούσῃ ζάλῃ τῶν ἐκκλησιῶν τοῦ Θεοῦ κυβερνήτης δεινότατος, ὡς ἔδειξε καὶ ὁ βραχὺς αὐτοῦ παρὰ τῇ ἐκκλησίᾳ τῇ Θεσσαλονικέων βίος, νῦν οἴχεται ἀναρπασθεὶς ἐξαίφνης, πένθος μὲν ἡμῖν μέγα καὶ Θεσσαλονικεῦσιν ἀφείς—οὐδεὶς γὰρ οὕτως ἐκείνην ἀναρτῆσαι τὴν πόλιν ἀρχιερεὺς αὐτῆς μνημονεύεται—μείζω δὲ τοῖς Παλαμήταις χαράν, ὧν ἐκείνην θᾶττον ἐλπίδος πάσης ἐκάθηρεν. ἀλλ' ἵνα μὴ τῷ μήκει πολὺ κατ' ἐπιστολὴν ὑπερβαίνωμεν μέτρον, ἀφέντες τι πλέον περὶ ἐκείνου λέγειν, αὐτά σοι τὰ ἐκείνῳ πεπραγ-

---

60: 35–36 Cf. Greg. Naz., *Epist*. VI, (PG, 37, 32A) || 39–40 cf. Matt. 25:27 || 41–42 Matt., 5:15 || 45–46 Sophocles, *Ajax*, 169

---

44 πρωτουργικοὺς Mn || 48 ἐλάνθανεν Mn || 56 ὑπερέτης Mn

self above friendship and close association with your Wisdom, nor do I admire Plato more with respect to wisdom, nor the most pious men with respect to piety, nor the most perfect men with respect to perfect character.

But if you have no confidence in me, remember the Cypriotes. Is not the divine Bartholomew here, or the admirable Kosmas, or the divine Blassios? And where is the most learned Leo? To all of them you are no less than the air they breathe, and they are no less proud of your Wisdom than Gyges was of his ring and no less opposed to the Palamites than anybody else. And so, entrust your discourses to the hands and souls and care of such men with confidence and do not hide the sacred treasure, but give the very "talent to the exchangers" and—I do not mention what is sad—do not put "the lamp" of the Church "under the meal-tub" of what is merely caution, but place it "on the lamp stand" which is the Church itself, that it may illuminate it and show up the thieves and show forth the man who kindled the light and praise God for Whom and by Whom it was originally kindled. For the Church prevails, even if jackdaws raise a clamor. "Afraid of the huge falcon," they will crouch for fear when you appear with your discourses, for they are crushed even when your appearance is only through your letters, just as the Trojans were by any of Achilles' weapons, if they could not escape detection.

The confidence that I already have in you and the cause of piety persuade me to write this to you, my most wise friend, or rather they compel me. And if I carry it too far, your Excellence would rightly deem me worthy of forgiveness, for the compelling force is clear: love and need for piety, which is in terrible distress.

I wish to write to you also about the most holy Hyakinthos, the Metropolitan of Thessalonica, but I hesitate, because I did not wish to be the messenger bringing such news to you. For that man was a bishop most worthy of the ecclesiastical dignity and standard and a most able skipper in the storm presently afflicting the Churches of God, as is shown by his short episcopate in Thessalonica. Now he is suddenly snatched away and gone, having left a great sorrow to me and the Thessalonians (for no other bishop of that city is said to have uplifted it so) and a greater joy to the Palamites, whom he cleared out of Thessalonica, exceeding all expectation. But in order not to prolong this letter beyond measure, I cease saying anything more about him and have sent you what he has written and done and what has

60

μένα καὶ γεγραμμένα καὶ τὰ περὶ ἐκείνου πεπόμφαμεν, ἐξ ὧν ἀκριβέστερον [fol. 5v] τὰ κατ' ἐκεῖνον εἴσεις. δῆλον δὲ ὅτι προσθήσει καὶ τὰ λειπόμενα ὁ καλὸς ἡμῖν φίλος καὶ ἀδελφὸς οὑτοσὶ καὶ ὁμοσχήμων Ἰώσηπος.

Ὁ δὲ αὐτὸς οὑτοσὶ καὶ περὶ τῆς κοινῆς καὶ μεγίστης συμφορᾶς τῶν Ῥωμαίων, μᾶλλον δὲ τῆς ἁπανταχοῦ γῆς Χριστιανῶν, τῆς κατὰ τὸν περιβόητον καὶ ἀμίμητον νεὼν τῆς παντουργοῦ Σοφίας ἀπαγγελεῖ σοι, περὶ ἧς ἴσως καὶ ἄλλοι σοι γράψουσιν· ἐξ ἧς εἰς πένθος, οἶμαι, θαυμαστὸν πεπτωκότα—πῶς γὰρ οὔ;—πάλιν παραμυθήσονται ἐπαγαγόντες τὴν τοῦ παντὸς καὶ ὧδε χριστιανικοῦ πυρίπνουν προθυμίαν καὶ σύμπνοιαν ἐπὶ τὴν τοῦ πεπτωκότος ἀνάστασιν, εἰ μὴ ταύτην ὁ Θεὸς παραλύσοι διὰ τὰς ἁμαρτίας ἡμῶν.

Πέπομφά σοι καὶ τῶν ἐμῶν ἐν ἰάμβοις ἑβδομήκοντα πρὸς τοῖς τριακοσίοις, τῆς τ' εὐσεβοῦς καὶ ἐκκλησιαστικῆς καὶ ὡρισμένης πάλαι τῶν περὶ Θεοῦ δογμάτων ὁμολογίας καὶ αὖ τῆς καινῆς καὶ δυσσεβοῦς καὶ Παλαμήτιδος ἔκθεσιν, πρὸς δὲ τούτοις ἄγει σοι καὶ ἑτέρους ἐμοὺς ἰάμβους οἵους καὶ περὶ ὧν οὐκ ἐμὲ δεῖ διδάσκειν, ἀλλ' αὐτὸς ἰδὼν εἴσει καί, εἴτε τι τὴν περὶ τὰ μέτρα ἀκρίβειαν τῶν ποιητικῶν ἰχνῶν ἔχεται, σὺ κρινεῖς ὁ περὶ πάντων δεινότατος, εἴτε καὶ τῶν θεολογικῶν κανόνων ἐν τούτοις οὐκ ἐξιστάμεθα καὶ τῶν ὀρθῶν ἐννοιῶν περὶ τἄλλα, καὶ κρινεῖς καὶ ἡμᾶς διδάξεις καὶ τὸ μὴ εὖ κείμενον ἐπανορθώσῃ.

Προσείρηνται καὶ οἱ φίλοι οὓς ἐκέλευες καὶ ἀντιπροσαγορεύουσι τὰ εἰκότα τὴν θαυμαστὴν κεφαλήν σου. ὑπεράγαταί σου μετὰ τῶν ἄλλων, καὶ πρὸ τῶν ἄλλων, τὴν σοφίαν, τὴν φιλοθεΐαν, τὴν μεγαλόνοιαν, τὴν περὶ πάντα ἀκρίβειαν, καὶ ἡ θεοφιλεστάτη βασίλισσα ἡ ἐπὶ τοῦ κανικλείου θυγάτηρ, ἡ νύμφη τοῦ βασιλέως τῆς τῶν Παλαιολόγων γενεᾶς τοῦ δευτέρου, γυνὴ τὴν φύσιν, οὐ γυνὴ τὸν τρόπον, τοῖς ἀνδρῶν γενναιοτάτοις ἐφάμιλλος τὰ κάλλιστα καὶ σπουδαιότατα καὶ θεοφιλέστατα· ἣν ἴσθι φρονοῦσαν ἐπὶ τοῖς σοῖς οὐχ ἧττον ἢ ὁ Κροῖσος ἐπὶ τοῖς χρήμασιν ἢ Σεμίραμις τῇ Βαβυλῶνι ἢ αὐτή ποτε τῇ ἁλουργίδι, οὐδενὶ παραχωροῦσα τοῦ ὑπὲρ εὐσεβείας διασπωμένης πάθους, οὐδὲ γὰρ τῆς περὶ ταύτην καὶ τὰ θεῖα δόγματα τῆς ἐκκλησίας συνέσεως· διὸ πᾶς ὁ εὐσεβείᾳ συνήγορος ἀντὶ παντός γε ταύτῃ καὶ φίλου καὶ ἀδελφοῦ καὶ πατρός, εἰ δὲ καὶ σοφὸς οὗτος εἴη καὶ τῶν ἄλλων πρωτεύων τὴν σύνεσιν, καὶ ὑπὲρ τοὺς εἰρημένους εἰς πρεσβείαν αὐτῇ καὶ ἀξίωσιν. ὡς οὖν, οἶμαι, δέον καὶ τοῦτο μὴ ἀγνοεῖν σε, δεδήλωκα.

---

73 ἐξῆς Mn || 77 παραλύσει (οι supra lin.) Mn || διὰ τὰς ἁμαρτίας ἡμῶν Mn[sv] || 89 ὑπεράγανται Mn

60

been written about him, from which you will learn about him more exactly. And Josephos, my good friend and brother and fellow monk, will obviously add the rest.

The very same man will tell you also about the common and immense disaster that befell the Romans, or rather Christians the world over, as regards the famous and inimitable Church of the all-creating Wisdom of God, about which others also will probably write to you. And, though on account of this ⟨disaster⟩ you will have fallen, I believe, into extraordinary mourning—for how can you avoid it?—they will again console you, adducing the fire-breathing zeal and unity of all Christians here and everywhere for the restoration of the fallen church, unless God brings it to naught because of our sins.

I have also sent you 370 of my *Iambics*, an exposition of the pious and ecclesiastical and long-defined confession of the doctrines about God and also of the new and impious and Palamite confession. In addition to these, he is also bringing you other *Iambics* of mine, concerning which I ought not to instruct you; but you will know when you see them, and, being an expert on everything, you will judge whether anything follows closely the poetic rules as far as metrical precision is concerned, and also whether or not I deviate therein from the theological canons or from the other correct notions about other things. You will both judge and instruct me and correct what is wrong.

I gave your greetings to the friends you indicated, and they, in turn, send proper greetings to their marvelous friend. Together with others, and before others, the Princess most beloved of God (the daughter of the Keeper of the Inkstand and daughter-in-law of the second emperor of the Palaiologan dynasty, a woman by nature but not in her manner, she who can compete with the most noble men in all that is best and most important and beloved of God) also exceedingly admires you for your wisdom, love of God, magnanimity and exact understanding of all matters. Know that she thinks of you no less than Croesus thought of money or Semiramis of Babylon or she herself of the purple at one time! For no one surpasses her in her passion for piety, which is being torn asunder, and her sagacity with regard to piety and the divine doctrines of the Church. For this reason, any advocate of piety is in fact as important to her as anyone, even friend and brother and father; and if he should also be wise and excel others in sagacity, he is to her even above the aforementioned in rank and dignity. I have made this known to you, because I did not think that you should be ignorant of it.

61. Sine titulo

Τὴν ὁμότροπον δυάδα καὶ τῷ αὐτῷ Θεοῦ πνεύματι συνδεδεμένην καὶ τῆς αὐτῆς σοφίας καὶ παιδεύσεως ἔμπλεων καὶ ἡνωμένως οἶμαι προσαγορεύειν οὐκ ἄλογον, ὅτι μὴ καὶ κρείττω λόγον ἔχων ἢ διῃρῆσθαι τοῖς γράμμασι τοὺς μὴ τοίνυν ῥηθεῖσι διῃρημένους· ὧν καὶ πάλαι μὲν εἶχον ἐρωτικῶς τά τε ἄλλα καὶ ὧν ἕνεκεν αὐτοῖς ἠγαπημένος οἶδα καὶ εὐεργετημένος, οὐ γὰρ ἐπελαθόμην ἐκείνων ὅτι μὴ καὶ ἐμαυτοῦ. ὑμεῖς δὲ ἴσως ἐκλέλησθε, τὸ γὰρ εὖ πάσχον τοῦ εὖ ποιοῦντος ἐνταῦθα μνημονικώτερον· διὸ καὶ αὐτοῖς μὲν ὑμῖν οὐκ ἐθάρρουν πω γράφειν διὰ τὴν τοῦ χρόνου διάστασιν, οὐκ ὀλίγην οὖσαν ἐξ οὗ καὶ τόπῳ διέστημεν, ἀμαυροῦν πεφυκότος τὰς διαθέσεις τῶν διῳκισμένων, ἐν οἷς δὲ πρὸς ἄλλους οἷς εἰώθην ἐπέστελλον καὶ ὑμῶν ἐμνημόνευον τῶν ἱερῶν κεφαλῶν.

Νυνὶ δὲ τοῦ καλοῦ καὶ ἀγαθοῦ Γαβριὴλ **πολλην ἀ**φέντος φωνὴν καὶ σφόδρα ἐξυμνηκότος ὑμᾶς καὶ ὁμοῦ καὶ ἰδίᾳ ἐπ' εὐσεβείᾳ καὶ δικαιοσύνῃ καὶ πίστει περὶ τὸν βασιλέα τὸν ἐκ Θεοῦ καὶ θεῖον—τὴν γὰρ ἁγνείαν ἐῶ, τίς γὰρ οὐκ οἶδε ταύτην;—καὶ διὰ πάντων τὴν ἰσχυρογνωμοσύνην καὶ βεβαιότητα τὴν ὑμετέραν, δι' ἣν καὶ δεινῶν τινων ὑμᾶς ἔφασκεν ἐλθεῖν εἰς πεῖραν [fol. 4v] ὑπὲρ τῆς ἀληθείας, καὶ οὐδὲν μᾶλλον ἄλλους οὕτω φανῆναι, τὸ δὲ πάντων θειότατον, τὸν μετὰ τοῦ θειοτάτου ἀρχιερέως ὑμῖν ἐκείνου θερμὸν ἀγῶνα ὑπὲρ τῆς εὐσεβείας καὶ τῶν θείων αὐτῆς ὅρων καὶ κανόνων καὶ νόμων, τί χρὴ καὶ λέγειν ᾗ με περὶ ὑμᾶς διὰ ταῦτα ἐξέμηνεν· οὐκ ἐμὲ μέντοι μόνον, ἀλλὰ καὶ πάντας οἷς ὑπὲρ εὐσεβείας ὑβριζομένης λύπη καὶ λυομένης ἀγὼν καὶ σῳζομένης χαρά, πρὸ δὲ ἁπάντων τὸν θειότατον ἡμῶν δεσπότην τὸν οἰκουμενικὸν πατριάρχην, τὴν κοινὴν ὑπόθεσιν ὡς ἐν ἀνθρώποις λέγω τῆς εὐσεβείας ἡμῶν, καὶ ἔτι τὸν βασιλέως οἶκον αὐτῷ βασιλεῖ καὶ δεσποίνῃ τῇ θείᾳ. οὗτος ἐξήγαγε κἀμὲ ἀπὸ τοῦ μόνον φιλεῖν καὶ θαυμάζειν ἐπ' ἐμαυτοῦ τὰ ὑμέτερα ἐπὶ τὸ καὶ γράψαι θαρρῆσαι ὑμῖν. καὶ γράφω δὴ τοῖς ἱεροῖς ἀνδράσι οὓς ὁ θεὸς ἑαυτῷ εἰς τὰς παρούσας χρείας ἐτήρησε καὶ πρὸ τούτων ἐξήσκησεν αἷς ἀνδρῶν ἔδει τοιούτων μὲν τὴν ἀρετήν, τοιούτων δὲ τὴν σοφίαν, ὥσπερ ξιφῶν θαυμαστῶν ἐπὶ τοὺς καινοὺς διαιρέτας τῆς πίστεως καὶ ὑβριστὰς τῆς θεότητος διὰ τῆς πολυθεΐας· ὧν εἷς εἶναι ἐθέλω καὶ παρ' ὑμῖν ἐσκηνῆσθαι τῷ πνεύματι, εἰ καὶ μέγα ἐμοὶ τοῦτο καὶ λέξαι καὶ οἰηθῆναι. μέγα μέν—πῶς γὰρ οὔ;—ἀλλὰ καὶ αὐτοῦ τοῦ

61: Mn 4r–4v. Ed. Karpozilos, *Letters*, 80–81, no. 5.

16 εἰδε Mn || 20 ἡμῖν Mn

61

61. No Addressee

I do not think that it is unreasonable to address together two people who have the same habits and are bound by the same divine spirit and filled with the same wisdom and learning, unless I have a better reason than to divide by my letter those who have not been divided by what I have mentioned. I have been fond of them for a long time, both for other reasons and because I know that they loved me and treated me kindly. For I did not forget these things, unless I forgot myself also. But you have probably forgotten, for in this case the beneficiary has a better memory than the benefactor. Therefore, I did not dare write to you personally until now, because of the distance of time, for it is not a short time since distance of place set us apart also, and this naturally tends to weaken the attachments of those who are separated, but in the letters which I sent to others with whom I was accustomed to corresponding I remembered your sacred names also.

But now that the good and noble Gabriel spoke out and praised you excessively, both together and separately, for your piety and justice and loyalty to the divine and God-given Emperor (and I shall not mention your purity, for who does not know it?) and your resolution and steadfastness throughout, for which he said that you experienced some troubles for the sake of truth, and that no other man exhibited such virtues more than you did, and the most divine of all, your fervent struggle with your late and most divine bishop in defense of piety and the sacred rules and canons and laws, what is the use of saying how, on account of these, he drove me mad with affection for you! Nay, not only me, but also all those who grieve when piety is insulted and fight when it is destroyed and rejoice when it is preserved, and above all our most divine lord the Ecumenical Patriarch, the common support—among men, I mean—of our piety and, besides, the Palace with the Emperor himself and the divine Empress. He also led me from just loving and admiring your achievements on my own to summon the courage to write to you as well. And I am writing indeed to the holy men whom God preserved for Himself, for the present emergencies, and before these he trained them in those things that befitted men of such virtue and wisdom, just as if they were marvelous swords against the new dividers of the faith and violators of the Divinity through polytheism. I wish to be one of you and encamp spiritually near you, though this is a big thing for me to say and to presume, a big thing indeed. How could this not be so?

Θεοῦ ναοὶ γενέσθαι εὐχόμεθα, ὅτι καὶ γίνεσθαι τοῦτο ἐπιτετράμμεθα· οἷς μία πίστις, εἷς Θεός, ἡ Τριάς, ὁ ὑπὲρ πάντα καὶ ἐν πᾶσι καὶ διὰ πάντων ἐν μιᾷ τῇ παναιτίῳ καὶ πρὸ τῶν ὅλων οὔσῃ καὶ ἀδιαιρέτῳ καὶ ἀφράστῳ θεότητι. ἀλλ' εἰ καὶ ὑμῖν ἡμῶν τις λόγος καί τινος ὑμῖν δι' ἡμῶν ὑπηρεσίας δέοι, κελεύετε καὶ πάντα μεθ' ἡδονῆς λειτουργήσομεν.

62. Sine titulo

Τῷ δεῖνι πρὸς ὃν ἡμῖν χθὲς καὶ πρῴην γεγραμμένην ἀνέγνως τὴν σὴν ἐπιστολὴν ἐκείνην, τὴν καὶ τἄλλα μὲν θαυμαστὴν καὶ γενναίαν, μάλιστα δ' ὅτι τῆς εὐσεβείας προὐμάχει, τότ' εὐθὺς ἐνετύχομεν καὶ τῆς ἐκείνου δι' ἣν πρὸς αὐτὸν ἀπέσταλκεν ἡ σὴ σοφία διακηκόαμεν, ἀναγνόντος ἐκείνου καὶ ἡμῖν οἰομένου χαρίζεσθαι τοῦτό γε. ἐγὼ δὲ ἐθαύμασα τὴν τοῦ ἀνδρὸς ἀπάτην, ἀνδρὸς τοσούτου τὸ δοκεῖν καὶ τὸ δίαρμα, καὶ ἥκισθ' ὑπ' ἀπορίας εἶχον ὃ χρήσωμαι. γράφει μὲν ἐκεῖνος τῷ Παλαμᾷ κἀκεῖνο ἐσπουδακέναι δοκεῖ τοῖς γράμμασιν ἀποστῆσαι τῆς μάτην πραγματείας τὸν ἄνθρωπον, τά τε ἄλλα συντιθεὶς οἷς ᾤετο δῆθεν τοῦ φιλονεικεῖν ἀποσπάσειν ἐκεῖνον, καὶ δὴ καὶ θανάτου πρὸς αὐτὸν μνημονεύων, ὃς ἂν ἐπιστῇ φιλονεικοῦντι καὶ τὰ νῦν αὐτῷ πράττοντι κακῶς αὐτὸν ἀπαλλάξει, ἰσχυρῶς διατείνεται, καὶ οὐχ ὡς φίλον τῷ κρείττονι· εἶθ', ὥσπερ ἐπιλαθόμενος τῶν εἰρημένων, ἐκεῖνο προστίθησιν ὃ μόνον ἐξήρκει καὶ παρ' ἑαυτοῦ κατοκνοῦντα τὸν ἄνθρωπον ἀκονῆσαι πρὸς τὸ φιλόνεικον καὶ τούτου διακαρτερῆσαι παρασκευάσαι χάριν ἐν τοῖς ἐσχάτοις δεινοῖς. γράφει μὲν γὰρ ὅτι μηδὲν ἀπᾷδον οὐδὲ κακὸν εὑρίσκει περὶ τὴν εὐσέβειαν ἐν τοῖς ἐκείνου λόγοις, ἀλλ' ὅμως ἀποστητέον αὐτῷ τῶν λόγων καὶ τῆς φιλονεικίας. ὁ δ' ἀντιγράφει πρὸς ταῦτα, σοφῶς γε τοῦτο καὶ προσηκόντως αὐτῷ—κἀκεῖνο γὰρ ἡμῖν τὸ γράμμα ἐπέδειξε—χάριτας ὁμολογῶν οἷς αὐτὸν ὁμολογεῖ μηδὲν ἀπᾷδον ἔχειν αὐτῷ τοὺς λόγους οὐδὲ κακὸν [fol. 58ᵛ] εἰς εὐσέβειαν, τούτου δὲ οὕτως ἔχοντος, οὐ δεῖν ἀφίστασθαί φησιν εἰκότως τῶν λόγων τῶν ὑπὲρ εὐσεβείας τὸν εὐσεβείᾳ φίλον, κἂν δέῃ πάσχειν τὰ ἔσχατα καὶ τέλος ἀποθανεῖν ὑπὲρ τῆς ἀληθείας.

Εἶτα πῶς οὐδὲν ἀπᾷδον ἐκεῖνος εἰς εὐσέβειαν γράφει πυν-

61: 36 I Cor. 3:16; II Cor. 6:16 || 37–38 Eph. 4:5–6

62: M 58ʳ–62ᵛ.

7 χρήσομαι M || 12 ἀπαλλάξειν M || 13 εἴθ' M

But we pray to become even "temples of God" Himself, because we have been allowed to become this, too. For us "there is one faith, one God," the Trinity, "Who is over all and in all and through all," in one divinity which is the cause of all and in existence before all and indivisible and inexpressible. But if you too should need a certain discourse of mine and a certain service through me, give the order, and I shall minister to everything with pleasure.

62. No Addressee

Immediately after you read to me that letter which you had just recently written to So-and-So (an admirable and noble letter in all other respects and above all because it defended piety), I met him by chance and heard his letter to the end; it was in response to this that your Wisdom wrote to him, for he read it to me, thinking that he was surely doing me a favor. And I marveled at the man's deceit, a man of such reputation and eminence, and hardly knew what to say. For he writes to Palamas and seems to have sought only one thing with his letter, namely, to deter the man from arguing in vain. For he summed up all the other reasons by which he presumably thought that he would draw him away from contentiousness, and above all he reminded him of death, which, he strongly maintains, will take him away wretchedly and not as a lover of virtue, if it comes upon him while he is quarrelling and doing what he does now. Afterwards, as if he forgot what he had said, he adds that which alone was enough, even if the man himself were hesitant, to provoke him to contentiousness and make him remain firm to the end under the worst sufferings for its sake. For he writes that he finds in his writings nothing improper or bad as far as piety is concerned, but that he ought to abstain, nevertheless, from writing and quarrelling. In response to this, Palamas writes wisely and in a manner befitting him (for he showed me that letter also) and thanks him for that part in which he admits that his writings have nothing improper or harmful to piety, but says rightly that, this being the case, a lover of piety should not abstain from writing in defense of piety even if it is necessary to suffer the worst and finally to die for truth.

Afterwards, when I asked how it is that Palamas writes nothing contrary to

62

θανομένων ἡμῶν, πλῆθος ὑπερκειμένας καὶ ὑφειμένας συναϊδίους δογματίζων θεότητας, μιᾶς οὔσης καὶ μόνης καὶ ἀμεροῦς ἐν τῇ Τριάδι μονάδος, ὡς μεμαθήκαμεν, διεφθαρμένας καὶ ὡς ἀληθῶς Παλαμναίας ἡμῖν ἐδίδου τὰς ἀποκρίσεις, μᾶλλον δὲ παντάπασιν ἀδιακρίτους, οὔτ' ἐκεῖνον αὖθις, οὔθ' ἡμᾶς ἔξω τοῦ πλημμελεῖν τιθείσας· ἡμᾶς μὲν ὅτι κτιστὸν τὸ τοῖς θείοις ἀποστόλοις ἐπιφανὲν κατὰ τὸ Θαβώριον ὄρος φῶς τῆς τοῦ Κυρίου μεταμορφώσεως, τὸν δ' ὡς ὅλως ὑπερκειμένην θεότητα ὀνομάζοντα, καίτοι γε ὑφειμένας ἔστιν εὑρεῖν, ἔφασκε, παρὰ τοῖς θείοις λόγοις, ἀλλ' ὑφειμένων οὐσῶν ὑπερκειμένην οὐ δίδωσι λέγεσθαι.

"Ποίας ταύτας φῂς τὰς ὑφειμένας," ἐπερωτῶμεν, "ὦ βέλτιστε;"

"Τὰς ἀγγελικάς," ἔφασκε, "καὶ ἀνθρωπίνας ὧν πάντως ὑπερέχειν τὸ θεῖον ἀπειράκις ἀπείρως."

"Εἶτα λέγεις ἀκτίστους κἀκείνῳ συναϊδίους ταύτας;" ἀνταπεδίδομεν, "πόθεν; ὡς γὰρ ὁ Θεὸς τῶν θεῶν, οὕτω καὶ τῆς θεότητος τῶν θεοτήτων ὑπερκειμένης, εἰ μὲν ἄκτιστοι καὶ συναΐδιοι τῷ πάντων ὑπερκειμένῳ οἱ ὑφειμένοι θεοί, καὶ ὁ τῶν ὑφειμένων ἀριθμὸς θεοτήτων ἄκτιστος καὶ συναΐδιος δήπου τῇ πάντων ὑπερεχούσῃ θεότητι· εἰ δ' ἐκεῖνοι μὴ ἄκτιστοι, οὐδ' αἱ τούτων θεότητες."

Ὁ δ' εἶχε μὲν πρὸς τοῦτο λέγειν οὐδέν, ἠρώτα δὲ περὶ τοῦ θείου φωτὸς τοῦ κατὰ τὸ Θαβώριον ὄρος μεταμορφουμένου τοῦ Χριστοῦ πεφηνότος, εἴτ' ἄκτιστον ἐκεῖνο, εἴτε κτίσμα δοξάζοιμεν. ἡμεῖς δὲ ὅτι διπλοῦν τὸν Χριστὸν ἐπιστάμενοι, ἐκ θεότητος καὶ ἀνθρωπότητος εἰς μίαν ὑπόστασιν συντεθειμένον, ὃ μὲν ἦν αὐτοῦ ἀνθρώπινον καὶ ἐνεργούμενον τοῦτο κτιστόν, ὃ δὲ θεότης καὶ παντουργὸν τοῦτ' ἄκτιστον δοξάζειν ἀπεκρινάμεθα· ὁμοίως γὰρ ἀσεβὲς τό τε κτιστὸν τὸ ἀγένητον καὶ τὸ κτιστὸν δοξάζειν ἀγένητον.

"Ὅλως δὲ τίς," ἔφημεν, "ἡ τῶν λόγων τούτων ἐρώτησις καὶ χρεία καὶ ἐπιχείρησις; [fol. 59ʳ] μιᾶς γὰρ οὔσης θεότητος τρισυποστάτου, πολλῶν δὲ κηρυττομένων νῦν παρὰ πάντας τοὺς ὅρους τῆς εὐσεβείας, ὁ ταῦτα κατερωτῶν δῆλός ἐστι κατὰ τῆς μονάδος τὸ πλῆθος ἐπισυνάγων."

"'Ἀλλὰ φῶς ἡ παραδειχθεῖσα θεότης ἐπὶ τοῦ ὄρους," φησί.

"Ναί," φημι, "τί οὖν ἑτέρα παρὰ τὴν θείαν φύσιν ἐκείνη καὶ

62: 27 cf. Palamam, *Epist. III ad Acindynum*, 15, Syngrammata, I, 306, 18–20; ed. Nadal, 252, 10–12 || 39 Maxim. Conf., *Capit. theol.*, 1, 49 (PG, 90, 1101A) = Palamas, *Dialexis*, 24, Syngrammata, II, 186, 26; *Epist. ad Gabram*, 5, Syngrammata, II, 332, 12 || 59 Greg. Naz., *Or.*40, 6 (PG, 36, 365A)

38–39 leg. ὑπερέχει?

62

piety, when he teaches of a multitude of "higher and lower" divinities which are coeternal, whereas there is one and only one indivisible monad in the Trinity, as we have learnt, he gave me dishonest and truly Palamnaian answers, or, rather, altogether indiscriminate ⟨answers⟩, placing in turn neither Palamas nor myself beyond fault; myself on the one hand, because I call "created" the light which appeared to the divine Apostles on Mt. Tabor during the Transfiguration of the Lord; and him on the other hand, because he speaks at all of a higher divinity. And yet, he said, lower divinities can be found in the Holy Scripture, but, whereas there are lower divinities, it does not condone speaking of a higher divinity.

"What are those that you call lower, my good friend?" I inquired.

"Those of the angels and men," he said, "to which God, no doubt, is 'infinitely' superior."

"Then you call them uncreated and coeternal with Him?" I retorted. "Whence? For, seeing that the divinity is higher than the divinities just as God is higher than the gods, if the lower gods are uncreated and coeternal with Him Who transcends all, the number of lower divinities is also uncreated and coeternal, I presume, with the all-transcendent divinity. But if the lower gods are not uncreated, neither are their divinities."

He had nothing to say to this, but, as regards the divine light which appeared while Christ was transfigured on Mt. Tabor, he was asking whether I believe it to be uncreated or created. And I answered that since I knew that Christ had two natures combining divinity with humanity in one hypostasis, whatever belonged to his human and activated nature I believed to be created, and whatever belonged to the divine and all-creating nature I believed uncreated, for it is equally impious to believe that the uncreated is created and the created uncreated.

"Actually," I said, "why ask questions and argue about these matters, and for what purpose? For, since there is one Divinity in three hypostases, and now there are many divinities being proclaimed against all the laws of piety, he who asks these questions obviously gathers together the multitude of divinities against the one."

"But," he said, " 'the divinity shown on the Mountain was a light.' "

"Yes," I said, "So what? Is it different from the divine nature, as well as

ὑφειμένη καὶ ἐνεργουμένη; οὐκοῦν δύο θεότητες συναΐδιοι, τοσοῦτον ἀλλήλων διάφοροι ὅσον ὁρατὸν ἀοράτου καὶ ἐνεργούμενον ἐνεργοῦντος, τὴν ἐσχάτην διαφορὰν καὶ ἀνομοιότητα καὶ ἀνισότητα; πῶς οὖν μία θεότης; πῶς δ᾽ ἁπλῆ; πῶς δ᾽ ἀόρατος; πῶς δ᾽ ἀμερὴς καὶ ἀδιαίρετος ἔθ᾽ ἡμῖν πρεσβευθήσεται; καὶ πῶς οὐ πάντ᾽ ἄνω κάτω γενήσεται, τούτων κεκρατηκότων, τὰ δόγματα τῆς εὐσεβείας; ἅπερ εἴ τις ἐθέλει, καταλιπὼν ὡς ἁπλῶς ἡμῖν παραδέδοται κεῖσθαι πρὸς τῶν θείων πατέρων, ἐρωτᾶν ἐρωτήσεις κατὰ τὰς οἰκείας ἑαυτοῦ φαντασίας, οὐκ ἂν φθάνοι πᾶσαν ἀσέβειαν ἀποτίκτων ἐντεῦθεν καὶ πᾶσαν διαγράφων εὐσέβειαν. νῦν γὰρ δὴ τὰ τοιαῦτα ἐρωτήματα, ‘τί τὸ κάλλος τοῦ Θεοῦ καὶ ἡ δόξα;’ ‘τί δὲ τὸ φῶς τὸ ἐν τῷ ὄρει φανέν;’ ‘τίς ἡ ζωή;’ ‘τίς ἡ δύναμις;’ ‘τίς ἡ ἐνέργεια;’ ‘τίς ἡ θεότης;’ καὶ τὰ τοιαῦτα πάντα τὸ πλῆθος ἡμῖν τῶν θεοτήτων ἐδημιούργησε, διαιρεθείσης τῆς ἐν Τριάδι μονάδος εἰς διαφόρους καὶ ἀνίσους καὶ ἀνομοίους δυνάμεις ἑλληνικῶς καὶ θεότητας, καὶ συντεθείσης αὖθις ἐκ πολλῶν καὶ διαφόρων κατ᾽ ἐσχάτην ἀσέβειαν τοῖς τολμηταῖς ἁπάντων, οὐκ ἀκούσασιν, ἢ μηδ᾽ ἀκοῦσαι θελήσασι, Δαμασκηνοῦ τοῦ θείου ἀνδρός, τῶν πρώτων καὶ θειοτάτων θεολόγων ὑστάτου καὶ τὴν θεολογίαν ἄριστα ἠκριβωκότος, ὅτι τὸ ἐκ πολλῶν καὶ διαφόρων συγκείμενον σύνθετόν ἐστι, τὸ δὲ θεῖον ἁπλοῦν καὶ ἀσύνθετον· εἰ οὖν τὸ ἄκτιστον καὶ ἄναρχον καὶ ἀΐδιον καὶ ἀγαθὸν καὶ δημιουργικὸν καὶ τὰ τοιαῦτά, φησιν, οὐσιώδεις διαφορὰς εἴποιμεν ἐπὶ Θεοῦ, τὸ ἐκ τοσούτων συγκείμενον σύνθετον ἔσται καὶ οὐχ ἁπλοῦν, ὅπερ ἐσχάτης ἀσεβείας ἐστί· καὶ διὰ τοῦτό φησι, μορφὴ καὶ οὐσία καὶ φύσις καὶ θεότης ἐπὶ Θεοῦ ταὐτόν ἐστιν· οὐδὲ τοῦ μεγάλου καὶ σοφοῦ Βασιλείου ὡς οὐκ ἐπ᾽ ἄλλο μὲν ἡ τοῦ ἀγαθοῦ προσηγορία χειραγωγεῖ τὴν διάνοιαν, λέγοντος, ἐφ᾽ ἕτερον δὲ ἡ τοῦ σοφοῦ, ἐπ᾽ ἄλλο δὲ ἡ τοῦ δικαίου, ἀλλ᾽ ὅσαπερ ἂν εἴπῃς ὀνόματα, ἕν ἐστι διὰ πάντων τὸ σημαινόμενον· κἂν Θεόν, [fol. 59v] φησιν, εἴπῃς, τὸν αὐτὸν ἐνεδείξω ὃν καὶ διὰ τῶν λοιπῶν ὀνομάτων ἐνόησας· οὐδὲ τοῦ μεγάλου Διονυσίου, μὴ ἕτερον εἶναι τὸ ἀγαθὸν καὶ ἄλλο τὸ ὂν καὶ ἄλλο τὴν ζωὴν ἢ τὴν σοφίαν, οὐδὲ πολλὰ τὰ αἴτια, καὶ ἄλλων ἄλλας παρακτικὰς θεότητας ὑπερεχού-

---

66 Gregorius Cyprius I, 61 (Leutsch-Schneidewin, II, 61) ‖ 80–86 Joan. Dam., *De fide orthodoxa*, 1, 9 (PG, 94, 833B–836A) ‖ 87–88 Joan. Dam., *Dialectica*, 41 (PG, 94, 608B) ‖ 88–94 Basil. Caes., *Epist.* 189, 5 (PG, 32, 689BC) ‖ 95–98 Dion. Areop., *De div. nom.*, 5, 2 (PG, 3, 816C)

---

66 ἀδιαίρετος scripsi: ἀόρατος M ‖ 91 εἴποις M ‖ 93 εἴποις M

62

lower and activated? Are there, then, two coeternal divinities as different from each other as visible from invisible and activated from activating, in the most extreme form of difference and dissimilarity and inequality? How then can there be one divinity? How can it be simple? How can it be invisible? How can we still worship it as being without parts and indivisible? And how can all the pious doctrines fail to be 'turned upside down,' if these prevail? And so, if a man wishes to ask questions according to the figments of his own imagination, having forsaken these pious doctrines as they were handed down to us by the holy Fathers to remain fixed, he will surely produce thereby all kinds of impiety and erase all piety. Indeed, now, questions such as 'What is the beauty and the glory of God?'; 'What is the light that appeared on the Mountain?'; 'What is the life?'; 'What is the power?'; 'What is the energy?'; 'What is the divinity?'—such questions created for us the multitude of divinities, by dividing the monad in the Trinity into different and unequal and dissimilar powers and divinities after the pagan manner, and putting it together again from many different ones; ⟨this was done⟩ by those men who dare everything most impiously. For they did not hear, or did not even wish to hear, Damaskenos the divine man, the last of the leading and most divine theologians and a completely thorough student of theology, who says: 'That which consists of many and different parts is composite, but God is simple and uncompounded. If, therefore,' he says, 'with regard to God, we call uncreatedness and being without beginning and timelessness and goodness and creativity and such things essential differences, that which is made up of so many things will be composite and not simple, which is the very characteristic of extreme impiety; and for this reason,' he says, 'with regard to God, form and essence and nature and divinity are the same thing.' Neither did they hear the great and wise Basil who says that 'The name good does not lead the thought to one thing, while ⟨the name⟩ wise to another and ⟨the name⟩ just to yet another; in fact, no matter how many names you may mention, they all mean the same thing. And even if you say God,' he says, 'you indicate the same God Whom you meant by the other names also.' And they did not even hear the great Dionysios who says that 'Goodness is not one thing and being another and life or wisdom another, nor are there many causes and other divinities which produce various di-

62

σας καὶ ὑφειμένας, καὶ σαφῶς οὑτωσὶ τὴν Παλαμναίαν πλάνην προκαταβάλλοντος τοῖς ὁπωσοῦν τοὺς λογισμοὺς ὑγιαίνουσι.

Φέρε δὴ τὴν ἐν τῷ ὄρει παραδειχθεῖσαν θεότητα τίς κτιστὴν καὶ τίς ἄκτιστον καὶ λέγει καὶ νομίζει, σκεψώμεθα· ἡμεῖς αὐτὴν ἐκείνην τὴν πάντων ὑπερκειμένην τοῦ Θεοῦ Λόγου θεότητα τὴν καὶ σεσαρκωμένην οἰόμεθα παραδειχθῆναι τότε τοῖς ἀποστόλοις, ἧς οὐδὲν ὑψηλότερον· παραδειχθῆναι μέντοι ὡς οἷόν τε ἦν ἰδεῖν ἐκείνους θεότητα, οὐ καθ' αὑτὴν δειχθῆναι ᾗ πέφυκε, τοῦτο γὰρ αἰνίττεται καὶ τὸ παραδειχθῆναι, οὐ γὰρ εἶναι δευτέραν θεότητα τῷ μεταμορφωθέντι, μονὰς γὰρ ἡ θεότης ἀπλήθυντος· οὔθ' ὡς μορφὴν οὐσιώδη καὶ δόξαν, ἀμόρφωτος γὰρ ἡ θεία φύσις καθ' αὑτὴν καὶ ἀνείδεος, διὸ μορφὴ καὶ φύσις ἐπὶ τοῦ θείου ταὐτόν ἐστι· οὔθ' ὡς ἄλλο τι παρὰ τὴν θείαν φύσιν, τὸ γὰρ ἐκ πολλῶν, φησι, καὶ διαφόρων συγκείμενον οὐχ ἁπλοῦν οὐδ' ἀσύνθετον· ἀλλὰ τὸ φῶς τὸ ἀληθινὸν ὃ φωτίζει πάντα ἄνθρωπον ἐρχόμενον εἰς τὸν κόσμον, ὁ τοῦ Θεοῦ Πατρὸς Λόγος, τὸ ἀπαύγασμα τῆς δόξης τοῦ Πατρός, ἡ δόξα ἧς πατὴρ ὁ Πατὴρ τῆς ἀπορρήτου δόξης, οὗτος αὐτὸν ὡς ἐνῆν τοῖς μαθηταῖς τοῖς ἑαυτοῦ παραδείκνυσιν, ὥς που καὶ ἡ χρυσῆ φησι γλῶττα περὶ τῶν πρὸ τῆς χάριτος τοῦ Θεοῦ θεαμάτων· ἐπειδή, γάρ φησιν, ἔμελλεν ὁ υἱὸς τοῦ Θεοῦ δι' ἀληθινῆς φανήσεσθαι σαρκός, ἄνωθεν αὐτοὺς προεγύμναζεν ὁρᾶν τοῦ Θεοῦ τὴν οὐσίαν ὡς ἦν αὐτοῖς δυνατὸν ἰδεῖν· τὴν οὐσίαν οὐχ ἑτέραν θεότητα, οὐ γάρ ἐστι δευτέρα μετὰ τὴν πρώτην· εἰ γὰρ ἦν, οὐκ ἂν αὐτὴν ἔφασκε σαφῶς οὑτωσὶ τοῦ Θεοῦ τὴν οὐσίαν, ἀλλ' ἐκείνην ὡς ἔοικε. ἀλλ' οὐδὲν προαιώνιον πλὴν Πατρὸς καὶ Υἱοῦ καὶ ἁγίου Πνεύματος, ὡς οἱ πατέρες διδάσκουσι· ταῦτα δ' ἡ θεία φύσις διαιρουμένη οὐ διαφόροις θεότησιν ἀλλ' ὑποστάσεσιν, ἣ μόνη, φησί, τῶν κτισμάτων ὑπερκειται, ὅθεν οὐδὲν προσκυνοῦμεν ὅπερ αὐτὸν ὑποβέβηκε.

Ταῦτα οἱ θεῖοι πατέρες· καὶ διὰ ταῦτα οὐδ' ἡμῖν τὰς τῆς θείας φύσεως ὑφειμένας θεότητας καὶ ἀπειράκις ὑφειμένας ἀπείρως τοῦ Παλαμᾶ, καὶ δὴ καὶ ἐνεργουμένας—τῆς ὑπερβολῆς

---

100 Greg. Naz., *Or.*40, 6 (PG, 36, 365A) || 109 Joan. Dam., *Dialect.*, 41, (PG, 94, 608B) || 110–112 Joan. Dam., *De fide orthod.*, 1, 9 (PG, 94, 833B) || 112–113 ἀλλὰ . . . κόσμον Joan. 1: 9 || 114 Hebr. 1:3 || 115 Eph. 1:17 || 117–120 Joan. Chrys., *In Joannem* XV, 1 (PG, 59, 98) || 123–124 locum non inveni || 126–128 cf. Epiphanius, *Adv. haeres.*, 3, 1, 27 (PG, 42, 609D) || 130–131 ἀπειράκις . . . ἀπείρως; Maxim. Conf., *Capit. theol.*, 1, 49 (PG, 90, 1101A) = Palamas, *Dialexis*, 24, Syngrammata, II, 186, 26; *Epist. ad Gabram*, 5, Syngrammata, II, 332, 12 || 130 ὑφειμένας: cf. Palamam, *Epist. III ad Acindynum*, 15, Syngrammata, I, 306, 18–20; ed. Nadal, 252, 10–12

vinities higher and lower,' and thus he clearly rejects, in advance, the Palamnaian delusion for those whose reasoning is at all sound.

"Indeed, let us reflect: who says and believes that the 'divinity which appeared on the Mountain' was created and who says it was uncreated? I believe that the very divinity of God the Logos, which is higher than everything and has been incarnated, was demonstrated to the Apostles at that time. Nothing is higher than this divinity. ⟨I believe⟩ that it was demonstrated, of course, in the way that it was possible for them to see the divinity; not that it was shown in itself, in its natural state—and that is what the word 'demonstrated' also suggests—for there was no divinity second to Him Who had been transfigured. For the Divinity is a monad without plurality. And ⟨it was not demonstrated⟩ as the essential form and glory, for the divine nature is in itself without form and figure; wherefore 'with regard to God, form and nature are the same thing.' Nor ⟨was it demonstrated⟩ as anything else different from the divine nature, for 'that,' he says, 'which consists of many different parts is neither simple nor uncompounded.' But 'the real light which enlightens every man born into the world,' the Logos of God the Father, 'the effulgence of the Father's splendor,' the glory whose father is the 'Father' of the ineffable 'glory,' showed Himself to His own disciples as it was possible for them ⟨to see Him⟩. Just as Chrysostom says somewhere about the visions of God before the era of grace: 'because,' he says, 'the son of God was to appear in real flesh, He prepared them from the beginning to see the essence of God as it was possible for them to see it'; the essence, not another divinity, for there is no second divinity after the first, because if there were, he would not call this, so clearly, the essence of God, but that one, as it seems. But 'Nothing exists before time, except the Father and the Son and the Holy Spirit,' as the Fathers teach; that is, the divine nature divided not into different divinities, but into hypostases. 'This divinity alone,' he says, 'is above all created things, therefore we do not worship anything which is below Him.'

"That is what the holy Fathers say, and for this reason we must not worship the divinities which are lower than the divine nature, and especially those of Palamas which are 'infinitely lower' and, indeed, even activated—what excessively un-

τῶν ἀθέων δογμάτων!—[fol. 60ʳ]προσκυνητέον, μίαν καὶ τὴν αὐτὴν ἀπαράλλακτον ἐν τριάδι προσώπων καὶ ὑποστάσεων προσκυνοῦσι μονάδα παντουργόν τε καὶ παντοδύναμον καὶ πανταχοῦ παροῦσαν, ἁπλῆν, ἀόρατον, ἀμέριστον, ἀδιαίρετον, ἄπειρον, ἄποιον, ἀνείδεον, ἀπερινόητον, νοουμένην μέντοι καὶ ὁρωμένην αὖθις οἷς εὐσεβὴς ἡ διάνοια, τὸν ἐφικτόν τε καὶ θεμιτὸν αὐτοῖς τρόπον καὶ ὡς αὐτοῖς δυνατόν, κατὰ τὸν εἰρηκότα. οἱ δὲ πυνθανόμενοι καὶ πολυπραγμονοῦντες, 'τίς ἡ θεία φύσις;' 'τίς ἡ ταύτης οὐσιώδης θεότης;' 'τίς δ' ἡ ζωὴ καὶ τί τὸ φῶς καὶ ἡ παραδειχθεῖσα ἐν τῷ ὄρει θεότης;' καὶ κτιστὴν ἡμᾶς τὴν θεότητα ταύτην συκοφαντοῦντες λέγειν, ἵνα σφίσιν ἀποδειχθῇ τὸ πλῆθος τῶν θεοτήτων καὶ διαιρεθῇ τὸ τῆς μονάδος χρῆμα καὶ ἡ μία προσκύνησις τῆς μιᾶς ἐν τριάδι θεότητος οἴχηται ταῖς ἐκκλησίαις, τί περὶ ταύτης κομψεύονται, μᾶλλον δὲ βλασφημοῦσιν; ἄλλη, φασίν, ἐστι παρὰ τὴν θείαν φύσιν, οὐχ ἑτέρα δὲ μόνον, ἀλλὰ καὶ ἀπειράκις ἀπείρως, πρὸς δὲ καὶ ἐνεργουμένη, ἀλλὰ καὶ ἀνούσιος καὶ καθ' αὑτὴν ἀνυπόστατος, ἔστι δ' αὐτὴ καὶ φυσικὴ καὶ οὐσιώδης αὐτῷ, ἀλλ' ὑπὲρ ταύτην ὅμως, φησίν, ἐστι τὴν θεότητα ὁ ἐν Τριάδι Θεός, ἡ τρισυπόστατος φύσις, ἀπειράκις ἀπείρως καὶ ὡς τῶν ἐνεργουμένων τὸ ἐνεργοῦν καὶ τῶν ἀνουσίων ἡ οὐσία καὶ τῶν ὀνομαζομένων τὸ ὑπερώνυμον. πῶς ἄν τις ἀκριβέστερον Ἀρείῳ καὶ Εὐνομίῳ συνηγορήσειε μεθ' ὑπερβολῆς ἁπάσης, ὦ πάντολμοι; πῶς γάρ, εἰπέ μοι, τῶν κτισμάτων ὑπέρκειται ὁ ποιητὴς τῶν ὅλων; οὐχ ὡς τῶν ἐνεργουμένων τὸ ἐνεργοῦν καὶ τῶν ὀνομαζομένων τὸ ὑπερώνυμον καὶ ἀπειράκις ἀπείρως; ὡσαύτως δὲ καὶ τῆς Χριστοῦ θεότητος τῆς οὐσιώδους αὐτῷ; τῆς ἀσεβείας! πῶς οὖν κτίσμα ὑμῖν ἡ τοῦ Χριστοῦ θεότης; ὧν γὰρ ὁμοίως καὶ κατὰ τὸν ἴσον λόγον ὑπερέχει τὸ θεῖον, τούτων πῶς οἷόν τε εἶναι τὰ μὲν κτιστά, τὰ δὲ ἄκτιστα; εἶτα μορφὴν Θεοῦ καὶ δόξαν οὐσιώδη καὶ φυσικὴν ταύτην λέγοντες καὶ ταύτην ὁρᾶν καμπάζοντες καθ' ἑαυτὴν ἀμέσως σωματικοῖς ὀφθαλμοῖς, πῶς Μασσαλιανῶν ἀπολείπεσθαι τὴν ἀσέβειαν οἴεσθε καὶ δοκεῖτε λανθάνειν χείρω φρονοῦντες καὶ διδάσκοντες εἶναι τὴν τοῦ Λόγου θεότητα καὶ τῶν πρώτων κτισμάτων, μᾶλλον δὲ τῶν

134–135 Joannis Chrysostomi *Liturgia* (ed. Brightman), 353, 13 || 138 cf. Joan. Chrys., *In Joannem* XV, 1 (PG, 59, 98) || 140–141 cf. Greg. Naz., *Or.* 40, 6 (PG, 36, 365A) || 150 et 170 Maxim. Conf., *Capit. theol.*, 1, 49 (PG, 90, 1101A) = Palamas, *Dialexis*, 24, Syngrammata, II, 186, 26; *Epist. ad Gabram*, 5, Syngrammata, II, 332, 12 || 151–152 Palamas, *De divinis operationibus*, 47, Syngrammata, II, 132, 27–28

---

144 οἴχεται M

62

godly doctrines!—because we worship one, exactly uniform monad in a triad of persons and hypostases, all-creating and omnipotent and 'omnipresent'; simple, invisible, without parts, indivisible, infinite, without qualities, without form, incomprehensible, yet to be apprehended spiritually and seen, on the other hand, by those of a pious mind, in the manner which is accessible and right and 'possible for them,' as he said. And as for those who inquire and ask with officiousness, 'What is the divine nature?' 'What is its essential divinity?' 'What is life and what is the light and the divinity which were shown on the Mountain?' and who falsely accuse me of saying that this divinity is created, so that their multitude of divinities may be proven and the monad divided and the single worship of the one Trinitarian divinity may be gone from the Churches, why are they inventing these subtleties or rather blasphemies about this divinity? They say that it is other than the divine nature and not only different but 'infinitely' ⟨different⟩ and, in addition, activated and without essence and hypostasis of its own, yet of the nature and essence of God. But the Trinitarian God, says he, the divine nature in three hypostases, is 'infinitely' above this divinity, and as the activating is in relation to the activated and essence to those deprived of essence and that which is above every name to those which are designated by name! O impudent men! How could one advocate more precisely and with all extravagance the cause of Arios and Eunomios? For, tell me, how does the Maker of all excel the creatures? Is it not just as the activating ⟨principle⟩ excels the activated and that which is above every name excels those which are designated by name, and infinitely so? And does He likewise excel the divinity of Christ which is of His own essence? What impiety! Surely, then, for you the divinity of Christ is created! For how can some of the things which God excels in like manner and in equal proportion be created and others uncreated? Moreover, when you call this the natural and essential form and glory of God and boast of seeing it in itself directly with your bodily eyes, how do you presume that you fall short of the Messalians in impiety, and think that you are not found out when you believe and teach that the divinity of the Logos is inferior to that of the first created beings, or rather of

62

ἀσωμάτων πάντων μέχρι ψυχῆς, ἃ πάντα πᾶσιν ἀόρατα πέφυκε σωματικοῖς ὀφθαλμοῖς;

Τίνων ἤ—διὰ τοῦ κτιστὴν λέγειν τὴν ἄκτιστον θεότητά τε καὶ δύναμιν καὶ σοφίαν καὶ ἀγαθό-[fol. 60ᵛ]τητα, καὶ αὖθις ἄκτιστα τὰ ἐνεργούμενα καὶ ὧν πάντως ὑπερέχει τὸ θεῖον ἀπειράκις ἀπείρως—ἀσέβεια καὶ ἀτιμάζειν Θεὸν τὸν τῶν ὅλων τεχνίτην διὰ τῶν ἀνίσων βαθμῶν τῆς θεότητος, ⟨ὦ⟩ ἄνθρωπος; ἡ ἐκκλησία τοῦ Θεοῦ, ἢ οἱ τῆς ἐκκλησίας ἀποστάται καὶ πάντα τολμηταὶ Παλαμῖται;"

Ἀλλ' οἱ νοσοῦντες τὴν ἀκοὴν τῆς ψυχῆς ἐκεῖνοι καὶ ὑπερήφανοι, δι' αὐτό γε τοῦτο τὸν τῦφον καὶ τὴν ὑπερηφανίαν καὶ πρὸς τούτοις τὸ πρὸς τὰς ἀρχὰς δυσμενὲς καὶ μικρόψυχον, τούτων οὐκ ἐπαΐουσιν· οὐκ ἔχοντες δὲ ὅπως ἀπογνώσονται καὶ ἀφήσουσι παντελῶς ἀναίτιον τὸν Παλαμᾶν ὑπὸ τῆς τῶν ἐλέγχων λαμπρότητος, οὐδ' ἡμᾶς ἀφιᾶσιν ἀνυπευθύνους εἶναι διὰ τὰ εἰρημένα—τὸν τῦφον καὶ τὸ δοκεῖν τινες εἶναι—μέσοι τινὲς εἶναι ποιούμενοι, †καθάπερ τοὺς Ἀνομοίους οἱ θεολόγοι φασὶ Βασίλειος καὶ Γρηγόριος, οὓς μέσους Ἀρείου τοῦ τῆς ἑτερουσιότητος καὶ τῶν τὸ ὁμοούσιον εὐσεβούντων τοῦ Λόγου γενόμενοι, ὅμοιον τὴν φύσιν, μέσον τι τῶν εἰρημένων ἐφήμισαν,† καὶ τούτῳ τὴν ἐκκλησίαν πᾶσαν ὡς πιθανῷ πως κατέσπασαν· οὐκ ἀποδοκιμάσαντες Ἄρειον, ἀλλὰ τοῦτο μὲν προσποιησάμενοι, τὸν δὲ βεβαιότερον καταστησάμενοι, τὸ γὰρ ὅμοιον αὐτοῖς, οὐ προστεθέν γε τὸ ἀπαράλλακτον, ἀνόμοιον πέφηνε. τοὺς γοῦν Ἀρείῳ φίλους καὶ συνηγόρους ἀνεθεμάτισαν, ὁ θεολόγος φησί, κατεγνωκότες αὐτῶν οὐκ ἀσέβειαν ἄμετρον, ἀλλὰ συγγραφὴν ἄπληστον.

Τοῦτο ποιοῦσι καὶ οἱ νῦν ἐφευρεταὶ τῆς μεσότητος, οἷς μὲν αὐτοῦ κατηγοροῦσιν οὐκ ἀναιροῦντες τὰ πονηρεύματα, λόγων γὰρ ἀπληστίαν κατηγοροῦσιν αὐτοῦ καὶ ἀσχολίαν βίου, οἷς δὲ ἡμῶν ἐπιχειροῦσι καθάπτεσθαι, συνιστάντες ἐκεῖνον καὶ βεβαιούμενοι· καὶ τὸ μὲν συμπέρασμα δῆθεν ἔσθ' ὅτε ἀποπεμπόμενοι, καὶ οὐδὲ τότε τὸ πᾶν, τὰς δὲ προτάσεις ὧν τὸ συμπέρασμα γέννημα ἐπιεικῶς ἀσπαζόμενοι, φαντασίαν ἐχούσας ἀλογίστοις ἀνθρώποις ἀληθοῦς τὸ φαινόμενον, ἀλλ' οὐκ ἀλήθειαν· πῶς γὰρ αἵ γε πάντας τοὺς ὅρους καὶ τὰς ἀρχὰς τῆς ὅλης θεολογίας ἀναγκάζουσι κατὰ τὴν Παλαμναίαν πλάνην ἐκλαμβανόμεναι; καὶ τοῦτο ἔστιν ὅ φησιν ὁ μέγας

---

179 cf. Basil. Caes., *Epist.* 212, 2 (PG, 32, 781B) ‖ 182 cf. Epiphanius, *Adv. Haer.*, 3, 1, 19 (PG, 42, 437D) ‖ 188–189 Greg. Naz., *Or.* 21, 23 (PG, 35, 1108B)

---

171 ⟨ὦ⟩ addidi ‖ 174 τύφον M ‖ 178 τύφον M ‖ 179–183 καθάπερ . . . ἐφήμισαν: non satis perspicio

62

all incorporeal beings down to the soul, which are all by nature invisible to all bodily eyes?

"Who, Sir, is guilty of impiety for saying that the uncreated divinity and power and wisdom and goodness is created, and, in turn, that the activated and those which God 'infinitely' excels are uncreated, and who insults God the Architect of all with unequal degrees of divinity? Is it the Church of God or is it the Palamites who have rebelled against the Church and are daring everything?"

But, since their moral hearing is failing and they are proud as well, those men do not listen to this because of this very reason—their arrogance and pride and, in addition to this, their hostility and pettiness towards the authorities. And since they cannot reject the accusation and set Palamas completely free of the charge because of the brilliancy of the arguments of refutation, they call me to account for the aforementioned reasons—their arrogance and high opinion of themselves. Because they assume that they hold a moderate position, just as the theologians Basil and Gregory say of the Anomoeans, who took an intermediate stand between the Arian doctrine that the Son was of a different substance from the Father and those who venerated the consubstantiality of the Logos, and who called ⟨Christ⟩ "like" ⟨the Father⟩ in nature, something midway between the expounded ⟨doctrines⟩. And by what seemed to be in one way or another plausible, they pulled down the whole Church. For they did not reject Arios, but while they pretended to do this, they confirmed him even more, since their term "like" without the term "exactly like" added to it means "unlike." At all events, the Theologian says that they anathematized the friends and advocates of Arios because they found them guilty not of "immeasurable impiety, but of insatiate writing."

That is what the present inventors of the moderate position are doing also, since by their accusations against him, they do not refute his wickedness, for they charge him with "insatiate writing" and activity, while by their attempts to upbraid me they confirm and establish him. And while sometimes they pretend to dismiss the conclusion, and even then not all of it, they accept sufficiently the premises which give birth to the conclusion and have, for non-thinking men, the image of what seems to be true, but ⟨have⟩ no truth. For how can they, since they violate all the laws and principles of the whole theology when interpreted according to the Palamnaian delusion! And this is what Basil the great says about these "moderate men"

62

Βασίλειος περὶ τῶν μέσων τούτων καὶ τῶν ἀπεναντίας, οἵ τε γὰρ τὸ ἄθεον τῆς ἀνομοιότητος δόγμα ταῖς ἐκκλησίαις ἐπάγοντες ἐπ᾽ ἐμὲ τὸν πόλεμον ἔχουσιν, οἵ τε τὴν μέσην ἐλαύνοντες, ὡς οἴονται, καὶ ἀπὸ μὲν τῶν αὐτῶν ἀρχῶν ἐκείνοις ὡρμημένοι, [fol. 61ʳ] τῇ δὲ τῶν λογισμῶν ἀκολουθίᾳ μὴ ἐφιέντες διὰ τὸ ὑπεναντίον ταῖς ἀκοαῖς τῶν πολλῶν, ἡμᾶς δυσχεραίνουσι.

Ταῦτα καὶ πάλαι καὶ νῦν, λόγῳ μὲν ἡμῖν ἱστορούμενα πρότερον, ἔργῳ δὲ νῦν ὥσπερ καὶ τότε γινόμενα καὶ φαινόμενα· τό τε γὰρ ἄθεόν ἐστι τῆς ἀνομοιότητος δόγμα, τὸ δόγμα τοῦ Παλαμᾶ, εἴ γε καὶ οὗτος ἀνομοίους δοξάζει καὶ ἀνίσους θεότητας ἐν τῇ Τριάδι, τό τε τῶν μέσων πρᾶγμα· ὑπάρξεις μὲν δέχονται συναϊδίους πλῆθος, ἀνίσους καὶ ἀνομοίους ἀλλήλαις καὶ τῷ παντὶ ὑπερκειμένῳ Θεῷ, ἐνεργείας καὶ χάριτας ἀποκαλοῦντες ταῦτα καὶ φῶτα τῷ Θεῷ συναΐδια, παρὰ τὴν θείαν φύσιν καὶ ὑφειμένα ταῦτα ἀπειράκις ἀπείρως, ὁρατὰ καθ᾽ ἑαυτὰ σωματικοῖς ὀφθαλμοῖς, ἄλλο τε μορφὴν φυσικὴν καὶ ἄλλο φύσιν καὶ ζωὴν ἄλλο καὶ σοφίαν ἕτερον, ἐπὶ Θεοῦ ἄνισα καὶ ἀνόμοια πράγματα τὴν ἐσχάτην ἀνομοιότητα· ταῦτα δὲ οὕτως ἔχειν ἰσχυριζόμενοι, θεότητά τε λέγεσθαι καὶ τὴν πάντων ὑπερκειμένην φύσιν καὶ αὖ τὴν ἐνέργειαν ἀποφαινόμενοι τὴν ὑφειμένην ἐκείνης ἀπειράκις ἀπείρως καὶ ἄκτιστον, καὶ οὕτως ἀπὸ τῶν αὐτῶν ἀρχῶν ὡρμημένοι τοῖς Παλαμίταις, δύο θεότητας ὅμως ἀπαρνοῦνται μὴ λέγειν διὰ τὸ ὑπεναντίον ταῖς ἀκοαῖς τῶν πολλῶν, ὡς ὁ μέγας ἔφη Βασίλειος.

Ἐγὼ δὲ ὁρῶ ἀδύνατον ὂν μηδετέρου μετέχειν ὅστις ὁμολογεῖ θεοσεβεῖν ὁπωσοῦν. εἰ δ᾽ ἄρα τοῦτο πάντως φιλονεικοίη τις, τοῦτον εὑρίσκω παντελοῦς ἀθεΐας ἀντιποιούμενον, ἀπὸ γὰρ ἐναντίας παντάπασι τὰ Παλάμια πρὸς τὰ τῆς ἐκκλησίας καὶ μέσον οὐδ᾽ ὁτιοῦν· ὁ μὲν γὰρ πολλάς τε καὶ διαφόρους ἐν τῇ Τριάδι θεότητας, ἡ δὲ μίαν καὶ ἀπαράλλακτον ὁμολογεῖ. ὁ τοίνυν ἡμᾶς κακίζων τοὺς μίαν ὁμολογοῦντας θεότητα αὐτομάτως τοῖς τὸ πλῆθος συμφέρεται λέγουσιν· ὁ δὲ ἐκείνους αὐτόθεν τοῖς τὴν μίαν ὁμολογοῦσιν ὁμοφωνεῖ· καὶ τὸ ἐκείνους μὴ ἀποδέχεσθαι ἡμᾶς ἐστιν ἀποδέχεσθαι, τὸ δὲ μὴ

200–206 Basil. Caes., *Epist.* 212, 2 (PG, 32, 781B) ‖ 209 Basil. Caes., *ibid.* ‖ 215 et 220 Maxim. Conf., *Capit. theol.*, I, 49 (PG, 90, 1101A) = Palamas, *Dialexis*, 24, Syngrammata, II, 186, 26; *Epist. ad Gabram*, 5, Syngrammata, II, 332, 12 ‖ 219–220 Palamas, *Epist. III ad Acindynum*, 15, Syngrammata, I, 306, 18–20; ed. Nadal, 252, 10–12 ‖ 221 Basil. Caes., *Epist.* 212, 2 (PG, 32, 781B) ‖ 222–223 Basil. Caes., *ibid.*

---

232 *ἐκείνους*] ἐκεῖνος M

62
and his opponents: "Both those who introduce into the Churches the ungodly doctrine of Anomoeanism wage war against me, and those who follow the middle road—as they believe—and start from the same principles but do not yield to the cogency of the arguments, because it offends the ears of the majority, are annoyed at me."

These things happened in the old days as well as today. Previously we were told about them, but now, just as at that time, they actually happen and come to light. For there is both the ungodly doctrine of Anomoeanism—the doctrine of Palamas—since he too believes that there are dissimilar and unequal divinities in the Trinity, and the matter of the "moderate." On one hand, they admit a multitude of coeternal beings, unequal and dissimilar both with respect to one another and God Who transcends everything, calling them energies and graces and lights coeternal with God, but different from the divine nature and "infinitely" lower; visible in themselves to bodily eyes; one a natural form, and another nature, and another life, and another wisdom, things which in the case of God are unequal and dissimilar to the extreme of dissimilarity. And, on the other hand, while they claim that this is so and declare that both the transcendent nature and the energy—which is "infinitely lower" than the nature and uncreated—are called divinity and thus "start from the same principle" as the Palamites, they nevertheless deny speaking of two divinities, "because it offends the ears of the majority," as Basil the Great said.

But I see that it is impossible for a man who admits being at all religious not to share either belief. And if, perhaps, someone should contest this, I consider him a defender of absolute atheism, for Palamas' doctrines are altogether opposed to those of the Church and there is no middle road whatsoever. For he acknowledges many different divinities in the Trinity, whereas the Church acknowledges one and exactly uniform. The man who reproaches me, therefore, when I acknowledge one divinity automatically agrees with those who speak of a multitude ⟨of divinities⟩. And he who ⟨reproaches⟩ them, obviously agrees with those who acknowledge one; and to reject them is to accept me, while to reject me is, in fact, to accept them, if a person

62

τὸ καθ' ἡμᾶς ἐκείνους αὐτόχρημα, εἰ κεκριμένως ἔχοι· τὸ δὲ μὴ καθ' ἡμᾶς, μήτ' ἐκείνους παντελὴς ἀθεΐα· τὸ γὰρ μήτε μίαν θεότητα, μήτε πολλὰς δοξάζειν, οὐδεμίαν ἐστὶ περιφανῶς δοξάζειν· τοῦτο δὲ ἀθεΐα. οὐκ ἐμὸς δὲ ὁ λόγος οὗτος, ἀλλὰ τῶν ἱερῶν πατέρων, [fol. 61v] ὅθεν ἡμῖν καὶ τοῦτο· καίτοι γε ἐμὸς μᾶλλον ἢ τοῦ πάλαι εἰρηκότος φανήσεται, ὁ δέ ἐστι Γρηγόριος ὁ Νυσσαέων, ἕτοιμος ἡμῖν, λέγων, καὶ σαφὴς ὁ λόγος· ὁ γὰρ καταγινώσκων τῶν μίαν λεγόντων θεότητα ἐξ ἀνάγκης ἢ τῷ πολλὰς λέγοντι ἢ τῷ μηδεμίαν συνθήσεται· οὐ γάρ ἐστι δυνατὸν ἕτερόν τι παρὰ τὸ εἰρημένον ἐπινοῆσαι. ἀλλ' οὔτε πολλὰς λέγειν συγχωρεῖ ἡ τῆς Γραφῆς διδασκαλία, †καὶ μίαν ὁμολογοῦντες† ὅτι ἐν αὐτῷ κατοικεῖ πᾶν τὸ πλήρωμα τῆς θεότητος. εἰ οὖν εἰς πλῆθος ἐκτείνειν τὸν ἀριθμὸν τῶν θεοτήτων μόνων τῶν τὴν πολύθεον πλάνην νενοσηκότων ἐστί, τὸ δὲ καθόλου ἀρνεῖσθαι τὴν μίαν θεότητα ἄθεον ἂν εἴη, τίς λόγος ἐστὶν ὁ διαβάλλων ἡμᾶς ἐπὶ τῷ μίαν ὁμολογεῖν τὴν θεότητα;

Πρὸς ταῦτα τί φησιν ὁ τῶν πολλῶν θεοτήτων προστάτης; εἶτ' ἐνεργείας ἐρεῖ καὶ δυνάμεις ἀκτίστους καὶ μορφὰς καὶ κάλλη καὶ ζωὴν καὶ σοφίαν καὶ πάντων τούτων ὑπερκειμένην φύσιν, καὶ οὕτω τὸ πλῆθος τῶν θεοτήτων ἀξιώσει πρεσβεύειν, τὸν δὲ μὴ πειθόμενον ἀσεβείας γράψεται; ἀλλὰ τὸ εἰς πλῆθος ἐκτείνειν τὸν ἀριθμὸν τῶν θεοτήτων μόνων τῶν τὴν πολύθεον πλάνην νενοσηκότων ἐστίν· ὅστις γε οὖν τὸν θεῖον Γρηγόριον ἐν τοῖς ἁγίοις ἄγει, πῶς ἔτι προσέξει τῷ Παλαμίτῃ βόθρῳ; καὶ ὅστις ἄλλο τι φρονεῖ περὶ τοῦ θείου τοῦδε, ἀλλότριος οὗτος τῆς Χριστοῦ ἐκκλησίας. πῶς ἂν οὖν ἡμεῖς τῷ τοιούτῳ πεισθείημεν; καὶ μὴν ὡς ὁ μήτε τῷ Παλαμᾷ προσέχων ἐπὶ τῷ πλήθει τῶν θεοτήτων, μήτε ἐπὶ τῇ τριλαμπεῖ μονάδι τοὺς ταῦτα ὑπερμαχοῦντας ἀποδεχόμενος, τὴν ἄκραν ἀθεΐαν οὗτος πεπρέσβευκεν, ὁ θεῖος ἀνὴρ ἀπεφήνατο. τεραστίων ἄρα τις ὁ μέγας οὗτος λογισμὸς καὶ τραγελάφων ἂν εἴη τερατωδέστερος, εἴ γε καὶ λογισμὸν αὐτὸν δεῖ προσειπεῖν, ἀλλὰ μὴ λογισμοῦ παντὸς ἔκπτωσιν καὶ ἀλογίαν ἄκραν. ἔ-

---

239–251 Basil. Caes., *Epist.* 189, 4 (PG, 32, 688C–D) ‖ 256 ἀσεβείας γράψεται cf. Platonem, *Euthyphro*, 5c ‖ 256–258 Basil. Caes., *Epist.* 189, 4 (PG, 32, 688D)

---

245 *καὶ . . . ὁμολογοῦντες* non satis perspicio; cf. Basil. Caes., *Epist.* 189, 4 (PG, 32, 688C): ἀλλ' οὔτε πολλὰς λέγειν ἡ θεόπνευστος συγχωρεῖ διδασκαλία, εἴπου καὶ μέμνηται, μοναχῶς τῆς θεότητος μνημονεύουσα· ὅτι ἐν αὐτῷ κατοικεῖ πᾶν τὸ πλήρωμα τῆς θεότητος ‖ 252 εἴτ' M

62

exercises his judgment. But to agree neither with me nor with them is absolute atheism, for to believe neither in one nor in many divinities is manifestly to believe in none, and this is atheism. This is not my saying but that of the holy Fathers, from whom I have taken this quotation, though it will seem to belong to me rather than to the man who said it long ago, and he was Gregory of Nyssa telling us: "The matter is easy and clear. For he who condemns those who maintain one divinity by necessity will agree with the person who maintains many or none; it is impossible to think of anything other than what I have stated. But neither does the teaching of the Holy Scripture permit us to maintain many divinities, and when we acknowledge one divinity, ⟨we acknowledge⟩ that the whole fullness of divinity dwells in it. Therefore if, on the one hand, it is characteristic only of those who suffer from the delusion of polytheism to extend the number of divinities to a multitude, and on the other, it would be atheistic to deny altogether the one divinity, what is the reason for slandering us because we acknowledge one divinity?"

What does the defender of many divinities say to this? Will he then speak of uncreated energies and powers and forms and beauties and life and wisdom and the nature which transcends all these, and thus demand that we honor the multitude of divinities and indict for impiety the man who does not believe this? But "to extend the number of divinities to a multitude is characteristic only of those who suffer from the delusion of polytheism." Therefore, how can any man who honors the divine Gregory as a saint pay attention to Palamas' muck? And whoever holds a different opinion about the Saint is alien to the Church of Christ. How then can we obey such a man? Indeed, the Saint proved that this man worships extreme atheism, when he neither adheres to Palamas concerning the multitude of divinities nor approves of those who defend the doctrines concerning the Monad that shines with triple brightness. This great reasoning, therefore, would be something more monstrous than monstrosities and "stag-goats," if indeed it deserves even to be called reasoning rather than departure from all reasoning and extreme want of reason. For

σται γὰρ ὁ παλαιὸς λόγος, πάντα ἐν πᾶσι, τὸ τοιοῦτον πρᾶγμα· ὁ γὰρ αὐτὸς καὶ πολύθεος ἔσται καὶ ἅμα μὴ πολύθεος δόξει, καὶ οὔτε τοῦτο, οὔτ' ἐκεῖνο πάλιν, ἀλλὰ παντάπασιν ἄθεος κατὰ τὰ εἰρημένα.

Ὁ μὲν οὖν ἀεὶ τῇ ἀληθείᾳ πολέμιος τοσαύτην ἀσέβειαν καὶ οὕτω παντοδαπὴν καὶ ποικίλην κἂν τῷ παρόντι—καὶ νῦν γε ὑπερβαλλόντως ὥσπερ εἰς τὸν ἔσχατον τῆς ἀσε-[fol. 62r]βείας ἀφικόμενος ὅρον—τῆς ἐκκλησίας τοῦ Θεοῦ τῆς ἁγίας κατέχεε· σὺ δ' ᾧ πολλὴ θειότης συνοικεῖ καὶ σοφία καὶ τὸ παρὰ πάντων διὰ ταῦτα αἰδέσιμον πρόσεστιν, ὅση σοι δύναμις βοήθει τῇ εὐσεβείᾳ πρὸς αὐτῆς εὐσεβείας. μίμησαι τοὺς μεγάλους ἐκείνους Βασίλειον καὶ Γρηγόριον, οἳ τὰς ἐρήμους ἀφέντες ἐπειδὴ χειμαζομένας ᾔσθοντο τὰς ἐκκλησίας αἱρετικῇ τρικυμίᾳ, καίτοι πρὸς μεγάλας καὶ σκληρὰς δυνάμεις ἀντιφέρεσθαι μέλλοντες, ὅμως ἔδραμον καὶ συνεπλάκησαν, οὐδὲν ὑπολογισάμενοι, τοῖς ἐναντίοις ἀνυποστάτοις εἶναι δοκοῦσι παντάπασιν· ἀλλ' ἐπειδὴ προθύμως καὶ φιλοκινδύνως ἀνθίσταντο, κατὰ γνώμην ἀπήλλαξαν, τρεψάμενοι τοὺς πολεμίους καὶ ὡς ἐχρῆν ἀμυνάμενοι, καὶ τὰς ἐκκλησίας τοῦ Θεοῦ τῶν πολυτρόπων θηρῶν ἐξελόμενοι καὶ τοῦ λοιποῦ μετ' ἀσφαλείας οἰκεῖν καταστήσαντες. καὶ σύ που κατ' ἐκείνους τὴν ἀρετὴν καὶ σοφίαν, ὦ ἄριστε, οἱ δὲ τῆς νῦν αἱρέσεως ἔξαρχοι καὶ οἱ τούτοις συνήγοροι καὶ πρὸς τούτοις οἱ μέσοι πρὸς τοὺς πάλαι πολεμίους οὐδένες· εἰ γὰρ καὶ ἡμῶν ὑπερέχουσι διὰ τὴν ἡμετέραν εὐτέλειαν, σοί γε οὐδ' ἀντιβλέψουσι διὰ τὸ σὸν ὑπερέχον τοῖς ἅπασι. τοὺς δὲ φίλους ὄντας ἀποστήσεις τῆς πλάνης, εἰ μετὰ παρρησίας αὐτῶν τὸ ἀμαθὲς ἐλέγξεις—εἰ καὶ σοφοὶ δοκοῦσι—καὶ καταστελεῖς τὸν τῦφον ὡς οἷόν τε, ὑφ' ὧν ταῦτα πάσχουσι. * * * μηδὲ τῆς πρὸς τὸν δεῖνα καὶ τὸν δεῖνα δυσμενείας καὶ ἔχθρας, μηδὲ τῆς εἰς ἄλλον ἐλπίδος καὶ χάριτος—ταῦτα δὴ λέγω τὰ τοῦ πονηροῦ καὶ κοσμοκράτορος ἔγγονα καὶ τῆς ἐνταῦθα γενέσεως—τὸ τῆς ψυχῆς ἀγαθὸν ἐπιτρέπων προεῖσθαι καὶ τὴν εὐσέβειαν, καὶ ταὐτὸ πάσχειν ταῖς Αἰσώπου μελίτταις αἵ, τοὺς κλέπτας ἀφεῖσαι τοῦ μέλιτος ἀθῴους ἀπηλλάχθαι τῶν κέντρων, τὸν γεωργὸν ἐκέντουν μετ' ἐκείνους ἐλθόντα πρὸς ἐπιμέλειαν· λέγω δὲ οὐκ ἐμαυτὸν γεωργόν, ἀλλὰ τὸν πατριάρχην, οὐκ ἂν δὲ ὀκνήσαιμι πλὴν ἐμαυτοῦ καὶ ἄλλον τοῦτο ὀνομάσαι ὃς ἔχει γεωργικῶς περὶ τὸ κοινὸν ἀγαθόν, τὴν εὐσέβειαν, καὶ πρὸς τοὺς ταύτην λυμαινομένους οὐκ ἀνεκτῶς.

---

268 I Cor. 15:28; Eph. 1:23 || 274–275 Basil. Caes., *Epist.* 212, 2 (PG, 32, 781B)

292–293 *ἐλέγξοις* M || 293 *τύφον* M || 294 post *πάσχουσι* lacunam statui

62

such a thing will be, as the old saying goes, "all things to all men," because the same man will be both a polytheist and appear at the same time not to be a polytheist, and again neither this nor that, but altogether an atheist, according to what we said.

The perennial enemy of truth now too—indeed, now excessively, just as if he had attained "the extreme limit of impiety"—poured against the holy Church of God so much ungodliness and of so many forms and varieties. But you, with whom dwells so much holiness and wisdom and to whom for this reason accrues the respect of all, come with all your strength to the assistance of piety for the sake of piety itself. Imitate those great men, Basil and Gregory, who left the wilderness because they sensed that the Churches were exposed to the tempest of heresy, and, though they were to oppose great and cruel powers, yet they rushed and tangled with the enemy who seemed to be altogether irresistible, without taking anything into account. But because they resisted eagerly and daringly, they acquitted themselves in accordance with their wishes, for they routed their enemies and defended themselves against them as it was necessary, and delivered the Churches of God from the wily beasts and caused them to live securely henceforth. And you, my excellent friend, are not far from them in virtue and wisdom, while the leaders of the present heresy and their advocates and, in addition to them, the moderates, are nothing compared with the enemies of old. For if they excel me on account of my insignificance, they shall not even look straight at you because you excel everyone. And you will draw away from error the others who are your friends, if you will openly rebuke their ignorance, even though they appear to be wise, and will restrain as much as possible their arrogance whereby they suffer these * * * neither because of ill-will and hostility towards so-and-so and so-and-so nor because of expectations and favors from another (I mean, of course, the progeny of this life and the evil one and ruler of this world), allow to neglect the good of the soul and piety, and suffer the same thing as the bees of Aesop, which, after allowing those who stole the honey to escape without attacking them with their stings, were stinging the farmer who came afterwards to take care of them. And I do not call myself the farmer but the Patriarch. And I would not hesitate to call by this name, besides myself, another man also who cultivates the common good, piety, and does not tolerate those who insult it.

Εἰ δὲ διὰ τὴν ἄγαν ἡσυχίαν ᾗ σύνει καὶ τὴν ἀπραγμοσύνην δυσχερῶς ταῦτα φέρεις, ἀλλ' ἡμῖν γε συγγίνωσκε, οὓς ταῦτα λέγειν βιάζεται τεμνομένη θεότης καὶ κτίσις προσκυνουμένη πάλιν καὶ τρέχειν ἐπὶ τοὺς δυναμένους τιμωρεῖν εὐσεβείᾳ, ὧν σπάνις ἐν τῷ παρόντι. σὺ δὲ κἂν πλείστων ὄντων ὁ κορυφαῖος ἦσθα, καὶ νῦν [fol. 62^{v}] βουληθεὶς πολλοὺς τοὺς ἑπομένους ἕξεις καὶ πάντας, οἶμαι, ὁπόσοις δείξεις πολεμῶν ἐρρωμένως ταῖς ἀναισχύντοις γλώτταις· τῆς γὰρ ἐκκλησίας τοῦ Θεοῦ μισούσης μὲν τὴν πλάνην ταύτην καὶ ἐλαυνούσης εἰς δύναμιν, ἀπορούσης δὲ τῆς κατὰ σὲ σοφίας καὶ ἀρετῆς καὶ γλώττης, εἰ μᾶλλον πνεύσοις—ἔπνευσας γὰρ δὴ καὶ προτοῦ καὶ πολλοῖς γε ἐκείνων ὥσπερ πνεῦμα ἰσχυρὸν κονιορτοῖς ἐγένου—νῦν δὲ καὶ σφοδρότερος πνεύσας, τὴν συρφετώδη ταύτην κουφότητα, κἂν ἄλλως ἔχειν τι δοκῇ καὶ βάρους, εἰσάπαξ διασκεδάσεις.

63. Τῷ θειοτάτῳ πατριάρχῃ κῦρ Ἰωάννῃ

Τολμήσω τι φθέγξασθαι ἀπὸ καρδίας μέσης πρὸς τὸ σὸν θεῖον ὕψος καὶ τοῖς θείοις λογίοις κεχρήσομαι τολμηρῶς μέν, οἰκείως δέ πως τῷ κατ' ἐμὲ κλυδωνίῳ ὑφ' οὗ νῦν χειμάζομαι. ἀπέστρεψας ἀπ' ἐμοῦ τὸ πρόσωπόν σου καὶ ἐγενήθην τεταραγμένος, πάντων ἐπ' ἐμὲ λυπηρῶν συρρεόντων, καὶ γλῶσσαι διάβολοι κατισχύουσι τῆς ἐμῆς ταπεινώσεως. ἀντὶ τοῦ ἀγαπᾶν με, ἐνδιέβαλόν με, ἐπεὶ κατεδίωκον ἀγαθωσύνην. ἐνέτειναν τόξον αὐτῶν τοῦ καταβαλεῖν πτωχὸν καὶ πένητά με. ἕως πότε ὑψωθήσεται ὁ ἐχθρός μου ἐπ' ἐμέ; ἵνα τί ὑπνοῖς δέσποτα; ἀνάστηθι καὶ μὴ ἀπώσῃ εἰς τέλος. ἀποκατάστησον τὴν ψυχήν μου ἀπὸ κακουργίας αὐτῶν, ἀπὸ λεόντων τὴν μονογενῆ μου.

Ἦ γὰρ οὐ λέων καὶ θηριώδης φύσις Μηνᾶς ὁ γειτονεύων ἐμοί; ὃς ἀντὶ τῆς βοηθείας ἧς αὐτοῖς συνηράμην, ὡς ἦν ἐμοὶ δυνατόν, καὶ τῆς εὐπρεποῦς καὶ νομίμου Χριστιανοῖς εὐλαβείας εἰς τὸν τὰ πάντα

63: 4–6 Ps. 29(30):7–8 ‖ 7 cf. Ps. 9:13; 21(22):21 et alii loci per multi ‖ 7–8 *ἀντὶ . . . με*: Ps. 108(109):4 ‖ 8–9 *ἐπεὶ . . . ἀγαθωσύνην*: Ps. 37(38):20 ‖ 9–10 Ps. 36(37):14 ‖ 10–11 *ἕως . . . ἐμέ*: Ps. 12(13):2 ‖ 11–12 *ἵνα . . . τέλος*: Ps. 43(44):23 ‖ 12–14 Ps. 34(35): 17–18

63: M 41^{v}–42^{r}.
8 *ἐνδιέβαλλον* M ‖ 15 *ἢ* M

And if, on account of the absolute peace and inactivity in which you live, you find these ⟨words⟩ annoying, please bear with me, for the division of the Divinity and the worship anew of the created world force me to say these things and to pursue those who can avenge piety and are now scarce. But even if there were many, you would have been the foremost, and now if you wished, you will have many followers, and I believe that you will be followed by all those to whom you will show that you are fighting bravely against the impudent tongues. For since the Church of God hates this deceit and is driving it out to the best of its ability, but is in need of your wisdom and virtue and eloquence, if you will blow more strongly—because you did before and were to many of them as a strong wind is to dust—but if you blow even more powerfully now, you will scatter once and for all this light rubbish, even though it may otherwise appear to carry some weight.

63. To the most divine Patriarch lord John

I will venture to utter a word to your divine Sublimity from the depth of my heart and I will use the Holy Scripture in a manner that is bold but, somehow, appropriate for the storm that is now buffeting me. "Thou didst take away thy face and I was troubled," since all sorrows are converging on me and slanderous tongues overpower "my lowliness." "Instead of loving me, they falsely accuse me, because I followed goodness. They have bent their bow to cast down poor and needy me. How long shall my enemy be exalted over me? Wherefore sleepest thou, my lord? Rise and do not cast me off forever. Deliver my soul from their mischief, my only-begotten one from the lions."

Truly, is not Menas, my neighbor, a lion and a ferocious creature? In return for the assistance I offered them, as best I could, and for reverence for God, proper and customary for Christians—God the Maker of all, the invisible, the incomprehensi-

πεποιηκότα Θεόν, τὸν ἀόρατον, τὸν ἀκατανόητον καὶ τοῖς ἀγγέλοις αὐτοῖς, ἀναιδείᾳ πάσῃ χρησάμενος πρῶτον μὲν ξίφει με ἀνελεῖν ἐπεχείρησεν, εὐπορῶν τυραννίδος ἧς ἤθελεν· ἐπεὶ δὲ αὐτῷ τοῦτο οὐκ εἰς πέρας ἐλήλυθεν ἄκοντι, τῆς παντοδυνάμου δεξιᾶς τοῦ φανεροῦ με φόνου ἐξαρπασάσης τότε καὶ τοῦτον ἀφελομένης τὴν ἐπιχείρησιν, οὐ παύεται πάντα κινῶν [fol. 42ʳ] ἐξ ἐκείνου καὶ κακουργῶν ἐπ' ἐμοί, καὶ οὐχ ἧττω μοι κακὰ παλαμώμενος ὁ παλαμναῖος ὄντως ἢ ὁ χαλκεὺς Ἀλέξανδρος τῷ θειοτάτῳ Παύλῳ.

Δίδωσί μοι γὰρ εἰπεῖν καὶ τοῦτο τὰ πράγματα τετολμηκέναι καθ' ἑκάστην φαινόμενα· πάντα δὴ κεκινηκὼς ἐφ' ἡμᾶς ἰταμώτατα—ὕβρεις, λοιδορίας, συκοφαντίας—ἴσχυσε νῦν τοσοῦτον, ὥστ' ἀποκλεῖσαί μοι τὴν θυρίδα ἐκείνην ἧς χάριν ἀνῆλθε δεῦρο ἡ κηδεμονικωτάτη περὶ ἐμέ σου ψυχή. καὶ ἡ μὲν ἀποκέκλειται, ἡ δὲ σὴ χάρις λέλυται, καὶ ἡ πρᾶξις ἀνῄρηται, ἡμεῖς δὲ ἐν ἀπορίᾳ τοῦ διοδεύειν ἔξω καὶ ὧν ἄνθρωπος χρῄζει, ὅστις ποτ' ἄν, κατὰ πᾶσαν ἀνάγκην ἐπισιτίζεσθαι. ἐπεγγελᾷ δὲ τούτοις ἅπασι Μηνᾶς καὶ ἐφήδεται καὶ ἀτεχνῶς ὀρχεῖται καί φησιν εὖγε, εὖγε. ταῦτα ἀντὶ τῶν πολλῶν ἐκείνων καὶ καλῶν, οἶμαι, λόγων ὑπὲρ τοῦ θειοτάτου βασιλέως καὶ τοῦ θεαυγεστάτου τῆς οἰκουμένης λύχνου; ταῦτα ἀντὶ τῆς εἰς τὸ θεῖον εὐλαβείας καὶ τοὺς θείους ὅρους τῆς εὐσεβείας ἀκραιφνοῦς καὶ ἀκηράτου στοργῆς; ἐγὼ δὲ ἐλπίζω μὲν ἐρεῖν, ἔχων τὸν ἐμαυτοῦ δεσπότην μετὰ Θεὸν ἀντιλήπτορα, ἐπεῖδεν ὁ ὀφθαλμός μου ἐν τοῖς ἐχθροῖς μου καὶ ἐν τοῖς ἐπανιστaμένοις ἐπ' ἐμὲ πονηρευομένοις ἀκούσεται τὸ οὖς μου· εἰ δὲ νικᾷ τὰ χείρω, καὶ ταῦτα ὑπομενῶ μετ' ἀγαθῆς ἐλπίδος, ῥωννύμενος τὴν ψυχὴν πρὸς τὸ φέρειν ὑπὲρ τῆς εὐσεβείας ταῦτα τῇ τοῦ Θεοῦ δυνάμει.

64. ⟨Τῷ σκευοφύλακι⟩

Ἆρ' ἐπελάθου τῆς φιλίας ἐκείνης ἣν πρῴην ἔχειν πρὸς ἡμᾶς ὡμολόγεις καὶ ἐσαεὶ τηρήσειν; ἀλλ' οὐ πιστεύω· οὐ γὰρ εὐμεταβόλοις ἔοικας καὶ ἀστάτοις ἀνδράσιν, ἀλλὰ σφόδρα τὸ φιλεῖν ἐρ-

---

19–20 cf. Josue 11:12; 3 Mac. 7:5 ‖ 25 II Tim. 4:14 ‖ 35 Ps. 34(35):25 ‖ 40–43 Ps. 91(92):11

28–29 *ἱταμώτατα* M

64: M 63ᵛ–64ʳ.

1 Titulum ex linea 8 supplevi

ble even to the angels themselves—it was he who endeavored first to "annihilate me by the sword," using every kind of shameless means, free as he was to make use of his tyranny at will. Since, then, he unwillingly failed to accomplish this ⟨design⟩ of his (for the almighty hand of God snatched me away at that time from flagrant murder and prevented his attempt), he has not ceased since then to stir everything up and do me harm and, as a truly murderous character, to devise against me schemes no less vicious than the ⟨schemes⟩ of "Alexander the coppersmith" against the most divine Paul.

The facts themselves, as they appear every day, give me the courage to say this as well. After he had shamelessly stirred everything up against me—insults, abuses, calumnies—he has at this point become so powerful that he closed up for me that little opening for which you, my protector, came up here. This, then, has been closed, and your favor has been undone and the deed annulled, while I am unable to go out and provide myself with the things that a man, whoever he may be, absolutely requires for sustenance. Menas, on the other hand, laughs at all this and rejoices and simply dances and says: "Good! Good!" Is this in return, I presume, for the many and beautiful things I said in honor of the most divine Emperor and the divinely shining Light of the inhabited world? Is this in return for my reverence for God and my pure and undefiled love for the sacred laws of piety? But I, with my lord as my protector after God, hope to say: "And mine eye has seen mine enemies and mine ear shall hear the wicked that rise up against me." Yet, if the worse prevails, I shall endure this, too, with good hope, fortifying my soul with the strength of God to bear it for the sake of piety.

64. ⟨To the Keeper of the Holy Vessels⟩

Did you really forget the friendship which you recently confessed that you had for me and which you were to keep forever? But I do not believe it! For you resemble not fickle and unstable men, but men who are very strong in friendship.

ρωμένοις. πῶς οὖν ὁ δεῖνα καθ' ἡμῶν στασιάζει, σοῦ ζῶντος καὶ δυναμένου μὴ μόνον ἐκεῖνον παιδεῦσαι μὴ ἀμαθαίνειν, ἀλλὰ καὶ τοὺς δι' ὑπεροχὴν οὐδ' ἀξιοῦντας προσαγορεύειν αὐτόν; ἀνα-[fol. 64r]στήτω δὴ νῦν γε σκευοφύλαξ ὁ βέλτιστος, ὁ μὴ πρότερον ἀναστὰς οὐκ οἶδα ὅπως κατὰ τῶν δυσσεβούντων, καὶ πεσεῖται αὐτίκα τὸ πονηρὸν τοῦ π ν ε υ μ α τ ι κ ο ῦ τούτου πνεῦμα, καὶ τὸ θεῖον Πνεῦμα θεραπευθήσεται· ὃ λυπεῖν οὗτος σπουδάζει διὰ τοῦ χείρονος, τὸ γὰρ τῆς πλεονεξίας καὶ στασιῶδες πνεῦμα πονηρόν ἐστι καὶ δαιμόνιον καὶ τῷ θείῳ πολέμιον.

65. Sine titulo

Τὴν μὲν πολλὴν καὶ ἀπέραντον φλυαρίαν τῶν Παλαμναίων καὶ καινῶν κηρυγμάτων οὐ ῥᾴδιον ἦν σοι ἐκγεγραφότα πέμψαι, ὡς ὑπεσχόμην πρῴην, ἄλλως τε καὶ τῆς σῆς πρὸς τὴν ὑπερφυᾶ καὶ παντουργὸν μονάδα ἑνώσεως οὐκ ἂν ἀνασχομένης εἰς ἀκαιρίαν πολλὴν καὶ διαίρεσιν ἑαυτὴν ἐπιδοῦναι. πολλὴ γοῦν ἐστι καὶ δεινῶς ἀόριστος ἀδολεσχία, πολλαχῇ παραπαίουσα καὶ εἰς οὐδὲν ὡρισμένον καθισταμένη· τοιοῦτο γὰρ ἥ γε τοῦ ψεύδους φύσις. ἃ δ' ἦν καὶ ἀναγκαῖα τὴν σὴν σοφίαν ἰδεῖν καὶ εὐσύνοπτα, ταῦτά σοι τῶν ἄλλων ἀπολαβόντες πεπόμφαμεν, τῷ γενναίῳ προβόλῳ μὲν τῆς εὐσεβείας ἡμῖν, πρηστῆρι δὲ τῆς δυσσεβείας ταύτης, ἐν οἷς πεφανέρωται τὰ δυσσεβήματα καὶ οὐδεμίαν ἔχει πρόφασιν, οὐδ' ὅλως ἀποφυγὴν τὸ μὴ οὐ πάντως οὕτω κείμενα δυσσεβέστατα εἶναι καὶ φανερῶς ἀντικείμενα τοῖς κειμένοις ἡμῖν τῆς εὐσεβείας ὅροις.

Τοῦτο δὴ πεποιήκαμεν μεθ' ἡδονῆς θαυμαστῆς, ὅτι σε τοιοῦτον ἡμῖν τῆς εὐσεβείας ἀνέδειξε νῦν ὁ Θεὸς προστάτην ἐν ἀπορίᾳ δεινῇ τῶν οὐκ ἀνεχομένων λαλιᾶς ἀλλοκότου λωποδυτούσης ἡμῖν τὰ ἐπιχώρια δόγματα τῆς εὐσεβείας καὶ ὧν ἐσμεν τρόφιμοι. σὸν οὖν ἐστι καὶ τῆς εὐσεβείας καὶ θαυμοστῆς σοφίας τὰ κακῶς εἰσκωμάσαντα ταῦτα τῇ ἐκκλησίᾳ Χριστοῦ κάκιον ἀνακεχωρηκότα καὶ ἀπολωλότα δεῖξαι.

Ἡμεῖς δὲ καὶ πρότερον ποιοῦντες ὅπερ ἐκέλευσας καὶ νῦν ἔτι τὴν κέλευσιν ἀσπασάμενοι, ἅτε καὶ συνήθη προστεταγμένην ἡμῖν,

---

64: 10 cf. I Cor. 2:15; Palamas, *Trias* 1, 3, 13, Syngrammata, I, 423, 4–7

65: Mn 8r. Ed. Uspenskij, *Synodikon*, 79; ed. Karpozilos, *Letters*, 95, no. 9.
2 post *καινῶν* scripsit et deinde delevit *δογμάτων* Mn || 18 leg. *καὶ τῆς σῆς εὐσεβείας*?

How, then, does that fellow agitate against me, while you are alive and able not only to teach him not to be ignorant, but even ⟨to teach⟩ those who because of their superiority do not even deign speak to him? And so let the excellent Keeper of the holy vessels rise now—I do not quite understand how he did not rise earlier against the impious!—and the evil spirit of this man "gifted with the Spirit" will fall down immediately, and the Holy Spirit will be honored. It is the Holy Spirit that he is seeking to hurt through the evil one, for the spirit of arrogance and sedition is evil and diabolical and hostile to the Holy Spirit.

65. No Addressee

It was not easy to copy and send to you the great, indeed infinite, nonsense of the Palamnaian and new doctrines that are being proclaimed, as I promised earlier. Besides, you who are united with the marvelous and all-creating Monad could not bear to indulge in such impropriety and division. It is indeed such terribly vague talk, foolish in many ways and settling down to nothing definite; for such is the nature of falsehood. But I separated from the rest what was intelligible as well as necessary for your Wisdom to see and sent this to you, our noble defender of piety and our flash of lightning against this impiety. In these excerpts the impious doctrines are revealed and they have no excuse and no escape from the fact that as they stand they are, without doubt, most impious and manifestly opposed to our established laws of piety.

I did this with extraordinary pleasure, seeing that God appointed you such a guardian of our piety now, at a time when there is a terrible dearth of men who do not put up with outlandish talk which robs us of our native doctrines of piety with which we have been nourished. It is up to you, then, and your piety and extraordinary wisdom to make these doctrines, which burst in wretchedly upon the Church of Christ, leave and come to an even more wretched end!

As for myself, having in the past done what you bade me do, now again I followed your bidding eagerly, inasmuch as it enjoins what is also my practice. I

ἠρεμοῦμεν παντάπασι πρὸς ἡμᾶς αὐτοὺς καθάπαξ ἐπεστραμμένοι, καίτοι τῶν λοιμῶν τούτων καθ' ἡμέραν τὴν νόσον τὴν ἑαυτῶν καταβαλλόντων διὰ τῆς πόλεως, ὥσπερ ἐπ' αὐτῷ γεγενημένων τούτῳ, ἐφ' ᾧ μήτε αὐτοὺς εὐσεβεῖν καὶ ἡσυχίαν ἄγειν, μήτε τοὺς ἄλλους ἐᾶν. ὁ δὲ βραβεύων ἡμῖν τὴν ἡσυχίαν τήνδε καὶ διὰ τέλους βραβεύσειας εἰς ἅπαν ἡμῶν τὸ δεινὸν ἀπαλλάξας.

66. Sine titulo

Ἔδει μέν, ὦ γενναῖε, μὴ νῦν ἀμφίβολον ἡμῖν τὴν εὐσέβειαν εἶναι, μηδὲ μετὰ τοσοῦτον χρόνον τῆς κατὰ σάρκα ἐπιδημίας Χριστοῦ καὶ τῆς δι' αὐτοῦ λαμψάσης τηλαυγῶς ἀληθείας καὶ τὰς ἀποστολικὰς ἀκτῖνας καὶ τὰς συνοδικὰς μαρμαρυγὰς ἐκείνας, προσδοκωμένης ἤδη τῆς προρρηθείσης μετασκευῆς τοῦ παντός, νῦν ἀμφισβητεῖσθαι πότερον μίαν θεότητα ἀπαράλλακτον ἐν τῇ θείᾳ Τριάδι ἢ πλῆθος θεοτήτων ἀνίσων καὶ ἀνομοίων προσκυνητέον, καὶ πότερον ἀνείδεος ὁ Θεὸς καὶ ἀόρατος, ἢ μεμορφωμένος καὶ ὁρατὸς αἰσθητῶς [fol. 6^{r}] τισι σωματικοῖς ὀφθαλμοῖς ἐν φυσικῇ καὶ οὐσιώδει μορφῇ, καὶ ταὐτὸ μορφὴ Θεοῦ καὶ φύσις καὶ μηδενὶ τῶν ὄντων καθ' ἑαυτὸ θεατόν, ἵνα μὴ σύνθετος ᾖ, ἢ σύνθετος ὁ Θεὸς ἐκ πολλῶν καὶ διαφόρων συγκείμενος, ἀοράτου καὶ ὁρατοῦ, ἀμεθέκτου καὶ μεθεκτῶν, ἐνεργοῦντος καὶ ἐνεργουμένων, ὑπερκειμένου καὶ ὑφειμένων ἀπειράκις ἀπείρως, οὗ τί γένοιτ' ἂν συνθετώτερον ἢ ἀσεβέστερον ἐπὶ τοῦ θείου φρονεῖν; ἔτι δὲ πότερον αὐτὸ τὸ θεῖόν ἐστιν ἐν ἡμῖν ἀοράτως τὸ καὶ δημιουργῆσαν ἡμᾶς καὶ συνέχον καὶ προνοούμενον, καὶ Θεοῦ ναός εἰσι τοῦ πάντων ὑπερκειμένου, ἢ ἑτέρας θεότητος ὑφειμένης ἐκείνου οἷς ἐνοικεῖν Θεὸς λέγεται; καὶ ὁ Θεὸς Λόγος ἐστὶ τὸ φῶς τὸ ἀληθινὸν ὃ φωτίζει πάντα ἄνθρωπον ἐρχόμενον εἰς τὸν κόσμον καὶ ὁ Πατὴρ αὐτοῦ καὶ τὸ Πνεῦμα τὸ ἅγιον, ἢ ἑτέρα

66: 10 cf. Joan. Dam., *Dialect.*, 41 (PG, 94, 608B) || 11 cf. Basil. Caes., *Adv. Eunom.* IV, 1 (PG, 29, 673B) || 13–14 ὑπερκειμένου καὶ ὑφειμένων cf. Palamam, *Epist. III ad Acindynum*, 15, Syngrammata, I, 306, 18–20; ed. Nadal, 252, 10–12 || 14 Maxim. Conf., *Capit. theol.*, 1, 49 (PG, 90, 1101A) = Palamas, *Dialexis*, 24, Syngrammata, I, 186, 26; *Epist. ad Gabram*, 5, Syngrammata, II, 332, 12 || 17 I Cor. 3:16; II Cor. 6:16 || 19 cf. Palamam, *Epist. III ad Acindynum*, 15, Syngrammata, I, 306, 18–20; ed. Nadal, 252, 10–12 || 18–19 II Cor. 6:16 || 19–21 Joan. 1:9

---

23 ἐπεστρα[μ]μένοι Mn || 26 αὐτοὺς Mn

66: Mn 5^{v}–7^{r}. Ed. Karpozilos, *Letters*, 87–89, no. 7.

4 ἐκεῖνας Mn || 9 σωματικοῖς] τικοῖς Mn

remain absolutely quiet and have turned inwards to myself once and for all, though these pests spread their disease daily through the city as if they were born for this very purpose, ⟨namely⟩, to allow neither themselves nor others to be pious and at peace. But may you who award me this peace as a prize award it permanently and remove the suffering from me altogether!

66. No Addressee

Our piety, my gallant friend, should not be ambiguous now, and, such a long time after the incarnation of Christ and the truth which shone far and brightly through Him, and the Apostolic rays and those synodic sparks, while the prophesied transformation of the Universe is presently expected, we should surely not now question whether we must worship one divinity without variations in the Holy Trinity or a multitude of unequal and dissimilar divinities; and whether God is without form and invisible or has a form and is visible, through the senses, to certain bodily eyes in His natural and essential form; and whether the form and the nature of God are the same thing and this in itself is not visible to any being lest He be composite, or God is composite, compounded of many and different elements, visible and invisible, capable of being shared and incapable of being shared, activating and activated, "higher and infinitely lower." What could be more compounded and impious to believe about God than this? And, further, whether God Himself is within us invisibly, He Who created us and sustains us and provides for us, and whether those in whom it is said that God dwells are "temples of the" all-transcendent "God" or of another divinity lower than God; and whether the "real light which enlightens every man born into the world" is God the Logos and His Father and the Holy Spirit, or another divinity which is some other light besides the Father and Son and

66

θεότης φῶς οὖσά τι ἕτερον παρὰ τὸν Πατέρα, τὸν Υἱόν, τὸ Πνεῦμα τὸ παντουργόν, καὶ ὑφειμένη τούτων ἀπειράκις ἀπείρως, ἄκτιστος δέ, εἶθ' ὁρατὴ σωματικοῖς ὀφθαλμοῖς, ἡ τοὺς ἁγίους φωτίζουσα καὶ φῶς αὐτοὺς ποιοῦσα κατὰ τὴν νέαν πλάνην; καὶ τί μὲν ἄκτιστον, τί δὲ κτιστόν, τὸ ὑφειμένον τῆς θείας φύσεως ἀπειράκις ἀπείρως καὶ ἐνεργούμενον καὶ ὁρατὸν σωματικοῖς ὀφθαλμοῖς ὡς ἡ καινότης λέγει, τοῦτο ἄκτιστον ὡς Παλαμᾶς ἀποφαίνεται, ἢ τὸ μηθ' ὑφειμένον, μήτ' ἐνεργούμενον, μήθ' ὁρατὸν αἰσθητῶς ὡς ἡ θεόφρων τοῦ Θεοῦ ἐκκλησία; καὶ τὸ μεταληπτὸν ἀλλ' οὐ μεταληπτικόν, καὶ τὸ θεοῦν, οὐ θεούμενον, καὶ τὸ μετεχόμενον, οὐχ ἑτέρου μετέχον, ἃ περὶ τίνος λέγεται, τοῦ πάντων ὑπερέχοντος Πνεύματος, ἢ τοῦ τῆς θείας ὑφειμένου φύσεως ἀπειράκις ἀπείρως καὶ ἐνεργουμένου καὶ ὁρατοῦ σωματικοῖς ὀφθαλμοῖς κατὰ τὴν Παλαμῆτιν πλάνην;

Ταῦτα τοίνυν οὐκ ἐχρῆν εἶναι τοῖς εὐσεβέσιν, ὡς ἔφην, ἀμφισβητήσιμα, μηδ' οὕτως εἶναι ἀμφιβόλους τοὺς ὅρους τῆς εὐσεβείας ὥσπερ ἐν νυκτομαχίᾳ τοὺς οἰκείους ἀλλήλοις. ἐπεὶ δὲ καὶ τἄλλα ὁρῶμεν ἀνατρεπόμενα—γῆν ἀστατοῦσαν, θάλατταν τοὺς ἑαυτῆς ὑπερβαίνουσαν ὅρους, τὰ θειότατα τῶν ἔργων διαλυόμενα, μηδὲ τῶν ἐνταῦθα οἰκειοτάτων αὐτῷ τοῦ Θεοῦ φειδομένου, τυραννίδων ἀτόπων ἐπαναστάσεις, Χριστιανοὺς Χριστιανοῖς ἐπάγοντας ὄλεθρον ἐκ τῶν ἀθεωτάτων—διὰ ταῦτα ἐφῆκεν ὁ Θεός, οἶμαι, καὶ εἰς τὴν ἐκκλησίαν τὴν ἑαυτοῦ τοσοῦτον πλάνον καὶ ὄλεθρον, μᾶλλον δὲ διὰ τοῦτον ἐκεῖνα. οἱ γὰρ θεότητα τέμνοντες εὐδοκιμοῦσι μᾶλλον τῶν μὴ τοῦτο τολμώντων, καὶ πάντ' ἄνω κάτω γίνεται· τὰ πάτρια δόγματα τῆς εὐσεβείας ὡς ἀσεβῆ διαβάλλεται, τὰ νέα καὶ πρόσφατα καὶ τοῖς κειμένοις ἀντίθετα ὡς εὐσεβῆ προσλαμβάνεται, τὸ τῶν Χριστιανῶν εἰπών τις ὅτι μία θεότης, ἁπλῆ, ἀόρατος, Κρονικός τις δοκεῖ καὶ Διιπολιώδης, πρὸς μέντοι καὶ δυσσεβὴς τοῖς Παλαμᾷ μεταπεισθεῖσι τὸ Ἑλληνικὸν ὅτι πολλαὶ καὶ διάφοροι καὶ ὁραταί. καὶ προσέσχον οἱ πολλοὶ καὶ ἐθαύμασαν ὡς θεόπτην τὸν λέγοντα, καὶ θεόπτην οἷον [fol. 6ᵛ] οὐδένα πω πεφηνέναι συνέβη, κνηθόμενοι τὴν ἀκοήν, κατὰ τὸν εἰρηκότα, καὶ τῶν πάλαι κειμένων ἐμπεπλησμένοι.

---

23 Maxim. Conf., *Capit. theol.*, 1, 49 (PG, 90, 1101A) = Palamas, *Dialexis*, 24, Syngrammata, II, 186, 26; *Epist. ad Gabram*, 5, Syngrammata, II, 332, 12 ‖ 26–27 *ibid.* ‖ 33–34 *ibid.* ‖ 46 Gregorius Cyprius I, 61 (Leutsch-Schneidewin, II, 61) ‖ 50 Aristophanes, *Nubes*, 984 ‖ 54 II Tim. 4:3

---

41 αὐτῷ Mn ‖ 50 διηπολιώδης Mn

66

the all-creating Spirit and "infinitely" lower than They, but uncreated, yet visible to bodily eyes, enlightening the saints and turning them into light, according to the new delusion. Nor should we ask what is uncreated and what created, or whether, as Palamas declares, this is uncreated: ⟨namely⟩, that which is "infinitely" lower than the divine nature and activated and visible to bodily eyes (as the new doctrine says), or ⟨whether it be⟩ that which is neither lower nor activated nor visible through the senses (as the godly-minded Church of God declares). And ⟨we should not ask⟩ about whom are all these things said—⟨namely⟩, that it can be partaken of but it does not partake, and that it deifies but it is not deified, and that it is shared but it does not share in anything—⟨whether they are said⟩ about the Spirit Which excels all or about that which is "infinitely" lower than the divine nature and activated and visible to bodily eyes, according to the Palamite delusion.

These things, as I said, should now not be questioned by the pious, nor should the laws of piety be so attacked by both sides just like friends in a night battle. But since we see that other things are also being turned upside down, that the earth quakes, the sea overflows, the sacred buildings are falling apart (and here God does not spare even His very own) strange tyrannies rise up, Christians bring destruction upon Christians by the hand of the most infidel, because of all this, I believe, God sent such delusion and ruin even upon His Church, or rather it was because of the delusion that he sent the calamities. For those who cut up the Divinity are more esteemed than those who do not dare to do this, and everything "is turned upside down." The ancestral doctrines of piety are falsely accused as impious; the new and recent ⟨doctrines⟩, ⟨which are⟩ opposed to the established ones are accepted as pious. If one cites the Christian doctrine that "There is one divinity, simple, invisible," he seems to be old-fashioned and "out-of-date" and, in addition, of course, impious to those who have been persuaded by Palamas to change to the pagan belief that there are many and different and visible ⟨divinities⟩. And the many heeded and admired Palamas as a God-seeing man and a God-seeing man such as had not happened to appear up to now, because "their ears are itching," as the saying goes, and they have had their fill of the old established doctrines.

66

Καὶ ταῦτα γίνεται διὰ πολλὴν τοῦ κωλύσοντος τὴν ἐρημίαν· ἐξ οὗ καὶ τὸ τῆς ἐκκλησίας κράτος μετὰ τῶν ἑαυτῆς δογμάτων δεύτερον τῶν καινοφώνων, μᾶλλον δὲ οὐδὲ δεύτερον, ἀλλά που ἀπεωσμένον. καὶ Χριστὸς μὲν βοῶν, ἐν ταῖς ἐσχάταις ἡμέραις ἐγερθήσονται ψευδόχριστοι καὶ τερατίαι λέγοντες· ἰδοὺ ὧδε ὁ Χριστὸς καὶ ἰδοὺ ἐκεῖ· ἀλλ' ὑμεῖς αὐτοῖς μὴ πεισθῆτε, μηδὲ πιστεύετε, οὐ πιστεύεται· οἱ δὲ λέγοντες "ἰδοὺ ὧδε θεότης ἄκτιστος, ὁρατὴ σωματικοῖς ὀφθαλμοῖς" ἡδέως πιστεύονται.

Ἆρ' οὖν οὐχὶ καὶ ὁ Χριστὸς τὰ δεύτερα φέρει παρὰ τούτοις τῶν καινοτόμων τῆς πίστεως; οἳ τὸν μὲν Χριστὸν καὶ τὸν αὐτοῦ Πατέρα καὶ τὸ Πνεῦμα τὸ ἅγιον, τὴν μίαν ἐν τοῖς τρισὶ θεότητα καὶ δύναμιν ἐξελαύνουσι τῶν ἑαυτῆς κτισμάτων ὥσπερ ἐξούλης δράκοντες, ἄλλους δὲ θεοὺς καὶ θεότητας δημιουργοὺς καὶ προνοητὰς τοῦ παντὸς καὶ δωροδότας πᾶσιν ἀντεπεισάγουσι. ταῦτ' οὐ θρήνων ἄξια; ταῦτ' οὐ δακρύων ἄξια; ταῦτ' οὐ τῶν γεγονότων καὶ γινομένων καὶ ἔτ' ἐσομένων περὶ ἡμᾶς χαλεπωτέρων, οἶμαι, τῶν πρότερον; ἀλλ' ἐπειδήπερ ἐσχάτη ὥρα ἐστί, κατὰ τὰς τοῦ Κυρίου προρρήσεις καὶ τῶν αὐτοῦ μαθητῶν, καθ' ἣν ἀντίχριστος ἔρχεται, ὑφ' οὗ καὶ τοὺς ἐκλεκτοὺς ἀκούομεν πλανηθήσεσθαι, οὗ προδρόμους εἶναι δεῖ τινας καὶ ὑπηρέτας, ἔδει δὲ καὶ αἱρέσεις ἐν ἡμῖν εἶναι, κατὰ τὸν εἰρηκότα, ἵνα οἱ δόκιμοι φανεροὶ γένωνται, οὐ σφόδρα ταρακτέον τοῖς ὁρωμένοις, οἶμαι, οὐδὲ μαλθακιστέον, ἀλλὰ καὶ μάλιστα νῦν ὁπλιστέον ἐπὶ τὴν ὕδραν ταύτην· δοτέον δὲ καὶ λόγον ἑτοίμως παντὶ τῷ γε ἡμᾶς αἰτοῦντι περὶ τῆς ἐν ἡμῖν ἐλπίδος, ὡς δεδιδάγμεθα.

Ἃ τοίνυν ἐκέλευσας ἐν ὡς οἷόν τε βραχέσιν ἐκθέμενος πέπομφα, σὺ δ' ἐπελθών, ὦ θαυμάσιε, τὰ δ' ἡμέτερα ταῦτα καὶ τἄλλα ἐπίσκεψαι κατὰ σχολήν, συνετώτατε, καὶ εἰ μὲν ὡς οἰκεῖα καὶ κοινὰ τῆς ἐκκλησίας δόγματα κρινεῖς τε καὶ ἀποδέξῃ, χάρις Θεῷ· εἰ δέ τι καὶ χρῇζον ἐνίδοις ἐπανορθώσεως, ἐπανόρθου καὶ ἡμεῖς ἡδέως ἀποδεξόμεθα. μόνον σῳζέσθω ἡμῖν ἡ πάντων αἰτία Τριὰς ἐν μονάδι θεότητος, καὶ μία θεότης ἐν τρισὶν ὑποστάσεσιν· ἀμερής, ἀδιαίρετος, ἀόρατος, ἀναφής, ἀκατάληπτος καὶ μόνη ἄκτιστός τε καὶ προ-

---

56–57 Demosthenes, *Philip.* I, 49 ‖ 59–62 cf. Matt. 24:22–27 ‖ 67–68 Greg. Naz., *Or.*40, 41 (PG, 36, 417B) ‖ 73 I Joan. 2:18 ‖ 74–76 Matt. 24:24 ‖ 76–77 I Cor. 11:19 ‖ 80–81 I Pet. 3:15

---

69 *δράκοντες* scripsi: *διώκοντες*: Karpozilos: δ[·]*άκοντες* Mn ‖ 73 *ὥρα*] *ἄρα* Mn: cf. I Joan. 2:18

66

And these things happen because "there is none to hinder them," for which reason even the head of the Church together with its doctrines are secondary to the innovators, or rather, not even secondary but thrust away somewhere. Even Christ is not believed when He cries out: "In the last days, false messiahs and impostors will come saying, 'Look, here is Christ,' and 'There he is,' but do not listen to them nor believe them"; but, on the other hand, those who say: "look, here is an uncreated divinity, visible to bodily eyes" are gladly believed.

Is it not true, then, that for these men even Christ takes a second place to the innovators of the faith who, just as if they were serpents of ejectment, expel Christ and His Father and the Holy Spirit, the "one divinity and power in three ⟨hypostases⟩," from Their own creation, and introduce instead other gods and divinities, creators and supervisors of the Universe and givers of gifts to all? Are not these things worthy of lamentation? Are they not worthy of tears? Is this not what has happened around us, and what is happening, and will still happen and will be harder to bear, I fear, than before? But since, according to the predictions of the Lord and His disciples,, "It is the last hour" when "the anti-Christ is coming," by whom we hear that "even the elect shall be deceived," whose forerunners and servants some men ought to be, and "dissensions among us were necessary, if only to show which of the members are sound," as he said, I believe that we must not be too disturbed by what we see, nor must we be remiss, but we must now above all take arms against this "many-headed serpent" and "be ready with our defense whenever we are called to account for the hope that is in us," as we have been taught.

I have sent you, therefore, what you requested, having explained them as briefly as possible. And you, my admirable friend, having studied these writings of mine, as well as the others, reflect on them at your leisure, O most sagacious man, and if you judge and accept them as familiar and common doctrines of the Church, thanks be to God; but if you perceive therein something which requires correction, correct it and I shall gladly accept it. Only, for our sake, let the Trinity, which is the cause of all, be preserved in unity of divinity and in a single divinity in three hypostases, admitting of no partition or division, invisible, intangible, incomprehensible, and the only uncreated and existing before time, creator of all, "present everywhere

αιώνιος, δημιουργὸς τῶν ὅλων, ἁπανταχοῦ παροῦσα καὶ τὰ πάντα πληροῦσα, ἁπλῆ, ἀόρατος, ἀνείδεος, ἀκατάληπτος, καὶ μηδενὶ τῶν ὄντων ἐκ φυσικῆς ἐμφάσεως γινωσκομένη, κατὰ τὸν εἰρηκότα· οὐδὲν ἑαυτῇ συναΐδιον ἐφελκομένη, οὐκ ἴσον, οὐ μεῖζον, οὐκ ἔλαττον, πᾶν ὅπερ ἔχειν λέγεται οὐσιωδῶς, ἐν μονάδι τοῦτο καὶ ὑπερηνωμένως καὶ ἀπαράλλακτον ἔχουσα· καὶ τῷ παντὶ ἑαυτῆς ἁπανταχοῦ παροῦσα καὶ ἐκτὸς πάντων οὖσα, καὶ πολλὰ μὲν καὶ διάφορα δι' ἑαυτῆς ποιοῦσα, αὐτὴ δὲ ἐν τῷ ποιεῖν τὰ πάντα μονὰς ἡ αὐτὴ καὶ τριὰς ὁμοῦ μένουσα· μονὰς θεότητος ἀπαράλλακτος, ἐνεργής τε καὶ παντοδύ-[fol. 7^{r}]ναμος, καὶ τριὰς ὑποστάσεων ταῖς τῶν προσώπων ἰδιότησιν ἀριθμουμένη ἀλλ' οὐ διαφόροις θεότησιν, ὡς μεμαθήκαμεν. ὑπὲρ ἧς νῦν στῆθι προθύμως εἰς ἀνομοιοτάτας διαιρουμένης μοίρας τε καὶ θεότητας, μᾶλλον δὲ ὑπὲρ τῆς ἐκκλησίας ἧς ἡ κατατομὴ καὶ διαίρεσις· θεότης γὰρ ἀπαθής τε καὶ ἀδιαίρετος, κἂν μυριάκις αὐτὴν ὁ Παλαμᾶς μεμηνὼς κατατέμνῃ, κἂν πάντες αὐτήν, μιμησάμενοι Παλαμᾶν, κατατέμνωσιν.

67. Τῷ Κορίνθου

Ζωὴ ἀληθὴς ἡ ἀλήθεια· ζῇ τοίνυν ἀληθῶς ὁ ταύτης περιεχόμενος, κἂν μυριάκις ἀποθανεῖν ὑπὸ τῶν μὴ φίλων τῆς ἀληθείας δόξῃ. ὅταν δὲ καὶ περὶ τοῦ ὄντος ἀληθοῦς, τοῦ Θεοῦ καὶ τῆς εἰς αὐτὸν εὐσεβείας, ὁ λόγος ᾖ, οὐ μόνον ζῆν τὸν πρεσβευτὴν τῆς ἀληθείας εἰκός, ἀλλὰ καὶ μετὰ δόξης θεοδωρήτου καὶ εἰρήνης καὶ πάσης ἄλλης εὐδαιμονίας πνευματικῆς· δόξα, γάρ φησι, καὶ εἰρήνη παντὶ τῷ προαιρουμένῳ τὸ ἀγαθόν. ἐγὼ μὲν οὖν κἀνταῦθα δόξαν ὁρῶ θαυμαστὴν τῷ τοῦ τῆς ἀληθείας ἀνενδότως ἀντεχομένῳ λόγου· εἰ δ' ἄρα τοῖς πολλοῖς καὶ πρὸς τὴν ἀλήθειαν ἀμβλυωποῦσι πονηρὸς εἶναι δόξοι, παρὰ Θεῷ γοῦν οὗτος μακάριος· μακάριοι, γάρ φησίν, ἔστε ὅταν ὀνειδίσωσιν ὑμᾶς καὶ διώξωσι καὶ ἐκβάλωσι τὸ ὄνομα ὑμῶν ὡς πονηρόν,

---

91–92 et 97 Joannis Chrysostomi *Liturgia* (ed. Brightman), 353, 13 || 93 cf. Maxim. Conf., *Capit. theol.*, 1, 1 (PG, 90, 1084A) || 101–102 cf. Sophronium, *Epist. syn. ad Sergium*, (PG, 87^{3}, 3156C)
67: 7–8 Rom. 2:10 || 12–13 Matt. 5:11; Luc. 6:22

67: M 40^{r}–40^{v}. Ed. A. Vassilikopoulou-Ioannidou, Ἀνέκδοτος ἐπιστολή, 92. || 13 ἐκβάλλωσι M

and filling everything," simple, invisible, without form, incomprehensible, and "unknown to any being by means of a natural manifestation"—as he said—pulling along nothing coeternal or equal or bigger or smaller, possessing as a supremely united and invariable monad whatever It is said to possess in essence, and not only being wholly present everywhere, but also being outside everything and performing alone many different functions, but in performing everything remaining the same, a triad and monad at the same time; a monad as to divinity, without variations, activating and omnipotent; and a triad as to hypostases "counted according to the properties of the persons but not according to different divinities," as we have learned. In Its defense rise now eagerly! Because It is being divided into most dissimilar degree and divinities; or rather, rise in defense of the Church whose mutilation and division this is, for the Divinity is unaffected and indivisible, even though Palamas, having gone mad, should cut it up ten thousand times; even though all men, imitating Palamas, should cut it up.

67. To the metropolitan of Corinth

True life is truth! And so the man who defends this has true life, even if he appears to be put to death countless times by the enemies of truth. But when the question is especially about the real truth, God and the reverence due to Him, not only is it right that the representative of truth should live, but also ⟨it is right that he should live⟩ with glory and peace granted by God as well as every other spiritual gratification. For he says: "There will be glory and peace for every well-doer." I see marvelous glory, then, even in this case, for the man who clings tenaciously to the word of truth; and if he should perhaps appear to be infamous to most people who are also nearly blind as to truth, nevertheless before God this man is blessed. For He says: "How blest you are when men hate you, when they outlaw you and bar your name as infamous," and all the rest that the Savior's saying adds as a promise to

καὶ ὅσα ἑξῆς ἐπάγει ὁ σωτήριος λόγος ἐπαγγελλόμενος οἷς ἕνεκεν αὐτοῦ ταῦτα παθεῖν συμβαίη.

Μακάριος οὖν εἶ σύ, θειότατε δέσποτα, ἕνεκεν αὐτοῦ καὶ γενναίως ἐνστὰς καὶ λοιδορηθεὶς καὶ οὐδαμῶς φροντίσας τοῦ πονηρὸς ἀκοῦσαι καὶ προπηλακισθῆναι καὶ οὕτως μιμήσασθαι τὸν πρῶτον ἀρχιερέα, ἐφ' ᾧ καὶ αὐτὸς ὑπ' ἐκείνου ἀρχιερεὺς προὐβλήθης καὶ οὐκ ἔψευσας τὸν προβαλόμενον. ὁρῶ δὲ ἐγὼ καὶ ταῦτα εἰς τοὐναντίον μεταπίπτοντα καὶ μεταπεσούμενα, ἰσχυρῶς καὶ γενναίως ἀντεχομένης τῆς ἀηττήτου σου ψυχῆς τοῦ λόγου τῆς ἀληθείας· μὴ γὰρ ὅτι εὐκαταφρόνητος καὶ πονηρός τις δόξεις τοῖς κατασπᾶν ἐγχειροῦσί σε τοῦ ἀχειρώτου τῆς ἀληθείας ἐρύματος, ἀλλὰ τούτοις μὲν καὶ φοβερός, τοῖς δὲ οἰκείοις τῆς ἀληθείας ἄλλος θεῖος ἀπόστολος, αὐτῇ δὲ τῇ ἀληθείᾳ ὅστις ἐστὶν ὁ Χριστός, ἕρμαιον ἐν τῇ παρούσῃ σπάνει τῶν τοιούτων ὑπέρλαμπρον.

Ἵστασο δή μοι, θεοειδέστατε δέσποτα, ἐν τῷ ἀσφαλεῖ τῆς εὐσεβείας λόγῳ ἀκλόνητος, καὶ τοὺς ἄλλους ἡμᾶς διὰ τῆς κατὰ σαυτὸν ἀνδρίας ὑπέρειδε. πρὸς σὲ νῦν μόνον μετὰ Θεὸν ὁρῶντος, ἐπὶ σοῦ τε ἀνέχοντος παντὸς τοῦ καθ' ἡμᾶς, μετρίου μέν, ἀνενδότου δέ, σὺν Θεῷ φάναι, πρὸς τὴν καινοτομίαν τῆς πίστεως ἐναντιώματος. καὶ οὕτως οὐ διὰ σαυτὸν μόνον, ἀλλὰ καὶ δι' ἡμᾶς καὶ τοὺς ἄλλους ὅσοι πρὸς σὲ βλέποντες [fol. 40v] τῆς ἀληθείας ἀντιποιήσονται, στεφανωθήσῃ παρὰ τοῦ τῆς εἰς αὐτὸν εὐσεβείας ἡμῶν ἀγωνοθέτου καὶ ἀθλοθέτου Χριστοῦ, ὅταν Θεὸς ἐν μέσῳ θεῶν ἑστὼς τῶν ἑαυτοῦ σπουδαστῶν πρὸς ἀξίαν ἑκάστῳ τῆς εἰς αὐτὸν ἀγάπης διανέμῃ τὰ γέρα.

68. Sine titulo

Εὖγε τῆς σῆς ὄντως φωτοφανείας, θαυμασιώτατε· βάλλ' οὕτως, ἵνα φῶς ἀληθῶς τοῖς ἐν Χριστῷ φίλοις γένοιο· μὴ κάμῃς ἑστὼς ἐπὶ τῆς κοινῆς ἀσφαλείας τῆς πίστεως· μὴ δῴης εἰς σάλον τὸν πόδα σου, μηδὲ προδῷς τὸ ἀκίνδυνον. μία κρηπίς, εἷς θεμέλιος ἀρραγὴς ἡ πάλαι προκειμένη τῆς εὐσεβείας παράδοσις, ὑπὲρ ἧς

---

19 Hebr. 3:1; 4:14; 5:5 || 26 cf. Joan. 1:17; 14:6 || 35–36 cf. Clemens Alex., *Liber Quis dives salvetur*, 3 (PG, 9, 608B–C) || 36–37 Ps. 81(82):1

68: 3–4 Ps. 120 (121):3

68: M 41v.

5 ἀραγὴς M

those who were to undergo these sufferings for His sake.

You are blessed, therefore, your most divine Grace, because for His sake you resisted courageously and were abused and did not at all mind being called infamous and being trampled in the mire, thus imitating the first archpriest. For this reason you were yourself appointed "archpriest" by Him and did not displease Him Who appointed you. But I see that things are changing and will change, as your invincible spirit clings strongly and courageously to the word of truth. For you will not appear as someone contemptible and infamous to those who attempt to pull you down from the unconquered bulwark of truth; not only this, but ⟨you will even appear⟩ formidable to these people, while to the friends of truth ⟨you will appear⟩ as another divine apostle, and to "truth itself, which is Christ," as a most illustrious rare gift in the present dearth of such gifts.

Therefore, your most godlike Grace, remain unswerving in the infallible word of piety and sustain the rest of us by your courage! Because all our modest but, with God's help, unyielding opposition to this innovation in the faith looks to you alone, after God, and it leans upon you. And thus not only for yourself, but also for me and for all the others who will fight for truth as they look ⟨at your example⟩, you will be crowned by Christ the "arbiter" and "judge" of our piety towards Him, when He will stand, "God in the midst of gods," and distribute the prizes to each of His followers according to the degree of one's love for Him.

68. No Addressee

Congratulations on your true illumination, my most admirable friend! Keep striking this way, that you may become truly the light of your friends in Christ! Do not be weary of standing on the common safety of faith. "Let not thy foot be moved" and do not forsake security. There is only one foundation, one unbreakable foundation stone: the tradition of piety established long ago, for which its

μέχρι αἵματος ἀγωνιστέον τοὺς ὄντως ἀκριβεῖς αὐτῆς φύλακας· καὶ τοσοῦτο μᾶλλον ὅσον ἂν δοκῇ τίς τι λέγειν εὐπρόσωπον καὶ οὕτως ἀπατῶν παρασύρει τοὺς πολλοὺς εἰς τὴν πλάνην· ἓν γὰρ δεῖ, φησι, φοβεῖσθαι, τὸ λύειν τὴν πίστιν ἐν τοῖς σοφίσμασι. σκόπει οὖν καὶ κίνει τὴν ἔν σοι Θεοῦ χάριν, ὅπως μὴ λάθῃ τι παρεμπεσὸν εἰς τὴν ἐκκλησίαν ἀλλόκοτον, καὶ τοὺς ἄλλους ὅπλιζε πρὸς τὴν τοιαύτην στρατείαν τοῦ πνεύματος.

69. Sine titulo

Τὸ στερρὸν καὶ ἀκλινὲς καὶ βέβαιον ἐν ἀγαθοῖς καὶ πᾶσι μὲν ἀξιάγαστον, ἐν δ' εὐσεβείᾳ καὶ τὸ θειότατον· καὶ τοσούτῳ μᾶλλον, ὅσῳπερ ἂν ἀνθέλκηται πρὸς τοὐναντίον σφοδρότερον τοῖς σπουδασταῖς ἐκείνου. ἐπεὶ καὶ ὁ κυβερνήτης τότε θαυμασιώτερος, ὁπόταν ἐν ἀμηχάνῳ τρικυμίᾳ καὶ ζάλῃ ἀκίνδυνον διασῴζῃ τὴν ναῦν ἐκ τοῦ κλύδωνος ἐν ᾧ πολλαὶ διελύθησαν. καὶ τὴν σὴν τοίνυν σοφίαν ἐν τῇ παρούσῃ τῆς ἐκκλησίας ζάλῃ θαυμαστῶς ὑπερέχειν τῶν κυμάτων ἀκούοντες μετὰ θαύματος χαίρομεν—τί γὰρ οὐ μέλλομεν;—εἰ καὶ ἴσον ἐστὶ σκότος φῶς γενέσθαι καὶ τὴν ἀλήθειάν ποτε τῷ ψεύδει συνενεχθῆναι.

70. Μαξίμῳ

Οἷον ἔδρασας, ἄριστε, καταλιπὼν μὲν τὴν πόλιν ἥ σε μάλα ἐθαύμαζε, καταλιπὼν δὲ τὴν ἑταιρείαν ἥ σου σφόδρα ἐξείχετο, καὶ ἀφελὼν αὐτοῖς τὸ βέλτιστον, τὴν εὖ ῥέουσαν γλῶτταν! τί ῥέουσαν εὖ; τὰς Ἀχελῴου Σειρῆνας, αἷς ἐκήλεις μὲν τοὺς φίλους τῇ ἀληθείᾳ, τοὺς δυσμενεῖς δὲ ἅμα φανεὶς ἐτρέπου καὶ τῆς εὐσεβείας προὐμά-

---

9–10 Greg. Naz., *Or.*25, 18 (PG, 35, 1224B)

69: 5–6 *ἀκίνδυνον . . . κλύδωνος* cf. Greg. Naz., *Or.* 42, 20 (PG, 36, 481C)

69: Mn 4r Ed. Karpozilos, *Letters*, 79, no. 3.

4 *κυβερνήτις* Mn ‖ 5 *ναῦ* Mn

70: M 62v–63v. Mn 7r–7v. Ed. Uspenskij, *Synodikon*, 77–79; ed. Loenertz, *Epistulae*, 102–104, no. 6; ed. Karpozilos, *Letters*, 91–93, no. 8.

1 Μαξίμῳ ⟨τῷ Καλοφέρῳ⟩ scr. Loenertz ‖ 2 *ἔδρασας*] *ἔπραξας* Mn ‖ 4 *αὐτοῖς*] *αὐτῆς* Mn ‖ 4–5 *τί ῥέουσαν εὖ*] *τὴν ῥέουσαν εὖ* Mn ‖ 6 *δὲ* om. Mn ‖ *δυσμενεῖς . . . ἐτρέπου*] *δυσμενεῖς ἀνῄρεις* Mn

truly strict guardians must fight unto death. And all the more so when someone appears to be saying something seemingly fair and thus carries away most people and leads them astray. For he says: "You must fear one thing: destroying the faith by sophistries."

Keep a lookout, then, and call forth the divine grace that is in you, so that nothing strange may find its way undetected into the Church, and arm others for such a spiritual campaign.

69. No Addressee

Firmness and stability and constancy in any virtue, indeed, are desirable characteristics, but in piety they are indeed quite divine; and much more so whenever ⟨piety⟩ is drawn towards its opposite with great vehemence by the proponents of that position. Indeed, even a helmsman is more to be admired when, in the midst of fierce waves and storm, he saves his ship unharmed from the billows in which many others have been lost. And so, when I hear that in the present storm of the Church your Wisdom wonderfully survives against the waves, I marvel—and why should I not?—even though it is as likely for the light to become darkness as it is for truth to be carried away by falsehood.

70. To Maximos

What an awful thing you did, my excellent friend, when you left the City which admired you so much, as well as the group of friends who depended on you so much. And you took away their greatest asset: your fine-flowing speech! How fine and fluent? The Sirens of Achelous, with whom you charmed the lovers of truth, while turning its enemies to flight as soon as you appeared, and defending

70

χεις οὐκ ἔλαττον ἢ Ἀχιλλεύς ποθ' Ἑλλήνων. ἡγούμην μέντοι καί σε τοσοῦτον ἔχειν ἐπὶ τῷδε τῷ πολέμῳ φρονήματος, ὥστε μηδενὸς ἂν ἀποδόσθαι τοῦτό γε, μηδὲ προέσθαι τὰς πατρικὰς ἀριστείας ὑπὲρ τῆς εὐσεβείας. τί γὰρ ἂν θεοφιλέστερον γένοιτο, τί δ' ἐπὶ γῆς ἐντιμότερον τοῦ δύνασθαι καὶ προθυμεῖσθαι γλώττας ἀργὰς ἀποφαίνειν δυσσεβεῖς τε καὶ κακοπράγμονας, καὶ δὴ καὶ ἀποτέμνειν τμητικωτάτῳ λόγῳ τὰς τμητικὰς τῆς θεότητος;

Νῦν δὲ ἀκούσαντες, οὐκ ἀληθῆ μέν, οἶμαι, ἀκούσαντες δ' οὖν, ὅτι μὴ μόνον σιγῇ τῆς ἀληθείας προὔδωκας τοὺς ἀγῶνας ἐκείνους ὧν μέγα κλέος παρὰ ταῖς ἐκκλησίαις, ἀλλ' ὅτι καὶ τοῖς Παλαμήταις ἱλαρὸς συνεγένου, καὶ αὐτῷ τῷ Παλαμᾷ, οὐ σὺν ὁμοίῳ τῷ σχήματι μεθ' οὗπερ αὐτὸν λίθον ἀπέφηνας πρότερον ἐν μέσοις τοῖς βασιλείοις, πῶς δοκεῖς ἠνιάθημεν; αὐτὸ τοῦτο τεκμήριον ἡγησάμεθα μέγιστον τοῦ μέλλειν τὸ κακὸν ἐπιδώσειν, τὴν τῶν αἱρέσεων ὕδραν, Ἡρακλέους ἀναχωρήσαντος πρὶν τὸ θηρίον ἀνῃρῆσθαι καθάπαξ. καὶ ἦμεν ἐν ἀπογνώσει τοῦ κατὰ σὲ δήπου κρείττονος. ὡς δέ τις ἧκεν ἀπαγγέλλων ὅτι σε Ἄθως ἔχει, ἡ ἱερὰ κορυφή, τὸ ἡμέτερον μέλημα, ἀναπεπνεύκαμεν· ὡς δὲ καὶ ἄλλος καὶ μάλα ἄλλος ἐπῆλθεν ἀπὸ τοῦ θείου Ὄρους μηνύοντες ⟨οὐχ ὅτι μόνον⟩ τοῖς ἱεροῖς Λαυριώταις ἐναρίθμιος εἶ καί σοι προσέχουσιν ἄσμενοι, [fol. 63r] ἀλλ' ὅτι καὶ τοῖς αὐτόθι τὰ Παλάμια νοσοῦσιν ἀντέπνευσας, καὶ περιέστησας αὐτοῖς θαυμαστῶς τὰς ἐλπίδας ἀντὶ τοῦ πεισθῆναι σφίσιν, ὅπερ ἠλπίκεσαν, πείσας αὐτοὺς τὰ κρείττω, τί χρὴ καὶ λέγειν πρὸς ἀκριβῶς λογιούμενον ἐν οἵαις ἦμεν τηνικαῦτα βακχείαις; ἐπ' ἐκείνοις δ' ἐλθόντων παρ' ὑμῶν οἵπερ ἧκον, καὶ μήτε γράμματα, μήτ' ἄλλως λόγους παρὰ τῆς σῆς σοφίας κεκομικότων ἡμῖν, μετέπιπτεν ἡ βακχεία πρὸς σκυθρωπότητα· καὶ γράφομέν σοι νυνὶ ναρκώσῃ καὶ δυσκινήτῳ χειρὶ καὶ γνώμῃ.

Ἀλλ' ὁ ἐν ἱερομονάχοις θαυμάσιος καὶ σὸς Ἀθανάσιος, ὁ τοῦ φιλαλήθους καὶ ἀρετῆς πάσης ἕνεκα τοῖς ἀρίστοις συντρέχων, ὁ τῶν φιλοσοφίας θεραπευτῶν τὰ πρῶτα, ὁ μάλιστα μὲν ἀνιαθεὶς ἁπάντων ἐπὶ τοῖς χείροσι τῶν περὶ σοῦ λεγομένων, μάλιστα δὲ πάντων ἡσθεὶς τῇ ἀμείνονι φήμῃ, οὗτος ἀναγκασθεὶς πρεσβεῦσαι παρὰ τὸν

70: 18 Cf. Homerum, *Il.*, 24., 611; Platonem, *Symp.*, 198c

---

13 *τμητικωτάτῳ λόγῳ*] *ἀντικειμένῳ ξίφει* Mn ‖ 15 *προὔδωκα* Mn ‖ 18 *μεθ' οὗπερ*] *μεθ' οὗ* Mn ‖ 18 *πρότερον* om. Mn ‖ ante *ἐν μέσοις* scr. *ἐμπεσὼν* Mn ‖ 19 *ἠνιάθημεν*] *διετέθημεν* Mn ‖ 23 *ἐπαγγέλλων* Mn ‖ *ὁ Ἄθως* Mn ‖ 24 *ἀναπεπνεύκαμεν*] *ἀναπεπηδήκαμεν* Mn ‖ 25 *οὐχ ὅτι μόνον* om. M: ex Mn supplevi ‖ 27 *τὰ Παλάμια*] *τὰ Παλαμᾶ* Mn ‖ 32 *σῆς* om. Mn ‖ 33 *σκυθροπότητα* Mn ‖ 33–34 *ναρκώσει* Mn ‖ 34 post *χειρὶ* scr. *τε* Mn ‖ *γνώμῃ*] *καρδίᾳ* Mn ‖ 36 *πάσης . . . συντρέχων*] *ἁπάσης ἀμφισβητῶν τοῖς ἄκροις* Mn ‖ 37 *πάντων ἀνιαθεὶς* Mn ‖ 39 post *ἀναγκασθεὶς* scr. *βασιλικῇ δυνάμει* Mn

70

piety no less than Achilles, at one time defended the Greeks! I thought, of course, that you too had so great a spirit for this war that you would not give it up for anything, nor betray the ancestral deeds of valor on behalf of piety. For what would be dearer to God, what more honorable on earth than to be able and eager to render idle the impious and mischievous tongues and, indeed, cut out with most cutting words ⟨the tongues⟩ which cut up the Divinity?

But you cannot imagine how I grieved when I heard recently—I do not, of course, believe it to be true—⟨I mean⟩ when I heard that you not only betrayed by silence those struggles for truth which are greatly renowned in the Churches, but you also happily associated with the Palamites and even with Palamas himself; your attitude was not the same as before, when you attacked him in the middle of the Palace and turned him into "stone." I thought that exactly this is the surest sign that the evil will increase, the many-headed serpent of heresies; for Heracles left before destroying the beast once and for all. And I had no hope of anyone who would be stronger than you in this respect. But when someone came reporting that Athos, the holy peak, detains you, my beloved friend, I recovered. And as another man and then again many others came from the Holy Mountain revealing not only that you are counted among the holy monks of Lavra and that they have gladly welcomed you, but also that you blew like an adverse wind against those men there who suffer from Palamas' disease, and admirably reversed their hopes and instead of being convinced by them, as they had hoped, you convinced them of what is best—what need is there even to say to a man who will exactly work it out ⟨for himself⟩ in what ecstasy I was then! But when those men arrived afterwards—the men who came from you and brought me neither a letter nor any other word from your Wisdom—then my ecstasy turned to gloom, and I am at this moment writing to you with a numb and heavy hand and heart.

But the admirable hieromonk and friend of yours Athanasios—he who competes with the best because of all possible virtue and his love of truth, and ⟨holds⟩ the first prize among the devotees of philosophy, and who was most of all annoyed by the bad rumors about you and most pleased by the good news—he delivered me from despair and gloom over you when he was compelled to go as an ambassador to

70

ἡγεμόνα τῶν Τριβαλλῶν, ὡς εἴσῃ, τῆς ἐπὶ σοὶ δυσελπιστίας ἡμᾶς καὶ σκυθρωπότητος ἔλυσεν. ἔφη γὰρ οὐδὲν τοσοῦτον εἶναι παρὰ σοί, οὐκ ἀλλοίωσιν, οὐ μέμψιν ἐκ παλαιῶν ἐγκλημάτων, οὐ προκειμένας ἐλπίδας, οὐ φόβον ἐπηρτημένον, ὅπερ ἂν οὐ διαλύσῃ φανεὶς τοῖς φιλίας φαρμάκοις καὶ Θεοῦ συνεργίᾳ· καίτοι λύπης μέντοι παλαιᾶς ἴσως ἂν ἴχνος εὑρεῖν παρὰ σοί, ὅπερ εὐθὺς ἐξαιρήσειν, ἢ καὶ ὁτιοῦν ἄλλο τῶν ἀπηριθμημένων, μετάθεσιν δὲ τῶν δογμάτων παντελῶς ἀπηγόρευεν· οὐ γάρ ἄν ποθ' ἕτερόν τί σε φρονῆσαι παρὰ τὰ πάλαι καὶ πάτρια περὶ τοῦ θείου, ἥκιστα δὲ ἁπάντων τὴν Παλαμῆτιν πλάνην, ὡς οὐ μόνον αἵρεσιν δυσσεβεστάτην οὖσαν καὶ πηγὴν τῶν αἱρέσεων, ἀλλὰ καὶ ἀλόγιστον καὶ ἀνοητοτάτην· γνώσει γὰρ ἀληθεῖ καὶ σοφίᾳ, ἧς ἐραστὴς σὺ καὶ τρόφιμος—οὐ Παλαμᾶς ὁ τεράστιος τὴν ἀλογίαν οὐχ ἧττον ἢ τὴν ἀσέβειαν—οὐδὲν ἀλογίας καὶ ἀφροσύνης ἀλλοτριώτερον.

Καίτοι ταῦτα μὲν λέγειν ἡμᾶς, ὡς οἶσθα, αὐτὸς Παλαμᾶς ἐξηνάγκασε περὶ αὐτοῦ, δυσσεβεῖς ἁπανταχοῦ κηρύττων, ἐπειδήπερ αὐτοῦ ταῖς πλάναις οὐκ ἐθέλομεν πείθεσθαι. ⟨εἰ δὲ⟩ τούτων ἀποστὰς κοινῇ μετὰ τῆς ἐκκλησίας τοῦ Θεοῦ τὰ πάτρια δόγματα πρεσβεύειν ἐπήνεσε, μάλα θαρρῶν ἀποφαίνομαι ὡς οὐδεὶς ἂν ἁπάντων ἔφθη Γρηγόριον, ἐμὲ τουτονὶ τὸν ἀνθρώπων ἐλάχιστον, [fol. 63v] εἰς φιλίαν καὶ θεραπείαν ἐκείνου, προσθείην δ' ἂν καὶ δουλείαν, οὐχὶ ψευδόμενος. ὁ γὰρ τοῖς ἄλλοις πρότερον ἀπηχθημένος ὑπὲρ αὐτοῦ καὶ πράξας οὐχ ἧττω πρὸς τοὺς αὐτοῦ δυσμενεῖς ἤπερ αὐτὸς πρὸς αὐτοῦ, πῶς οὐχὶ δῆλός εἰμι οὔτε δυσχερὴς ὤν, ἀλλ' ἕτοιμος πρὸς καταλλαγάς, ἂν ἀφῇ τὴν καινότητα, οὔτε ἰδίας ἕνεκα διαφορᾶς ἢ φθόνου τὴν ἀρχὴν διενεχθεὶς πρὸς τοῦτον, ἀλλ' ὑπὲρ εὐσεβείας τοῦ κοινοῦ πάντων τῶν εὐσεβῶν ἀγαθοῦ; ὅπερ, οὐκ οἶδ' ὅ τι παθόντες, οἱ πλεῖστοι προΐενται, οἱ μὲν φιλίας καὶ χάριτος τῆς πρὸς τὸν πεπλανημένον, ἀντὶ τοῦ καὶ τούτῳ χαρίσασθαι διὰ τῆς ἐπιστροφῆς καὶ τῇ ἀληθείᾳ τῷ μὴ προδοῦναι ταύτην, οἱ δὲ δυσμενείας τῆς πρὸς τὸν πατριάρχην τὸν ἁγιώτατον, οἱ δὲ τῆς πρὸς ἡμᾶς, οἱ δ' οὐκ οἶδ' ὧντινων προφάσεων καὶ βαράθρων, πλῆθος θεοτήτων ἀνίσων καὶ ἀνομοίων, ἀντὶ τῆς ἀμερίστου μονάδος τῆς ἐν τρισὶν ὑποστάσεσιν, καὶ ἀντὶ τοῦ ἀοράτου καὶ ἀνειδέου Θεοῦ, μεμορφωμένον φυσικῇ καὶ οὐσιώδει μορφῇ καὶ ὁρατῇ σωματικοῖς ὀφθαλ-

---

40 *τῶν* om. Mn ‖ *εἴσῃ*] *εἴσε* Mn ‖ 44–45 *μέντοι*] *μέν τι* Mn ‖ 49 *δυσσεβεστάτην* om. Mn ‖ 50 *καὶ ἀλόγιστον*] *καὶ* om. Mn ‖ *ἀλλόγιστον* Mn ‖ 51–53 *οὐ* Παλαμᾶς . . . *ἀλλοτριώτερον*] *οὐδὲν ἀλογίας καὶ ἀφροσύνης ἀλλοτριώτερον ἧς* Παλαμᾶς *ὁ τεράστιος* Mn ‖ 54 *ἡμᾶς λέγειν* Mn ‖ *ὡς οἶσθα* om. Mn ‖ 56 *πλάναις*] *καινοφωνίαις* Mn ‖ *εἰ δὲ* ex Mn supplevi: *οὐδὲ* M ‖ 58 *ἐπήνεσε*] *ἠθέλησε* Mn ‖ 61 *πρότερον* om. Mn ‖ 62 *πρὸς*] *ὑπὲρ* Mn ‖ 73 *τοῦ* om. Mn ‖ 73–74 *μεμορφωμένον* om. Mn ‖ 74 *οὐσιώδη* Mn

70

the king of the Serbians, as you will know. For he said that as far as you are concerned there is nothing so serious, neither change, nor discontent from old grievances, nor present expectations, nor impending fear, that he could not dissolve it when he comes with the charms of friendship and the help of God. Though he said that one might, perhaps, find in you a trace of old annoyance or whatever else I ennumerated, which he will remove immediately, he completely excluded a doctrinal change. For he said that you would never believe anything different from the old and ancestral doctrines about God, least of all the Palamite delusion; for not only is it a most impious heresy and source of heresies, it is also absurd and foolish. And to true knowledge and wisdom, of which you are a lover and nursling, but not Palamas whose absurdity is no less monstrous than his impiety, nothing is more alien than absurdity and folly.

And yet, as you know, Palamas himself has forced me to say these things about him by everywhere proclaiming me impious because I do not wish to listen to his delusions. But if he abstained from them and consented to honor the ancestral dogmas in common with the Church of God, I say with great confidence that of all people none would overtake Gregory—myself, the lowliest of men—in love and care for him, and I would even add slavery without lying. For it must be obvious that I who previously became hateful to others for his sake and did no less to his enemies than he did on his own account, I am not difficult, but ready for reconciliation if he abandons his innovation, for I did not quarrel with him in the first place because of a personal difference, but for the sake of piety, the common good of all pious men. And I do not know what befell most men, that they betray it: some do so for the sake of friendship and favor to the deluded man, instead of doing a favor both to him by correcting him and to truth by not betraying it; others ⟨do so⟩ because of their hostility to the most holy Patriarch; others because of their hostility to me; and as for the rest, I know not for what pretexts and ruin they chose a multitude of unequal and dissimilar divinities rather than the indivisible Monad in three hypostases; and in place of the invisible and formless God, one who has a form, natural and essential and visible to bodily eyes; and in place of the God Who is "present every-

μοῖς, καὶ ἀντὶ τοῦ παντα χοῦ παρόντος ἀμιγῶς καὶ ἀσχέτως ὡς ἀπείρου καὶ ἀσωμάτου, μὴ δυνάμενον παρεῖναι καθ' ἑαυτὸν ἁπανταχοῦ καὶ πᾶσιν ὥσπερ τὰ σώματα, καὶ ὅλως ἀντὶ τῶν θεοπρεπῶν καὶ παλαιῶν δογμάτων ἀνθῃρημένοι τὰ ἀτοπώτατα καί, ὡς εἰπεῖν, γραωδέστατα. ὧν σὺ καταπτύσας, εἴπερ τις, καὶ καταγελάσας ἀξίως τῆς μοχθηρίας αὐτῶν καὶ τοὺς ἁλισκομένους τοῖς τοιούτοις κατελεήσας, καὶ πολλούς γε ἀνασπάσας τοῦ τοσούτου βαράθρου διὰ τῆς χρυσῆς γλώττης, ὥσπερ σειρᾶς, μὴ καταισχύνῃς ἐκεῖνα διὰ τῶν τελευταίων, ἀλλ' ὥσπερ πέπλον εὐσεβείας εἰς τέλος τὸν χαριέστατον ἐξύφανον τῷ Θεῷ δι' ὁμοίας τῆς γλώττης καὶ φέρων ἀνάθες διὰ χρόνου παντὸς σωθησόμενον καὶ ταῖς εὐσεβέσι γλώτταις ὑμνηθησόμενον.

71. Sine titulo

Ἀεὶ σὺ παρ' ἡμῖν ἔμφυτος, καὶ οὐδὲν ἐκεῖνο δύναται τὸ [fol. 67v] φίλτρον ἀποσβέσαι, κἂν πολλὰ πάνυ κατά σου κατὰ τούτου συντρέχῃ· ὥστ' ἐν ἔθει πολλῷ σου γεγονότες τοῦ φίλτρου, κἂν εἰ ἐβουλήθημεν, οὐκ ἂν ἐδυνήθημεν ἐξελεῖν τῆς καρδίας· ἔθος γὰρ χρόνιον εἰς φύσιν μεθίσταται, ὡς τῶν σοφῶν αἱρεῖ λόγος, εἰ καὶ παρὰ σοὶ τοῦτο πρὸς ἡμᾶς ἐμαράνθη καὶ ὁ λόγος οὗτος διέπεσεν, οὐκ οἶδ' εἴθ' ὑπὲρ φύσιν, εἴτε παρὰ φύσιν ἐληλυθότι, δυοῖν γὰρ δὴ θάτερον.

Ἔγωγ' οὖν διὰ τὸ τῆς σῆς κράτος παρ' ἐμοὶ συνηθείας οὔτε δύναμαι μὴ γράφειν πρὸς τὴν σὴν βαθυτάτην τὰ πρὸς ἐμὲ σιωπήν, οὔτε μὴ δεδιέναι περὶ σοὶ μή τι παραπολαύσῃς τῆς τοῦ καιροῦ κακίας, καὶ ὅπως μὴ τοῦτο γένοιτο εὔχεσθαι τὰ δυνατά μοι· καίτοι γε εἰδὼς ὡς ἔστιν ὅτε λυσιτελούντως ὁ Θεὸς ἐπάγει τὰς συμφορὰς τοῖς οὕτως ἐπιτηδείοις παρὰ Θεοῦ σωφρονίζεσθαι, ἀλλ' ὅμως εὔχομαί σε μηδενὸς ἐλθεῖν εἰς πεῖραν ἀνιαροῦ, εἰ καὶ πυνθάνομαι τοῖς ἐμοῖς ἐφήδεσθαι λυπηροῖς καὶ δὴ καὶ συλλαμβάνειν τοῖς ἵν' ἐγὼ τεθναίην

---

75 Joannis Chrysostomi *Liturgia* (ed. Brightman), 353, 13 82 Homerus, *Il.*, 8, 19 82–83 Homerus, *Il.*, 6, 90 et 271

71: 4–5 Georgides, *Gnomologion*, ed. Boissonade, *Anecdota Graeca*, I, 32

---

78 post *ἀτοπώτατα* scr. *καὶ ἀμαθέστατα* Mn ‖ 81 *βάθρου* Mn ‖ 82 post *χρυσῆς* scr. *σου* Mn ‖ 83–84 *ἀλλ' ὥσπερ . . . χαριέστατον*] *ἀλλ' ὥσπερ πέπλον εὐσεβείας ἐξύφηνεν τῷ Θεῷ εἰς τέλος δι' ὁμοίας τῆς γλώττης τὸν χαριέστατον* Mn ‖ 84 *ἐξυφάναι* M ‖ 85 *ἀνέθες* Mn

71: M 67r–67v.

where" unmixed and unrelated, being infinite and incorporeal, one who cannot, just as with bodies, be present by himself everywhere and in everything; and in short, instead of the godly and old doctrines, they chose the most absurd doctrines, only befitting old women, so to speak. At these you more than anyone else spat and jeered in a manner worthy of their wickedness, and you felt great pity for those who were succumbing to them, and by your golden tongue, just as if it were a rope, you pulled up many from so deep a pit. Do not put those deeds to shame by your latest conduct, but finally weave for God with the same tongue the "loveliest robe" of piety, as it were, and bring it and dedicate it to be forever preserved and praised by pious tongues.

71. No Addressee

You are part of me forever, and nothing can extinguish that love, even if, as far as you are concerned, too many things conspire against it. And so, since I have become greatly accustomed to loving you, even if I wanted to I would not be able to drive this love out of my heart. For as the saying of the sages goes, "An old habit becomes second nature," though your love for me died away and this saying failed. I do not know whether this happened because you have gone above and beyond nature, or ⟨because you have gone⟩ against it; certainly it is because of one of these alternatives.

At all events, because of the strength of my close association with you, I cannot fail to write in response to your most profound silence towards me, nor can I avoid fearing for you, lest you share some fruits of the wickedness of the times, so I pray as much as I can that this may not happen. Although I am aware that at times God brings misfortunes for a good purpose to those who are capable of being chastened by God; nevertheless, I pray that you may not experience any grief, though I hear that you rejoice at my sorrows and, in fact, even assist those who endeavor that

ἐκτόπως ἐσπουδακόσιν. ὃ δεινὸν ὄν, οὐκ ἂν ἦν οὕτω δεινόν, εἰ μὴ ὑπὲρ τῆς κοινῆς εὐσεβείας ἐπολεμούμην ἀνδράσιν ὧν αὐτὸς κρείττω με φρονεῖν καὶ λέγειν ἐμαρτύρησας οὐκ ὀλιγάκις. ἀλλὰ καὶ οὕτω λόγοις μὲν ὢν μεθ' ἡμῶν ἐφωράθης, νυνὶ δὲ οὐδὲ λόγοις, ἔργῳ δὲ μετ' ἐκείνων οἳ Θεὸν ἀτιμάζοντες διὰ τῶν ἀνίσων βαθμῶν τῆς θεότητος, καὶ πολεμοῦντες θεότητι τῷ κατατέμνειν αὐτὴν εἰς ἐκτόπους ἀνομοιότητας, καὶ τῇ κτίσει λατρεύοντες παρὰ τὸν κτίσαντα διὰ τῆς καὶ τὸ τῶν Ἑλλήνων ὑπερβαλλούσης πολύθεον πολυθεΐας, καὶ ἡμῖν πολεμοῦσιν ἐπειδὴ μὴ σὺν αὐτοῖς τῷ Θεῷ πολεμεῖν ἀνεχόμεθα.

Σὺ δ' εἰ μὲν συκοφαντῇ ταῦτα ψεύσταις καὶ βασκάνοις ἀνθρώποις, τί μὴ δηλοῖς ἡμῖν γράμμασι; εἰ δ' ἀληθῶς οὕτως ἔχεις, ὡς ἡ φήμη σε πρὸς ἡμᾶς ἀπαγγέλλει, θρηνοῦμέν σε τῆς ἀπωλείας, ἀλλ' οὐ μακαρίζομεν τῶν ἐλπίδων ἐφ' οἷς δουλεύεις δυσσεβέσιν ἀνθρώποις.

72. Sine titulo

Ἐν οὐκ ὀλίγῃ τιθέμενος φροντίδι σοι καθομιλῆσαι παρ' ἡμῖν ὄντι πρῴην, ἀφείλου τῷ τάχει τῆς αὖθις ἀποδημίας καὶ τὸ μετρίως σοι συγγεγονέναι. καὶ ὃν ἀπολαβόντες ἐκ τῆς μακρᾶς ἀποδημίας ἐκείνης ἧ Τριβαλλοῖς ἐνετρίβης ἐχαίρομεν, τοῦτο αὖθις ἡμᾶς ἀφελομένη Θεσσαλονίκη λυπεῖ, τά τε ἄλλα εὖ διαθέσθαι τοὺς φίλους δυνάμενον τῇ συνουσίᾳ, καὶ τὸ μέγιστον, συνεργὸν ἡμῖν ὄντα τὸν προθυμότατον ὑπὲρ τῆς εὐσεβείας, ἣν οἶδεν ἀτόπους μὲν ἀνθρώπους καὶ κομιδῇ δυσσεβεῖς ἐσπουδακότας καὶ νῦν, ὑπὲρ τοὺς πάλαι δυσσεβεῖς, ἀνατρέπειν, ἡμᾶς δὲ περιέπειν καὶ ταύτης προκινδυνεύειν, ὥσπερ εἰκὸς τροφίμους.

Ἀλλὰ ταύτην ἡμῖν τὴν ὠφέλειαν καὶ αὐτόθι παρέξεις—ἔξεστι γάρ σοι—τοῖς Παλαμίταις δείξας [fol. 52r] ὡς ἔστι τις γνήσιος τῆς ἐκκλησίας υἱὸς καὶ τρόφιμος τῆς εὐσεβείας, ὁ τὴν εἰς ταύτην ὕβριν οὐκ ἀνεχόμενος. ἀγγέλλονται γὰρ οὗτοι δεῦρο πάντα ποιοῦντες ἐκεῖ καὶ θορυβοῦντες ὑπὲρ τῶν ἀσεβεστάτων μὲν τοῦ Παλαμᾶ δογμάτων, κατὰ δὲ τῶν κειμένων τῆς εὐσεβείας ὅρων τοῖς τοῦ θείου σπαράκταις ἐξευρημένων. εἰ τοίνυν τοῖς μὲν φιλοθέως ἀντὶ τούτων ἐπάξει, Ἀντώνιον δὲ ἀγαπήσεις τὸν ἱερὸν τουτονὶ καὶ ἡμέτερον, τὸν

23–24 Rom. 1:25

72: M 51v–52r. Ed. Loenertz, *Epistulae*, 104–105, no. 7.

I should die in exile. This is terrible. But it would not have been so terrible, if I had not been persecuted for the cause of the common piety by men in comparison with whom you personally avowed, not a few times, that I believe and say better things. But even so you appeared in your words to be on my side, whereas right now not even your words ⟨are on my side⟩, and in your actions you are with those who dishonor God through the unequal degrees of divinity and who wage war against the divine nature by cutting it up into strange dissimilarities, ⟨men⟩ who "have offered reverence and worship to created things instead of to the Creator" by their polytheism which exceeds even that of the pagans, and who wage war against me because I cannot bring myself to wage war with them against God.

If, then, these are false accusations brought against you by lying and slanderous men, why do you not prove this to me by ⟨writing⟩ a letter? If, on the other hand, you feel this way, as they report to me, I lament your loss, but I do not congratulate you on the hopes for which you serve impious men.

72. No Addressee

I was really anxious to be with you every day while you were here recently, but by departing again so quickly you deprived me of your company for even a moderate length of time. And Thessalonica pains me by snatching away again the man whom I rejoiced to receive back from the long stay abroad—during which you became acquainted with the Serbians—a man who can please his friends with his company in every other respect, but most important of all, a man who is my most zealous assistant in defense of piety, which he knows that some absurd and altogether impious men are seeking to overthrow now, ⟨trying⟩ even more than the impious men of old, while I strive to honor piety and bear the brunt of battle for its defense, as is fitting for one fostered ⟨by piety⟩.

But you can render me this service even where you are, for it is within your power, if you show the Palamites that there is a genuine son of the Church fostered by piety who does not tolerate the insolence against her. For it is reported that they are doing everything there to raise a clamor in favor of Palamas' most impious doctrines and against the established rules of piety which have been devised against those who ⟨try⟩ to rend the Divinity asunder. If, therefore, for the sake of these rules you will march piously against the Palamites and, on the other hand, treat with affection this holy friend of mine, Anthony, the best of hieromonks on account of his

ἱεροδιακόνων τὰ κράτιστα, πάσης ἀρετῆς καὶ παιδεύσεως ἕνεκα καὶ τῆς ὑπὲρ τῆς εὐσεβείας σπουδῆς, ἣν πολλὴν καὶ θαυμαστὴν κατὰ τῶν βεβήλων τούτων καὶ ἀνιέρων δογμάτων πεποίηται καὶ νῦν ἐπιδείκνυται, ἀνθ' ὧν ἁπάντων καὶ τῆς ἱερωσύνης ἠξίωται παρὰ τῇ πασῶν τῶν ἐκκλησιῶν ὑψηλοτάτῃ μητρὶ καὶ τῆς ὅλης ἱερωσύνης πηγῇ, ταῦτα ποιήσας, τὸ πᾶν ἡμῖν κεχαρισμένος ἔσῃ· χάριν δὲ νῦν αἰτῶν σε ταύτην ἐπιμελέστατα, οἶδ' ὅτι χάριν ὁμολογήσεις μοι, ἐπειδὰν ὁμιλήσῃς οἰκείως τῷ διακόνῳ τοῦ Πνεύματος.

73. Τῷ Ἴσαρι

Ὁ μὲν σὸς πρὸς ἡμᾶς τῆς διαθέσεως τρόπος οὐδαμῶς ἡμῖν ἐπέτρεπε γράψαι σοι, ὁ δ' ἡμέτερος πρὸς σὲ οὔπω σιωπᾶν ἡμῖν συνεχώρησεν, ἀλλ' ὡς οἷόν τε ἀνακαλεῖσθαι τέως ἐπιχειρεῖν τὴν παρὰ πᾶσιν ὑμνουμένην ἡμῶν ἐκείνην καὶ θαυμαστὴν φιλίαν, τὴν ἄτυφον, τὴν καθαράν, τὴν ἄδολον, τὴν ἀνυπόκριτον. εἰ μὲ οὖν ἐπανήκοι· εἰ δὲ μή, τότε εἰκότως σιγήσομαι, καίτοι γε ἡμεῖς μὲν σιγήσομεν, ὁ δὲ ἀκριβὴς τῶν πραγμάτων ἔλεγχος, τὸ παρὰ σοὶ συνειδός, καὶ σιωπώντων ἡμῶν οὐ σιγήσεται τὸ μὴ οὐ τὴν σὴν περὶ ἡμᾶς ἀδικίαν ἐλέγχειν, πάντων ἀδίκων ἀδικωτάτην οὖσαν.

Ἐκεῖνο δὲ εἰδέναι δεῖ τὸν θαυμάσιον Ἴσαριν ὡς ὁ μὲν ἕνεκά του κέρδους μὲν ἑαυτοῦ πάντως, ζημίας δὲ ἡμετέρας, τὴν περὶ ἡμᾶς ἀδικίαν προείλετο, τὸ δέ ἐστιν ἐναντίον· οὐ γὰρ κέρδος αὐτῷ περιέσται, οὐδὲ μικρὸν ἐντεῦθεν, ἀλλ' ἡ μεγίστη ζημία, οὐδὲ μᾶλλον ἡμᾶς ἢ αὐτὸν ζημιώσει, τοῦ γὰρ εἰς φιλίαν τοσαύτην ὁμοῦ καὶ τὸν Θεὸν ἁμαρτεῖν οὐδὲν οὔτε χεῖρον, οὔτε μᾶλλόν ἐστιν ἐπιζήμιον τῷ γ' ἐξημαρτηκότι.

Ἃ δέ μοι ταυτί σοι κατηνάγκασε γράψαι ὁ ἐμοὶ μὲν ἀγαπητὸς ἀδελφὸς ἐν Κυρίῳ, αὐτῷ δὲ τῷ Κυρίῳ διάκονος, ἀπαγγελεῖ σοι καθ' ἕκαστα, εἰ πρᾴως αὐτοῦ καὶ μακροθύμως [fol. 52v] ἐθελήσαις ἀκοῦσαι.

74. Sine titulo

Σοὶ τὸν ἡμέτερον Ἀντώνιον τὸν τοῦ Χριστοῦ διάκονον ἀπεσταλκότες πρῴην, σοὶ καὶ νῦν τὰ πρὸς αὐτὸν ἀπεστάλκαμεν

73: M 52r–52v.

74: M 47r–47v. Ed. Loenertz, *Epistulae*, 105–107, no. 8.

education combined with all possible virtue as well as zeal for piety which he displayed, ⟨a man who⟩ is still displaying this ⟨zeal⟩ greatly and admirably against these profane and ungodly doctrines, and for all these reasons he was even deemed worthy of the priesthood by the most sublime mother of all Churches, the source of all priesthood—if you do so, you will grant me the greatest favor. And when I ask you most anxiously for this favor, I know that you will be grateful to me when you become closely acquainted with the deacon of the ⟨Holy⟩ Spirit.

73. To Isaris

Your disposition towards me in no way permitted me to write to you, whereas my disposition towards you did not allow me to remain silent any longer, but made me attempt recently to recall as much as possible that admirable friendship of ours which was praised by everyone: the gentle, the pure, the genuine, the sincere friendship. May this return! If it does not, then I shall be justified in keeping silent. But, in fact, though I keep silent, that strict judge of facts, the conscience that is in you, even if I keep silent, will not cease to condemn your injustice to me as the most unjust of all injustices.

The admirable Isaris, then, should realize one thing, namely, that he certainly chose to do me this injustice for some profit of his own and to my detriment. But the outcome will be the opposite; for no profit, not even a small one, but rather the greatest damage, will accrue to him from this. Nor will he injure me more than himself, for no sin that a man commits is worse or more damaging to himself than the sin against such a great friendship as well as against God.

My beloved brother in the Lord and the Lord's own deacon will tell you in detail what forced me to write this to you, if you care to listen to him with kindness and forbearance.

74. No Addressee

I recently sent you my friend Anthony, the deacon of Christ, and now I have sent you my letter addressed to him—since I am fortunate to have you there in my

ἡμέτερα γράμματα, ἐπειδή σε ἀνθ' ἡμῶν αὐτῶν εὐτυχοῦμεν αὐτόθι, ὡς ἄν, εἰ μὲν αὐτὸν ἔτ' ἐκεῖ τὰ γράμμαθ' εὕροι διάγοντα, διὰ τῆς σῆς εὐμενείας λαβεῖν αὐτῷ ταῦτα γένηται καὶ μὴ διαπεσεῖν πως· εἰ δὲ μὴ φθάσαι τοῦτον, τοῖς ἄλλοις ἐμφανισθῇ τῶν φίλων. χρήσιμον γάρ, καὶ μάλιστα τὰ τοῦ Κυπρίου φιλοσόφου γράμματα οἷς ὄντως φιλόσοφος ἀνὴρ καὶ ζηλωτὴς εὐσεβείας τελεώτατος δείκνυται, τὴν Παλαμναίαν νόσον παντὸς μᾶλλον ἐκ τῆς ὑπερορίας βάλλων καὶ σχετλιάζων καὶ βοῶν "ὢ τῆς ἀσεβείας!" τοῖς γράμμασιν ἐπὶ τῷ πλῆθος θεοτήτων ἀνίσων εἰσάγοντι καὶ τῷ μηδενὶ ταῦτα μέλειν τῶν τῇδε λόγοις ἐμβριθέσιν ἀνελεῖν [fol. 47v] τὸ παράπαν, ἀλλ' ἡσυχάζειν μὲν τοὺς ἐν λόγοις δοκοῦντας τὰ μέγιστα δύνασθαι, τὸ δὲ δόγμα καθάπερ ἰὸν ἐπιβόσκεσθαι τὸ ποίμνιον τοῦ Χριστοῦ, ἕνα δὲ μόνον—ἐμὲ δὴ λέγων—ζῆλον θεῖον ἀναλαβόντα ἀντιστῆναι τῷ δόγματι καλῶς μὲν καὶ ὀρθῶς, μαλακωτέρως δέ, φησιν, ἢ ὡς ἔδει πρὸς τοὺς τοιούτους ἀντιστῆναι τῶν λόγων. ᾧ δὴ καὶ μᾶλλον ἥσθην ἢ εἴ με μηδεμίαν ἔφασκεν ὑπερβολὴν ἀφεῖναι τοῦ τοιούτου πολέμου. καίτοι γε οὐκ εἰδότος ἐστὶν ὁ λόγος ὅλον τὸ ἡμέτερον πρᾶγμα· οὐ γὰρ ἂν ᾤεθ' ἡμᾶς μαλακῶς ἀντιστῆναι τῷ δόγματι τούς γε μέχρις αἵματος ὑπὲρ τοῦ ὀρθοῦ καὶ εὐσεβοῦς κινδυνεύσαντας. ἀλλ' ὅμως χάριν ἔχω τοῦ λόγου θαυμαστὴν τῷ Λαπίθῃ—τοῦτο γὰρ ὄνομα τῷ φιλοσόφῳ—ἐπὶ τῷ λόγῳ τούτῳ, αἰσχύναντι τοὺς διὰ τοῦτο φιλονεικίαν ἐπεγκαλοῦντάς μοι· οὓς οὐ δεῖν φησιν οὕτως ἔχειν περὶ τῆς εὐσεβείας, μηδὲ περιορᾶν φθειρομένην τὴν ἐκκλησίαν—πάντα γὰρ εἶναι πρὸς ἓν τοῦτο πάρεργα Χριστιανοῖς—καὶ ταῦτα τοῦ δυσσεβοῦντος ἀμαθοῦς ἄγαν ὄντος καὶ μηδὲ τὰς πρώτας ἀρχὰς τῆς φιλοσοφίας εἰδότος, μηδὲ τί ἐστιν ἐπιστήμη καὶ ὅπως γίνεσθαι πέφυκεν ἐπισταμένου, ὡς αὐτὸς ἐξ αὐτῶν τοῦ Παλαμᾶ τῶν λόγων μαρτυρεῖ μαθεῖν ὁ φιλόσοφος.

Δεῖ δὴ ταῦτα καὶ τοὺς αὐτόθι λόγων τροφίμους καὶ εὐσεβείας ἰδεῖν καὶ θαυμάσαι μὲν τὴν σοφίαν, θαυμάσαι δὲ τὴν εὐσέβειαν καὶ τὴν ἑκατέρωθι τοῦ ἀνδρὸς εὐεξίαν καὶ ῥώμην καὶ τὸν ἀγῶνα τὸν ὑπὲρ εὐσεβείας καθ' ὃν οὐ μόνον αὐτὸς πῦρ πνεῖ κατὰ τῶν δυσσεβούντων, ἀλλὰ καὶ τοὺς ἐνθάδε δυνάμει διαφέροντας λόγων ἐπὶ τὸν κατὰ τούτων πόλεμον παρακαλεῖ καὶ θαυμαστῶς συγκροτεῖ. τοιοῦτον ἄρα ψυχὴ ἧς διὰ βάθους ἦλθε σοφία τε καὶ εὐσέβεια. διὸ χρὴ δήπου ταῦτα καὶ ἰδεῖν καὶ θαυμάσαι τοὺς ὑμετέρους σοφούς· τὰ γὰρ καλά, καὶ μάλισθ' ὑφ' ὧν τὸ θεῖον δοξάζεται καὶ εὐσεβεῖται, θαυμάζεσθαι δίκαια. ἰδόντων μὲν οὖν καὶ ἄλλοι ταῦτα, ἰδέτω δὲ καὶ ὁ θαυμάσιος Μάγιστρος καὶ ὁ σοφὸς Κυδώνης καὶ ὁ ἱερὸς καὶ θεῖος ἐν

---

38 ἡμετέρους M

74

place—so that if it should find him still there, it may not get lost somehow, but that it may be possible for him to receive it through your kindness; and so that if it should not reach him, it may be shown to other friends. For it is very valuable; especially the letter of the Cypriote philosopher in which he is shown to be truly a philosopher and a most accomplished champion of piety. More than anyone else he attacks from abroad the Palamnaian disease and expresses his indignation and exclaims in his letter "O what impiety!" at the man who introduces a multitude of unequal divinities and at the fact that none of the men here cares to refute these doctrines with serious writings; those who appear to be our most capable men of letters keep quiet, while this doctrine feeds upon Christ's flock like poison; and one man alone—namely myself—took up the divine zeal to resist this doctrine well and correctly, but in a manner that is milder, as he says, than is required for resistance to such writings. I rejoiced indeed at this remark, more so than if he had said that I had carried the war to the extreme. And yet this is the remark of a man who does not know everything about me, for he would not have thought that I oppose this doctrine mildly; I who risked even my blood for the sake of the correct and pious ⟨doctrines⟩. But I am most grateful for this remark to Lapithes (for this is the philosopher's name), because he put to shame by this remark those who accuse me of contentiousness because of this ⟨resistance⟩. These men, he says, should not take this attitude with regard to piety, nor should they neglect the Church when it is being destroyed. For with Christians all other matters are secondary to this one, and especially when the perpetrator of impiety is extremely ignorant and unacquainted with even the first principles of philosophy, not knowing what knowledge is and how it is naturally formed, as the philosopher himself testifies that he learned from Palamas' very writings.

It is obviously necessary that learned and pious men over there see this letter also and admire the man's learning and piety and his soundness and vigor in each of these ⟨qualities⟩, as well as his struggle for piety in which he not only breathes fire against the impious, but also encourages and admirably organizes for the war against them those men here who are distinguished for their literary prowess. Such indeed is a soul deeply penetrated by learning and piety! For this reason it is surely necessary that your learned men both see and admire this ⟨letter⟩, because good things and especially those through which the Divinity is glorified and revered have a right to be admired. And so, let others see it also. Let the admirable Magistros see it and the sage Kydones and the holy and divine hieromonk Matthew, who practices

ἱερομονάχοις Ματθαῖος ὁ ἐν τῇ τοῦ θεσπεσίου Ἰσαὰκ ἱερωτάτῃ μονῇ τὴν ἀρετὴν μετιών· σὺν οἷς καὶ ὁ θεσπέσιος δικαιοφύλαξ Βρυέννιος, αἰσχύνης δὲ ἕνεκα τῆς ἑαυτοῦ καὶ ὁ τῶν θεοτήτων πλῆθος τεθαυμακὼς Χαρατζᾶς καὶ εἴ τις ἄλλος αὐτῷ παραπλήσιος.

75. Μαξίμῳ ἢ Ἰγνατίῳ

Εἰ ἐκ τοιούτων προφάσεων εἰς ἔχθρας αἱ φιλίαι μετέπιπτον, οὐκ ἂν ἦν οὐδαμοῦ παρ' ἀνθρώποις φιλία. οἶμαι μὲν οὖν μηδένα εἶναι ἀνθρώπων, μηδὲ γενέσθαι πώποτε τοῖς φίλοις παντελῶς ἀνεπίληπτον· ἀνθρώπου γὰρ φύσις οὐκ ἀναμάρτητος, φέρουσι δὲ ἀλλήλων οἱ φίλοι ῥᾷον τὰ ἁμαρτήματα ἢ τὰς εἰς ἀλλήλους εὐεργεσίας οἱ δυσμενεῖς· τὰ μὲν γάρ, τῇ φύσει τῇ κοινῇ τῶν ἀνθρώπων ὡς εἰκὸς λογιζόμενοι, ἀνύποπτα κακοηθείας εἶναι νομίζουσι, τὰ δὲ οὐκ ἄνευ ὑποψίας τοιαύτης. διὸ δὴ καὶ Παῦλός φησιν ὁ νομοθέτης θεοφιλοῦς τοῖς ἀνθρώποις καὶ τοῦ βελτίστου βίου, ἀλλήλων ἀνέχεσθε, καὶ ἀλλήλων τὰ βάρη βαστάζετε· καὶ Πυθαγόρας ὁ Σάμιος, μὴ ἔχθαιρε φίλον σὸν ἁμαρτάδος οὕνεκα μικρῆς.

Ὁ τοίνυν εὐσεβὴς καὶ ἐκ τοιούτων γενόμενος πῶς καταδέξεται καὶ τῆς Πυθαγόρου τοῦ δυσσεβοῦς ἀρετῆς ἀπολείπεσθαι, καὶ διὰ μικροψυχίαν ἀπ' εὐτελοῦς αἰτίας, ἄρδην ἀνατρέψαι πολυετῆ φιλίαν ἣν πολὺς μὲν χρόνος, οὐχ αἱ τυχοῦσαι δὲ ἀφορμαὶ συνειλόχασιν; εἰ δὲ καὶ εὐσέβεια τὸ μάλιστα ταύτην συστῆσαν εἴη, καὶ λυομένης ταύτης συμβαίνει τὴν εὐσέβειαν αὐτὴν πλημμελεῖσθαι τῷ τὴν συνήθειαν λύοντι, τί τις ἂν εἴποι; δι' ἣν γὰρ καὶ αἱ δυσμένειαι λύονται τοῖς εὐφρονοῦσι καὶ ἄλυτοι φιλίαι συνίστανται, οὕτω φιλέχθρως καὶ φιλαιτίως ἔχειν ὡς μηδὲ ταύτης φείσασθαι, ἀλλ' ὥσπερ χειμάρρουν συγκατασῦραι μετὰ τῆς συνηθείας, πῶς οὐχὶ πάνδεινον; καὶ ὁ μὲν Θεμιστοκλῆς καὶ Ἀριστείδης ὁ Λυσιμάχου, διαφορᾶς οὐκ ὀλίγης συνεστηκυίας αὐτοῖς, ἐσπείσαντο ἐπιόντος τοῦ Μήδου καὶ ἀμνηστίαν ἀλλήλοις τῶν πρῴην ἐγκλημάτων παρέσχοντο, εὖ καὶ καλῶς

75: 10–11 ἀλλήλων ἀνέχεσθε Eph. 4:3; Col. 3:13 ‖ 11 Gal. 6:2 ‖ 12–13 Hierocles, *Carmina aurea*, VII, 6–8 (ed. F. Mullach, *Fragmenta philosophorum graecorum* [Paris, 1876]), I, 428

75: M 76ᵛ–77ʳ.
16 ἀνατρέψας M ‖ 23 συγκατασύραι M ‖ 25–26 ἀμνηστεῖαν M

asceticism in the most holy monastery of the divine Isaak, and together with them the divine *dikaiophylax* Bryennios, and—to his own shame—Charatzas who admires the multitude of divinities, and anyone else like him.

75. To Maximos or Ignatios

If friendships changed into enmities for such pretexts, friendship would not exist anywhere among men. Indeed, I do not believe that there is or ever was a man completely blameless towards his friends (for human nature is not faultless), but friends tolerate each other's faults more eagerly than enemies do each other's expressions of kindness. For they rightly attribute the former to the common nature of men and think that they are free of suspicion of malice, whereas the latter are not free of such suspicion. For this reason, indeed, Paul, who ordained for men the life which is best and most dear to God, says: "Be forbearing with one another, and help one another to carry these heavy loads"; and Pythagoras of Samos says: "Do not hate your friend because of a small error."

How, then, will a pious man born of pious parents deign to fall short of the generosity of even the pagan Pythagoras and, because of pettiness due to a trivial reason, completely destroy a friendship of many years which was established over a long time and not just on chance occasions? Moreover, if piety should be what really founded ⟨the friendship⟩, and if when it is broken the man who breaks the relationship happens to offend piety itself, what could one say? For sensible men break up even their enmities for the sake of ⟨piety⟩ and establish unbreakable friendships. Is it not horrible, therefore, to be so hostile and censorious as not to spare even piety but, just like a torrent, to sweep it away along with friendship? Even Themistocles and Aristeides the son of Lysimachos (though the difference that existed between them was not a small one) made up their quarrel and forgave each other their former grievances before the approaching Persians, because they suspected correctly that

ὑποπτεύσαντες μὴ τὸ διάφορον αὐτῶν εὐχειρώτους παράσχοι τῷ βαρβάρῳ τοὺς Ἕλληνας· ἡμῖν δὲ τῆς εὐσεβείας πολεμουμένης καὶ τῶν ψυχῶν, οὐ τῶν σωμάτων—ὡς αὐτὸς παντὸς μᾶλλον ἐπίστασαι ὁ καὶ διαφερόντως ἀμυνόμενος τοὺς πολεμίους τούτους—σὺ τοσαύτην ἀνέλαβες πρὸς ἡμᾶς τὴν δυσμένειαν, οὐδὲν ἔχων ἐγκαλεῖν λόγον ἔχον, ὥστε που καὶ αὐτὴν τὴν εὐσέβειαν [fol. 77ʳ] βλάπτειν ἧς χθὲς καὶ πρῴην προεκινδύνευες. καὶ πῶς ἄν τις τοῦτ' ἄξιον εἶναι φαίη τῆς εὐφυΐας τῆς σῆς καὶ πρὸς ἀγαθῆς σοι δόξης;

Ἀλλ' εἰ μὲν μικρὸν μέν, ἦν δὲ ὅμως ἡμαρτηκώς τι περὶ σὲ καί μοι τὸ συνειδὸς ἠνώχλει, παρῃτούμην ἂν καὶ προσῆκον ἂν ἦν εἰρῆσθαι τὰ εἰρημένα μοι. νῦν δὲ οὐδ' ἔστιν ὅ τι σύνοιδα ἐμαυτῷ περὶ τὴν σὴν ἀγχίνοιαν ἡμαρτηκώς, πλὴν εἰ λέγεις ἁμάρτημα τοὺς ἐπαίνους ἐκείνους οὓς εἰκότως ἐκείνῳ τῷ ῥεύματι τῆς γλώττης ἐγὼ περιετίθουν τῆς σῆς, οὓς σὺ μέν, ὡς ἔοικε, μετριοφρονῶν καὶ μηδὲν μέγα οἰόμενος περὶ σαυτοῦ, εἰρωνείαν ὑπείληφας, ἐγὼ δὲ ὁρῶν ὅσον ἐστὶ τὸ χρῆμα καὶ οἵαν ἔχεις ἐν τῷ στήθει τήν τε τῶν λόγων πηγὴν κἀν τῇ γλώττῃ τὴν εὔροιαν, εἰκότως οὕτως ἐθαύμαζον, ὥστε σοι δόξαι σκώπτειν, ἀλλ' οὐ θαυμάζειν τὴν δύναμιν, πρᾶγμα καὶ ἄλλως τῆς ἐμῆς ἀλλότριον φύσεως, μὴ ὅτι πρὸς λόγους χαρίεντας καὶ ξένον ὡς ἀληθῶς τὸ γόνιμον ἔχοντας, καὶ τὸ μέγιστον, ὑπὲρ τῆς εὐσεβείας καὶ αὐτῶν ἡμῶν ῥέοντας. μὴ τοίνυν νικάτω μικροψυχία παρὰ σοὶ τοιαύτην φορὰν ἀγαθῶν καὶ τοσαύτην, μηδὲ δύο τοσαῦται καὶ τοιαῦται δυνάμεις, εὐσέβεια καὶ φιλία, ὑπὸ τοιούτου πάθους ἡττάσθωσαν· σχέτλιον γὰρ ὄντως τοῦτό γε καὶ τῆς σῆς, εἴπερ τινός, ἀνάξιον φύσεως.

76. Μαξίμῳ τῷ Καλοφέρῳ

Τὸ μὲν ἐμοὶ χαλεπαίνειν καὶ μέμφεσθαι καὶ πᾶν ὁτιοῦν ἢ λέγειν ἢ καὶ ποιεῖν με φλαῦρον, ἀνδρὸς ἂν εἴη πρᾶγμα ἢ ἀδικοῦντος, ἂν ταῦτα πράττῃ τόν γε πράττειν οὐ δίκαιον, ἢ μὴ φιλοσοφοῦντος μὴ μέντοι μηδ' ἀδικοῦντος, ἂν ἀμύνηται τὸν προηδικηκότα. τὸ δὲ ἀμύνεσθαι μὲν ἐθέλειν τὸν δυσμενῆ, οὐ μᾶλλον δὲ ἐκεῖνον ἢ ἑαυτὸν οἷς ἀμύνοιτο βλάπτειν περὶ τὰ καιριώτατα, σὸν ἰδεῖν τίνος ἂν εἴη [fol. 45ʳ] πρᾶγμα. σὺ τοίνυν δυσμενῶς ἐμοῦ μεμνημένος, ὡς ἔοικεν, εἶτα δι' ἐμὲ καὶ τὴν καλὴν ὁμολογίαν προδιδούς, ἧς ἀρτίως προ-

---

28 *βαρβάρῳ* scripsi: *βαράθρῳ* M

76: M 44ᵛ–45ᵛ. Ed. Loenertz, *Epistulae*, 107–108, no. 9.

their quarrel might render the Greeks an easy prey to the barbarians. But in our case, when war is waged against piety and against our souls rather than our bodies (as you yourself know better than anyone else, since you resist these enemies exceptionally), you have assumed such a hostile attitude against me, without being able to accuse me of anything serious, that you are somehow harming even the very piety for which you so recently sustained the brunt of battle. And how can one say that this is worthy of your intelligence and that it adds to your good reputation?

And if, indeed, I had committed an offense against you, even a small one, and if my conscience was bothering me, I would have given up, and it would have been fair to say to me all that was said to me. But now I do not even know myself what offense I committed against your Sagacity, unless you call an offense those praises with which I properly adorned that well-known fluency of your tongue. Being modest, as it seems, and having no conceit about yourself, you assumed that they were ironical, while I, seeing what a great talent this was and what a fountain of eloquence you have in your breast and what fluency in your tongue, properly showed so much admiration, that I appeared to you to be mocking, not admiring, your ability, a thing which even in other circumstances is alien to my nature, to say nothing of mocking graceful speech and its truly wondrous abundance and—something which is most important—speech flowing in the interest of piety and our own. May pettiness, therefore, not prevail over so fine and great an abundance of virtues in you! Do not let two such noble and great forces, piety and friendship, be defeated by such a passion! For this, indeed, is truly wicked and unworthy of your character, more than of anyone else's.

76. To Maximos Kalopheros

To be angry with me and find fault with me and either say or even do all sorts of malicious things against me would be the behavior either of an unjust man (if he does these things to a person who does not deserve them) or of one who is not a philosopher, but who is not unjust either, if he retaliates against a man who wronged him first. But it is up to you to consider who would behave so as to wish to retaliate against an enemy and by this retaliation to injure himself more than the enemy in

76

ἵστασο καὶ πάλαι παρὰ τῶν θείων πατέρων κεκληρονόμηκας, σκόπει μὴ ἐμὲ μὲν ἧττον ἧς ἀμυνόμενος, σαυτὸν δὲ τελεώτατα βλάπτων, καὶ ταῦτα ἑκών, διὰ μικροψυχίαν. εἰ μὲν γὰρ ἐξ ἀγνοίας καὶ ἀμαθίας τὰ τοιαῦτα ἡμάρτανες, ἧττον ἂν ἦν τὸ δεινόν· νῦν δέ, εἴπερ τις, τὴν ἀλήθειαν εἰδὼς καὶ πολλοὺς μὲν ἀγῶνας ὑπὲρ αὐτῆς ἀνύσας, πολλοὺς δὲ καὶ μέλλων καὶ κομιδῇ προθυμούμενος, ἐκτὸς τοῦ μικροψυχεῖν διὰ φαύλας αἰτίας, εἶτα διὰ τοῦτο μὴ μόνον τοὺς εὐσεβεῖς ἀγῶνας, ἀλλὰ καὶ τὴν ὁμολογίαν αὐτήν, ὡς λέγεται, παραιτούμενος τῆς εὐσεβείας, καὶ φιλονεικίαν ὀνομάζων τὸ ἡμέτερον πρᾶγμα, οὐκ οἶδ' ὅ τι δεινὸν καταλείπεις νομίζειν, οὐδ' ὅπως ἐμὲ μᾶλλον ἢ σαυτόν, ὅπερ εἶπον, ὑπολαμβάνεις κακοῦν. εἰ δὲ μηδὲ σαυτὸν μόνον, ἀλλὰ καὶ πολλοὺς ἄλλους συνεμπεσεῖν ποιήσεις εἰς τὸν αὐτόν σοι βόθρον, περὶ τὸ θεῖον ὄντως τοῦ πταίσματος, τίς τούτῳ θρῆνος τῷ πταίσματι καὶ κοπετὸς ἱκανὸς γένοιτ' ἄν ποτε;

Οὐ ταῦτα ἦν, ὦ θαυμάσιε, τὰ τῇ σῇ φύσει πρέποντα· οὐχ οὗτος ἧς αὐχεῖς ἐπιστήμης φυσικὸς καὶ οὐσιώδης καρπός, ἀλλὰ τῆς ἐναντίας, καὶ ἀπειράκις ἀπείρως διαφέρων ἐκείνου. δεῖ γάρ με διαλεχθῆναί σοι ἀπὸ τῆς καινῆς φιλίας καὶ ἀστεΐσασθαί γε πρὸς τὴν καινήν σοι χάριν, εἰ καὶ θρηνῶ τρόπον ἕτερον. ἀλλ' ἐγὼ λυπηρός τις καὶ ὑπερόπτης τῶν φίλων καὶ τῶν ἑλκτικῶν ἰύγγων ἀμέτοχος, αἳς τοὺς πολλοὺς ἡ καινότης θηλύνουσα καινὸν ἐργαστήριον ἀσεβείας ἐδημιούργησεν, ὅ φησιν ὁ θεολόγος * * * οὔπω λέγω τοῦτο μὲν ἀρετήν, ἐκεῖνο δὲ κακίαν εἶναι δοκεῖν τοῖς ἱεροῖς πατράσι, καὶ τοῖς οἷος σὺ τὴν εὐφυΐαν καὶ παίδευσιν αἰσχρὸν αἱρεῖσθαι ὅλως τὸ δεύτερον. ἀλλ' εἰ δίκην ἐγὼ δίκαιος διὰ τοῦτο διδόναι, οὐ παραιτοῦμαι· ὑβριζέσθω Γρηγόριος—ὅπερ οὖν δὴ καὶ πάσχει—καὶ προπηλακιζέσθω καί, εἰ βούλει, τυπτέσθω, καὶ ὅλως πᾶσαν τὴν δοκοῦσαν δίκην τιννύτω τοῖς ἀδικεῖσθαι νομίζουσι, μὴ μαθὼν γλωττοστροφεῖν καὶ πᾶσιν ἡδὺς εἶναι καὶ δημοχαρὴς ὑπὲρ τὸν Ὀδυσσέα, ἀλλ' ἁπλοῦν ἦθος καὶ ἀποίητον φέρων καὶ μόνου τοῦ εὐθέος φροντίζων, καὶ τιμῶν μὲν τοὺς φίλους καὶ ἀγαπῶν, εἴπερ τις, κολακεύειν δὲ ἀφυὴς ὤν, εἴπερ τις. εἰ ταῦτα ἀπαίδευτα, καὶ ἀδικήματα περὶ τοὺς φίλους ἐμά, ἐμὲ μέν, ὡς εἶπον, ἀπαιτείτωσαν οἱ φίλοι τὴν ἐπὶ τούτοις δίκην· Θεὸς δὲ [fol. 45v] μὴ ἀδικείσθω, μηδ' ὁ τῆς εὐσεβείας λόγος, μηδ' ὁ γενναῖος καὶ σοφὸς ἡμῖν Μάξιμος· ἄλογον γάρ, ἵν' εὐφήμως εἴπω, καὶ αὐτὸς ὁ ἔσχατος τῆς ἀδικίας ὅρος.

---

26 Maxim. Conf., *Capit. theol.*, 1, 49 (PG, 90, 1101A) = Palamas, *Dialexis*, 24, Syngrammata, II, 186, 26; *Epist. ad Gabram*, 5, Syngrammata, II, 332, 12 || 30 Greg. Naz., *Or.* 27, 9 (PG, 36, 24A) || 38 Aristophanes, *Nubes*, 792

---

31 ante οὔπω lacunam statui

76

most important matters. Now it seems that because you have been holding a grudge against me, you betrayed on my account the good faith which you supported recently and inherited from the holy Fathers long ago. Yet beware lest you retaliate less against me, while injuring yourself completely—and willingly, at that—because of pettiness! For if you had committed these errors out of ignorance and inexperience, it would have been a smaller misfortune. But, as it is, when you know the truth better than anyone else, and you carried on many struggles for its sake and were ready and altogether eager for many others (for you were far from pettiness which is provoked by trivial reasons), thereafter because of pettiness you give up not only the pious struggles but also, as they say, the very confession of piety, and you call my attitude contentiousness, I know not what horrible thing you leave ⟨one⟩ to believe, nor, as I said, how you assume that you injure me more than yourself. But since your error concerns the Divinity, if you will cause not only yourself but many others also to fall into the same pit with you, what lament and gesture of sorrow would ever be sufficient for this error?

These things did not become your character, my admirable friend! This is not the natural and essential product of the learning that you boast of, but of the opposite, and it is "infinitely" different from that product. For I must talk to you in terms borrowed from your new friendship and make witticisms appropriate to your new gratification, even though I lament after another fashion. But I am a troublesome man, and overbearing with friends, having no share of the magic charms with which the new doctrine "enervates" the majority and renders them "a new workshop of impiety," as the Theologian says * * * I do not yet say that the holy Fathers consider the former to be a virtue and the latter a vice, and that it is altogether disgraceful for men who are like yourself in intelligence and education to choose the latter. But if I am bound to be punished for this, I do not beg for pardon! Let Gregory be insulted (which is what he in fact suffers now) and trampled in the mud and beaten, if you wish, and, in short, pay every penalty that appears right to those who believe themselves wronged, because he did not learn to "talk glibly" and to be pleasant to everybody and more popular than Odysseus, but has a simple and unaffected character and cares only for what is right and honors his friends and loves them more than anyone else, but more than anyone else lacks a natural talent for flattery. If these are rude things and offenses of mine towards my friends, let the friends, as I said, demand punishment for them. But let God not be wronged nor the principle of piety nor my noble and wise Maximos. For this is absurd, to put it politely, and the extreme limit of injustice.

76

Εἰ μὲν οὖν οὐ κακῶς ταῦτα λέγεται, πεπαύσθω τὰ νῦν ὑπὸ σοῦ κηρυττόμενα, καὶ φανείτω πάλιν Ἀχιλλεὺς ἐν τοῖς Ἕλλησι μετὰ τῶν ὅπλων· εἰ δ' οὐκ εὐφυῶς οὐδὲ πεπαιδευμένως, διδότω δίκην καὶ τούτων Γρηγόριος, ἀλλὰ μὴ ὁ τῆς ἀληθείας ἀτιμαζέσθω λόγος. πάντως δὲ πεπαύσθω Θεὸς βλασφημούμενος τῇ κακῇ παλινῳδίᾳ τοῦ γενναίου Μαξίμου, καὶ μηδ' αὐτὸς ἐπαινούμενος ὁ τὴν παλινῳδίαν ᾄδων.

76

And so, if what I say is not wrong, cease what you are now proclaiming and let Achilles appear among the Greeks with his armor! But if I speak neither cleverly nor in a well-bred manner, let Gregory be punished for this also, but let the principle of truth not be dishonored! At all events, let God no longer be blasphemed through the wicked recantation of the noble Maximos, and let the man who sings this recantation cease being praised!

COMMENTARY

1.

Having read a letter of Gregoras which dealt with astronomy, Akindynos writes from Thessalonica to congratulate the author and initiate a correspondence with him.

Addressee: Nikephoros Gregoras in Constantinople.

Date: February–April 1333; see commentary on lines 5–6 *infra*.

Guilland (*Correspondance*, 275) assigns this letter to between 1325 and 1330 but gives no reason for this date. Beyer (*Antirrhetica I*, 56) correctly notes that it was written after Barlaam's unsuccessful debate with Gregoras in the capital; see commentary on lines 41–42 *infra*.

2 Βαλσαμὼν ὁ γενναῖος: A Thessalonian known from a letter he addressed to Gregoras expressing his admiration for the renowned polymath and his desire to meet him; see Gregoras, *Hist.*, I, LXXXIX–XC; French résumé in Guilland, *op. cit.*, no. 10, 277. Guilland (*ibid.*, 304) identifies him tentatively with Stephen Balsamon, the recipient of three letters of Michael Gabras; see Fatouros, ed., *Die Briefe des Michael Gabras*, nos. 12–13 and 289.

Another contemporary Balsamon bore the first name of Nikephoros and is attested as *oikeios tou basileos* in 1327; see *Actes de Chilandar*, nos. 116, 289.

5–6 *τὴν σὴν ἐκείνην ἐπιστολὴν τὴν περὶ τῶν ἐν οὐρανῷ τοὺς ἀγνοοῦντας διδάσκουσαν*: Guilland thought that this was probably the letter to the metropolitan of Apros in which Gregoras criticized those who abused astronomy through their ignorance; see *Correspondance*, 275 and 189–93. However, it is more likely that Akindynos had read the letter to Kaloeidas in which Gregoras referred to his prediction of two eclipses of the sun; see *ibid.*, no. 35, 147–55. Akindynos alludes to this when he writes that even the sun and the moon and the stars proclaim the fame of Gregoras as they appear and disappear at his command; see Letter 2, lines 17–19; and Beyer (*Antirrhetika I*, 57) who also sees in this statement an allusion to Gregoras' letter to Kaloeidas.

Gregoras wrote in that letter that shortly after the eclipse of the sun on 30 November 1331 he had asked his opponent (*sc.*, Barlaam) to predict the date of the next eclipse, but, since he failed to receive an answer for a

whole year, he felt free to break his silence and divulge to Kaloeidas that the next solar eclipse would occur near noon on 14 May of the first indiction (i.e., 1333); see *Correspondance*, 151, lines 11–14, 153, lines 10–14; Polemis, Ἀντιλογία, 53–54; J. Mogenet-A. Tihon, *Barlaam de Seminara, traités sur les éclipses de soleil de 1333 et 1337* (Louvain, 1977), 155. Therefore, since Gregoras' letter can be dated to the end of 1332 or the beginning of 1333, ours must be assigned to the spring of 1333 and, more precisely, before May, because Akindynos alludes to Gregoras' successful prediction of the solar eclipse of May not in this but in the following letter; see Letter 2, lines 17–19.

10–11 *τό τε τῆς ἑρμηνείας Ἑλληνικόν*: Akindynos must be commending Gregoras for the purity and correctness of his language. In his *Rhetoric*, Aristotle discusses purity (*ἑλληνίζειν*, "good Greek") as an element of good style (cf. *Rhet.*, III, 5, 1407a, line 19–1407b, line 10), but later writers went even further, making it one of the principal rhetorical precepts; see, for example, Dionysius of Halicarnassus who in his *Commentaries on the Ancient Orators* cites Lysias as a model orator because of his use of the pure Attic language (cf. H. Usener-L. Rademacher, eds., *Dion. Halic. Quae extant* [Teubner, 1899, repr. 1965], V, 9, line 11–10, line 3) and Apthonius who includes it among the four virtues of narrative prose; see *Progymnasmata*, 2, ed. L. Spengel, *Rhetores Graeci* (Leipzig, 1854) (hereafter, Spengel, *Rhet. Gr.*), II, 22, lines 10–12: *ἀρεταὶ δὲ διηγήματος τέσσαρες, σαφήνεια, συντομία, πιθανότης, καὶ ὁ τῶν ὀνομάτων ἑλληνισμός.*

11 *τὸ τῶν λέξεων ἀνθηρόν*: cf. Hermogenes, *Progymnasmata*, 10, ed. Spengel, *Rhet. Gr.*, II, 16, lines 35–36: *ἂν ἀνθηρὸν τὸ πρᾶγμα, ἔστω καὶ ἡ λέξις τοιαύτη.*

12–13 *ποικιλίαν ἐνθυμημάτων ἐκ τῶν Πλάτωνος θησαυρῶν*: Literally a thought or consideration, an enthymeme is an argument or, technically, a rhetorical syllogism drawn from probable premises; see Aristotle, *Rhet.*, 1355a, lines 6–13, and Hermogenes, *Περὶ εὑρέσεως*, III, 8, ed. Spengel, *Rhet. Gr.*, II, 219–22.

There is no variety of arguments drawn from the Platonic treasures in Gregoras' letter to Kaloeidas, unless one might say that the author echoes Socrates when he says that he will disregard his opponents, whom he calls sophists, because "he who claims to be wise must live for himself and not for the opinion of the many"; see Guilland, *Correspondance*, 147, line 21 and 155, lines 6–8; Plato, *Crito*, 44c–48b.

26 *τοῦ Θηβαίου ποιητοῦ*: The lyric poet Pindar who was born in Cynoscephalae near Thebes in Boeotia.

28–32 *καὶ πολλ᾽ ἕτερα τῆς σῆς . . . γλώττης δημιουργήματα παρ᾽ ἐμοί σοι συνῆκται . . . εἴπερ ἃ πέπομφας Ἰωσὴφ ἐκείνῳ τῷ μακαρίτῃ . . . διὰ μνήμης ἔχεις*: The reference is to Gregoras' treatise on the method for calculating the date of Easter which, according to its superscription in *Vaticanus Gr. 1086*, fol. 75r, was addressed to Joseph the Philosopher; cf. Gregoras, *Hist.*, I, XLVIII and LXXI note 2: Πρὸς *τὸν σεβασμιώτατον* Ἰωσὴφ *περὶ τοῦ* Πάσχα, *ἀπόδειξις ὅπως ἐσφάλη πρὸ χρόνων καὶ ὅπως δεῖ ποιεῖσθαι τὴν τούτου διόρθωσιν*. This treatise has been inserted in Gregoras' *History* (VIII, 13:I, 364, line 3–372, line 18) and was also published by M. Bezdeki in "Nicephori Gregorae Epistulae XC," *Ephemeris Dacoromana*, II (1924), no. XX.

It is not possible, however, to determine which were the many other works of Gregoras which Akindynos says here that he possessed.

On Joseph the Philosopher's association with Gregoras, see Guilland, *Correspondance*, 338–42; on his life and works, see D. Stiernon, «Joseph le philosophe, moine byzantin, mort vers 1330,» *Dictionnaire de Spiritualité*, vol. 8 (Paris, 1974), cols. 1388–92.

31–32 *διά τοῦ θεσπεσίου καὶ σοφοῦ* Παλαμᾶ: Palamas, who was then living in Berroia, had gone to Constantinople on the occasion of his mother's death; see Philotheos, *Encomium*, cols. 572B–573B; Meyendorff, *Introduction*, 58. Since, according to Akindynos, he returned shortly after the death of Joseph the Philosopher which occurred in 1330, his trip can now be dated to that year; see commentary on line 33 *infra*.

32 *πρὸ γὰρ δυοῖν ἐτοῖν τοῦτό γε*: The information that Akindynos was writing two years after the death of Joseph corroborates J. Treu's conjecture that Joseph died *ca.* 1330; see "Der Philosoph Joseph," *BZ*, 8 (1899), 33. For if we are correct in assigning this letter to the first months of 1333, Joseph must have died at the end of 1330.

33 *τὸν φιλόσοφον*: For the various meanings of the term "philosopher" as used by the Byzantines to denote a monk, scholar or rhetorician, see F. Dölger, "Zur Bedeutung von *φιλόσοφος* in byzantinischer Zeit," *Byzanz und die europäische Staatenwelt* (Ettal, 1953), 197–208.

40 *λέγω δὴ τοῖς*Ἕλλησιν: Akindynos alludes here to the coterie of intellectuals who regarded themselves as the cultural heirs of the ancient Greeks; see S. Runciman, *The Last Byzantine Renaissance* (Cambridge, 1970), 20–21. That Akindynos gives to the word "Hellene" a purely cultural connotation is evident from Letter 2, lines 11–12, where he writes to Gregoras: "It is the beauty and the power of your works which proclaim you great all over the earth, and persuade each man not to honor any of the Hellenes (such as are now Hellenes) above their own author."

Akindynos' correspondent Nicholas Kabasilas uses this word in exactly the same sense in the letters to his father, where he refers to the learned Thessalonians as "the sons of the Hellenes" or the "Hellenes among us"; see P. Enepekides, ed., "Der Briefwechsel des Mystikers Nikolaos Kabasilas," *BZ*, 46 (1953), Letter 1, lines 17–18 (Ἡ δὲ ἐπιστολὴ σοὶ μὲν ἴσως κεχαρισμένη φανεῖται τὸν πατέρα φιλοῦντι, οὐκ' οἶδα δὲ εἰ καὶ τοῖς Ἑλλήνων υἱέσιν) and Letter 4, line 18 (μὴ φανεὶς οὕτως ἔχων [*sc.*, ὁ πρὸς τὸν μάρτυρα λόγος] λυπήσει τοὺς ἐν ἡμῖν Ἕλληνας).

41–42 *πολλοὺς τῶν ἐν λόγοις . . . λυπεῖ*: The allusion is to Barlaam and his unsuccessful debate with Gregoras, which took place in Constantinople in the winter of 1331–32. Gregoras refers to this date in his *History* (XI, 10: I, 555, line 20–556, line 17) and describes it in his dialogue *Florentios*. On the chronology of the debate, see Leone, "Alcune osservazioni sul Florentios di Niceforo Gregora," *Byzantino-Sicula II*, Miscellanea di Scritti in memoria di G. Rossi Taibbi (= *Quad. dell' Instit. di Studi Bizantini e Neoellenici*, 8 [Palermo, 1975], 335–36; and Beyer, "Eine Chronologie," no. 27, p. 134.

2.

Akindynos is delighted at Gregoras' promise to be his friend, and he assures his distinguished correspondent that he is not a base flatterer, but a sincere admirer of his.

Addressee: Nikephoros Gregoras in Constantinople.

Date: Summer of 1333, after the solar eclipse of 14 May 1333 to which Akindynos alludes in this letter; see commentary on lines 17–19 *infra*.

2–4 *Οὐδὲν θαυμαστὸν ἴσην* Κλεοδήμῳ *σε δόξαν ἀποφέρεσθαι . . . ὄρνιθάς τινας ἑαυτὸν ᾄδειν ἐδίδασκε*: In answer to Akindynos' effusive praise of his works, Gregoras wrote that his fame was just an act of God, whereas a certain Kleodemos was justly famous because he had taught some birds to sing his praises. Gregoras' letter to Akindynos—the only surviving one—has been published by A. Mustoxydes-D. Schinas Byzantios in Συλλογὴ *ἀποσπασμάτων ἀνεκδότων ἑλληνικῶν μετὰ σημειώσεων* (Venice, 1817), VIII, no. 2, 4–7. (I regret that I have not been able to consult this hard to obtain edition and have studied this letter from a photocopy of *Vat. Gr. 1086*, fols. 120ʳ–121ʳ.) For a French résumé of this letter, see Guilland, *Correspondance*, no. 20, p. 10.

As already commented by Beyer (cf. *Antirrhretika I*, 57 note 261),

this story is from Aelian's *Historia Varia* (14, 30), where Anno the Carthagenian, and not Kleodemos, is said to have been so excessively vain that he purchased a great many birds and taught them to sing "Anno is a god." It was, however, a wasted effort because once the birds were let free, they reverted to nature, forgetting the lesson that Anno taught them in captivity. This anecdote is also cited by Niketas Choniates who tells the story exactly as Aelian (cf. *Historia*, ed. Bonn, 565; rec. J. A. Van Dieten [Berlin, 1975], I, 431), whereas Gregoras writes that Kleodemos' trick was successful and made him famous; see *Vatic. Gr. 1086*, fol. 120^r: Ἐγένετο τις ἀνὴρ Καρχηδόνιος, Κλεόδημος ὄνομα, ὃς τῶν ὀρνίθων ὁπόσοι πρὸς τὴν τῆς ἀνθρωπίνης φωνῆς ἐξικνοῦνται μίμησιν πλείους ξυνηθροικὼς καὶ ὥσπερ ξυνωμοσίαν ἐλάσας, μέγαν εἶναι θεὸν ἐδίδασκε λέγειν Κλεόδημον. οἳ δὴ καὶ ὀψὲ τοῦ χρόνου τῆς ξένης ἐκείνης Ἀκαδημίας ἀπολυόμενοι, καθάπερ τινὲς αὐτοφυεῖς τῆς Κλεοδήμου σοφίας αἱρεσιῶται, ᾖδον ἀνά τε Λιβύην καὶ Αἴγυπτον σκιδνάμενοι μέγαν θεὸν τὸν Κλεόδημον· κἄπειτα ἦσαν μισθοὶ τελεσιουργοὶ τῷ καινῷ διδασκάλῳ οἱ τῶν ἀκουότων ἔπαινοι καὶ θειασμοί.

17–19 *ἥλιος αὐτὸς καὶ σελήνη καὶ ἄστρα κατὰ τὴν σὴν ὑφήγησιν . . . ἐκλείποντά τε καὶ πάλιν φαινόμενα καὶ ὡς ἔχει κινούμενα*: An eclipse of the sun occurred, just as Gregoras had predicted in his letter to Kaloeidas (cf. commentary on Letter 1, lines 5–6), on 14 May 1333; see Th. von Oppolzer, *Kanon der Finsternisse*, *Akademie der Wissenschaften, Mathematisch-Naturwissenschaftliche Classe*, 52 (Vienna, 1877), 244 and table 122; V. Grumel, *Chronologie*, 467.

84 *βασιλέα δὲ τὸν θειότατον*: Andronikos III whose favor, as Beyer points out (cf. *Antirrhetika I*, 57), Gregoras apparently had won by then, since he could take the liberty of reading to him and praising the letter of Akindynos. The latter admits that it was a compliment to Gregoras and his extraordinary prestige that the emperor would condescend to listen to a letter by an unknown author like himself; see lines 90–93.

87–88 *οὐδὲν οὕτως οἰκεῖον ὡς λόγοι τῇ βασιλείας φύσει*: The view that love of learning ought to be the attribute par excellence of a ruler goes, of course, back to Plato (cf. *Republic*, V, 17, 473d), but Akindynos may here be quoting his own teacher Thomas Magistros, who wrote to Andronikos II: *Δεῖ δή σοι λόγων μάλιστα πάντων, ὦ βασιλεῦ, μᾶλλον δὲ μετὰ πάντων τῶν ἄλλων καὶ λόγων ἐξ ἀνάγκης σοι δεῖ, ὡς μόνην ταύτην οὖσαν καλλίστην καὶ τελεωτάτην καὶ διὰ πασῶν, ὡς εἰπεῖν, ἁρμονίαν*. See Περὶ *βασιλείας*, PG, 145, col. 493B.

3.

Akindynos congratulates Gabras on his discourse against a certain fashionable hairstyle.

Addressee: Perhaps John Gabras, the recipient of Letter 32 and possibly Letter 31, or Michael Gabras, as suggested by Karpozilos (*Letters*, 100). On the Gabrades, see commentary on Letter 32 *infra*.

Date: Before 1341. Karpozilos is of the opinion that this letter and Letter 32 are not addressed to the same Gabras because they "differ substantially in content and style," and because in this case the addressee is "in no way connected with the Palamite controversy." Without excluding the possibility that this letter may be addressed to Michael Gabras, I believe that the lack of any reference to the dispute has to do with the letter's date rather than with the recipient's attitude towards the religious controversy. Judging from the pattern of Akindynos' correspondence during the conflict, it is highly unlikely that if he were writing at that time, Akindynos would have failed either to urge his correspondent to put his literary gifts to the service of the cause or—in the case of John Gabras, author of an anti-Palamite tract—to remind him of the service rendered by his eloquence in the past. See, for example, his similar appeals to other men of letters in Letter 15, lines 13–18; Letter 34; Letter 42, lines 2–37; Letter 43; Letter 52, lines 1–40, 99–101; Letter 62, lines 305–17; Letter 70, lines 79–86. Akindynos considered the defense of the faith as the ultimate goal of true learning (cf. Letter 41, lines 39–45). He reminded his learned friends of the fate of the servant who hid the talent given him by his master, and insisted that when questions of dogma were at stake silence was a sin and neutrality impossible, unless one was an atheist. See Letter 41, lines 198–203; Letter 30, lines 172–77; Letter 27, lines 60–66; Letter 41, lines 155–83 and Letter 62, lines 225–51.

I believe, therefore, that this letter, which contains no allusion whatsoever to the dispute, was written before 1341.

2 *τὸν περὶ τῆς κόμης λόγον*: This work is known only from Akindynos' letter. Michael Gabras wrote several discourses, but they did not survive. Their titles are known from his correspondence; see Fatouros, *Die Briefe des Michael Gabras*, 25–26; Kourouses, Μανουὴλ Γαβαλᾶς, 3, 8. Of the writings of John Gabras (cf. commentary on Letter 32), nothing has survived.

On Byzantine hairstyles, see Ph. Koukoules, "Περὶ κομμώσεως τῶν Βυζαντινῶν," Ἐπ. Ἑτ. Βυζ. Σπ., 7 (1930), 3–37.

4.

Letter of encouragement to a friend of exemplary wisdom and piety who is suffering unjustly.

Addressee: An unidentified bishop or ecclesiastical archon; see commentary on line 1 *infra*.

Date: 1336(?) Karpozilos (*Letters*, 97) does not suggest a date for this letter, but associates it with the liquidation of the anti-Palamite party, thus implying that it was written after 1347. Without ruling out this possibility, I believe that this letter is unrelated to the controversy, because, unlike similar letters of consolation dating from 1347–48, it does not contain any explicit reference to the dispute; see, for example, Letters 67–69. It is, therefore, possible that it was addressed to the archdeacon Bryennios, the *sakelliou* of the metropolis of Thessalonica, who in 1336 was falsely accused of not believing in the resurrection; see commentary on Letter 58.

1 *σῆς θεοφιλείας*: In the fourteenth century this form of address was no longer restricted to metropolitans, but could also denote an ecclesiastical archon of the second class, such as a *protonotarios*, *logothetes*, *referendiarios*, or *hypomnematographos*; cf. Darrouzès, *Offikia*, 123–24. In private correspondence these formalities were, of course, less strictly observed. Akindynos, for instance, addresses as *θειότατε δέσποτα* both the Patriarch and the metropolitan of Corinth (cf. Letter 37, line 4; Letter 67, line 16) and as *σοφώτατε δέσποτα* the archdeacon Bryennios, who was at the time the *sakelliou* and *dikaiophylax* of the metropolis of Thessalonica; see Letter 58, line 1.

13 *Ἡρακλέους λεοντῆς*: The killing of the Nemean lion was the first labor performed by Heracles; see Hesiod, *Theogony*, 326ff; Sophocles, *Trachiniae*, 1091ff; Diodorus Siculus, *Bibliotheca historica*, IV, 11, 3ff; Apollodorus, *Bibliotheca*, II, 5, 1ff. Afterwards the hero used the lion's skin as his armor and the head as his helmet; see H. Hunger, *Lexikon der Griechischen und Römischen Mythologie* (Vienna, 1969), 164.

5.

Akindynos relays Barlaam's answer to Palamas' criticism of his anti-Latin writings and tactfully suggests that Palamas should find this satisfactory.

Addressee: Gregory Palamas at the hermitage of St. Sabbas on Mt. Athos; see Meyendorff, *Introduction*, 67–68.

Date: Summer or early fall of 1336. The present letter is in reply to the letter which Palamas sent to Akindynos in late May or early June of 1336; see page xii and note 22 *supra*.

Loenertz assigns this letter of Akindynos to 1335–36 on the assumption that Palamas read Barlaam's anti-Latin treatises in 1335, shortly after they were composed; see "Dix-huit lettres," 86 and note 3.

Akindynos was probably still in Thessalonica when he wrote this letter, although no certain conclusion can be reached on the basis of the available evidence. Palamas provides only the information that Akindynos and Barlaam were together at the time and that they sent their replies to him with the Thessalonian Neilos, probably the monk Neilos Triklinios, the correspondent of Barlaam; see Α΄ Πρὸς 'Ακίνδυνον, *Συγγράμματα*, I, 203, lines 15–17; Β΄ Πρὸς 'Ακίνδυνον, *Συγγράμματα*, I, 222, lines 5–10. The hypothesis in favor of Thessalonica is supported by the testimony of Philotheos, who writes that Barlaam left Thessalonica for the capital shortly after his quarrel with Palamas over the anti-Latin treatises; cf. *Encomium*, PG, 151, col. 584D.

3–4 *καί σου πρότερον τὴν μακρὰν ἐκείνην σιωπὴν δυσχεραίνων*: Prompted by the *pourparlers* for union in the early spring of 1335, Palamas wrote his anti-Latin or *Apodictic Treatises*, which he sent to Akindynos, receiving in return a rather critical reply (cf. p. xii *supra*). Thereafter, Palamas kept silent for a long time and, as Sinkewicz correctly points out, this "long silence" indicates that it was after Pentecost of 1336, and not of 1335, that he again wrote to Akindynos; see "A New Interpretation," 496.

8 *τοῦ ἐκ Σικελίας*: As Loenertz notes, Barlaam is here called a Sicilian because his native Calabria had been part of the Kingdom of Sicily; see "Dix-huit lettres," 87 note 1. Palamas also refers to Barlaam as a Sicilian; see, for example, Τριὰς 2, 1, 1, *Συγγράμματα*, I, 465, line 11.

8 *λόγους*: Meyendorff assumes that the copy of Barlaam's anti-Latin writings which Palamas received shortly before writing to Akindynos contained a collection of six treatises which form a separate entity among Barlaam's twenty-one anti-Latin treatises. He also notes, however, that Palamas might have been originally familiar only with treatise XVII, which deals exclusively with the propriety of applying formal logic to theological arguments; cf. "Les débuts de la controverse hésychaste," *Byzantion*, 23 (1953), 103 note 3 and 108 note 3 (=Meyendorff, *Hesychasm*, *Study* I). See also Sinkewicz ("A New Interpretation," 499) who argues convincingly in favor of the latter hypothesis.

9–11 *ὃ καὶ αὐτὸς οὐκ ἐσίγησας . . . λόγους*: See Palamas, Α΄ Πρὸς 'Ακίνδυνον, *Συγγράμματα*, I, 203, lines 5–14, where he admits that

what prompted him to break his silence was Barlaam's book *Against the Latins*.

25–29 *ἡ ἐκ τῆς ἀρχῆς ἀρχή . . . ἀπολογίας αὐτῷ*: As Sinkewicz points out ("A New Interpretation," 497–98), Barlaam refers to this patristic quotation only in his first Greek discourse, where he is simply explaining, not espousing, the Latin position; see *Συμβουλευτικὸς περὶ ὁμονοίας πρὸς Ῥωμαίους καὶ Λατίνους* Βαρλαὰμ *μοναχοῦ*, ed. C. Giannelli, "Un progetto di Barlaam Calabro per l'unione delle Chiese," *Miscellanea G. Mercati*, III, Studi e Testi, 123 (Vatican City, 1946), 193, lines 13–17. Sinkewicz (*op. cit.*, 489–94) cites valid reasons for dating this discourse to the theological discussions of 1335, and believes that Palamas had this particular work in mind when he complained to Akindynos about Barlaam's use of this quotation from Gregory of Nazianzus.

42–45 Περὶ *μέντοι τῆς ἀποδείξεως . . . κομπάζουσιν*: The reference is to Barlaam's anti-Latin treatise XVII; see commentary on line 8 *supra*.

42–43 *περὶ τῆς κατ'* Ἀριστοτέλη *. . . τοὺς λόγους πεποίημαι*: See Aristotle, *Analytica posteriora*, 71b, line 17–72a, line 14.

47–50 *ἀπόδειξις ἡ ἐξ ἀνάγκης . . . ὁμολογουμένων*: See *ibid.*, 71b, lines 17–20 and 73a, line 24.

50 *ἀπόδειξις δὲ ἡ διαλεκτική*: See *idem*, *Analytica priora*, 65a, lines 35–37.

50–51 *ἡ κατὰ ῥητορικὴν πιθανότητα*: See *idem*, *Analytica posteriora*, 71a, lines 9–11, and *Rhetorica* 1355a, lines 6–14.

53–54 *ἣν ᾔδειν . . . ἀπόδειξιν*: i.e., the apodictic syllogism as defined by Aristotle in the *Analytica posteriora*, 71b, line 17–72a, line 14.

56 *τοῖς τῆς εὐσεβοῦς μοίρας*: i.e., the Eastern Orthodox theologians: a periphrasis.

60–61 *εἰ δέ τῳ φίλον . . . πρώτην ἀπόδειξιν*: See Palamas, Α´ Πρὸς Ἀκίνδυνον, *Συγγράμματα*, I, 213, lines 7–10: Ἡ*μεῖς δὲ οὐκ ἐξ ἐνδόξων ἐπὶ τὸ θεολογεῖν ὁρμώμεθα ἀρχῶν, ἀλλ' ἀμεταπείστως περὶ ταύτας ἔχομεν, θεοδιδάκτους οὔσας· πῶς οὖν οὐκ ἀποδεικτικόν, ἀλλὰ διαλεκτικὸν τὸν τοιοῦτον συλλογισμὸν ἐροῦμεν;*

69 *φιλοσόφοις*: On the use of this term by Byzantine writers, see commentary on Letter 1, line 33 *supra*.

6.

Akindynos describes the pleasure with which he read the addressee's discourse against those who accused him of avoiding holy orders.

Addressee: The hesychast Ignatios, spiritual director of the princess Irene-Eulogia Choumnaina Palaiologina(?). Two clues, the association of the addressee with the Princess (cf. commentary on line 7 *infra*) and his alleged refusal to accept holy orders (cf. commentary on line 3 *infra*), suggest that the unknown addressee might have been the monk Ignatios, tentatively identified by Laurent with the scholarly hesychast who became Choumnaina's spiritual adviser sometime between 1332 and 1338; see "La direction spirituelle à Byzance," 64–68.

Ignatios was a respected hesychast whose prestige greatly increased when he declined his unanimous promotion to the episcopate and confirmed his decision by oath; see Barlaam, *Epist. V*, *Epistole Greche*, 315, lines 8–11.

Date: 1337–41: After Akindynos' arrival at Constantinople and before the controversy, to which there is no allusion in this letter.

3 *τὴν ἱερωσύνην φεύγεις*: *ἱερωσύνη* may mean either the priesthood or the episcopate; see J. Darrouzès, *Epistoliers byzantins du Xe siècle* (Paris, 1960), 294 note 44.

7 *θαυμασία βασίλισσα*: The princess Irene-Eulogia Choumnaina Palaiologina, daughter of the imperial chancellor Nikephoros Choumnos and widow of the despot John, son of Andronikos II from his second marriage to Yolanda-Irene of Montferrat. For the basic facts of her life, see J. Verpeaux, "Notes prosopographiques sur la famille Choumnos," *Byzantinoslavica*, 20 (1959), no. 17, 260–61.

The title *basilissa* applied at the time to the wife of the despot, while that of *despoina* was reserved for the empress; see N. B. Tomadakes, Βυζαντινὴ ἐπιστολογραφία (Athens, 1969–70), 144. In Letter 60 (lines 91–92), Akindynos again refers to Irene-Eulogia by the same title: *ἡ θεοφιλεστάτη βασίλισσα, ἡ ἐπὶ τοῦ κανικλείου θυγάτηρ, ἡ νύμφη τοῦ βασιλέως*. . . . For other references to Irene-Eulogia as *basilissa* in contemporary sources, see Kourouses, Μανουὴλ Γαβαλᾶς, 189 note 1a.

6 Irene-Eulogia was the founder and abbess of the convent of *Φιλάνθρωπος Σωτὴρ* in Constantinople; see Laurent, "Une princesse byzantine au cloître," *EO*, 29 (1930), 29–60; Janin, *La géographie ecclésiastique*, 541–44. During the controversy her convent became the nucleus of resistance to Palamism, and the Princess herself became the

target of Palamite wrath. Palamas' *Seventh Antirrhetic* contains a vehement diatribe against this defiant woman who engaged in theological discussions and wrote letters attacking the Palamite doctrines; see *Συγγράμματα*, III, 466–70. Kalothetos also frequently attacks the wealthy princess in his writings, claiming that her money had bought Akindynos and his venal followers (cf. commentary on Letter 41, lines 194–95), and blaming her for Akindynos' lapse into heresy; see *Πρὸς τοὺς Βαρλααμίτας*, *Συγγράμματα*, 175, lines 464–72. For more on Choumnaina and her anti-Palamite activity, see my article, "Irene-Eulogia Choumnaina Palaiologina, Abbess of the Convent of Philanthropos Soter in Constantinople," *Byzantinische Forshungen*, 9 (1983).

Irene-Eulogia remained faithful to Akindynos until her death *ca.* 1356, and, according to Gregoras (*Hist.*, XXIX, 21: III, 238), her partisans revered her grave as miracle working. Her name figures on the list of prominent anti-Palamites (Mercati, *Notizie*, 223, no. 26). For Akindynos' praise of Choumnaina's intelligence and piety, see Letter 60, lines 90–100.

11–12 *τῆς καθαρότητος*! *τῆς γλυκύτητος . . . καὶ σεμνότητος*: Clarity, sweetness, and dignity or nobility of expression are among the elements of good style valued by rhetorical theorists; see Hermogenes, *Περὶ ἰδεῶν*, I, 3, ed. Spengel, *Rhet. Gr.*, II, 275–81; 357–64; 287–96; Aristeides, *Περὶ πολιτικοῦ λόγου*, ed. Spengel, *op. cit.*, 459–69; 499–500; *idem*, *Περὶ ἀφελοῦς λόγου*, ed. Spengel, *op. cit.*, 530–32; 534–35.

21–29 *ὃ δὲ τοῦ λόγου διαφερόντως ἐθαύμασα . . . ἓν ἀντὶ πλήθους ἀπόχρη τῇ χρείᾳ τῆς ὑποθέσεως*: Conciseness was also regarded as an essential of vigorous style; cf. Aristeides, *Περὶ πολιτικοῦ λόγου*, ed. Spengel, *op. cit.*, 500; Demetrius, *Περὶ ἑρμηνείας*, I, 7; II, 103; III, 137; Loeb (London–New York, 1965), 300, 366, 388.

7.

As a sincere and well-meaning friend, Akindynos begs his correspondent to stop his abuse of the monks, which may prove detrimental to him and those associated with him.

Addressee: Barlaam. Though he is not here mentioned by name, the references to the addressee's mission to the West (line 8) and to his attack against the

hesychasts (lines 78–95) indicate that this letter was addressed to Barlaam in Thessalonica (line 30).

Date: Late autumn of 1339 to early autumn of 1340: after Barlaam's return from Avignon, which he left shortly before 9 September 1339 (cf. *Acta Benedicti XII, 1334–42*, ed. A. L. Taŭtu, Fontes, III, vol. VIII [Vatican City, 1958], no. 42, 80), and before his arrival at Constantinople in October 1340; cf. Palamas, *Theophanes* (*Συγγράμματα*, II, 222, lines 13–15), where it is stated that Barlaam arrived at the capital seven months before Palamas, i.e., seven months before May 1341.

8–9 *τῆς μεγάλης παρ' Ἰταλοὺς πρεσβείας*: At the beginning of 1339, Barlaam was sent by Andronikos III on a confidential mission to Robert the Wise of Sicily, to Philip VI of France, and to Pope Benedict XII at Avignon to appeal for military aid against the Turks: see Barlaam's two Latin orations for the Union of the Churches, PG 151, cols. 1332C–1338C and 1338C–1340B; *Acta Benedicti XII*, ed. Taŭtu, no. 42, 80–85; no. 43, 86–95; Palamas, *Τριὰς* 3, 1, 4, *Συγγράμματα*, I, 618, lines 16–18.

12–13 *ὁπόσον οὐδ' Ἡρακλῆς ἐκεῖνος τοὺς ὑπ' αὐτοῦ δεθέντας*: Perhaps an allusion to the Kerkopes, the knavish dwarfs who attempted to rob the sleeping Herakles of his weapons and were consequently caught by him and fastened head down on the opposite ends of a pole; see Apollodorus, *Bibliotheca*, II, 6, 3; Diodorus Siculus, *Bibliotheca historica*, IV, 31, 7.

29–30 *εἴ τις ἐκ Βυζαντίου . . . τοῖς ἐν Θεσσαλονίκῃ*: Barlaam was obviously in Thessalonica at the time.

34 *ὁ γενναῖος Γεώργιος*: Possibly George of Thessalonica, the friend of Barlaam who accompanied him to the West in the summer of 1341 and shared with him some funds provided by the papal treasury in August of that year and in March of 1342; see K. H. Schaefer, *Die Ausgaben der apostolischen Kammer unter Benedikt XII, Klemens VI, und Innocenz VI (1335–1362), Vatikanische Quellen zur Geschichte der päpstlichen Hof und Finanzverwaltung 1316–1378, Görres Gesellschaft* (Paderborn, 1914), III, 138, 157; and G. Mercati, *Notizie sulla vita di Simone Atumano*, Studi e Testi, 30 (Rome, 1916), 28–29 note 3.

78–79 *μήπω σε πεπαῦσθαι . . . βλασφημίας καὶ μάχης*: Barlaam renewed his attack against the hesychasts after reading Palamas' second *Triad*, which was written during his absence in the West; see Meyendorff, *Introduction*, 72.

96–113 *Ἃ τοίνυν . . . ὄλεθρον*: see Herodotus, *Hist.*, III, 39–44; 120–26.

100–1 *ὥσπερ ἰατρῶν παῖδες τὴν εὐεξίαν, οὐκ εἶναι ἀσφαλεστάτην*: cf.

Basil. Caes., *Ad Adolescentes*, PG, 31, col. 584C: *ἐγὼ δὲ καὶ σφαλερὰν εἶναι τὴν ἐπ' ἄκρον εὐεξίαν ἰατρῶν ἤκουσα.*

107 *διαλυτήρια*: not in lexica.

115 *ἂν ἄρα καὶ καταδέχῃ τὸ κοινὸν τοῦτο λέγω*: an allusion to Barlaam's vanity. For similar ironical remarks, see lines 65–66 and 120–21.

127–28 *τοῖς ἑαυτοῦ τοιαῦτα . . . καὶ τῶν ἐκείνου νόμων*: Akindynos accuses Barlaam of insulting not only the hesychasts but also the divine laws. In the following letter, he qualifies this statement by explaining that it is uncanonical to call someone a heretic before he has been so declared by a synod; see Letter 8, lines 17–18.

8.

While not strongly opposed to Barlaam on matters of doctrine, Akindynos reiterates his opposition to Barlaam's meddlesome interference against the hesychasts and warns him that his efforts to prove Palamas a heretic will be futile and disastrous.

Addressee: Barlaam in Constantinople.

Date: November/December 1340: Barlaam had already presented his charges against Palamas; see lines 7–9. On the date of Barlaam's arrival in the capital, see commentary on Letter 7.

1–3 *Ἃ γέγραφάς μοι . . . καὶ ἀπὸ στόματος εἶπες*: This exchange of letters obviously followed a recent conversation between the two friends. In his *Report* Akindynos wrote that when Barlaam came to Constantinople to present his charges against Palamas, he asked him for his cooperation, but he refused to support him. At the meeting with the Patriarch, Akindynos criticized Barlaam's writings and tried both by word of mouth and in writing to persuade Barlaam to withdraw his charges. See *Report*, 86: *ἐπὶ τούτοις οἴκαδε ἀναχωροῦμεν καὶ μετὰ ταῦτα καὶ λόγοις ἁπλῶς τοῖς ἐκ στόματος, καὶ λόγοις ἄλλως συντεταγμένοις, ἐγὼ μὲν ἀντεκείμην ἐκείνῳ . . .*

3–7 *ὅτι δὲ κἀγώ σοι τὰ περὶ θεολογίας . . . περιεργάζεσθαι*: Akindynos expresses here his first doubts about Palamas' doctrine of the divine grace, but, since he is acquainted with it only through Barlaam's writings, he questions the accuracy of his interpretation of this doctrine; see also *Letter* 9, lines 46–47 and 67–71; Letter 10, lines 197–99.

7–9 *ἀπίθανον γὰρ ἐκεῖνον . . . αἱρετικὸν φανῆναι, ὃ σὺ σπουδάζεις*

. . . τὴν ἐκκλησίαν πεῖσαι: see Akindynos, *Report*, 86: ἧκε μὲν ὁ Βαρλαὰμ ἐνταῦθα πρὸς τὴν μεγάλην ἁγιωσύνην σου . . . φέρων λόγους τε οἰκείους κατὰ τοῦ Παλαμᾶ καὶ τοῦ τρόπου τῆς ἡσυχίας τῶν μετιόντων ταύτην καὶ μεγάλα ἐγκλήματα κατ' αὐτοῦ περὶ τῆς εὐσεβείας. Barlaam accused Palamas of being a ditheist and a follower of John of Blachernai, a priest condemned for Bogomilism under Alexios I Komnenos (Anna Komnena, *Alexiad*, X, 1); see Palamas, Γ' Πρὸς 'Ακίνδυνον, Συγγράμματα, I, 296, line 1; (ed. Nadal, "La première redaction," 250, line 6) Τριάς III, 1, 7; 2, 3; 3, 4; Συγγράμματα, I, 621, lines 14–15; 657, lines 18–20; 682, line 29.

Akindynos considers the condemnation of Palamas for heresy an improbability, because of the man's widespread reputation for piety; see lines 15–16 and Letter 9, lines 74–75 where Akindynos again warns Barlaam that the Church will not pay equal attention to him and to Palamas.

17–18 πρὸ γὰρ ψήφου συνοδικῆς . . . οὐ κανονικόν: See the thirteenth canon of the first and second synods of Constantinople (Rhalles-Potles, II, 688–89), which aimed at stemming the growth of schismatic factions in the Church and enjoined that no lower clergyman could accuse his bishop of heresy and refuse to remain in communion with him before the bishop had been found guilty by a synod.

9.

To Barlaam's contention that Akindynos could not persuade him because he did not argue from premises acceptable to him, Akindynos answers that demonstration and instruction are also conducive to persuasion. He claims to have persuaded Barlaam in that manner and proceeds to show how the events themselves have proven him right.

Addressee: Barlaam in Constantinople.

Date: Winter of 1340–41. Letters 8–10 are consecutive and were written after Barlaam's arrival at Constantinople in October 1340; see commentary on Letter 8. This and the next letter are probably the λόγοι which Akindynos claims to have written during that period in his effort to restrain Barlaam; see commentary on Letter 8, lines 1–3.

1–13 Τὴν μὲν τοῦ συλλογισμοῦ φύσιν . . . ὁμολογεῖν ἐθέλεις: At the conclusion of the last letter, Akindynos asked Barlaam to listen to him because he was trying to persuade him as a true and sincere friend (Letter 8, lines 13–16). In return, Barlaam must have given him a lesson in logic, reiterating what he had previously written to Palamas, namely, that in or-

der to persuade someone you must argue from premises acceptable to him; see Barlaam, *Epist. I*, *Epistole Greche*, 238, line 217; 249, lines 488–91. (A. Fyrigos' *Barlaam Calabro Epistole a Palamas* [Rome, 1975] was unfortunately unavailable to me.)

16–17 *εἰ ἅ σοι δοκοῦσιν . . . ὥσπερ τις ὢν Σωκράτης*: In his letter to the hesychast Ignatios, Barlaam claimed that, just as Socrates, he too was driven by a desire to seek out truth, and in the process he inevitably made many enemies; *Epist. V*, *Epistole Greche*, 319–23. Akindynos repeatedly refers to Barlaam's intellectual conceit, which he holds responsible for his involvement in various disputes; see lines 17–20, 28–29, 81–82, 96–97, of this letter and Letter 10, lines 27–29, 33–34, 42–43, 49, 117–19 and 318–24. In the discourse he addressed to the Patriarch against Akindynos, Kalothetos also remarks ironically on the vanity of Barlaam. Having been treated by the Emperor and other notables in Constantinople like another Hermes—says Kalothetos—Barlaam began to look at others like an "elephant looks at mosquitoes." See *Συγγράμματα*, 236, lines 25–31.

19–20 Ναζιραίοις: The hesychasts; see Suidas, *Lexicon*, *s.v.* The Nazarites or Nazirites were persons consecrated to God through special vows; cf. Numbers 6:1–21 and A. Barbieri, *New Catholic Encyclopedia*, vol. 10, col. 287.

21–25 *λέγοντας ἀπὸ φιλίας γνώμης . . . τὰς τούτων αἰτίας*: See *Letter* 7, lines 78ff.

29 *λογοις μακροῖς*: The lost treatise Κατὰ Μασσαλιανῶν. Its title and context are known from Palamas' refutation in the *Third Triad* (*Συγγράμματα*, I, 615–94). The title is also cited in Philotheos' *Encomium* (PG, 151, col. 589D) and the synodal *Tome* of 1341 (PG, 151, col. 632C; Miklosich-Müller, I, 205).

33–34 *σὺ δ'ὥσπερ τινὰ φῇς . . . θεολογεῖν*: A reference to Barlaam's charges of heresy against Palamas; see commentary on Letter 8, lines 7–9.

34–47 *οὕτω παρὰ τοὺς χαρακτῆρας . . . παρόντος τοῦ διαβαλλομένου*: Note Akindynos' defense of the hesychast method of prayer. He declares that Barlaam's attacks against the monks are an expression of his contentious spirit, and consequently he questions the validity of his accusations against Palamas' theology. For similar expressions of doubt, see commentary on Letter 8, lines 3–7.

48 *ὀκνῶ καὶ δέδοικα περὶ σοὶ μᾶλλον . . . καθ' οὗπερ ἧκες*: Akindynos reiterates here the fears he expressed in his previous letters con-

cerning the consequences of Barlaam's dispute with the hesychasts and their highly respected leader; see Letter 7, lines 114–30 and Letter 8, lines 13–24.

50 *μεθ' ὑποκρίσεως*: Barlaam claimed originally that his attack was not directed against the enlightened hesychasts, but against their simple and uneducated colleagues, whose practices and beliefs shocked him when he first became acquainted with them; see his letter to the hesychast Ignatios, *Epist. V*, *Epistole Greche*, 323–24.

52–54 *καί τινα αἵρεσιν . . . κλόνον σπλάγχνων . . . ἐκωμῴδησας*: when Barlaam lodged his first complaint with the Synod he ironically styled the hesychasts "men-with-their-souls-in-the navel"; see Palamas, Β΄ Πρὸς Βαρλαάμ, Συγγράμματα, I, 288, lines 18–20: *ἀλλὰ καὶ πικρὸς αὐτοῖς ἐπὶ συνόδου κατέστη κατήγορος, 'ὀμφαλοψύχους' ὀνομάζων αὐτούς*. See also Barlaam's letter to Ignatios, *Epist. V*, *Epistole Greche*, 323, 117–26: . . . *ἐν οἷς διαζεύξεις τινὲς τερατώδεις καὶ αὖθις συζεύξεις νοῦ πρὸς ψυχὴν παρεδίδοντο, δαιμόνων τε πρὸς αὐτὴν συνουσιώσεις καὶ φώτων διαφοραί πυρρῶν τε καὶ λευκῶν· καὶ νοεραί τινες εἴσοδοί τε καὶ ἔξοδοι διὰ τῶν ῥινῶν ἅμα τῷ πνεύματι γινόμεναι, παλμοί τε περὶ τὸν ὀμφαλὸν συμβαίνοντες· καὶ τελευταῖον συνάφεια ἐντὸς τοῦ ὀμφαλοῦ τοῦ ἡμετέρου δεσπότου πρὸς τὴν ψυχὴν ἐν αἰσθήσει καὶ πληροφορίᾳ καρδίας γινομένη καὶ τοιαῦτ' ἄττα, ἃ τῷ ἐπιτηδεύοντι, ἀναγκαῖόν μοι δοκεῖ ἢ εἰς καθαρὰν μανίαν τελευτῆσαι ἢ εἰς φρονήματος μὲν πλήρωσιν, κένωσιν δὲ φρονήσεως.*

57 *τὴν Μασσαλιανῶν δυσσέβειαν*: The Messalians were convicted in 431 by the council of Ephesos for claiming to apprehend physically the essence of God; see *Acta conciliorum oecumenicorum*, ed. E. Schwartz, I, I, VII, 117.

58–61 *εἶτα συνθεὶς πάντας τούτους τοὺς λόγους . . . ἤγαγες εἰς τὴν ἁπασῶν ταύτην ἐκκλησιῶν μητέρα*: It is evident from this statement that Barlaam had already published his treatise *Against the Messalians* and presented his charges against Palamas and the monks before the Patriarch at Constantinople.

66–67 *ὅτι σὺ μὲν ἦρξας πολέμου . . . ἀμύνειν πολεμουμένοις προθυμηθείς*: Following Barlaam's first charges against the hesychasts, Palamas left his hermitage on Mt. Athos and returned to Thessalonica where for three years prior to his departure for Constantinople in the winter of 1341 he undertook the defense of his fellow-monks (see Philotheos, *Encomium*, PG, 151, col. 592C–D; Meyendorff, *Introduction*, 71). The

fruits of his endeavors were the *Triads* and the *Hagioretic Tome*; see Meyendorff. *Introduction*, 71–74.

68–69 *τὰ πρὸς τὸ δόγμα ἐκείνου μόνον τὸ περὶ τοῦ ὑπὸ τὴν θείαν φύσιν ἀκτίστου καὶ ὑπερουσίου Θεοῦ καὶ ληπτοῦ σωματικοῖς ὀφθαλμοῖς*: This is Akindynos' first explicit reference to the Palamite doctrine of the divine grace for which Barlaam accused his opponent of ditheism.

69–70 *ἃ φῇς ἐκεῖνον γράφειν*: Obviously, Akindynos had not yet received Palamas' letter, and the latter's doctrine of the divine energies was known to him through Barlaam's writings.

69–75 *εἰ μὲν τὰ πρὸς τὸ δόγμα ἐκείνου . . . καὶ διὰ τἆλλα πάντα*: Akindynos remarks that Barlaam would have done better to concentrate on the charge of ditheism against Palamas which, if accurate, would be far more serious than the charge of Messalianism against the monks. However, he again emphasizes how difficult it would be to convince the Church of Palamas' guilt.

81 *ᾤου ληρεῖν μὲν ἐμέ*: Barlaam obviously dismissed his friend's warnings as nonsense; see also Letter 10, lines 11–12; 309–10.

91–92 *γαληνῶς ἔχουσαν τὴν ἐκκλησίαν . . . κατασείετε*: Akindynos accuses both Barlaam and Palamas of disturbing the peace of the Church by their dispute. In his letter to Dishypatos he again expresses the fear that this dispute might cause a serious rift in the Church (Letter 12, line 53).

93–94 *οὐκ ἀνεκτὸν ἡγησάμην . . . ἄλλους παρακαλέσαι*: See Akindynos, *Report*, 86; and p. xiv *supra*.

102–4 *τά γε μὴν ἐν Βερροίᾳ . . . λελυπηκότα τινάς*: Barlaam obviously wrote to Akindynos that his activity in defense of Palamas and the monks had displeased their mutual friends in Berroia, Thessalonica and Constantinople. That Barlaam enjoyed at the time the support of his fellow-literati is confirmed by Patriarch Neilos of Constantinople. See his *Encomium* of Palamas (PG, 151, col. 668A). Kalothetos also admits that Barlaam had succeeded, prior to the synod of June, in rousing "nearly everyone" against Palamas and the monks. See *Κατὰ τοῦ 'Ακινδύνου πρὸς τὸν πατριαρχην . . .*, *Συγγράμματα*, 238, line 85.

108–9 *εἰ ἐκ τῶν ἐμοὶ δοκούντων . . . τὸν διαλεκτικῶς ἐπιχειροῦντα πείθειν*: See Barlaam, *Epist. III*, *Epistole Greche*, 313, lines 830–32 (*τοῦτο γάρ ἐστι τὸ διαλεκτικῶς πρός τινας διαλέγεσθαι, τὸ ἐξ ὧν αὐτοὶ συγχωροῦσι ποιεῖσθαι πρὸς αὐτοὺς τὸν λόγον*), and Aristotle, *Anal. Post.*, 81b, lines 18–22.

10.

Akindynos elaborates on certain statements in his last letter which Barlaam found objectionable.

Addressee: Barlaam in Constantinople.

Date: Winter-spring of 1341. Loenertz assigns this letter to 1340–41 because he does not study it in conjunction with Akindynos' other letters to Barlaam, and therefore assumes that it antedates Barlaam's formal denunciation of Palamas; cf. "Dix-huit lettres," 87.

2 *φιλόσοφον*: On this term, see commentary on Letter 1, line 33 *supra*.

2 *περιεργίᾳ*: See Letter 8, line 6, where Akindynos uses the same word to describe Barlaam's activities against the monks; also lines 177–78 of this letter where he calls Barlaam's writings on the hesychast method of prayer the work of a meddlesome and mischievous man.

12–14 *νομίζω τοίνυν ἤ τοι φιλοδοξίᾳ . . . ἀνδράσιν ἐπηρεάζειν*: See Letter 9, lines 13–20.

17–29 *ὅτε πρῶτον ἐλθὼν . . . ἀμαθὴς ὢν ἠλέγχθης*: Barlaam first visited the capital in 1330. This is the inference from Gregoras' statement that Barlaam upon his arrival in Constantinople failed to pay a visit to Theodore Metochites who had recently returned from exile; see *Florentios*, 421–27. On the date of Metochites' return from exile, see I. Ševčenko, *Études sur la polémique entre Théodore Métochite et Nicéphore Choumnos* (Brussels, 1962), 8 note 2. For Barlaam's unsuccessful debate with Gregoras, to which Akindynos refers here, see commentary on Letter 1, lines 41–42.

As Loenertz (*op. cit.*, 83) notes, the testimony of Akindynos proves that Gregoras did not lie when he claimed to have won a brilliant victory against Barlaam.

30–31 *τὰς πρώτας εἰρωνείας τοῦ Παλαμᾶ κατετόξευες*: See Barlaam's ironical comments on Palamas' contemplative pursuits in the first letter he addressed to him (*Epist. I*, *Epistole Greche*, 229, lines 1–11; 231, lines 50–53.

37 *Λαπίθου τοῦ Κυπρίου*: On the Cypriot George Lapithes, see commentary on Letter 42 *infra*.

39–40 *ἀπορίας τινάς . . . καὶ ζητοῦντος λύσιν*: Barlaam's answers to Lapithes were recently published, but they do not justify Akindynos' accusation that they were insulting and sarcastic. Only in one instance Barlaam implies that the Cypriot was unfamiliar with the tenets of Platonism, and at the end he notes with a touch of irony that he will be indebted to

his wise correspondent if he can find better solutions to these difficult problems and enlighten him too; see R. E. Sinkewicz, "The Solutions Addressed to George Lapithes by Barlaam the Calabrian and their Philosophical Context," *Mediaeval Studies*, 43 (1981), III, 6, p. 208; IV, 16, p. 215; V, 8, pp. 216–17.

Lapithes' queries were published by Tsolakes, but now Sinkewicz points out that what Tsolakes mistook for excerpts from Lapithes' letters to Barlaam, are actually the latter's summaries of Lapithes' arguments; see Tsolakes, *Γεώργιος Λαπίθης*, 93–94; Sinkewicz, *op. cit.*, 154.

56–58 *ὥστε οὐκ ἂν ἀδικοίην ἐπηρεαστήν σε . . . καὶ Θεοῦ*: See Letter 7, lines 127–28.

61–71 *καίτοι τί με συκοφαντεῖς . . . οὐκ ἐπιστήμονας*: See Letter 9, lines 1–11.

89 *ὁ δεῖνα δὲ εἰ κακῶς θεολογῶν φωρᾶται*: i.e., Palamas.

89–90 *ἄλλος οὗτος ὁ λόγος καὶ μετ' ὀλίγον εἰρήσεται*: See lines 197–208 of this letter.

93–94 *εἰπών, ἀσυνέτως . . . τοὺς* Ναζιραίους *λέγειν*: See Letter 9, line 55. Ναζιραῖοι are the hesychasts; see commentary on Letter 9, lines 19–20.

97–106 *φθόνῳ γάρ σε κινούμενον . . . γένωνται κατεγνωσμένοι*: See Letter 7, lines 84–92.

110–12 *σὺ μὲν ἦρξας πολέμου . . . οὐ παροπτέος αὐτοῖς . . . ταῦτ' ἐπὶ λέξεως ἔγραψα*: This is an exact quotation from Letter 9, lines 65–67.

124–25 *κατασκευάζοντα τὰς* Μασσαλιανῶν *ἐπὶ τούτοις ἐννοίας*: See commentary on Letter 9, lines 29 and 57 *supra*.

130 *τριῶν ἐτῶν ἢ τεττάρων ὑμῶν . . . ταῦτα νεανιευσαμένων*: Akindynos' testimony supports the view that Palamas and Barlaam began their dispute over the hesychasts in the spring of 1337.

134–36 *ἡγούμενον . . .* Μαξίμου *περὶ τούτων δογμάτων*: For the passages from St. Maximos' *De caritate* which Barlaam adduced against the hesychast method of prayer, see Meyendorff, *Introduction*, 201.

145–47 *τὸν μέγαν* Ἐπιφάνιον *λέγοντα . . . ἀντιπίπτοντες*: This passage is not from Epiphanios, but from John of Damaskos, who states that the members of this sect opposed all religious studies and emphasized instead the importance of good deeds; see De *haeresibus*, 88; PG, 94, col. 757A. We do not know, however, when and where they lived and what their importance was; see G. Bareille, *DTC*, 6^2, cols. 1433–34.

152–53 *ἡ γνωστὴ παρ' ἐκείνῳ ἑτέρα αἱρετικῶν φατρία*: The Gnostics; see Epiphanios, *Adv. haeres.*, II, XXVI, PG, 41, cols. 329D–364B.

195–96 *ὁμοίως γὰρ κακίζω καὶ τὰς ἐκείνου κατά σου φιλονεἰκους στρατείας, τάς γε πρὸ τῶν περὶ προσευχῆς*: In the original dispute over the use of apodictic reasoning in matters of theology, Akindynos was inclined to agree with Barlaam. He suggested that Palamas should accept Barlaam's explanations and not imperil such a divine blessing as friendship; see Letter 5, lines 64–72.

197–99 *κἀκείνου τὸν ἄκτιστον θεόν . . . εἰ τοῦτ' ἀποφαίνεται*: See Letter 9, lines 68–69.

199–200 *καί σου τὸ κτιστὸν τῆς θεουργοῦ χάριτος—εἰ καὶ σὺ τοῦτο λέγεις*: In his third *Triad*, Palamas affirmed that Barlaam declared the divine grace to be created and for this reason accused of impiety all those who did not share his views; see Τριὰς 3, 1, 3, Συγγρ., I, 617, 21–24 (*Τίνος οὖν χάριν τὴν τοῦ πνεύματος χάριν ἄκτιστον αὐτός τε φάναι οὐ πείθεται καὶ τοὺς πειθομένους δυσσεβεῖς ἀποφαίνεται καὶ πάντα λίθον . . . κινεῖ πᾶσι ταύτην ὑποδεῖξαι κτιστήν . . .*); Τριὰς 3, 1, 5, Συγγρ., I, 620, lines 6–8 (*Ἐγὼ δ' ἐκ τούτων καὶ τῶν τοιούτων οὐχ ὑπ' ἀγνοίας, ἀλλ' ὑπὸ κακονοίας, κτιστὴν αὐτὸν ἀποφαίνεσθαι τὴν θεοποιὸν ὑπενόησα χάριν τοῦ πνεύματος*).

Akindynos here asserts his impartiality by refusing to listen to the accusations that his two friends were hurling at each other. Later, during the controversy, he recalled how he objected to the innovations of both parties in the dispute, but noted his partiality for Palamas because he was a friend and fellow-Byzantine; see *Antirrhetic V*, *Monac. Gr. 223*, fol. 321[v] (*καὶ ἦμεν ἡμεῖς καὶ τότε τῶν μετὰ τῆς ἐκκλησίας ἑκατέρου μὲν τὴν καινότητα φυλαττομένων καὶ ἀποδοκιμαζόντων, τούτῳ δ' οὖν ὅμως μᾶλλον προσκειμένων διὰ τὸ σύνηθες καὶ ὁμόφυλον*).

205–6 *ὥστ', εἰ σὺ διὰ τοῦτο Κύριλλος, ὡς ἀπεκόμπασας, πρὸς ἐκεῖνον Νεστόριον*: Barlaam evidently compared himself with Cyril and Palamas with Nestorios, the two famous opponents in the Christological controversy of the early fifth century.

Nestorios, patriarch of Constantinople (428–31), was accused of heresy by Cyril, the patriarch of Alexandria (412–44), for contending that the Holy Virgin was the mother of Christ (Christotokos) and not the mother of God (Theotokos), since she was herself a human being. He was condemned and deposed at the council of Ephesus in 431.

237 *σκηνεργάται*: This word is not in the dictionaries. It is found only in a text of unknown authorship entitled *Λαβύρινθος ἥνπερ Σολομὼν ἐτεκτήνατο*, in which time (*χρόνος*) is called *σκηνεργάτης*; see M. Berthelot-C. E. Ruelle, eds., *Collection des anciens alchimistes grecs* (Paris, 1888), III, 40, 14; C. D. Buck-W. Petersen, *A Reverse Index of Greek Nouns and Adjectives* (Chicago, 1945), 546.

Akindynos uses it in reference to Homer and other poets excluded from Plato's ideal state because they were "imitators by means of words." I have, therefore, translated it as "actors" (stage performers).

304 *ὁ Λυγκεύς*: An Argonaut and a member of the Calydonian boar hunt, Lynceus was fabled for his extraordinary vision; see Pindar, *Nemean Odes*, X, 62; Apollonius Rhodius, *Argonautica*, I, 53; Apollodorus, *Bibliotheca*, III, 10, 3. See also *Appendix proverbiorum*, III, 71 (Leutsch-Schneidewin, I, 430).

318 *Ταῦτα αὖ πάλιν λέγοντες, Ἡράκλεις*: A marginal note in the manuscript explains that Akindynos used this form of address as a rebuke because Barlaam had referred to himself as Heracles when writing to him; see *critical apparatus*, 318.

329–31 *ἅ γέγραφά σοι . . . γαλήνην ἀγούσῃ θεοχορήγητον*: See Letter 9, lines 90–100.

334–36 *οὕτως καὶ Ἄρειος μὲν εἶχε πρός τούς Ἀθανασίου . . . Εὐνόμιος δὲ πρὸς τοὺς τοῦ . . . Βασιλείου, Νεστόριος . . . τοῦ θείου Κυρίλλου*: Akindynos tells Barlam that he is not disturbed if his arguments fail to convince him. Neither were the notorious heretics of old persuaded by their orthodox opponents.

Athanasios, patriarch of Alexandria (328–35; 346–55; 361–62; 363–65; 366–73), directed most of his voluminous writings against the doctrines of Arios, the Alexandrian presbyter who was condemned at the first ecumenical council in 325 for teaching that the Father and the Son were not consubstantial.

Basil, bishop of Caesarea in Cappadocia (370–79), refuted Eunomios, the doctrinal successor of Arios, who taught that the Son was unlike (*anomoios*) the Father. His doctrine was condemned at the second ecumenical council in 381.

On Cyril and Nestorios, see commentary on lines 205–6 *supra*.

11.

Akindynos writes to Palamas that the patriarchal letter which he is sending to him is the result of his own conciliatory efforts.

Addressee: Gregory Palamas, somewhere in the vicinity of the capital, since he is reported to have arrived a few days later; see Akindynos, *Report*, 87 (*ἔπεμψα τῷ Παλαμᾷ τὸ γράμμα, καὶ μετά τινας ἡμέρας ἥκει καὶ ὁ Παλαμᾶς*). It is possible that this letter reached Palamas in Adrianople, as Darrouzès suggests (no. 2205).

Date: Spring 1341.

2–3 *τὰ μὲν ἐμοὶ σπουδασθέντα . . . διώκοντα*: Akindynos refers to his refusal to support Barlaam, his criticism of Barlaam's writings in the presence of the Patriarch, and his subsequent efforts to restrain Barlaam by writing to him repeatedly. See commentary on Letter 8, lines 1–3.

5–6 *ἔστιν οὖν ἐκείνων τῶν σπουδασμάτων καὶ τὸ παρόν*: Unlike the previous summons, this patriarchal letter was addressed directly to Palamas as a result of Akindynos' personal appeal to the Patriarch; see p. xv *supra*.

6–7 *προλαβόντων τῶν δοκεῖν ἐμοὶ λυπηρῶν . . . γραμμάτων*: The reference is to the first patriarchal summons, which was addressed to the Church of Thessalonica and had already been sent by Barlaam; see p. xv *supra*. This summons must have reached Thessalonica no later than January 1341, because Kalothetos says that when summoned, the monks left that city immediately, although it was "the height of the winter;" see Πρὸς *τὸν πατριάρχην*, *Συγγράμματα*, 238, lines 70–75. See also Darrouzès, no. 2204.

9 *ἣν δὲ μεγάλην ἐπιστολὴν καὶ γενναίαν ἀπέστειλας*: Palamas' third letter to Akindynos; see note 44 of my introduction *supra*. Akindynos received this letter after writing to Palamas to inquire whether Barlaam's charges against his doctrine of the divine grace were true or false. See Akindynos, *Antirrhetic V* (*Monac. Gr.* 223, fol. 244r): *Γράφων γὰρ πρὸς ἐμὲ ἀπὸ τῆς Θεσσαλονίκης καὶ συνιστὰς τὴν ὑφειμένην θεότητα, ἐπεσταλκότα περὶ ταύτης αὐτῷ τῆς θεολογίας ἐντεῦθεν, ὡς ἄρα οὐκ ἔρρωται καὶ εἰ αὐτοῦ ὡς ἀληθῶς εἴη τὸ δόγμα τοῦτο πυθόμενον ἢ συκοφαντοῖτο τῷ Βαρλαάμ, ἐπὶ τούτοις τοίνυν ἐπιστέλλων πρὸς ἐμὲ δεῦρ' ἐκεῖθεν, "πυνθάνει," τοίνυν φησίν, "εἰ χάριτι τοῦ ἀκτίστου τετύχηκεν ἡ χάρις αὕτη· ἀλλ' ἔσται χάρις χάριτος, καὶ ταύτης πάλιν ἄλλη, καὶ τοῦτο ἐπ' ἄπειρον.»* *Ibid.* (fol. 344v): *'Ακούσας γὰρ περὶ αὐτοῦ τὴν ἀρχὴν ὡς ἄρα μὲν δύο κηρύττοι θεότητας ἀκτίστους, ὀνομάζοι δὲ τὴν μὲν φύσιν, τὴν δὲ χάριν αὐτῆς, γράφω μὲν πρὸς αὐτὸν καὶ ἠπόρουν πῶς ἡ χάρις χάριτι ἄκτιστος, δέχομαι δὲ παρ'αὐτοῦ ἐπιστολὴν ἐξ ἧς ἐκεῖνά ἐστι ἃ νῦν παραγέγραμμαι.*

11–16 *διελθὼν δὴ ταύτην ἐπιστατικῶς . . . καταστήσεται γνώμη*: Akindynos politely praises Palamas' letter, but hints at their future disagreement when he proposes to discuss Palamas' views at their forthcoming meeting.

12.

Serious rumors of an impending Scythian invasion compel Akindynos to write to the monk Dishypatos advising him to leave his mountain retreat and seek the safety of the capital. The escalating dispute between Barlaam and their mutual friend Palamas also requires his presence at Constantinople where Palamas has been summoned by the Patriarch to appear and account for the charges brought against him by Barlaam.

Addressee: David Dishypatos at the monastery of Paroria in Bulgaria. Akindynos implies that Dishypatos' hermitage was somewhere in the Balkan mountains when he remarks that he would be free to return to his solitude on Haimos if the barbarian threat did not materialize; see line 66. Being more specific, Philotheos writes in his *Encomium* of Palamas that Dishypatos was at the time at a mountain retreat on the border between Thrace and the Scythians (Bulgaria), where Gregory of Sinai had founded a monastery (PG, 151, col. 597B). On the basis of this information, Loenertz identified this monastery with Paroria which was established by Gregory in Mesomilion, near Sozopolis, with the support of the Bulgarian czar John-Alexander; see "Dix-huit lettres," 89–90; Laurent, "L'assaut avorté," 150.

A member of a noble family related to the Palaiologi, the monk David Dishypatos was acquainted with all three protagonists in the controversy. Barlaam included him among the hesychasts from whose acquaintance he had benefited (cf. *Epist. V, Epistole Greche*, 323, lines 110–13) and addressed to him two letters at the outset of the dispute; see *Epist. VI and VII, Epistole Greche*, 325–27 and 329–30. At the height of the controversy, Dishypatos emerged as an active supporter of Palamas. His polemical works against Akindynos include an iambic poem (cf. Dishypatos, *Poem*); a discourse addressed to Nicholas Kabasilas (cf. Dishypatos, Λόγος); and a brief history of the origins of the dispute, which he presented to the empress shortly before the fall of Kalekas; cf. *Ἱστορία διὰ βραχέων ὅπως τὴν ἀρχὴν συνέστη ἡ κατὰ τὸν* Βαρλαὰμ *καὶ* Ἀκίνδυνον *αἵρεσις*, ed. M. Candal, "Origen ideologico del palamismo en un documento de David Disípato," *Miscelánea Comillas*, I (Santander, 1943), 489–525 = *OCP*, 15 (1949), 85–125. On Dishypatos and his role in the hesychast controversy, see Beyer, "David Disypatos als Theologe und Vorkämpfer für die Sache des Hesychasmus (ca. 1337–ca. 1350), *JOB*, 24 (1975), 107–28.

Date: Late spring, 1341; Palamas had been summoned to appear at the council of 10 June and was momentarily expected in Constantinople; see line 36.

2 *Σκυθῶν*: Loenertz has identified these Scythians with the Mongols of the

Golden Horde whose ruler Ozbeg-Khan had married an illegitimate daughter of Andronikos III. Their threatened attack, according to Loenertz, was averted through the skillful diplomacy of John Kantakouzenos, who is known to have sent the father of Demetrios Kydones on a successful mission to the Mongol court in the spring of 1341. See "Dix-huit lettres," 90–91; also Laurent's detailed commentary ("L'assaut avorté," 148–53), in which he argues convincingly that the Scythians in question were the Mongols of the Golden Horde and not the Bulgarians, as suggested by Meyendorff (*Introduction*, 79 note 55).

4–5 *βασιλέως μὲν θυγατρός, γυναικὸς δὲ τοῦ Σκύθου*: As already commented by Loenertz, this princess was an illegitimate daughter of Andronikos III whose marriage to the Mongol Ozbeg-Khan is attested by the Arabian traveler Ibn Battuta (*Voyages d'Ibn Battuta*, ed. C. Defrémery-P. R. Sanguinetti [Paris, 1854], 393–94, 412–14); see "Dix-huit lettres," 90. See also Laurent, "L'assaut avorté," 147, 151–52, 153–54.

5–6 *παρωξύνθαι καὶ μανῆναι τὸν βάρβαρον*: See Laurent's interesting hypothesis that the Mongols were motivated by vengeance provoked by the diversionary tactics of the Byzantines who in 1340, in an effort to spare Thrace from the Turkish razzias, must have encouraged the hordes of Umur Pasha to attack the rich Mongol territories on the Black Sea ("L'assaut avorté," 153–57).

6 *ἓξ μυριάδας*: According to Laurent, these large numbers of troops are an additional indication that Akindynos is here referring to the Mongols and not to the Bulgarians who could not at the time mobilize such forces; "L'assaut avorté," 152.

7 *Ἴστρον*: The Danube.

26–35 *δειλίαν γὰρ ἐγνωκώς . . . καὶ διὰ τοῦτο πεσών*: Note the rare prosopographical details: Akindynos confesses to an excessive fear of the sea and also to his inability to suffer physical hardship.

30 *Ταναΐδος*: The river Don in Russia.

37 *μεταπέμπεται γὰρ αὐτὸν γράμμασιν . . . Βαρλαάμ*: See commentary on Letter 11 *supra*.

39–40 *διὰ τὸ χώραν αὐτῷ . . . ἰσχυρίζεσθαι*: An allusion to Palamas' doctrine of the divine grace with which Akindynos became directly acquainted after reading the last letter that Palamas sent him before leaving for the capital; see commentary on Letter 11, lines 9 and 11–16.

40–41 *ὅ σοι καὶ πρότερον ἔγραψα*: This letter has not survived.

45–46 *μὴ πάντα αὐτῷ συναινέσαντας . . . ὑποψίαν ἀντιδιακειμένων*: Palamas suspected Akindynos of agreeing with Barlaam on the question

of the demonstrability of the divine realities; see Palamas' second letter to Akindynos, *Συγγράμματα*, I, 220, line 8–221, line 7.

46–48 *εἰ ⟨καὶ⟩ τὰ σαφεστάτου φίλου νῦν ἐγὼ . . . νομίζεσθαι*: The evidence from this letter, as well as from the preceding letters to Palamas and Barlaam, shows that Akindynos gave an accurate account of the preliminaries of the council of June 1341 in the *Report* he presented to the Patriarch and the Synod in the spring of 1343; see *Report*, 86–88.

50–52 *ἀφ' ὧν πρὸς ἐμὲ ἄρτι γέγραφε . . . κρατύνουσαν*: See commentary on Letter 11, line 9.

55–60 *ὡς ἂν δὲ ἡμῖν δοκεῖ . . . ἐναντίων καθαίρεσιν*: The text is here corrupt, and, as Loenertz notes, we can only guess at the meaning (Laurent, "L'assaut avorté," 159 note 47, where the grammatical commentary is by Loenertz). Akindynos concludes that both adversaries are to be corrected, but not in a humiliating manner which would increase their stubbornness and provoke a rift in the Church.

61 *ἐλθών*: Dishypatos arrived at Constantinople three days after Palamas; see Philotheos, *Encomium*, PG, 151, col. 597C.

67 *τοῦ νοσεῖν ἀνεθεῖσι*: I do not know whether the reference is to a temporary or a chronic ailment. Neither Akindynos' correspondence nor his *Report* contain any other allusion to a sickness. However, the inference from some statements by his opponents is that Akindynos suffered from epilepsy.

In his *First Antirrhetic*, Palamas says that the Akindynist party was led by some epileptics (although he uses the plural, it is unlikely that there could have been more than one); see Συγγράμματα III, 73, line 25–74, line 13: Ἡ *δὲ φατρία οὐκ ἀγενής. Ἔστι μὲν γὰρ οὓς ἐπιληψία κατὰ περιόδους ἁλισκομένους ἔχει τῆς σελήνης—ἐπιτηρεῖ γὰρ ὁ δαίμων τὸν καιρόν, κατὰ τὸν Χρυσόστομον πατέρα, τοῦ πείθειν ἕνεκεν τοὺς ἀνοήτους ὡς τῶν οὐρανίων ἐξῆπται τὰ καθ' ἡμᾶς—οἱ δ' ὑπόλοιποι, τὸν τρόπον οὐ λίαν εἰσὶν ἀποδέοντες αὐτῶν, ὑπὸ γὰρ τοιούτοις ἀξιοῦσι ζῆν. Ὅταν τοίνυν μὴ δοκῇ τῷ δαίμονι, τὰς ἐν ἐγκεφάλῳ διεξόδους τοῦ ψυχικοῦ πνεύματος ἐμφράττοντι καὶ λυμαινομένῳ τὰς ἐκεῖθεν προϊούσας ἐνεργείας, σπασμὸν ἐνεργάζεσθαι τοῖς συνεκτικοῖς τοῦ σώματος μορίοις, κἀντεῦθεν ῥιπτεῖν καὶ συμπνίγειν ἐπὶ γῆς αὐτούς, ἀνὰ τὴν πόλιν περιάγει πᾶσαν, νῦν μὲν ἐπ' αὐτὰς ἄγων τὰς ἀγορὰς καὶ τὰς τριόδους, νῦν δ' ἐπὶ τοὺς ἄρχοντας, καὶ ἐπ' αὐτοὺς αὐτῶν τοὺς οἴκους, ὡς καὶ τὰς συζύγους περιβομβήσειαν, ἐκεῖνα λέγοντας ἃ καὶ μικρόν τις ἐπιστήσας γνοίη ἂν διανοίας ὄντα δαιμονιώδους ὄντως καὶ κατηλογημένης, καὶ μηδ' εἰδυίας ἑαυτῇ γοῦν ἀκολούθως προϊέναι.*

In his *Fourth Antirrhetic*, Kalothetos calls Akindynos another Barlaam, "though worse than Barlaam as far as physical ailments and wicked deeds are concerned" (*Συγγράμματα*, 160, lines 26–27: *ὅσῳ καὶ δεινότερος τοῖς φυσικοῖς ἀρρωστήμασι καὶ κακουργήμασι*). Then, speaking of Akindynos' followers, Kalothetos writes (*ibid.*, 164, lines 150–54): *Σὺ δ' ἐπὶ τούτοις μεγαλοφρονεῖς καὶ ὅτι σύστημα φατρίας πονηρᾶς συνεστήσω ὀλίγῃ μάζῃ καὶ ἀργυριδίοις, οὐκ εἰδὼς ὅτι καὶ πρὸ σοῦ ὁ Μωάμεθ ἐκεῖνος, ὃς καὶ κατὰ τὰς σεληνιακὰς ἐκλείψεις πάσχων κατὰ σὲ ἐκ θείας ἐνεργείας ἔλεγε ταῦτα πάσχειν.* Depending on how we punctuate—whether we place the comma before or after *κατὰ σὲ*—we can translate this passage as follows: And you are proud of them and of having gathered a wicked faction by means of a little barley bread and a few coins, because you do not know that the notorious Mohammed did the same before you. He who, even when suffering during the lunar eclipses, said, as you do, that he was suffering this by an act of God / when suffering during the lunar eclipses, as you do, said that he was suffering this by an act of God.

According to the first reading, we can still interpret Kalothetos' statement to mean that Mohammed attributed even his epileptic seizures to an act of God, just as Akindynos attributed his following to an act of God. The second reading, on the other hand, permits no doubt that Akindynos was an epileptic.

Moreover, Kalothetos often calls Akindynos mentally disturbed; see, for example, *Πρὸς Γρηγόριον τὸν Στραβολαγκαδίτην*, *Συγγράμματα*, 373, line 119; 375, lines 173, 183; 376, lines 207–8 (*τοῦ παρακεκινημένου τὰς φρένας Ἀκινδύνου· παραπλήξ· παράφρων· ὁ τὰς φρένας παρακεκινημένος Ἀκίνδυνος*)· Such expressions are undoubtedly a *topos* in polemical literature, but it must be noted that Kalothetos does not use them in reference to Barlaam.

Still the evidence is inconclusive. It is hard to believe that if Akindynos suffered from epilepsy, his opponents would have failed to be more specific or make more extensive use of such a powerful weapon against him, seeing that the Church considered epileptics to be the victims of the devil, and not of the moon, as ordinary people believed. See, for example, John Chrysostom, *In Matth.*, 3 (PG, 58, col. 562); Theophylact of Bulgaria, *Ennar. in evang. Matth.*, 5 and 17 (PG, 123, cols. 185C and 332B); Euthemios Zegabenos, *Comment. in Matth.*, 17 (PG, 129, col. 488D).

13.

Akindynos appeals to his correspondent to change his present distressing attitude and thus preserve peace and their friendship.

Addressee: Palamas in Constantinople(?).

This letter is found in the Escorial manuscript together with three others which are beyond doubt addressed to Barlaam (Letters 7–9). However the following internal evidence points to Palamas as the addressee:

1) The general tone of this letter is more obsequious than that of Akindynos' letters to Barlaam. Though such forms of address as *ἡ σὴ ἱερότης, ἡ σὴ θειότης* do not appear in this letter, their absence does not necessarily indicate that the letter is not addressed to an ecclesiastic like Palamas, because Akindynos is not consistent in his use of these terms. They occur in his second letter to Palamas (Letter 11, lines 2 and 7), but not in the first (Letter 5). Moreover, the description of the addressee as a man of intelligence, character, and power (line 17) comports with Akindynos' opinion of Palamas' moral stature and high ecclesiastical and social prestige (Letter 8, lines 15–16; Letter 9, lines 63–64, 74–75; Letter 42, lines 48–50), but it is hardly compatible with his portrait of Barlaam as an arrogant and impulsive man (cf. commentary on Letter 9, lines 16–17).

2) Akindynos seems to be pleading for himself rather than for a third party (lines 6–9), as would have been the case if he were asking Barlaam to withdraw his charges against the hesychasts.

3) He alludes to favors which he knew well how to repay (lines 4–5). Palamas had been kind to him during his visit to Mt. Athos, and Akindynos repaid him by personally interceding with the Patriarch on his behalf before the Council of June.

4) The addressee seems to be a man with a large following whose views would be influenced by his decision (lines 9–17).

It is, therefore, possible that Akindynos addressed this letter to Palamas during the short period between the councils of June and July 1341 when he sought unsuccessfully to convince his former spiritual father to eliminate from his writings the terms that he found objectionable concerning the doctrine of the divine grace; see p. xvii *supra*. The phrase *παρακαλεῖ σε Θεὸς ὑπὲρ οὗ παροικοῦμεν ἐνταῦθα καὶ τὴν αἴτησιν ταύτην ποιούμεθα* (lines 6–7) may even be a reference to Akindynos' visit to the monastery of Athanasios I on Xerolophos, where he and the Palamites held a conference shortly before the council of July in an attempt to settle their differences; see pp. xvii–xviii *supra*.

Date: Shortly before the council of July 1341(?).

7–8 *αὐτὸ τὸ πρᾶγμά σοι . . . ἀμφοῖν ὂν ἐπωφελὲς ὁμοίως*: Akindynos may here be alluding to the matter of his reconciliation with Palamas, which would be to the benefit of both. In his *Report*, he mentions the Patriarch's eagerness to put an end to the dogmatic dispute and reconcile the adversaries prior to the council of July; see *Report*, 88.

10–11 *ἄν δέ τις μείνῃ τῆς οἰκείας σκληρότητος οὐκ ἀφιστάμενος*: In the quarrel that preceded the synod of July, Kalothetos and other hesychasts sided with Palamas and repeatedly tried to convince Akindynos that he was wrong; see Kalothetos, *κατὰ τοῦ Ἀκινδύνου πρὸς τὸν κατριάρχην κῦρ Ἰωάννην*, *Συγγράμματα*, 240, lines 130–37.

14.

Akindynos wishes to initiate a correspondence with Kabasilas whose learning and character he greatly admires.

Addressee: The Mystic Nicholas Kabasilas Chamaëtos. On his career and works, see the prosopographical survey in Dennis, *The Letters of Manuel II Palaeologus*, xxx–xxxiv; and C. Tsiparnlis, "The Career and Writings of Nicolas Cabasilas," *Byzantion* 49 (1979), 411–27.

Although he later became a defender of Palamism, Kabasilas retained a neutral attitude at the start. This is attested by the discourse which David Dishypatos addressed to him early in the dispute in an attempt to draw him to the Palamite camp; see Dishypatos, Λόγος. Whether Akindynos' desire to establish contact with Kabasilas represents a similar attempt cannot be ascertained, because his letter contains no reference to the controversy or, for that matter, to Kabasilas' piety, which does not even figure among the virtues that endeared him to Akindynos.

Date: Autumn 1341–spring 1342, while Akindynos was still restrained by the patriarchal injunction against written polemics; see p. xxii *supra*. Even if this letter has nothing to do with the dispute, it could not have been written before 1340, because, as Loenertz and Ševčenko convincingly argue, Kabasilas was born *ca.* 1320, and it is hard to imagine that this letter which describes Kabasilas as a learned man and a talented writer was addressed to a teenager; see Loenertz, "Chronologie de Nicolas Cabasilas," 205–6; Ševčenko, "Nicolaus Cabasilas' Correspondence," 53–55.

Kabasilas must still have been in Thessalonica when this letter was written. He left his native city in 1347 when he was invited by the vic-

torious Kantakouzenos to join him in the capital; see Loenertz, *op. cit.*, 207–8.

2–5 *εἰ σφόδρα φιλοῦντες . . . ἀναρμοστίαν ἤθους καὶ γνώμης κατηγορήσομεν*: A marginal note in the manuscript shows that a later reader found fault with the syntax of this sentence and attempted to correct it; see *apparatus*, 2.

3–4 *τὸ μὲν ἔχοντα, τὸ δὲ μετὰ πάσης ἐπιμελείας ἀθροίζοντα*: This phrase, as Ševčenko observes (*op. cit.*, 53 note 4), is an indication that Kabasilas was still a young scholar "partly in possession of learning and partly diligently collecting it."

17 *τὰ γὰρ ἡμέτερα οὐχὶ τῶν ἐρωμένων*: The corrector of the letter's opening sentence obviously agreed with Akindynos' evaluation of his own style.

15.

Though Styppes has neglected him, Akindynos is proud of his friend's growing literary reputation and urges him to use his talents for the defense of piety.

Addressee: Although the addressee is otherwise unknown, his family name is not. In 1042, when Zoe married Constantine IX, the ceremony was performed by the *protopresbyteros* Stypes of the New Church; cf. Kedrenos, Hist., II, 542, lines 17–18. A century later, during the reign of John II Komnenos, a Leo Styppes was patriarch of Constantinople (1134–43); see V. Grumel, "La chronologie des Patriarches de Constantinople de 1111 à 1206," *REB*, 2 (1944), 252; *idem*, *Chronologie*, 436; and P. Wirth, "Leon Styppes oder Styppeiotes?" *Byzantinische Forschungen*, 3 (1968), 254–55.

Styppes was probably a former student of Akindynos or a young friend indebted to him for some favor; see lines 8–9.

Date: Autumn–spring 1342: only one cautious appeal for resistance to Palamas; see lines 16–18.

16.

Akindynos begs a justice-general to be impartial and hear him too, just as he heard his opponent.

Addressee: A justice-general; see lines 2–3, in which Akindynos states that the addressee had been entrusted by the Emperor with straightening the reins of justice. The target of Akindynos' veiled accusations of favoritism (lines 7–10) was probably Nicholas Matarangos, whom Palamas praised for censuring his opponents; see Πρὸς Δανιὴλ Αἴνου, *Συγγρ.*, II, 388, lines 12–16.

Matarangos was one of the original four judges appointed in 1329 as a result of the judiciary reform of Andronikos III. He was the only one found innocent of the charges of bribery brought against these judges in 1337; see P. Lemerle, "Le juge général des Grecs et la réforme judiciaire d'Andronic III," *Mémorial Louis Petit* (Paris, 1948), 304; 309–10. At the proposed date of this letter (autumn 1341–spring 1342), Matarangos was probably still in office, since in an act of Kutlumus dating from February 1341 he signs as the justice-general; see *Actes de Kutlumus*, ed. P. Lemerle, *Archives de l'Athos*, II (Paris, 1945), 88–89 (Lemerle, "Le juge général . . . ," 309).

It is highly improbable that Akindynos addressed this letter to the Palamite Nomophylax Symeon who has been tentatively identified by Meyendorff with the unknown nomophylax and justice-general sent to summon Palamas to the Palace in the summer of 1342 (cf. *Introduction*, 367). Meyendorff's identification has also been accepted by Lemerle; cf. "Documents et problèmes nouveaux concernant les juges généraux," *Δελτίον τῆς Χριστιανικῆς Ἀρχαιολογικῆς Ἑταιρείας*, Δ′ [1964–65], 34). Certain disparaging comments in Gregoras' *History* regarding the nomophylax Symeon, biased though they may be, leave little doubt that he had never been a justice-general. For, writing after Symeon's death, Gregoras describes him as a destitute opportunist to whom "accrued the dignity of nomophylax" (*Hist.*, XXVI, 45: III, 111: *Οἶσθα δὴ πάντως καὶ Συμεὼν ἐκεῖνον, ᾧ τοῦ νομοφύλακος προσεγεγόνει ἀξίωμα ἐν τῇ τῶν πραγμάτων ζάλῃ, ὃς τοῖς παλαμίταις καὶ στόμα καὶ γλῶττα καὶ νόμος ἦν, καὶ στρατηγὸς τῇ παρανόμῳ φάναι καθίστατο φάλαγγι, ἅτε μᾶλλον ἐλλόγιμος ἢ κατ' ἐκεῖνον ὑπάρχων τὸν θίασον· πένης δ' ἄλλως ὢν καὶ λιμῷ τὸν βίον στρατηγούμενος, κολακείᾳ τοὺς ἐν δόξῃ μετῄει παντοδαπῇ, βίου πρόφασιν ἐπιτηδεύων καὶ ζωῆς πορισμὸν ἑαυτῷ καὶ παισὶ καὶ συζύγῳ καὶ ὅλῃ φάναι συλλήβδην οἰκίᾳ*). Had Symeon attained an even higher office, would Gregoras have failed to mention it? Furthermore, a justice-general could not have been indigent, since we know from the same Gregoras that in order to protect them from temptation the emperor provided these justices with ample annual revenues; see *Hist.*, IX, 9, 5: I, 438, lines 3–7; Lemerle, "Le juge général . . . ," 296.

Neither could the jurist Harmenopoulos have been the recipient of this letter, because he did not become a justice-general until the second

patriarchate of Philotheos (1364–76); see J. Verpeaux, "Un témoin de choix des oeuvres de Constantin Harménopoulos: le Vaticanus Ottobonianus Gr. 440," *REB*, 21(1963), 231. Moreover, we know from Akindynos that Harmenopoulos was closely allied with the anti-Palamites until 1347 when he condemned both factions for disturbing the peace of the Church; see p. xxxii *supra*.

Date: Autumn 1341–spring 1342; the lack of invective against Palamas indicates that Akindynos was not yet allowed to engage in polemics. See also commentary on lines 17–19 *infra*.

2–3 *τὰς αὐτοῦ τοῦ δικαίου . . . ἡνίας ἐνεχειρίσθης ὀρθοῦν*: According to Gregoras, the aim of the judiciary reform instituted by Andronikos III in 1329 was to improve the standards of justice which suffered from an "incurable and endemic disease." See *Hist.*, IX, 9, 5: I, 437–38; Lemerle, "Le juge général . . . ," 295–96.

17–19 *οἱ δόξαντες ἐνταῦθα κατακεκρίσθαι . . . κατακρημνησθῶσιν*: Akindynos is obviously alluding to his condemnation in July 1341. His statement suggests that he was still in disgrace.

27–28 *φίλους μὲν ἀλλήλοις ὑπάρξαντας . . . ὁμόπνους*: For similar references to his friendship with Palamas and the hesychasts, see Letter 5, lines 19–21; Letter 26, lines 48–50; Letter 27, line 170; Letter 28, lines 37–38; Letter 49, lines 40–42; and *Third Antirrhetic*, *Monac. Gr.* 223, fol. 198[r] (*ἀλλὰ θρηνήσωμεν τὸν εἰς τοσοῦτο βάραθρον ἐκπεπτωκότα πλάνης, φίλον ἡμῖν γεγονότα καὶ ἀδελφὸν ἐν τοῖς μάλιστα* . . .). See also Joseph Kalothetos, who writes that prior to the controversy Akindynos honored the hesychasts above all (*Λόγος ἀντιθετικὸς κατὰ τοῦ 'Ακινδύνου*, *Συγγράμματα*, 98, line 522) and asserts that he and Akindynos were friends in their youth (*Πρὸς τοὺς Βαρλααμίτας*, *Συγγράμματα*, 182, lines 669–70).

29–30 *τῆς ἀληθείας ἧς οὐδὲν προτιμότερον . . . κατὰ τὸν μέγαν Παῦλον*: A misquotation of I Cor. 13:13, where love, and not truth, is cited as the supreme virtue.

17.

After reading Gregoras' encomium of the empress Theophano, Akindynos congratulates the author and commends him in particular for his denunciation of the religious conflict and for his views on the inability of men to attain a vision of the divinity through the senses.

Addressee: Nikephoros Gregoras.

Date: Winter 1341–spring 1342. The moderate tone of this and the following letter to Gregoras suggests that they were written before the fall of 1342 when Akindynos was allowed to write freely against Palamas following the latter's condemnation; see commentary on Letter 25, line 11. Guilland (*Correspondance*, 282) dates it to 1345–50.

1 Τῷ φιλοσόφῳ: On this term, see commentary on Letter 1, line 33.

2–4 *Ἐκείμην ἐν ἀσθενείᾳ . . . φάρμακον τῆς ἀσθενείας ἀπαλλακτήριον*: Under the restrictions imposed on him by the patriarchal injunction in the immediate aftermath of the council of July, Akindynos' position was indeed very weak, as he later confessed to the Cypriot Lapithes (Letter 42, lines 108–40). It is not surprising, therefore, that he expressed such enthusiasm about this work by Gregoras which appeared to him to contain certain views favorable to his own anti-Palamite stand; see commentary on lines 11–15 *infra*.

4–6 *ὁ δὲ ἦν ποίημα τῆς σῆς . . . σοφίας . . . κόσμημα δὲ τῆς . . . βασιλίδος Θεοφανοῦς*: The first wife of Leo VI (886–912), Theophano was renowned for her piety. She died young and was canonized by the Orthodox Church. Her memory is celebrated on the 16th of December; see K. Doukakes, *Μέγας Συναξαριστὴς πάντων τῶν ἁγίων τῶν καθ' ἅπαντα τὸν μῆνα Δεκέμβριον ἑορταζομένων* (Athens, 1896), 398. Her *vita* by an anonymous author and her encomium by Gregoras have been published by E. Kurtz; cf. "Zwei Griechische Texte über die Hl. Theophano, die Gemalin Kaisers Leo VI," *Mémoires de l'Académie impériale des Sciences de St. Pétersbourg, Classe historico-philologique*, VIIIe série, vol. III[2] (1898), 2–24 and 25–45 respectively.

For the dates of Theophano's marriage and death, see G. P. Majeska, "The Body of St. Theophano the Empress and the Convent of St. Constantine," *Byzantinoslavica* 38 (1977), 14.

9–10 *ἐν ᾧ τῆς ἐκκλησιαστικῆς κατεύχῃ τρικυμίας ⟨καὶ⟩ ζάλης*: See Gregoras, *Encomium*, ed. Kurtz, 45, lines 4–8: *τούς τε τῆς ἐκκλησίας ἱεροὺς θεσμοὺς καὶ νόμους εἰλικρινεῖς καὶ ἀκιβδήλους καὶ αὐτοὺς τὸν ἅπαντα διατήρησον χρόνον· καὶ πᾶν εἴ τι νόθον ἔθος καὶ ἀληθείας πόρρω που πλανώμενον τὴν αὐτῆς εὐκοσμίαν καὶ ὡραιότητα συγχεῖ καὶ ταράττει διενοχλοῦν, εἰς βυθούς τε καὶ πυθμένας ἀπωλείας πέμψον ὑποβρύχιον.*

11–15 *τὸ πεφυκὸς δέχεσθαι τὰς τυπωτικὰς θεοπτίας καὶ ὄψεις κάλλιστά σοι πεφιλοσοφημένον . . . ἐξελέγχεις*: Despite Guilland's claim that the text of the *Encomium*, as it now stands, does not justify Akindynos' comments (cf. *Correspondance*, 282 note 7), a careful perusal of this work shows that it contains certain statements which could be interpreted as a refutation of the hesychasts' claim to perceive with their eyes the

uncreated light of the Transfiguration. For, in relating how Theophano's birth was announced to her aged and childless parents by a messenger from the Holy Virgin who appeared to them in their sleep, Gregoras does say that no human being while awake and fully alert could communicate with the divinity, because only in sleep or in a state of ecstasy is the human mind released from the fetters of the senses; see *Encomium*, 31, lines 23–28: *οὐ γὰρ ἂν εἴη γρηγοροῦντι καὶ φρονοῦντί τινι τῶν ἀνθρώπων θεόθεν γενέσθαι μέλλοντος δήλωσιν, ἀλλ' ἢ κατὰ τοὺς ὕπνους ἠρεμοῦντος τοῦ τῶν αἰσθητηρίων ὑλικοῦ καὶ συρφετώδους κλύδωνος, ἢ πεπονθότος περιτροπήν τινα καὶ ἔκστασιν τοῦ νοῦ· ὑπέστρωσε γὰρ ὁ Θεὸς τῷ ἡγεμονικῷ τὸ φανταστικὸν πνεῦμα καθάπερ τι κάτοπτρον ἢ βιβλίον ὑπὸ τοῦ νοῦ θεωρούμενόν τε καὶ ἀναγινωσκόμενον.*

Gregoras may also be making an anti-Palamite allusion—as Beyer suggests (*Antirrhetika I*, 110)—when, at the end of the *Encomium*, he prays to the Saint to intercede with Christ her "bridegroom" Whom she now sees directly and clearly and not in "riddles and mirrors, as it were"; see *Encomium*, 44, lines 10–13: *Σὺ δέ, μακαρία, ἵλεως ἡμᾶς ἐποπτεύοις ἄνωθεν· νῦν γὰρ οὐχ ὡς ἐν ἐσόπτροις οὐδ' ὡς ἐν αἰνίγμασι βλέπεις ὃν ἐπόθεις νυμφίον Χρίστόν, ἀλλ' ἀμέσως καὶ καθαρῶς ἐντυγχάνεις αὐτῷ.*

The *Encomium* also contains a reference to civil strife (cf. p. 44, lines 23–27: *οὐ γὰρ μόνον βορρᾶς καὶ νότος, 'Ασία τε ἅμα καὶ Εὐρώπη δυσμενῆ καὶ ἀνήμερον τὴν ὁρμὴν πεποίηνται κατ' αὐτῆς . . . ἀλλ' ἤδη καὶ αὐτὴ πρὸς ἑαυτὴν σφόδρα ἐκπεπολέμωται . . .*), on the basis of which E. Kurtz (*op. cit.*, p. VIII) dated it to 1328–29, the years of the conflict between Andronikos II and his grandson. Akindynos' letter, however, helps us assign this work to the civil war of the forties.

18.

Akindynos returns to Gregoras his encomium of Constantine the Great and his discourse against the Latins and compliments him for his ideas and his style. This time he perceives in Gregoras' arguments against the Latins another refutation of Palamite theology.

Addressee: Nikephoros Gregoras.

Date: Autumn 1341–spring 1342; see commentary on Letter 17. Guilland (*Correspondance*, 276) dates it to 1335–40, but gives no reason for this date.

2 Βασιλικὸς ὁ λόγος: This unpublished encomium of Constantine the

Great is preserved in codex *Berolinensis Hamilton Gr. 453* (fols. 8^{r}–62^{v}); see Guilland, *Correspondance*, 276 note 2; C. De Boor, *Handschriftenverzeichnisse der königlichen Bibliothek zu Berlin* (Berlin, 1897), vol. 11, II, 233–34. For a résumé of this discourse, see Guilland, *Essai sur Nicéphore Grégoras* (Paris, 1926), 190–92.

19–20 Περὶ δὲ τοῦ πρὸς Λατίνους καὶ κατὰ τῶν . . . τολμώντων: This is the speech that Gregoras made in 1334 before the Patriarch and some of the more prominent bishops who had asked for his advice on the forthcoming *pourparlers* with the papal legates just arrived in Constantinople; see Gregoras, *Hist.*, X, 8: I, 501, line 12–502, line 10; Beyer, *Antirrhetika I*, 59. It is found in his *History* (X, 8: I, 502, line 10–520, line 1) and has also been published separately by M. Paparozzi; see Περὶ τοῦ μὴ δεῖν ἀκαίρως καὶ ἀπερισκέπτως θεολογεῖν κατ' ἐξουσίαν τοὺς βουλομένους, καὶ κατὰ Λατίνων: Λόγος συμβουλευτικὸς πρὸς τὴν θείαν καὶ ἱερὰν σύνοδον περὶ τοῦ μὴ προσδέχεσθαι μήτε Λατίνους εἰς διαλέξεις τὰς περὶ θεολογίας, μήτε καινοφωνοῦντας ἄλλους, "Un opusculo di Niceforo Gregoras sulle condizioni del dialogo teologico con i Latini," *Atti del Convegno storico interecclesiale*, III (Padua, 1973), 1331–59.

22–24 τοὺς τυφλοὺς τὴν ψυχὴν . . . τοῦθ' ὅπερ εἰσὶ δείκνυσι: As already commented by Beyer ("Nikephoros Gregoras als Theologe," *JÖB*, 20 [1971], 175), Gregoras' discourse has nothing to do with the Palamite controversy which it antedates. However, since its main emphasis is on the incomprehensibility of God, Akindynos could interpret it as favorable to his own anti-Palamite thesis, just as he did at the synod of July 1341 when the Patriarch ordered the reading of a passage of St. Basil concerning the impossibility of knowing God; see p. xix *supra*.

24–25 εἰς ἐρημίας ἀποπεπλανημένους καὶ βάραθρα: According to Beyer (*Antirrhetika I*, 66) the image of those "who have strayed away into the wilderness" is taken up by Gregoras in his first *Antirrhetic*.

27–28 τὸ ὄντως φιλόσοφον οὗ τὸ κεφάλαιον . . . ἐπιστήμων εὐλάβεια: Akindynos often wrote to his learned correspondents that true philosophy was "correct theology"; see Letter 19, lines 8–12; Letter 41, lines 41–45; Letter 42, lines 15–22.

Gregoras shared this view which goes back to Philo and the early Church fathers who considered learning and philosophy as ancillary to the true wisdom of God; see Philo, *De congressu*, 14; Clement of Alexandria, *Stromat.*, 1, 5, PG, 8, cols. 717C–D–719A, 728A–B; Eusebius, *Demonstr. evang.*, I, 6, PG, 22, cols. 61D–64A; Beyer, *Antirrhetika I*, 126 note 10.

35 τῇ δέλτῳ: For the use of this term to denote a book in Byzantine Greek,

see B. Atsalos, *La terminologie du livre manuscrit à l'époque byzantine* (Thessalonica, 1971), 106–12.

19.

Akindynos congratulates the learned addressee for his outspoken opposition to Palamas.

Addressee: Unknown. Obviously a man of letters, since Akindynos writes that his arduous pursuit of philosophy brought forth the finest fruit which was his excellence in theology; see lines 5–12.

Date: Spring of 1342. The tone of this letter is bolder than that of the preceding ones, but there is no mention of the condemnation of Palamas in the summer of 1342.

8–9 *ἀσφαλοῦς θεολογίας . . . οὖσαν καρπὸν τῆς ὅλης φιλοσοφίας*: See commentary on Letter 18, lines 27–28.

20.

Akindynos congratulates a learned physician for his reported anti-Palamite stand.

Addressee: Despite the biographical details provided by Akindynos, it is impossible to identify the recipient of this letter. He was obviously a physician and a scholar (see lines 1–6). A native of Constantinople, he had spent some time in Thessalonica and on Mt. Athos, but was presently living abroad (see lines 66–71).

If Akindynos were not speaking of a monk, as his reference to his correspondent's pious exertions on the Holy Mountain implies (lines 68–69), the remaining evidence could point to George Chrysokokes, a contemporary physician, scholar, and astronomer who was at that time living in Trebizond. Practically nothing is known about Chrysokokes' life, except that in the early 1340s he was in Trebizond pursuing studies in astronomy and mathematics; see U. Lampsides, "George Chrysococcis, le médecin et son oeuvre," *BZ*, 38 (1938), 315–16. He wrote several treatises on geography and astronomy, but all the manuscripts which contain his works give him the title of *ἰατρός*; see *ibid.*, 315 and note 4. Neither is he designated as a monk in codex *Vaticanus Palatinus* 7, which

he finished copying in 1336 and signed simply as George Chrysokokes; see A. Turyn, *Codices Graeci*, 137.

The Palamite Joseph Kalothetos cites a physician among the few staunch Akindynists, but he does not mention his name. Instead, he refers to him ironically as a "Galen inexperienced in medicine": Οὐδένας γὰρ ἄλλους οἶδα συμφρονοῦντας αὐτῷ, εἰ μὴ Νίφωνάς τινας καὶ Γαληνοὺς ἀνασκήτους ἰατρικῆς (Λόγος τρίτος κατὰ τοῦ κινδυνεύσαντος Ἀκινδύνου, Συγγράμματα, 144, lines 81–82).

It is possible that this individual and the addressee of this letter are the same person.

Date: Late spring of 1342: Akindynos openly attacks Palamas, but does not refer to the latter's condemnation in the summer of 1342.

2–3 *καὶ πολλῶν ἄλλων ὡς ἀληθῶς ἀντάξιον*: A quotation from Homer, *Iliad*, 11, 514, referring to the Thessalian healer and fighter Machaon, the son of Asclepius.

21–22 *ὥσπερ Ἀθανάσιος ὁ μέγας κατὰ τῆς Ἀρείου . . . μανίας*: See commentary on Letter 10, lines 334–36 *supra*.

61 *ὁ καλὸς καὶ ἀγαθὸς ἡμῖν ἀδελφός . . . Μαλαχίας*: Unknown. Probably a fellow-monk, since Akindynos calls him "brother." On the term *ἀδελφὸς* as used among ecclesiastics, see J. Darrouzès, *Epistoliers byzantins du Xe siècle* (Paris, 1960), 397, *s.v.*

66 *καὶ τὴν ἐπὶ σοὶ τελεωτάτην ἑορτὴν ἑορτάσαιμεν*: I do not know what Akindynos means by this "most perfect feast" in honor of the addressee. Is he, perhaps, expressing a wish that his correspondent be ordained?

21.

Akindynos explains to his supporter Hierotheos that he did not write his treatise on the divine grace out of contentiousness, but because of Palamas' doctrinal innovations.

Addressee: The Thessalonian monk Hierotheos to whom Akindynos addressed in 1347 a lengthy refutation of the jurist Harmenopoulos' contention that both parties in the hesychast dispute were equally guilty of disturbing the peace of the Church; see *Address to Hierotheos*.

Hierotheos is also known from the correspondence of Thomas Magistros who, in a letter to the *epi tou sakelliou* Trikanas described how devotedly Hierotheos nursed him during a serious illness; see PG, 145, col. 417C–D. When Hierotheos retired to Mt. Athos, Magistros ex-

pressed pain and bewilderment at his friend's sudden decision to leave the city; see *Τῷ ἐμῷ Ἱεροθέῳ ἀνακεχωρηκότι πρὸς τὸν Ἄθω*, ed. E. Martini, "Una lettera del retore Teodulo (Thomas Magistros) al monaco Ieroteo," *Miscellanea Ceriani* (Milan, 1910), 435–47. Referring to their close association and mutual affection, Magistros writes that Hierotheos thought of him as a father and protector and guardian (cf. *ibid.*, 438, line 10–439, line 25), which leads to the conclusion that Hierotheos, like his friend Akindynos, was probably a student of that notable Thessalonian grammarian and rhetorician; see commentary on Letter 56.

Date: Late spring of 1342. The cautious tone of this letter, in which Akindynos carefully explains the reasons that compelled him to write his dogmatic treatise, and the absence of any reference to the condemnation of Palamas indicate that it was written before the anti-Palamite synods of the summer and fall of 1342, which were followed by Akindynos' unrestricted polemics against Palamas; see commentary on Letter 25, line 11.

This hypothesis is supported by the testimony of Palamas who writes in his second *Antirrhetic* that hardly a year after the publication of the synodal tome of 1341 Akindynos sent to Thessalonica some of his writings in which he again questioned the uncreated character of the divine light of the Transfiguration; see *Συγγράμματα*, III, 89, line 10–90, line 6.

Karpozilos (*Letters*, 78) assigns this letter to between 1343 and 1344 because Palamas' third and fifth *Antirrhetics*, in which he refutes parts of Akindynos' treatise on the divine grace, are dated to that period.

6–7 *τὸν . . . περὶ τῆς χάριτος λόγον*: A treatise on the divine grace has not survived. The evidence from this letter, however, confirms B. Phanourgakes' hypothesis that Akindynos wrote such a work, since Palamas refers to it in his *Antirrhetics*; see *Ἄγνωστα ἀντιπαλαμικὰ συγγράμματα τοῦ Γρηγορίου Ἀκινδύνου*, *Κληρονομία*, 4 (1972), 295–99.

51–52 *ὡς ἡ κοινὴ ἔννοια . . . τῆς ἐκκλησίας παρέλαβε*: See *Synodikon*, ed. Gouillard, 51, line 98: *Οἱ προφῆται ὡς εἶδον . . . ἡ ἐκκλησία ὡς παρέλαβεν . . .*

22.

Akindynos congratulates his correspondent for writing to Thessalonica in support of the true faith.

Addressee: An unidentified supporter. Perhaps a native of Thessalonica and a man

of importance, since his letters allegedly had a considerable effect in that city; see lines 6–7.

Date: Spring 1342. The internal evidence is too vague for a precise dating of this letter, but its moderate tone assigns it to the early period.

23.

Akindynos praises his correspondent's writings on behalf of God and His dogmas.

Karpozilos, *Letters*, no. 12

Addressee: An unidentified supporter.

Date: This letter, which is similar in tone to Letter 22, must also be assigned to the same period: spring of 1342.

24.

Akindynos hails the *megas doux* as the defender of God and country.

Addressee: Alexios Apokaukos in Constantinople.

From 20 November 1341 to 11 June 1345 the title of *megas doux*, chief admiral of the fleet (cf. R. Guilland, "Études de titulature et de prosopographie byzantines: Drongaire de la flotte, grande drongaire de la flotte, duc de la flotte, mégaduc," *BZ*, 44 [1951], 222), was held by Alexios Apokaukos; see *Chronica*, I, Chronicle 8, §36, p. 82; §44, p. 84; commentary, *ibid.*, II, 253–54; 263.

By his obsequious flattery of the *megas doux* in this letter, Akindynos obviously hoped to endear himself to Apokaukos who, despite his political differences with Palamas, had on occasion shown his sympathy for the hesychast leader. Early in 1342, when Palamas refused to cooperate with the Patriarch's political schemes, Apokaukos intervened and protected him from Kalekas' wrath (cf. Πρὸς *Φιλόθεον*, *Συγγρ.*, II, 532, lines 8–12); and in the autumn of the same year, he heeded Palamas' appeal and removed the guard of soldiers that the Patriarch had stationed at the monastery where he was confined following his return from Heracleia and his condemnation by the Synod (Πρὸς *σεβασμιωτάτους Γέροντας*, *Συγγρ.*, II, 513, lines 20–23).

In the controversy over Akindynos' ordination, Apokaukos sided with the Empress against the Patriarch, and it was only after Sabbas Lo-

garas' intercession on behalf of Akindynos that he relented; see commentary on Letter 51. Palamas later claimed him as a proponent of his doctrines (Ἀ*ναίρεσις γράμματος* Ἰ*γνατίου*, Σ*υγγρ.*, II, 639, lines 6–10), but, as both Meyendorff (*Introduction*, 123) and Weiss (*Kantakuzenos*, 117–20) agree, Apokaukos' interest in the dispute was purely political, and it appears that any show of favor on his part towards Palamas was but an aspect of the political rivalry between him and the Patriarch.

Date: End of 1342; see commentary on lines 7–8 *infra*.

2–4 *στρατηγῶν ἀπαλλάττεις πραγμάτων τὴν βασιλείαν καὶ ἀντιμεθίστης τὰ δεινὰ τοῖς βαρβάροις . . . ἀεὶ πάσχει*: Though Akindynos is here very vague, he may be referring to specific events that occurred in the last six months of 1342. In the summer of that year, Apokaukos led two successful naval expeditions against Kantakouzenos and his allies in Macedonia and Thrace and was enthusiastically received by the Patriarch and the people upon his return to Constantinople; see Kantakouzenos, *Hist.*, III, 40–46: II, 243–81; Gregoras, *Hist.*, XIII, 1–2: II, 634–36; *Chronica*, I, Chronicle 8, §§ 37 and 38, p. 82; commentary *ibid.*, II, 254–55.

Following Kantakouzenos' failure to capture the city of Serres in the early fall, Apokaukos marched against the Kantakouzenists in Didymoteichos, but was forced to abandon the siege and proceed in a hurry to Adrianople to ward off an attack by the "Scythians" (Mongols) who had suddenly overrun Thrace; see Kantakouzenos, *Hist.*, III, 51: II, 301.

The Mongols, then, must be the forever troublesome barbarians to whom Akindynos is here alluding. See Letter 12, where he describes to Dishypatos in terror the news of an impending "Scythian" invasion, which has been correctly identified by Laurent as an attack planned by the Mongols of the Golden Horde in the spring of 1340.

4 *τὸ ἡμέτερον γένος*: For other contemporary writers using *γένος* in a nationalist sense, see I. Ševčenko and J. Featherstone, *Two Poems by Theodore Metochites* (Hellenic College Press, Brookline, 1981), 6 note 10.

4–5 *ἐπανήκων . . . τὴν ἐκκλησίαν κρατύνεις*: An allusion to the condemnation of Palamas in the fall of 1342; see commentary on Letter 25, line 11.

Akindynos could maintain that Apokaukos was one of those responsible for the condemnation of Palamas, since he had done nothing to prevent it, and it was only after Palamas wrote to him and complained that he responded by removing the guard; see commentary on addressee *supra*.

7–8 *ἐκπλεῖς . . . ἐπὶ τὰ πρόσθεν ἔργα*: In the last months of 1342,

Apokaukos sailed with the fleet for Amphipolis, where he was to meet with the Serbian king. The purpose of that meeting was to lure Stephen Dushan away from Kantakouzenos, but Apokaukos' plan fell through when Stephan Hrelja, the Serbian magnate who was acting as an intermediary, died suddenly on 27 December 1342; Kantakouzenos, *Hist.*, III, 54: II, 32–34; 327–28. For the date of Hrelja's death, see P. Schreiner, "La chronique brève de 1352," *OCP*, 31 (1965), 344.

25.

This is a covering letter accompanying the tract which Akindynos wrote, at the command of the Patriarch, in refutation of Palamas' *Dialogue of an Orthodox with a Barlaamite*.

Addressee: The Patriarch of Constantinople, John XIV Kalekas (1334–47)

Date: January–February 1343. This letter alludes to the expulsion of Isidore from the Church of St. Sophia on Christmas Day 1342, but contains no reference to Palamas' stay as a refugee at the same church from 11 February to 11 April 1343; see commentary on lines 22–25 *infra* and on Letter 27, line 171.

4 *θαρρεῖν δὲ οὐκ εἶχον, ἰδιώτης ὢν διδασκαλικῆς ἀξίας*: The sixty-fourth canon of the Quinisext Synod forbade anyone below the rank of bishop to discuss questions of dogma (Rhalles-Potles, II, 453–54). The Tome of 1341 specifically referred to this canon and prohibited all such discussions; see PG, 151, 681C and 692A–B; Miklosich-Muller, I, 203–4.

4 *ἰδιώτης*: In contemporary usage, this term denoted a monk who was not ordained; see J. Darrouzès, *Offikia*, 157 note 3; I. Ševčenko, "Anti-Zealot Discourse," 86 note 24; *idem*, "Alexios Makrembolites' Dialogue," 190 note 18. Because of his status as a plain monk, Akindynos lacked authority—was an *idiotes*—in doctrinal matters. In his Fifth *Antirrhetic*, he makes a similar pun when he refers to some of Palamas' opponents as *ἐν τοῖς ἰδιώταις τὸν λόγον, οὐχ ἰδιῶται τὴν γνῶσιν* (*Monac. Gr. 223*, fol. 352^{v}).

11 *καὶ τὰ μὲν ἔργα ἑαυτῇ*: In the early summer of 1342, when Palamas, who had been accused by the Patriarch of collusion with Kantakouzenos, suddenly left the capital, Kalekas convoked a synod which condemned him *in absentia* and decreed that his works composed after August 1341 were to be burnt (Akindynos, *Report*, 90–91; Letter 42, lines 145–53; Meyendorff, *Introduction*, 103). In the autumn of the same year, Palamas

was brought under escort from his hermitage in Thracian Heraclea to the Palace in Constantinople and was again condemned without a hearing by an assembly of bishops and senators presided over by the Empress. Subsequently, he was first kept in the Palace and then, after a short confinement in an unidentified monastery, he was transferred through the intercession of the *megas doux* Apokaukos to the monastery of Christ the Incomprehensible (*τοῦ Ἀκαταλήπτου*), near the patriarchal residence. He remained there until 11 February 1343 when he escaped to the Cathedral of St. Sophia, from which he was expelled two months later and removed to a Palace prison; see Akindynos, *Report*, 91 Letter 42, lines 153–56; Palamas, *Πρὸς σεβασμιωτάτους γέροντας*, *Συγγρ.*, II, 513, lines 9–27; *Ἀναίρεσις γράμματος Ἰγνατίου*, *Συγγρ.*, II, 637, lines 28–29, 639, lines 1–3; Philotheos, *Encomium*, PG, 151, col. 603A–C; Meyendorff, *Introduction*, 104–5, and commentary on Letter 27, line 171.

11–15 *τοὺς δὲ λόγους ἡμῖν ἐφῆκε . . . τὸν παλαμναῖον ὄντως διάλογον*: The reference is to Akindynos' *Dialogue of the Impious Palamas with an Orthodox*, which is a refutation of his opponent's *Dialexis of an Orthodox with a Barlaamite*. The surviving fragment of the *Dialogue* (*Marc.* Gr. 155, fols. 91^{v}–98^{v})—which covers less than half of Palamas' *Dialexis* (*Συγγράμματα*, II, 161, line 1–171, line 22)—shows that Akindynos copied faithfully each paragraph from his opponent's work and then he proceeded to refute it. The scrupulousness with which Akindynos quotes Palamas in his refutatory works has been emphasized by Nadal; see "La rédaction première," 243–47 and, especially, 245 note 2, where he refers to the *Dialogue*.

15 *παλαμναῖον*: Literally, one guilty of violence, a murderer; hence: abominable; see Liddell-Scott, *s.v.* Akindynos often uses this pun to which his opponent's name so conveniently lent itself. For the sake of accuracy I have transliterated Παλαμναῖος when used as an epithet noun. Thus: "Palamnaian bane," not "Palamite" or "abominable bane" (cf. line 22 of this letter). For other examples, see Index *infra*.

22–25 *τοὺς αὐτῆς φυτευτας ἐκκηρύκτους ποιήσας . . . τεμένη*: Akindynos refers here not only to Palamas, but also to his friend Isidore, the later patriarch of Constantinople. As the bishop-elect of Monemvasia, Isidore attended the first synod which Kalekas convoked against Palamas in the summer of 1342 and incurred the Patriarch's wrath by his vigorous defense of Palamas; cf. Akindynos, *Report*, 91.

According to Akindynos, Isidore's loyalty to Palamas cost him both his episcopacy and his priesthood. On Christmas Day 1342, at the Cathedral of St. Sophia, the Patriarch demanded from him a public denunciation of the Palamite dogmas before accepting him to communion. When he refused, he expelled him from the Church and excommunicated him;

see *Antirrhetic V* (*Monac. Gr. 223*, fols. 351[v]–352[r]): *Οὐ μὴν ἀλλὰ καὶ ὁρῶμεν δὴ τοὺς ταῦτα καινοφωνοῦντας ὑφ' ὑμῶν εἰργομένους ἱεροτελεστίας . . . τὸν δὲ τούτου θιασώτην Ἰσίδωρον τάς τ' ἀρχιερατικὰς ἀφαιρεθέντα ψήφους καὶ τὴν ἱερωσύνην αὐτὴν καὶ ὅλως τὴν κοινωνίαν ὑμῶν. οὐκ αὐτὸν ἐπὶ τούτοις τῆς μεγάλης ἐκκλησίας μέλλοντα σὺν ὑμῖν ἱερουργεῖν ἐξεβάλετε, πάσης παρούσης τῆς πόλεως, τῶν γενεθλίων τοῦ Χριστοῦ τελουμένων, καὶ οὐκ ἡ αἰτία φανερὰ διὰ πάντων ἐλήλυθεν; ἀπαίτησις γὰρ ὑμῶν πρὸς ἐκεῖνον ὑπῆρχεν ἐν μέσῃ τῇ ἐκκλησίᾳ παρεσκευασμένων πρὸς τὴν ἱερουργίαν, κἀκείνου συμπαρασκευαζομένου, μᾶλλον δὲ αἱρέσεως πρότασις, ἤ τοι ἀποκηρύξαι τὰ Παλάμια δόγματα ἐγγράφως καὶ διαρρήδην· εὐθύς . . . ἢ τοῦ μεθ' ὑμῶν καὶ ὅλως ἱερουργεῖν ἐκπεσεῖν καὶ τῆς ἄλλης μεθ' ὑμῶν ἱερᾶς κοινωνίας· τοῦ δὲ μὴ βουληθέντος τὴν μιαρὰν τῶν Παλαμίων δογμάτων ἕξιν ἀποβαλέσθαι, τὸ λοιπὸν ὑμεῖς ἐπεξείργασθε, καὶ τοῦτον ἐκβαλόντες τοῦ ὑμετέρου κλήρου καὶ πάντα ἀφῃρημένοι ὧν τοὺς ἐπὶ πονηροτάταις αἱρέσεσιν ἑαλωκότας ἐκπίπτειν οἱ θεῖοι νόμοι κελεύουσι, πᾶσι φανερὸν αὐτὸν ὑπάρχειν αἱρετικὸν κατεστήσατε.*

See also Letter 30, lines 50–55, the anti-Palamite declaration of 1347 (PG, 150, col. 880C), and the synodal act of Isidore's deposition on 4 November 1344, which states that Isidore had been already forbidden to officiate at the liturgy because of his agreement with Palamas (Mercati, *Notizie*, 200).

This public humiliation, however, was not followed by any immediate disciplinary measures against Isidore, because in April 1343 he attended, though for the last time, a session of the Permanent Synod in his capacity as bishop-elect of Monemvasia; see Miklosich-Müller, I, 237.

26.

Akindynos writes to an old acquaintance with whom he had not been in touch for almost ten years. He informs him of his quarrel with Palamas and of the latter's condemnation.

Addressee: An Athonite monk(?) See commentary on lines 1 and 40–44 *infra*.

Date: January–February 1343. This letter dates from the early part of the controversy, since Akindynos assumes that his correspondent might not have heard about it yet; cf. lines 63–64. The reference to the expulsion of Palamas and Isidore from the Church helps assign it to the beginning of 1343; see lines 60–61.

1 *ὁ μὲν τῆς ἀπουσίας χρόνος δεκαετὴς ὢν ἤδη που*: The letter's desti-

nation was probably Mt. Athos, where Akindynos had retired for a short time at the beginning of the previous decade; see pp. x–xi *supra*.

10–11 *δικαιοσύνης, ἀνδρίας, σωφροσύνης, φρονήσεως*: The four cardinal virtues; see Diogenes Laertius, *Περὶ Πλάτωνος*, *De clarorum philosophorum vitis*, III, 90–91.

40–44 *ὁ . . . θαυμάσιος Σεναχηρεὶμ καὶ ὄντως σὸς ἀδελφός . . . παραστήσει ταῦτα*: The addressee and the carrier of this letter were obviously monks. Senacherim is probably to be identified with the monk Senacherim who between 1328 and 1330 sent to the exiled Metochites in Didymoteichos some fine wine from Stagira in Macedonia; see Metochites' letter to "Sir Methodios Senacherim the Monk," ed. and trans. by I. Ševčenko, "Theodore Metochites, the Chora, and the Intellectual Trends of his Time," Appendix II, *The Kariye Djami, IV, Studies in the Art of the Kariye Djami and its Intellectual Background* (ed. P. A. Underwood, Princeton, 1975), 86–89.

The Senacherim were a prominent family of Epirotan origin; see A. Meliarakes, *Ἱστορία τοῦ βασιλείου τῆς* Νικαίας *καὶ τοῦ δεσποτάτου τῆς* Ἠπείρου (Athens, 1898), 50, 64. On the Senacherim in the first half of the fourteenth century, see F. Dölger, *Aus den Schatzkammern des heiligen Berges* (Munich, 1948), no. 19, 63–64.

48–50 *ὑπὸ τῶν πρῴην μὲν φίλων καὶ φιλικῶν . . . πειραθέντων*: A reference to his former friendship with Palamas and his intervention on his behalf before the council of June 1341; see pp. xiii–xvi *supra* and commentary on Letter 16, lines 27–28 *supra*.

50–52 *εἶτα μὴ μόνον πᾶσαν διαβολὴν . . . ἑτοίμως κεκινηκότων*: See p. xix note 62 *supra*.

60 *καὶ ἡμᾶς συναπαχθῆναι σφίσι βεβιασμένοι*: Akindynos is here alluding to the statement of submission that he was forced to sign shortly before the synod of July 1341; see p. xviii *supra*.

60–61 *ὁ μὲν πρότερον, ὁ δ' ὕστερον ἀπελήλαται τῆς ἐκκλησίας*: See commentary on Letter 25, lines 22–25.

67–68 *τοὺς τὰ πρῶτα δοκοῦντας εἶναι τῶν εὐσεβῶν*: Palamas and his fellow-hesychasts.

27.

Akindynos urges the addressee to continue to serve the fight against heresy through his exceptional learning and reputation. He elaborates on Palamas' principal doctrinal errors and encloses some of his own polemical literature.

Addressee: An unidentified supporter. Described as a scholar of extraordinary reputation and an active anti-Palamite, he obviously lived in Thessalonica or its environs, since the delivery of this letter was entrusted to the Thessalonian Isaris and the Berroian Andronikos Tzimiskes; see line 3.

Date: Late February 1343; cf. commentary on line 171 *infra*.

2 *ὁ θαυμάσιος Ἴσαρις*: The Thessalonian landowner George Isaris, as identified by Loenertz, "Dix-huit lettres," 93. Portrayed here as a trusted friend of Akindynos, he later changed his attitude and incurred the indignation of Akindynos who accused him of betraying his principles for personal profit; see Letter 73, lines 11–12. Isaris was evidently an old acquaintance of Akindynos, perhaps even a student of his, since Akindynos claims to have helped him achieve excellence and honor "through the works of the wise men of old" (Letter 59, lines 52–53). Akindynos' complaint that his friend had abandoned him is substantiated by a synodal act of September 1350 which shows that Isaris was with Palamas on Mt. Athos at the second trial of Niphon (the *Protos* of the Holy Mountain accused of Bogomilism) which took place during Palamas' visit to Mt. Athos in the last months of 1347; see PG, 152, col. 1309B; Miklosich-Müller, I, 298. For Isaris' career and his rise successively to the rank of eparch, *megas primikerios*, and great constable, see Loenertz, "Dix-huit lettres," 93–94; V. Laurent, "Une nouvelle fondation monastique de Choumnos: La Néa Moni de Thessalonique," *REB*, 13 (1955), 115 notes 2 and 4.

2 *ὁ γενναῖος Ἀνδρόνικος*: Probably the hetaeriarch Andronikos Tzimiskes mentioned in Letter 28, lines 14–15. According to Philotheos, Tzimiskes had studied grammar with Akindynos in his native Berroia. He later became a staunch supporter of his teacher and remained faithful to him long after the latter's death. But the miraculous cure of his fatally ill son, one of Palamas' several posthumous miracles, finally converted Tzimiskes to Palamism; see *Encomium*, PG, 151, cols. 651A–652A.

Philotheos describes Tzimiskes as "well-born and wise" (PG, 151, col. 651A), and Akindynos writes in the spring of 1343 that he was a hetaeriarch (Letter 28, line 14), i.e., a court official whose duty was to summon the lower dignitaries to the presence of the emperor. This office ranked sixty-second in Ps.-Kodinos' list of dignities; see *Traité des Offices*, 139 and 186; see also P. Karlin-Hayter, «L'hétériarque. L'évolution de son rôle du De Cerimoniis au traité des Offices,» *JÖB*, 23 (1974), 101–43.

Unknown is the relationship of Andronikos to his contemporary John Tzimiskes who was an *ἀπογραφεὺς* (surveyor) for the theme of Thessalonica; cf. P. Lemerle, *Philippes et la Macédoine orientale à*

l'époque chrétienne et byzantine, Recherches d'histoire et d'archéologie (Paris, 1945), I, 231–32, 235–36.

72 *τὰς βεβήλους καινοφωνίας περιίστασο*: My translation of this passage from 2 Tim. 2:16 does not follow the *New English Bible*, because the latter reads *κενοφωνίας* and translates: Avoid empty and worldly chatter.

141–148 *παρ' ἡμῶν μὲν αὐτῶν οὐδὲν τέως εἰπεῖν . . . φυλαττόμενοι*: An allusion to the patriarchal injunction of 1341 forbidding the prolongation of the doctrinal controversy and Palamas' defiance of this injunction; see p. xii *supra*.

149–156 *κελεύσαντος ἡμῖν τοῦτο ποιῆσαι τοῦ . . . πατριάρχου . . . καὶ τῶν πολλῶν ὀλίγα παρ' ὑμᾶς κατεπέμψαμεν*: Since Akindynos speaks here of many refutatory treatises, he is obviously referring not only to his *Dialogue of the Impious Palamas with an Orthodox*, which he presented to the Patriarch at the beginning of 1343 (cf. commentary on Letter 25, lines 11–15), but also to his *Antirrhetics*, which were also written at Kalekas' behest; see p. 24 note 82 *supra*.

162–163 *συνοδικῇ ψήφῳ δὶς κατεκρίθη . . . πρὸς καῦσιν*: See commentary on Letter 25, line 11.

170 *ἀδελφὸς ὢν ἡμῶν καὶ φίλος*: See commentary on Letter 16, lines 27–28 *supra*.

171 *ἀλλ' ἔτι φεύγει καὶ κρύπτεται*: In his *Report* (p. 92), Akindynos again uses the word *φυγὰς* in alluding to Palamas' presence as a refugee in St. Sophia. Palamas wrote that he was expelled from that church in midspring after a stay of two months, and Meyendorff correctly assigned this event to April–May 1343; see *Ἀναίρεσις γράμματος Ἰγνατίου*, *Συγγράμματα*, II, 637, lines 28–29; 639, lines 1–3; Meyendorff, *Introduction*, 104. I believe, however, that the exact date of the expulsion of Palamas and his companions from St. Sophia is provided by Kantakouzenos, who writes that the Patriarch arrested many men who had sought asylum at the Cathedral and sent them to prison on "Good Friday, the very day that Christ was arrested by the Jews"; cf. *Hist.*, III, 51: II, 300. Since Easter occurred that year on 13 April (cf. Grumel, *Chronologie*, 261), Palamas was expelled from St. Sophia on 11 April. Our letter, therefore, must have been written between 11 February and 11 April 1343. I am even inclined to be more specific and suggest late February as the probable date, since Palamas was still a refugee in St. Sophia when Akindynos received news from Andronikos Tzimiskes, the carrier of this letter, after his arrival in Berroia; see Letter 28, lines 14 and 33–34.

Loenertz assigns this letter to between May 1342 and April 1343,

noting that it was written after the two anti-Palamite synods and before Palamas' imprisonment in the Palace; see "Dix-huit lettres," 91 and 92.

28.

Akindynos congratulates his correspondent on his anti-Palamite stand.

Addressee: An unidentified supporter in Berroia, since his opposition to Palamism was known to Akindynos through the letters of the Berroian Andronikos Tzimiskes; see lines 14–15.

Akindynos had friends in that Macedonian city where he had spent some time as a teacher. According to Palamas, it was to them and to his friends in Thessalonica that Akindynos sent his first polemical writings when he did not yet dare to circulate them in Constantinople; see *Ἀντιρρητικὸς* 2, 2, 8, *Συγγράμματα*, III, 89, line 29–90, line 6.

Late March–early April 1343; before Palamas' expulsion from St. Sophia and after the arrival in Berroia of Andronikos Tzimiskes, the carrier of Letter 27; see lines 14–15 and 33–34 and commentary on Letter 27, line 171 *supra*.

11 *πρωτονοτάριος ὅδε . . . ἐμοὶ πεφιλημένος ἀεὶ*: Probably Michael Kaballaropoulos, known as deacon *protonotarios* from a synodal act of 1341; see Miklosich-Müller, I, 223. He is the addressee of Letter 29, where he is described as a staunch supporter of Akindynos. The *protonotarios*, head of the patriarchal secretaries, ranked first in the second of the five classes of ecclesiastical officials; see J. Darrouzès, *Offikia*, 548–49.

13–14 *τῶν δ' ἐπεσταλκότων Ἀνδρόνικός ἐστιν ὁ Τζυμισκῆς*: See commentary on Letter 27, line 2.

29–30 *καὶ τοῖς ἐν βασιλείοις, μάλιστα . . . τῇ δεσποίνῃ*: The second anti-Palamite synod, in the fall of 1342, was held at the Palace in the presence of the Empress-mother Anna of Savoy; see Palamas, *Πρὸς σεβασμιωτάτους γέροντας*, *Συγγρ.*, II, 513, lines 10–12; Akindynos, *Report*, 91.

The widow of Andronikos III and mother of John V, Anna was the daughter of Amadeus V of Savoy. In February 1326 she became the second wife of Andronikos III, changing her name from Joanna to Anna; see U. V. Bosch, *Kaiser Andronikos III. Palaiologos. Versuch einer Darstellung der byzantinischen Geschichte in den Jahren 1321–1341* (Amsterdam, 1965), 106–7. Following the death of her husband on 15 June 1341 and until the coronation of John VI Kantakouzenos on 21 May 1347, she acted as regent for her young son John V; see F. Dölger, "Zum Kaisertum der Anna von Savoyen," *Παρασπορά* (Ettal, 1961), 208–21. She

died in Thessalonica *ca*. 1365, after acting as governor of that city for twelve years; see R. J. Loenertz, "Chronologie de Nicolas Cabasilas," 216–20. According to the Synodikon of Orthodoxy (cf. ed. Gouillard, 101–3, lines 869–73), Anna died a nun under the name of Anastasia. This evidence, as G. Mercati points out, discredits the theory of Franciscan historians that Anna reverted to Catholicism before her death; see Mercati, *Notizie*, 150 note 4; also Gouillard, *op. cit.*, 101 note 343, who shares Mercati's view.

During the controversy, Anna supported the Patriarch's religious policy until the end of 1344 when the Palamites convinced her that the ordination of Akindynos was in direct defiance of the decisions of the council of June 1341, which had been presided over by her late husband; see pp. xxiv note 84 and xxvi–xxviii *supra*. On Anna in general, see D. Muratore, *Una principessa Sabauda sul trono di Bisanzio, Giovanna di Savoia imperatrice Anna Paleologina* (Chambéry, 1906); C. Diehl, "Anne de Savoie, femme d'Andronic III," *Impératrices de Byzance* (Paris, 1959), 275–95; M. Candal, "La confésion de fé antipalamítica de Gregorio Acíndino," *OCP*, 25 (1959), 228–40.

31–34 *ὁ ταῦτα τολμήσας . . . τῆς τοῦ Θεοῦ Σοφίας κατέφυγε*: Akindynos writes in his *Report* that because Palamas continued his intense polemical activity even after his confinement to the monastery of Christ the Incomprehensible (Ἀκαταλήπτου), the Patriarch ordered him to appear before him and denounce his doctrines, but he ran away to the safety of St. Sophia *Report*, 91–92). For the length of Palamas' stay at that church, see commentary on Letter 27, line 171.

37–38 *ὡς οὐδ' ἡμεῖς ἐν μετρίᾳ . . . λύπῃ . . . φίλων ἡμῖν καὶ συνήθων*: See commentary on Letter 16, lines 27–28 *supra*.

39–43 *ὅθεν καὶ προὐκαλεσάμεθα . . . ἐχομένους συνθήκης*: For attempts on both sides to reach a reconciliation between June and July 1341, see pp. xvii–xviii *supra* and commentary on Letter 13.

51 *οὐ μεταδίδωσι σφίσιν ἱεροτελεστίας*: In a letter dating from the spring of 1343, Palamas also wrote that the Patriarch had excommunicated all those who agreed with Akindynos' opponents; see Πρὸς Παῦλον Ἀσάνην, Συγγρ., II, 366, lines 32–34: *καὶ γὰρ ἀφορίζει καὶ ἀποκηρύττει καὶ λόγῳ καὶ γράμμασι τοὺς ὁμοφρονοῦντας τοῖς τῷ Ἀκινδύνῳ καὶ ὁπωσοῦν ἀντιλέγουσι*. For the date of this letter, see P. Chrestou, Συγγράμματα, II, 287.

According to the Short Chronicle of 1352, the Patriarch pronounced these excommunications in October 1342; see *Chronica*, I, Chronicle 8, § 39, p. 83; commentary, *ibid.*, II, 258. Although the Chronicle erroneously associates this event with the devastating earth-

quakes which occurred a year later, its chronology regarding the excommunications is obviously accurate, as Ševčenko already noted; see "Anti-Zealot Discourse," 167 note 164; *idem*, "Alexios Makrembolites' Dialogue," 192.

29.

Akindynos praises his correspondent's piety and acclaims him as one of the foremost defenders of the true faith.

Addressee: The deacon *protonotarios* Michael Kaballaropoulos who brought Akindynos the news from Berroia; see commentary on Letter 28, line 11.

Date: April 1343; soon after Kaballaropoulos' return from Berroia; see commentary on lines 22–31 *infra*.

14–18 *ἤδη μὲν οὖν τις ὡς εὐδαίμονας . . . εὐφημίαν ἀπέλαυσε*: The story of Cleobis and Bito, the sons of a priestess of Hera at Argos. According to legend, when their mother ran the risk of arriving late at the sanctuary during the festival of Hera because the team of oxen that were to draw her chariot had not returned from the fields, the youths put the yoke on their own necks and drew their mother's chariot all the way to the sanctuary, nearly five miles away. When they arrived at the festival they were enthusiastically acclaimed by their fellow-citizens, and after taking part in the festivities they fell asleep in the temple, passing into the realm of heroes. At the beginning of the sixth century, the Argives set up their statues at Delphi.

Herodotus relates this story in connection with the visit of the Athenian statesman Solon to the court of the Lydian king Croesus. When asked to name the happiest of the mortals, Solon mentioned first the Athenian Tellus and second Cleobis and Bito (*Hist.*, 1, 31).

22–31 *οὐ μόνον πρὸς ἀπόντα . . . βλέπειν αὐτοπροσώπως*: Kaballaropoulos was obviously back in Constantinople, since Akindynos explains that so great was his admiration for him that he felt compelled to write him letters, even when he was not away, and he expresses the wish to see him often in person.

30.

Akindynos congratulates his correspondent for showing his impartiality by listening to both opponents before deciding who is at fault, but cautions him against the dangerous doctrines of Palamas, which must be resisted by all the pious.

Addressee: An unknown acquaintance in Constantinople. The information on line 73, which identifies Akindynos' friend Gabras with John Gabras, the correspondent of Palamas, also helps us to identify the addressee of this letter with the "follower of Akindynos and former student of Barlaam" whose visit to Palamas is described in the latter's letter to Gabras; see commentary on lines 73–77 *infra* and *Συγγράμματα*, II, 325, lines 20–24.

According to Palamas, this man went to see him in the monastery where he was held prisoner, bringing with him Akindynos' *Dialogue of the Impious Palamas with an Orthodox*. Palamas reports in detail the debate which ensued and claims to have completely won over his visitor. Akindynos, on the other hand, presents this man as a Palamite (cf. lines 4–5) who after debating with both opponents became convinced of Palamas' impiety.

Date: Spring 1343. Palamas wrote to Gabras after the addressee's visit sometime between Christmas 1342 and 11 February 1343 (see commentary on lines 49–54 *infra*). The contents of his letter were communicated to Akindynos by Gabras, and Akindynos in turn wrote this letter.

18–20 *τὰς ὑπὲρ ὧν ἠσέβησεν ἀπολογίας . . . θεογονίαν μὴ παραδέχεσθαι*: Akindynos complains that Palamas accused him of impiety because he refused to accept his doctrine of the divine energies for which Palamas had been charged with ditheism and in defense of which he wrote his tracts.

40–41 *συκοφαντεῖσθαι διισχυρίζεται*: For Palamas' charges that Akindynos was falsifying his writings through deliberate deletions, additions, and misinterpretations, see *Περὶ θείων ἐνεργειῶν*, *Συγγράμματα*, II, 135, lines 14–18; *Πρὸς Γαβρᾶν*, *Συγγρ.*, II, 328–29; 334–35; 337–38; 340, lines 24–25; 348, lines 5–6; Meyendorff, *Introduction*, 92–93.

49–54 *οὐδ' ἂν αὐτὸς ἐφρουρεῖτο . . . οὐδ' ἂν ὁ Ἰσίδωρος . . . ἱερωσύνης καθῄρητο . . . ἐκκλησιαστικῆς κοινωνίας ἐξέπεσε*: Isidore had obviously been expelled from the Church when the addressee visited Palamas at the monastery where he was confined from the fall of 1342 to 11 February 1343. Since Isidore was publicly expelled from St. Sophia on Christmas Day, this visit must have taken place sometime between 26 December 1342 and 11 February 1343; see commentary on Letter 25, lines 11 and 22–25, and note that here too Akindynos explicitly states that Isidore was both deposed and excommunicated.

64–68 *ἐκθέμενοι τοίνυν τά τε ὑπαίτια δόγματα . . . δίδομεν*: Palamas describes how his visitor had underlined the important arguments in Akindynos' *Dialogue* and ironically styles the whole treatise "malicious gossip" (*λέσχη*) see *Πρὸς Γαβρᾶν*, *Συγγράμματα*, II, 326, lines 24–26; 351, line 20; 354, line 13.

73–78 *νῦν δέ μοι Γαβρᾶς ὁ θαυμάσιος, τὸ μέγα χρῆμα τῆς φιλίας, ἀπήγγειλεν ὡς ἐπειδὴ σὺ ταῦτα αὐτῷ προσαγάγοις . . . τὴν μὲν Ἀρείου καὶ Εὐνομίου καὶ Σαβελλίου καὶ ὅ τι ἕτερον ἀσεβὲς ὀνομάζει*: This passage reveals that Gabras was the man who reported to Akindynos the particulars of the addressee's visit to Palamas. Since this visit forms the topic of Palamas' letter to John Gabras (*Συγγρ.*, II, 325–62), he and the correspondent of Akindynos—his great friend, as he calls him here—must be the same person. Furthermore, in his letter to Gabras, Palamas accuses Akindynos of committing the same errors as Arios and Eunomios and Sabellios, just as Akindynos claims here that Gabras informed him; see *Συγγρ.*, II, 356, lines 6–9; 359, lines 3–23.

93 *Ὠκεανοῦ καὶ Τηθύος*: Oceanus and Tethys were the children of Uranus and Gaea and the progenitors of the gods; see Hesiod, *Theogony*, 133, 136; Homer, *Iliad*, XIV, 201, 302; Aristotle, *Metaphysics*, 983b, 30; Greg. Naz., *Or.* 31, PG, 36, col. 152A. Akindynos alludes here to his opponent's alleged polytheism when he remarks that only from pagan theogony can Palamas produce evidence in support of his belief in the uncreated energies of God.

31.

Akindynos congratulates the addressee for writing an anti-Palamite treatise and requests a copy of it.

Addressee: John Gabras(?). Any of Akindynos' correspondents who wrote against Palamas could have been the recipient of this letter. He hailed the support of Gabras, Logaras, and Lapithes with the same enthusiasm, exclaiming over the rare combination of character and learning which they brought to the cause. There is a strong probability, however, that this letter was sent to Gabras, since in the manuscript it stands before the letter addressed to Gabras in which Akindynos acknowledges receipt of Gabras' anti-Palamite tract; see Letter 32.

Date: If this letter is addressed to Gabras, it must date from the summer of 1343, since Letter 32, which is consecutive, can be dated on internal evidence to the late summer or autumn of that year.

5 *ὁ πονηρὸς γεννήτωρ τῶν πονηρῶν ἐγγόνων*: The devil.

32.

Akindynos waxes enthusiastic over Gabras' anti-Palamite tract and tells the author how favorably it was received in the capital.

Addressee: John Gabras in Thracian Aenos; see commentary on lines 46–48 *infra*.

In the mid-fourteenth century we know of the following Gabrades: 1) Michael Gabras, author of a voluminous correspondence (ed. Fatouros, *Die Briefe des Michael Gabras*) and of several discourses which have not survived; see Fatouros, *op. cit.*, 25–26; 2) John Gabras, the brother of Michael and author of a discourse on the presentation of the Virgin (ed. Boissonade, *Anecdota Graeca* [Paris, 1832], III, 71–111); 3) John Gabras, to whom Palamas addressed a letter in 1343 (*Συγγράμματα*, II, 325–62); 4) A Gabras known only by his last name, who was the correspondent of Akindynos (Letters 3 and 32 and possibly 31) and author of an anti-Palamite tract refuted by Joseph Kalothetos; see *Λόγος ἀντιθετικὸς εἰς τὸν τοῦ Γαβρᾶ λόγον*, *Συγγράμματα*, 269–81; 5) The Palamite monk Gabras who predicted before 1347 the elevation of Palamas' friend Isidore to the patriarchal throne; see Philotheos, *Vita Isidori*, 107–8.

The possibility that the last three Gabrades might be the same person was first suggested by Meyendorff (*Introduction*, 358). His conjecture is partly confirmed by Letter 30 which proves beyond doubt that John Gabras was indeed the correspondent of both Palamas and Akindynos (see commentary on Letter 30, lines 73–78). After Palamas' unsuccessful attempt to draw him to his side (cf. *Πρὸς Γαβρᾶν*, *Συγγρ.*, II, 361–62), Gabras published the anti-Palamite tract which forms the topic of our letter. Thereafter, however, the name of Gabras disappears from Akindynos' correspondence, and the possibility that he might have converted to Palamism and assumed the monastic habit is supported, in my opinion, by the following evidence:

a) A careful reading of the pertinent passage in the *Vita Isidori*, where Philotheos relates the prophecy of Gabras regarding Isidore's elevation to the patriarchal throne, reveals that the name of the clairvoyant monk was Ἰωαννίκιος, the monastic equivalent of Ἰωάννης: *Ἰωαννίκιος τις τῶν τὰ μοναχῶν, μᾶλλον δὲ τῶν τῆς μοναδικῆς πολιτείας τὰ ὑψηλά τε καὶ θεωρητικώτατα καλῶς τε καὶ κατὰ λόγον φιλοσοφούντων· τὸν Γαβρᾶν οἶδ' ὅτι πάντες γινώσκετε, πλὴν ὀλίγων, οἱ μὲν ἀκοῇ, οἱ δὲ καὶ αὐτῇ πείρᾳ μεμαθηκότες· ἐπίσημος καὶ γὰρ ὁ ἀνὴρ δι' ἀρετῆς παντοίας περιουσίαν* (*Vita Isidori*, 107–8).

b) The portrait that Philotheos paints of the monk Gabras as a man highly respected for his intellectual and moral excellence is consistent

with what we know about John Gabras from the other sources; see lines 10–13 of this letter; Palamas, *Πρὸς Γαβρᾶν*, *Συγγρ.*, 2, 362, lines 1–6; Kalothetos, *Λόγος ἀντιθετικὸς εἰς τὸν τοῦ Γαβρᾶ λόγον*, *Συγγράμματα*, 269, lines 1–5.

It must also be noted that Gabras' name does not appear on the anti-Palamite list (cf. Mercati, *Notizie*, 222–23), although this does not necessarily prove that he changed camps, because the name of as prominent an anti-Palamite as Kyparissiotes does not figure on that list either.

The relationship of John Gabras to the contemporary man of letters Michael Gabras and his brother John is unknown. The latter, as Kourouses has shown (cf. *Μανουὴλ Γαβαλᾶς*, 43–44), died in 1319, long before the controversy, and cannot be identified with his homonym involved in that conflict.

On the Gabras family—Pontian landowners known from the second half of the tenth century—see A. Bryer, "A Byzantine Family: The Gabrades, ca. 979–ca. 1653," *University of Birmingham Historical Journal*, 12, 2 (1970), 164–87; A. Bryer, S. Fassoulakis, D. M. Nicol, "A Byzantine Family: the Gabrades. An Additional Note," *Byzantinoslavica*, 36 (1975), 38–43 (=A. Breyer, *The Empire of Trebizond and the Pontos* [London, 1980], Studies IIIa and IIIb).

Date: Late summer or autumn 1343, since Akindynos complains that he had been subjected to the insults of the Palamites for two years; see lines 7–8.

3–4 *τοιοῦτον ἄνδρα ἐτόλμησεν ὑβρίσαι καθάρματα*: For Palamas' reaction to Gabras' treatise, see his letter to the Nomophylax Symeon which begins: *γράμματα πρῴην ἔπεμψας ἡμῖν τὰ φερωνύμως γαῦρα* (*Συγγρ.*, II, 394). The ingenious interpretation of this pun on Gabras' name is due to I. Ševčenko; see "Nicolaus Cabasilas' Correspondence," 51–52.

11 *μήτε γένους φιλοτιμίᾳ*: See Palamas, *Πρὸς Γαβρᾶν*, *Συγγρ.*, II, 362, lines 4–6: . . . *τὸ εὐσεβεῖν ἄνωθεν ἐκ προγόνων, οἷά τινα κλῆρον ὑπερκόσμιον ὄντως ἐφ' ὑμᾶς . . . καταβαίνοντα κεκτημένοις*· See also Kalothetos, *Λόγος ἀντιθετικὸς εἰς τὸν τοῦ Γαβρᾶ λόγον*, *Συγγράμματα*, 269, lines 1–4: *Ὁ παρὼν οὗτος, ὃς καθ' ἡμῶν τρόπαιον ἐγεῖραι φιλονικεῖ, οὗ τὸ ὄνομα παρείσθω, οὐ τῶν ἐκ βαράθρου οὐδὲ τῶν ἐξ ἁμάξης, οὐδὲ τῶν ἐξ ὑπερωρείας ἢ ἀκρωρείας τινός, ἀλλά τις τοῦ χοροῦ τῶν τελούντων ἐς λόγους καὶ γένους εὖ ἥκων καὶ εὐλαβείας καὶ συνέσεως.*

33–35 *τοὺς δὲ τὴν πλάνην ταύτην . . . ῥαθυμότερον ἔχοντας*: Perhaps an allusion to Gregoras.

35–36 *Ἀλέξανδρον τὸν Μακεδόνα Τιμόθεος*: The celebrated musician Timothy of Miletus (ca. 450–360 B.C.) was not a contemporary of Alex-

ander the Great. Yet he is cited by many authors as Alexander's favorite flutist; see, for example, Basil of Caesarea, *Ad adolescentes*, PG, 31, col. 580A; Anna Comnena, Ἀλεξιάς, *προοίμιον* I, IV; Suidas, *Lexikon*, *s.v.* Timotheos.

40–42 *τοῖς σοι κατὰ τῆς* Παλαμναίας . . . λόγοις: This treatise has not survived; see its refutation by Kalothetos, *op. cit.*

42–43 *ἡ δὲ θειοτάτη βασιλὶς ἡμῶν καὶ βασιλέως . . . μήτηρ*: The empress Anna of Savoy. Akindynos usually refers to her as *Despoina*, reserving the title *Basilissa* for Eulogia Choumnaina; see commentary on Letter 6, line 7. In his Fifth *Antirrhetic*, Akindynos praises both the Empress and the Princess for supporting Kalekas in his fight against Palamas and against insists on the widespread opposition to Palamism among ecclesiastical and lay circles (*Monac. Gr. 223*, fol. 352[v]): Καὶ *εἰ μὴ χεὶρ Θεοῦ ἀνέστησέ σου τὴν θαυμαστὴν γνώμην . . . καὶ εἶδες οἷ πρόεισι τὸ παρὸν τοῦτο κακόν, καὶ ἰδὼν ἐπέσχες . . . συναιρομένης σοι τῆς ὄντως εὐσεβεστάτης καὶ θειοτάτης δεσποίνης, ᾗ δίκην Λυδίας λίθου τό τε κίβδηλον ὀξέως μάλα συνῄσθετο καὶ κατέγνω καὶ συνεσπούδασέ σοι καθελεῖν τὸ ἐπαιρόμενον τοῦτο κατὰ τῆς θείας ὑπεροχῆς καὶ γνώσεως ὕψωμα, ἐφ' ᾗ καὶ πᾶς ὁ τῶν θείων ἀρχιερέων καὶ τῶν περὶ σὲ τῆς ἐκκλησίας κύκλος, ὁ τῶν περὶ τὴν βασιλικὴν οἰκίαν θεοφιλῶν, ὁ τῶν ἱερῶν κατάλογος, ὁ τῶν μοναζόντων, τῶν τε μιγάδων καὶ τῶν μετὰ τοῦ ἀπλανοῦς καὶ ἀτύφου τὸν τοῖς πολλοῖς ἀκοινώνητον ἀσπαζομένων βίον· οἱ περὶ λόγους καὶ τὰ μαθήματα, οἱ ἐν τοῖς ἰδιώταις τὸν λόγον, οὐκ ἰδιῶται τὴν γνῶσιν, ἐῶ δὲ τὴν βασίλισσαν ἐκείνην ἢ θᾶττον ἂν τὸ ζῆν προεῖτο καὶ ἥδιον, κἂν εἰ μυρίας μὲν οὖν εἶχε ζωάς, προεῖτ' ἂν ἑτοιμότατα πρότερον ἢ τῆς παρούσης ἀνασχέσθαι καινοτομίας· ἥτις δὲ αὕτη τὴν ἀρετὴν καὶ γνῶσιν καὶ θεοσέβειαν οὐκ ἐμὸν ἄρτι λέγειν.*

46–50 *τοῦ τῶν ἄλλων κύκλου . . . ἐντεθραμμένοις*: This statement identifies Gabras with the "self-educated or, rather, uneducated theologian" who wrote to Palamas that not only all the wise men at Aenos, but also, according to a letter he had received from Akindynos, the leading class in the capital as well as the monks were in agreement with the anti-Palamites; see Πρὸς Δανιὴλ Αἴνου, *Συγγρ.*, II, 375, line 23; 387, lines 5–10: *Φησὶ δὲ καὶ τοὺς παρ' ὑμῖν σοφοὺς ἅπαντας συμφθέγγεσθαι καὶ συναινεῖν, ᾧ πολλοῦ δέω πείθεσθαι· μεταπείθει γάρ με τὸ πρὸς αὐτὸν τοῦ 'Ακινδύνου γράμμα δι' οὗ καὶ αὐτὸς ἰσχυρίζεται τούς τε ἐλλογιμωτέρους τῶν ἐνθάδε καὶ τοὺς ἡσυχίᾳ προσανέχοντας καὶ τοὺς ἄλλους ἁπλῶς πάντας συμφωνοῦντας ἔχειν.*

This evidence also confirms Chrestou's view that in his letters both

to the Nomophylax Symeon and to Daniel of Aenos, Palamas argues against Gabras (cf. Συγγρ., II, 288), and it leaves no doubt that the author of the anti-Palamite tract and the Gabras who corresponded with both Palamas and Akindynos were the same person. Furthermore, since Gabras informed Palamas about the situation at Aenos, it is safe to assume that he was there at the time; see also Chrestou (*op. cit.*, 283, 288) who shares this view.

In his recent edition of seventeen letters of Akindynos, A. Karpozilos correctly identified the addressee of this letter with John Gabras, the correspondent of Palamas. He bases his identification, however, simply on the similarities in the portrait that Akindynos, Palamas, and Kalothetos paint of Gabras; see Karpozilos, *Letters*, 114.

33.

Akindynos describes the joy that he experiences when he receives one of the addressee's rare letters, begs him not to deny him this unique pleasure, and sends him some of his polemical works.

Addressee: Thomas Magistros in Thessalonica(?)

The description of the addressee as an ecclesiastic (cf. lines 1 and 23), leading man of letters (line 16), and teacher of Akindynos (line 31) points to Thomas Magistros. On this scholar-monk, see commentary on Letter 56.

Date: Spring–fall 1343. A more precise date cannot be postulated. The reference to the refutatory treatises which were presented to the Patriarch during the first months of 1343 provides only a *terminus post quem*; see p. xxiv note 82. On the other hand, references to the condemnation of Palamas and to the expulsion of Isidore from the Church, common in the letters dating from the spring of 1343 (cf. Letter 26, lines 58–61; Letter 27, lines 169–71; Letter 28, lines 33–34; Letter 30, lines 49–55), are missing here, and this may indicate that some time had elapsed since the events of the winter of 1342, and they were no longer news.

Karpozilos does not suggest a date for this letter; cf. *Letters*, 98.

7 Ὀλυμπίου νέκταρος: Nectar was the drink of the gods; see, for example, Homer, *Iliad*, 4, 3; 19, 347; *Odyssey*, 5, 93; 9, 359.

8 Καλλιόπης πέπλος: I have not been able to find another reference to the robe of Calliope. The *peplos* of Athena was the elaborately embroidered robe which was carried in procession at the Panathenaea and then draped around the statue of Athena Polias on the Acropolis; see Plato,

Euthyphro, 6c; Aristotle, Ἀθηναίων πολιτεία, 49, 3; 60, 1. A robe as a votive offering to Athena is also mentioned in the *Iliad* (6, 269–304) where Hecuba, acting on the advice of Hector, takes to the temple of Athena a precious robe as a gift.

Perhaps what Akindynos means here is that the addressee's letter was a masterpiece fit to adorn Calliope, the most noble of the Muses and patroness of epic poetry and rhetoric; see Hesiod, *Theogony*, 80, and Plutarch, *Quaestionum convivalium*, 9, 14, *Moralia*, IV, ed. C. Hubert (Leipzig, 1971), 322 and 330.

26–31 *ὧν δὲ ἡμῖν . . . ἔδοξε συνεισενεγκεῖν . . . τοῦ πατριάρχου κελεύσαντος . . . μικρ᾽ ἄττα πεπόμφαμεν*: On the tracts that he wrote at the Patriarch's behest, see p. xxiv note 82 *supra*.

37–38 *τὸ γὰρ ψεῦδος μόνον τοῦ ὄντος ἐστέρηται*: See John of Damaskos, *Dialectica*, I, PG, 94, col. 529A: Τὸ *γὰρ ψεῦδος ἕτερον οὐδὲν ἢ τὸ μὴ ὂν καθέστηκεν.*

34.

Akindynos reminds Logaras that it was his intervention which stirred the Patriarch and the Court against Palamas and begs him to continue the fight against heresy.

Addressee: Sabbas Logaras. A personage who had considerable influence with the members of the Regency (cf. lines 39–43 and Letter 51), a man of letters (cf. Letters 35 and 36), and possibly a monk (cf. line 39), Sabbas may tentatively be identified with the Logaras (first name unknown) who bore the title *epi ton anamneseon* and was an equally prestigious figure, since he addressed a personal appeal to Andronikos III on behalf of the General Justices condemned for bribery in 1337; see S. K. Lampakes, Ἐπιστολὴ *τοῦ ἐπὶ τῶν ἀναμνήσεων Λογαρᾶ πρὸς τὸν* Ἀνδρόνικον Γ΄ *ἀφορῶσα εἰς τὴν καταδίκην τῶν καθολικῶν κριτῶν*, Ἐπ. Ἑτ. Βυζ. Σπ., 42 (1976), 397–407. He is also known from two letters that the metropolitan Matthew of Ephesos addressed to him in 1339; see M. Treu, *Matthaios metropolit von Ephesos. Über sein leben und seine schriften. Programm des Victoria-Gymnasiums zu Potsdam* (Potsdam, 1901), 50–51, 53–56; S. Kourouses, Μανουὴλ Γαβαλᾶς, 262–65; D. Reinsch, *Die Briefe des Matthaios von Ephesos im Cod. Vind. Theol. Gr. 174* (Berlin, 1974), 175–82. In the second of these letters there is a phrase which, as Kourouses points out, may indicate that Logaras had recently

become a monk; see Kourouses, *op. cit.*, 265; Reinsch, *op. cit.*, *Epist.* 56, lines 102–3: *ὃ νῦν ἐπηλυγάσω θειότερον σχῆμα*. This evidence could further identify him with Akindynos' correspondent, since our letter also contains what may be an allusion to the addressee's monastic status; see lines 39–40: *εἰ μὴ διὰ τῆς σῆς ἀπὸ τῆς ἡσυχίας, ὥσπερ τινὸς ἐπιβλέψεως, τῆς φορᾶς ἀνεκόπη*. On the basis of this particular evidence, Meyendorff had originally identified Sabbas Logaras with the well-known ascetic Sabbas of Vatopedi (*Introduction*, 106–7 note 55). He has now revised his opinion and kindly brought to my attention that according to the superscription of the fragment of Sabbas' *vita* in *Marcianus Gr. 155* (fol. 199[r]), the surname of this monk was Tziskos; see p. xxxvii *supra*.

The other Logaras known to have lived during this period is Philip Logaras, known from the correspondence of Michael Gabras who addressed to him a total of twenty-eight letters between 1320 and 1327; cf. Fatouros, *Die Briefe des Michael Gabras*, I, 60. A close friend of Gabras, whose literary interests he shared, he was a layman of unknown occupation, but, according to Gabras, he was closer than he to Andronikos the Elder; see Fatouros, *op. cit.*, *Epist.* 198, lines 8–10; *Epist.* 449; *Epist.* 220, lines 32–33; Lampakes, *op. cit.*, 399. M. Treu and D. Reinsch identify him with the *epi ton anamneseon* Logaras, but, as Lampakes points out, the available evidence is not sufficient to make this identification indisputable; see Treu, *op. cit.*, 50; Reinsch, *op. cit.*, 35–36; Lampakes, *op. cit.* 399.

The *epi ton anamneseon* could be either a civil or an ecclesiastical official. The duties of the former were to bring to the emperor's attention the names of the men who distinguished themselves in military campaigns and other endeavors so that they would be properly rewarded. In the mid-fourteenth century this office had become a titular dignity; see Ps.-Kodinos, *Traité des Offices*, 185–86; R. Guilland, "Observations sur la liste des dignitaires du Pseudo-Kodinos," *REB*, 12 (1954), 58–68; "Sur quelques titres du Bas Empire byzantin: le mémorialiste, *ἐπὶ τῶν ἀναμνήσεων*, le myrtaite et le tatas," *JÖB*, 16 (1967), 147–52.

For evidence that this title was also held by ecclesiastical officials, see Darrouzès (*Offikia*, 357 note 3) who cites the example of a fourteenth-century patriarchal act whose *prooimion* is signed by an *epi ton anamneseon*. We do not know, therefore, whether Logaras was a Palace or a Church dignitary. But if he was the imperial *epi ton anamneseon*, he must have retired before 1342, because in the autumn of that year that office was held by a certain Skoutariotes who was sent to conduct an inquiry into Palamas' activities in Heraclea and escort him back to Constantinople; see Palamas, *'Αναίρεσις γράμματος 'Ιγνατίου*, *Συγγρ.*, II, 638, lines 2–3.

Date: 1343–44; see commentary on line 42 *infra*.

18 *καινοῖς θεολόγοις*: Borrowing the phrase from patristic polemics (cf., for example, Greg. Naz., *Or.* 29, 10, PG, 36, col. 88A), Akindynos and Palamas referred to each other as "the new theologian"; see, for example, Akindynos, Letter 42, line 150, and Palamas, Πρὸς Γαβρᾶν, Συγγρ., II, 353, line 6.

36–37 *δυσσέβεια . . . φῦσα μὲν ἐν τῇ Θεσσαλονίκῃ*: Akindynos is not referring here to hesychasm in general, but to Palamas' defense of it. His *Triads* and his third letter to Akindynos, in which he explained to him for the first time his doctrine of the divine grace, were written in Thessalonica; see Meyendorff, *Introduction*, 71 and 77.

42 *γενναιοτάτου πρωτοσεβαστοῦ*: The title of *protosebastos* was held from January 1342 to the spring of 1344 by John Gabalas. A friend of Kantakouzenos and a member of an embassy sent by him to negotiate with the Empress after the coup d'état in the autumn of 1341, Gabalas defected to Kantakouzenos' enemies and was rewarded successively with the titles of *protosebastos* and *megas logothetes*; cf. Kantakouzenos, *Hist.*, III, 22: II, 138–39.

In the spring of 1344, according to Gregoras, while Apokaukos was preparing to leave for Thrace accompanied by the Patriarch and the young Emperor John V, he left Gabalas in charge of the government after securing his loyalty by promising to give him his daughter in marriage (*Hist.*, XIV, 3, 7: II, 701). However, when Gabalas later perceived that the *megas doux* had no intention of keeping his promise and that he planned to marry his daughter to young John V, he alerted the Empress who immediately recalled the Patriarch and her son to the capital (*Hist.*, XIV, 5, 7–8: II, 710–11; *Chronica*, I, Chronicle 8, § 43, p. 83; commentary *ibid.*, III, 259–60. He then advised the Empress to open negotiations with Kantakouzenos (Kantakouzenos, *Hist.*, III, 72: II, 437), but his intrigues finally cost him the favor of the *megas doux*, and, fearing for his life, Gabalas sought asylum at the Church of St. Sophia and even assumed the monastic habit (Kantakouzenos, *Hist.*, III, 80: II, 497; Gregoras, *Hist.*, XIV, 9, 1: II, 726–27). Later he was caught trying to escape from the monastery of Pammakaristos and was thrown in jail (Kantakouzenos, *Hist.*, III, 80: II, 498). His subsequent fate is unknown, although, as Loenertz conjectures, he might have been a victim of the massacre that followed the murder of Apokaukos on 11 June 1345 ("Dix-huit lettres," 95).

As already commented by Loenertz (*ibid.*), the career of Gabalas helps us postulate a more precise date for our letter. Since Akindynos refers to him here by his lower title, he must have been writing before Gabalas' elevation to the rank of *megas logothetes*. Loenertz suggests

October 1344 as a *terminus post quem* for this letter, on the basis of two acts dating from October and November 1344 and signed by the *megas logothetes* John Raoul, whom he identifies with John Gabalas. But I believe that we can propose an even earlier date on the evidence of Kantakouzenos who, in relating the events of the summer of 1344, refers to Gabalas by the title of *megas logothetes*. It is very possible that Gabalas was promoted to that office in the spring of that year when, according to Gregoras, Apokaukos handed him the government: *τούτων δ' οὕτω ῥυέντων καὶ τὴν τῶν δημοσίων αὐτῷ μὲν εὐθὺς ἐγχειρίζει πραγμάτων, αὐτὸς δ' ἄρας ἐκ Βυζαντίου σύν γε πατριάρχῃ καὶ τῷ βασιλεῖ τάχιστα ἐχώρει πρὸς Πείρινθον* (Gregoras, *Hist.*, XIV, 3, 8: II, 702).

Therefore this letter must have been written before the spring of 1344 and after the winter of 1342–43, since the Patriarch, the Empress, the *megas doux* Apokaukos and the *protosebastos* are all said to have risen against Palamas (lines 40–43), and Akindynos exhorts Logaras to engage in written polemics against his opponents (lines 30–31, 45–52). Logaras indeed responded to Akindynos' plea by two written attacks against Palamas; see commentary on Letter 35.

The titular dignity of *protosebastos*, which was created by Alexios I Komnenos for his brother Adrian and his brother-in-law Taronites, ranked fifteenth in Ps.-Kodinos' list of dignities; see Anna Comnena, *Alexiad*, III, IV; L. Stiernon, "Notes de titulature et de prosopographie byzantines: Sébaste et Gambros," *REB*, 23 (1965), 227; Ps.-Kodinos, *Traité des Offices*, 137 and 175; R. Guilland, *Recherches sur les institutions byzantines* (Amsterdam, 1967), 283.

On the Gabalades, a prominent family from Asia Minor, see Kourouses, Μανουὴλ Γαβαλᾶς, 299–300 and 319, where the author tentatively identifies John Gabalas with the son of Manuel Gabalas, the later metropolitan Matthew of Ephesos.

35.

Akindynos agrees with Logaras' criticism of Palamas' literary style, but finds this the least of his opponent's errors.

Addressee: Sabbas Logaras; see commentary on Letter 34.

Date: End of 1343–autumn of 1344. At the end of the previous letter, Akindynos prayed that God might inspire Logaras to become more actively involved in the struggle against Palamism. Logaras apparently responded to his plea by two prompt attacks on Palamas (cf. Letter 36, lines 2–3). The

first, a criticism of Palamas' literary style, forms the subject of this letter, while the second, a polemical tract, is discussed in Letter 36. All three letters to Logaras are consecutive and antedate the ordination of Akindynos and the ensuing disturbances which prompted Logaras' intervention on Akindynos' behalf (cf. Letter 51).

3 *ἄτεχνον αὐτοῦ*: Palamas admitted that his style was lacking in Attic elegance (see Α' *Πρὸς 'Ακίνδυνον*, *Συγγρ.*, I, 219, lines 21–22; *Πρὸς Γαβρᾶν*, *Συγγρ.*, II, 325, lines 5–8), but pointed out that he was writing out of necessity and not for exhibition; see *Τριὰς* 3, 1, 2, *Συγγρ.*, I, 616, line 30–617, line 10. On the other hand, according to Kalothetos, Akindynos was proud of his mastery of grammar and thought of himself as the only expert on style; see Kalothetos, *Πρὸς τοὺς αὐτοὺς Βαρλααμίτας*, *Συγγράμματα*, 211, lines 202–5.

36.

Akindynos congratulates Logaras on his anti-Palamite discourse.

Addressee: Sabbas Logaras.

Date: Spring–summer 1344; see commentary on Letter 35.

14–16 *εἰ ταῦτα εὐλαβουμένου λέγειν . . . παρρησίας τοξεύματα*: Logaras must have described his work as a mild attack against Palamas, though Akindynos seems to find it vehement enough.

37.

Akindynos denounces the polemical activity of the Palamite monk Mark Kyrtos who had recently escaped to Chios from Thessalonica and written to the Patriarch against him.

Addressee: The Patriarch of Constantinople John XIV Kalekas (1334–47).

Date: Summer 1343–spring 1344; see commentary on lines 46–48 *infra*.

6–23 *Μᾶρκος ἐκεῖνος . . . συνέκυψε καὶ κατεκλάσθη, μᾶλλον ἢ φαίνεται κατὰ τὸ σῶμα*: Akindynos employs here the manner indirect to allude to Mark's surname which was Kyrtos (hunchback) when he refers repeatedly to his physical deformity and contrasts him with the woman in the Gospel who was "bent double." The hesychast monk Mark Kyrtos is known from a note on fol. 1^v of *Coisl. Gr. 288* as the donor of

that manuscript to the Athonite Lavra. He is also, as Meyendorff correctly concluded, the monk Mark (last name unknown) to whom are assigned the works contained in that manuscript and among which is found the letter to the Patriarch which Akindynos mentions here (lines 46–48); see Meyendorff, *Introduction*, index, p. 420. D. Stiernon has rejected Meyendorff's identification on the ground that none of the sources cited by him mentions Mark's surname; see "Bulletin sur le Palamisme," *REB*, 30 (1972), 270. However, as Ševčenko also points out, the name Kyrtos with its connotation of hunchback can easily be inferred from Akindynos' references to the physical and moral crippling of Mark; see "Society and Intellectual Life in the Fourteenth Century," 72 and note 11, where he too identifies Mark Kyrtos with the author of the treatises and letters against Akindynos in *Coisl. Gr. 288* and with the Palamite monk Mark mentioned by Palamas in his refutation of Ignatios of Antioch (*Συγγρ.*, II, 634).

Meyendorff further identifies Kyrtos with Mark the disciple of Gregory of Sinai (*Introduction*, 63, 75, 78), but this identification can be only tentative. Kallistos, the biographer of Gregory, was Mark's closest friend and fellow-disciple, and he describes him as a model of piety and humility, but says nothing about his physical disability or, for that matter, about his polemical activity in defense of hesychasm. The only evidence that might connect him with Kyrtos is a reference to a serious illness which forced Mark to leave Gregory's *skete* and seek the relative comfort of the Athonite Lavra, where he was so highly esteemed by the monks that he was not allowed to leave; see *Vita S. Gregorii Sinaitici*, ed. I. Pomjalovskij, *Zapiski de la Faculté historico-philologique de St. Pétersbourg*, 35 (1896), 20–22.

7 *Θερσίτης*: See Homer, *Iliad*, 2, 211–77. Eloquent, but ugly, lame, and arrogant, Thersites annoyed the leaders of the Achaeans with his effrontery. He was finally suppressed by Odysseus who thrashed him publicly for insulting Agamemnon.

8–10 *εἰπεῖν . . . ἐκεῖνον τὸν στιχουργόν . . . τοῦ Σατὰν δίφρος*: I do not know who was the "versifier" who made this sarcastic remark about Kyrtos.

32–34 *διαφυγὼν τὰς Θεσσαλονικέων χεῖρας . . . καὶ ἄπιστος*: Mark must have been expelled from Thessalonica by the anti-Palamite Zealots as a partisan of Kantakouzenos. Akindynos implies that there were political reasons when he insists on Mark's disloyalty to the Emperor John V; see also lines 38–39.

34–35 *νῦν κακῶς τὴν Χῖον καταλαβών*: Palamas provides a *terminus ante quem* for Mark's arrival at Chios when he writes in his refutation of Igna-

tios of Antioch (*Συγγρ.*, II, 634, lines 12–23) that Kalekas wrote to the metropolitan of Chios to take disciplinary action against Mark before the arrival of Ignatios in the capital, i.e., before the summer or fall of 1344 (*ibid.*, 629, lines 3–4; 634, lines 2–7). Karpozilos contradicts himself when he says that Mark was expelled from Thessalonica during the anti-Palamite persecution conducted by metropolitan Hyakinthos (fall 1345–spring 1346) and then admits that Kalekas wrote against him to the metropolitan of Chios in 1344; see Karpozilos, *Letters*, 113.

35 *οὐ μετρίως ταράττει καὶ συγκυνᾷ τὴν νῆσον*: Palamas implies that Mark was quite successful in Chios, where the natives disregarded the Patriarch's letter against him and openly denounced Kalekas; see *Ἀναίρεσις γράμματος Ἰγνατίου*, *Συγγρ.*, II, 634, lines 17–19.

39–40 *τοὺς ἀμφότερα ἡμᾶς . . . καθαροὺς . . . ἀποκηρύττει*: In addition to Mark's letter to the Patriarch, *Coisl. Gr. 288* contains two anti-Akindynist treatises by Mark, both addressed to the emperor; see fols. 3^{r}-212^{v} and 213^{r}-221^{r}. These two works, however, date from a later period, and the emperor is obviously John Kantakouzenos and not the young John V, as originally suggested (Meyendorff, *Introduction*, 413). In the *prooimion* of the first treatise, Mark not only refers to the emperor's zeal for justice and piety which has been known to the whole world for a long time, but specifies that the sovereign has manifested this zeal by personally refuting the "adversaries and calumniators of the pious" and showing them to be guilty of Barlaam's heresy; see fol. 3^{r}: *Δηλοῖ δὲ τοῦτο καταφανέστατα, ὑπὲρ αὐτὸν δήπου σχεδὸν τὸν ἥλιον, καὶ ὁ νῦν ἐνθεώτατος ζῆλος τοῦ θείου σου κράτους, μεθ' οὗ τοῖς ἀντιθέτοις καὶ τὴν συκοφάντιν γλῶτταν προπετῶς κατὰ τῶν εὐσεβούντων ἀποτολμῶσι κινεῖν, διαλεκτικῶς συμπλεκόμενος, ὑπερφυῶς ἀνατρέπεις καὶ ἀτεχνῶς αὐτοὺς ἀπελέγχεις κατὰ Βαρλαὰμ αἱρετίζοντας.*

In the second treatise, he refers repeatedly not to Akindynos but to his followers, and ends by exhorting the emperor to drive them away along with their new supporter Nikagoras (the latter is undoubtedly Gregoras. In his *Antirrhetic* against Gregoras, the Palamite Kalothetos also refers to him by this pseudonym, which Gregoras used in *Florentios*; see Kalothetos, *Συγγράμματα*, 303–41, *passim*); see fol. 218^{v}: *Εἰς οἷον βυθὸν ἀπωλείας . . . κατηνέχθησαν οἱ τοῖς τοῦ Ἀκινδύνου καὶ Βαρλαὰμ πειθόμενοι· οὐ μόνον δὲ οὗτοι, ἀλλὰ καὶ οἱ τοῖς τοιούτοις συγκαταβαίνοντες ταῖς αὐταῖς αὐτοῖς εἰσιν ὑπόδικοι καταδίκαις.* Fol. 220^{v}: *Καὶ οὐκ ἔστιν οὐδεὶς τῶν ἁπάντων, εἰ μόνον εὐσεβεῖν ἐθέλοι . . . ὃς οὐκ ἂν εἰκότως τοὺς τὰ τοῦ Ἀκινδύνου καὶ Βαρλαὰμ φρονοῦντας ἐκτρέποιτο καὶ φεύγοι ὁπόση δύναμις . . . δεῖ δὲ τοὺς θεοσεβεῖν ἑλομένους ἄρχοντας ἐκ μέσου ποιεῖσθαι τὰ*

σκάνδαλα . . . Fol. 221^{r}: *Εἰ δὲ καὶ* Νι*καγόρας ἢ ὁστισοῦν τῶν ἁπάντων ἀρτιφανὴς ἐγεγόνει συναιρετίζων ἐκείνοις ἢ συναιρόμενος, καὶ τοῦτον ἀπωθεῖσθαι χρεὼν καὶ ἐκτρέπεσθαι.*

I believe, therefore, that these treatises are not aimed against Akindynos but against his successors, and must antedate the council of 1351, judging from Mark's appeal to the emperor to eradicate the heresy and from the implication that Gregoras had just begun his anti-Palamite campaign.

45 *καὶ πάλαι μὲν ἐξ ὅτουπερ ἔγνων τὴν πονηρὰν αὐτοῦ φύσιν*: Akindynos must have known Mark since his unhappy sojourn on Mt. Athos.

46–48 *αὐτὸν ἤκουσα γεγραφέναι . . . κατὰ τῆς εὐσεβείας γράμμα*: This letter has been preserved in *Coisl. Gr. 288*, fols. 291^{r}–306^{r} and *Lavra 1779 (M 88)*, fols. 184^{r}–198^{r}; see Meyendorff, *Introduction*, 413.

According to Palamas, Akindynos wrote to Thessalonica shortly after presenting his *Report* to the Patriarch and the synod (spring 1343) that the council of July was a satanic affair; see Palamas, Ἀ*ντιρρητικὸς* 6, 2, 5, Σ*υγγρ*., III, 382, lines 11–23. In his letter to Patriarch Kalekas, Mark protests against this specific remark of Akindynos and thus helps us establish the spring of 1343 as the *terminus post quem* for his letter to Kalekas; see *Coisl. Gr. 288*, fols. 305^{r}–305^{v} *αὐτὸς γὰρ πρός τινα τῶν ἑαυτοῦ καὶ ἡμέτερον φίλον, μεθ' ὧν αὐτῷ γράφει καὶ διαλέγεται, καὶ τοῦτο τὸ ψεύδους γέμον καὶ φαυλότατον ῥῆμα προστίθησιν· ἡ δὲ γενομένη περὶ τούτου, φησίν, ἐξέτασις καὶ διάλεξις οὐ πνευματικὴ μᾶλλον γέγονεν ἢ σατανικὴ καὶ οἵαν ἐβούλετο ὁ καὶ θεοκτόνος διάβολος.*

On the other hand, Palamas also informs us that Kalekas had written to the metropolitan of Chios to take disciplinary action against Mark before the summer/fall of 1344; see commentary on line 35 *supra*. Therefore our letter, which is subsequent to the letter of Mark but prior to that of the Patriarch, must have been written sometime between the summer of 1343 and the spring of 1344.

Mark's letter to the Patriarch—which begins with an allusion to his illness (*Coisl. Gr. 288*, fol. 291^{r}: *ζῶ καὶ αὐτός . . . τῷ σώματι μὲν ὑγιαίνων μετρίως*)—is a refutation of Akindynos' charges against Palamas' doctrines, but it also contains some interesting evidence on the synod of July 1341; see p. xviii and note 59 *supra*.

56 *ἡ πολυκέφαλος ὕδρα*: The allusion is to the Lernaean hydra, the water-serpent with nine renascent heads, slain by Heracles; see Hesiod, *Theogony*, 313; Sophocles, *Trachiniae*, 574, 836; Euripides, *Heraclidae*, 950; *idem*, *Ion*, 191, Apoll., *Bibl*., 2, 5, lines 2–6.

Akindynos refers again to the "hydra" of heresy in his next letter to the Patriarch (Letter, 38, line 34), in Letter 66, line 80 and in his letter to

Maximos Kalopheros, whom he likens to Heracles (Letter 70, line 20). Conversely, Palamas sees himself as Heracles and his opponent as the many-headed hydra ('Ἀντιρρητικὸς I, 1, *Συγγρ.*, III, 39, lines 7–9), while Kalothetos calls Akindynos' doctrines a revival of the many-headed hydra of the old heresies (Ἕτερος . . . *κατὰ τῶν αὐτῶν Ἀκινδύνου καὶ Βαρλαὰμ τῶν κακοδόξων*, *Συγγράμματα*, 119, line 270). Finally, Gregoras in his *Antirrhetics* makes use of the same metaphor in reference to Palamism; see Beyer, ed., *Antirrhetika I*, 1, 6, 155, line 10.

113 Κουρᾶς: Unknown. Obviously another Palamite monk.

137 Δαυίδ: Probably David Dishypatos, the friend and follower of Palamas (cf. commentary on Letter 12) or, as Beyer conjectures (cf. *Antirrhetika I*, 107), the Athonite monk David who was accused of Bogomilism together with George of Larissa, Joseph of Crete, Moses the painter, and Job; see commentary on Letter 52, lines 59–60.

38.

Akindynos writes to the Patriarch that the Palamites, emboldened by his absence, have again started to agitate.

Addressee: The Patriarch John XIV Kalekas in Heracleia (Thrace); see commentary on lines 2–10 *infra*.

Date: May–August 1344; see commentary on lines 1–10 *infra*.

2–10 *Ἔδει μὲν ἡμᾶς παρόντας . . . τῶν θείων νόμων ἐνστάσεως*: On Kalekas' absence from the capital during the summer of 1344, see p. xxv *supra*.

8–10 *μήτε δὲ τὴν σὴν . . . κεφαλὴν οἴκοι μένειν . . . ἐνστάσεως*: Akindynos attributes the Patriarch's trip to religious reasons, but Gregoras claims that Apokaukos left the capital accompanied by the young emperor John V and Patriarch Kalekas because his plan was to marry John V to one of his daughters; see Gregoras, *Hist.*, XIV, 3: II, 702.

10–11 *μήθ' ἡμᾶς ἀφείσης ἀκολουθεῖν σοι τῆς ἀσθενείας ἡμῶν*: Akindynos alludes to his insignificant position which prevented him from accompanying the Patriarch; see Letter 42, line 141, where he refers to himself in the same terms: *ἡμετέραν ἀσθένειαν*.

35–37 *καὶ νῦν ἀδείας τινὸς . . . καταβαλέσθαι σπέρμα*: According to Kantakouzenos (*Hist.*, III, 72: II, 437), the advisers of the Empress sought to convince her to come to terms with him while the Patriarch and

Apokaukos were absent from the capital. Akindynos' complaints about the resurgence of Palamism as well as the reaffirmation of his personal loyalty to Kalekas and the Emperor (see lines 16–18) support Kantakouzenos' testimony.

37–38 *ὥσπερ καθεύδοντος τοῦ γεωργοῦ διὰ τὴν ἀπουσίαν*: Here, as well as in Letter 62, line 301, Akindynos calls the Patriarch *γεωργός*.

In the New Testament parables, the vine-growers who killed the servants sent to them by their master and finally the master's son are called *γεωργοί* (Matt. 21:33–36; Luke 20:9–17; Mark 12:1–2). In patristic literature, however, the term is used in reference to Christian teachers (Justin, *Apol.*, I, 44, 13, PG, 6, col. 396C); the Apostles (Macarius, *Hom.* 28, 6, PG, 34, col. 713D); God the Father (Origen, *Com. in Joan.*, PG, 14, col. 300A); or Christ (Clemens, *Protrepticus* 11, PG, 8, col. 232C; Origen, *Contra Celsum*, 6, 62, PG, 11, col. 1281A). See G. W. H. Lampe, *A Patristic Greek Lexicon* (Oxford, 1961), *s.v.*

43–46 *ὁ δίκαιος καὶ ἀληθινὸς βασιλεὺς . . . μέτεισι τῆς ἀπειθείας*: Young John V, whom the Palamites had betrayed by siding with Kantakouzenos.

39.

Akindynos reproaches an old friend and supporter for his defection to the Palamite camp.

Addressee: Probably George Isaris in Thessalonica. The betrayal of their old friendship (lines 47–48) and the implication that the addressee had changed his allegiance for other than religious reasons point to that former student and friend whose disloyalty Akindynos bemoaned until the end; see commentary on Letter 27, line 2.

Date: Winter 1343–autumn 1344. Akindynos declares that the anti-Palamites have nothing to fear, since the Patriarch and the court are on their side; see lines 62–64.

62 *ἀκινδύνως . . . εὐσεβεῖν*: This may be a pun on his name.

40.

Akindynos expresses pain and disbelief at the alleged defection of an enthusiastic supporter.

Addressee: Unknown. He was apparently an ecclesiastic (cf. commentary on lines 219–20 *infra*) who lived in Thessalonica, since he is reported to have succumbed to Charatzas; see commentary on line 2 *infra*. Akindynos describes him as a friend who had strongly encouraged his fight against Palamas (cf. lines 105–12).

Date: Spring–fall 1344. Akindynos mentions here for the first time the name of Charatzas, which appears with increasing frequency in the letters dating from the winter to the autumn of 1345. But since, unlike those letters, this does not contain a reference to the patriarchal tomes of 1345, we must assume that it was written before his ordination.

Karpozilos dates this letter to "sometime after the synod of November 4, 1344," on the assumption that Akindynos refers to that synod when he says that the new doctrines have been condemned by the Palace, the Senate, the Patriarch, his synod, and the monks (lines 127–34). However, similar statements are found in his Fifth *Antirrhetic* (see commentary on Letter 32, lines 42–43 *supra*) and in his letter to Gabras (Letter 32, lines 42–48), and they refer to the unanimous condemnation of Palamism rather than to a specific synod. Furthermore, if Akindynos were writing after the synod of 4 November 1344, would he have failed to add the names of the Patriarchs of Antioch and Jerusalem to those who condemned Palamas, or to mention the deposition of Isidore? See, for example, Letter 50, lines 124–34.

2 *ὃς Χαρατζᾶς ὀνομάζεται*: This ardent Palamite who persecuted the followers of Akindynos during the summer of 1345 (Letter 57, lines 10–11; Letter 58, lines 5–6) is otherwise unknown, unless he is to be identified with a Charatzas who was officer of the guards (*πριμικήριος τῶν ἐξκουβιτώρων*) in Constantinople *ca*. 1352; see PG, 152, col. 1327A; Loenertz, "Dix-huit lettres," 99. Such an identification is not unlikely in view of Akindynos' picture of the man as lacking in theological training and as being among those unable to distinguish even "what lies in front of their feet . . . , let alone the incomprehensible" (lines 5 and 123–24).

156–57 *τῆς εὐσεβείας* Τελχίν: An allusion to Palamas. Sons of the Earth or the Pontus and ancient inhabitants of Crete, the Telchines taught men the arts and crafts. Skillful workers in metal, they were envied by their fellow-artisans who accused them of being spiteful sorcerers. Thus their name became associated with destruction; see Diodorus Siculus, *Bibliot. histor.*, 5, 55, 3; Suidas, *Lexikon, s.v.*

In his *Antirrhetics*, Gregoras also calls the Palamites "more shameless than any Telchin"; see Beyer, ed., *Antirrhetika I*, 1, 6, 155, line 1.

215–19 *ἃ πρὸς τὴν θείαν . . . ἀνήνεγκα σύνοδον . . . ἐν οἷς εἰσι τούτων . . . ἔλεγχοι πρὸς τῶν θείων . . . πατέρων*: I do not believe that

Akindynos is referring here to a refutatory discourse that he read at the synod of November, as Karpozilos comments (*Letters*, 108), but to the *Report* he presented to the Patriarch and the Permanent Synod in the spring of 1343, which, just as he says here, contains a whole anti-Palamite florilegium; see p. xxiv note 83 *supra*.

219–20 *σου τὴν ἱερότητα*: The addressee was obviously an ecclesiastic, but we do not know of what rank, since Akindynos uses this form of address in writing to the hieromonk Palamas (Letter 11, line 2) and to the archdeacon Bryennios (Letter 58, line 25); calls the bishop of Corinth *ἱερὸς* (Letter 52, line 41) and the hieromonk Matthew *ἱερώτατος* (Letter 50, line 105).

41.

Akindynos thanks his correspondent for his support which makes even his present persecution preferable to a life of leisure. He also asks him to send the patriarchal tome against the Palamites to the Athonite monk Trikanas and the others who refused to align themselves with either side in the dispute and to persuade them that in this case neutrality is possible only for atheists.

Addressee: Branas. See line 204: *χάρις δὲ καὶ τῷ γενναίῳ* Βρανᾷ . . . Akindynos acclaims Branas for his piety and learning which were an object of admiration in all Thessalonica (lines 2–3), but no such figure by the name of Branas is known from contemporary sources. A George Branas lived in Thessalonica ca. 1327, for he is known to have attended at the time a court hearing in that city along with certain other prominent Thessalonians; see the fragment of an act published by S. Lindstam, "Ett i Mitylene förövat övergrepp på några resande till Thessalonike," *BZ*, 25 (1925), 47. For the Branades—first names unknown—who owned land in Chalkidike in the 1320s, see the *Prosopographisches Lexikon der Palaiologenzeit*, fasc. 2 (Vienna, 1977), nos. 3157 and 3158.

Akindynos' correspondent was obviously a layman, since he addresses him only as *γενναῖος*. He was a staunch and active anti-Palamite (cf. lines 20–31), and he had a brother who shared his convictions (cf. lines 205–6).

Date: Winter–spring 1345; see commentary on line 37 *infra*.

14 *τοῦ γὰρ Παλαμᾶ καὶ τῆς αὐτοῦ φατρίας*: Akindynos (cf. also Letter 47, lines 23, 26) and Palamas (cf., for example, 'Αντιρ., I, 8, 50, Συγγρ., 3, 73, lines 24, 25) use the word *φατρία*—a party without principles (cf. Demetrakos, *Lexikon, s.v.*)—when referring to the opposite

faction. Other fourteenth-century writers, however, use it in a positive sense in reference to religious groups, just as the words ἑταιρεία and σύστημα; see Weiss, *Kantakouzenos*, 139.

15–20 *καὶ τῶν τῆς εὐσεβείας . . . ψυχροῖς δὲ τὴν εὐσέβειαν*: Akindynos alludes here to Gregoras (cf. Letter 42, lines 30–31, and his appeal to Gregoras in Letter 43) and to all those who claimed to be neutral. Calling upon the testimony of Gregory of Nyssa, Akindynos declared that such men had no other option but to be atheists, since they sided neither with the Church nor with those whom she condemned; see lines 48–60 and 155–83.

37 *ὁ διωγμὸς οὑτοσί*: This is the only time Akindynos refers openly to the persecution that followed his ordination. On the events of the winter of 1344–45, see pp. xxvi–xxviii *supra*. According to the Palamites, he was beaten and imprisoned, but succeeded in escaping; see notes 106 and 112 *supra*.

41–45 *τοῦτο φιλοσοφίας καρπός . . . πολὺν κάματον*: See commentary on Letter 18, lines 27–28.

48 Τρικανᾶς: Iakobos Trikanas, abbot of the Athonite Lavra from *ca.* 1350–66/7. For the details of his career, see D. Papachryssanthou, "Hiérissos, métropole éphémère au XIVe siècle," *Travaux et Mémoires*, 4 (1970), 396–97.

In his defense of his brother Prochoros, Demetrios Kydones describes Trikanas as a Palamite hostile to Prochoros and instrumental in his excommunication by Patriarch Philotheos. He paints a portrait of a weak and irresolute man, which is not inconsistent with Akindynos' description of Trikanas as one of the "undecided"; see *Against Philotheos*, Mercati, *Notizie*, 320–21.

49 Χαρατζᾶς: See commentary on Letter 40, line 2.

50–51 *μήτε μετὰ* Κλεοβούλου, *μήτε μετὰ* Καλλιάδου *τετάχθαι—τῷ μὲν τοὺς* Παλαμίτας, *τῷ δὲ ἡμᾶς αἰνιττόμενος*: Kleoboulos and Kalliades are pseudonyms by which Trikanas must have referred to Palamas and Akindynos. In the same manner, the Palamite Kalothetos surnamed Barlaam Thrasymachos and Akindynos Glaukophanes; see, for example, ⟨Κατὰ Ἰωάννου Καλέκα⟩, Συγγράμματα, 283–301, *passim*; Κατὰ Νικηφόρου Γρηγορᾶ, Συγγράμματα, 303–41, *passim*.

57–60 *οὓς ἑαυτῆς ἀποκόψασα . . . προὐνοήθη*: Akindynos is referring to the deposition of Isidore on 4 November 1344 and the condemnation of the Palamites announced by the tomes of Kalekas and Ignatios of Antioch; see Mercati, *Notizie*, 199 and 202; PG, 150, 891D–894C.

160–72 *ὁ καταγινώσκων . . . τοῦτο δέ φησι . . . ὁ θεῖος* Γρηγόριος *ὁ*

Νυσσαέων: This passage is found in St. Basil's letter to the physician Eustathios; see PG, 32, 688 C–D; Loeb, III (London-New York, 1926–1934), 54 and 56; and ed. Y. Courtonne (Paris, 1957), II, 135. Akindynos assigns this letter to Gregory of Nyssa, as do some of the MSS which have preserved it; cf. PG, 46, 235; PG, 32, 684D note 81.

186–89 *πέμψας καὶ τὸν ἱερὸν αὐτοῖς λόγον . . . ὁ πατριάρχης*: Akindynos asks Branas to send the encyclical of Kalekas (PG, 150, 891D–894C) to Trikanas and the others who remained uncommitted.

194–95 *Τίς ἡμᾶς χωρίσει ἀπὸ τῆς ἀγάπης τοῦ Θεοῦ*: Kalothetos answered this query by an attack against Akindynos' friend and supporter, Eulogia Choumnaina: *'Αλλὰ τί ποτ' ἂν σε τῆς τοῦ Χριστοῦ ἀγάπης καὶ τοῦ δεσμοῦ ἀπαγάγοι; μᾶλλον δὲ τίς ἠδυνήθη ἀπαγαγεῖν σε; γυνὴ κατὰ γῆν εὐγενής, βάρος ἀργυρίου, λιπαραὶ τράπεζαι, μαγείρων μαγγανεύματα, θρύψις σαρκός, οἶνος ἀνθοσμίας, βίος κατερραστωνευμένος . . .* (*Λόγος τρίτος κατὰ τοῦ κινδυνεύσαντος 'Ακινδύνου*, *Συγγράμματα*, 143, lines 49–55.

42.

Akindynos welcomes enthusiastically his new supporter and gives him a brief history of the controversy, but avoids any reference to his ordination and subsequent persecution. He confesses, however, that he may have to seek refuge in Cyprus.

Addressee: George Lapithes in Cyprus. A wealthy landowner and scholar of varied interests (cf. Gregoras, *Hist.*, XXV, 8–12: III, 27–34; Kyrres, *'Η Κύπρος καὶ τὸ ἡσυχαστικὸν ζήτημα*, 23–24), Lapithes must have become interested in the dispute through the group of anti-Palamite Cypriots in the capital led by the later metropolitan Hyakinthos of Thessalonica; see Letter 44, lines 37–47, and Letter 60, lines 23 and 33–35. He developed into an ardent anti-Palamite whose zeal inspired Akindynos until the end and won the admiration of another determined opponent of Palamas, the Princess Eulogia Choumnaina-Palaiologina; see Letter 74, lines 6–30, and Letter 60, lines 89–99. But the polemical tracts he had promised to send and for which Akindynos was so anxiously waiting did not arrive; see Letter 46, lines 22–23; Letter 47, lines 22–24 and Letter 60, lines 7–13. There is evidence that he wrote them, but they have not survived and neither have his letters to Akindynos; see commentary on Letter 60, lines 7–8 *infra*. On Lapithes' other works, see Guilland, *Correspondance*, 344–46, and Tsolakes, *Γεώργιος Λαπίθης*, 85.

According to Gregoras, Lapithes' wish to visit him in Constantinople was not fulfilled because of the final victory of Palamism; see *Hist.*,

XXV, 14: III, 37–38. This information as well as the fact that Lapithes' name appears on the list of anti-Palamites (Mercati, *Notizie*, 223, no. 16) is sufficient evidence that he remained firm in his ideological position. The asumption that Lapithes was eventually converted to Palamism (Guilland, *Correspondance*, 344; Beck, *KTL*, 722) stems from Guilland's erroneous translation of one of Akindynos' letters to Gregoras (*Correspondance*, 282–83). Contrary to Guilland's interpretation, Akindynos fervently defends the orthodoxy of Lapithes and emphasizes the Cypriot's opposition not only to Palamas but also to the doctrines of the Latins under whose sway he was forced to live; see commentary on Letter 44 *infra* and Tsolakes, Γεώργιος Λαπίθης, 87.

Date: January–February 1345. Since Letter 46, which followed Lapithes' answer to this letter, can be dated on internal evidence to between March and April 1345, this letter must have been written at least two months earlier; see commentary on Letter 46, lines 92–96 *infra*.

12–15 *δοκεῖν . . . βουλεύματα*: I am here following the translation of H. W. Smyth, *Aeschylus: The Seven against Thebes*, Loeb, I (London-New York, 1922), 371.

19–21 *ἡ γὰρ πρώτη καὶ κορυφαία φιλοσοφίας ἕξις . . . ἐπιστήμη*: See commentary on Letter 18, lines 27–28 *supra*.

28–31 *τοὺς παρ' ἡμῖν καὶ σοφοὺς . . . ἥρω καὶ τῆς νίκης ἐπώνυμον*: Akindynos writes here in response to a letter that Lapithes had sent to the Cypriot monk Hyakinthos expressing his dismay at the apathy of his friend Gregoras and criticizing what he considered to be the mild polemics of Akindynos, with whom he had had no personal contact; see Letter 44, lines 37–47.

31–32 *μαλθακώτερον δὲ . . . διατεθέντας*: Akindynos again hints at his dissatisfaction with Gregoras' silence.

38–39 *ὃν φῂς τοῦ δέοντος μαλθακώτερον ἀντιλέγειν τῷ δόγματι*: See Letter 44, lines 46–47.

45 *λανθάνειν ζῶντα*: See Epicurus, *Fragm.* 551; Basil of Caesarea, *Epist.* 9, PG, 32, col. 272B: *τὸ λαθεῖν βιώσαντες ἐν τοῖς πρώτοις τῶν ἀγαθῶν ἄγομεν.*

47 *διαχυτικὸν ἡ παρρησία*: See Agathon, *Apophthegmata*, 1, *Apophthegmata patrum*, PG, 65, col. 109A: *οὐκ ἔστιν ἕτερον πάθος χαλεπώτερον τῆς παρρησίας.*

48–50 *τοῖς καινοῖς θεολόγοις, μεγάλοις . . . ἀρετῇ καὶ σοφίᾳ*: Akindynos contrasts his own low status with Palamas' social prominence and, as in his letters to Barlaam, stresses the man's moral and intellectual prestige.

54 *γράμματος ἐκκλησιαστικοῦ*: The synodal tome of 1341.

57 *ὥσπερ ὁ Ἄρειος τοῖς κατὰ Σαβελλίου*: Sabellios was the Libyan presbyter condemned in the early third century for teaching that the persons of the Trinity are only aspects of the same Being; see Epiphanios, *Adv. haer.*, LXII, PG, 41, cols. 1052A–1061C. Arios defended his own doctrine on the grounds that he did not wish to commit the same error as Sabellios; see his letter to Alexander the Patriarch of Alexandria, Epiphanios, *Adv. haer.*, LXIX, PG, 42, col. 213A–B: Οἴδαμεν ἕνα θεόν, *μόνον ἀγέννητον, μόνον ἀΐδιον . . . οὐδ' ὡς ὁ Σαβέλλιος, ὁ τὴν μονάδα διαιρῶν, υἱοπάτορα εἶπε.*

60 *καὶ ἀκινακαι εἱλκύσθησαν καὶ αἷμα ἡμῶν ἐρρύη*: See p. xix and note 62 *supra*.

105 *οἱ μὲν ἔγραφον ὑπὲρ τῆς ἀσεβείας . . . λόγους*: In the year following the synod of July 1341, Palamas wrote his *Apology*, the *Dialogue between an Orthodox and a Barlaamite*, and *Theophanes*; see Συγγράμματα, II, 69–163, 163–218, 218–62. On the dates of these works, see Meyendorff, *Introduction*, 101; Chrestou, Συγγρ., II, 45–59.

108 *ἡμῖν δὲ οὐδὲ γρύζειν ἐξῆν*: cf. Palamas, Πρὸς Φιλόθεον, Συγγρ., II, 528, lines 14–18: *Καὶ ταῦτα πρὸ τῆς ἐμφυλίου στάσεως . . . σχεδὸν μηδὲ γρύζειν* Ἀκινδύνου *παρρησίᾳ τολμῶντος . . .*

114–18 *τοῖς μὲν καθάπαξ πεπεισμένοις ἐκείνοις . . . ἐνέπεσον*: Akindynos admits that the number of Palamas' followers and those who remained undecided was considerable.

125–27 *τοῖς δ' ὡς ἰδιώταις ἡμῖν . . . ἐπιχειρεῖν ἐδόκει*: See commentary on Letter 25, line 4.

132–34 *εἰς τοὐμφανὲς οὐκ ἐγράφομεν . . . κρύφα . . . ἐποιοῦμεν*: Palamas writes that during this period Akindynos confined his polemical activity in Constantinople to oral propaganda and dared to send his writings only to his faraway friends in Berroia and Thessalonica; see Ἀντιρρητικὸς 2, 2, 8, Συγγρ., III, 89, line 29–90, line 6. See also his letter to Gabras, where he writes that Akindynos kept his writing under lock and key and showed them only to a few trusted friends; Palamas, Συγγρ., II, 354, lines 20–23.

137–40 *τρεχόντων ἡμῶν ἀεὶ πανταχόσε . . . οὐδ' ἀναπνεῖν ἐχόντων*: According to Palamas, Akindynos and his party were at the time running all over town disseminating their propaganda against him; see Ἀντιρρητικὸς 1, 8, 50, Συγγρ., III, 73, line 11–74, line 13.

142–46 *ὁ μὲν θειότατος ἡμῶν δεσπότης . . . Παλαμναίαν πλάνην*: Akindynos implies that Kalekas' duties as regent during the civil war prevented him from attending to the Palamite heresy earlier.

146–56 *ἀκολουθούσης αὐτῷ προθύμως . . . καὶ νῦν αὐτὸν ἔχει*: See Akindynos, *Report*, 90–92. Akindynos diplomatically stops his account of the controversy at the imprisonment of Palamas and makes no mention of his own ordination and subsequent punishment.

166–67 Τῶν *δὴ γεγενημένων ἡμῖν προχείρως καὶ σχολιαστικῶς . . . πεπόμφαμεν*: Akindynos sent Lapithes his refutation of the third letter that Palamas wrote to him in the spring of 1341; see commentary on lines 202–3 *infra*, and Letter 46, lines 41–51. He insists that his refutations of Palamas were written in haste and in the form of commentaries because Lapithes had criticized his mild manner of attacking such a serious heresy; see commentary on lines 28–31 *supra*.

167–69 *εἰργασμένοι μὲν καὶ τινας σπουδαιοτέρους, οὔπω δὲ καιρὸν εἰληφότες τῆς αὐτῦν παρρησίας διὰ τὰ εἰρημένα*: The reference is to his five antirrhetic treatises (*Monac. Gr.* 223, fols. 124^{v}–363^{v}); see note 82 of my introduction. Concealing the fact that he was under persecution and unable to send out these vehement invectives, he claims that they did not see the light of publicity because of the Tome's injunction against doctrinal polemics and the fear of disturbing the peace of the Church.

175–78 *παροξυσμῷ δὲ καὶ τῶν ὁμοίων . . . περιουσίᾳ λόγων*: Another allusion to Gregoras.

178–79 *ὀλίγαι σου συλλαβαί*: Lapithes' letter to Hyakinthos; see commentary on lines 28–31 *supra*.

184 *ὥστε σε καὶ ἀξιοῦμεν χώραν ἡμῖν ἑτοιμάσαι ἀποστροφῆς*: An indisputable proof that he was in serious trouble.

192–202 Τ*ήν γε μὴν ἐπιστολὴν . . . τῆς ἱερᾶς συνόδου*: See Akindynos, *Report*, 87–88.

199 Ν*αζιραίων*: The monks; see commentary on Letter 9, lines 19–20.

202–3 *ἀνθ' ὧν μοι ταῦτα ἔγραψεν ἅπερ . . . νῦν σοι πέπομφα μετρίως ἀνασκευάσας*: This refutation of Palamas' letter has been preserved in *Monac. Gr. 223*, fols. 32^{r}–51^{r}. An excerpt has been published by Uspenskij in *Synodikon*, 85. As shown by Nadal, this treatise has also preserved the original version of Palamas' third letter to Akindynos; see p. xv note 44 *supra*.

215–16 *κατ' ἐρημίαν ἐλέγχων ἐρρωμένων τῆς πλάνης. ὅπερ οὖν εὖ συνιδὼν καὶ αὐτὸς ἀποφαίνῃ*: Lapithes had written to Hyakinthos that Akindynos' fight against Palamas was weak; see Letter 44, lines 46–47.

218–19 *καὶ κλεινῶν ἀνδρῶν ὧν ἂν εἶεν οἱ λόγοι*: Lapithes wrote that the illustrious Gregoras was the man to refute Palamas; see Letter 44, lines 42–43.

43.

Akindynos exhorts Gregoras to become the leader of the opposition to Palamas and tells him that he should not take second place to Lapithes in the fight for piety.

Addressee: Nikephoros Gregoras in Constantinople.

Date: Early spring 1345. It is most likely that Akindynos wrote to Gregoras at the same time he wrote to Lapithes, i.e., after reading the latter's letter to Hyakinthos in which the Cypriot criticized Gregoras' silence and Akindynos' weak polemics; see commentary on Letter 42, lines 28–31 *supra*. Guilland assigns this letter to 1345–47; see *Correspondance*, 281.

2–3 Νύττω σε . . . ἐφ' ἅ σε νύττειν παρακαλεῖ Λαπίθης: See Letter 44, lines 41–43. Besides this letter, Akindynos addressed to Gregoras an appeal in verse in which he again begged his famous friend to end his silence; see the Introduction to Gregoras' *History*, XIX and LXXIII–LXXIV. His other iambic poem which refers in exuberant tones to Gregoras' writings and struggle for Christ (cf. *ibid.*, XXX and LXXIV) must date from the end of 1346–47 when Gregoras, who was told by the Empress to put down in writing his views on Palamas' doctrines, composed his first *Antirrhetics*; see Gregoras, *Hist.*, XV, 7: II, 769–70; Beyer, *Antirrhetika I*, 111; *idem*, "Eine Chronologie," no. 44, p. 136.

3–4 ὃν οὐ δεύτερον εἶναί σου στρατηγόν, ἀλλὰ πρῶτον: See Letter 44, line 43.

12–13 Παυσανίας ἐπὶ τοὺς Μήδους τοῖς Ἕλλησιν: Pausanias, the Spartan regent, led the combined Greek forces to victory against the Persians at the decisive battle of Plataea in 479 B.C. After capturing Byzantium in 478, he entered into secret negotiations with the Persian king, was accused of Medism, and died a refugee at the sanctuary of Athena Chalcioecus on the Spartan Acropolis *ca.* 471. See Herod., V, 32 and IX, 10–88; Thucyd., I, 94–96 and 128–34; II, 71 and 72; III, 58.

13 Φίλιππος Θηβαίοις ἐπὶ τὰς πύλας: Philip II of Macedonia (382–336 B.C.) defeated the allied Boeotian and Athenian forces at the battle of Chaeroneia in 338, disbanded the Boeotian League, and reduced Thebes to a single city-state with a Macedonian garrison; see Diod. Sicul., XVI, 87–88; Plut., *Phocion*, XVI, 4; Polyb., V, 10.

Akindynos tells Gregoras that if he assumes the leadership in the fight for the faith, he will acquire more glory than the two illustrious pagan generals, one of whom secured the independence of Greece by dealing the final blow to the Persian invaders, while the other established the Macedonian supremacy in Greece by crushing the Thebans and their famous "Sacred Band."

44.

Akindynos assures Gregoras that it was not he who informed Lapithes about the controversy and fervently defends Lapithes' orthodoxy.

Addressee: Nikephoros Gregoras in Constantinople.

Date: Spring 1345. In the previous letter, Akindynos wrote to Gregoras, at the instigation of Lapithes, to assume the leadership of the fight against Palamas. When Gregoras answered by repeating Palamas' accusations against Lapithes, Akindynos wrote back in defense of his new supporter. I believe, therefore, that this letter dates from the spring of 1345 and, more precisely, just before the appointment of Hyakinthos to the metropolis of Thessalonica in the late spring of that year, for Akindynos refers to him here simply as *ἱερὸς Ὑάκινθος* and not as *θεῖος ποιμήν*, *πανίερος δεσπότης*, *θειότατος ἀρχιερεύς*, as he did after his promotion to the episcopacy. See Letter 56, line 70; Letter 57, line 29; Letter 60, line 23; Letter 61, line 20.

Guilland dates this letter to 1350 (*Correspondance*, 282) and Tsolakes to between 1345 and 1347 (Γεώργιος Λαπίθης, 90).

2–15 Τῆς *ἀναισθησίας . . . ἡγεμονίαις οὐκ εὐσεβέσιν εἰσί*: Gregoras must have provoked this angry declamation by some reference to Palamas' denunciation of both Akindynos and his new Cypriot supporter. For Akindynos exclaims here at the insolence of his opponent who questioned the piety of Orthodox Christians because they lived in distant lands or under foreign rule and who refused to recognize that their support, added to that of the Church of Constantinople, completely vindicated Akindynos.

6–7 *τὸν Παλαμᾶν ἀποβάλλεσθαι καὶ ἀναθεματίζειν*: See the encyclical of Kalekas against Palamas and his followers (PG, 150, cols. 891C–894A). Arsenios of Tyre (Mercati, *Notizie*, 205) agrees with Akindynos that Palamas was excommunicated and anathematized, but the word "anathema" is not found in the encyclical, and a separate excommunication of Palamas is not known from that period. As Darrouzès convincingly argues, the excommunication of Palamas and his adherents, published by Allatius (PG, 150, cols. 863D–864A), was issued shortly before February 1347 against the members of the Synod who were planning his deposition. See Darrouzès, no. 2265.

7 *ἀλλὰ καὶ τὰς πορρωτάτω*: Akindynos is referring to the Patriarchs Ignatios of Antioch and Gerasimos of Jerusalem, who confirmed Kalekas' anti-Palamite decisions in the winter of 1344–45; see commentary on Letter 50, lines 109–10 and 125–26.

9 *ὑφ' ἑτέροις μὲν ἡγεμόσι τελοῦντας, εὐσεβεῖς δὲ ὁμοίως*: An allu-

sion to Lapithes. Cyprus was then under the rule of the French House of the Lusignan.

18–23 *ὅτι πάντες αὐτοῦ τὴν ἀσέβειαν ᾔσθηνται . . . μεστὴ μὲν Ἀντιόχεια καὶ Κύπρος . . . μεστὴ δὲ Ἀλεξάνδρεια, μεστὴ δὲ καὶ αὐτὴ Ῥώμη τῆς τῶν ἀσεβημάτων ὑπερβολῆς τῶν τούτου, μεστὰ δὲ πάντα*: Akindynos does not say here that Palamism had conquered the Empire and all these cities, as Guilland translates it (*Correspondance*, 282), but that Palamas inveighed against the whole world, because his impiety was notorious the world over. He makes a similar statement in his *Address to Hierotheos* (195–96) concerning the widespread opposition to Palamas.

At the time, the eastern patriarchates were presided over by anti-Palamite prelates. Not only Ignatios of Antioch and Gerasimos of Jerusalem, but also Gregory of Alexandria was an outspoken critic of Palamas, according to Agathangelos, the friend of Gregoras who traveled in the Middle East shortly after Kantakouzenos' victory in 1347 (Gregoras, *Hist.*, XXII, 5: III, 9–10). Like Akindynos, Agathangelos claimed that the previously unknown Palamas had become notorious because rumors of his spurious doctrines had reached Syria and Egypt and Cilicia (*ibid.*, XXV, 4: III, 23).

Cyprus, in addition to Lapithes, had contributed to the Akindynist party one of its stalwarts, Hyakinthos of Thessalonica, around whom gathered a group of Cypriot anti-Palamites in the capital; see Letter 60, lines 33–35, and Kyrres, Ἡ *Κύπρος καὶ τὸ ἡσυχαστικὸν ζήτημα*, 25–27, 30.

Rome must have known about the dispute since the summer of 1341 when Barlaam returned to Italy and became a bishop of the Catholic Church a year later; see commentary on Letter 46, line 96. Furthermore, according to Akindynos, Palamas himself sent his emissaries to the Genoese in Galata and his writings to the Grand Master of the Hospitallers in Rhodes, trying to win their support; see Letter 44, lines 71–73.

Finally, the opposition to Palamas among the Orthodox outside the Empire is also noted by Gregoras, who writes that after Isidore's elevation to the Patriarchal throne many bishops and presbyters from the churches of Antioch, Alexandria, Trebizond, Cyprus, Rhodes, Bulgaria and Serbia wrote to Constantinople anathematizing both Palamas and Isidore; see Gregoras, *Hist.*, XV, 10: II, 786–87.

24–25 *μεθ᾽ ὧν οὑτοσὶ καὶ ἀκέφαλος*: Since the whole Church—all five patriarchates—were against the Palamites, Akindynos declares that they were a sect without a recognized head.

At the end of the fifth century, *akephaloi* was the term for the strict Monophysites who refused to recognize the authority of the patriarch of

Alexandria Peter Mongos, because he had accepted Zeno's *henoticon* (act of union) in 428; see N. Matsoukas, *'Ακέφαλοι, Θρησκευτικὴ καὶ 'Ηθικὴ 'Εγκυκλοπαιδεία* (Athens, 1962), 1, cols. 1199–1200. The fathers of the synod of 787 called the iconoclastic council of 754 *akephalos* because no patriarchate was represented at that council; see J. D. Mansi, *Sacrorum Consiliorum Nova et Amplissima Collectio* (Florence-Venice, 1758–98), 13, 207d.

25 *οὐκ 'Ακινδύνῳ πεπεισμένων*: Palamas obviously accused Akindynos of having involved Lapithes in the dispute. The Palamite Kalothetos, indeed, complained that Akindynos had roused the whole world against his opponents through his polemical activity; see *Λόγος τρίτος κατὰ τοῦ κινδυνεύσαντος 'Ακινδύνου*, *Συγγράμματα*, 141, lines 14–15.

38 *ἱερὸν 'Υάκινθον*: Hyakinthos, a hieromonk at the monastery of Hodegetria in Constantinople and later metropolitan of Thessalonica (*ca.* late spring 1345–spring 1346). He was a Cypriot (cf. Kalothetos, ⟨*Κατὰ 'Ιωάννου Καλέκα*⟩, *Συγγράμματα*, 298, lines 418–19, and the anonymous Palamite in Mercati, *Notizie*, 221 note 2) and must be identified with the "Reverend Father Hyakinthos" who carried Gregoras' letters to Lapithes in Cyprus before the controversy (Gregoras, *Hist.*, XCII). Hyakinthos was appointed to the metropolitan throne of Thessalonica in the late spring of 1345 (cf. Letter 52, lines 48–50), succeeding Makarios, who most probably died in the autumn of 1344; see commentary on Letter 50, lines 91–92.

The persecution of the anti-Palamite Zealots in the summer of 1345 prevented Hyakinthos from taking possession of his see until the fall of that year when the Zealots regained control of the government in Thessalonica; see commentary on Letter 58, lines 7–13. His episcopate lasted less than a year. Akindynos mourns his sudden death in a letter to Lapithes written shortly after the collapse of the dome of St. Sophia on 19 May 1346 (cf. commentary on Letter 60, line 60) and praises him for having cleared Thessalonica of Palamism during his brief tenure. See Letter 60, lines 61–63; also the reference to Hyakinthos' fight against the Palamites in Letter 61, lines 20–21, and in the *Address to Hierotheos*, 193.

Akindynos' testimony is confirmed by an anonymous Palamite who denounces Hyakinthos as the persecutor of bishops and monks who had remained faithful to the synod of 1341 (Mercati, *Notizie*, 221 note 2) and by Kalothetos who calls him a fierce thunderbolt that struck Thessalonica (*op. cit.*, 297, lines 390–94).

On Hyakinthos' possible role in the secularization of monastic property in Thessalonica, see Ševčenko, "Anti-Zealot Discourse," 168 and Kyrres, *'Ο Κύπριος ἀρχιεπίσκοπος Θεσσαλονίκης 'Υάκινθος*, 109–21.

46–47 *τούτῳ μαλακίαν ἐξονειδίζει πρὸς τὸν ἀγῶνα τοῦτον*: See Letter 42, lines 38–39, where Akindynos quotes this criticism of his own resistance to Palamism.

65–66 *οἱ κατὰ ταύτης αὐτῷ γεγενημένοι λόγοι, οὐ τῆς τοῦ Παλαμᾶ γε ὄντες ἀτονίας καὶ ἀθεΐας μεστοί*: These anti-Latin discourses are not among the surviving works of Lapithes listed by Guilland (*Correspondance*, 344–45) and Tsolakes (*Γεώργιος Λαπίθης*, 85). They were obviously against the Latin doctrine of the procession of the Holy Spirit, because Akindynos compares them with Palamas' anti-Latin treatises (*Συγγράμματα*, I, 23–175) and says that they were much more vehement.

71–72 *τοὺς Γαλατηνοὺς τούσδε*: The Genoese in Galata.

72–73 *καὶ εἰς Ῥόδον . . . τῷ μαΐστορι καὶ τοῖς ἐκεῖ Λατίνοις*: The office of the Grand Master of the Hospitallers in Rhodes was held from 1321 to 1346 by Hélion de Villeneuve of Provence. During his tenure, the Hospitallers were active in the anti-Turkish Christian League and participated in its two expeditions against Smyrna in 1334 and 1344; see J. Delaville Le Roulx, *Les Hospitalliers à Rhodes jusqu' à la mort de Naillac (1310–1421)* (Paris, 1913), 51–100; P. Lemerle, *L'Émirat d'Aydin, Byzance et l'Occident* (Paris, 1975), 91–100; 180–203.

78–79 *καὶ διελέγχειν . . . ὅποι σφάλλοιντο τῆς εὐσεβείας*: According to Agathangelos, who visited Lapithes in Cyprus, the Cypriot scholar retained cordial relations with the French lords of the island, but being well versed in Latin, he debated with king Hugh IV and his learned entourage on matters of dogma; see Gregoras, *Hist.*, XXV, 9–10: III, 29–30.

45.

Akindynos thanks the bearer of Lapithes' letter from Cyprus and expresses regret at having missed his visit.

Addressee: Unknown. Perhaps one of the Cypriots mentioned in Letter 60, lines 34–35.

Date: March to April 1345, since Akindynos' answer to the letter brought by the addressee dates from March to April 1345; see commentary on Letter 46, lines 92–96.

7–9 *ἀντιπονήσομεν δὲ καὶ αὐτοὶ μετ' οὐ πολὺ . . . τὴν παρὰ σὲ πορείαν*: Akindynos' promise to return the addressee's visit "before long" indicates that he was still in hiding but expected to be able soon to circulate freely.

46.

Akindynos thanks Lapithes effusively for his flattering letter and inspiring support, but tells him that due to recent local disturbances he was unable to send him the polemical literature that he requested.

Addressee: George Lapithes in Cyprus; see commentary on Letter 42.

Date: March–April 1345; see commentary on lines 92–96 *infra*.

2 *τὴν προτέραν ἐπιστολήν*: Lapithes' letter to Hyakinthos; see Letter 44, lines 37–38.

5–6 *οὐ γὰρ οὕτω τὰ Ἀχιλλέως ὅπλα . . . Τρῶας κατέσειε*: See Homer, *Iliad*, 16, 40–43; 20, 40–46.

9–12 *οὐχ ἅπερ ἐμοὶ μόνον γράφεις, ἀλλὰ καὶ . . . παρακαλεῖς*: Lapithes must have written to Gregoras and other leading literary figures, urging them to take a stand against Palamism.

22 *τοὺς λόγους οὓς ἔτι δημιουργεῖν ἐδήλους*: In his previous letter Akindynos had speculated on the decisive role that Lapithes' own polemical tracts could play in the dispute (Letter 42, line 181). His correspondent wrote back that he had been working on such discourses, but a year later Akindynos was still waiting for them (Letter 60, lines 7–12) and there is no evidence that they ever arrived.

41–46 *Ἀπαιτῶν δ' ἡμᾶς ἔτι λόγους . . . θορύβων . . . ἀνάμεστον*: Akindynos again conceals his persecution from Lapithes, but his lame excuses about the lack of time and the local disturbances which prevented him from satisfying the Cypriot's request for more of his own writings as well as those of Palamas and Barlaam reveal that he was still in hiding.

49–51 *ἡ πρὸς ἐμὲ τοῦ ἀνδρὸς ἐπιστολὴ . . . σοι πεμφθεῖσα*: See Letter 42, lines 192–93.

92–96 *Ὅ γε μὴν Βαρλαὰμ ὅτι μὲν ἥμαρτέ τι . . . δόγματα*: According to Palamas, Akindynos made this statement to Lapithes less than four months after the annulment of his ordination when he had signed a document denouncing the doctrines of Barlaam. See p. xviii note 106 *supra*. Therefore this letter must have been written between March and April 1345, since Akindynos was ordained sometime between November of 1344 and January of 1345; see p. xxvii note 103 *supra*.

96 *τῷ νῦν λατινισμῷ*: After his return to Italy in the summer of 1341, Barlaam became a Catholic and in October of the following year he was appointed bishop of Gerace in Calabria by Pope Clement VI; see *Acta Clementis VI, 1342–1352*, ed. A. L. Taŭtu, Fontes III (Vatican City, 1960), vol. 9, no. 10, 20–22.

47.

Since his previous letter missed the earlier ship to Cyprus, Akindynos sent it on the next one, adding an explanation for the delay and taking the opportunity to enclose his refutation of Palamas' *Dialexis*, which he had been unable to procure before, as well as the patriarchal tomes against Palamas.

Addressee: George Lapithes in Cyprus; see commentary on Letter 42.

Date: April–May 1345; soon after Letter 46, which had missed the previous ship to Cyprus; see lines 2–3.

3–4 *ἅ σοι τότε μὴ δύνασθαι πέμψαι ἐγράφομεν*: See Letter 46, lines 41–46.

5–20 *διάλογον τοῦ Παλαμᾶ . . . ἐφ' οἷς ἐστι καὶ ἡμέτερα σχόλια ἀντιρρητικὰ πρὸς ταῦτα κατὰ τὸ σχέδιον*: If *κατὰ σχέδιον* is to be taken literally, we must assume that Akindynos sent Lapithes a copy of Palamas' *Dialexis* with an improvised commentary. If, on the other hand, this phrase is just a banal expression of modesty, prompted by Lapithes' criticism of Akindynos' mild polemics, the reference must be to Akindynos' *Dialogue of the Impious Palamas with an Orthodox*, which contained the text of Palamas' *Dialexis* and Akindynos' refutatory comments, described here as "impromptu," "offhand." I am inclined to believe the latter, seeing that in his first letter to Lapithes, Akindynos remarked that his first tracts were written hastily, without preparation, and in commentary style, and described his refutation of the *Third Letter* of Palamas as belonging to that group and being moderate in tone; see Letter 42, lines 135–37, 166, 203. He also explained to his correspondent that it was the Patriarch who had ordered him to restrict himself to commentaries; see *ibid.*, lines 160–63.

20 *λόγους γὰρ οὐκ ἦν εὐχερὲς ἀποστεῖλαι*: His inability to send Lapithes his *Antirrhetics* indicates that he was not yet free.

23 *δυσσεβῆ φατρίαν*: On Akindynos' use of this term, see commentary on Letter 41, line 14.

26–30 *πυνθάνομαι γάρ τινας . . . πρὸς τὴν σὴν σοφίαν*: Lapithes' entrance in the arena against Palamas apparently provoked a Palamite reaction. But I do not know of any work by a Palamite author written against Lapithes or addressed to him. A letter by Kalothetos addressed to the Cypriot monks who were visiting the capital and had asked him for information on the dispute does not even mention Lapithes' name. See Kalothetos, *Πρός τινας μοναχοὺς ἐλθόντας ἐ Κύπρου καὶ ζητήσαντας ἁπλῷ λόγῳ μαθεῖν τίνα τὰ παρ' ἀμφοτέρων τῶν μερῶν λεγόμενα*, *Συγγράμματα*, 385–94. Are the four letters by a Cypriot Palamite

(*Chalc. Panagh. 157*, fols. 284ʳ–291ᵛ), which, according to Meyendorff (*Introduction*, 408), may be addressed to Hyakinthos of Thessalonica, addressed instead to Lapithes? I do not know because I have been unable to consult them.

37 *κἂν δάκνῃ τινὰς ὁ λόγος*: The allusion is to Gregoras.

49–53 *'Επεί σοι ἔδει καὶ τοὺς πατριαρχικοὺς ἀποσταλῆναι τόμους . . . 'Αντιοχείας*: The patriarchal encyclical (PG, 150, cols. 891D–894C) and the tome of Ignatios of Antioch; see commentary on Letter 50, lines 109–10.

57 *γενναίων ἐγγόνων*: The anti-Palamite treatises that Lapithes was writing; see Letter 46, lines 22–23.

48.

Akindynos congratulates the Metropolitan of Philadelphia on his recent anti-Palamite discourse.

Addressee: Makarios Chrysokephalos, metropolitan of Philadelphia (1336–82).

Makarios came to Constantinople in February 1345 (cf. his autograph note in *Marcianus Gr.* 452, fol. 251ᵛ; most recent transcription in Passarelli, *Macario*, 31 note 26), and in April of the same year he attended a meeting of the Permanent Synod; see Miklosich-Müller, I, 242–43.

Akindynos hailed his support, but Makarios' opposition to Palamas was shortlived. In September 1346 he countersigned a letter of protest against the Patriarch, which was addressed to the Empress by six members of the Synod whom Kalekas kept away from any activity (PG, 151, col. 770D; Darrouzès, no. 2263), and on 23 October 1346 he signed a confirmation of the Tome of 1341 which he had not originally signed. See Passarelli, *op. cit.*, 33 note 32.

Makarios signed also the Tomes of 1347 (Meyendorff, ed. "Le tome synodal de 1347," 225) and 1351 (PG, 151, col. 762A) which established the victory of Palamism, though, according to Arsenios of Tyre, he adopted a critical attitude at the council of 1351. See Passarelli, *op. cit.*, 37 note 55.

Date: Spring of 1345 to summer of 1346; after the arrival of Makarios in the capital in February 1345 and before his denunciation of Kalekas in September 1346.

4–5 *καὶ ῥεῦμα προχέων ἀπὸ τῆς γλώττης θαυμάσιον*: Makarios' eloquence is equally extolled by Sophianos, another of his correspondents,

who addresses him as teacher of the Church and proclaims him superior to Manuel Holobolos and Sophonias the commentator of Aristotle. See R. Walther, "Ein Brief an Makarios, den Metropoliten von Philadelpheia," *JÖB*, 22 (1973), 228, line 1; 229, lines 29–33. Another letter addressed to the Metropolitan by Makarios Paradeissas is also a tribute to his exceptional talent as an orator; see Walther, "Weiter Briefe an Makarios den Metropoliten von Philadelpheia (1336–1382)," *JÖB*, 23 (1974), 219, line 39–220, line 67.

On Makarios' career and literary activity as an ecclesiastical orator, hagiographer, author of catenae and an anthology of excerpts and proverbs from the works of classical and Byzantine writers, see Passarelli, *Macario*, 24–43 (with earlier bibliography).

9–10 *καί γε πρότερον μέγας ὢν ὑπέρμαχος τῆς ἀληθείας*: Akindynos is alluding to the fact that Makarios had not signed the Tome of 1341.

22–23 *ὁ ἐμὸς πατὴρ καὶ τῆς μονῆς τῆς καθ' ἡμᾶς προστάτης*: I do not know what monastery Akindynos has in mind here. Kalothetos does not name the monasteries with which he claims that Kalekas rewarded Akindynos so that he could play host to his followers; see Πρὸς Γρηγόριον . . . *Στραβολαγκαδίτην*, *Συγγράμματα*, 378, lines 253–54. Known centers of anti-Palamite activity were Choumnaina's double monastery of Christ Philanthropos (Janin, *Géographie ecclésiastique*, 541–44) and the monastery of Hodegetria (*ibid.*, 208–16), headquarters of the anti-Palamite Patriarch of Antioch and residence of Hyakinthos until his elevation to the metropolitan throne of Thessalonica (cf. commentary on Letter 52, line 50). To these, as Tsames suggests (Kalothetos, *Συγγράμματα*, 378 note 1), may be added the monastery of Christ the Incomprehensible (Janin, *op. cit.*, 518–20), where Palamas was confined in the autumn of 1342 (Akindynos, *Report*, 91), and the monastery of St. Stephen the Protomartyr (Janin, *op. cit.*, 493), where the anti-Palamite synod of July 1347 was held (Gregoras, *Hist.*, XV, 10: II, 786).

26 'Ο Βιζύης: The metropolitan of Bizye in eastern Thrace. The name of this prelate is unknown, but he is to be identified with the metropolitan of Bizye who fled to Constantinople when the citizens of that city decided to surrender to Kantakouzenos' forces in the winter of 1344; see Kantakouzenos, *Hist.*, III, 79: II, 492. His signature does not appear on the Tome of 1347, but he must have been allowed to retain his position, for he is listed as a member of the Synod in September 1347; see Miklosich-Müller, I, 270; Darrouzès, no. 2291. However, his loyalty to the new emperor and the patriarch remained suspect, because in December 1348 Isidore ordered the metropolitan of Bizye to perform the liturgy in the presence of the patriarchal archon George Perdikes in order to clear him-

self of suspicion. See Miklosich-Müller, I, 284–85; Darrouzès, no. 2303; nos. 2305–6.

49.

Akindynos wonders why he has not heard from this old friend for such a long time.

Addressee: Tzakonopoulos: unknown, probably a monk, since Akindynos is sending him this letter with Brother Atouemes (line 54) and asks him to convey his regards to Brother Makrenos who is staying with him (line 58). Akindynos might have known him from Mt. Athos or Thessalonica, for he speaks of their earlier friendship and remarks that Tzakonopoulos knows his old association with Palamas (lines 3–6 and 41–49).

Date: Spring 1345. Akindynos mentions both the expulsion of the Palamites from the Church (lines 38–39) and also his correspondence with Lapithes (lines 7–10), which began in the winter of 1345. He says nothing, however, of the appointment of Hyakinthos to the metropolis of Thessalonica.

5 *μουσείων*: Since late antiquity, in accordance with the Alexandrian tradition, the term *mouseion* applied to institutions of higher learning. See Isidore of Pelusium, *Epist.* 334, PG, 78, col. 1529B (*οὐδὲ πάντες οἱ ἐν μουσείοις φοιτήσαντες ῥήτορες*); Ph. Koukoules, *Βυζαντινῶν βίος καὶ πολιτισμός* (Athens, 1948), A', 48.

Under Andronikos II the university of Constantinople was known as the *Mouseion*. It was later renamed *Katholikon Mouseion* when Manuel II reorganized this institution at the end of the fourteenth century; see F. Fuchs, *Die höheren Schulen von Konstantinopel im Mittelalter* (Leipzig, 1926), 59, 72; L. Bréhier, *La civilisation byzantine* (Paris, 1950; reprint, 1970), 403, 405.

7–9 *ὅτε καὶ οἱ πρὸς τοῖς ἐσχάτοις . . . λόγοις φιλοφρονοῦνται*: Clearly a reference to Lapithes who wrote from distant Cyprus urging Akindynos to a more spirited fight and promised to send him an anti-Palamite tract of his own. See Letter 42, lines 38–39, and Letter 46, line 22.

43–44 *ἐκκλησιαστικοῖς αὐτῶν διῃρημένοι θριγγοῖς*: Since the Palamites had been excommunicated, Akindynos could not associate with them. The Tenth Apostolic Canon punished with excommunication anyone who even prayed at home with an excommunicated individual, and the Eleventh Apostolic Canon prescribed that any cleric who prayed with a de-

posed cleric was subject to the same punishment; see Rhalles-Potles, II, 14–15. See also the second canon of the synod of Antioch and the thirty-third of Laodicea which forbade associating or praying together with excommunicated persons, heretics, or schismatics (Rhalles-Potles, III, 126 and 198).

54–55 *ἀδελφὸς Ἀτουέμης, γέμων ἁπάσης σοφίας . . . ὑπὲρ τὴν ἡλικίαν*: This young partisan of Akindynos is to be identified with Theodore Atouemes who was present at the council of 1351 and is described by Arsenios of Tyre as a man wiser than his age; see *Tome*, *Vat. Gr. 2335*, fol. 2r (Mercati, *Notizie*, 223 notes 8–9; Meyendorff, *Introduction*, 142 note 71).

His name figures on the list of anti-Palamites (Mercati, *Notizie*, no. 15, p. 223) and in the dialogue on dogmatic theology written by Philotheos of Selymbria, in which he appears as one of the Akindynists debating against the Palamites; see *Patmiacus 366*, fol. 369r (Mercati, *Notizie*, 223 note 15, and 246).

Philotheos Kokkinos, who like Akindynos and Arsenios of Tyre comments on Atouemes' wisdom, implies that he might have been converted to Palamism. See *Encomium*, PG, 151, col. 633C: *Εἰσὶ δ' οἱ τῶν ἡμετέρων καὶ τὸν ἐν σοφίᾳ προὔχοντα παρ' ἐκείνοις Ἀτουέμην ἐκεῖνον, ὃν δὴ καὶ μεταβεβλῆσθαί φασιν ὕστερον καλῶς πρὸς τὰ κρείττω . . .*

It must be noted that Akindynos alone calls Atouemes *ἀδελφός*. None of the other sources designate him as a monk. In his letter to the bishop of Carpasia in Cyprus, Kantakouzenos mentions a *cubicularius* Atouemes who after the final victory of Palamism in 1351 settled in Cyprus; see Darrouzès, "Une lettre inédite de Jean Cantacuzène relative à la controverse palamite," *REB*, 17, 1959, 17, line 4. I do not know what the relationship of this man to Theodore Atouemes was. In fact, I am inclined to believe that they were the same person, since Philotheos does not appear to be sure of Theodore's conversion to Palamism and, as already mentioned, he is included among the unrepentant anti-Palamites.

58 *ἀδελφὸν Μακρηνόν*: Probably a monk; otherwise unknown. The name Makrenos appears in several contemporary documents. In the 1330s a Constantine Makrenos was *domestikos ton thematon* and surveyor (*ἀπογραφεὺς*) in Macedonia. See A. Guillou, ed., *Les archives de St. Jean Prodrome sur le mont Ménécée* (Paris, 1955), no. 27, 95–96; no. 29, 98–99; J. Lefort, ed., *Actes d' Esphigménou* (Paris, 1973), no. 19, 133–34; P. Lemerle, *Philippes et la Macédoine orientale à l'époque chrétienne et byzantine* (Paris, 1945), 234–36. A priest Demetrios Makrenos of the metropolis of Ainos is mentioned in an act of Kutlumus in 1313; cf. Lemerle, ed., *Archives de l'Athos*, 2 (Paris, 1945), no. 8, 53.

Finally, a peasant George Makrenos and his son Demetrios appear in an act of Xeropotamou dating from 1312; cf. J. Bompaire, ed., *Archives de l'Athos*, 3 (Paris, 1964), no. 16, 124.

50.

Akindynos expresses his disbelief at the alleged defection of Matthew, a hitherto devoted and active supporter.

Addressee: An ecclesiastic, since he is called *ἱερώτατος* (cf. line 105). He is most probably the hieromonk Matthew of the monastery of Kyr-Isaak in Thessalonica whose name figures amongst those of other learned Thessalonians in Letter 74 (lines 41–42); see Loenertz, *Epistulae*, 97 note 5; "Dix-huit lettres," 103.

According to Akindynos, Matthew had been an early opponent of Palamas (lines 2–8) and had as a result suffered abuse by the Palamites (lines 84–85). He had acted as liaison between the Patriarch and the metropolitan of Thessalonica (lines 90–92) and had expressed his approval of Akindynos in his correspondence with him as well as with the Princess Eulogia Choumnaina (lines 99–107). His defection, about which Akindynos is here complaining, is confirmed by the friendly tone of a letter which Kalothetos addressed to him—probably during the persecution of the Palamites in Thessalonica (fall 1345–spring 1346)—extolling his wisdom and urging him to remain firm in the face of adversity. See Kalothetos, Πρὸς *τὸν ἐν ἱερομονάχοις σοφὸν τὰ θεῖα ἐν* Θεσσαλονίκῃ *καὶ σεβάσμιον κῦρ* Ματθαῖον, Συγγράμματα, 395, lines 17–19; 396, lines 44–48.

As first suggested by Meyendorff (*Introduction*, 124 note 138; 137 note 47), Matthew is to be identified with the jurist Matthew Blastaris whose works include two anti-Palamite treatises. See Meyendorff, *Introduction*, 413–14; G. Theocharides, Ὁ Ματθαῖος Βλάσταρις *καὶ ἡ μονὴ τοῦ κῦρ'*Ἰσαάκ *ἐν* Θεσσαλονίκῃ, *Byzantion*, 40 (1970), 442 note 1. This identification is corroborated by the evidence that Blastaris had been a monk at the monastery of Kyr-Isaak in Thessalonica; see Theocharides, *op. cit.*, 437–42, and commentary on Letter 74, lines 41–42. On Blastaris, author of the *Syntagma*, a nomo-canonical collection which was translated into Serbian soon after its publication and exercised a profound influence on the development of law in the Slavic countries, see Theocharides, *op. cit.*, where a detailed bibliography is cited.

Date: Spring 1345. Because Akindynos refers here to the rumor that the Patriarch had been deposed (lines 121–23), Loenertz assigns this letter to May

1346 when Kalekas was deposed by a synod of dissident bishops in Adrianople; see "Dix-huit lettres," 101–2. I have opted for an earlier date, because I believe that Akindynos is here informing his correspondent about a series of recent events which had occurred in the course of the previous winter, such as his own ordination, the severe Palamite reaction, the condemnation of Palamas and his followers, the deposition of Isidore and the election of Isidore's successor (lines 111–40). Furthermore he hints at his own persecution, which was apparently nearing the end, since he assures Matthew that, contrary to Palamite rumors, he was not destroyed, nor was the Patriarch deposed (lines 120–28). Finally, he mentions the dispatch of the patriarchal tomes (line 140), just as he does in other letters dating from the spring of 1345; see Letter 41, lines 187–88; Letter 47, lines 49–53.

29 *Μακεδονίου*: Macedonios, patriarch of Constantinople (342–48 and 350–60), was the leader of the *Pneumatomachi* who taught that the Holy Spirit was subordinate to the Father and the Son. He and his followers were condemned by the second ecumenical council in 381.

90 *κορυφαίου τῆς ἐκκλησίας κράτους*: Patriarch Kalekas.

91–92 *Τῷ μακαρίτῃ Θεσσαλονίκης ἐκείνῳ μητροπολίτῃ*: Makarios of Thessalonica (1342–44?). On 26 March 1342, Makarios, then abbot of Lavra, arrived in the capital with an Athonite delegation which had been sent by Kantakouzenos to negotiate peace with the Empress. See Kantakouzenos, *Hist.*, III, 34: II, 209; Darrouzès, no. 2228. Sometime between April and June of the same year, Kalekas appointed Makarios metropolitan of Thessalonica and sent him as an ambassador to Serbia to try to persuade Kantakouzenos to surrender. See Kantakouzenos, *Hist.*, III, 35, 52: II, 212, 306–9; Darrouzès, no. 2228. Nothing more is known about Makarios, except that he died in office in Thessalonica. See Philotheos, *Encomium*, PG, 151; Darrouzès, no. 2247.

The correspondence of Akindynos shows that Makarios died before the spring of 1345 when Kalekas appointed Hyakinthos to succeed him; see commentary on Letter 44, line 38. It is highly probable that he died as early as the autumn of 1344 and that his death precipitated the ordination of Akindynos, whom the Patriarch intended to place on the metropolitan throne of Thessalonica. For this view, see Kyrres (who accepts, however, Meyendorff's assumption that Makarios was deposed), *Ὁ Κύπριος ἀρχιεπίσκοπος Θεσσαλονίκης Ὑάκινθος*, 93–94; Darrouzès, nos. 2247 and 2256 (p. 205).

As shown by Darrouzès (no. 2247), there is no evidence to support the assumption that Makarios was deposed because of his Palamite sympathies (Meyendorff, *Introduction*, 106 note 53). I arrived independently at the same conclusion as Darrouzès. However, I do not see a hint

at Makarios' disloyalty to the Palamites in the passage from Kalothetos' letter to Gregory Stravolangadites (*Συγγράμματα*, 373, lines 138–41) quoted by Darrouzès; see no. 2247. The *φιλολαυριώτης*, to whom Kalothetos alludes in this passage, is not Makarios, but Palamas whom some of his fellow-Lavriotes critized for having left the Lavra and engaged in polemics. A careful perusal of the whole paragraph shows that Kalothetos is defending Palamas against a charge of contentiousness, and for this reason he emphasizes that the defense of the faith is a more sacred duty than the defense of one's country. See Kalothetos, *op. cit.*, 373, line 133–374, line 146: 'Αλλ' *εἰ μὲν καλὸν καὶ δίκαιον καὶ τοῦ παντὸς κρίνετε τὸ προμαχεῖν τῆς εὐσεβείας καταπεπονημένης ὑπὸ τῶν ἀντικαθισταμένων αὐτῇ, πῶς οὐ δίκαιοί εἰσι καὶ τοῦ παντὸς ἄξιοι οἱ τῆς εὐσεβείας κραταιῶς ὑπερμαχοῦντες;* Εἰ *γὰρ πολλοῦ κρίνεται τὸ ἑλέσθαι τινὰ ὑπὲρ πατρίδος προκινδυνεῦσαι, πόσον ἂν εἴη τὸ ὑπὲρ τῆς ἐκκλησίας τοῦ* Χριστοῦ *τοῦτο παθεῖν;* Εἰ *δέ τινες φιλοπαλάμονες ὄντες, ὥσπερ ἐκεῖνος φιλολαυριώτης, καὶ τοῦτον οὐκ ἀφιᾶσιν αἰτίας τῷ μὴ προσεδρεύειν ἔτι τῇ ἱερᾷ* Λαύρᾳ, *φθάνουσιν ἑαυτοὺς συγγνώμης πάσης ἀποστεροῦντες.* 'Εοίκασι *γὰρ δοξάζειν τὰ ἡμέτερα ἠρτῆσθαι ἀπὸ λεπτοῦ τινος μίτου καὶ μὴ τῆς πάντα συνεχούσης καὶ συνδεούσης προνοίας.* Καὶ *γοῦν οὐδεὶς λύχνον ἅψας ὑποκάτω κλίνης τίθησιν, οὐδὲ πόλις κρυβῆναι δύναται "ἐπάνω ὄρους κειμένη".* Ἔδειξε *γὰρ οὗτος συμπλακεὶς τοῖς ἀντιπάλοις, τίνα μὲν λεόντων σπαράγματα, τίνα δὲ πιθήκων μιμήματα.*

That not all Lavriotes approved of Palamas' conduct is evident from the attitude of Iakobos Trikanas, the later abbot of Lavra, who assured Akindynos' friend Branas early in 1345 that he sided neither with Palamas nor with Akindynos; see Letter 41, lines 48–52. See also Letter 62, lines 18–20, where Akindynos cites another of the "undecided" who approved of Palamas' doctrines, but not of his polemical activity.

As for Makarios, he must have kept a "low profile" in the dispute, because he is ignored by the polemicists on both sides.

102 *θαυμαστῇ βασιλίσσῃ*: The Princess Eulogia Choumnaina Palaiologina; cf. commentary on Letter 6, line 7.

106–8 *ὅτι με . . . ἐπανέστησαν τῇ ἐκκλησίᾳ καμοί*: See pp. xxvi–xxviii *supra*.

109 *συνόδῳ κατ' αὐτῶν παντελεῖ χρησαμένῃ*: See p. xxvii note 104 *supra*.

109–10 *παρόντος αὐτῇ καὶ τοῦ* 'Αντιοχείας: Ignatios of Antioch, whose name appears on the anti-Palamite list; see Mercati, *Notizie*, 223, no. 34. An Armenian convert to Orthodoxy, Ignatios came to Constantinople in the autumn of 1344 to obtain the necessary confirmation of his election to the

patriarchal throne of Antioch. See Kalothetos, *Κατὰ Καλέκα*, *Συγγράμματα*, 298, line 418; Palamas, *Ἀναίρεσις γράμματος Ἰγνατίου*, *Συγγράμματα*, II, 634, lines 2–7. While in the capital, he countersigned the act registering the deposition of Isidore the bishop-elect of Monemvasia on 4 November 1344; see Mercati, *Notizie*, 199–200; Darrouzès, no. 2250. According to our letter, he was present at the synod which the Patriarch convoked when the Palamites opposed the ordination of Akindynos. Before returning to his see shortly thereafter, Ignatios handed Kalekas his written agreement with the synodal decision against Palamas; see Arsenios of Tyre, *Tome*, Mercati, *Notizie*, 205. This document has not survived, but its context is known from Palamas who wrote a lengthy refutation of it, denouncing its author as a liar who, without having ever met him, repeated Kalekas' accusations against him; see Palamas, *op. cit.*, 628, line 31–629, line 24.

According to Kyparissiotes (*Palamiticae transgressiones*, PG, 152, col. 736A–B), Ignatios died following a cruel persecution. However, as both Meyendorff (*Introduction*, 146 note 93) and Darrouzès (no. 2415) convincingly argue, there is no evidence that Ignatios died either under persecution or in Cyprus, where, according to an unidentified source, the long arm of his persecutors finally caught up with him. The friendly tone of a letter addressed to him by Patriarch Kallistos in 1356, in which the Patriarch complains that Ignatios had not answered his letters, indicates that his attitude towards Constantinople was cool, but relations were not severed. See Miklosich-Müller, I, 378–82; Darrouzès, no. 2397. The date of Ignatios' death is not known, but another letter which Kallistos sent to him ca. 1359–61 shows that he was still on the throne at the time. See Miklosich-Müller, I, 410–11; Darrouzès, no. 2415.

110 *καὶ ἄλλων Ἀσιανῶν ἐπισκόπων*: These were probably some bishops in the entourage of Ignatios. In the account of his visit to the Patriarch of Antioch, Agathangelos says that Ignatios showed him the tome that he issued against Palamas while in Constantinople, pointing out that it was countersigned by the bishops and presbyters in his diocese. See Gregoras, *Hist.*, XXV, 5: III, 24.

115–20 *κἄν τι πάσχωμεν . . . οὐδὲ οὕτως ἀνῃρέθημεν*: Akindynos was obviously writing at the end of his persecution, when he was fairly sure of the outcome.

115–16 *πάσχομεν . . . μετὰ τῆς ἐκκλησίας*: An allusion to the Patriarch's serious quarrel with the other members of the Regency.

123–24 *ὑπὸ γὰρ ἐπισκόπων ἐπ' αἰτίᾳ καθαιρεῖται τοιαύτῃ*: See the seventy-fourth Apostolic Canon, which prescribed that if any charges had been brought against a bishop by trustworthy individuals, that bishop

ought to be summoned to appear before the other bishops (Rhalles-Potles, II, 93–94), and the twelfth canon of the council of Carthage, according to which a quorum of twelve bishops could sit in judgment of another bishop if it was not feasible to convoke a synod (Rhalles-Potles, III, 322). See also Zonaras' commentary on the fourth canon of the council of Antioch (Rhalles-Potles, III, 133: *οἱ μὲν ἐπίσκοποι ἐπὶ ἐγκλήμασι κατηγορούμενοι, συνόδου δέονται δικαζούσης*).

125–26 *τοῦ Ἱεροσολύμων*: Gerasimos of Jerusalem (1341/2–49). A Palestinian monk, Gerasimos had gone to Constantinople under Andronikos III to contest the election of his compatriot Lazaros to the patriarchal throne of Jerusalem. While the case was being investigated, the emperor died, and Kalekas confirmed the appointment of Gerasimos instead of the Kantakouzenist Lazaros, who fled to Kantakouzenos after the latter's return to Didymoteichos in 1343, and in May 1346 crowned him emperor in Adrianople. See Kantakouzenos, *Hist.*, IV, 14: III, 91–93; III, 92: II, 564–65; Meyendorff, *Introduction*, 11 note 70.

In 1349 Kantakouzenos deposed Gerasimos and reinstated Lazaros; see P. Wirth, "Der Patriarchat des Gerasimos und der zweite Patriarchat des Lazaros von Jerusalem," *BZ*, 54 (1961), 319–23.

126 *καὶ τῶν μητροπολιτῶν ἁπάντων*: Kalothetos accused the Patriarch of having bribed some of the bishops to approve the ordination of Akindynos; see Πρὸς *τὸν ἐν μοναχοῖς αἰδέσιμον Σάββαν*, *Συγγράμματα*, 364, lines 26–28.

130–32 *τὸν μὲν ἐξελόντες . . . ἕτερον ἀντεισήγαγον*: Akindynos is here referring to the deposition of Isidore, the bishop-elect of Monemvasia, on 4 November 1344 (Mercati, *Notizie*, 199–200; 202; Darrouzès, no. 2250) and the appointment of his successor Iakobos Koukounares; see Letter 52.

133–34 *τὸν δὲ καὶ εἱρκτῇ παραδόντες . . . οὐδὲν ἧττον φρουροῦσι*: Palamas was confined to the Palace prison from 11 April to February 1347 when he was freed by the Empress and sent on a mission to the victorious Kantakouzenos, who had just entered the capital. See commentary on Letter 27, line 171; Kantakouzenos, *Hist.*, III, 99: II, 612–13; Meyendorff, *Introduction*, 105 and 120.

134–38 *καὶ πέμπει δὴ βασιλεὺς ὁ θειότατος μετὰ τῆς μητρός . . . καὶ δυσσέβειαν ὁμολογοῦντες εἶναι*: In the late fall of 1344 an imperial *prostagma* was sent to Mt. Athos, assuring the monks that Palamas was kept in prison for reasons of impiety. This document has not survived but, according to Palamas, it was contemporary with the Patriarch's letter to the Athonites, which gave the same reasons for Palamas' incarceration (cf. Palamas, Β′ Πρὸς Μακάριον, *Συγγράμματα*, II, 539, lines

11–15). This patriarchal letter is dated November 1344; see Miklosich-Müller, I, 238–42; Darrouzès, no. 2251.

Palamas is telling the truth when he says that the imperial writ preceded the ordination of Akindynos (*op. cit.*, 540, lines 2–4), for there is no doubt that the Empress would not have complied with Kalekas' wishes after their quarrel over the ordination of Akindynos.

For other references to the imperial *prostagma*, see Kalekas, *Encyclical*, PG, 150, col. 893A; Gregoras, *Hist.*, XV, 9: II, 780–81; Meyendorff, *Introduction*, 111 note 73.

140 *λόγοι καὶ γνῶμαι τοῖς θειοτάτοις πατριάρχαις*: Kalekas' *Encyclical* (PG, 150, cols. 892A–894C), and perhaps also his *Interpretation of the Tome* (PG, 150, cols. 900B–903B), and the tome of the Patriarch of Antioch (cf. commentary on lines 109–10).

140–41 *ἐνεχθέντες ἢ ἐδίδαξαν*: We know from his letter to Branas that Akindynos had already sent the patriarchal encyclical to Thessalonica; see Letter 41, lines 186–89.

142 *Βρυεννίου*: On Bryennios, see commentary on Letter 58.

51.

Akindynos thanks Logaras for saving him from his recent ordeal and vows his eternal gratitude to him and to the *megas doux*.

Addressee: Sabbas Logaras; see commentary on Letter 34 *supra*.

Date: Middle of May to beginning of June 1345. When Akindynos last wrote to Lapithes (Letter 47) sometime between April and May, he was still in hiding. His reconciliation with the *megas doux* must have occurred shortly thereafter, for on 11 June 1345 Apokaukos was murdered. On the correct date of his death, see the authograph note by Makarios Chrysokephalos in *Marcianus Gr.* 452, fol. 215^{v} (Passarelli, *Macario*, 32 note 29). See also *Chronica*, II, 263, for P. Schreiner's commentary on all other sources on the murder of Apokaukos.

2 *Ὅτε τοῦ μεγάλου χειμῶνος καταλαβόντος ἡμᾶς τελέως*: Akindynos is here referring to his persecution in the winter of 1344–45, which was literally for him a stormy season.

22 *τὸ μέγα δήπου καὶ πρᾶγμα καὶ ὄνομα*: That Akindynos is here alluding to the *megas doux* is confirmed by line 43 where he spells out Apokaukos' title.

25 *ἀλλ' ὅμως ἥκιστα πάντων ταύτης ὄντες ἄξιοι τῆς ὑποψίας*: Despite

a lacuna in the text, it is evident from what follows that Akindynos had been accused of disloyalty to the *megas doux* and that Logaras helped clear him of such suspicion. For he stresses here his loyalty to Apokaukos and points out that it was not inspired by opportunism but by pure piety; see lines 26–36.

The opposition of Apokaukos to Akindynos' ordination is confirmed by a letter of Kalothetos to the monk Sabas, in which he describes how vigorously the *megas doux* protested to the Patriarch on that occasion; see Kalothetos, Συγγράμματα, 366, lines 96–98.

52.

The Metropolitan's letters to Akindynos, Lapithes, and the bishop of Corinth are worthy of the anti-Palamite tracts he composed before his elevation to the episcopate. He should also write to his compatriots, the Thessalonians, and their newly-appointed metropolitan Hyakinthos. They need the benefit of his letters because their city, where Isidore and Palamas resided for so long, has been infected with Messalianism.

Addressee: Iakobos Koukounares, metropolitan of Monemvasia (1344–47). His full name is known from the letter he addressed to Patriarch Isidore shortly after Isidore's election in May of 1347. See PG, 152, col. 1293A; Miklosich-Müller, I, 271; Loenertz, *Epistulae*, 89 and note 1; "Dix-huit lettres," 97.

A Thessalonian by birth (cf. line 52), he was appointed to the metropolis of Monemvasia after the deposition of Isidore on 4 November 1344. Akindynos describes him as a polemicist who received the episcopal throne as a reward for his writings against Palamas (cf. lines 8–14) and who, after his appointment, did not confine his polemical activity to his own diocese, but encouraged through his letters such fellow-Akindynists as the metropolitan of Corinth and the Cypriot Lapithes (cf. lines 34–43).

Koukounares did not, however, remain loyal to Akindynos until the end. Shortly after the elevation of Isidore to the patriarchal throne, he wrote to him congratulating him and praising Kantakouzenos' conciliatory policy (cf. PG, 152, col. 1293A–D; Miklosich-Müller, I, 271), but he apparently failed to win the forgiveness of his former opponent. A synodal act shows that in September 1348 the metropolitan of Patras was transferred to the see of Monemvasia; see PG, 152, col. 1294A–C; Miklosich-Müller, I, 274–75. This document contains no reference to Koukounares, but, according to Philotheos, he was deposed and died

shortly thereafter. See *Vita Isidori*, 95, lines 24–29 (ᾧ δὴ καὶ κατὰ πόδας τὰ τῆς δίκης ἐπηκολούθησε, χειρὶ θείᾳ καὶ μικροῖς τισι γράμμασιν ἀποφάσεως, συνδιαρραγείσης τε καὶ συγκαταλυθείσης αὐτῷ τῇ προστασίᾳ καὶ τῆς ζωῆς αἴσχιστα . . .). His name appears on the list of anti-Palamites; see Mercati, *Notizie*, 223, no. 40.

Date: Late spring or early summer 1345; after 4 November 1344, when Koukounares succeeded Isidore as the metropolitan of Monemvasia and before Hyakinthos of Thessalonica took possession of his see; cf. commentary on line 50. As Kyrres suggests (Ὁ Κύπριος ἀρχιεπίσκοπος Θεσσαλονίκης Ὑάκινθος, 101–2), this letter must have been written in May or June 1345, since Koukounares had had time to become established in his diocese and to write to his various distant friends. Moreover, the confident and exuberant tone of this letter, as well as the lack of any reference to Akindynos' persecution indicates that it was written when that ordeal was over.

Loenertz assigns this letter to between 1344 and 1346.

8–10 *ἠγώνισαι μὲν λόγοις λαμπροῖς καὶ γενναίοις ἐνταῦθα κατὰ τῆς Παλαμᾶ δυσσεβεστάτης πλάνης*: Philotheos confirms this when he says that the metropolitan's shameful end was a retribution for his impious writings and for his fury and insolence against Isidore; see *Vita Isidori*, 95, lines 25–29.

15–16 *κινδυνεύοντα τὸν τῆς Πελοποννήσου προεστηκότα θρόνον τὸ Παλαμναῖον ἀναδεδέχθαι κακόν*: The ascendancy of the church of Monemvasia began in the early Palaiologan era, when the harbor of Monemvasia in the southeastern Peloponnese was regarded as a valuable base for the reconquest of the rest of the peninsula from the Latins.

In June 1301 Andronikos II conferred the title of exarch of all the Peloponnese to the metropolitan of Monemvasia and established his jurisdiction over several bishoprics, including those of Kynouria, Maina, Modon, and Coron (cf. Miklosich-Müller, V, 155–61; for the correct date of this chrysobull, see St. Binon, "L'histoire et la légende de deux chrysobulles d' Andronic II en faveur de Monemvasie. Macaire ou Phrantzès?" *EO*, 37 [1938], 278–311). At the same time Andronikos endowed the metropolis of Monemvasia with extensive properties consisting of whole villages with *paroikoi*, farms, vineyards, forests, and orchards; see Miklosich-Müller, V, 161–65.

Before their quarrel in the spring of 1342, Kalekas had offered this important metropolis to Palamas and, upon his refusal, he appointed to it Palamas' closest friend, Isidore Boucheiras, the future patriarch; see Palamas, Ἀναίρεσις γράμματος Καλέκα, Συγγράμματα, II, 618, line 39–619, line 18. Thus in the next two years the church of Monemvasia

was under Palamite control. For, although Isidore was not consecrated, he did not refrain from governing his diocese, as attested by his biographer and the disciplinary charges brought against him at his deposition on 4 November 1344. See Philotheos, *Vita Isidori*, 88, lines 26–28 (*καὶ τὴν ἤδη λαχοῦσαν αὐτὸν ἐκκλησίαν ἐκείνην, κατὰ θείους δηλαδὴ θεσμούς, ἐν χεροῖν εἶχε καὶ πατρικῶς τε καὶ διδασκαλικῶς κἀνταῦθα διατρίβων ἐκείνης προὐκάθητο*); Mercati, *Notizie*, 199 (*ἐλαλήθη περὶ τοῦ ὑποψηφίου τῆς ἁγιωτάτης μητροπόλεως Μονεμβασίας, ἱερομονάχου Ἰσιδώρου, ὥς τινας τῶν τοῦ κλήρου τῆς αὐτῇ ἐκκλησίας τετίμηκε προβιβασμοῖς ἐκκλησιαστικῶν ὀφφικίων, μνημονευόμενος δὲ καὶ ὡς εἴθισται καὶ νενόμισται μνημονεύεσθαι τοὺς ἀρχιερεῖς μετὰ τὴν χειροτονίαν* . . .).

Furthermore, Isidore developed close ties with the large colony of Monemvasiote merchants and sailors in the capital, the majority of whom, according to Philotheos, were transformed into a «pious fraternity» around their spiritual leader; see *Vita Isidori*, 89–90.
see *Vita Isidori*, 89–90.

20 *τὸ Δωριέων γένος*: Philotheos also refers to the Monemvasiotes as Dorians; see *Vita Isidori*, 88, line 5; 89, lines 2, 15.

34 *οἷς τῷ Κορινθίων ποιμένι πέμπεις ἐκεῖσε*: On Hyakinthos of Corinth, see commentary on Letter 67. He was obviously not in Corinth but somewhere in the vicinity, because that city belonged to Frankish Morea and was at the time under the suzerainty of the young Angevin prince Robert of Taranto and his mother Catherine of Valois, the titulary Latin empress of Constantinople. See A. Bon, *La Morée franque; Recherches historiques, topographiques, et archéologiques sur la principauté d'Achaie (1205–1430)* (Paris, 1969), 208–9. The Latins had installed a Catholic archbishop in Corinth since 1212; see Bon, *op. cit.*, 68; 93–94. *Ca.* 1340 the Catholic primate of that city was a certain Iakobos; see R. Janin, "Corinthe," *Dictionnaire d'histoire et de géographie ecclésiastique*, vol. 13, col. 879.

34–35 *Λαπίθῃ*: See commentary on Letter 42.

37–40 *ὅ γέ φασιν Ἀλέξανδρον τὸν Μακεδόνα ὑπὸ τῆς Ἀντιγενίδου μούσης . . . ὥρμα εὐθὺς ἐφ' ὅπλα*: Antigenides, the Theban flute player and composer, lived before the time of Alexander, probably in the late fifth or early fourth century. See Plutarch, *De musica*, 21, *Moralia*, IV, 1138b; *idem*, Demetrius Poliorcetes, I; Leonidas, *Epigrammata*, *Anthologia Palatina*, V, 206 (205), eds. P. Waltz-J. Guillou (Paris, 1960), II, 93; Suidas, *Lexikon*, *s.v.* Antigenides.

43 *καὶ ἀνέγνωμεν καὶ ἐθαυμάσαμεν*: It is not clear whether Akindynos

received copies of Koukounares' letters to Lapithes and Hyakinthos of Corinth from the recipients or from the author himself. The latter seems more probable.

48–49 Ὑάκινθος ὁ θαυμάσιος: See commentary on Letter 44, line 38.

54–55 ὁ τῆς μονῆς οἰκήτωρ Ὁδηγητρίας τῆς παναγοῦς Θεομήτορος: This monastery was located in the center of the city, near and to the east of St. Sophia; see Janin, *Géographie ecclésiastique*, 208–16. Since 1288, when it was assigned to Cyril of Antioch (cf. Pachymeres, *De Andronico Palaeologo*, II, 7: II, 123), it had been used by the patriarchs of Antioch as their headquarters in Constantinople. During the controversy it became a focus of anti-Palamite activity, since both Ignatios of Antioch (cf. commentary on Letter 50, lines 109–10) and Hyakinthos of Thessalonica who, according to our letter, resided there before his elevation to the episcopate, were fierce anti-Palamites.

50 οὗτος γὰρ νῦν ἀρχιερεὺς Θεσσαλονίκης κεχειροτόνηται: The newly ordained metropolitan of Thessalonica did not take possession of his see until the early fall of 1345 when the Zealots had regained control of the government in Thessalonica; see commentary on Letter 58, lines 7–13.

53–54 παρὰ τὸ χρονίους ἐκεῖ διατετριφέναι τὸν Παλαμᾶν τε καὶ τὸν Ἰσίδωρον: Palamas went to Thessalonica for the first time in 1325 when the Turkish incursions forced him to quit his hermitage on Mt. Athos, but he remained only for a year. See Meyendorff, *Introduction*, 53; G. Chionides, Ἱστορικὰ προβλήματα καὶ μνημεῖα ἐκ τῆς παραμονῆς τοῦ ἁγ. Γρ. Παλαμᾶ εἰς τὴν περιοχὴν Βερροίας, Γρηγόριος ὁ Παλαμᾶς, 50 (1967), 283. He returned in the winter of 1337/8 to undertake the defense of his fellow-hesychasts against the accusations of Barlaam and stayed until the winter of 1341, when he was summoned to the council of 10 June at Constantinople; see Meyendorff, *Introduction*, 71.

Isidore, on the other hand, was born in Thessalonica of Chian parents (cf. Philotheos, *Vita Isidori*, 55–56) and spent his youth there, first as a teacher of grammar and later as a lay member of a monastic group under the tutelage of Gerasimos, a disciple of Gregory of Sinai (cf. *ibid.*, 63 and 71). When Gerasimos died, Isidore retired to the Holy Mountain and joined the circle of hesychasts around Gregory of Sinai (*ibid.*, 76–77). However, the Turkish incursions forced him to seek the safety of Thessalonica at the same time as Palamas, and thereafter he remained in his native city for several years as the spiritual director of a group of monks and lay people from all walks of life; see *Vita Isidori*, 77–80; Isidore, *Testament*, Miklosich-Müller, I, 287–88; Meyendorff, *Introduction*, 53. *Ca.* 1335 he paid another brief visit to the Holy Mountain,

where he received the monastic tonsure from the hands of Palamas and at his insistence was ordained deacon (see Philotheos, *Vita Isidori*, 81–82; *idem*, *Encomium*, PG, 151, col. 581D; Meyendorff, *Introduction*, 53 note 53). Isidore was among the first to resist Barlaam's attacks on the monks, and it was at his invitation that Palamas went to Thessalonica in the winter of 1337/8 to undertake their defense and stayed with him until they both left for the capital in the winter of 1341; see *Vita Isidori*, 84–86; *Encomium*, 592C–D; Meyendorff, *Introduction*, 71.

59–60 *αὕτη τοίνυν ἡ αἵρεσις νῦν ἀνεφάνη μετ' αἰσχίστων ἔργων ἑτέρων καὶ εἰκονομαχίας ἐν Ὄρει τῷ ἱερῷ καὶ τῇδε κἀν τῇ Θεσσαλονίκῃ*: Akindynos refers here to the Bogomil heresy, whose emergence in Thessalonica and Mt. Athos is attested by other contemporary sources. Gregoras cites a tome which the Athonites sent to the Synod at Constantinople with charges of Bogomilism against the monks Joseph the Cretan, George of Larissa, Moses the painter, Isaak, David, and Job; cf. Gregoras, *Hist.*, XIV, 7: II, 718–19; *idem*, *Antirrhetika I*, 1, 2, ed. Beyer, *Antirrhetika I*, 131–32. Like Akindynos, Gregoras mentions iconoclasm and other strange practices among the offenses of these heretics. See *Hist.*, XIV, 7: II, 719, lines 3–6 (. . . *καὶ ὅτι τὰς θείας λάθρα συντρίβοντες κατακαίουσιν εἰκόνας· καὶ ὅτι τὸ τοῦ διδασκάλου σεμνύνοντες οὖρον τοῖς ἐδέσμασιν αὐτῶν ἐπιρραίνουσι· καὶ ὅτι τὴν ἔνσαρκον καὶ θείαν οἰκονομίαν οὐδαμῇ προσίενται*).

It was probably at this time that the first charges of Bogomilism were pressed against Niphon, the later Protos of the Holy Mountain, because the synodal act of 1350, which confirms his innocence, states that he was first accused at the time when certain individuals on Mt. Athos were found guilty of Messalianism. See Miklosich-Müller, I, 296, lines 13–16.

According to another source, the *Life of St. Theodosios of Trnvo*, this outbreak of Bogomilism in the mid-fourteenth century had its origin in Thessalonica from where it spread to Mt. Athos and thence to Bulgaria. See commentary on lines 69–75 *infra*.

60 *εἰκονομαχίας*: The Bogomils rejected the veneration of icons as idolatry, and for this reason they allegedly honored the iconoclastic emperors and especially Constantine Kopronymos; see Euth. Zegabenos, *Panoplia dogmatica*, XXVII, PG, 130, col. 1308D; H. C. Puech-A. Vaillant, *Le traité contre les Bogomiles de Cosmas le prêtre; traduction et étude* (Paris, 1945), 70–72.

The hesychasts, as Meyendorff points out, were accused of iconomachy because they disapproved of the sumptuous decoration of churches; see *Introduction*, 57.

61–68 Γεώργιος ἐκεῖνος . . . ἀπηλάθη τοῦ θείου Ὄρους: Loenertz has identified this George with the Athonite Bogomil George of Larissa known from Gregoras; see *Epistulae*, 91, ad apparatum 51; "Dix-huit lettres," 98, and commentary on lines 59–60 *supra*. It must be noted, however, that although Gregoras refers repeatedly to George of Larissa in his *Antirrhetics* (cf. Beyer, ed., *Antirrhetika I*, I, 1, 2, 1–2; I, 1, 4, 1; I, 2, 5, 1), he mentions neither of the incidents related here by Akindynos, namely, that George had in the past fled from Thessalonica to escape the wrath of the people and that he had been punished by branding. Furthermore, he does not associate him, as our letter does, with Isidore but with Palamas, maintaining that the latter was the disciple of George of Larissa while on Mt. Athos and that he fled from there to the cosmopolitan city of Thessalonica before his heresy was detected.

In any event, if we accept the hypothesis that both Akindynos and Gregoras are referring to the same George, we must conclude that he fled from Thessalonica to Mt. Athos before 1338 and was expelled from there in 1344/45, because, as Beyer convincingly argues, Gregoras' reference to the flight of Palamas from the Holy Mountain must not be associated with his first visit to Thessalonica in 1325, but with his second visit when he undertook the defense of the hesychasts; see *Antirrhetika I*, 105–6. Therefore, George's escape to Mt. Athos and his association there with Palamas must be assigned to the period between Palamas' return to the Holy Mountain in 1331 and his departure in the winter of 1337/8.

67 σταυροειδῶς ἐστίχθη καυτηρίαις τὸ πρόσωπον: The Bulgarian czar (John-Alexander, 1331–71) is said to have inflicted the same punishment upon the Athonite Bogomils who fled to Trnvo and tried to spread their heresy there. He ordered them branded on the forehead and expelled from his kingdom; see V. S. Kiselkov, *Zitieto na sv. Teodosij Tirnovski kato istoričeski pametnik* (Sofia, 1926), 17 (as cited in E. Werner, "Spätbogomilisch-adamitische Spekulationen und Pratiken in religionshistorischer Sicht," *Byzantine Studies*, 1 [1974], 42).

69–75 ὧν ἄρχουσα ἡ Πορινὴ . . . σὺν Παλαμᾷ τῷ σοφῷ: G. Weiss ingenuously suggested that Πορινή is a conflation of Εἰρήνη and πορνεία (*Kantakuzenos*, 154 note 1004). Therefore, as Loenertz originally noted (*Epistulae*, 91, ad apparatum 58), this female leader of the heretics in Thessalonica must be identified with the Thessalonian nun Irene who, according to the *vita* of St. Theodosios of Trnvo, converted her fellow-citizens to Bogomilism by pretending to be orthodox and through some monks who were her disciples infected both the Holy Mountain and Trnvo with her heresy. See Kallistos (or pseudo-Kallistos?), *Life of St. Theodosios of Trnvo* (text in Slavonic), ed. V. N. Zlatarski, "Žitie i

žizn Prepodobnago otca našego Feodosija," *Sbornik za umotvorenija, nauka i knižnina*, 20 (Sofia, 1904), 19–20 (as cited in Meyendorff, *Introduction*, 55 note 63; Werner, "Spätbogomilisch . . . ,"41.)

Porine's friendship with Isidore and Palamas probably dated from 1325–26 when they were both together in Thessalonica. Isidore was then a layman but, according to his biographer, he had under his tutelage a mixed group of monks and lay people; cf. Philotheos, *Vita Isidori*, 77–80. His activities at that time were later strongly criticized by his enemies who accused him of teaching strange doctrines, holding clandestine meetings, and not abstaining from food and drink at the prescribed times; cf. the anti-Palamite declaration of July 1347 in PG, 150, col. 882A; Meyendorff, *Introduction*, 54.

Akindynos, of course, contends that the two leading hesychasts were Porine's disciples, and his portrait of this female arch-heretic is similar to that which Gregoras paints of the Athonite Bogomils, George of Larissa and Joseph of Crete, whom he calls the tutors of Palamas: they spent most of their time drinking strong wine and feasting. See Beyer, ed., *Antirrhetika I*, I, 1, 4, 1; Meyendorff, *Introduction*, 57 note 69. note 69.

78–79 *τὸν διάλογον δέξαι τὸν ἐχιδναῖον*: Akindynos sent Koukounares his own *Dialogue*, which not only refuted Palamas' *Dialexis* but it also cited the full text of that work; see commentary on Letter 25, lines 11–15.

53.

Akindynos comforts a worried follower with news of the happy ending of his ordeal.

Addressee: Unknown.

Date: Summer 1345. Akindynos has emerged victorious from his persecution.

9–12 *τότε μὲν ἑώρταζον . . . τῷ τῆς ἡδονῆς ἐκτόπῳ καὶ ἀκρατεῖ*: The Palamites were obviously not exaggerating when they described how adverse was the official reaction to the ordination of Akindynos and how severe his punishment. See p. xxviii, notes 105 and 106 *supra*.

11–12 *πρὸς τῷ μηδέν τι βλάψαι καὶ λαμπρότερον ἔδειξε τὸ καθ' ἡμᾶς ἡ ἐπήρεια*: This confirms Meyendorff's view that Akindynos became more powerful in the immediate aftermath of his persecution; see *Introduction*, 114.

54.

Akindynos writes to the imperial private secretary to request the appointment of a friend to the imperial chancery.

Addressee: Manuel Kinnamos. His first name is known from an imperial συμβόλαιον with Venice, which he signed in August 1343 in his capacity of μέγας οἰκονομιαστής; see F. Dölger, *Regesten der Kaiserurkunden des oströmischen Reiches von 565–1453, Corpus der griechischen Urkunden des Mittelalters und der neueren Zeit*, Abteilung I (Munich, 1965), 5, 9–10, no. 2891. According to Kantakouzenos, Kinnamos held the same title in the winter of 1342 when he and his associates, the *megas doux* Apokaukos and the *protosebastos* Gabalas, appropriated the largest part of the Kantakouzenos family property in Constantinople. See Kantakouzenos, *Hist.*, III, 36: II, 23 (. . . καὶ Κιννάμου τοῦ μυστικοῦ τῶν βασιλικῶν χρημάτων τότε ταμίου ὄντος καὶ πολλῶν ἑτέρων εὐνούχων οἳ παρεδυνάστευον . . .). After the murder of Alexios Apokaukos in June 1345, Kinnamos, who was by then promoted to the rank of *mystikos*, assumed the reins of the government together with the Patriarch and Isaak Asen and remained in charge until the fall of the regency in February 1347. See Kantakouzenos, *Hist.*, III, 89: II, 549; III, 97: II, 599. But he must have then taken advantage of the political amnesty granted by Kantakouzenos, for he seems to have retained his position under the new regime, since in September 1349 he signed with the title of *mystikos* a renewal of the imperial treaties with Venice. See Miklosich-Müller, III, 114–20; Dölger, *Regesten*, 21–22, no. 2952.

The *mystikos*, whose office ranks thirty-first in Ps.-Kodinos' list of dignities (cf. *Traité des Offices*, 138), was in charge of the emperor's secret correspondence; see Dölger, *Byzantinische Diplomatik. 20 Aufsätze zur Urkundenwesen der Byzantiner* (Ettal, 1956), 64.

Date: Summer–winter 1345(?) Kinnamos must have been promoted to the office of *mystikos* sometime between August 1343 and June 1345, but since we do not know when, I have tentatively assigned this letter to the period immediately following the end of Akindynos' persecution, when both he and Kinnamos were at the height of their power.

12 Εὐφημιανός: A Theodosios Euphemianos is attested as the scribe of folios 137–184 of codex *Ambrosianus H 52 sup.*, which is dated July 1347; see Turyn, *Dated Greek Manuscripts*, 1, 130. Perhaps, it is the same man or a younger relative.

28 Μανασῆς: Unknown.

55.

To an ecclesiastic who was angry because Akindynos could not grant him a certain favor.

Addressee: An unidentified bishop or ecclesiastical archon; see commentary on line 1 *infra*.

Date: Summer 1345. The independent tone of this letter and the fact that a favor was requested from him by a ranking clergyman or archon indicate that Akindynos was at the height of his power, which by his own admission he achieved after the end of his persecution. See commentary on Letter 53, lines 11–12.

1 *θεοφιλέστατε δέσποτα*: On this form of address, which in the fourteenth century was no longer restricted to metropolitans, but could also be used in reference to an ecclesiastical archon, see commentary on Letter 4, line 1 *supra*.

56.

Akindynos wonders why Magistros, who fully approved of his opposition to Palamas, has been silent for so long. He begs his old teacher not to treat him so cruelly and tells him that he spoke of him to the new metropolitan who is presently arriving to take possession of his see and promised him that he will find in Magistros a principal supporter in his struggle to eradicate Palamism.

Addressee: The Thessalonian philologist and rhetorician Thomas Magistros, also known as the monk Theodoulos; see Loenertz, *Epistulae*, 95, and "Dixhuit lettres," 100. On Magistros in general, see Guilland, *Correspondance*, 348–53. (Guilland mistakenly assumes that Magistros died *ca.* 1330. Akindynos' correspondence shows that he was still alive in 1347; see *Letter* 74, line 41.) On his works, see Krumbacher, 548–50, 554–56; Beck, *KTL*, 704–5; F. W. Lenz, *Fünf Reden Thomas Magisters* (Leiden, 1963), VII–XVIII.

Date: Autumn 1345. Metropolitan Hyakinthos, who is about to arrive in Thessalonica (cf. line 70–71), took possession of his see after the defeat of the Kantakouzenists in Thessalonica in the summer of 1345; see commentary on Letter 58, lines 7–13.

Loenertz ("Dix-huit lettres," 100) dates this letter to between 1345 and 1346. Kyrres (Ὁ Κύπριος ἀρχιεπίσκοπος Θεσσαλονίκης, 102) believes that it was written in June of 1345, after Hyakinthos' ordination and while he was waiting for the turbulence to subside in Thessalonica.

2–4 *Τὴν τοῦ φοίνικος ἡμῖν ἐμιμήσατο φύσιν, . . . ὥσπερ Ἰνδοῖς ἐκεῖνος καὶ Αἰγυπτίοις ἐπιδημῶν*: According to the Egyptian legend related by Herodotus, the phoenix was a sacred bird resembling an eagle in appearance, but with gorgeous plumage. Every five hundred years it flew to Egypt from its native Arabia, carrying its dead parent all plastered up in myrrh and deposited it in the temple of the Sun in Heliopolis; see Herodotus, *Hist.*, II, 73.

The phoenix did not visit India, as Akindynos thought, but was, according to some sources, a native of that land or of Ethiopia, from where it made its rare appearances in Egypt. See Philostratus, *Vita Apollonii*, III, 49; Heliodorus, *Aethiopica*, VI, 3; Achilles Tatius, *Τὰ κατὰ Λευκίππην καὶ Κλειτοφῶντα*, III, 25. See also Turk's article in W. H. Roscher's *Ausfürliches Lexikon der griechischen und römischen Mythologie* (Leipzig, 1902–9, 3[2], col. 3450ff.

5–6 *τοῦ Νείλου φύσιν αὐτὸν μεμιμῆσθαι ἠθέλομεν, ἐπετείως ἡμᾶς τοῖς γράμμασιν ἄρδοντα*: Another allusion derived from Herodotus; see *Hist.*, II, 9, where he describes how the Nile rises every year during the summer solstice.

6–7 *ὁ δ', οἶμαι, γράφειν ἡμῖν καὶ παντελῶς ἀπεῖπεν*: If I am correct in assuming that Letter 33 was also addressed to Magistros, Akindynos must not have heard from him for two years.

8–9 *τὰ ὕστατα ἐπιστέλλων ἡβῶντί τινι πρὸς τοῦτο τοὖργον ἐῴκει*: see Letter 33, lines 8–9.

13–14 *ὃν αὐτὸς πολλάκις ληροῦντα πρότερον καὶ σαφῶς πεπλανημένον ἀπέδειξας*: I do not know of any anti-Palamite writings of Magistros. His letter to Hierotheos (the friend and correspondent of Akindynos; cf. commentary on Letter 21 *supra*), in which he deplores the latter's decision to retire to Mt. Athos and maintains that the wilderness is no more conducive to spiritual salvation than life in the city, may be construed as an indictment of the fundamental tenets of hesychasm, but it is not an attack on Palamas' theology. See *Τῷ ἐμῷ Ἱεροθέῳ ἀνακεχωρηκότι πρὸς τὸν Ἄθω*, ed. E. Martini, "Una lettera del retore Teodulo (Thomas Magistros) al monaco Ieroteo," *Miscellanea Ceriani* (Milan, 1910), 438–47. Martini (*ibid.*, 437–38) comments that the author, like other Byzantine men of letters, was indirectly attacking hesychasm and its most prominent exponent, Palamas, but he suggests no date for this letter, and there is no evidence that it was written during the controversy.

Even if Magistros did inveigh against Palamas early in the dispute, Akindynos' complaints about his long silence (cf. commentary on lines 6–7 *supra*) indicate that he later adopted an apathetic stand. As Mercati observes (cf. *Notizie*, 513), Magistros could not have been a prominent anti-Palamite or such a pillar of Palamism as the Patriarch Philotheos would not have boasted of being his student. See the address to Philotheos of Demetrios Kydones (ed. Mercati, *Notizie*, 302–3) who, it must be noted, though bitterly anti-Palamite, says nothing about Magistros' opposition to Palamism, but even scoffs at his competence to teach theology and asserts that this skilled rhetorician who had lost his eyesight since childhood could no more be a theologian than he could see.

As for the identification of Magistros with the hieromonk Theodoulos named in the anti-Palamite list, which Loenertz tentatively proposes, it must remain hypothetical until more evidence is available. See Mercati, *Notizie*, 223, no. 13; Loenertz, "Dix-huit lettres," 110 note 4.

18–19 *εἰ δὲ δειλία τῶν πονηρῶν στομάτων ἃ ῥεῖ χειμάρρων δίκην ἐπὶ τοὺς οὐ τῇ καινῇ πίστει ταύτῃ προσρέοντας*: Perhaps an allusion to the persecution of the anti-Palamites in Thessalonica during the summer of 1345; see commentary on Letter 57, lines 10–11.

34–35 *τὴν Ἀρείου μανίαν καὶ τὴν Μακεδονίου*: See commentary on Letter 10, lines 334–36 and Letter 50, line 29.

40 *τί δ᾽ οὐχὶ καὶ Σαβελλίου*: See commentary on Letter 42, line 57.

43–44 *τί δὲ ουχὶ καὶ Μασσαλιανός*: See commentary on Letter 9, line 57.

70 *τοῦ θείου ποιμένος*: Hyakinthos of Thessalonica, on whom see commentary on Letter 44, line 38.

75–76 *ὁ πατὴρ καὶ διδάσκαλος*: Akindynos must have studied with Magistros during his early years in Thessalonica. This is the only reference to such an association between them.

57.

Akindynos knows of the addressee's piety through the letters that he wrote to others in Constantinople inveighing against the violence of the Palamite Charatzas. But the latter's sway is over now. The new metropolitan will prove this and will honor the addressee for his piety.

Addressee: An unidentified Thessalonian; probably a man of letters, since Akindynos praises his literary prowess and graceful style (cf. line 3).

Date: Autumn 1345, after the defeat of the Kantakouzenists in Thessalonica; see commentary on lines 25–28 *infra*. Loenertz assigns this letter to between 1345 and 1346 ("Dix-huit lettres," 99) and Kyrres to after 1 September 1345, when the Zealot regime was restored (Ὁ Κύπριος ἀρχιεπίσκοπος Θεσσαλονίκης . . . , 102).

9 Χαβάρων: Chabaron's name figures on the list of prominent anti-Palamites; see Mercati, *Notizie*, 223, no. 25. He is probably to be identified with the Chabaron who in 1343 made a donation to the monastery of Φιλανθρώπου Σωτῆρος, which belonged to Akindynos' most loyal supporter, the Princess Eulogia Choumnaina Palaiologina. See Miklosich-Müller, I, 324; Mercati, *Notizie*, 511; Loenertz, "Dix-huit lettres," 100.

10–11 *καὶ Χαρατζᾶς ὁ πάντολμος ἐκακίζετο ἀνθ' ὧν τοῖς εὐσεβέσιν ὑμῖν θηριωδῶς ἐπετίθετο*: On Charatzas, who is probably to be identified with a later officer of the guards in Constantinople, see commentary on Letter 40, line 2. His persecution of the Akindynists in Thessalonica must have occurred during John Apokaukos' abortive attempt to hand the city over to Kantakouzenos during the summer of 1345; see Loenertz, "Dix-huit lettres," 99.

Sometime before the assassination of the Grand Duke Alexios Apokaukos on 11 June 1345, his son John, the governor of Thessalonica, took complete control of the government in that city by murdering his colleague Michael Palaiologos, the head of the Zealot party. Apokaukos granted considerable freedom to Kantakouzenos' followers immediately, but he did not feel free to declare openly for the enemy of his father until after the latter's death. He then convoked an assembly and with its approval he sent two emissaries to Berroia to negotiate with Manuel Kantakouzenos. No sooner, however, did the ambassadors return with news of Manuel's agreement, than Andrew Palaiologos, a former Zealot who had promised to cooperate with Apokaukos, withdrew his support and incited a bloody uprising. Apokaukos and his associates were cruelly massacred and the Zealots regained control of the government. See Kantakouzenos, *Hist.*, III, 93 and 94: II, 568–82; Gregoras, *Hist.*, XIV, 10: II, 740–41.

According to the short chronicle of Thessalonica, Apokaukos was killed in the year 6853, in other words, as Loenertz points out, before the first of September when the new year (1346) started. See *Chronicon breve Thessalonicense*, ed. Loenertz, *Correspondance*, I, 174; Loenertz, "Note sur une lettre de Démétrius Cydonès à Jean Cantacuzène," *BZ*, 44 (1951), 405–8 (reprinted in Loenertz, *Byzantina et Franco-Graeca* (Rome, 1970), 279–83; *Chronica*, I, Chronicle 49, § 5, p. 351; commentary, *ibid.*, II, 263–64.

It was, therefore, during the short period of Kantakouzenist influ-

ence between the spring and late summer of 1345 that the Palamites were allowed to persecute their opponents in Thessalonica.

25–28 *τὴν ἐκείνου νίκην καὶ τὴν θρασύτητα ἧτταν ἐκείνου . . . νῦν περιφανῶς ἀποδείκνυσιν οὖσαν*: His assertion that Charatzas had been definitely defeated shows that Akindynos was writing after the Zealot victory.

29–30 *ὁ δὲ πανίερος ἡμῶν μὲν δεσπότης, ὑμέτερος δὲ ποιμήν, φανεὶς παρ' ὑμῖν καὶ τοῦτο δείξει καλῶς*: Obviously, the new metropolitan Hyakinthos (cf. commentary on Letter 44, line 38) had not yet taken possession of his see.

58.

Akindynos has heard of Bryennios' courageous resistance to Palamism and considers it fitting that someone who had been his teacher and friend since childhood should also be his ally in the fight for piety. Now that the new metropolitan has arrived, he too will seek Bryennios out and rely on his assistance for the eradication of Palamism in Thessalonica.

Addressee: Bryennios, an official of the metropolis of Thessalonica. He is mentioned with the title of *sakelliou* in an Athonite act dating from April 1329 (cf. *Actes de Chilandar*, no. 118, 246) and in a patriarchal act of October 1336, registering his acquittal of false charges of impiety (a man named Chionios had accused Bryennios and certain other Thessalonians of not believing in the resurrection); see PG, 152, cols. 1220B–1223D; Miklosich-Müller, I, 174; Darrouzès, no. 2174; Loenertz, "Dix-huit lettres," 99 note 2. He is also designated by the same title in the superscription of a letter that he wrote to Gregoras *ca*. 1325–30, after receiving from him one of his panegyrics of Andronikos II; see Gregoras, *Hist.*, I, XC–XCI; French résumé in Guilland, *Correspondance*, 275–76, no. 7. According to this letter, Bryennios had met Gregoras during a visit to Constantinople and had been his admirer ever since.

Although Guilland does not suggest it, Bryennios may also be the recipient of a letter of Gregoras which is addressed to the "*Sakelliou* in Thessalonica" and which shows that it was through him that Gregoras initiated a correspondence with Magistros; see Bezdeki, ed., "Nicephori Gregorae Epistulae XC," *Ephemeris Dacoromana*, II (1924), no. LXII; French résumé in Guilland, *Correspondance*, 16, no. 29.

By 1345 Bryennios had also been appointed to the office of *dikaiophylax*. Akindynos refers to him as either *sakelliou* or *dikaiophylax* in Letter 50 (lines 141–42) and as *dikaiophylax* in Letter 74 (line 43). The

title of *sakelliou* or *sakellion* ranks fifth in the first class of ecclesiastical *offikia*. Its jurisdiction extended over the episcopal prison, the management of women's monasteries, and other church property; see Darrouzès, *Offikia*, 551, 556, 558, and 561. The title of *dikaiophylax*, which originally denoted an imperial legal magistrate, was from the time of Michael VIII Palaiologos borne also by ecclesiastical officials in Constantinople and the provinces; see Darrouzès, *op. cit.*, 109–10.

According to our letter, Bryennios was Akindynos' teacher and had befriended him since he was a boy (see line 27). He was apparently a loyal supporter, though his name does not appear in the anti-Palamite list published by Mercati (*Notizie*, 222–23).

Date: Late fall–winter 1345, after the restoration of the Zealot government and the arrival of Hyakinthos in Thessalonica; see commentary on lines 7–13. Loenertz dates this letter to between 1345 and 1346 (cf. "Dix-huit lettres," 98), and Kyrres assigns it to the end of 1345, noting that it was written after the arrival of the metropolitan, therefore after Letters 56 and 57 (Ὁ *Κύπριος ἀρχιεπίσκοπος Θεσσαλονίκης* . . . , 102).

5–6 *ὅτε Χαρατζᾶς ἔπνει σφοδρῶς ὁ δεινὸς Παλαμίτης κατὰ τῆς εὐσεβείας*: On the period of Charatzas' influence in Thessalonica, see commentary on Letter 57, lines 10–11.

7–13 *καὶ ἄλλως τῆς Χαρατζᾶ μανίας λελωφηκυίας, ἧκε θαυμαστὸς ὑμῖν τῆς ἐκκλησίας τῆς ὑμετέρας ποιμὴν . . . ἐξελῶν αὐτῆς τὴν Παλαμῆτιν νόσον*: According to this information, Hyakinthos arrived in Thessalonica when the "fury" of the Palamite Charatzas had already subsided, in other words, after the victory of the anti-Palamite Zealots. The new metropolitan, just as Akindynos predicted, proved a determined persecutor of his opponents; see commentary on Letter 44, line 38.

13 *ἀγαθοῦ ποιμένος ἐρημίᾳ*: Thessalonica had been without a metropolitan since the spring of 1345, when the local disturbances prevented Hyakinthos from taking possession of his see, or perhaps even earlier, if we are to accept the hypothesis that Kalekas intended to make Akindynos metropolitan of Thessalonica when he ordained him at the end of 1344. See commentary on Letter 50, lines 91–92.

20–22 *οὐ γὰρ Θεμιστοκλεῖ μὲν καὶ Ἀριστείδῃ . . . πρὸς ἀλλήλους διάφορα*: The reference is to the well-known reconciliation of the two Athenian political enemies shortly before the battle of Salamis in 480 B.C.; see Herodotus, *Hist.*, VIII, 78–81; Plutarch, *Themistocles*, XII; *idem*, *Aristeides*, VIII.

59.

Akindynos was happy to hear that Isaris escaped the terrible fate that befell his allies in Thessalonica and hopes that he will learn from this misfortune that if one betrays friendship and piety for the sake of worldly profit, he runs the risk of losing everything.

Addressee: The Thessalonian George Isaris who in the spring of 1343 had carried a letter of Akindynos to another mutual friend and supporter in Thessalonica. See commentary on Letter 27, line 2.

A wealthy landowner, Isaris apparently joined the Kantakouzenist party in Thessalonica (cf. Letter 39, which is probably also addressed to him) and as a result nearly lost his life during the terrorism that erupted in that city at the end of the summer of 1345. See commentary on lines 24–27.

Date: Autumn–winter 1345, after the massacre of the Kantakouzenists by the Zealots in Thessalonica. See commentary on lines 24–27. Loenertz, who does not note Akindynos' allusion to that event, dates the letter to between 1345 and 1346; see "Dix-huit lettres," 101.

9–10 *διὰ . . . μανίαν ἐρωτικὴν δόξης κενῆς καὶ χρημάτων*: Shortly before his death, Akindynos again complained that Isaris had betrayed him for material advantages: see Letter 73, lines 11–13. On the successful career of Isaris, who became an *oikeios* of both Stephan Dushan and John Kantakouzenos, see Loenertz, "Dix-huit lettres," 93 and notes 2–3.

24–27 *'Εγὼ δὲ . . . ὅτι τὰ ξίφη διέφυγες*: His vague remarks about the "disaster" and the "swords" from which Isaris escaped leave no doubt that Akindynos is here alluding to the atrocities of the bloody Zealot uprising during which many wealthy Thessalonians lost their lives and property. See Kantakouzenos, *Hist.*, III, 94: II, 580–81; Gregoras, *Hist.*, *XIV, 10, 15: II, 740–41; Demetrios Kydones, Occissorum Thessalonicae Monodia*, PG, 109, cols. 639A–652D (English translation by J. W. Barker in *Essays in Memory of Basil Laourdas* [Thessaloniki, 1975], 291–300); *idem*, *Ad Ioannem Cantacuzenum oratio prima*, ed. Loenertz, *Correspondance*, I, 5, lines 5–37. See also Kydones' reference to these events in some of his letters, ed. Loenertz, *Correspondance*, I, no. 7, lines 59–62; no. 77, lines 20–23; no. 87, lines 10–12. On the date of this massacre and on John Apokaukos' coup d'état which provoked this counter-rebellion, see commentary on Letter 57, lines 10–11.

47 *τῶν* Κροίσου *χρημάτων*: The wealth of Croesus, the last king of Lydia (*ca.* 560–546), was proverbial. See Herodotus, I, 30; 50–54; Gregory of Cyprus, *Centuria*, III, 15 (Leutsch-Schneidewin, II, 87).

51–52 *εἴ τί σοι, καὶ ἡμεῖς πρὸς τοῦτο συνετελέσαμεν παλαιῶν ἀνδρῶν καὶ σοφῶν . . . λόγοις*: Akindynos was a teacher of grammar; see p. x *supra*. Isaris must have been one of his students in Thessalonica.

52–53 *παλαιῶν ἀνδρῶν καὶ σοφῶν . . . λόγοις*: See Basil of Caesarea, *Ad adolescentes*, PG, 31, col. 565A: *καὶ τοῖς ἐλλογίμοις τῶν παλαιῶν ἀνδρῶν δι' ὧν καταλελοίπασι λόγων, συγγινομένοις ὑμῖν.*

60.

Delighted though he was to hear from Lapithes after such a long time, Akindynos was painfully disappointed when he did not receive as well the anti-Palamite discourses which his Cypriot supporter had promised him. He begs him, therefore, to send his urgently needed polemics to his fellow-Cypriots in Constantinople—in case he is afraid to send them to him—and tells him the tragic news of the sudden death of metropolitan Hyakinthos of Thessalonica and of the recent collapse of the dome of St. Sophia. He also sends him the writings of Hyakinthos and 370 iambics of his own.

Addressee: The Cypriot George Lapithes; see commentary on Letter 42.

Date: Early summer 1346. Akindynos was obviously writing soon after the collapse of the dome of St. Sophia on 19 May 1346, since he assumes that Lapithes had not heard about it yet and remarks that others will write to him about that tragic event (cf. lines 70–73).

Loenertz dates this letter to September 1346 on the assumption that the troubles of which Akindynos is here complaining (cf. lines 13–14) refer also to the formal protest which six bishops signed against the Patriarch in September of that year; see "Dix-huit lettres," 103. Karpozilos notes that it was written after 19 May, but does not propose a more precise date; see *Letters*, 85.

3–4 *τί δ' ἡμᾶς περιεῖδες τοσοῦτον χειμαζομένους χρόνον οὐδὲ πυρσῷ θαρρύνας*: Akindynos apparently had not heard from Lapithes since the spring of the previous year; see commentary on Letter 46.

7–8 *αὐτοὺς δὲ τοὺς λόγους οὔπω δεξάμενοι*: In the spring of 1345 Akindynos had asked Lapithes to write a refutation of Palamas' doctrines, and he had promised to do so (see commentary on Letter 46, line 22). But we do not know whether he kept his promise, since the Letters contain no further reference to Lapithes' polemical tracts. There is evidence, however, that he wrote them, because Gregoras affirms that his friend Agathangelos saw them when he visited Lapithes in Cyprus. See *Hist.*, XXV, 13, 14: III, 37, lines 3–9.

13 *ἡ δ' αἰτία τῆς ἀτυχίας ἡμῖν κυκεῶνες πραγμάτων*: This host of troubles started early in 1346 when the Empress took an active interest in the dogmatic dispute and demanded a personal doctrinal statement from the two protagonists as well as from the Patriarch (cf. pp. xxx–xxxi *supra*). Other severe blows were the sudden death of Hyakinthos of Thessalonica (cf. lines 54–63) and the decision of the dissident bishops gathered at Adrianople for the coronation of Kantakouzenos on 21 May to depose the Patriarch on the grounds that he had ordained condemned heretics; see p. xxxi *supra*.

22–23 *τοῖς μετὰ τὸν . . . Ὑάκινθον φίλοις*: The Cypriot Hyakinthos of Thessalonica was a long time friend of Lapithes, and it was through him that Lapithes came in contact with Akindynos; see commentary on Letter 44, line 38. The other friends were probably the Cypriots mentioned in the present letter, lines 34–35.

33–34 *ὁ θεῖος* Βαρθολομαῖος: Unknown. Probably a monk at the monastery of Hodegetria, where Hyakinthos had also been a resident.

34 Κοσμᾶς *ὁ θαυμάσιος*: Unknown.

34 *θεσπέσιος* Βλάσιος: Unknown.

35 *Λέων ὁ λογιώτατος*: Perhaps the sage Leo who is mentioned in a letter of Gregoras to the Cypriot Athanasios Lependrenos. See Guilland, *Correspondance*, no. 156, p. 259, lines 6–16; Kyrres, Ἡ Κύπρος *καὶ τὸ ἡσυχαστικὸν ζήτημα*, 26, 30.

Loenertz, following Guilland (*Correspondance*, 258 note 1), tentatively identifies Gregoras' friend Leo with a Cypriot scholar and bibliophile of the same name who resided in Constantinople and is known from an anonymous fourteenth-century correspondence; cf. E. Rein, "Die Florentiner Briefsammlung (codex Laurentianus S. Marco 356)," *Annales Academiae Scientiarum Fennicae*, ser. B, XIV, 2 (Helsinki, 1915), 57–59 (For the identification of the author of this correspondence with George Oinaiotes, see Kourouses, Μανουὴλ Γαβαλᾶς, 109). According to Loenertz, Leo must have returned to Cyprus after the final victory of Palamism, because Gregoras, who wrote to Lependrenos after 1351, complained that Leo wrote to others in Constantinople but not to him. See Loenertz, "Un Pachymère, auteur des lettres du San Marco 356?" *BZ*, 53 (1960), 291 and note 5.

36–37 *καὶ τὴν σὴν αὐχοῦσι σοφίαν οὐχ ἧττον ἢ τὸν δακτύλιον* Γύγης: According to the story in Plato's *Republic* (II, 3, 359d–360c), Gyges was a shepherd in the service of the king of Lydia when he accidentally discovered a ring which allowed him to become invisible when worn with the bezel turned toward the palm. With the aid of this ring Gyges entered the royal chamber, and after seducing the queen he killed her husband and

seized the throne. See also Cicero, *De Officiis*, III, 38. Akindynos and other Byzantine writers (cf., for example, Kalothetos, *Βίος πατρ. Ἀθανασίου*, *Συγγρ.*, 471, lines 601–2) are probably copying Gregory of Nazianzus, *Or.* 43, 21 (PG, 36, col. 524B): *ἡμῖν δὲ τὸ μέγα πρᾶγμα καὶ ὄνομα, Χριστιανοὺς καὶ εἶναι καὶ ὀνομάζεσθαι· ᾧ πλέον ἐφρονοῦμεν ἢ τῇ στροφῇ τῆς σφενδόνης ὁ Γύγης.*

42 *ἐπὶ τὴν λυχνίαν τίθει, τὴν ἐκκλησίαν αὐτήν*: For *λυχνία* as a figure of the Christian church, see Rev. 1:12, 20.

60 *νῦν οἴχεται ἀναρπασθεὶς ἐξαίφνης*: The death of Hyakinthos of Thessalonica was obviously very recent. It must, therefore, have occurred in the late spring of 1346.

62–63 *μείζω δὲ τοῖς Παλαμήταις χαράν, ὧν ἐκείνην θᾶττον ἐλπίδος πάσης ἐκάθηρεν*: On Hyakinthos' anti-Palamite activity in Thessalonica, see commentary on Letter 44, line 38.

69 *Ἰώσηπος*: Unknown. Probably the monk mentioned in the anti-Palamite list; see Mercati, *Notizie*, 223, no. 21.

70–72 *περὶ τῆς κοινῆς καὶ μεγίστης συμφορᾶς τῶν Ῥωμαίων . . . νεὼν τῆς παντουργοῦ Σοφίας*: On the night of 19 May 1346 the dome of St. Sophia, which had been weakened by earthquakes during recent years, partially collapsed. The eastern arch suddenly gave way pulling down the half-dome which rested on it as well as a section of the central dome. The debris covered part of the sanctuary and destroyed the iconostasis and the ambo. See Gregoras, *Hist.*, XIV, 2: II, 698, lines 8–11; XV, 2: II, 749, line 10–751, line 20. On the correct date, see the autograph note by Makarios Chrysokephalos in *Marcianus Gr.* 83, fol. 229^{v} (Passarelli, *Macario*, 33 note 29); *Chronica* I, Chronicle 7, § 10, p. 65; commentary *ibid.*, II, 265; and Kourouses, *Αἱ ἀντιλήψεις περὶ τῶν ἐσχάτων τοῦ κόσμου*, 229 note 1, where various other sources on the collapse and the damage done to the church are cited.

This calamity was the subject of two laments, one by Alexios Makrembolites and the other by an unknown author. Both have been edited with a detailed commentary by Kourouses, *op. cit.*, 235–39 and 247–49.

75–76 *ἐπαγαγόντες τὴν τοῦ παντὸς καὶ ὧδε χριστιανικοῦ πυρίπνουν προθυμίαν καὶ σύμπνοιαν ἐπὶ τὴν τοῦ πεπτωκότος ἀνάστασιν*: The zealous and concerted efforts of the Constantinopolitans to restore their city's most holy and magnificent monument are affirmed by Gregoras who describes how all citizens, regardless of their station in life, rushed crying to the ruins and began to clear the rubble. Even noble ladies in all their finery were seen lifting heavy stones; see Gregoras,

Hist., XV, 2: II, 750. The repairs, which started immediately, were not completed, however, until the end of 1353 when Kantakouzenos finally levied the money required to finish the restoration of the central dome. See Kantakouzenos, *Hist.*, IV, 4: III, 30, lines 5–15; Gregoras, XXVIII, 39: III, 201, line 22–202, line 3; Kourouses, *op. cit.*, 229–30. The Grand Duke Simeon of Moscow had already sent a considerable sum for that purpose, but according to Gregoras, Kantakouzenos spent it on wages for his Turkish mercenaries. See Gregoras, *Hist.*, XXVIII, 34–36: III, 190, line 10–200, line 9; XXXVI, 31: III, 516, line 12; 517, line 11; Kourouses, *op. cit.*, 229–30.

76–77 *εἰ μὴ ταύτην ὁ Θεὸς παραλύσοι διὰ τὰς ἁμαρτίας ἡμῶν*: In a letter written after the deposition of Kalekas in February 1347, Akindynos again alludes to the collapse of the dome of St. Sophia and holds the victory of his opponents responsible for this sign of divine retribution; see Letter 66, lines 40–41. Even the enlightened Gregoras writes in his *History* that the cathedral was damaged because the Palamite council of 1341 was held there (*Hist.*, XXII, 3: III, 6, lines 16–19; Kourouses, *op. cit.*, 228 note 5) and compares the gap in the dome to an open mouth protesting against the Palamite victory; see Gregoras, *Hist.*, XV, 2: II, 749, line 10–750, line 12; Kourouses, *op. cit.*, 243–44. Makrembolites, on the other hand, appears to assign the guilt to the anti-Palamites and interprets the collapse as a sign of the approaching end of the world; see *Εἰς τὴν ἁγίαν Σοφίαν*, 237, line 41; 235, lines 3–5.

78–79 *Πέπομφά σοι καὶ τῶν ἐμῶν ἐν ἰάμβοις ἑβδομήκοντα πρὸς τοῖς τριακοσίοις*: To my knowledge, these iambics have not survived. Akindynos' iambic poem against Palamas consists of 510 iambic trimeters; cf. PG, 150, cols. 843A–861A.

91–92 *ἡ θεοφιλεστάτη βασίλισσα*: The Princess Irene-Eulogia Choumnaina Palaiologina; see commentary on Letter 6, line 7.

96 *ὁ Κροῖσος ἐπὶ τοῖς χρήμασιν*: The Lydian king Croesus (*ca.* 560–546 B.C.) thought of himself as the happiest of mortals because of his immense wealth and was annoyed at Solon, the Athenian sage, when he told him that no man could be considered happy before his life had come to an end; see Herodotus, *Hist.*, I, 30–33; Plutarch, *Solon*, XXVII.

96 *Σεμίραμις τῇ Βαβυλῶνι*: This Assyrian queen (*ca.* 800 B.C.) was, according to Herodotus, one of the rulers credited with building the celebrated walls and temples of Babylon; see *Hist.*, I, 184.

96–97 *αὐτή ποτε τῇ ἁλουργίδι*: The Princess Irene-Eulogia was the widow of the Despot John Palaiologos, son of Andronikos II; see commentary on Letter 6, line 7.

61.

News of the addressees' resistance to Palamism and their support of their late metropolitan pleased the Patriarch and the Court and encouraged Akindynos to write to them and reestablish contact after a long time.

Addressees: Unknown; probably two monks, since Akindynos says that their chastity was renowned (cf. line 16). He mentions that they had been kind to him once (during his stay on Mt. Athos?) and that, although he had not written to them directly, he remembered them in his letters to mutual friends (cf. lines 5–12).

Date: Summer–autumn 1346; after the death of Hyakinthos of Thessalonica and before the Patriarch abandoned Akindynos; see commentary on line 20 *infra*.

13 Γαβριήλ: Unknown; probably another monk.

15–18 *πίστει περὶ τὸν βασιλέα τὸν ἐκ Θεοῦ καὶ θεῖον . . . δι' ἣν καὶ δεινῶν τινων ὑμᾶς ἔφασκεν ἐλθεῖν εἰς πεῖραν*: The addressees, who were politically loyal to John V and religiously opposed to Palamas, must have suffered during the brief rule of the Kantakouzenists in Thessalonica in the summer of 1345. See references to that persecution in Letter 57, lines 10–11 and Letter 58, lines 5–6.

20 *μετὰ τοῦ θειοτάτου ἀρχιερέως ὑμῖν ἐκείνου*: The reference is to Hyakinthos of Thessalonica who must already have been dead, because the word *ἐκεῖνος* often accompanies the names of deceased persons. On this specific usage, see D. Sophianos, "'Ὁ *βίος τοῦ* Εὐθυμίου *πατριάρχου* Κωνσταντινουπόλεως (†917)) *καὶ ὁ χρόνος συγγραφῆς αὐτοῦ*," Ἐπ. Ἑτ. Βυζ. Σπ., 38 (1971), 295 note 6.

Since Hyakinthos died in the spring of 1346 (cf. commentary on Letter 60, line 60), this letter must date, at the earliest, from the summer of that year. On the other hand, it could not have been written later than the end of 1346 because the Patriarch is reported to be still in power; see lines 25–27, where Akindynos assures his correspondents that news of their loyalty delighted the Patriarch as well as the emperor and his mother. I would opt for the earlier date, in view of Akindynos' offer to be of any service to the addressees, which indicates that he could still exercise some influence and had not yet been abandoned by Kalekas; see lines 40–41 and Letter 63.

62.

Akindynos describes the conversation that he had with a mutual acquaintance who remained neutral in the dispute, refusing to side either with him or Palamas. He inveighs against such men whom he compares to the semi-Arians and pleads with the addressee to persuade these arrogant and opportunistic friends to side with piety and the Church.

Addressee: An unidentified supporter; someone from Constantinople, since he and Akindynos had recently met and conversed (cf. lines 1–2). Probably a monk or a retired dignitary; see lines 275–291 and 305–17, where Akindynos reminds him of his past services to the cause and urges him to imitate the Cappadocian Fathers and, leaving his retreat, to take an even more active part than before in the fight against heresy. The evidence points to Sabbas Logaras; see commentary on Letter 34.

Date: Autumn–winter 1346: the Patriarch is under attack, but still in power; see lines 300–01.

1 Τῷ *δεῖνι*: Unknown. Obviously someone of importance who had recently written to Palamas objecting to his contentiousness but not to his doctrines (cf. lines 7–19). At his meeting with Akindynos he read to him a copy of this letter, thus provoking his anger and the long invective against those who refused to take sides in the dispute.

1–3 *πρὸς ὃν ἡμῖν . . . γεγραμμένην ἀνέγνως τὴν σὴν ἐπιστολὴν . . . , τὴν καὶ τἄλλα μὲν θαυμαστὴν . . . μάλιστα δ' ὅτι τῆς εὐσεβείας προὐμάχει*: Like Akindynos, the addressee must have rebuked this unaligned friend for condemning only the contentious spirit of Palamas and not his theology.

19–25 *ὁ δ' ἀντιγράφει . . . χάριτας ὁμολογῶν οἷς αὐτὸν ὁμολογεῖ μηδὲν ἀπᾷδον ἔχειν αὐτῷ τοὺς λόγους . . . ἀποθανεῖν ὑπὲρ τῆς ἀληθείας*: I do not know of any surviving letter of Palamas in which he thanks his correspondent for expressing approval of his writings and vows to continue the fight until death.

171 *⟨ὦ⟩ ἄνθρωπος*: On the vocatival use of the nominative in connection with *ἄνθρωπος*, see R. Schneider and G. Uhlig, eds., *Apollonii Dyscoli quae supersunt* (Leipzig, 1878–1910), II, 301.

173–271 Ἀλλ' *οἱ νοσοῦντες τὴν ἀκοὴν τῆς ψυχῆς . . . ἄθεος κατὰ τὰ εἰρημένα*: For similar denunciations of those who refused to align themselves with either of the contending parties, holding them both equally guilty of disturbing the peace of the Church, see Letter 41, lines 155–83, and the *Address to Hierotheos*, 195, lines 15–24 and 198, lines 13–22,

where Akindynos again asserts that neutrality is possible only for atheists and serves no other purpose but further to divide the Church.

179–83 *μέσοι τινὲς εἶναι ποιούμενοι, καθάπερ τοὺς Ἀνομοίους οἱ θεολόγοι φασὶ Βασίλειος καὶ Γρηγόριος . . . ὅμοιον τὴν φύσιν, μέσον τι τῶν εἰρημένων ἐφήμισαν*: The text of this passage appears suspect, for even if we correct the errors in syntax (reading: *οἳ μέσοι . . . γενόμενοι* instead of *οὓς μέσους . . . γενόμενοι*) Akindynos' statement fails to make sense, since it attributes to the Anomoeans the doctrine of their opponents the Homoeans.

The *μέσοι*, to whom Akindynos compares the unaligned, were not the Anomoeans or Eunomians—extreme Arians who taught that there was no resemblance between the Father and the Son, since one was the creator and the other a creature (cf. Epiphanios, *Adv. Haeres.*, 76, PG, 42, cols. 516C–640A)—but the Homoeans or semi-Arians, as Epiphanios calls them (cf. *ibid.*, 73, PG, 42, cols. 400C–473B), who introduced the term *homoios* (like the Father), as a compromise between *anomoios* and *homoousios*. In their writings quoted here by Akindynos, Basil of Caesarea and Gregory of Nazianzus called Homoeanism *τὸ τῆς μεσότητος δόγμα*, emphasizing the insidious character of this moderate form of Arianism which created a further rift in the Church by opposing both the orthodox party and the Anomoeans.

185–87 *τὸ γὰρ ὅμοιον αὐτοῖς, οὐ προστεθέν γε τὸ ἀπαράλλακτον, ἀνόμοιον πέφηνε*: See Basil of Caesarea, *Epist. IX*, PG, 32, col. 272A: *Εἰ δέ τις τοῦ ὁμοίου τὸ ἀπαράλλακτον ἀποτέμνοι . . . ὑποπτεύω τὸ ῥῆμα ὡς τοῦ μονογενοῦς τὴν δόξαν κατασμικρύνον.*

204–5 *τῇ δὲ τῶν λογισμῶν ἀκολουθίᾳ μὴ ἐφιέντες*: I have borrowed the translation of this phrase from R. J. Deferrari, *St. Basil: The Letters*, Loeb, III (London–New York, 1926–34), 221.

265–66 *τραγελάφων*: An imaginary animal, the "goat-stag" was used in introductory treatises on philosophy as a term to which no reality corresponds. See Elias, *Prolegomena philosophiae* (*Commentaria in Aristotelem Graeca*, XVIII, 1 [Berlin, 1900]), 3, lines 7–8; David, *Prolegomena philosophiae* (*Comment. in Arist. Gr.*, XVIII, 2 [Berlin, 1904]), 1, lines 16–17, as cited in I. Ševčenko, "The Definition of Philosophy in the Life of St. Constantine," *For Roman Jacobson* (The Hague, 1956), 450 note 5. See also Gregory of Nazianzus, *Or.* 25, 6 (PG, 35, col. 1205B): *σκινδαψοί τινες . . . καὶ τραγέλαφοι.*

278–80 *μίμησαι τοὺς μεγάλους ἐκείνους Βασίλειον καὶ Γρηγόριον, οἳ τὰς ἐρήμους ἀφέντες . . . αἱρετικῇ τρικυμίᾳ*: Basil of Caesarea and his friend Gregory of Nazianzus left their hermitage by the river Iris in Pontos to become the leaders of the resistance against the Arian heresy and

the Emperor Julian's attempt to restore paganism. See Gregory the Presbyter, *Vita S. Gregorii Theologi*, PG, 35, 304B–C, and Gregory of Nazianzus, *Or.* 43, 29, PG, 36, cols. 536B–540A.

291–301 *τοὺς δὲ φίλους ὄντας ἀποστήσεις τῆς πλάνης . . . ἀλλὰ τὸν πατριάρχην*: If the addressee of this letter is Sabbas Logaras, this could be an appeal to him to exercise his influence at Court in favor of the Akindynists, just as he had done twice before; see Letter 34, lines 40–44; Letter 51; and lines 313–16 of this letter, where Akindynos reminds the addressee that he had attacked the Palamites successfully in the past.

298–300 *Αἰσώπου μελίτταις . . . ἐλθόντα πρὸς ἐπιμέλειαν*: See Aesop, Μελιττουργός, ed. K. Halm, *Fabulae Aesopicae collectae* (Leipzig, 1872), no. 289, 141.

300–01 *λέγω δὲ οὐκ ἐμαυτὸν γεωργόν, ἀλλὰ τὸν πατριάρχην*: For Akindynos' use of the word *γεωργὸς* to denote the patriarch, see commentary on Letter 38, lines 37–38.

63.

Akindynos is in despair because the Patriarch has turned away from him and the Palamite Menas, his old and implacable enemy, does not even allow him to go out and procure for himself the absolute necessities of life. He complains of the ingratitude of church and state and begs the Patriarch to come to his rescue.

Addressee: The Patriarch of Constantinople, John XIV Kalekas (1334–47).

Date: Last months of 1346 to January of 1347. It is evident from Akindynos' pleas for help that the Patriarch was still in power when this appeal was addressed to him; see lines 4–14. It must, therefore, have been written shortly before his deposition when—as Meyendorff suggests (cf. *Introduction*, 118 note 110)—Kalekas abandoned his troublesome protégé because he was himself fighting for survival.

Weiss' proposal to date this letter to 1341, after the synod of July (cf. Weiss, *Kantakuzenos*, 121), is not tenable, because Akindynos speaks here of his services to Patriarch and Emperor, a claim he could not have made in 1341; see lines 35–37.

15 *ἡ γὰρ οὐ λέων καὶ θηριώδης φύσις* Μηνᾶς *ὁ γειτονεύων ἐμοί*: It is possible that this fierce persecutor of Akindynos was the hesychast Menas to whom, according to the anti-Palamite sources, Palamas wrote a letter concerning the psycho-physical method of prayer; see Kyparissiotes, *Palamiticae transgressiones*, I, PG, 152, col. 683C; Ps.-Kydones, *Adversus Palamam*, PG, col. 154, 840D; Mercati, *Notizie*, 281; Meyen-

dorff, *Introduction*, 398, and notes 86 and 87. The hesychast Menas is also known as the author of an ascetic work containing instructions to the monks for the period of the Great Lent; see Meyendorff, *Introduction*, 398, and note 88.

16 *ὃς ἀντὶ τῆς βοηθείας ἧς αὐτοῖς συνηράμην*: Akindynos refers to his support of the hesychasts prior to the council of June 1341 and complains of Menas' ingratitude.

19–20 *πρῶτον μὲν ξίφει με ἀνελεῖν ἐπεχείρησεν*: Menas was apparently the monk who attempted to assassinate Akindynos at the synod of July; see *supra*, p. xix and note 62.

20 *εὐπορῶν τυραννίδος ἧς ἤθελεν*: Akindynos implies that in July 1341 Menas could act against him with impunity because the patron of the Palamites, the then Grand Domestic and later usurper Kantakouzenos, was in power. In his fifth *Antirrhetic*, Akindynos claimed that in the immediate aftermath of the council of July the Palamites harassed him and proclaimed him condemned because they enjoyed the powerful support of Kantakouzenos; see note 66 of my introduction.

24–25 *παλαμώμενος ὁ παλαμναῖος*: Note the pun; for other instances, see commentary on Letter 25, line 15.

29–31 *ἴσχυσε νῦν τοσοῦτον, ὥστ' ἀποκλεῖσαί μοι τὴν θυρίδα ἐκείνην ἧς χάριν ἀνῆλθε δεῦρο ἡ κηδεμονικωτάτη περὶ ἐμέ σου ψυχή*: It appears that Akindynos had been confined to a monastery under Palamite control. The Patriarch had obviously made an effort to improve his living conditions but, as his power was waning, his orders were defied.

43 *εἰ δὲ νικᾷ τὰ χείρω, καὶ ταῦτα ὑπομενῶ μετ' ἀγαθῆς ἐλπίδος*: We can only guess that Kalekas must have heeded Akindynos' desperate appeal and helped him escape, for in the farewell address to his followers, written before his death in the spring of 1348, Akindynos intimated that he had been in hiding for much more than a year, in other words, before February 1347 when the Patriarch was deposed. See *Marc. Gr. 155*, fol. 32ʳ: *Χαίρετέ μοι . . . διαφερόντως ὑμεῖς, ὦ θειότατοι, οἵ μοι τοὺς διωγμοὺς . . . ἐπεκουφίζετε καὶ τὸν ὅλον ἐνιαυτὸν καὶ πολὺ τούτου πλέον ὡς ἡμερῶν ἑβδομάδα ἐδείξατε . . .*

64.

Akindynos appeals to his old friend the skevophylax for help against a troublesome enemy.

Addressee: I was unable to identify the skevophylax to whom this letter is ad-

dressed. George Perdikes who signed the tome of 1351 as skevophylax must have been appointed to that office after the death of Akindynos, for in 1348 he held the title of *epi ton sekreton*; see Miklosich-Müller, I, 285; Darrouzès, no. 2306; *idem*, *Offikia*, 140.

The skevophylax was third in rank in the first class of patriarchal officials known as *exokatakoiloi*. He was in charge of the liturgical vessels, vestments, and books; see Darrouzès, *Offikia*, 314–18.

Date: End of 1346–47.

2–3 Ἆρ' ἐπελάθου τῆς φιλίας ἐκείνης ἣν πρῴην ἔχειν πρὸς ἡμᾶς ὡμολόγεις καὶ ἐσαεὶ τηρήσειν: The skevophylax was, apparently, one of those friends who abandoned Akindynos after the Patriarch lost interest in him.

5 πῶς οὖν ὁ δεῖνα καθ' ἡμῶν στασιάζει: An unknown Palamite. Perhaps Menas whom Akindynos describes as his tormentor in his letter to Kalekas; see Letter 63, line 15.

9–10 τὸ πονηρὸν τοῦ πνευματικοῦ τούτου πνεῦμα: In his first *Triad*, Palamas referred to Barlaam, in Pauline phraseology, as ψυχικὸς (unspiritual) and to the hesychasts as πνευματικοὶ (men gifted with the Spirit); see 1 Cor. 2:14–17; Τριὰς I, 3, 12–13, Συγγράμματα, I, 422, lines 10–26; 423, lines 3–10. Akindynos, therefore, ironically styles his enemy a "man gifted with the evil spirit."

65.

Unable to satisfy his correspondent's request for a full copy of Palamas' works, Akindynos sends him a synopsis. He hails this new supporter and promises to follow his advice and remain quiet, though his opponents who are infesting the City with their heresy do not leave him in peace.

Addressee: Unknown. Although he was not a new acquaintance, since he had advised Akindynos in the past (cf. line 21), the addressee was obviously someone who had just decided to take a stand against Palamas (cf. lines 14–15) and probably to write and refute his doctrines, since he wished to familiarize himself with all of his works.

In the spring of 1345 Lapithes had made a similar request, and Akindynos, who was again under persecution, was able to send him only his *Dialogue* and his refutation of Palamas' third letter; see Letter 42, lines 192–205; Letter 46, lines 41–51; Letter 47, lines 5–6.

Was the addressee also someone from abroad? The fact that Akindynos deems it necessary to tell him that the Palamites are spreading their

disease all over the City and do not allow him to remain in peace suggests that he was not a resident of Constantinople; see lines 24–25. Finally, because he addresses him only as "Your Wisdom" (cf. line 8), I believe that he is writing to a layman and not to an ecclesiastic.

Date: Spring–winter 1347: the Palamites are already victorious and spreading their heresy all over Constantinople; see lines 24–25. Karpozilos dates it between the months immediately preceding Kalekas' deposition and 1347 (*Letters*, 96).

22–23 *ἅτε καὶ συνήθη προστεταγμένην ἡμῖν, ἠρεμοῦμεν παντάπασι πρὸς ἡμᾶς αὐτοὺς καθάπαξ ἐπεστραμμένοι*: In order to defend himself against charges of contentiousness, Akindynos often emphasized his preference for peace and solitude, his chosen lot as a monk (cf. Letter 42, lines 43–46). It was for the sake of piety, he wrote, that he was drawn away from his peaceful existence as painfully as a man driven by force from his own beloved land. See *Ἑτέρα ἔκθεσις καὶ ἀνασκευὴ τῶν τοῦ Παλαμᾶ πονηροτάτων αἱρέσεων*, *Monac. Gr. 223*, fols. 66ʳ–66ᵛ (excerpt edited by Uspenskij in *Synodikon*, 93): *εἰ οὖν ἐξῆν ἡμῖν σιωπῶσιν ἡσύχως διάγειν . . . οὐκ ἂν ᾑρούμεθα πράγματα καὶ πόνους καὶ συνεχεῖς κινδύνους οὓς ὑπομένομεν, τοὺς ἐλέγχους ἀνῃρημένοι τῆς ἀσεβείας ταύτης, ἀντ' ἐλευθέρας ζωῆς καὶ ἀπράγμονος ἧς ἐξ ἀρχῆς ἀντ' ἄλλου παντὸς ἠγαπήσαμεν καὶ ἧς ἀποσπώμενοι . . . οὕτω βαρυαλγοῦμεν ὥσπερ οἱ κομιδῇ φιλοπάτριδες τῆς πατρίδος βιαίως ἐξελαυνόμενοι.*

The sincerity of such statements made to justify his polemical activity is, of course, subject to skepticism, but the regret he expresses in his farewell address at the loss of a peaceful life is undoubtedly honest. For his touching adieu to the quiet hill where he lived and which he claims to have chosen because it allowed him to lead a peaceful and inconspicuous existence, see note 141 of my introduction *supra*.

66.

In response to his correspondent's request, Akindynos sends him a brief exposition of his as well as his opponent's doctrines and urges him to champion the cause of piety.

Addressee: Unknown; someone who was yet undecided and had asked for more information on the doctrinal dispute before committing himself to the support of Akindynos. The latter obviously respected his judgment, because

he asked him to make any corrections he considered necessary in his writings, provided that he did not violate the unity of the Holy Trinity; see lines 86–88.

Date: March–November 1347: after the Patriarch's deposition and before his death on 29 December 1347; see commentary on lines 56–58. Karpozilos (*Letters*, 90) assigns this letter to the end of 1346.

5 *προσδοκωμένης ἤδη τῆς προρρηθείσης μετασκευῆς τοῦ παντός*: Akindynos frequently called his opponents the "false prophets" whose rise Christ had foretold as a sign of the "last times"; see Matt. 24:23–25; Luke 17:22–23; and Letter 37, lines 124–31; Letter 39, lines 74–81; Letter 49, lines 23–24.

The final victory of Palamas and Kantakouzenos, preceded as it was by such ominous events as the violent earthquakes, the collapse of the dome of St. Sophia, and the devastating Turkish incursions—to all of which Akindynos alludes in this letter (see lines 37–42)—further convinced him that the end of the world was imminent. His contemporary, Alexios Makrembolites, expressed a similar view in his lament on the collapse of St. Sophia's dome; see Makrembolites, *Εἰς τὴν ἁγίαν Σοφίαν*, 235, line 1–238, line 48. For the tendency of the Byzantines to interpret natural disasters, religious controversies, and political upheavals in retributive and eschatological terms, see Kourouses, *Αἱ ἀντιλήψεις περὶ τῶν ἐσχάτων τοῦ κόσμου*, 211–23.

39 *γῆν ἀστατοῦσαν*: In the early 1340s Constantinople was hit by two severe earthquakes. The first and more violent one occurred on 18 October 1343; see *Chronica*, I, Chronicle 9, § 10, p. 93; Chronicle 87, § 1, p. 612; Chronicle 113, § 1, p. 681; (Chronicle 8, § 39, p. 83, gives the incorrect date of 1342); commentary *ibid.*, II, 258. See also Gregoras, *Hist.*, XIV, 2: II, 694, lines 13–14; 20–22; Makrembolites, *Dialogue*, 203, line 7; *idem*, *Εἰς τὴν ἁγίαν Σοφίαν*, 236, lines 22–26.

The second earthquake followed a year later, on 6 November; see *Chronica*, I, Chronicle 87, § 2, p. 613; commentary *ibid.*, II, 260.

38–39 *θάλατταν τοὺς ἑαυτῆς ὑπερβαίνουσαν ὅρους*: For references to the destructive tidal waves which accompanied the earthquake of October 1343, see Gregoras, *Hist.*, XIV, 2: 694, lines 13–15; 695, lines 5–13; Makrembolites, *Dialogue*, *ad apparatum, Variae lectiones*, *Titulus*; *idem*, *Εἰς τὴν ἁγίαν Σοφίαν*, 236, lines 26–28; and *Chronica*, I, Chronicle 9, § 10, p. 93; Chronicle 87, § 1, p. 612; Chronicle 113, § 1, p. 681; commentary *ibid.*, II, 258.

40 *τὰ θειότατα τῶν ἔργων διαλυόμενα*: On the collapse of the dome of St. Sophia, see commentary on Letter 60, lines 70–72.

41–42 *τυραννίδων ἀτόπων ἐπαναστάσεις*: The allusion is to the victory of Kantakouzenos in February 1347 and his recognition as co-emperor. Akindynos had used the word "tyranny" before to describe Kantakouzenos' usurpation of the imperial authority; see the passage from his Fifth *Antirrhetic*, cited in note 66 of my introduction.

If this is also an allusion to the "class war" in Thessalonica, as Karpozilos assumes (cf. *Letters*, 89), then Akindynos would be more likely to consider the loyalist Zealots as the representatives of the legitimate regime and their Kantakouzenist opponents as the usurpers. This is, at least, the conclusion to be drawn from his reaction to the expulsion from Thessalonica (probably by the Zealots) of the Palamite monk Mark Kyrtos and to the narrow escape of the landowner Isaris from the massacre of 1345. The former he pronounced impious as well as disloyal to the emperor (Letter 37, lines 32–39), and of the latter he said that he incurred the wrath of God because he betrayed his religious convictions for the sake of material advantages (undoubtedly, his alliance with the Kantakouzenists); see Letter 59, lines 1–10 and 24–29.

42–43 *Χριστιανοὺς Χριστιανοῖς ἐπάγοντας ὄλεθρον ἐκ τῶν ἀθεωτάτων*: Akindynos alludes to Kantakouzenos' alliance with the Turks during the civil war or perhaps, more specifically, to two attacks against Constantinople by Kantakouzenos and his Turkish allies. Like Akindynos, the short chronicle of 1352 mentions in the same breath these attacks and the collapse of the dome of St. Sophia, although, as P. Schreiner points out, these events were not contemporary. The first of these abortive attacks was launched shortly after the murder of the megas *doux Apokaukos* (11 June 1345), and the second one followed a few months later, in the fall of 1345; see *Chronica*, I, Chronicle 8, § 45, p. 84; commentary *ibid.*, II, 261–62 (especially, Schreiner's fully documented commentary in "La chronique brève de 1352," *OCP*, 31 [1965], 363–65).

45–46 *οἱ γὰρ θεότητα τέμνοντες εὐδοκιμοῦσι μᾶλλον τῶν μὴ τοῦτο τολμώντων*: Further evidence that this letter was written after the Palamite victory in February of 1347.

50 *Διιπολιώδης*: The Dipolieia was an ancient Attic festival celebrated each year at the beginning of the summer in honor of Zeus Polieus, the protector of the city, whose altar was on the Acropolis. The particular ceremony of the Dipolieia was the Bouphonia, the slaying of the ox, which tradition associated with the first animal sacrifice; see Pausanias, *Attica*, I, 24, 4 and 28, 10.

By the time of Aristophanes, the antiquated ritual of the Bouphonia was considered so out-of-date that he used the term *Διιπολιώδης* in the sense of "old-fashioned," "archaic"; see *Nubes*, 984; H. W. Parke, *Festivals of the Athenians* (Ithaca, New York, 1977), 162–67.

57–59 *τὸ τῆς ἐκκλησίας κράτος . . . ἀπεωσμένον*: The allusion is to the Patriarch. Akindynos uses the same *periphrasis* when he refers to him in Letter 38, lines 31–32, and Letter 50, lines 89–90.

Since Kalekas is reported to be in disgrace, this letter was written after his deposition on 8 February 1347 and before his death, which occurred in prison in Constantinople on 29 December 1347; see *Chronica*, I, Chronicle 11, § 3, p. 106; commentary *ibid.*, II, 273.

In March 1347, after Kalekas repeatedly rejected Kantakouzenos' proposal that he submit to a new trial, the senior emperor confirmed his deposition, and he was exiled to Didymoteichos. But due to his rapidly deteriorating health he was recalled to Constantinople for treatment and died shortly thereafter. See Kantakouzenos, *Hist.*, IV, 3: III, 24–25; *idem*, *Prostagma*, PG, 151, col. 772A–B; G. T. Dennis, "The Deposition of Patriarch John Kalekas," JÖBG, 9 (1960), 51–55.

67.

Akindynos congratulates the Metropolitan for his fortitude in the face of harsh persecution and tells him that he is the only support of the modest but intransigent opposition to Palamism.

Addressee: Hyakinthos of Corinth (1343–47?). His name is known only from the anti-Palamite list; see Mercati, *Notizie*, 223, no. 39.

In April 1343, at the alleged request of the Orthodox population of Corinth, Kalekas transferred to the metropolis of that city the archbishop of Kos, who was at the time residing in Constantinople because his island diocese was under Latin control; see Miklosich-Müller, I, 234. Corinth was also ruled by Latin princes, the French Angevins, and had had a Catholic bishop since 1212; but Hyakinthos went, if not to Corinth, at least to the vicinity, as attested by Akindynos' letter to the Metropolitan of Monemvasia and by the fact that Hyakinthos' signature does not appear on the acts of the Permanent Synod after April 1343. See commentary on Letter 52, line 34, and Vassilikopoulou-Ioannidou, Ἀνέκδοτος ἐπιστολή, 94–95.

Hyakinthos was a staunch Akindynist. Iakobos of Monemvasia admired his anti-Palamite ardor (cf. Letter 52, lines 41–43) and Kalothetos regarded him as one of the most active anti-Palamite appointees of Kalekas, together with Ignatios of Antioch, Hyakinthos of Thessalonica, Iakobos of Monemvasia, and the metropolitan of Lacedaemon. See Kalothetos, ⟨Κατὰ Ἰωάννου Καλέκα⟩, Συγγράμματα, 299, lines 423–27 (*ἀλλ' ἐκεῖνοι μὲν ἠλλάξαντο τὴν ἑαυτῶν, ὢ συμφορᾶς,*

ἀσέβειαν τῆς προεδρίας τῶν ἐκκλησιῶν καὶ δῆλον καὶ τὰ χειρόγραφα αὐτῶν κατὰ τῆς ἀκτίστου καὶ ἀϊδίου χάριτος καὶ οἱ ἐξορκισμοὶ καὶ οἱ ἀφορισμοί, οὓς τῷ προέδρῳ καὶ φροντιστῇ τῶν ἡμετέρων ψυχῶν ἐνεχείρισαν).

Nothing more is known about Hyakinthos, but we can infer from this letter of Akindynos that he remained loyal to him and was persecuted by his victorious opponents; see lines 16–18, and Meyendorff (*Introduction*, 131 note 15), who is also of the opinion that the metropolitan of Corinth was deposed because of his loyalty to Akindynos.

Date: Summer–winter 1347. Hyakinthos must have been deposed after the election of the Palamite patriarch Isidore on 17 May 1347 (on this date, cf. Miklosich-Müller, I, 256; Darrouzès, no. 2273). Isidore's first task was to appoint new metropolitans; see Darrouzès, no. 2279, where these appointments are dated to between May and August 1347.

Vassilikopoulou dates this letter to 1344 because she assumes that, due to the adverse conditions prevailing in Latin-occupied Corinth, Hyakinthos was anxious to leave his diocese, and, therefore, Akindynos wrote to encourage him to remain there and continue the fight against Palamism; see Vassilikopoulou, *op. cit.*, 96.

The following evidence, however, argues against such an assumption: (a) This letter is not addressed to someone who is wavering in his loyalty or in his devotion to duty, but to a man whose firmness and courage in the face of persecution evoked the admiration of Akindynos; (b) Akindynos admits that the modest but intransigent opposition to Palamism looks now to Hyakinthos as their only support after God (cf. lines 30–32). Such a statement would have been incongruous in 1344 when Akindynos boasted that the Patriarch and the Palace and all the eminent ecclesiastics and laymen in the capital were on his side; see Letter 32, lines 40–47, and Letter 40, lines 125–34. Indeed, the absence of any reference to Kalekas and the Court in this letter is a further indication that it was written after the Palamite victory.

68.

To a loyal supporter.

Addressee: Unknown.

Date: Spring of 1347–beginning of 1348: after the Palamite victory and before Akindynos' death in the spring of 1348.

1 *Εὖγε τῆς σῆς ὄντως φωτοφανείας*: A pun on the hesychasts' claim to see the divine light of the Transfiguration.

4 *μηδὲ προδῷς τὸ ἀκίνδυνον*: A pun on his own name. According to his adversaries, Akindynos maintained that even his name indicated that his was the safe and correct doctrine; see p. ix and note 5 *supra*.

69.

Another letter of encouragement to an unwavering supporter.

Addressee: Unknown.

Date: The same as that of the previous letter.

5–6 *ἀκινδυνον διασῴζῃ*: Another pun on his name.

70.

Akindynos deplores the departure from Constantinople of Maximos, one of the most eloquent opponents of Palamism. He is even more disturbed by contradictory rumors about him. Some report that he is now befriending Palamas, and others that he is at the Athonite Lavra continuing his propaganda against Palamas. His own silence tends to confirm the worst fears of Akindynos, although the hieromonk Athanasios has reassured him of Maximos' loyalty. He begs Maximos, therefore, to adhere to his convictions and put his eloquence in the service of piety.

Addressee: As already commented by Loenertz (*Epistulae*, 102, and "Dix-huit lettres," 108), Maximos is to be identified with Maximos Laskaris Kalopheros, the addressee of Letter 76, who was the scion of a noble family and a member of the imperial court; see Loenertz, "Pour la biographie de Jean Lascaris Calophéros: À propos de deux publications récentes," *REB*, 28 (1970), 130–31.

In 1347, shortly after Kantakouzenos' victorious entrance into Constantinople, Maximos retired to Mt. Athos, which was then under Serbian control, and became a monk at the monastery of the Great Lavra (cf. lines 23–26). Neither Akindynos nor Demetrios Kydones (cf. *Letter to Kalopheros*, ed. Loenertz, *Correspondance*, I, no. 72, p. 104), who was equally surprised at his friend's sudden decision to embrace the monastic life, hints at the reasons which prompted it. It seems, however, that Maximos left the capital following a quarrel with Kantakouzenos, and before retiring to Mt. Athos he had sought refuge in Latin territory (probably Galata). This is to be inferred from a document that he signed in Constantinople in September 1350 promising, in return for the amnesty granted to him through the intercession of the Patriarch (the newly

elected Kallistos), never again to defend the doctrines of Akindynos nor those of the Latins; never to seek refuge either in Latin territory or outside the borders of the empire; and never to intrigue against the Emperor nor insult him; see Miklosich-Müller, I, 295; PG, 152, cols. 1307D–1308B; Darrouzès, no. 2315; Loenertz, "Dix-huit lettres," 107; A. K. Eszer, *Das abenteuerliche Leben des Johannes Laskaris Kalopheros*, Schriften zur Geistesgeschichte des östl. Europa, 3 (Wiesbaden, 1969) (hereafter, Eszer, *Kalopheros*), 9.

While on Mt. Athos, Maximos met with Palamas (cf. lines 16–17), and before long he changed his convictions and accused Akindynos of contentiousness (cf. Letter 76, lines 18–19). He had, therefore, given up his opposition to Palamism more than two years before he formally renounced the doctrines of Akindynos. On the other hand, despite his promise to Kantakouzenos, he remained a Latinophrone. In 1355 he wrote to Pope Innocent VI at Avignon, confirming the sincere intentions of John V Palaiologos to heal the schism and received a papal letter of thanks (cf. O. Halecki, *Un empereur de Byzance à Rome* [Warsaw, 1930], 43–44; 45 and note 1; Loenertz, "Dix-huit lettres," 110; Eszer, *op. cit.*, 166, no. 2); and in 1365, though he was by then a *protosynkellos* of the patriarchate of Constantinople, he embraced Catholicism and was congratulated by Urban V; see Halecki, *op. cit.*, 94–95; 363, no. 5; Loenertz, *op. cit.*, 110; Eszer, *op. cit.*, 19. Finally, Maximos is most probably to be identified with Maximos Laskaris, the Catholic abbot of the monastery of St. Diomedes in Constantinople to whom Pope Gregory XI recommended his legates in 1374; see Halecki, *op. cit.*, 95 note 1; 294 and note 1; Loenertz, *op. cit.*, 110; Eszer, *op. cit.*, 20.

Date: November–December 1347: after the arrival of Palamas on Mt. Athos in the fall of 1347 (cf. commentary on lines 16–17) and before the death of Kalekas (cf. commentary on lines 68–71).

5 *τὰς Ἀχελῴου Σειρῆνας*: See Apollonius Rhodius, *Argonautica*, IV, 893, where the Sirens are called daughters of the river Achelous and the Muse Terpsichore.

9–10 *μηδὲ προέσθαι τὰς πατρικὰς ἀριστείας ὑπὲρ τῆς εὐσεβείας*: Perhaps an allusion to the Kalopheros' claim to be descendants of the Lascarids, the founders of the empire of Nicaea where the Byzantine church and state were reborn after the catastrophe of 1204; see Loenertz, "Pour la biographie de Jean Lascaris Calophéros," 130–31.

15–16 *προὔδωκας τοὺς ἀγῶνας ἐκείνους ὧν μέγα κλέος παρὰ ταῖς ἐκκλησίαις*: It is not clear whether Akindynos implies here that Maximos was famous for his anti-Palamite activity or alludes, in general, to his ancestors' championship of Orthodoxy. Probably the former, since in his final letter to Maximos he reminds him of his many struggles on behalf of

truth (cf. Letter 76, lines 14–15), and in the closing paragraph of the present letter he says that Maximos more than anyone else jeered at the Palamite doctrines and with his eloquence saved many from falling into that heresy; see lines 79–82.

16–17 *ἀλλ' ὅτι καὶ τοῖς Παλαμήταις ἱλαρὸς συνεγένου, καὶ αὐτῷ τῷ Παλαμᾷ*: Palamas retired to Mt. Athos after the Zealot government prevented him from taking possession of the see of Thessalonica to which he had been appointed immediately after Isidore's election to the patriarchate on 17 May 1347; see Philotheos, *Encomium*, PG, 151, cols. 613B–614D. On the evidence of his biographer, we can establish 8 September as the *terminus ante quem* of Palamas' abortive attempt to take possession of his diocese. Philotheos tells how the paralytic daughter of a Palamite priest in Thessalonica was miraculously cured on that day (the feast day of the nativity of the Holy Virgin) in response to her father's prayers for a sign from Heaven in favor of Palamas who was being unjustly driven away. And he adds that, although the miracle was widely proclaimed, the new metropolitan left the city which had rejected him and proceeded slowly to the Holy Mountain which he reached after many days because he was ill (see *ibid.*, 614B–D). He must, therefore, have arrived there some time in October, and our letter, which was written after the news of his meeting with Maximos reached Constantinople, must date from November at the earliest. Loenertz assigns it to between October and December 1347; see "Dix-huit lettres," 106.

17–19 *οὐ σὺν ὁμοίῳ τῷ σχήματι μεθ' οὗπερ αὐτὸν λίθον ἀπέφηνας πρότερον ἐν μέσοις τοῖς βασιλείοις*: This confrontation between Palamas and Maximos "in the middle of the palace" must have occurred after Palamas' release from the palace prison where he remained until the Empress freed him and sent him on an embassy to Kantakouzenos shortly after the latter's entrance into the capital on 2 February 1347; see Kantakouzenos, *Hist.*, III, 99: II, 612–13; Meyendorff, *Introduction*, 120.

20 *τὴν τῶν αἱρέσεων ὕδραν*: See commentary on Letter 37, line 56 *supra*.

35–40 *ὁ ἐν ἱερομονάχοις θαυμάσιος καὶ σὸς Ἀθανάσιος . . . ἀναγκασθεὶς πρεσβεῦσαι παρὰ τὸν ἡγεμόνα τῶν Τριβαλλῶν*: Athanasios must have taken part in the embassy which Kantakouzenos sent to the Serbian king Stephan Dushan (1331–55) shortly after his own coronation and the wedding of his daughter Helena to John V at the end of May 1347; see Kantakouzenos, *Hist.*, IV, 4: III, 30–32; Loenertz, "Dix-huit lettres," 108. He is probably the same Athanasios to whom Gregoras wrote an account of his own mission to Serbia under Andronikos II (see Guilland, *Correspondance*, 31–51, no. 12; 303; Loenertz, *ibid.*). Other than to imply that Athanasios had taken a similar journey, Gregoras' letter sheds no light on the identity of this personage. But the fact that an

anti-Palamite was chosen by Kantakouzenos as his emissary to Serbia indicates that Athanasios was no ordinary monk, as Weiss rightly observes (cf. *Kantakouzenos*, 127), and shows that Akindynos' description of Athanasios as a philosopher par excellence is not merely a banal expression of flattery (cf. lines 36–37). Akindynos, of course, implies that Athanasios was unwilling to serve the usurper, for he writes that he was forced to go on this mission and in another version of this letter preserved in *Monac. Gr. 223* (fols. 7^r–7^v) he adds that he was forced by "the imperial authority"; see ad apparatum 39.

Athanasios, whose name appears on the list of anti-Palamites (cf. Mercati, *Notizie*, 223, no. 9), was one of the leading representatives of the anti-Palamite party at the council of 1351, together with Gregoras, Atouemes, and Dexios. See Arsenios of Tyre, *Tome, Vat. Gr. 2335*, fol. 2^r, as quoted in Mercati, *Notizie*, 223 notes 8–9; Meyendorff, *Introduction*, 142 note 71.

Athanasios may be the recipient of two letters of Akindynos, Letters 72 and 74.

40 *τῶν* Τριβαλλῶν: The Serbians; cf. George Chrysococces, Περὶ ἐπωνυμίας *πόλεων καὶ τόπων*, ed. U. Lampsides, "George Chrysococcis, le médecin, et son oeuvre," *BZ*, 38 (1938), 322, no. 6; K. Amantos, Τὰ ἐθνολογικὰ εἰς τοὺς Βυζαντινοὺς συγγραφεῖς, Ἑλληνικά, 2 (1929), 103.

42 *μέμψιν ἐκ παλαιῶν ἐγκλημάτων*: Some dispute or disagreement must have existed between Kalopheros and Akindynos, for he alludes to it also in lines 44–45 (*καίτοι λύπης μέντοι παλαιᾶς ἴσως ἂν ἴχνος εὑρεῖν παρὰ σοί*), and in his final letter to Kalopheros he accuses him of having betrayed the cause because of his personal animosity towards him; see Letter 76, lines 1–12.

42–43 *οὐ προκειμένας ἐλπίδας, οὐ φόβον ἐπηρτημένον*: Perhaps an allusion to Kalopheros' quarrel with Kantakouzenos. Akindynos speculates that hopes for an amnesty or fear or persecution might be the motives for his friend's purported change of allegiance.

61–63 *ὁ γὰρ τοῖς ἄλλοις πρότερον ἀπηχθημένος ὑπὲρ αὐτοῦ . . . ἥπερ αὐτὸς πρὸς αὐτοῦ*: Akindynos refers here to the preliminaries of the council of 10 June 1341, when by defending Palamas and the hesychasts he displeased Barlaam and some of his other friends; see Letters 7–9, and especially Letter 9, lines 101–4, and Letter 10, lines 191–92.

68–70 *οἱ μὲν φιλίας καὶ χάριτος τῆς πρὸς τὸν πεπλανημένον . . . οἱ δὲ δυσμενείας τῆς πρὸς τὸν πατριάρχην τὸν ἁγιώτατον, οἱ δὲ τῆς πρὸς ἡμᾶς*: Convinced of the infallibility of his beliefs, Akindynos attributed the attitude of his opponents to other than dogmatic reasons.

Even at the height of his power he claimed that those who opposed him did so either out of hostility towards him or friendship for Palamas, but not because of serious doctrinal objections; see Letter 40, lines 135–37.

The reference to the Patriarch indicates that Kalekas was still alive when Akindynos wrote this letter. For the date of his death, see commentary on Letter 66, lines 57–59.

81–82 *διὰ τῆς χρυσῆς γλώττης, ὥσπερ σειρᾶς*: The allusion is to Homer's *Iliad*, 8, 19–26, where Zeus challenges the other gods to test their power—or lack thereof—by trying to pull him down from Mt. Olympus with a golden rope. Gregoras also uses this allegory in his Ἀντιλογία; see P. L. M. Leone, ed. "Nicephori Gregorae 'Antilogia' et 'Solutiones Quaestionum,'" *Byzantion*, 40 (1970), 481, line 53. See also the earlier edition by Polemis, Ἀντιλογία, 64, lines 9–11, and p. 70, where the editor discusses Michael Psellos' use of the allegory of the *χρυσῆ σειρὰ* and traces Gregoras' indebtedness to him.

83–84 *ὥσπερ πέπλον εὐσεβείας . . . τὸν χαριέστατον*: Another allusion to the *Iliad*; see *ibid.*, 6, 86–92 and 269–71, where Hecuba is advised to offer her loveliest robe to the temple of Athena in order to propitiate the goddess and save the city of Troy.

71.

Although the addressee does not write to him and even associates with those who are anxious to see him die in exile, Akindynos retains his old affection for him and wishes him well.

Addressee: The evidence points to the Thessalonian landowner George Isaris, the student and friend of Akindynos, who in the summer of 1345 joined the Kantakouzenists in Thessalonica and nearly lost his life during the Zealot uprising; see commentary on Letter 27, line 2, and on Letter 59. During Palamas' stay on Mt. Athos—between September 1347 and September 1348 (cf. commentary on Letter 70, lines 16–17)—Isaris met with him and accompanied him to the second trial of Niphon, the *Protos* of the Holy Mountain accused of Messalianism; see PG, 152, cols. 1309B; 1310A; Miklosich-Müller, I, 298; Loenertz, "Dix-huit lettres," 93.

In his final letter to Isaris, Akindynos wrote that he had recently made an attempt to remind him of their once sincere friendship (cf. Letter 73, lines 4–5). Our letter probably represents this attempt.

Date: November–December 1347. This and the previous letter must be contemporary. Their destination was Mt. Athos, and they were probably carried

thither by the hieromonk Athanasios who, on his return from a mission to Serbia, had made a brief stop at Constantinople and brought Akindynos news of Maximos Kalopheros; see commentary on Letter 70, lines 35–40.

11–12 *μή τι παραπολαύσῃς τῆς τοῦ καιροῦ κακίας*: If this is an allusion to the hostility of the Zealots towards the Kantakouzenists and the Palamites, it would further support the hypothesis that this letter is addressed to Isaris.

72.

Upon his return from a trip to Serbia, the addressee stopped over briefly, and Akindynos complains that he did not have time to enjoy his company. He is consoled, however, by the thought that Thessalonica needs this able supporter just as much, because the Palamites are seeking to establish their heresy there. He also recommends to his correspondent another devoted supporter, the deacon Anthony.

Addressee: The information that the addressee is a Thessalonian who had gone on a long trip to Serbia helps identify him with the hieromonk Athanasios who was sent by Kantakouzenos on a mission to Stephen Dushan in the summer of 1347; see Loenertz, *Epistulae*, 104; "Dix-huit lettres," 105; and commentary on Letter 70, lines 35–40.

Date: End of 1347, shortly after the return of Athanasios to Thessalonica (cf. lines 2–5); therefore shortly after Letter 70, which is to be dated between November and December 1347. Loenertz assigns both these letters to between October and December 1347; see "Dix-huit lettres," 105–6.

14–16 *ἀγγέλλονται γὰρ οὗτοι δεῦρο πάντα ποιοῦντες ἐκεῖ καὶ θορυβοῦντες ὑπὲρ τῶν ἀσεβεστάτων μὲν τοῦ* Παλαμᾶ *δογμάτων*: This is probably an allusion, as Loenertz suggests, to Palamas' unsuccessful attempt to take possession of his see in the early fall of 1347; see Loenertz, "Dix-huit lettres," 105; Meyendorff, *Introduction*, 134–38.

18–20 *Ἀντώνιον δὲ ἀγαπήσεις τὸν ἱερὸν τουτονὶ καὶ ἡμέτερον, τὸν ἱεροδιακόνων τὰ κράτιστα . . . ὑπὲρ τῆς εὐσεβείας σπουδῆς*: Probably the hieromonk Anthony Phoinikes known from the anti-Palamite list (cf. Mercati, *Notizie*, 223, no. 6) and from Kalothetos' third *Antirrhetic* against Akindynos, where the author describes him as the well-trained disciple of a "holy father" and bemoans his loss to Akindynos. See Kalothetos, *Λόγος τρίτος κατὰ τοῦ κινδυνεύσαντος Ἀκινδύνου*, *Συγγράμματα*, 144, lines 83–86 (. . . *καὶ τέλος, βαβαί, καὶ Φοίνικας Ἀντωνίους, ὅπερ ἰδὼν οὐκ ἀδακρυτὶ τὴν συμφορὰν ἤνεγκα· ὅς εὖ*

καὶ ὡς ἔδει τραφεὶς παρὰ τῷ ὁσίῳ τούτου πατρί, νῦν ἅρπαγμα γέγονε, φεῦ τοῦ πάθους, τῷ ἀγρίῳ τούτῳ συΐ).

22–24 *ἀνθ' ὧν ἁπάντων καὶ τῆς ἱερωσύνης ἠξίωται παρὰ τῇ πασῶν τῶν ἐκκλησιῶν ὑψηλοτάτῃ μητρὶ καὶ τῆς ὅλης ἱερωσύνης πηγῇ*: Loenertz conjectures that the deacon Anthony might be that "other Akindynos" whom Kalekas attempted unsuccessfully to appoint to the metropolis of Thessalonica shortly before his own deposition; see Loenertz, "Dix-huit lettres," 105, and the Tome of 1347, PG, 152, col. 1278C; ed. Meyendorff, "Le tome synodal de 1347," 217 (*ὡς δ' ἡ κατὰ Θεσσαλονίκην ἐκκλησία χρείαν εἶχε προέδρου, ὁ δὲ τὴν δυσσέβειαν Ἀκίνδυνον ἄλλον ὑποψήφιον ἐποιήσατο, μαθοῦσα τοῦτο πάλιν ἡ τῆς εὐσεβείας, εἴπερ τις, προστάτις καὶ θεοσεβεστάτη βασιλὶς πάλιν ὀνειδίζει τὸν πατριάρχην καὶ παραινεῖ τῶν τοιούτων ἀποσχέσθαι τελείως ὡς δυσσεβῶν συνοδικῶς ἀναπεφηνότων*).

Loenertz' hypothesis is supported by two sources he does not quote: the *Encomium* of Philotheos and Kalothetos' diatribe against Kalekas. Philotheos provides the interesting detail that this "other Akindynos" was a monk and deacon from the close entourage of Akindynos (PG, 151, col. 611D). Kalothetos, on the other hand, leaves no doubt that this man was Hyakinthos' intended successor, and not Hyakinthos himself, for the following reasons: a) Kalothetos is writing after Hyakinthos' death; see ⟨Κατὰ Καλέκα⟩, Συγγράμματα, 297, lines 390–95: *Τί δ' ἂν εἴποις περὶ τοῦ ἐκ Κύπρου Θεσσαλονίκης χρηματίσαντος, ὃς ἐνέσκηψε τῇ ἐκκλησίᾳ Θεσσαλονικέων, ὥσπερ τις σκηπτός . . . ἀλλ' ἡ θεία δίκη παραπόδας αὐτῷ τὴν δίκην ἐκήνεγκε.* b) Kalothetos implies that Kalekas' attempt to appoint this man was both recent and unsuccessful; see *ibid.*, 299, lines 437–39: *Τί δὲ συναπελάβετό σοι καὶ εἰς τὸν ψηφισθέντα σοι πρώην ὀλίγου καὶ καταψηφισθέντα Θεσσαλονίκης ἡ ἁγία ἡμῶν αὐγούστα καὶ οἱ ἐν τέλει;*

73.

Akindynos accuses Isaris of having betrayed their friendship as well as God out of selfish interests.

Addressee: George Isaris; see commentary on Letter 27, line 2; and Letters 59 and 71.

Date: End of 1347; contemporary with Letter 72. Both letters were destined for Thessalonica, and their carrier was obviously the deacon Anthony; see lines 18–19 and commentary on Letter 72, lines 18–20.

74.

Akindynos asks his correspondent to give the enclosed letters to the deacon Anthony whom he had recently recommended to him. He also asks that the letter of Lapithes in which he deplores the lack of a more vigorous resistance to Palamism be shown to the learned men in Thessalonica.

Addressee: Most probably the hieromonk Athanasios in Thessalonica to whom Akindynos had recently recommended the deacon Anthony; see commentary on Letter 72 and Loenertz, "Dix-huit lettres," 108–9.

Date: End of 1347–beginning of 1348, shortly after Letter 73; see lines 1–2 (*σοὶ τὸν ἡμέτερον Ἀντώνιον . . . ἀπεσταλκότες πρῴην*) and Loenertz, "Dix-huit lettres," 109.

1 *Ἀντώνιον τὸν τοῦ Χριστοῦ διάκονον*: On the deacon Anthony, see commentary on Letter 72, lines 18–20 and 22–24.

7–21 *καὶ μάλιστα τὰ τοῦ Κυπρίου φιλοσόφου γράμματα . . . μέχρις αἵματος ὑπὲρ τοῦ ὀρθοῦ καὶ εὐσεβοῦς κινδυνεύσαντας*: For Lapithes and his first letter to Hyakinthos, in which he criticized the apathy of Gregoras and the mild polemics of Akindynos, see commentary on Letter 42, lines 28–31.

23–24 *ἐπὶ τῷ λόγῳ τούτῳ αἰσχύναντι τοὺς διὰ τοῦτο φιλονεικίαν ἐπεγκαλοῦντάς μοι*: An allusion to his former supporters, Harmenopoulos and Kalopheros, who had both recently accused Akindynos of contentiousness. See *Address to Hierotheos*, 188–89 and Letter 76, lines 18–19.

26–29 *καὶ ταῦτα τοῦ δυσσεβοῦντος ἀμαθοῦς ἄγαν ὄντος . . . μηδὲ τί ἐστιν ἐπιστήμη καὶ ὅπως . . . πέφυκεν ἐπισταμένου*: Palamas' learned adversaries sought from the beginning to treat him as an ignorant monk. In the first letter that he addressed to him, Barlaam commented that, judging from his arguments on dialectic syllogisms, Palamas spoke the truth when he claimed to have completely forgotten the secular sciences and attained the true wisdom; see Barlaam, *Epistole Greche*, 262, lines 847–52. Later on, the polymath Gregoras wrote that if Palamas made his doctrinal errors out of ignorance and not willingly, then he was an illiterate; and he proposed to teach him elementary grammar so that he might attain a proper understanding of the Scriptures. See Gregoras, *Hist.*, XXX, 20: III, 282–83. See also Kalothetos' *Antirrhetic* against Gregoras (*Συγγράμματα*, 308, lines 116–29), where the author states incorrectly that Gregoras was the only leading anti-Palamite to call Palamas ignorant and uneducated.

Yet, despite the assertions of his opponents and his own repudiation of the wisdom of the world, Palamas was the beneficiary of a classical education, and he proudly reminded Gregoras that no lesser figure than Theodore Metochites himself had admired his excellent understanding of Aristotelian philosophy. See the passage from his First *Antirrhetic* against Gregoras in *Coisl. Gr. 100*, fol. 236[r] (as cited by Meyendorff, *Introduction*, 47 note 15), and Philotheos, *Encomium*, cols. 559D–560A. For Logaras' disparaging comments on Palamas' style, see commentary on Letter 35, line 3.

41 *ὁ θαυμάσιος* Μάγιστρος: Thomas Magistros; see commentary on Letter 56.

41 *ὁ σοφὸς* Κυδώνης: It is not possible to identify with any degree of certainty the sage Kydones, who is here included among the learned men in Thessalonica to whom Akindynos wished that the letter of Lapithes be shown. Mercati maintains that Akindynos is referring to Demetrios Kydones whose name appears accompanied by the epithet *σοφὸς* in another anti-Palamite document, an anonymous letter preserved in *Vat. Gr.* 678 (B), fol. 30[v]; see *Notizie*, 128–29; 129 note 1; and 501. Loenertz (cf. "Dix-huit lettres," 109), however, hesitates to endorse fully such an identification, and although he does not state his reasons, they are not difficult to guess. For it does, indeed, seem unlikely that Demetrios, who was at the time in the service of Kantakouzenos and had been himself an enemy and vociferous critic of the Zealot regime, would venture a visit to Thessalonica while it was still under Zealot control. See Loenertz, "Démétrius Cydonès I: De la naissance à l'année 1373," *OCP*, 36 (1970), 49–51; and Kydones' first address to Kantakouzenos (ed. Loenertz, *Correspondance*, I, 5, lines 5–37), where he describes how he escaped the massacre of 1345 because he happened to be away on a mission imposed on him by the Zealots and how during his absence from Thessalonica his enemies destroyed his family possessions and forced him to become an émigré.

It is, of course, possible that, like his friend Nicholas Kabasilas, Demetrios might have accompanied Palamas to Thessalonica when the latter sought unsuccessfully to take possession of his see in the autumn of 1347 (cf. Loenertz, "Chronologie de Nicolas Cabasilas," 208–9). But there is no evidence to support this hypothesis.

In addition to being a partisan of Kantakouzenos, Demetrios was closely connected with Palamas' foremost associate, Patriarch Isidore, who had been a friend of the Kydones family in Thessalonica and the teacher of Demetrios. See the letter which Demetrios wrote to Isidore in 1346 when he was a destitute refugee seeking the consolation of his for-

mer teacher (ed. Loenertz, *Correspondance*, I, no. 43). But, despite his association with such leading representatives of Palamism and despite his own later anti-Palamite stand, Demetrios does not seem to have taken an interest in the religious dispute. Neither his letters to Isidore (*Correspondance*, I, no. 43 and no. 86) nor any of his other contemporary letters contain any references to the controversy.

As for Kydones' brother, Prochoros, the well-known anti-Palamite, he must have been too young in 1347 to be designated by Akindynos as *σοφός*. See Kydones' first address to Kantakouzenos, where he complains that his mother's widowhood and the youth and inexperience of his siblings made their life in Thessalonica during the civil war even more difficult (*Correspondance*, I, 5, lines 2–4: *ἥ τε τῆς μητρός χηρεία καὶ τὸ τῶν ἀδελφῶν οὕτως ἄωρόν τε καὶ ἄπραγμον* . . .).

Another learned Kydones who might have been a contemporary of Demetrios and a fellow-Thessalonian was the "philosopher" George Kydones, known from an epitaph he composed in memory of Demetrios Kassandrenos, a prominent Thessalonian who accompanied Matthew Kantakouzenos to the Peloponnese in 1361. See D. Bassi's edition of this epitaph (from codex *Ambros. Gr. D 538*, fol. 306^r) in "Sette epigrammi greci inediti," *Rivista di filologia e d'istruzione classica*, 26 (1898), 394. The date of Kassandrenos's death is not known, but it must have occurred in Mistra after April 1362, because the manuscript of Plutarch's *Parallel Lives* (*Ambr. Gr. D 538*) which he had ordered from Manuel Tzycandyles was completed in Mistra on 7 April 1362, and, as A. Turyn notes, there is nothing in Tzycandyles' subscription of this MS to indicate that Kassandrenos had already died; see Turyn, *Dated Greek Manuscripts*, I, 229.

We can, therefore, assume that the "philosopher" George Kydones was a member of the intellectual milieu at Mistra in the 1360s. His relationship, if any, to Demetrios Kydones is, of course, unknown, although F. Tinnefeld convincingly argues that he may be identified with George the Philosopher, a physician with a penchant for traveling to whom are addressed several letters of Demetrios Kydones; see Tinnefeld, "Georgios Philosophos: Ein Korrespondent und Freund des Demetrios Kydones," *OCP*, 38 (1972) 145 note 2. George the Philosopher appears to have been an anti-Palamite (see Kydones, *Correspondance*, no. 31, lines 71–72, and no. 110, line 51; Tinnefeld, *op. cit.*, 150–51 and note 1). But even if Tinnefeld's hypothesis is correct, his identification with the Kydones mentioned in our letter remains highly conjectural.

Finally, a Manuel Kydones is mentioned in a chrysobull of John V as a member of the imperial chancery in Thessalonica in 1350. Nothing else, however, is known about him; see Loenertz, "Démétrius Cydonès I:

De la naissance . . . ," 53, and the edition of this chrysobull by Eszer, *Kalopheros*, 162.

41–42 *καὶ ὁ ἱερὸς καὶ θεῖος ἐν ἱερομονάχοις Ματθαῖος ὁ ἐν τῇ τοῦ θεσπεσίου* 'Ισαὰκ *ἱερωτάτῃ μονῇ τὴν ἀρετὴν μετιών*: This information supports the hypothesis that the hieromonk Matthew, a former follower of Akindynos (cf. commentary on Letter 50), is to be identified with the jurist Matthew Blastaris, who was a disciple of the monk Isaak and a resident in the latter's monastery in Thessalonica. See G. Theocharides, 'Ο Ματθαῖος Βλάσταρις *καὶ ἡ μονὴ τοῦ κῦρ*-'Ισαὰκ *ἐν* Θεσσαλονίκῃ, *Byzantion*, 40 (1970), 439–42, where all pertinent evidence is analyzed and bibliography cited. In this carefully documented study, Theocharides maintains that the monastery of Theotokos Peribleptos, located in the center of Thessalonica and also known as the monastery of kyr-Isaak, was founded by metropolitan Iakobos who occupied the throne of Thessalonica from *ca*. 1290 to *ca*. 1310 and who, according to the Synodikon of Thessalonica, later embraced monasticism under the name of Isaak; see Theocharides, *op. cit.*, 442–50.

First mentioned in an Athonite act of 1314 (cf. *Actes de Chilandar*, no. 27, 31), this monastery was still in existence in 1548, according to an inventory notice on a manuscript of Photios' *Bibliotheca* (codex *Monac. Gr. 30*); see Theocharides, *op. cit.* 450; 453–54.

Theocharides believes that this monastery has survived and is the present-day church of St. Panteleimon, a fourteenth-century structure located in the center of Thessalonica, near the arch of Galerios, and known during the Turkish occupation as Issakie-Djami; see Theocarides, *op. cit.*, 454–58.

43 *δικαιοφύλαξ* Βρυέννιος: See commentary on Letter 58.

44 Χαρατζᾶς: See commentary on Letter 40, line 2.

75.

Akindynos fears that his correspondent has misunderstood his sincere admiration for his eloquence, for he cannot imagine in what other way he could have offended him. He begs him, therefore, not to allow such pettiness to destroy their friendship and damage their sacred cause.

Addressee: According to its superscription, this letter was intended for either Maximos or Ignatios, two men who must have suddenly and without obvious reason turned against Akindynos. As Loenertz has commented (cf. "Dixhuit lettres," 108), Maximos is probably Maximos Lascaris Kalo-

pheros, whose eloquence Akindynos had recently praised effusively (cf. Letter 70, lines 4–5 and 82) and who was already reported to be in the company of Palamas on Mt. Athos (see *ibid.*, lines 16–17).

The identity of Ignatios, on the other hand, cannot be established. The monk Ignatios who was one of the anti-Palamite representatives at the council of 1351 and whose name appears on the list of anti-Palamites was obviously a loyal supporter and, therefore, could not have abandoned Akindynos. See Arsenios of Tyre, *Tome, Vat. Gr. 2335*, fol. 2[r] (cited by Mercati, *Notizie*, 223 note on nos. 8–9; Meyendorff, *Introduction*, 142 note 71); Mercati, *Notizie*, 223, no. 8. Unless, of course, his quarrel with Akindynos was strictly personal and did not affect his attitude towards Palamism. But this hardly seems probable, because Akindynos here implies that his friend had defected when he says that his hostility towards him "does not even spare piety, but sweeps it away like a torrent along with friendship" (cf. lines 22–23).

In the 1320s and 30s a hieromonk Ignatios was a *dikaios* (substitute for the abbot) of the monastery of Hodegetria in Constantinople, according to the subscriptions of two manuscripts copied at his expense. In 1327 Ignatios, then a former *dikaios*, commissioned a Menology of Symeon Metaphrastes (codex *Laurenzianus Gr. 11. 1*, fol. 245[r] [cited in Turyn, *Dated Greek Manuscripts*, 164]); and in 1336 Ignatios, now a *Dikaios*—obviously reappointed, as Turyn concludes (*op. cit.*, 166)—commissioned a gospel (codex *Parisinus Gr. 311*, fol. 382[v] [cited in Turyn, *op. cit.*, 166]).

Was Ignatios still alive in 1347 and was he an Akindynist, since he held an important position at the monastery of Hodegetria which was a centre of anti-Palamite activity during the controversy? We do not know.

As for Laurent's identification of the hesychast Ignatios with the spiritual director of Eulogia Choumnaina-Palaiologina and the philosopher-monk Ignatios mentioned in the anti-Palamite list (cf. commentary on Letter 6), that too must remain conjectural until more contemporary sources come to light.

Date: End of 1347–beginning of 1348; after Letter 70 in which Akindynos deplores the departure of his extremely eloquent supporter Maximos Kalopheros.

23–25 *καὶ ὁ μὲν Θεμιστοκλῆς καὶ Ἀριστείδης ὁ Λυσιμάχου . . . ἐσπείσαντο ἐπιόντος τοῦ Μήδου*: In the letter to his teacher Bryennios, Akindynos wrote that in this most important struggle against heresy even personal feuds ought to be forgotten, and he cited again this well-known example of the two patriotic Athenian statesmen. See commentary on Letter 58, lines 20–22.

76.

Akindynos begs his former friend not to allow his personal animosity towards him to jeopardize his own salvation and that of many other men who might follow him.

Addressee: Maximos Laskaris Kalopheros, recipient of Letter 70 and probably Letter 75; see commentary on Letter 70.

Date: Beginning of 1348; after Letters 70 and 75 and before the death of Akindynos sometime before May 1348. Loenertz dates it between 1347 and 1348; see "Dix-huit lettres," 109.

8–12 *σὺ τοίνυν δυσμενῶς ἐμοῦ μεμνημένος . . . μικροψυχίαν*: See commentary on Letter 70, line 42.

14–15 *καὶ πολλοὺς μὲν ἀγῶνας ὑπὲρ αὐτῆς ἀνύσας*: See commentary on Letter 70, lines 15–16.

26–28 *ἀλλὰ τῆς ἐναντίας, καὶ ἀπειράκις ἀπείρως διαφέρων . . . καινήν σοι χάριν*: Note the irony; Akindynos borrows his opponent's phraseology in writing to this new convert to Palamism.

32–34 *οὔπω λέγω τοῦτο μὲν ἀρετήν, ἐκεῖνο δὲ κακίαν εἶναι δοκεῖν τοῖς ἱεροῖς πατράσι . . . τὸ δεύτερον*: The preceding lacuna in the text makes it impossible to determine the antecedents of *τοῦτο* and *ἐκεῖνο* which the holy Fathers considered to be a virtue and a vice respectively. Flattery seems to be the sin which Akindynos refuses to commit, since in the following sentence he declares that he loves his friends but would rather suffer than flatter them.

47–48 *φανείτω πάλιν Ἀχιλλεὺς ἐν τοῖς Ἕλλησι μετὰ τῶν ὅπλων*: See Homer, *Iliad*, 19, 360–400.

INDICES

I: PROPER NAMES

II: TERMS and VOCABULARY

*Distinguishes unattested or rare words

III. CITATIONS

Bible

UNIDENTIFIED

IV: INCIPITS

CORPUS FONTIUM HISTORIAE BYZANTINAE

SERIES WASHINGTONIENSIS, EDITOR JOHN M. DUFFY

DUMBARTON OAKS TEXTS

De Administrando Imperio
Constantine VII Porphyrogenitus
Gyula Moravcsik | R. J. H. Jenkins
CFHB 1 • DOT 1

Nicholas I, Patriarch of Constantinople: Letters
R. J. H. Jenkins | L. G. Westerink
CFHB 6 • DOT 2

Nicholas I, Patriarch of Constantinople: Miscellaneous Writings
L. G. Westerink
CFHB 20 • DOT 6

The Correspondence of Athanasius I, Patriarch of Constantinople
Alice-Mary Talbot
CFHB 7 • DOT 3

The Letters of Manuel II Palaeologus
George T. Dennis
CFHB 8 • DOT 4

The Synodicon Vetus
John Duffy | Thomas S. Parker
CFHB 15 • DOT 5

Letters of Gregory Akindynos
Angela Constantinides Hero
CFHB 21 • DOT 7

The Correspondence of Leo, Metropolitan of Synada and Syncellus
M. P. Vinson
CFHB 23 • DOT 8

Three Byzantine Military Treatises
George T. Dennis
CFHB 25 • DOT 9

Nikephoros, Patriarch of Constantinople: Short History
Cyril Mango
CFHB 13 • DOT 10

The Correspondence of Ignatios the Deacon
Cyril Mango | Stephanos Efthymiadis
CFHB 39 • DOT 11

The Taktika *of Leo VI*
George T. Dennis
CFHB 49 • DOT 12

The Life of Patriarch Ignatius
Nicetas David
Andrew Smithies | John M. Duffy
CFHB 51 • DOT 13

COMMENTARIES

De Administrando Imperio*: A Commentary*
R. J. H. Jenkins

A Critical Commentary on the Taktika *of Leo VI*
John F. Haldon